MIRACLES OF THE SAINTS

The Blessed Virgin Mary Surrounded by Saints. *Medieval icon by unknown artist from 1370. Vatican Museum. Left: St. Onuphrius of Egypt, hermit; St. Nicholas of Myra; on the right: St. Bartholomew the Apostle; St. John the Evangelist.*

MIRACLES OF THE SAINTS

HENRYK BEJDA

SOPHIA
INSTITUTE PRESS

Translated into English by Anna Pietrus and Katarzyna Fejklowicz.

First published in the Polish language as *Cuda Wielkich Świętych* by Fronda PL Sp. z o.o., ul. Łopuszańska 32, 02-220 Warszawa.

Cover by Perceptions Studios.
Cover image: *The Virgin Mary with the Apostles and Other Saints* by Fra Angelico (Alamy KGD1EN).

Sophia Institute Press
Box 5284, Manchester, NH 03108
1-800-888-9344
www.SophiaInstitute.com

Hardcover ISBN 978-1-64413-820-5
ebook ISBN 978-1-64413-821-2
Library of Congress Control Number: 2024944414

Contents

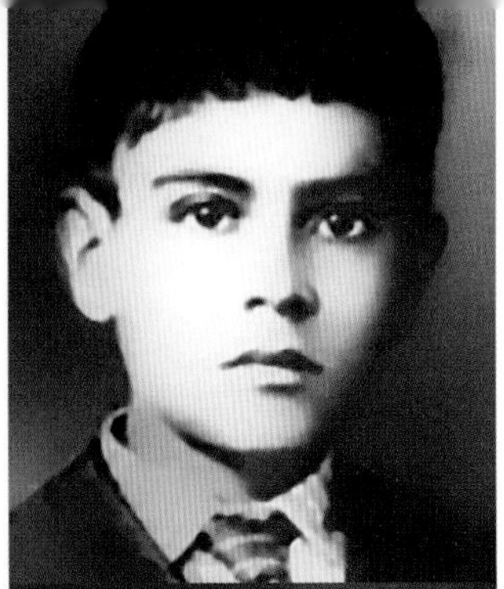

भारत
INDIA
100

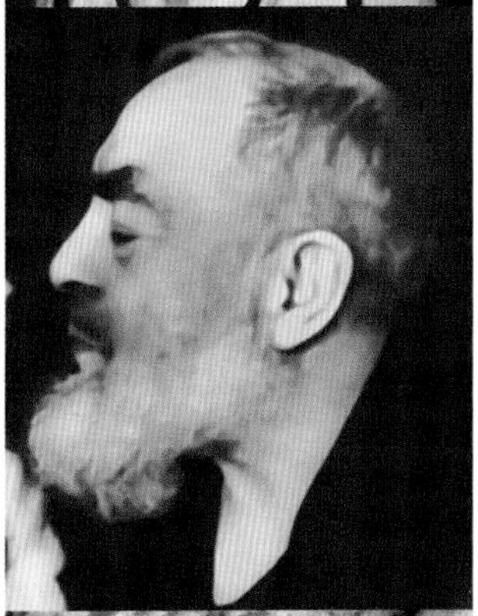

Doctors of Souls and Bodies

We associate saints with miracles. For centuries, as confirmation of someone's holiness, the Church requires not only a recognition of heroic virtues, but also miraculous healings confirmed by doctors and theologians.

A miracle performed by God through the intercession of a person could therefore be called a kind of heavenly seal, confirming that a given person is already in Heaven. Although the pope can perform canonizations without fulfilling the requirement for a miracle, there have been only a few such cases in the history of the Church (including John XXIII). Saints usually have at least two obvious miracles—confirmed by science—and many graces attributed to their intercession. And many of the saints are openly called "miracle workers." This book talks precisely about saints and the miracles attributed to them.

This publication is the fruit of many years of passion—exploring everything related to saints and miracles—carried out together with my invaluable collaborators in various publications. For this book's needs, I refreshed and reworked some of my old texts, usually expanding them with additional information; but many texts were created completely from scratch—I dealt with some of the saints and many miracles for the first time. Absolutely countless are the number of sources I reviewed during the course of writing. In addition to a few contemporary books and press publications regarding saints, I also looked through many miracles in old Latin, Italian, Spanish, German, English, Czech, Hungarian, and Old Polish folios from the nineteenth, eighteenth, seventeenth, and even sixteenth centuries (a great nod to internet libraries!); I studied formal decrees regarding miracles posted in the Holy See's official gazette, *Acta Apostolicae Sedis*; I reviewed files and descriptions of beatification processes and canonization in the invaluable multi-volume *Acta Sanctorum*; I contacted healed people or their families; I benefited from the help of members of religious congregations; and so forth. My goal was clear: to collect as much information as possible—to gather legends and anecdotes and establish the facts, always trying to find the truth (although in some cases it wasn't that easy)—and to describe all this in an understandable, and interesting way. Have I succeeded?

Judge for yourself.

You may also be wondering which criteria guided me in the selection of saints for this study. First of all was the desire to show the universality of the Church, its presence at all ends of the world. I tried to introduce saints from all continents and from as many countries as possible. Secondly, with this selection I wanted to demonstrate that everyone is called to holiness, regardless of skin color, nationality, age, abilities, or profession. Therefore, you will find here both great sages—Doctors of the Church—and evangelical simpletons, martyrs and confessors, clergy and lay people, adults and children.

One more note: the miraculous help that the saints—as the Church Triumphant, i.e. people already in Heaven—provide to the Church Militant, i.e. people still on pilgrimage on earth, makes fully visible to us one of the dogmas we profess: the truth about *communio sanctorum*, i.e. the communion of saints. Therefore, let us remember that each of us in difficult times can turn to them—the saints—for help.

Henryk Bejda
AMDG

◀ Saints and Doctors of the Church, *unknown, France, 1490–1500. Phoenix Art Museum, USA.*

From the Publisher

The maps accompanying the chapters—depending on editorial needs—show the saint's birthplace, customarily associated with their name, the area of their missionary activity, if they came from another country (e.g. Ireland for St. Patrick), and the place of death.

Beatification painting by Stanisław Baj, depicting 108 Polish martyrs in World War II.

Author's Thanks

I dedicate this work to my beloved wife Marta and our three wonderful daughters: Zosia, Hania, and Lusi.

The number of people who, to a lesser or greater extent, contributed to the creation of this book is so great, it would be impossible to list them all. Thank you to all, and a special thanks is deserved by those who made the most substantial contributions. This includes: my daughter Zosia; Agnieszka Rzemieniec; Roland Kauth; Maronite brothers; the editor of the quarterly *Alma Mater*, Fr. Marinus Parzinger, OFM Cap.; L'abbe Laurent Biselx, FSSPX; Fr. Emmanuel Charles McCarthy; Bob Gutherman; Sr. Diana Papa, OSC; Albertine Sisters from Krakow; Jolanta Zakrzewska; Fr. Artur Świeży, SDB; Damien Cash; Sr. Constance, LSP; Fr. Stanisław Groń, SJ; and Sr. Elżbieta Siepak, ZMBM.

Words of thanks are due to those who helped my research on the subject of the saints and the miracles attributed to them—the late Dr. Eng Antoni Zięba, Malgosia (my current "boss"), and Mietek Pabis, as well as Grazyna Kich and Fr. Robert Wróblewski—my longtime colleagues of the monthly publication *Cuda i Łaski Boże* ("Miracles and God's Grace"); also those who at that time (*Cuda i Łaski Boże* appearing from 2004 to 2020) helped in the preparation of the individual issues and articles that I use today.

I would also like to thank those who indirectly contributed to the creation of this work: my sincere friends Łukasz and Ola Kudlicki, Jarek and Joanna Szark, Waldek and Dorota Maliszewski, whose dedication and help I could always count on, Tomek Balon-Mroczka and Halina Marchut from the publishing house Rafael, who were the first to publish my works, Sr. Gaudiosa Dobrska, CSDP, and other Sisters of the Divine Shepherd and Sisters from other religious congregations who continuously supported and offered words of encouragement, my parents-in-law and Mrs. Ania for helping us in our everyday life—not always a bed of roses—as well as my parents who, I believe, are looking out for me from above, Dorota Kościołek, and Mr. Roman Zakrzewski. I would also like to thank all the good people from the Fronda Publishing House (original Polish press) and many others who—due to human limitations—I simply have forgotten to mention. I wish the readers a pleasant and fruitful reading.

Henryk Bejda

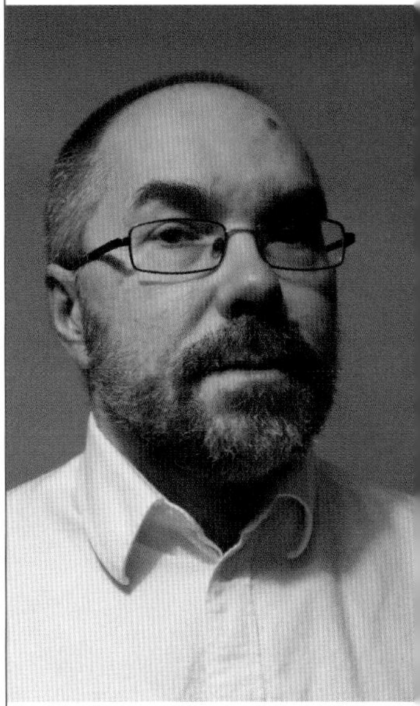

St. John Paul II beatified the 108 Polish martyrs in Warsaw on June 13, 1999. The beatified were:

- *three bishops,*
- *fifty-two diocesan priests,*
- *twenty-six priest religious,*
- *three seminarians,*
- *seven monastic brothers,*
- *eight nuns,*
- *nine lay people.*

S. SILVESTER

Miracles of the Saints

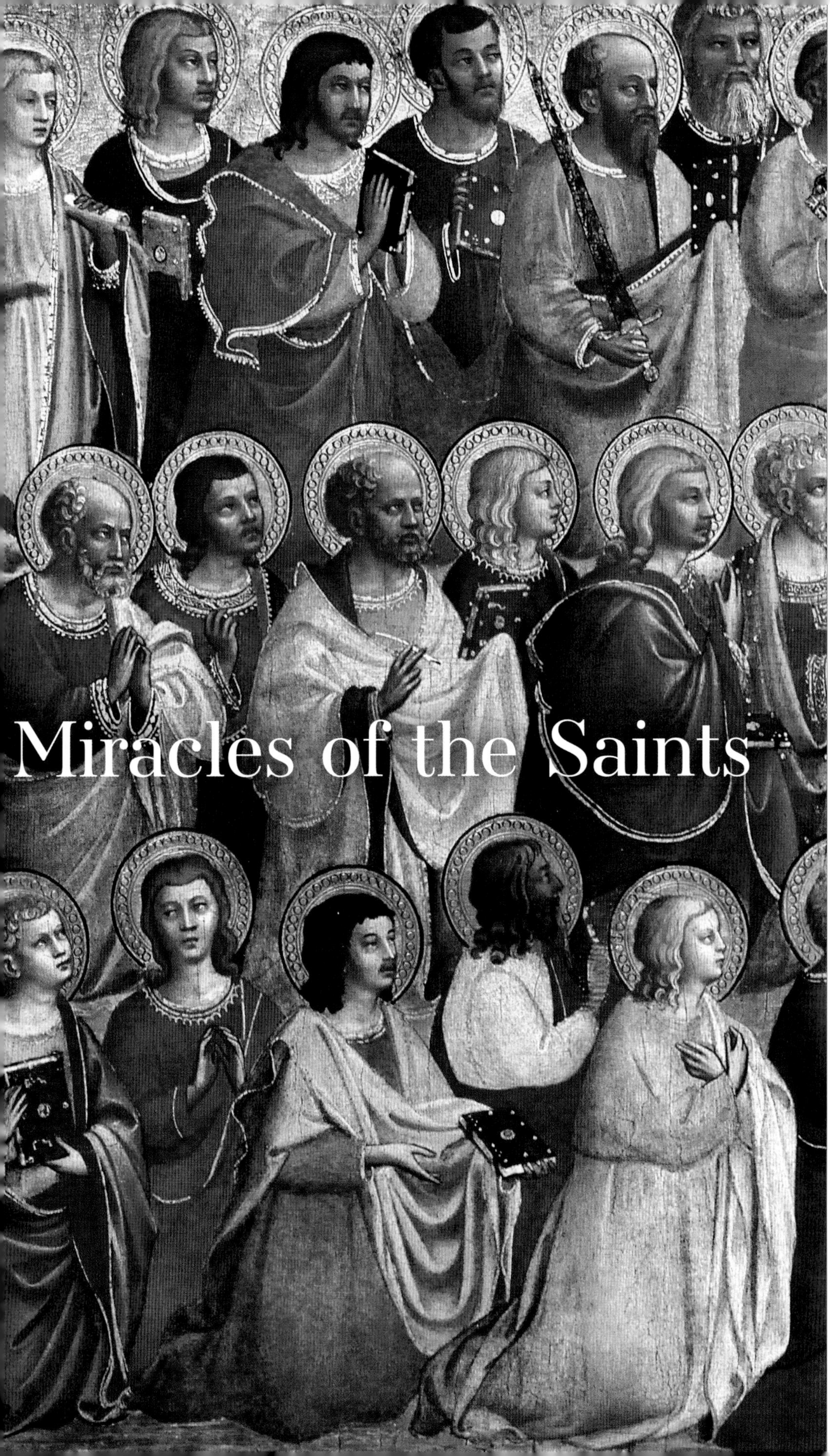

The Virgin Mary with the Apostles and Other Saints *by Fra Angelico.*

Aurelia and Enrico, the parents of the holy visionary.

A LIVING ICON OF CRUCIFIED JESUS

St. Gemma Galgani

An Italian mystic from the city of Lucca in Tuscany, Italy, St. Gemma is the most beautiful of saints. Though she went to the Lord when she was only twenty-five years old, during her short life, she received the gifts of stigmata and prophecy from God, had mystical ecstasies, was tormented by Satan, and shared in the Lord's Passion every week through her own personal suffering. Because of her companionship with the suffering Christ, St. Gemma has been called the Daughter of the Passion, the Flower of Christ's Passion, and a living icon of Jesus.

Gemma, whose name means jewel, was the fifth of eight children born to Enrico Galgani, a chemist from Borgonuovo, and his wife, Aurelia. Her mother and her first teachers—the Sisters Oblates of the Holy Spirit—instilled in her heart fervent piety, deep love for Jesus and Mary, love of the Cross, and a desire for a deep understanding of the Lord's Passion and Heaven.

When Gemma was seven years old, Jesus spoke to her during Mass and asked her to give Him her mother, who was sick with tuberculosis. Gemma agreed. Soon after this vision, thirty-nine-year-old Aurelia died. Unfortunately, the death of Gemma's mother was only the first in a series of tragic events: her father grew sick and died, the family lost their fortune, her beloved brother died, and Gemma and her siblings were forced to wander from place to place, fully dependent on the kindness of relatives and strangers.

Gemma Galgani at the age of seven with her sister Angelina.

Gemma herself was also frequently sick. At the age of nineteen, she suffered from meningitis, which caused her to experience paralysis of her arms and legs, spinal curvature, and total deafness. She offered her illness and pain to God as reparation for the pain she caused Him, for the conversion of sinners, and for the souls in Purgatory. Gemma also did not abandon hope of healing and turned to the then-Venerable Passionist, Gabriel of Our Lady of Sorrows (Francesco Possenti), for assistance. Through his intercessions, she was miraculously cured of her ailments. (See the chapter dedicated to St. Gabriel to learn more of this story.)

From an early age, Gemma felt called to religious life. She rejected two marriage proposals and tried to join various religious orders, but she was turned away because of her poor health. She then decided to live like a nun in the world and made private vows of chastity, obedience, and poverty.

God blessed Gemma with numerous mystical gifts. She experienced ecstasies and saw and spoke with Jesus and the Virgin Mary. She had the gift of prophecy and would see saints and her guardian angel in visions.

On June 8, 1899, the feast of the Sacred Heart, at the age of twenty-one, Gemma received the stigmata. For the next year, from Thursday night until Friday afternoon, wounds would appear on her hands, feet, and side. She also often experienced the wounds from the crown of thorns and the scourging. While Gemma experienced these physical pains, she would enter into a state of ecstasy as she shared in the Lord's Passion.

In early 1903, Gemma fell sick with tuberculosis. When Holy Week began, her suffering became more intense, and she went home to the Lord on Holy Saturday.

MIRACLES OF HEALING LEG AILMENTS

Those who witnessed Gemma's life and death were awestruck by her holiness. Since her death, many Catholics have

As a child, Gemma attended the school of the Sisters Oblates of the Holy Spirit, where Bl. Elena Guerra was the Superior General.

Lucca, Italy, a small Tuscan city located near Florence and Pisa.

Statue of St. Gemma Galgani in Madrid's Cathedral.

asked for her intercession and have received miraculous answers to their prayers.

Maria Menicucci of Vitorchiano, in Italy, suffered from severe pain in her right knee for many years. She applied bandages and various ointments to her knee and even traveled to Italian spas for relief, but nothing soothed her pain. Her doctors diagnosed her with synovitis, a debilitating inflammation of the membrane that surrounds various joints. This type of long-term inflammation can lead to degeneration of the entire joint. Maria struggled with this pain for nineteen years, and by the time she received her diagnosis, her condition was nearly incurable. Finally, in 1907, one doctor in Pistoia, Italy, where Maria was staying with relatives, suggested a surgery that would not completely heal Maria but would, he hoped, bring her some relief. Before she could have the surgery, Maria turned to the Handmaid of God Gemma Galgani for help. She began a novena to Gemma asking that she be healed. She also obtained a relic of the saint and applied it to her affected knee. On the ninth day of her prayers, Maria felt the pain leave her knee. She could even go up and down stairs without feeling any pain. Her extraordinary and instantaneous cure was confirmed by two physicians who had personally treated her, as well as by three others who investigated the case on behalf of the Sacred Congregation of Rites.

Seventy-six-year-old Fr. Ulysses Fabrizi also had leg problems. He not only suffered from varicose veins but also a venous ulcer, an open sore caused by poor blood circulation in the legs. Fr. Fabrizi's ulcer was resistant to treatment and only got worse over time. Eventually, it grew in size to twelve by seven centimeters (about five by three inches) and was so inflamed and painful that Fr. Fabrizi's doctors became concerned that it would become infected and endanger his life. And so on the afternoon of November 26, 1919, they decided that they would send the priest to Rome to see a specialist who could take more radical measures to save his life. But Fr. Fabrizi was concerned about making the journey: not only was he sick and in pain, but he was also elderly, and he feared he would not survive the journey. So he prayed: "My Gemma, heal this wound; before I die, I would like to see you raised to the altars, and then I will die happy." The night passed peacefully, as never before, and in the morning, when Fr. Fabrizi's bandages were removed to be changed, the doctors realized that his wound had disappeared. The place where it had been before was covered with thin, undamaged skin, and the only trace of the dangerous ulcer was a slight reddening. Fr. Fabrizi knew that Gemma's prayers had healed him. He said the *Te Deum* in thanksgiving and went to celebrate Mass. Medical experts unanimously said later that it was a miracle.

The Vatican likewise approved these two healings as miracles, and so Gemma Galgani was declared Blessed in 1933, only thirty years after her death.

A YOUNG GIRL HEALED

The two miracles needed for canonization were approved in 1939. They happened in the same town—in Lappano, Italy, in the Calabria region—and they were received by two people with the same last name who were, regardless, not related to each other.

Ten-year-old Elisa Scarpelli fell ill with cancerous ulcers on her face and neck in September 1932. Doctors bent over backwards to help her, but nothing helped: compresses and ointments were of no use, and surgical attempts to get rid of the ulcers failed.

Yet on May 14, 1933, the day when Gemma was declared Blessed, Elisa felt compelled to ask her for her help. Around eleven o'clock in the morning, Elisa removed the bandages that were covering her ulcers and applied an image of Gemma to her face. "Gemma, look at me and have pity on me; please cure me," she said desperately

Church of St. Gemma Galgani in Rome.

Church of San Michele in Foro, Italy, where Gemma received the Sacrament of Confirmation.

➤ *The entryway of Gemma Galgani's home.*

Crude furnishings in the bedroom of the great saint.

but full of faith and hope. She removed the image, touched her face, looked in the mirror, and screamed in shock: the wounds had healed instantly, and the tumors and lesions had disappeared! Disturbed by her screams, Elisa's mother came running. She saw her daughter completely healed and was speechless!

The miraculous, immediate healing from a disease that doctors couldn't cure was attributed to God Himself and the intercession of the newly Blessed Gemma.

SHE WILL HEAL YOU TOO!

Elisa's healing made a great impression on the residents of Lappano and the surrounding area. So when Maria Scarpelli heard of Elisa's healing, she ran to her father and begged him, "Father, let us ask Bl. Gemma for help. She cured our neighbor Elisa, why wouldn't she heal you too?"

Maria was the only daughter of Natale Scarpelli, a farmer who had been suffering from health problems since 1918. Like Fr. Fabrizi, Natale suffered from varicose veins in his legs. While they were operated on successfully at one point, on April 3, 1935, Natale injured his left leg in an accident. His leg then became covered with blue, painful, festering wounds and ulcers. He couldn't stand the pain, which was increasing day by day, and on May 18, 1935, he finally went to the doctor. The doctor prescribed medication, but unfortunately, it didn't help. The wound and the ulcer also started to spread and grew in size to about nine square centimeters (about three and a half square inches).

Natale was completely unable to walk or work and was confined to his bed. As a result, the Scarpelli family found themselves in a very difficult financial situation. And so Maria Scarpelli decided it was time to ask Blessed Gemma for help. The family obtained relics and began to pray for her intercession for Natale's healing. During these prayers, on May 30, Maria took the relics in her hand and made the sign of the cross over her father's bandaged sores. He grew tired and fell asleep.

The next morning, Natale's leg was healthy. The pain had stopped, and after he removed his bandages, he saw new, pink skin in place of his extensive sores. Natale's legs were still covered with varicose veins, but they didn't cause him severe suffering. The overjoyed farmer immediately got out of bed. From then, he was able to walk normally and return to work.

As a result of these two miracles, Gemma was canonized by Pope Pius XII on May 2, 1940.

HE CONVERTED AND GAVE HIS SOUL TO GOD

We also find spiritual transformations among the many miracles and graces received through the intercession of St. Gemma. The saint is a successful specialist in bringing hardened sinners to God. Although these conversions are often greater miracles than physical healings, they are scientifically immeasurable, and so they are not taken into account during the processes of beatification and canonization.

Medical back brace of St. Gemma Galgani.

Portrait and commemorative inscription on the wall of the house where the visionary died.

Relics of St. Gemma Galgani.

Habit of Gemma Galgani.

Statue of Gemma in the Church of Santa Maria del Pi in Barcelona.

But one of these conversions made a great impression on the pope himself—St. Pius X. Sr. Gesualda of the Holy Spirit recounts this amazing story in her biography of St. Gemma Galgani, *Gemma Galgani: Un fiore di Passione nella citta del Volto Santo* (*A Flower of the Passion in the City of the Holy Face*), which was published before the outbreak of World War II. Sr. Gesualda writes:

> *In 1907, in a hospital in Lucca, there was a sick man who was not only a great sinner but also hostile toward religion and completely devoid of faith. The hospital sisters and Capuchin fathers tried to touch his heart by all means possible, but it was in vain. At last, to avoid scandal, they stopped trying. They could not, however, accept the thought that this soul would be lost, and so one of them decided to summon the saintly parish priest, Fr. Benassini, to come see the sick man. Witnesses of the patient's brutal behavior toward the nuns and Capuchins advised the priest not to expose himself to this kind of treatment, but he did not back down and spoke confidently. Yet the priest's kind words infuriated the patient even more.*
>
> *"I never believed in these lies and threats," he said angrily, "and your Christ, I don't know who He is! What's all this talk about souls, about Heaven, about Hell! Please leave me alone and let no one bore me with this ridiculous talk!"*
>
> *The man even wanted to spit in the priest's face, and Fr. Benassini retreated in sadness. But when he returned home, his eyes fell on* the Life of Gemma, *which he had recently begun to read. The sight of the book revived his hopes: he knelt down and, with tears in his eyes, invoked the Servant of God for help. Then he called for his chaplain and told him to go to the hospital with a woman who was a friend of the patient. And so, around 11:00 p.m. the woman went inside while the priest waited in front of the hospital. Meanwhile, Fr. Benassini prayed fervently in his house.*
>
> *As soon as the sick man saw his acquaintance, something miraculous happened: he asked her to bring him a priest. He then confessed with deep contrition. Tears flowed from the priest's eyes when he raised his hand to absolve the repentant man and give him to Jesus. Then he hurried to fetch the viaticum and holy oils. The patient received these two sacraments, and around 4:00 a.m., he began to die. At last, the repentant sinner gave his soul to God.*

1265–1345

His humility and patience were so great that he was called the second Job.

PATRON SAINT OF CANCER SUFFERERS

St. Peregrine Laziosi

The Italian Servite led a truly holy life, but he is mainly known for the miracle he experienced on his own skin. In Italy, the famous San Pellegrino is almost as popular as St. Rita of Cascia and St. Jude Thaddeus, and he is regarded as a powerful intercessor for people suffering from cancer, AIDS, foot ailments, and other incurable diseases.

Schönbühel. Monastic church of St. Rosalia from 1669. Chapel of St. Peregrine from 1737.

Pilgrimage Church of Maria Langegg. St. Peregrine in the side altar.

The 60-year-old Servite friar had been suffering for some time from a large wound that had formed on his right leg. Apparently, you could see the bone through it, and those who saw this wound would weep in pity. Peregrine's infected leg was swollen and black. It looked gangrenous, and many people thought his days were numbered. It was believed to be cancer. Whether this was indeed the case, we cannot be sure today. The diagnoses of the fourteenth century were quite different from those that modern physicians make. The characteristic feature of this wound was the unbearable stench that accompanied it, as a result of which even his fellow friars avoided him, including those who had to take care of him. Peregrine himself was disgusted by it. The wound was very painful, and the ostracism he received from the other friars—although he understood why—made him very sad. Nevertheless, the illness was extremely uncomfortable, and Peregrine suffered so much that he was called "the second Job." He did not feel sorry for himself, however, enduring this disease as if it were but a slight cold. He accepted "God's will" as an expression of God's extraordinary love, with unchanging, constant serenity, with faith in the words of St. Paul, "strength being made perfect in weakness." Perhaps he also thought of the words "a thorn in the flesh," which wounded the great apostle. He believed with certainty that it was a God-sent trial, proof of God's supernatural love.

STANDING FOR THIRTY YEARS

St. Peregrine's biographer, Nicolò Borghese, gave the probable cause of the wound: severe forms of mortification. One that's especially unimaginable consisted of him never sitting down for thirty years. Day after day and night after night, he did everything standing up. He ate standing up, prayed only slightly kneeling. Only from time to time, when overcome by exhaustion, did he lean against a stone wall or a choir stall. How did he sleep? Of course, he had to sleep every now and then, but he didn't use a bed. Instead, he would lay down on the bare ground. Practicing

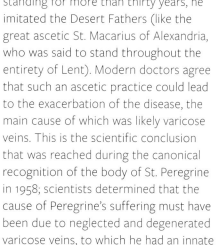

Peregrine was 60 years old when a cancer appeared on his leg. He prayed ardently for healing. Jesus appeared to him and healed him.

Basilica of St. Peregrine in Forlì. (Italian: Basilica di San Pellegrino Laziosi, also known as di Santa Maria dei Servi di Forlì.)

standing for more than thirty years, he imitated the Desert Fathers (like the great ascetic St. Macarius of Alexandria, who was said to stand throughout the entirety of Lent). Modern doctors agree that such an ascetic practice could lead to the exacerbation of the disease, the main cause of which was likely varicose veins. This is the scientific conclusion that was reached during the canonical recognition of the body of St. Peregrine in 1958; scientists determined that the cause of Peregrine's suffering must have been due to neglected and degenerated varicose veins, to which he had an innate

⮝ Gate of St. Peregrine Laziosi in the Vatican.

➤ His liturgical feast day is celebrated on dies natalis (May 1). He is revered as the patron saint of cancer sufferers.

predisposition. The severe mortification imposed by Peregrine, consisting of constantly staying in an upright position, largely contributed to the deterioration of their condition. Due to the lack of proper treatment and emerging bacterial infections, the wound was in a state of constant aggravation and smelled unbearably. Modern physicians were also able to accurately locate it—at the bottom, on the inner part of the right leg. It was found that the friar's feet also suffered as a result of the disease. Looking at them, the researchers determined that Peregrine was forced to only walk on the heel of his right foot and that he suffered additional stiffness because of this. Whatever disease tormented Peregrine—be it a cancerous lesion or just a gangrenous, hard-healing wound—and regardless of what its cause was, the prognosis was very bad. The Servite was in danger of dying.

AN UNUSUAL NIGHT

Most likely in 1325, Dr. Paolo Salazio came to the cell to examine Peregrine. He concluded that the leg couldn't be cured with the medical resources available at that time and that an untreated wound could gradually infect the rest of the body and threaten not only Peregrine's health, but also his life. The diseased leg had to be amputated immediately.

The night before the scheduled surgery, Peregrine prayed for a long time. He thought about what was about to happen, and he was certainly afraid of what lay ahead. Who else could he turn to? All that was left was God Himself. He decided to turn to the Savior. He dragged himself with great difficulty to the monastery chapter house, to the place where there was a fresco depicting the crucified Jesus—the work of the master Giuliano da Rimini.

Once he got there, he began to pray with great faith and hope in God's help:

> *O Redeemer of man, to wash away our sins You willingly submitted Yourself to the torment of the Cross and a bitter death. When You were on earth among Your people, You healed many of them from various diseases: You cleansed the leper, You gave sight to the blind, who said: "Jesus, thou Son of David, have mercy on me." Please Lord, My God, free my leg from this incurable evil, because if You do not do it, it will have to be cut off.*

Despite the unbearable pain, he prayed fervently until finally, exhausted by the battle between soul and body, he fell asleep. That's when he saw him. He saw the Savior coming down from the Cross and leaning over to him. Jesus touched his sick leg, speaking to him and, suddenly—oh, a miracle!—all the pain stopped.

Peregrine woke up and was speechless with surprise. His leg didn't hurt anymore.

He looked at it. It was healthy, as if it were someone else's. The nasty, festering wound was gone; indeed, there was not even the slightest trace that a wound had ever been there. Up to this point, his skin was black and gangrenous, but now it was as bright and healthy as a baby's. Having the images of the dream still in his mind, Peregrine soon came to the conclusion that the extraordinary help he received from the Savior was not a dream at all, but something real. Extremely happy, but at the same time mentally and physically exhausted, the friar returned to his cell and fell asleep. He slept as if he were dead—the way that someone who was kept awake by intense pain for months, for years, night after night, might sleep. When he woke up, he looked at his leg and was probably surprised again to see that it was, indeed, perfectly healthy.

A GREAT MIRACLE

In the morning, the doctor entered Peregrine's cell to perform the amputation. He had the necessary tools and ointments with him. Peregrine, however, told him to return home. He explained that he had already seen a doctor who restored him to health: a doctor who told him that He was the only one who bestows people with good or bad health, who takes care of both their bodies and their souls, the only one who gives sight to the blind, cleanses lepers, heals paralytics, and raises the dead; that He is a doctor who doesn't know what fatigue is, who doesn't know what disgrace is, who for our salvation didn't hesitate to accept the most terrible kind of death. "The One who told me this healed me, doctor," Peregrine said. The doctor was probably convinced that the patient was talking nonsense, trying to avoid a painful procedure at all costs. He wasn't surprised: Amputation is no joke. He would have gladly spared him from it, had he not been convinced of its necessity. "Show me that leg! If I don't cut it off, you'll die," he threatened. "Doctor, heal yourself!" Peregrine replied. "I no longer need your medical expertise; the prince of physicians and the originator of the work of our salvation removed all my weaknesses with His power. Look, let me show you what kind of doctor I had," he said, pointing to the sick limb. Salazio was amazed at what he saw! "Imagine that! I have seen it so many times." He couldn't comprehend what had occurred. "There was a nasty wound here, the shank was black from gangrene ... and now? The leg is clean, healthy. There is no trace of a wound, tumor, or cancer on it."

The doctor also found no sign of any surgical intervention on the leg and came to the only rational conclusion available: *a miracle had happened*. It couldn't be otherwise. "This is something miraculous!" he said to his assistants.

The news of the great miracle performed by God on His faithful servant spread throughout the city like lightning. People glorified God and began to venerate

Albrecht Dürer, Job [and his wife], *Jabach Altarpiece. Nuremberg.*

⮝ *Medal of St. Peregrine.*

⮟ *Siena. Piazza del Campo.*

Peregrine himself. The healed one, with even greater energy, followed the path of the Lord, longing for the joys that God has prepared for those who keep His commandments. Both the healed one and the people who witnessed this extraordinary event were fully aware that it was done by Christ Himself, "the healer of the soul and body" as St. Ignatius of Antioch called Him.

PHILIP BENIZI AND A MARIAN APPARITION

Here's a little bit more about Peregrine. He was born around 1265 (or maybe five years earlier) in Forlì, an Italian town between Ravenna and Florence, to the wealthy and famous Laziosi family. Together with his family and the many wealthy residents of Forlì, he belonged to the Ghibellines, an anti-papal political party. As an eighteen-year-old, he struck in the face the pro-papal Servite Fr. Philip Benizi, who shortly after the bloody clash of the Guelphs with the Ghibellines was seeking forgiveness and reconciliation with the pope, leading to his expulsion from Forlì.

Philip did not repay young Peregrine with the same treatment. Even though he was insulted and beaten, he did not react with anger. He let all insults pass by. He turned the other cheek and prayed for the aggressor and for all those who were after him and who didn't want peace. He gave a great example of Christian conduct: he repaid evil with good and forgiveness. Peregrine was greatly impressed by this conduct. He was moved by Philip's humility, patience, and kindness. He felt guilt and regret immediately. The next day, he caught up with the banished friar, fell on his knees before him, sincerely apologized to him, and begged his forgiveness. The pious Servite

greeted him with love. He forgave him. This played a part in the eventual conversion of St. Peregrine.

According to Borghese, the Marian apparition St. Peregrine later experienced did even more to change his attitude, leading him to choose the path of monastic life, serving God and people.

Peregrine—as Borghese claims—after thinking about what happened and meeting with Fr. Philip Benizi, who despised worldly vanity and saw mortal life as nothing but filth and darkness, began to think about the path he would follow to achieve salvation.

For this reason, he went to the local church and, praying before the image of the Mother of God, begged her to show him the way of salvation. The Blessed Virgin appeared to him and instructed him to travel 120 miles to Siena and join the Order of Servants of Mary—the Servites. He obeyed her command. After spending a few years in Siena, Peregrine returned to Forlì around 1320 and stayed there until the end of his life. He desired to serve and suffer alongside the poor and the afflicted.

MARIAN PENITENT

St. Peregrine's spirituality was characterized by deep Marian devotion, prayerful contemplation, severe penance, and fasting. His inspiration for prayer and contemplation was meditation on God's Word, and he was constantly reading the Bible. The practice of not sitting for more than thirty years, which had disastrous results, was perhaps only one of the many mortifications with which he burdened his body.

Peregrine also led an active life outside the walls of the monastery: he visited the poor and the sick, comforted them, helped them, and converted sinners. Shunning politics, he became "everything to everyone." The residents of Forlì were moved by his generosity during the plague that hit the town in 1323. The Servite was also exceptionally patient and humble. It's been said that he had the ability to miraculously multiply wheat and wine. During his thirty years in the monastery, Peregrine became an example of a truly holy life for everyone—both friars and lay people. He was a good brother to everyone, and most likely—like St. Francis of Assisi—he never became a priest. He died of a fever in holiness in 1345, at the age of 80.

HOLINESS CONFIRMED BY MIRACLES

The sanctity of the friar was confirmed by numerous miracles performed through his intercession. It was thanks to them that, in 1609, Pope V beatified the Italian

The Church of St. Peregrinus in the Vatican.

Relic of St. Peregrine.

Servite, and in 1726, his great devotee, Pope Benedict XIII, proclaimed him a saint.

Borghese mentioned three miracles, noting that he chose them among many.

When the saint's body was still exposed in the monastery choir, representing an "attractive relic" for the poor, a blind beggar appeared at his side. He begged with all his heart to have his eyesight restored, and his prayers were answered. Experiencing an extraordinary grace, he shouted with joy and declared that he could see very well. He thanked God and Peregrine and left happy.

The second miracle involved freeing a Forlì woman possessed by one or more evil spirits. Satan, who took over the woman, made her have superhuman strength—she broke all the shackles and chains she was bound with. Lured by the news of the miracles taking place, the family led the possessed woman to Peregrine's relics in the church. When the woman touched them, the evil spirit came out of her with a "terrifying roar." Before he left, however, he declared that he had been driven out by "the prayers of St. Peregrine." The freed woman thanked God and Peregrine, returning home happy.

The third miraculous healing, described by Borghese, happened to a man who fell from a tree. The man climbed a very tall tree but slipped and fell down. He suffered so much damage to his internal organs that there was no hope of survival for him. He called upon Bl. Peregrine for help and was healed.

▲ *He devoted himself entirely to pastoral work, in silence and solitude.*

➤ *Francesco Antonio Bondi,* Glory of St. Peregrine Laziosi, *plafond in the Basilica of St. Peregrine.*

LEG SPECIALIST

Several miracles (selected from 342 miracles and graces that occurred in Città di Castello, which competed with Forlì as the center of the cult of Peregrine) contributed to the elevation of Peregrine to sainthood. Significantly, all three involved healing diseases of the legs (including two from limb cancer).

Alessandro Baccadori, born in 1690, experienced one of these healings. At the age of 4, Baccadori became a cripple. Three years later, in a church of the Conventual Franciscans near his home, Alessandro prayed for healing to St. Anthony. He hoped the great Franciscan would come to his aid, but his pleadings went unanswered. Looking for another intercessor, one day the boy went to the church of the Servites in Città di Castello and knelt before the altar of Bl. Peregrine. He asked him for the grace of healing that St. Anthony did not obtain for him. He wanted to walk normally. He'd had enough of using crutches. After the prayer, feeling that something strange was happening to him, he threw the crutches in front of the altar and independently—quickly and without any support—returned home. Alessandro's father couldn't believe what he saw. "Dad, dad, my crutches are now with Fr. Peregrine, I gave them to him for safekeeping!" his son exclaimed happily. There were many more miracles similar to this one. They happen to this day, and crowds of pilgrims still come to the most important site of the cult of St. Peregrine: the Basilica of St. Peregrine in Forlì.

Relic of St. Peregrine.

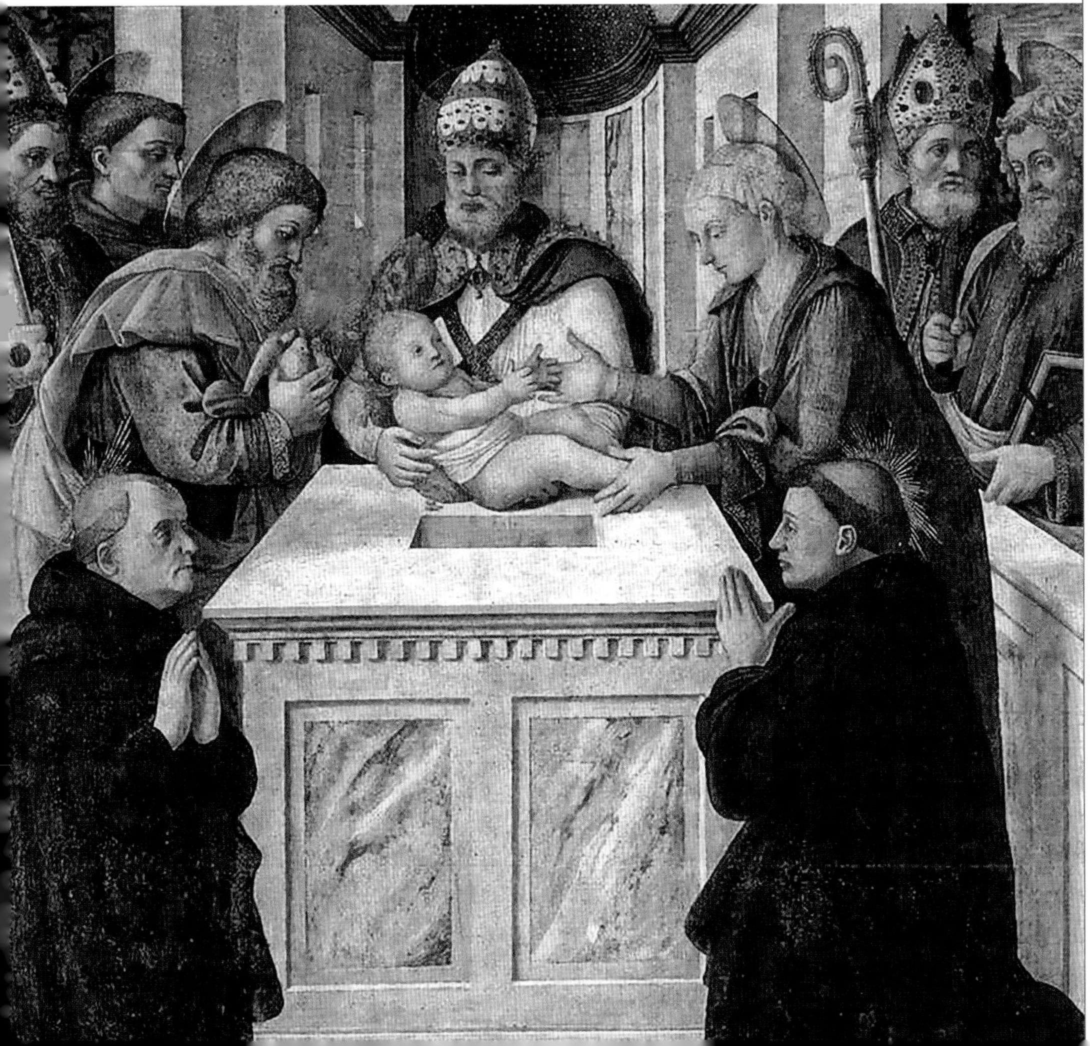

The Presentation in the Temple, *painting by Filippino Lippi (St. Peregrine is on the bottom right).*

1891–1942

➤ *Edith Stein's family home at 38 Nowowiejska Street in Wrocław.*

Edith Stein was born into a Jewish family in the Odrzańskie suburb.

➤ *Portrait of St. Teresa Benedicta of the Cross based on the commonly-called passport photo that was issued when entering the Cologne Carmel around 1938.*

⮝ *St. Teresa Benedicta of the Cross, a contemporary icon from St. Martin Church in Bad Bergzabern.*

PATRONESS OF EUROPE

St. Teresa Benedicta of the Cross

Born Edith Stein, St. Teresa Benedicta of the Cross was a Jewish convert to Catholicism, a doctor of philosophy, a Carmelite nun, and, above all, a tireless seeker of truth. She is one of the Patronesses of Europe and a Doctor of the Church. She offered her life to God three times: as an atonement for the Jewish people's unbelief, for the salvation of Germany, and for peace in the world. She was murdered by the Germans in the Auschwitz concentration camp on August 9, 1942.

"When you look through the prism of faith, you don't see coincidences. Everything has perfect meaning and connection in the face of God" (Edith Stein).

Edith Stein was born on October 12, 1891, on Yom Kippur, the Jewish holiday of penance and atonement for the sins of the nation. She was the eleventh and youngest child of a Jewish merchant family residing in Wrocław (then German Breslau). Her father died before she was two years old. Her mother faithfully followed Jewish religious practices, but Edith abandoned the faith and considered herself a radical atheist at the age of fourteen.

Extremely intelligent and talented, Edith began studying history and psychology at the University of Wrocław in 1911. "My longing for truth was a single prayer," she wrote in her memoirs. Soon after, she moved to Göttingen and became a student of Edmund Husserl, philosopher and founder of phenomenology. It was during her studies that she made friends with the

philosopher Max Scheler, who was the first lecturer to introduce her to the "world of God" and the Catholic Faith.

Edith also began a friendship with Anna Reinach, whose husband died on the front during World War I. She admired the young widow's spiritual strength, calmness, and serenity, as well as her perspectives on death. While for Edith, death was the greatest catastrophe and the final end to life, for the Christian Anna Reinach, it was merely a transitional stage on the way to God. "That was the moment my unbelief collapsed ... and Christ shone forth: Christ in the mystery of the Cross," Edith wrote years later. While perusing Anna's library,

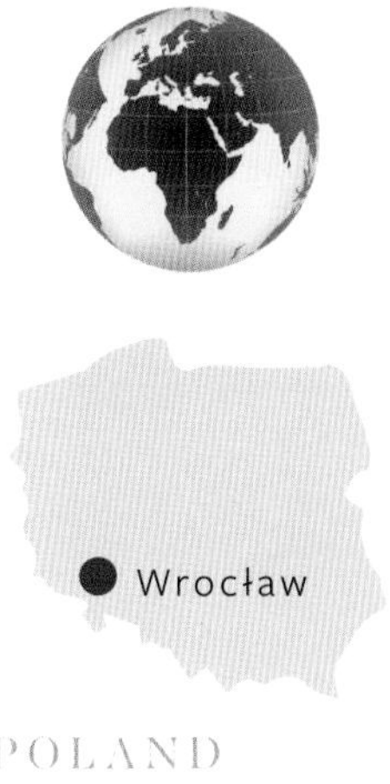

University of Göttingen Library, where Edith Stein studied.

The Great Hall of the University of Göttingen.

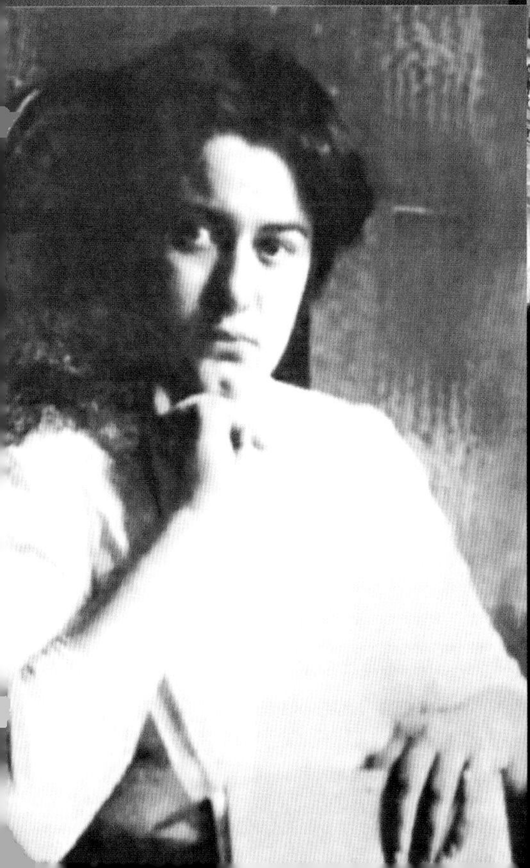

Edith Stein as a student. Wrocław, around 1913.

After defending her thesis with Husserl, Edith Stein met Max Scheler, who introduced her to the "world of God" and the Catholic faith.

The most well-known photo of Edith Stein at the exhibition devoted to her in a museum located in Lubliniec. This town has adopted Edith Stein as its patroness.

On August 2, 1942, Edith Stein and her sister were arrested by the Nazis. After a short stay in transit camps, both Carmelite nuns were transported to the Auschwitz concentration camp and murdered, most likely upon their arrival, on August 9, 1942.

Edith also discovered St. Teresa of Ávila and her famous autobiography, *The Book of My Life*. Edith was so captivated by reading the autobiography that she read it from cover to cover in one night. "This is the truth!" she told herself at dawn.

Thirty days later—after completing a retreat based on the Spiritual Exercises of St. Ignatius—Edith decided to become Catholic. She knew the truth and wanted to be faithful to it. She was baptized on January 1, 1922, and received the Sacrament of Confirmation on February 2. Immediately after her Baptism, she wanted to join the Discalced Carmelites, but her spiritual directors persuaded her to wait, and so she instead devoted herself to pedagogy.

Edith taught, gave lectures, and translated the works of Sts. Thomas Aquinas and John Henry Newman, and in 1932, she became an associate professor at the German Institute for Scientific Pedagogy in Münster. She lost her job, however, as a result of the anti-Jewish decrees of the Nazis. She then had the opportunity to go to South America, but she did not go; and a year later, she joined the Carmelite Order in Cologne, taking the name Teresa Benedicta of the Cross.

In the fall of 1938, Edith, together with her sister Rosa, who had also been baptized and who served as a convent portress in the Cologne Carmel, were moved to Echt in the Netherlands in order to escape the Nazi persecution of Jews in Germany. Nevertheless, she and her sister were arrested by the Nazis on August 2, 1942. After a short stay in transit camps, both Carmelite nuns were transported to the Auschwitz concentration camp and murdered, most likely upon their arrival, on August 9, 1942.

Edith Stein was beatified as a martyr in 1987. In that case, a miracle wasn't required, but it was necessary for her to become a saint. And this miracle happened—in America.

A CHILD IN THE HOSPITAL

Mary Margaret Buman and Emmanuel Charles McCarthy were married in 1966. Fifteen years later, on August 9, 1981, in Damascus, Syria, Patriarch Maximos V Hakim ordained Emmanuel as a Catholic priest of the Melkite rite, which allows for the ordination of married men and married men with children.

In March 1987, the couple went on a week-long trip to Rome. It was their first trip together without children in more than twenty years. They left their twelve children home in Brockton, Massachusetts, located near Boston; the eldest, already adult daughters were to take care of the younger children. While the parents were away, however, the children came down with the flu.

On Friday evening, March 20, 1987, the McCarthys returned home. They had plans to take the children to a conference held by the Needham Peace and Justice Group where Fr. McCarthy was meant to teach on Christian peace and nonviolent conflict resolution. The parents arrived in Brockton around 8 p.m., and they had not even made it to the front door of the house when their children ran out to meet them, informing them that their eldest daughters had just taken two-and-a-half-year-old Teresa Benedicta to the local hospital because she had been behaving strangely and having convulsions.

What had happened? None of Teresa's siblings knew.

SHE HAD SWALLOWED PILLS LIKE CANDY

Young Teresa Benedicta's parents rushed to the hospital. There they learned that their child was severely poisoned. The

The unloading ramp in Auschwitz and entrance gate to the Nazi death camp.

⮝ *A women's striped uniform from the Auschwitz concentration camp. The yellow Star of David is perfectly visible.*

doctors told them that the girl's blood contained sixteen times the lethal dose of acetaminophen, and to make the situation worse, the poisoning occurred probably twenty hours earlier.

Fr. and Mrs. McCarthy didn't understand or realize the seriousness of the situation at first. The doctors' words sounded serious, but their daughter still looked reasonably well, though she was unusually drowsy and had confused-looking eyes. They wondered how Teresa could have consumed so much medicine.

One explanation emerged. While the children had been sick with the flu, they had taken Tylenol, a brand name medicine whose main ingredient is acetaminophen. The box of Tylenol the family had at home contained packets of medicine that were easy to open. The medicine was hidden, but little Teresa must have seen one of the older children reaching for it. Then, secretly, thinking it was candy, she reached for the medicine and ate handfuls of it. Even the smallest overdose of this drug can be deadly, let alone such a huge dose. When Teresa became ill, her siblings thought at first that she, like the others, had succumbed to the flu, but soon she had begun to behave strangely, so they rushed her to the hospital.

HER SITUATION GREW WORSE

While still at the hospital in Brockton, Fr. and Mrs. McCarthy began to pray for their daughter's health, and Fr. McCarthy gave her the Anointing of the Sick. Teresa's doctor realized that the Brockton hospital could not deal with such a serious case,

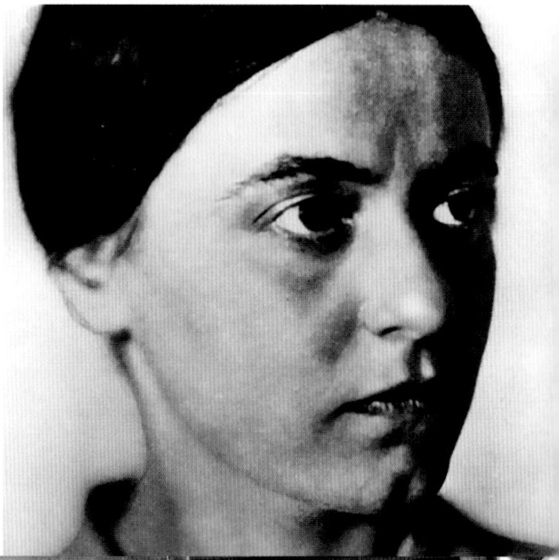

⮞ *The interior of the barracks in Auschwitz. Two-story bunks arranged in rows.*

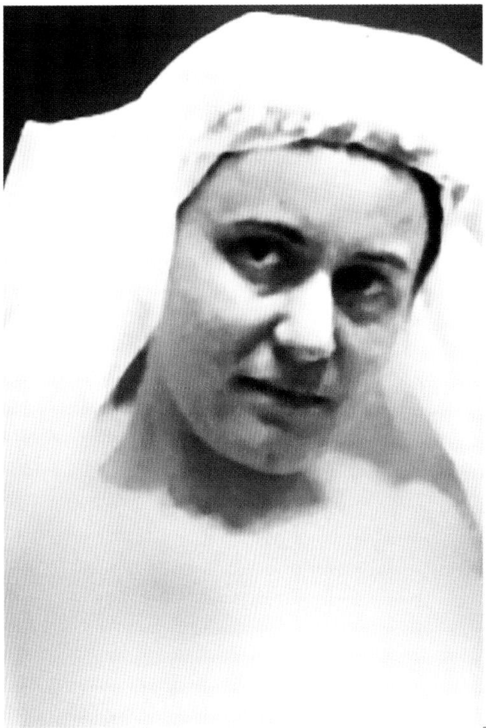

equivalent of not sixteen but nineteen lethal doses of the drug!

The tests were repeated several times during the night, but the results were only getting worse.

A TOUGH DECISION

Saturday morning brought more bad news. Teresa was unconscious. She was motionless, not responding to anything. Her kidneys started failing. The McCarthys brought her favorite teddy bear, and even though she was unconscious, they read Teresa her favorite book and, most importantly, prayed fervently. Next to the child's hospital bed, they placed an icon that they had brought from Rome, and on the bed linens they placed a cross combined with the Star of David, a symbol worn by members of the Edith Stein Guild.

◄ *Edith behind the convent gate at the Carmel.*

▼ *"My longing for truth was a single prayer."*

so he called for an ambulance to take the little girl to Massachusetts General Hospital in Boston, one of the best hospital facilities in the United States.

There was no room for the child's parents in the ambulance, so they had to get to the next hospital on their own. At the time, neither of their cars was working properly, but they somehow made it to Boston in a car with only one working gear. On the way there, they prayed Rosary after Rosary. The rest of the children, who were at home and had been informed of what was happening with their sister, were doing the same thing.

Hour after hour, the condition of the child, who was placed in the intensive care unit, worsened. After further tests, it turned out that Teresa was in critical condition—her liver was five times its normal size, and the results of the examinations done in Brockton had been interpreted too optimistically by doctors. In little Teresa's case, she swallowed the

Selection at the ramp in Auschwitz.

In February 1997, after nine years of tedious and difficult scientific study and investigation, a specially appointed board acknowledged that the healing of Teresa Benedicta McCarthy could not be explained by science. When the decree on the miracle was announced, the road to the canonization of Edith Stein was opened.

On Saturday at 11 p.m., Fr. and Mrs. McCarthy went home to rest. They were exhausted because they had been up for two days straight after a tiring flight from Europe. Meanwhile, they had to make another difficult decision. Fr. McCarthy was meant to leave the next night, March 20, to lead a three-day nonviolence retreat in North Dakota. About eighty people were waiting for him there, and spreading the message of nonviolence was his life mission. "What should I do," he said, struggling with his thoughts. "Should I leave my dying daughter and go? Or stay and be by her side?" The decision was not an easy one, because on the one hand his duties were calling him, and on the other—he wanted to watch over his sick child. He knew, however, that he was unable to help his daughter, and he could pray for her no matter where he was.

Still weighing his options, Fr. McCarthy headed for bed just after midnight. As he approached the bed, he found an open book beside it. He picked the book up to place it back on the bookshelf. But when he looked at the open page, one sentence caught his attention like a glowing neon sign: "Take care of my affairs and I of yours." These were the words Jesus said to the great Spanish Carmelite, St. Teresa of Ávila. He had his answer! "I'll go to North Dakota to do Jesus' business!" he decided.

Little did he know that things were going to get even more complicated. At 3:45 a.m., the hospital called to tell the family that Teresa had developed an additional infection that the doctors had been unable to stop. They were also told that the child's liver could no longer be saved. Fr. and Mrs. McCarthy were terrified.

The phone call had woken them up, and the parents got no more sleep that night. They once again considered Fr. McCarthy's retreat, but they finally decided once and for all that he would go. "You should do it," Mrs. McCarthy said, "because it looks as if something or someone is desperately trying to prevent you from going."

A NECESSARY TRANSPLANT

In the morning, Mary McCarthy drove her husband to the airport and went to the hospital. There, she found Teresa conscious but on a ventilator. She had already been given morphine and muscle relaxants. Half an hour later, Mrs. McCarthy was informed that her daughter's liver was completely destroyed and a transplant was needed. Doctors from the transplant team added that Teresa was first on the waiting list and that they would perform the operation as soon as they could get a suitable organ. The operation was tentatively scheduled for 11 a.m. on Monday, in the hopes that they would find a donor by then.

The doctors, however, were blunt: a liver transplant is a very difficult operation, and the chance of the body accepting the organ was about 50 percent, maybe even less in this case. What's more, even if the body didn't reject the implanted organ, the child would have to struggle with various health problems for the rest of her life. But in Teresa's case, there was no other medical alternative.

PRAYING TO EDITH STEIN

Fr. and Mrs. McCarthy had nothing left to do but pray and wait. They decided that in this difficult moment, they would call upon Edith Stein for help. And so while their daughter was fighting for her life, the McCarthys called all their friends, asking them to join them in prayer for the health of their child through the intercession of Edith Stein. They made dozens of phone calls, and the urgent request for prayers for a toddler girl who was balancing on the edge of life and death spread like wildfire. Fr. McCarthy also shared his prayer request with his retreat group at the end of the retreat.

Why did the parents choose Edith Stein to be their daughter's patron? It's simple—it was her religious name that little Teresa Benedicta carried.

Fr. and Mrs. McCarthy had chosen this name before their daughter had been born. In 1984, three years after his ordination,

Edith Stein.

Edith Stein's father's grave in a Jewish cemetery in Wrocław.

Female prisoners of the Birkenau women's camp.

during a retreat he led as Spiritual Director at the Melkite seminary in Newton, Massachusetts, Fr. McCarthy had become aware of the strange coincidence of the dates of his ordination and the death of Edith Stein, then a little-known handmaid of the Lord. In addition, Fr. McCarthy had already made a commitment to fast for the forty days leading up to August 9 because it was also the anniversary of the American bombing of Nagasaki, Japan, in 1945.

Once he discovered Edith Stein, Fr. McCarthy began to study all of her works and related publications that were translated into English, and he became enraptured with her message of nonviolence. He shared his passion with his wife, and the two were so captivated by the holiness and depth of thought of Sr. Teresa Benedicta of the Cross that they decided their unborn daughter would be named after her.

And so little Teresa was born on August 8 at 8:15 p.m.; in Europe, in Auschwitz, it was 2:15 a.m. on August 9. The delighted parents kept such knowledge close to their hearts as a sign from God.

➤ *A close-up of the monument of St. Teresa Benedicta of the Cross erected in Cologne.*

⮝ *Alois Plum's stained-glass window in the Church of the Heart of Jesus in Kassel. In the adjacent window, there is a portrait of St. Maximilian Kolbe.*

A CANCELED OPERATION

As prayers were being sent to Heaven on Monday morning, something extraordinary happened in the Boston hospital. The transplant team informed Mrs. McCarthy that there was still no liver available, but there were signs indicating that Teresa's liver had started working again. They also said that even if a liver finally did become available, they would cancel the operation.

The girl was disconnected from the devices preparing her for the transplant.

IT WAS A MIRACLE

Teresa still didn't move, and people were beginning to worry if she had suffered some kind of neurological damage. However, on Tuesday night, when her father returned from the retreat, the girl began to move her fingers and toes.

On Wednesday morning, Teresa's doctors reported that there was a high level of creatinine in Teresa's blood, which meant that the girl's kidneys were damaged and only working at 15–20 percent. But the girl's body continued to fight, and by Saturday, her creatinine level dropped to a normal range. Her kidneys were functioning properly again!

What's more, the child's liver returned to a normal size (although earlier the doctors had predicted that it would take up to a year for it to shrink!), and Teresa's body began to operate as a normal three-year-old's. The doctors and nurses were amazed. Some of them stated outright that a miracle had happened. Dr. Ronald E. Kleinman, Teresa's lead physician, was also convinced of the extraordinary nature of this case. Mr. and Mrs. McCarthy had no doubts about it either.

Teresa Benedicta left the hospital on April 5 completely healthy and without any medication. Additional examinations, which she underwent five years later, showed no trace of poisoning.

Yes, it was a miracle! Praise the Lord!

APPROVED MIRACLE

In February 1997, after nine years of tedious and difficult scientific study and investigation, a specially appointed board acknowledged that Teresa's healing could not be explained by science. The decree on the miracle was announced, and the road to the canonization of Edith Stein was opened.

Earlier, the Holy See had had to grant a special dispensation for the healing to be recognized as a canonization miracle, as it had taken place before the beatification of the handmaid of the Lord but after a decree proclaiming "the martyrdom and the heroic virtue" of the nun. Despite these obstacles, however, in 1998, Bl. Teresa Benedicta of the Cross was officially named a saint.

Selection at the Auschwitz-Birkenau ramp.

Daily roll call of female prisoners at Auschwitz-Birkenau.

St. Edith Stein memorial plaque in Prague, Czech Republic.

WHAT HAPPENED AFTER THE MIRACLE

Fr. McCarthy spoke more than thirty-two years after this miracle and less than two months after the death of his wife, Mary. When asked how this event affected their family, whether it changed anything in their lives, he answered: "I don't know. From the beginning, we were a family that took our faith in Jesus as Lord, God, and Savior very seriously. From the day we were married, our family went to Mass every day; and then, until the children left home to go to college or work, we all attended Sunday Mass together. Twelve of our living children (one child died shortly after birth) still attend Sunday Mass with our twenty-two grandchildren, and some still attend Holy Mass daily. Our family life after the miracle kept the same rhythm as before. Of course, the miracle must have had a personal impact on everyone, but I can't say how it affected their life choices."

THE COMB

"And what about Teresa Benedicta McCarthy? Is St. Teresa Benedicta of the Cross still present in her life? Does she have any thoughts about her, or did something in her biography particularly appeal to her?" I asked.

In response, I received an article from Fr. McCarthy written by Teresa for a Catholic women's magazine—one text in which, ten years ago, the now thirty-four-year-old woman, who avoided the media and publicity, revealed the inside story of her relationship with the saint. In this beautiful and uplifting testimony, she wrote about—a comb. She referred to an icon that had hung in her house since childhood

on which, among many other attributes of St. Teresa Benedicta of the Cross, was depicted a comb. It was this detail that caught little Teresa's special attention. She had asked her father what the comb meant, and he replied that it was related to a story from a Nazi camp.

On the way to Auschwitz, Edith Stein had been detained in the German transit camp Westerbork. There, she had shown great calmness and, like an angel, had circulated among mothers who, close to madness and submerged in apathy and despair, had stopped taking care of their own children. The Carmelite took care of their children; she bathed them, combed their hair, fed them, and took care of their other needs. She amazed everyone with her kindness.

For a long time, however, little Teresa could not understand how, in this ocean of misfortunes, it was possible to care about such insignificant matters as combing a child's hair. Where was the heroism here? Was it important for children to die with perfect hair? She finally understood this simple gesture—as she admitted in the aforementioned article—many years later, when she herself fell ill and was unable to care for her body. She was grateful to her sister for washing and combing her hair. She now saw the icon differently and understood the meaning behind Edith Stein's simple action.

Today, Teresa Benedicta McCarthy works in health services, dealing with hospital computers. At least once in her work, she has combed the hair of a seriously ill patient. Teresa has learned empathy and compassion from her patron saint. She understands that what seems insignificant can be of great importance because there is love in such simple gestures, and, as St. Teresa Benedicta of the Cross said, only great love remains.

A monument in front of St. Martin Church in Bad Bergzabern.

A monument of St. Teresa Benedicta of the Cross erected in Cologne.

Church of St. Michael the Archangel in Ołbin, a suburb of Wrocław. Edith Stein, who lived nearby on Nowowiejska Street, visited this church from 1922–1933. Her chapel is located on the left side of the church.

St. Edith Stein Church in Wilkowice.

Queen Hedwig, Aleksander Lesser's engraving.

GODMOTHER OF LITHUANIA

St. Hedwig, Queen of Poland

Hedwig (Jadwiga) was crowned the king of Poland, the only monarch of the land! (The Polish Crown was always appointed king.) She fervently worshipped God as Supreme Lord, and she devotedly served others and her country. She was born in Hungary, but she gave her heart to Poland. When she died at the age of twenty-five, her people already considered her a saint due to the many miracles and graces that God sent through her merciful hands.

Józef Haller (1873–1960), a distinguished Polish general of the famous Blue Army, had a great devotion to Queen Hedwig, whom he considered to be his holy patron even before she was officially beatified. It is to her he turned for help in 1939, when his beloved mother, Olga, fell ill and suffered from paralysis and pneumonia. The general and his wife prayed in their home in Warsaw, begging for Olga to be healed, and then left for Krakow, where she was staying in the hospital. After visiting his mother, the general went to the Wawel Cathedral, where the remains of the queen were kept. There, he prayed before the Black Crucifix, where

Black Crucifix of Queen Hedwig—a wooden figure of Christ spread out on the Cross, from the fourteenth century, property of St. Hedwig Andegaweńska, king of Poland.

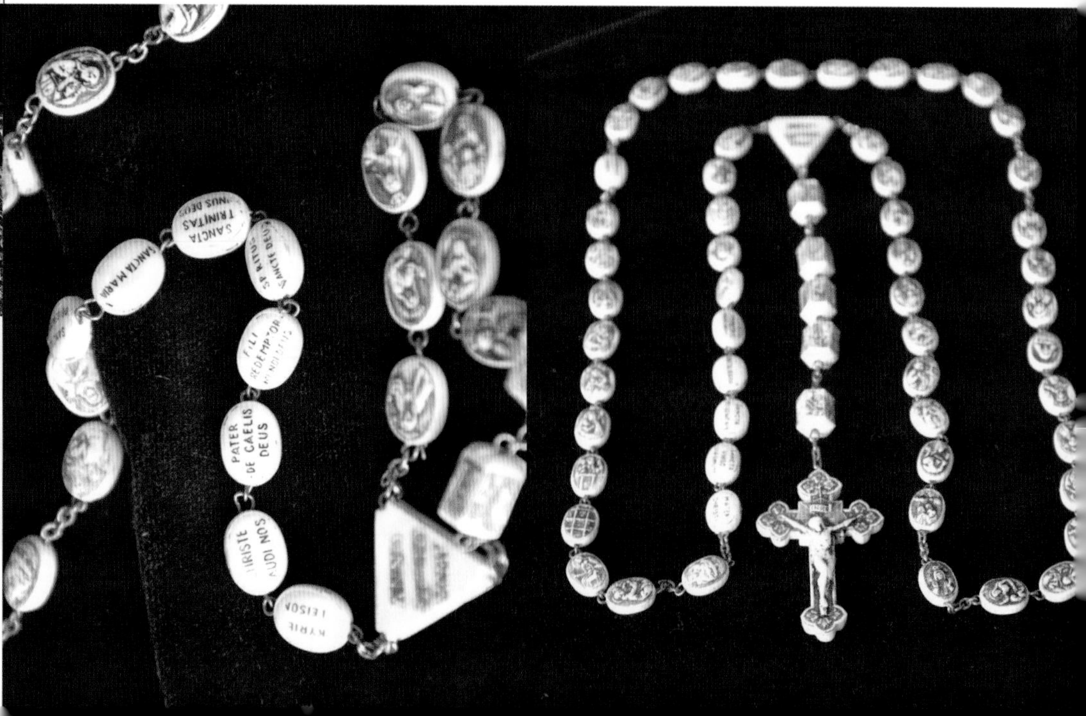

General Haller's rosary from the collection of the Licheń Museum.

St. Hedwig had liked to pray, attended Holy Mass, received Communion, and laid flowers at the foot of the main altar. General Haller begged for mercy for his mother: "Queen Hedwig ... faithful daughter of God ... united with God in prayer ... exemplary royal spouse ... caretaker of the poor ... funder of Churches and monasteries ... Apostle of Christ's Faith ..." After each invocation, he repeated the words "pray for us"—and his prayers were answered.

The next day, to Olga's doctor's surprise, both her paralysis and the accompanying pneumonia were completely gone. The general's miraculously healed mother was able to return home on the same day to Jurczyce, near Krakow.

DO WHAT YOU SEE!

Princess Hedwig (in Polish, Jadwiga) was born in Buda, in Hungary (now part of Budapest), in 1374. She was the third and youngest daughter of Ludwik (Louis I), King of Hungary and Poland, and Elizabeth of Bosnia, his Queen Consort.

At the age of ten, Hedwig moved to Krakow, then the capital of Poland, and was crowned monarch of Poland.

Queen Hedwig was very pious: she participated in Holy Masses and devotions, read the Bible (she especially liked the Book of Psalms), submitted herself to strict fasting, and spent much of her time in prayer, especially before the Black Crucifix of Wawel Cathedral. Day and night she knelt before this wooden Gothic crucifix, entrusting her joys and worries to the Savior, in whose presence she always found solace for her soul. Once, she heard Jesus speak to her. According to old folios, the Crucified Christ "stretched out His hand to Hedwig, as if to bless her, when she prayed before Him," and Christ advised the twelve-year-old Hedwig to marry Jagiełło, the Grand Duke of Lithuania. This marriage would make way for Lithuania to become Christian and unite into one state with Poland, but young Hedwig must have had some reservations. Not only was the Grand Duke twenty-four years older than her, but she had been engaged to William of Habsburg, a young Austrian Duke with

◄ *Józef Męcina-Krzesz,* Queen Hedwig, *Museum of the Warsaw Archdiocese.*

▼ *Władysław Ciesielski*—Baptism of Lithuania.

⮝ *Jan Matejko,* The Baptism of Lithuania (*History of Civilization in Poland, the Jagiellonian Era, the Baptism of Lithuania, 1387 AD*).

whom she had likely been in love! Yet the Crucified, selfless Lord spoke to her: *Fac quod vides*—"Do what you see"—he said. And so the saintly girl took up her cross, died to herself, and married the Duke.

THE WISE AND GOOD RULER

Hedwig's marriage to Jagiełło came as a personal sacrifice, but she agreed to the marriage for the sake of Poland and Christianity. And so the child queen became quickly known as a true statesman who put the good of her country above her own interests.

Thanks to this marriage, Lithuania, which popes, kings, Teutonic Knights, and Orthodox Christians had tried to convert for more than a century, was finally baptized. Jagiełło became one of the most outstanding Polish rulers, "the most Christian prince," and the famous conqueror of the Teutonic Knights, German monks who, under the guise of missionary activity, had committed all sorts of wickedness.

Hedwig, although very young, actively participated in political life. She negotiated for peace and helped to strengthen Poland's reputation in Europe. It was also thanks to her strenuous efforts and the sale of her personal jewelry that the University of Kraków, one of the oldest universities in Europe, was restored, and she and her husband successfully petitioned Pope Boniface IX to sanction the foundation of a faculty of Theology at the school. Their contribution to academia was memorialized in the new name of the school: to this day, it is called Jagiellonian University.

Educated and intelligent, beautiful and good, humble and gentle, the queen cared for the good of the Church and the faithful. She established a college of sixteen psalmists in the cathedral to sing hymns to God day and night. She listened to her people's problems and solved them with love and mercy. She gave money to hospitals and orphanages and cared for the poor. She supported missionaries evangelizing Lithuania and Ruthenia, and she gave generously to the Church.

PILLAR OF THE CHURCH, ANCHOR OF THE WEAK

Unfortunately, Hedwig did not live long. She died on July 17, 1399—a few days after the birth and death of her daughter, Elizabeth Bonifacia—most likely from postpartum infection.

Soon after her death, Hedwig was venerated and honored as a saint among her people. Word spread of her life, deeds, and even miracles performed during her lifetime. According to one story, for example, Hedwig had once thrown her mantle over a drowned man, and he came back to life! As one historical account states, “She was the wealth of the clergy, the dew of the poor, the pillar of the Church, the honor of the nobility, the pious guardian of the people, mother of the poor, refuge of the needy, the guardian of the orphan, the anchor of the weak, the protector of all her subjects ... mirror of purity, humility, and simplicity.”

Although efforts toward her beatification and later canonization began as early as

Portrait of Queen Hedwig Andegaweńska by Marcello Bacciarelli.

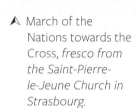

March of the Nations towards the Cross, *fresco from the Saint-Pierre-le-Jeune Church in Strasbourg.*

Founding of the Academy in Krakow, *1361–1399/1400 AD—the seventh painting from the series* History of Civilization in Poland *by Jan Matejko.*

Józef Simmler, Oath of Queen Hedwig.

St. Hedwig Andegaweńska's sarcophagus in the Wawel Cathedral, made by Antoni Madeyski, 1902, in Rome.

Insignia taken from the tomb of Queen Hedwig.

1426, Hedwig was officially beatified by one of her greatest devotees, Pope John Paul II, in 1979. Hedwig was considered Blessed, but for her to be called a saint, a miracle had to happen.

AN EAR INFECTION TURNS SERIOUS

In December 1949, a twenty-six-year-old woman from Warsaw, Anna Rostafiński-Romiszowska, was suffering from tonsillitis, after which her right ear began to hurt. She received penicillin injections at first, but her ear showed no improvement. At the end of July of the following year, her illness worsened, and she developed a serious middle ear infection (acute otitis media). The infection was accompanied by swelling and pain in her ear, dizziness and loss of balance, nausea, malaise, and partial hearing loss.

After several months of unsuccessfully attempting to treat the ear at home and then in a hospital in Warsaw, Anna's condition continued to deteriorate. It was suspected that the infection was spreading to the inner ear, and the doctors feared that it would spread to her bones. Anna was referred to a reputable otolaryngology clinic in Kraków for surgical treatment.

On August 10, 1950, Anna reported to the clinic and was examined by Professor Jan Miodoński, an outstanding specialist and the national consultant in the field of otolaryngology. The doctor acknowledged that Anna should be admitted, but due to the lack of space, she had to wait.

Anna had been intending to attend events in Kraków on August 14 to celebrate the one hundredth anniversary of the birth of her grandfather Jan Rostafiński, a well-known professor of botany at the Jagiellonian University. After the ceremonial Holy Mass, Anna's father told Prelate Rudolf van Roy, the provost of the Collegiate Church of St. Anne at that time, about her problems. The priest, who was a postulator in the beatification process of Queen Hedwig and was spreading her cult, gave Mr. Rostafiński a relic—a piece of the shroud in which Hedwig's remains were wrapped during the transport of her body from her sarcophagus to her coffin in 1949. Fr. van Roy recommended that the sick daughter hold the relic, with faith, to her aching ear. At the same time, a novena was initiated to heal the girl.

Hedwig's relic certainly pleased the father and his daughter because the family had been devoted to her cult for years. Anna and her mother had read Bishop Władysław Bandurski's book *Hedwig, Holy Queen on the Polish Throne* and had used it as a model for behavior; Anna even called the book her "life catechism." Anna prayed and held the relic to her ear, just as she had been instructed.

Anna was finally admitted to the hospital on August 16. The next morning, when she applied the relic to her ear, after months of ineffective treatment, the sick woman felt substantially better. The pain in the ear and beyond the ear disappeared and, what's more, Anna was able to hear well. She told her doctor. Thorough examinations and x-rays revealed that the condition did not go beyond the middle ear, and her hearing had returned to normal. The planned operation was canceled, and Anna was released from the hospital a day later. From then on, she never had any problems with her ear or hearing.

A MIRACLE!

This extraordinary story was revisited forty-four years later, when the Church was seeking a miraculous healing to contribute to the canonization of Queen Hedwig. The Church discovered the story of Anna's illness, and three independent specialists were asked to reexamine the case. Among them was Dr. Adam Miodoński, an outstanding neuroanatomist and laryngologist and professor at the Jagiellonian University Medical College. In an interview with the Kraków journalist Zbiegniew Świechów, Dr. Miodoński reported:

> *As a doctor, I can say that a cure in similar cases can be achieved through careful local treatment, i.e. through frequent cleaning of the external ear canal from secretions accumulating in it along with the perforation site in the eardrum (if possible) with the simultaneous use of antibacterial drugs..., anti-inflammatory and anti-edematous drugs, with simultaneous careful observation of the patient.... However, for general and local symptoms to disappear completely with hearing returning to normal limits, a few weeks must pass.... Therefore, the sudden recovery of Miss Anna Romiszowska, as a believer, I consider it to be a miracle.*

What's more, the professor added that "if we were to encounter a case of a middle ear infection similar in its course to the case of Miss Anna Romiszkowska today, it would also take a few weeks, maybe two or three weeks, to be completely cured. Therefore, even today, an immediate, sudden cure is not possible, as it was in the case of Miss Anna Romiszowska."

Other specialists and Vatican experts had no objections, and the miracle was approved. On June 8, 1997, in Kraków, John Paul II canonized Queen Hedwig.

St. Hedwig's altar from the Church of the Assumption of the Blessed Virgin Mary in Wilno (Vilnius, Lithuania).

Dymitr of Goraj Stops Hedwig from Breaking the Door at Wawel Royal Castle—*painting by Jan Matejko.*

➤ *A modern-day image of John Macías, created based on his relics. The saint in the order served as porter, but over time, thanks to his involvement in helping the poor and sick, he earned the title "Father of the Poor."*

FATHER OF THE POOR

St. John of Rice (Macías)

The Spaniard John Macías (1585–1645) is not widely known. His cult is spread mainly across his native country and Peru, where he died and where his remains are located. He is also venerated by the Dominicans and people associated with the Order of Preachers. It was because of this Dominican friar that one of the strangest miracles in the history of the Church took place. The main character in this story is not a healed person, but a few grains of rice.

It was January 23, 1949. Like every Sunday in the Church of Santa María Magdalena in the town of Olivenza in Extremadura (a region of Spain bordering Portugal), a small meal was being prepared for the local poor and children from a nearby orphanage. While the priest was celebrating Holy Mass in the Church, the cook, Leandra Rebollo Vázquez placed a large ten-liter pot of water on the stove, lit a fire under it, and went to the pantry to get some rice. When she entered, she was speechless. The pantry was empty. Only a handful of rice grains were scattered on

➤ *Convent of Santo Domingo in Lima, where the relics of St. John Macías are kept.*

Church of Santa María Magdalena in Olivenza.

the floor. Most likely, thieves broke into the pantry in the middle of the night, stealing everything there was to eat. In one of the bags, María noticed a hole. She scooped up the grains. Very little was left—less than a kilogram. What was the poor woman supposed to do? With tears in her eyes, she threw the pitiful remains into the large pot. "Blessed John Macías, help! The poor will go without dinner today!" she cried with a sigh to the fellow Spaniard whom she venerated. It didn't take long for the results of this prayer to become apparent.

MANY WELL-FED PEOPLE

After fifteen minutes, the boiling rice began to multiply, until it was pouring out from the large pot. To rescue the situation, the rice was moved into a second smaller eight-liter pot, but after a moment—even without stirring—the rice began to escape once more. María started to look for another dish. The unusual

Castle in Olivenza.

A nineteenth-century lithograph of the Lima Cathedral where the relics of John Macías are kept.

The interior of the Convent of Santo Domingo in Lima.

phenomenon was also witnessed by the parish priest's mother, who helped her in the kitchen, and the seminarian J.V. Ferrer.

The miracle, which supposedly went on for four hours, was extraordinary and incredible. How could this happen? How could 154 people (95 poor people from the city, 17 boys and 42 girls from the orphanage) be fed to fullness on what was originally such a meager portion of uncooked rice? The miracle ended when the pastor Luis Zambrano Blanco arrived in the evening. He came in the company of María Gragera Vargas Zúñiga, headmistress of the Instituto Secular Hogar de Nazaret, a pious charity founded by him in 1935. The priest, seeing what was happening, ordered the pots to be taken off the fire. Only when this was done did the rice stop multiplying.

Starting in 1961, twenty witnesses in connection with the miraculous multiplication event were questioned, and two grains of the aforementioned rice, preserved by witnesses as "relics," were also put under the microscope (these were found to be just ordinary rice). In 1974, this miracle was declared inexplicable and canonically approved, paving the way for the canonization of the Spanish Dominican by Pope Paul VI on September 28, 1975.

GOD OF THE HUNGRY

The rice miracle was written in an issue of *New Scientist* magazine on April 8, 1982. It was also described by the outstanding Italian journalist Vittorio Messori in his column in the the Italian Catholic daily newspaper *Avvenire*. He used it as an example that can help us rediscover Christian materialism, which we usually forget about, to focus on incorporeal spirituality. "We think of the God of the Bible as though He has nothing to do with the body, as if He is merely some abstract Supreme Being like that of the Masons, a Pure Spirit that does not look at the materiality of the body, and whose function is to point out to us noble human values, to give moral guidelines that will lead to universal agreement." Messori argues that the God of the Bible is different—He is a God who heals, "rebuilds jaws and restores the tongue," using "signs that are corporeal, tangible, like the relics whose cults need to be rediscovered as a powerful antidote to the threatening movement of contemporary Gnosticism." In reference to the miracle we are describing, Messori adds that

He is a God who plays a part even in the preparation of meals. He is therefore a God who, through the intercession of his saints, also takes care of the empty bellies of the Spanish peasants, as He once did with bread and fish for five thousand hungry people from Galilee. He is a God of flesh and blood, reconciled in an incomprehensible way with the materiality of our everyday life. We are far from the cold, impassive, moralistic God, the mere guarantor of general values.

There is no better summary.

LOVE GIVEN TO THE POOR

It is also significant that John Macías—a human, who was cheerful and interested not only in the spirit but also in the material—was a simple evangelist. He came from a poor but very religious family in Ribera del Fresno. At the age of 25, he left for South America, where, after years of working in Peru, he joined the Dominicans as a lay brother, not ordained, working in the fields and gardens, looking after animals and serving as the door-keeper for more than twenty years. He loved the Virgin Mary and fervently prayed for the souls in Purgatory.

God noticed that this pious porter from Lima, a friend of St. Martin de Porres, was well known for his great care for the poor, sharing with them everything he had or received and organizing a place for them. Every day he gave out food to about two hundred hungry poor people who came to the gate. It was his love for the poor that was emphasized in the canonization homily by Pope Paul VI:

> *John Macías is an admirable and eloquent witness to evangelical poverty. As a young orphan he used his own shepherd's wages to help other poor shepherds, sharing his faith with them. Inspired by his patron, St. John the Baptist, he emigrated, but he did not go for the sake of riches, as did so many others. He went to carry out God's will. Both as porter and shepherd he quietly lavished his love on the needy, while at the same time he taught them to pray. As a friar, he made his vows an eminent form of love for God and neighbor, for he "wanted only God for himself." In his porter's lodge he combined an intense life of prayer and penance with direct help to others and the distribution of food to large crowds of poor people. He denied himself food to satisfy the hungry.*

◄ *The figure of St. John Macías is dressed in vestments in accordance with the liturgical season.*

▲ Convent of Santo Domingo in Lima, photo from the beginning of the twentieth century.

1874–1949

➤ *St. Laura's father died, leaving a young wife and three children behind. In addition, under passed laws (aimed at the Church and Catholics) all of the family's property was confiscated.*

⮝ *St. Laura Montoya wanted to bring the good news to those who knew almost nothing about Jesus—the Colombian Indians, considered by many to be savages.*

➤ *St. Laura Montoya on a ceramic wall, Jericó, Antioquia, Colombia.*

THE APOSTLE OF COLOMBIA

St. Laura Montoya

Jericó, Antioquia. Those who think this is in the Middle East would be mistaken. The town and department with such names are in Colombia. The first Colombian woman recognized as a saint by the Church was born in Jericó. Sr. Laura Montoya (1874–1949) was a mystic and apostle of the Colombian Indians. One of the people she healed was an anesthesiologist.

Laura Montoya was born into a wealthy religious family. Colombian Catholics, however, did not have an easy life back then. A civil war was raging in the country, and Laura's father, who was a doctor and a merchant—defending faith and homeland—took part in it. When he died, Laura was only two years old. He left behind a young wife and three children. In addition, new laws (aimed at the Church and Catholics) led to the confiscation of all of the family's property.

Forced to wander, the impoverished family had to ask relatives for help. Laura gained enough knowledge to become a teacher at the age of 19. By teaching in many different institutions, she gained a lot of experience and recognition over time. Laura combined work with religious practices. She prayed without ceasing and had mystical experiences and apparitions. At the age of six, she saw God and got to know Him. She believed that every action, if it was to be effective and bear fruit, must be based on a prayerful foundation.

AMONG THE EMBERÁ INDIANS

Over time, she felt a need to bring the good news to those who knew almost nothing about Jesus—the Colombian Indians, considered by many to be savages. For this purpose, in 1914, she founded a

new religious order: the Congregation of the Missionary Sisters of the Immaculate Virgin Mary and Saint Catherine of Siena. Although her mission was not recognized or accepted, Sr. Laura prayed and found five bold, courageous women, burning with love for God, ready to live like the poor inhabitants of the forests and to lead them to God. On May 5, she set off with them to Dabeiba on her great missionary expedition to live among the Emberá Indians and share their fate, preaching to them Christ's truth about salvation. Over time, sisters infected with the missionary charism of Sr. Laura began to arrive, and the hierarchs and secular members of Colombian society—having become convinced how much good they were sowing—began to look at them with a more favorable eye.

DECORATED WITH THE CROSS OF CHRIST

For the last nine years of her life, the ailing Sr. Laura moved around in a wheelchair, but she continued to look after the well-being and development of the community and those under her care. She never lost her sense of humor or humility. When the president of Colombia presented her with the Grand Cross of the Order of Boyacá (the highest civilian decoration in Colombia) for her exceptional service in social work, she laughed that she had become a "knight" and said that the only cross she wanted to wear was the cross of Christ, and that she already wore it.

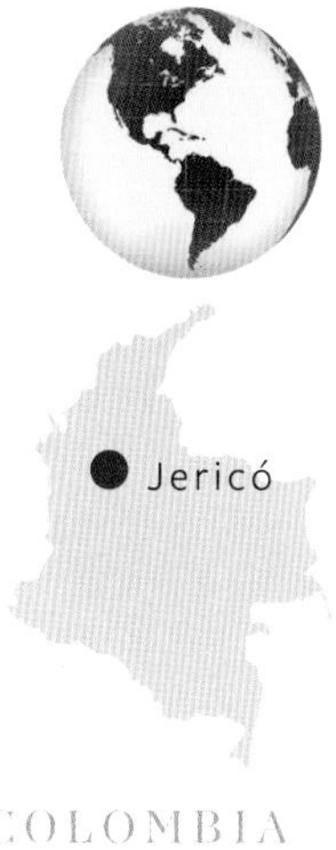

▲ *The religious order founded by Laura Montoya, commonly known as the "Lauritas," spread the faith of Christ in 21 countries in America, Africa, and Europe.*

◄ *Jericó, Antioquia, in Colombia.*

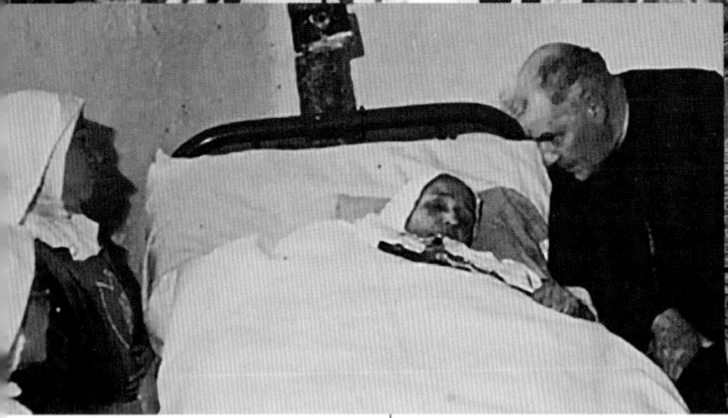

▲ *After a long and serious illness, she died leaving a thriving congregation of 467 sisters working in 90 branches in 3 countries.*

▲ *Mass of Thanksgiving to celebrate the canonization of Laura Montoya in the Cathedral of Medellín.*

After a long and serious illness, she died, leaving behind a thriving congregation of 467 sisters working in 90 branches in 3 countries. The religious order founded by Laura Montoya, commonly known as the "Lauritas," is active to this day, spreading the faith of Christ and sowing good seeds in 21 countries in both the Old World and the New World. It's also worth mentioning that Sr. Laura was a great writer and thinker. She wrote more than 30 books and 2,800 letters. She also wrote poems, and her extensive autobiography *Histories of the Mercies of God in a Soul* is considered a gem of religious literature. Colombian clergymen are making efforts to give her the honorable title of Doctor of the Church. She would then become the fifth woman—after Teresa of Ávila, Catherine of Siena, Thérèse of Lisieux, and Hildegard of Bingen—in this elite group of 37 people.

CANCER LEFT NO TRACE

Fifty-five years after her death, Mother Laura was beatified by St. John Paul II. It became possible after the healing of Herminia Gonzales Trujillo—the mother of one of the Lauritas—was recognized as a miracle. In 1993, the 86-year-old Herminia was diagnosed with cervical cancer. She suffered from severe pain and constant bleeding. In such a serious state, she went to the convent in Belencito. She entered the room where Sr. Laura had died and, during fervent prayer, asked her for help. At that very instant, the pain and bleeding stopped. Three years later, the gynecologist examining her confirmed that there was no trace of the cancer.

A MIRACULOUSLY CURED DOCTOR

A few years later, in 2004, a 33-year-old doctor, Carlos Eduardo Restrepo Garcés, was admitted to the Las Americas Clinic in Medellín, Colombia. He had struggled with a debilitating connective tissue disease since his youth, the effects of which were rheumatoid arthritis and lupus. Year after year, the disease wreaked more and more havoc on Carlos's body. Eventually, he developed polymyositis, a rare disease of the connective tissue that causes chronic inflammation and muscular weakness. Within eight months, the disease left the young doctor disabled and bedridden. He was unable to perform the simplest of tasks. His heart and kidneys suffered.

Experiencing severe chest pain, he took 60 immunosuppression drugs a day and the maximum dose of the opioid painkillers he had been prescribed. On January 13, 2005, he ran a fever and an endoscopy was performed, revealing the cause of the pain and fever. It was esophageal perforation, which led to mediastinitis—a severe, life-threatening condition that develops in the chest area. As a doctor himself, he knew very well that his life was hanging by a thread. Surgery became necessary (and, due to his illnesses, it would have be performed without anesthesia), but the chances of him surviving it were small.

Expecting the worst, Dr. Restrepo received the Sacrament of the Anointing of the Sick. He also said goodbye to his relatives and friends. Being a man of faith, he thought of Bl. Sr. Laura Montoya. Why her? He doesn't know. He didn't know her very well, but due to her recent beatification, the nun was very popular in Colombia. Images of her appeared in many places, and she was even honored on postage stamps. The doctor evoked her image in his imagination and, praying for her intercession, made a deal with her: "Mother Laura, get me out of this, and I promise that I will do everything in my power to raise you to the glory of the altars," he promised. He slept soundly that night.

"The next day, at 7 a.m., the change was immediate," Restrepo later told another doctor—Dr. Jose Ricardo Navarro—in an interview for *InfoSCARE*, an institutional publication aimed at the Colombian Society of Anesthesiology and Resuscitation (SCARE).

> *They told me they stopped all immunosuppressants. On the third day, they confirmed that they would not operate on me and they would protect my stomach from an abscess. After ten days I was still able to walk without autoimmune drugs. Do you understand? Without immunosuppressants! I was even able to take a bath. A month and a half later I was out of the hospital and able to walk. I had a central venous catheter and was taking antibiotics. After twelve hours the fever disappeared and after fifteen days—after follow-up examinations—it turned out that the perforation was already sealed; something that was impossible had happened.*
>
> *On May 2, three months after leaving the hospital, I was performing anesthesia there once again.*

Before he left the hospital, Dr. Restrepo visited the convent—walking on his own two feet, which until then was impossible—to tell the Lauritas about the grace he had received and to thank his blessed savior.

Dr. Restrepo's complete and immediate healing was carefully analyzed and finally approved as a miracle. On this basis, on May 12, 2013, Pope Francis raised the Colombian nun to the dignity of the saints. And Dr. Restrepo, after studying in Canada and England, is an outstanding anesthesiologist who, knowing fully well what suffering and pain is, now helps others cope with it.

Colombian clergymen are making efforts to give her the honorable title of Doctor of the Church. She would then become the fifth woman—after Teresa of Ávila, Catherine of Siena, Thérèse of Lisieux, and Hildegard of Bingen—in this elite group of 37 people.

1894–1941

TWO CROWNS

St. Maximilian Maria Kolbe

St. Maximilian Maria Kolbe, a Polish Franciscan who gave his life for a fellow prisoner, is known all over the world today. From his childhood to his monastic life and until his martyr's death, he was a true warrior of God, a knight in the service of God and the Blessed Virgin Mary—madman of the Immaculate.

He wanted to be "the greatest saint," and that's who he became. He lived in the twentieth century, but his life—following the example of saints from the Middle Ages—was an intricate tapestry interwoven with various miracles and "wonders." Today, from Heaven, he continues to help those who ask him.

He was born in Zduńska Wola, a textile town in central Poland, into a family of weavers. He had four brothers and was baptized with the name Raymond. When he was 10, his mother asked him what he would do with his life. The question troubled the little boy. Two years later, he asked the Mother of God during prayer in the Church of St. Matthew in Pabianice. He had a vision. He saw the Blessed Virgin holding two crowns in her hands—one white (symbolizing purity) and the other red (symbolizing martyrdom). "Which one do you choose?" she asked. He chose both.

Young Maximilian from the time of his studies in Rome.

The home in Zduńska Wola, where Maximilian was born.

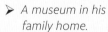

A museum in his family home.

Twelve-year-old Raymond had a vision. He saw the Blessed Virgin holding two crowns in her hands—one white (symbolizing purity) and the other red (symbolizing martyrdom). "Which one do you choose?" She asked. He chose both.

Monumental icon of two crowns. Church of the Sacred Heart of Jesus in Warsaw (Falenica).

▲ *Knight of the Immaculata, a magazine founded by St. Maximilian, is still published today.*

MAXIMILIAN'S FINGER AND WATER FROM LOURDES

Feeling called to religious life, the teenage Mundek (as his parents called him) joined the Franciscans. From the age of 13, he attended the junior seminary of the Conventual Franciscans in Lviv, and then moved to Kraków, where he studied philosophy and theology.

In 1912, already going by Maximilian, he went to Rome to receive a higher education and to become a priest. Two years later, he experienced God's grace firsthand. In a letter to his mother he wrote that he nearly lost a finger on his right hand. He developed something resembling an abscess. The doctor was unable to treat it and finally said that the bone itself was beginning to become infected, and a minor surgical curettage of the bone would be necessary. The rector of the Franciscan college in Rome urged him to use water from Lourdes, telling him a story from when he was a little boy and, thanks to water from Lourdes, he healed his leg and saved himself from surgery. He added that when he miraculously recovered, the doctors were speechless with amazement, and one of them converted and built a church. The young seminarian heeded his superior's advice. He put his finger in the water. "And what happened?" Maximilian later wrote. "The day after, I was told by the surgeon of the hospital that surgery was no longer necessary. After a few medications it was completely healed. Glory be to the Lord God, and also to the Immaculata."

KNIGHTS AND "BULLETS"

In 1917, Maximilian witnessed a large anti-Church demonstration in Rome marking the anniversary of Martin Luther's revolt. The demonstrators waved black flags on which Lucifer stomps upon St. Michael the Archangel; they glorified Satan, attacking the Church, the Mother of God,

➤ *Church in Niepokalanów, devoted to the Blessed Virgin Mary the Immaculate, the Omni-mediatress of All Glories.*

and Christ. The young seminarian from Poland became a fierce enemy of the ideas behind Freemasonry and atheism, but on the other hand he felt sorry for the people lured in by these false doctrines. To help in the battle against the forces of darkness, Maximilian founded the Militia Immaculatae—the Knights of the Immaculata. "To win the whole world for Christ through the Immaculata" was the goal of this newly formed organization, which, like a mustard seed, soon grew into a powerful tree—a network of about four million people around the world today. Following the example of their spiritual master, the Knights of the Immaculata fight the enemies of Christ and the Church with daily prayers, shielding themselves with Miraculous Medals, the design of which is based on Marian apparitions experienced by the French nun Catherine Labouré in the nineteenth century.

In 1918, Br. Maximilian was ordained a priest. A year later, he was back in Poland.

A FINANCIAL MIRACLE

After returning to Kraków, Fr. Kolbe taught at the Higher Theological Seminary of the Archdiocese and, in 1922, started publishing *Knight of the Immaculata.* Then something extraordinary happened—a financial miracle. Fr. Kolbe describes it as follows: "When paying the printing house for the January issue of the *Knight of the Immaculata,* we needed 500 Mp [Polish Mareks, the currency]. That same day, on the altar of the Immaculate Conception of the Blessed Virgin Mary, a letter with the inscription 'For you, the Immaculate' was found and inside the missing amount of 500 Mp. Is it just a coincidence?" There were many times when Fr. Maximilian undertook various works without having money for them. Mary always miraculously provided him with the means he needed.

GIVE HIM FIVE MORE YEARS!

That same year, Fr. Kolbe moved to Grodno, where he had to administer sacraments to the dying Fr. Kusta. The priest confided in him that he would like to live a little longer to finish the construction of the church. Fr. Kolbe knelt down and began to pray aloud, "Mother of God, give him five more years of life, I beg you! And if it can't be otherwise, take my life instead!" The priest recovered, lived another five years, and oversaw the completion of the church.

▲ *Maximilian Kolbe with the monastic fire service in Niepokalanów and at the Royal Castle with President Mościcki.*

▼ *The Small Daily—an authoritative newspaper with a large circulation.*

MAŁY DZIENNIK

Dziś 16 str

Trzecia Rzesza otoczyła naród czeski „opieką"

Tysiące Czechów już w obozach koncentracyjnych

ODWOŁANIE AMBASADORA ANGIELSKIEGO

Nareszcie Francja wyciąga wnioski z wypadk

Możności szybkich decy

▲ *Mary watched over St. Maximilian in a special way in the works he undertook for her glory. The photos show preparations for the trip to Japan and working in the printing house in Niepokalanów.*

▼ *St. Maximilian with the Franciscans in the monastery in Japan.*

A KNIGHT IN SPACE

In 1927, in Teresin near Warsaw, he founded the Niepokalanów monastery, to which he moved his entire thriving publishing house. He became the first guardian of the new monastery.

He made Niepokalanów (the name means "City of the Immaculata") into a great media center. There were times when he would print a million copies of the daily paper that he founded.

Fighting for the cause of God, he was open to every technical innovation that could allow him to reach the widest possible audience with the good news. He was an inventor himself. As a young boy, he built telegraphs and sound-recording devices. He was interested in mathematics, physics, fortifications, and military tactics. He founded a radio station in Niepokalanów and seriously thought about starting a television station as well and planned to establish a film studio. He built a shortwave radio station with the call sign of SP3RN. To deliver magazines to recipients as quickly as possible, he had plans to construct an airport.

To evangelize and convert, he was even willing to fly into space. When he was a seminarian in Rome, he developed plans to build a spaceship—an "ethereoplane." He even sent an article full of mathematical calculations, graphs, and drawings to the Italian scientific journal *Scienza Per Tutti*. It was supposedly a well-thought-out invention. "Every means, every new invention . . . let it be used in the service of evangelization," he would often repeat. Today, his *Knight of the Immaculata* appears in twenty languages around the world.

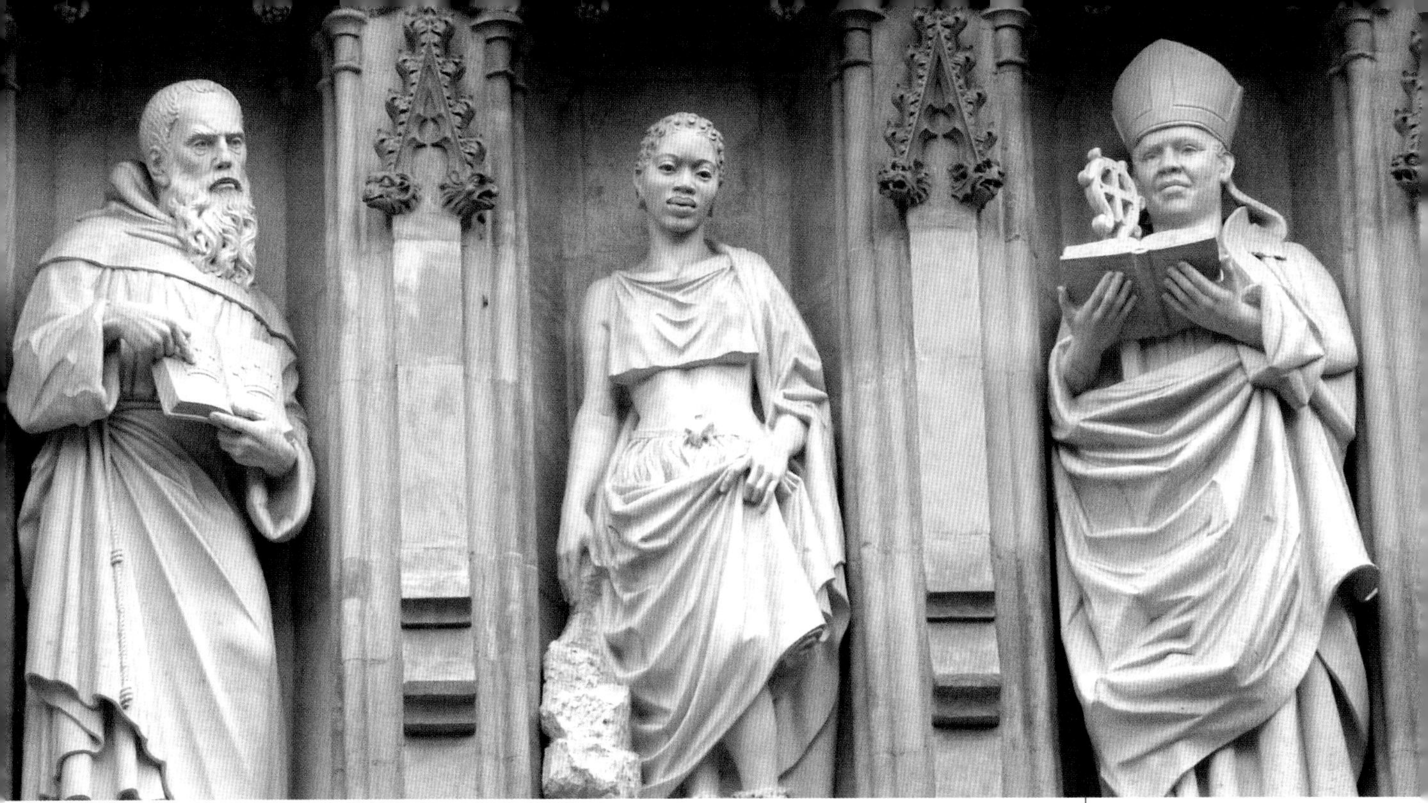

JAPANESE WONDERS

He traveled a lot. One day he was riding a train with several foreign-looking passengers. He wanted to talk to them but couldn't find a common language. When he finally managed to communicate somehow, it turned out they were Japanese and, to his horror, knew nothing about Jesus. Wishing to remedy this, in 1930 he went to Japan, where he founded a monastery in Nagasaki, still in operation today, opened a seminary, and began publishing the *Knight of the Immaculata* in Japanese. Thanks to him, many Japanese people became Catholics. It was in Japan where Fr. Kolbe gained inner certainty that he was guaranteed Heaven. However, he kept the details of this apparition a secret.

One of the missionaries in Japan wondered why Fr. Kolbe built his Japanese Niepokalanów not in the city center but on its outskirts. "You will see that the Immaculate wants to reign here and has chosen the best place for herself," Fr. Kolbe replied. Everything became clear when the atomic bomb was dropped on Nagasaki in 1945. The city center was obliterated in fires hotter than the surface of the sun, while at the monastery, the only damage was a few broken windows. During the explosion, Japanese professor and doctor Paul Nagai was also injured. At that time, he invoked the help of Fr. Maximilian and later testified that he had been healed by him from a severe hemorrhage.

THE IMMACULATE IS THE BEST DOCTOR

One might think that with so many undertakings and so much traveling, Fr. Kolbe enjoyed good health, but nothing could be further from the truth. He held on miraculously, to the astonishment of doctors. He had been suffering from tuberculosis since his youth. Several stays in the sanatorium didn't help much. He was often overcome by fever and had frequent hemorrhages. In 1920, one of his lungs was removed. Although doctors recommended absolute rest, Fr. Kolbe was constantly on the move, working and creating, even when he was forced to lie in bed. "This is clearly an unexplainable

Great martyrs of the Holy Church immortalized on the façade of Westminster Abbey. First on the left: St. Maximilian Kolbe.

The gate of the Auschwitz camp and the cell where St. Maximilian died.

case in the medical field: four-fifths of the lungs are affected by tuberculosis, almost motionless, and a continuous high fever. If he was an ordinary sick person, he would have to lie in bed," said Professor Nagai, who examined him in 1935. Seeing his astonishment, Fr. Kolbe took out a rosary and said he was given strength through the Immaculate. "It seems that some people think I already have one foot in the other world. One foot perhaps, but not the right hand, which is writing to you, or the left hand, which is holding the paper," he joked in a letter to Niepokalanów.

A HEROIC ACT OF LOVE

In 1936, Fr. Kolbe returned to Poland for good, once again becoming the guardian of Niepokalanów. After being arrested by the Germans in 1941, he was imprisoned in Pawiak Prison in Warsaw, and then in the Auschwitz concentration camp. Giving his life for a fellow prisoner—a father of a family—he died on August 14, 1941, finished off with a phenol injection in a starvation cell. His martyrdom was a great heroic act of love for God and neighbor.

"Do not worry about me, mother. Where I am is full of happiness."

The mother of St. Maximilian.

HE CAME TO HIS MOTHER

After his death—in August 1941—Fr. Kolbe appeared to his mother, who was then residing in the convent of the Felician Sisters in Kraków. During the morning prayer she heard a knock on the door, Maria Kolbe wrote in a letter to the Franciscans of Niepokalanów. After a moment she saw her son in a habit. He was smiling and surrounded by light. The woman asked if the Germans had let him go. The figure then crossed the room and approached the window saying, "Do not worry about me, mother. The place I'm in is full of happiness." She understood then that her son was dead, and was informed later that same day of his murder.

SEAMSTRESS FROM SASSARI

The fact that Fr. Maximilian Kolbe was recognized as a martyr and "released" from the need to confirm his holiness with miracles was decided decades later by John Paul II. Until then, to be beatified, the Franciscan needed two miracles attributed to his intercession. Both happened in Italy, eight and nine years after his death.

Angela Testoni, a seamstress from Sassari—the second largest city on the

Italian island of Sardinia—came from a poor but pious family. She lost her mother and sister and had to work hard from a young age. She was 29 when she began to suffer from frequent abdominal pains and would often vomit. After a year and a half of self-treatment, Angela decided to go to the doctor. He suspected peritonitis or some other disease of the digestive system, but he could not determine exactly what was underlying her problems. He prescribed the young woman medication, but there was no improvement. Her abdomen still hurt and the pain grew ever more intense. In 1946, Angelina wanted to go to the seaside. Before going, she underwent further tests. A disturbing diagnosis thwarted her plans: peritonitis, and even worse, tuberculosis of the left lung. Instead of going to the seaside, the woman went to the hospital in Sassari and then to the sanatorium in Bonorva.

After two years of relative peace, Angela found herself in the hospital again. Treatment did not work, and in August 1948, she began to suffer from nearly constant vomiting. It was hard to bear. At the end of 1948, she was referred for another X-ray. Instead of getting better, things only grew worse. It turned out that the tuberculosis was also attacking her intestines. After half a year, the patient couldn't eat or drink. Her condition was considered hopeless, and death was thought to be imminent. The only medications she was prescribed from then on were painkillers. According to the doctors, it was simply too late for any form of treatment: a woman with such advanced pulmonary and intestinal tuberculosis had no chance of survival.

The young seamstress confided in her confessor about her serious health problems. The Franciscan consoled her as best he could and told her to ask God for help through the intercession of God's servant Maximilian Maria Kolbe. The sick woman began to pray, but the Franciscan deemed that she wasn't praying enough. He

St. Maximilian Kolbe died, finished off by executioners, after two weeks spent in the death block of Auschwitz.

➤ *"Every means, every latest invention . . . let it be used in the service of evangelization," he repeated. Today, his work* Knight of the Immaculata *appears in twenty languages around the world.*

⮟ *The façade and interior of the Church of Santa Maria de Belém.*

told her to pray more because he wanted at all costs "to see the miracle with [his] own eyes." And he did. "For a long time, I had kept a picture of God's servant under my pillow," Angela Testoni later reported.

> *I started to call on the servant of God from time to time [for healing], as well as to obey Father Augustin. On July 24, 1949, around noon, Father Picchedda, who had been encouraging me to recite the prayer from the picture kept under the pillow, placed it on my stomach and gave me a blessing. That same afternoon, I became aware that the abdominal pains had disappeared, and I began to feel with certainty that I could now eat without a problem. In fact, the following day I ate several times.*
>
> *In the first few days, out of cautiousness, I followed a diet, but after a week I ate everything. On the night of July 24, I slept soundly for the first time, and after three or four days, I got out of bed. On August 2,*

on my name day, I started helping household members, including in the kitchen. And, on the Feast of the Assumption of the Blessed Virgin Mary, I went to church to attend Holy Mass. I have felt fine ever since.

The healing was sudden, scientifically inexplicable, and—most importantly for the woman—permanent. It was clearly a miracle. In 1970, this was confirmed by all the doctors of the nine-person commission investigating this healing.

Angela Testoni, who the doctors said would die at 36, lived 47 years longer! She probably would have lived even longer if not for the car accident that killed her. The old woman died on September 15, 1996, on the feast of Our Lady of Sorrows, when she was with her friend, returning from the Holy Mass celebrated in the Church of Santa Maria de Belém in Sassari.

The woman loved St. Maximilian with all her heart. She became a model of faith and perseverance in the devotion to the Immaculata for the inhabitants of Sardinia, based on the guidance of the Polish Franciscan martyr.

HEALED ARISTOCRAT

The second person miraculously healed was an Italian aristocrat, the Marquis Francesco Luciani Ranier from the province of Marche. It was 1948 when Francesco, then 50, began to complain of pain in his legs. He was initially diagnosed with arthritis, but in late December 1948, the doctor examining him noticed a small wound on his right foot. The legs swelled, and the wound not only did not want to heal, but—what's worse—it suppurated and became enlarged, and new infection clusters appeared. In the middle of 1950, as a result of progressive necrosis and gangrene, which according to the doctors was due to progressive atherosclerosis, the marquis had his right leg amputated to the knee. The patient's condition still did not improve after the amputation, and it was decided to perform another one. This time, a part of the man's leg was cut off above the knee.

Fr. Angelo Fiori, the guardian of the Monastery of Franciscan Fathers in Penne, soon found out about Ranier's disease. In a letter to the sick man's wife, the friar assured her he would pray for him, and asked the whole family to pray for a healing through the intercession of the Servant of God Maximilian Kolbe. He attached an image of Fr. Kolbe with a prayer to the letter. The married couple began to say it every day, in the morning and in the evening. When Francesco could no longer read, his wife read it and then

He founded a radio station in Niepokalanów and seriously thought about television (he participated in the first television broadcast, which took place in 1938 in Berlin) and [planned to establish] a film studio. He built a short-wave radio station with the call sign of SP3RN. To deliver newspapers to recipients as quickly as possible, he had plans to construct an airport.

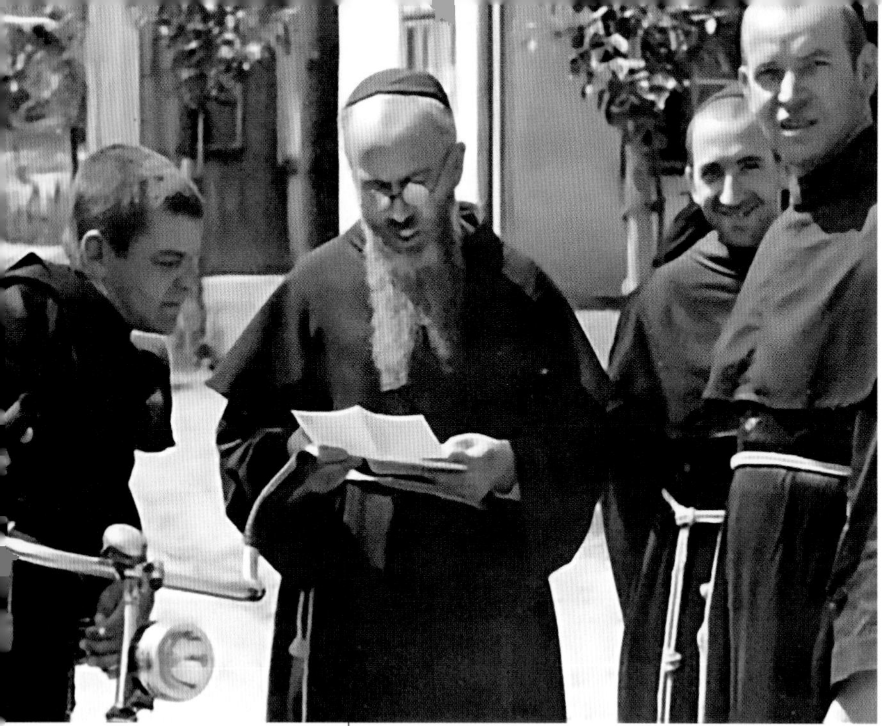

On June 14, 1971, a decree issued by Pope Paul VI was announced approving both miracles attributed to the intercession of Fr. Maximilian. Four months later, the pope beatified him. The fact that Fr. Kolbe is in Heaven was confirmed by John Paul II in 1982, [when he] officially recognized him as a saint.

placed the picture under the pillow on which the sick man was lying.

A few days after the second amputation, Ranier developed a high fever, complained of a loss of feeling in his left arm, became delirious, and lost consciousness. Soon after, he stopped recognizing those closest to him. He feverishly ranted, moving his hands as if he were conducting an orchestra. The doctor's diagnosis sounded like a death sentence: sepsis. Today this word still evokes fear, let alone in the 1950s. It became clear to both the doctors and the family that the sick man was dying, that he would live only a few more days, maybe a week at most.

And then Fr. Fiori stepped in again. Upon hearing the condition of the Marquis was critical, he initiated in his monastery a *triduum* of prayers for his healing. Although the family also stormed Heaven with prayers, they transported the dying man just in case to Porto San Giorgio, where the family tomb was located. "In Porto San Giorgio, in the sick man's room, the Holy Rosary was recited every evening. I also saw in this room a picture of Father Maximilian M. Kolbe, to whom my mother entrusted herself," Francesco's son later reported.

On the afternoon of August 4, 1950, the doctors caring for the man stated that the sick man had only a few hours left to live. "That evening, when we gathered for the rosary, my mother read a prayer to Fr. Maximilian," recounted the son of the sick man. "The picture of the Servant of God caught my special attention that evening because I was present when it was placed under the sick man's pillow. It was about 9:00 or 9:30 in the evening. Then we went to bed and my mother stayed to watch over my father. The medical prognosis turned out to be poor." The hours passed and the marquis was still alive and still struggling with death. His body was not giving up. On the morning of August 5, the sick man's condition improved slightly, only to deteriorate again in the evening. A doctor—Francesco's son-in-law—was called in to give a sedative injection. After the injection, the patient calmed down. That night turned out to be life-changing. We can imagine the astonishment on the faces of the family members—and also the doctors—when, the following morning, Francesco Ranier was healthy. He was calm and fully conscious. He sat on the bed, ate the breakfast given to him with a ravenous appetite, and then stated that he felt well. He was seated in an armchair, at his request. The two attending physicians, though both atheists, agreed that the "healing seemed to be a miracle." "I don't believe in saints much, but someone very powerful had to intervene in this case," one of them said. The miracle was evident, but it still had to be confirmed by medical consultants and a theological commission. And that's what happened. During the process of certifying this healing, which took place in 1964, Francesco Ranier also spoke: "I believe, since the moment of healing, that I received a miracle through the intercession of the Servant of God, Maximilian Kolbe. That's why I received

Holy Communion in thanksgiving the next day. My condition now is completely normal. I sleep well, I eat better, I don't complain about any pain."

On June 14, 1971, a decree issued by Pope Paul VI was announced approving both miracles attributed to the intercession of Father Maximilian. Four months later, the pope beatified him. The fact that Father Kolbe is in Heaven was confirmed by John Paul II in 1982, when he officially recognized him as a saint.

For us Catholics, the recommendations directed to us by this great saint are still valid:

Do not miss any opportunity to further the Kingdom of the Immaculata in souls, and through that, the Kingdom of the Heart of Jesus: with your pen, your words, your example, with suffering, with humiliations.

Let each person consider his environment of relatives, friends, colleagues, the place of residence, as the territory of his mission to win hearts over to the Immaculate, and use all influences and abilities for this purpose.

For us Catholics, the recommendations directed to us by this great saint are still valid: "Do not miss any opportunity to further the Kingdom of the Immaculata in souls, and through that, the Kingdom of the Heart of Jesus: with your pen, your words, your example, with suffering, with humiliations, etc." "Let each person consider their environment of relatives, friends, colleagues, the place of residence, as the territory of their mission to win [hearts] over to the Immaculate, and use all influences and abilities for this purpose."

Personal items used by St. Maximilian.

Monument of St. Maximilian Kolbe in front of the basilica in Niepokalanów.

➤ St. John the Evangelist *by Peter Paul Rubens.*

➤ St. John the Evangelist. *Orthodox icon.*

Miraculous Resurrectors

Resurrecting the dead, alongside healing the sick, cleansing lepers, and casting out evil spirits, was among the commands the Lord Jesus gave to the twelve apostles when He sent them on missions. The Savior Himself performed at least three resurrections: of Lazarus of Bethany, already lying in the tomb; of the son of the widow of Naim, carried on the stretcher; and of the daughter of Jairus, the synagogue supervisor, who had been considered dead. The gift of raising the dead was bestowed by God on the first apostles and many saints of the Church.

The Apostle Peter, the first pope, who had been present when Jesus resurrected the daughter of Jairus, resurrected a disciple named Tabitha, which means Gazelle, in Joppa. She did much good and gave generous alms. "About that time she became sick and died, and her body was washed and placed in an upstairs room. Lydda was near Joppa; so when the disciples heard that Peter was in Lydda, they sent two men to him and urged him, "Please come at once!" Peter went with them, and when he arrived he was taken upstairs to the room. All the widows stood around him, crying and showing him the robes and other clothing that Dorcas had made while she was still with them. Peter sent them all out of the room, then got down on his knees and prayed. Turning toward the dead woman, he said, "Tabitha, get up." She opened her eyes, and seeing Peter, she sat up. He took her by the hand and helped her to her feet. Then he called for the believers, especially the widows, and presented her to them alive. This became known all over Joppa, and many people believed in the

➤ St. Peter *by Peter Paul Rubens.*

Lord (Acts 9:37–42). In the New Testament, we can also find the miracle of resurrection performed by the "Apostle of the Nations," St. Paul, who was not one of the Twelve. It happened during his apostolic seven-day stay in Troas when he met with his brothers in faith on Sunday for the "breaking of bread" and then spoke to them all night long. "There were many lamps in the upstairs room where we were meeting."

Seated in a window was a young man named Eutychus, who was sinking into a deep sleep as Paul talked on and on. When he was sound asleep, he fell to the ground from the third story and was picked up dead. Paul went down, threw himself on the young man, and put his arms around him. "Don't be alarmed," he said. "He's alive!" Then he went upstairs again and broke bread and ate. After talking until daylight, he left. The people took the young man home alive and were greatly comforted (Acts 20:8–12).

The youngest, beloved disciple of Jesus, the apostle and evangelist St. John, also raised the dead. He spent the last years of his life in Ephesus. One legend recounts how on one occasion idolaters dragged him to the local temple of Diana (Artemis), forcing him to make an offering to her. John stated that he would make such an offering on the condition that they, having called upon the name of Diana, would tear down the church of Christ. However, he demanded that they would believe in Christ if he, by God's power, would tear down the temple of the pagan goddess. The pagans agreed to this. After John's prayer, the pagan temple fell apart until only its foundations remained, and the statue of Diana crumbled into tiny pieces. However, the priest Aristodemus started another riot, demanding that the apostle drink poison and survive to confirm that Christ is truly God. In front of the apostle, and in the presence of the proconsul, two convicts were killed with this poison. John took the

St. John the Evangelist, *painted by El Greco.*

Bad Säckingen, St. Fridolin of Säckingen with Resurrected Ursus, *a sculpture on the pediment of the church.*

⮝ *Fridolin heard a voice telling him to go to the grave of Ursus in Glarus and call him as a witness. The opposing party, Landolf, must have been very surprised when Fridolin appeared in court accompanied by his deceased brother.*

cup, made the sign of the cross, and drank all of it. As expected, it did him no harm, and all who saw this began to praise God. All except Aristodemus, who demanded another miracle: the resurrection of the two convicts who had been killed by the poison. The apostle then gave him his cloak to lay it on the dead, in his name and the name of Christ. When the convicts were resurrected in the name of Jesus, the pagan priest and proconsul finally believed. They and their families were baptized, and they built a church in honor of St. John.

THEY WERE RESURRECTED TO TESTIFY TO THE TRUTH

Three very similar resurrections were made by saints: Fridolin, Stanislaus, and Anthony. In all of these cases, resurrected people were to testify to the truth. St. Fridolin of Säckingen (who died in 538) was, according to tradition, an Irish Benedictine monk and a missionary.

He was born into a wealthy family from Ireland, and having given his wealth to the Church and the poor, he devoted himself to preaching the gospel in Ireland and France, and eventually became the apostle of the Upper Rhine (Upper Baden in present-day Germany). He also probably reached Switzerland, where he converted two knights—brothers Ursus and Landolf—to Christianity. Ursus died childless. Before his death, he donated a large fortune and a piece of land situated in the canton of Glarus to Fridolin. However, when it came to executing Ursus's last will, Landolf, although he had previously agreed to it, refused to recognize its validity. The case went to court in Rankweil. Unfortunately, Fridolin had no witnesses to confirm the validity of his claims. Not knowing what to do or how to defend his right to the property, which was, after all, the property of the Church, he knelt on a stone in the Gastra forest and began to pray. Strangely, the stone then began to melt under his knees and elbows (this stone, with matching indentations, today is situated in the chapel of the basilica in Rankweil). Then Fridolin heard a voice telling him to go to the tomb of Ursus in Glarus and call him as a witness. The resurrected man confessed the truth, and the ashamed Landolf not only recognized the legitimacy of the last will but also gave Fridolin his own property. After visiting the court, Fridolin escorted Ursus back to his resting place. To this day, in many paintings and sculptures, Fridolin is depicted in the company of a friendly skeleton.

More than five hundred years later, a similar case was recorded in Poland, where in 1074 Bishop St. Stanislaus of Szczepanów (1040–1079) reportedly resurrected the knight Piotr Strzemieńczyk of Janiszewo (Piotrowin) to testify for him before the royal tribunal. This case was about confirming the bishop's acquisition of a certain village. The truth was also attested to by a certain murdered aristocrat whose corpse was placed in the Lisbon garden of Martin, the father of St. Anthony of Padua. Because the murdered man, who had been resurrected by the saint, himself testified to the innocence of the accused Martin, the latter was cleared of the charge of murder (more on this miracle on pp. 189–190). Anthony of Padua himself reportedly performed at least a dozen resurrections.

BROUGHT BACK TO LIFE TO BE RECONCILED WITH GOD

St. Malachy of Armagh, St. Francis of Assisi, and St. Philip Neri raised the dead so that they could be reconciled with God before they died again. Known for the papal prophecies attributed to him, Irish prophet and bishop St. Malachy of Armagh (1094–1148) was for some time the Benedictine abbot of Bangor (now North Down in Northern Ireland).

The story of the resurrection that was described by the Polish hagiographer Father Piotr Skarga, quoting St. Bernard of Clairvaux, happened during that period.

> *The woman, while dying not far from the Bangor Monastery, asked him to give her the holy oil, and he, having visited her, postponed it until the next day, because everyone thought that it was already evening. At night, the woman died. Malachy came, complaining of himself that she had died without the holy oil, and raising his hands to Heaven, he said: "Lord, I have done foolishly, I have sinned, I have postponed it, not the one who wished to receive it." He then declared before all that he would not rest, and that he would return to her and pray all night, with his disciples saying the psalms. In the morning, the Lord God heard him. The dead woman opened her eyes and, scratching her head, sat down on the bed. Seeing Malachy, she piously greeted him. The weeping turned into joy and great admiration. Malachy gave her the holy oil, knowing that in this sacrament sins are forgiven and that praying with faith saves the sinner. The woman recovered and lived a little longer. Having fulfilled the penance given by Malachy, she fell asleep in the Lord.*

A slightly different story happened in the life of St. Francis of Assisi. Among the several miraculous resurrections performed by God "for the sake of the merits" of this saint was the resurrection of a woman, "noble by birth, and even nobler by virtue," from the town of Montemarano near Benevento.

"This woman," wrote Thomas of Celano, "had a special devotion to St. Francis and offered him her reverent service. She fell gravely ill and, having reached the end, shared the fate of all mortal beings. She died around sunset. The funeral was postponed until the next day so that a large number of people dear to her could gather."

At night the priests came to sing exequies and eve along with psalms. A cluster of people of both sexes stood around, praying.

> *Suddenly, in front of everyone, a woman got up on the bed and called out to one of the priests present, her godfather, saying: "Father, I want to confess, hear my sin! For*

Statue of St. Malachy.

St. Francis. Fragment of the painting St. John the Evangelist and St. Francis *by El Greco.*

St. Malachy of Armagh.

I have died and was destined for a heavy prison because I have never confessed the sin that I will now confess to you. But St. Francis, whom I have always venerated as much as possible, asked that I be allowed to return now to my body, and after confessing the sin I would earn forgiveness. And, having revealed it to you, before all those witnesses, I shall hasten to the promised eternal rest." Thus, trembling, before a trembling priest, she confessed, received absolution, peacefully went to bed, and happily died.

➤ *Stained-glass window depicting the life of St. Francis de Sales.*

Fabrizio de' Massimi had been a regular penitent and good friend of St. Philip Neri for many years. With his first wife Lavinia de Rustici, he already had five daughters, and when she was about to give birth again, Fabrizio went to Philip to ask him to pray for his wife. The founder of the Oratory then predicted that this time she would give him a son, and asked him to name him Paolo. Of course, it happened just as Philip had predicted. Paolo then became the saint's favorite student and a good and very pious boy.

On January 10, 1583, the boy, then 14, became seriously ill with malaria. Lavinia had passed away a few years before. He was running a high fever nonstop for sixty-five days, and Philip, along with other fathers, visited him every day. When the boy was on the verge of dying on March 16, they sent for the saint so he could arrive as soon as possible if he wanted to see him still alive. Unfortunately, upon arriving at the Roman church of St. Jerome, the messenger found Philip celebrating Mass and decided that he could not disturb him. Meanwhile, the boy died after receiving the Sacrament of Anointing of the Sick, which was administered to him by a priest from his parish. Philip arrived half an hour after the servants had already prepared to wash Paolo's body and wrap it in a sheet. Philip then entered the room where the dead body was, and throwing himself on the edge of the bed, "prayed for seven or eight minutes with the usual palpitation of his heart and trembling of his body. He then took some holy water and sprinkled the boy's face, and put a little into his mouth." After this he "breathed in his face," as described by Pietro Giacomo Bacci, "laid his hand upon his forehead, and called twice with a loud and sonorous voice: 'Paolo, Paolo!' upon which the youth, as if awakening from a deep sleep, immediately opened his eyes and said, in reply to Philip's call, 'Father!' and immediately added, 'I forgot to mention a sin, so I should like to go to confession.'" Philip asked everyone to leave the room, put the crucifix in the boy's hand, heard his Confession, and then gave him absolution. Then, after the return of the household members, the saint talked to Paolo for about half an hour about his deceased relatives, his mother and his sister Julia. At the time, the boy seemed to be "in perfect health." The saint knew, however,

⮟ *Herm with the skull of St. Martin, Basilica of St. Martin in Tours.*

St. Margaret of Hungary is also famous for miraculous resurrections.

Celebration of the feast of St. Rose in her hometown of Viterbo.

that this was just temporary, and after some time asked Paolo if he was ready to die. "Yes, I will gladly do so, especially since I will then be able to see my mother and sister in Heaven," the young boy replied. Philip then blessed him. "Go then, be blessed and pray to God for me," he said, and immediately after these words, "with a calm face and without the slightest movement, Paolo died in Philip's arms." Evidence of this miracle, as Father John Pabis noted, is that the room in which it happened was turned into a chapel.

THERE WERE MANY RESURRECTORS

The resurrections attributed to the intercession of St. Martin of Tours called *trium mortuorum suscitator magnificus*, or "the great resurrector of the three dead," are particularly famous. One of them involved a catechumen, who was being prepared by him for Baptism. The saint took the catechumen's dead body to his cell and did what the biblical prophets Elijah and Elisha used to do in such cases: he stretched over his "dead limbs" and, praying fervently, breathed new life into the dead body. While living in Liguge, in a similar manner Martin resurrected a man who had hanged himself. Later, when he was already a bishop, near Chartres he resurrected a young boy at the plea of his distraught mother. Martin prayed for this miracle with the boy in his arms in the middle of a field in the presence of a huge crowd of pagans, which resulted in many conversions.

Many resurrections (mainly of drowned people) were reportedly performed by Polish saints: St. John Cantius (he was credited with twenty-six resurrections) and St. Hyacinth of Poland (at least fifty were mentioned, and one was even included in the Bull of Canonization).

Among the greatest resurrectors is undoubtedly the bishop of Geneva, St. Francis de Sales. He has been credited with as many as thirty-seven resurrections!

Among the evident miracles that made Francis de Sales a saint was the resurrection of the teenager Jerome Genin, who, having drowned in a stream, was already lying in a coffin and had even begun to "stink," and another drowned person, a nine-year-old girl named Françoise de Pesse.

Legends describing the life and miracles of St. Nicholas of Myra mention a great many resurrections. One of the most incredible was the resurrection of three boys (or students) bestially murdered by a butcher (or innkeeper). The bishop of Myra was also famous for resurrecting a man killed by a cart, a child who died in a fire, and an infant who was boiled alive while bathing by an irresponsible mother who, having forgotten about him, went to the church to attend the episcopal consecration of St. Nicholas.

An unusually spectacular resurrection was performed through the intercession of St. Elizabeth of Hungary. A girl who had been dead for more than thirty days, the daughter of a Hungarian couple from Esztergom who had traveled with her body to the tomb of St. Elizabeth in Germany, was healed even before they reached Marburg.

An English woman, a great venerator of the Hungarian princess, was also resurrected at the tomb of St. Elizabeth. In Cologne, on the other hand, a man who had been hanged and already declared dead was resurrected thanks to prayers through the intercession of this saint. St. Elizabeth's relative, St. Margaret of Hungary, is also famous for her miraculous resurrections.

An Italian saint, St. Rose of Viterbo (1235–1252) died when she was only seventeen years old. She led a life of penance, suffering, and self-mortification for sinners. She was a Franciscan nun from the Third Order. When she was just three years old and was praying in the morning in front of the home statue of the Mother of God, her mother informed her that her aunt Maria had died. "Mom, why are you crying? Didn't you tell me that Jesus raised the son of the widow of Naim? Didn't He raise Lazarus, who had been dead for four days? Why would Jesus, who listened to the mother and sisters of Lazarus, be deaf to our pleas? Surely He will listen to us too, if we pray fervently here," Rose said, and then went to her aunt's house and prayed for a miracle. The relative, who had been considered dead for many hours, came back to life!

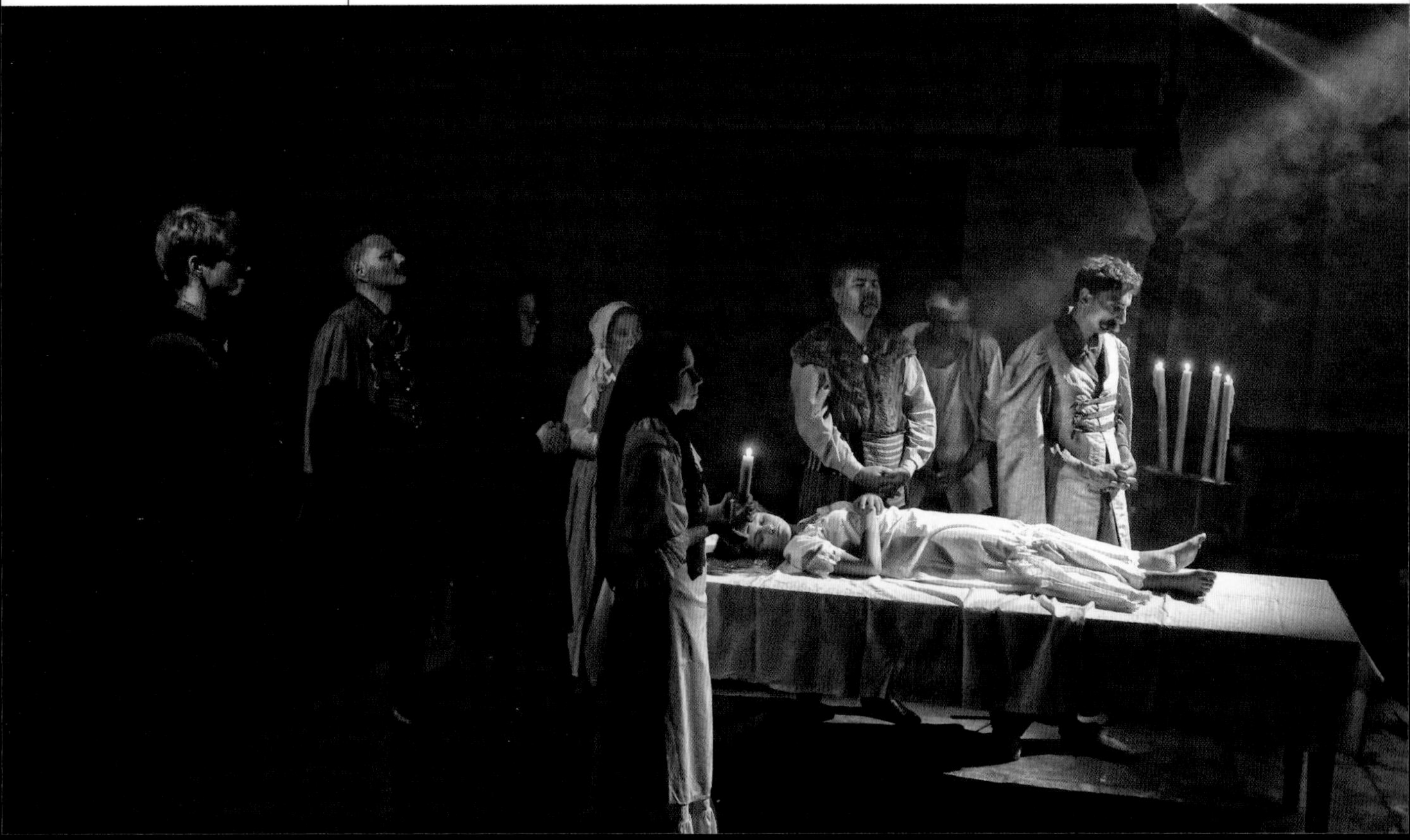

Film depicting a reenactment of Stanislaus Papczyński's resurrection of the daughter of Mrs. Raciborska at the altar in the cenacle in Góra Kalwaria.

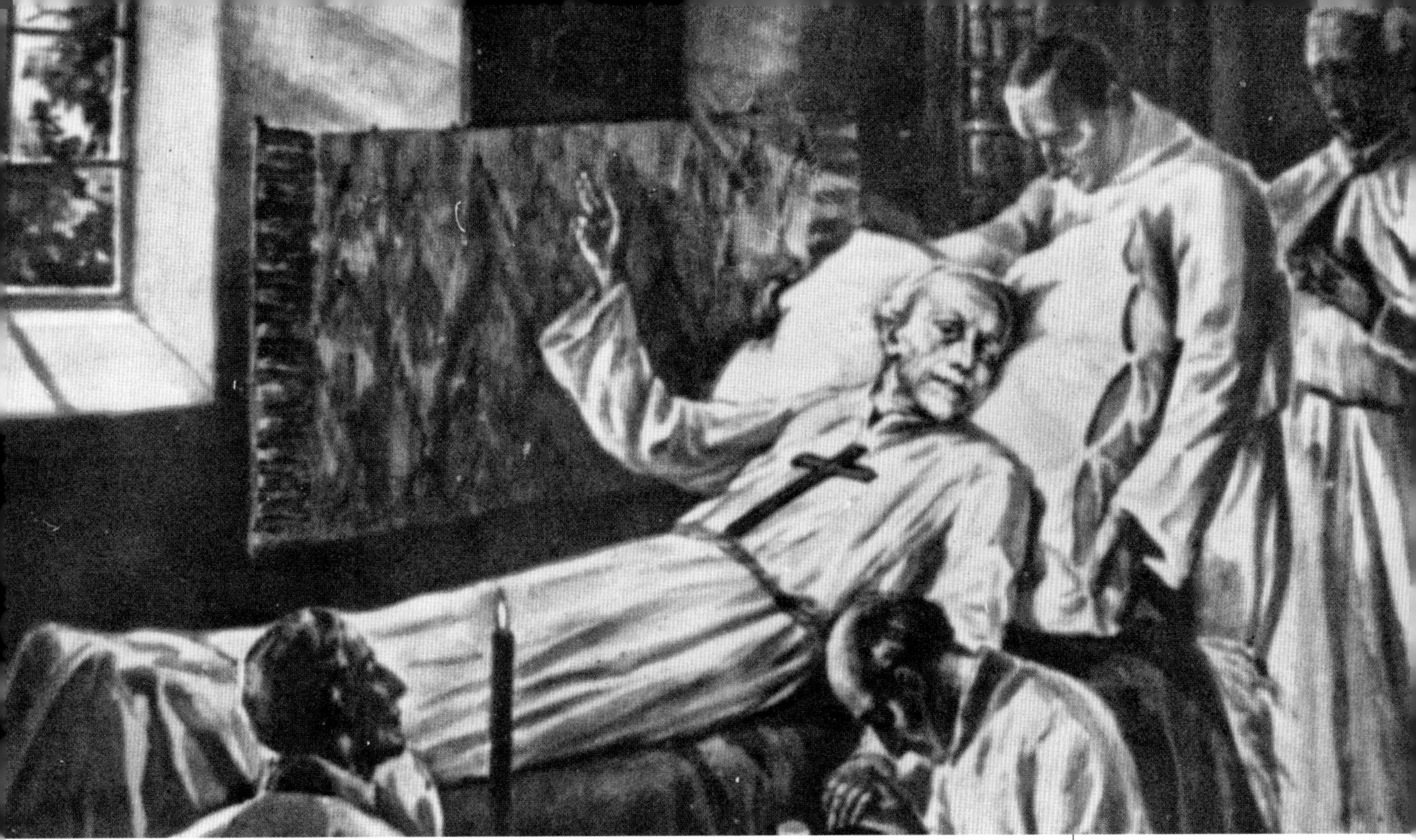

▲ *Father Papczyński on his deathbed.*

We can find resurrections (sometimes many of them) with even more detailed descriptions in the biographies of a great many saints, including the following: St. Benedict of Nursia, the Apostle of Ireland St. Patrick, St. Dominic, St. Paul of the Cross, St. Salvador of Horta, St. Colette of Corbie, St. Vincent Ferrer, St. Louis Bertrand, St. Francis Xavier, St. Francis of Paola, St. Bernard of Clairvaux, St. Margaret of Città di Castello, St. Ignatius of Loyola (he resurrected a man who hanged himself after losing a lawsuit), St. John Bosco, St. Prince Casimir Jagiellon, St. Jadwiga of Poland, and many, many more.

RESURRECTIONS STILL HAPPEN

However, those who would think that resurrections are only a thing of the past, that they were perhaps a result of people not being able to fully distinguish death from lethargy or temporary unconsciousness, would be mistaken. Indeed, miraculous resurrections still happen today. Evidence of this can be found, for example, in the officially recognized miracles that contributed to the beatification or canonization of three nuns: María de las Maravillas de Jesús, Teresa of Jesus of the Andes, and Maria Crescentia Höss.

The canonization of María de las Maravillas de Jesús was made possible thanks to a miraculous healing that occurred in 1998 in a small town in northern Argentina. Eighteen-month-old Manuel had fallen into a pool filled with muddy water, and when they pulled him out, he seemed to be dead. At the hospital, they believed he was already in a state of clinical death. However, when the physicians saw the boy's mother praying, they began to resuscitate Manuel, and after thirty minutes, what seemed absolutely impossible suddenly became real. Not only did the boy come back to life, but after awakening from the coma, despite the dire prognosis, he recovered completely and immediately!

Two miracles, thanks to which the Chilean Carmelite nun Teresa of Jesus of the Andes was canonized, were immediately declared

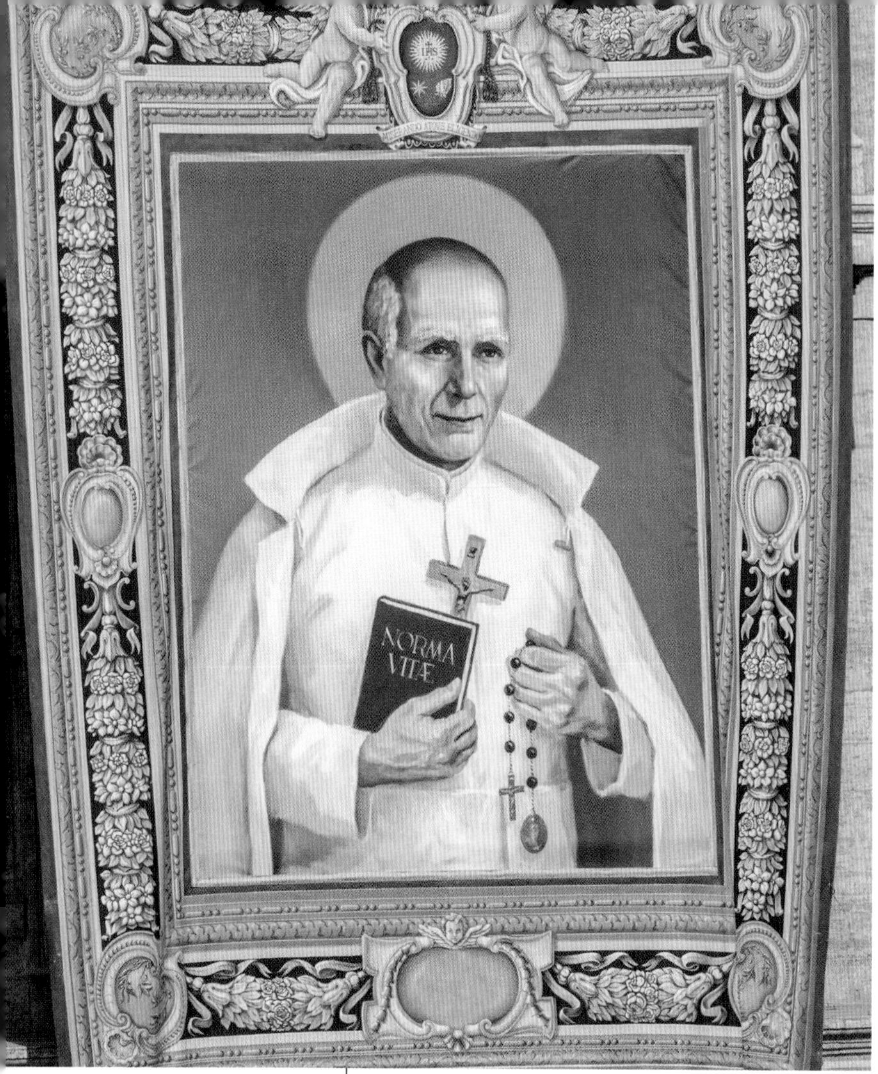

whirlpool. The friend died, whereas Margit was rescued (after forty-five minutes spent underwater!). "Clinically dead," Margit was taken to the hospital, where they managed to restore her vital functions. However, she remained in a coma, and doctors diagnosed her with extensive brain damage due to ischemia. After intense prayers through the intercession of Maria Crescentia, the girl woke up and, despite the poor medical prognosis, she quickly and completely recovered.

The spectacular miracle of "resurrecting a dead child in the mother's womb" contributed to the beatification of Marian Father Stanislaus Papczyński.

It happened in 2001. Barbara Markowska, a young woman, found out she was pregnant again (she conceived a year before but was not able to carry the child to term due to miscarriage). According to Fr. Wojciech Skóra, MIC, the General Postulator,

> *Already during the first weeks of pregnancy, she was informed of the danger of losing her baby. The young mother was hospitalized. An effective therapy was used. Her health improved. Based on an ultrasound done on the last day of her hospital stay, the fetus's heart rate was captured and its size was determined.*

The joy, however, did not last long. The very next day, there were already symptoms indicating that there was a risk of miscarriage.

Another ultrasound brought sad news. Because the heart rate had stopped and the fetus had shrunk, the doctor concluded that the baby was dead. He recommended that the mother discontinue taking medication to support the pregnancy. Another test performed the next day confirmed the previous diagnosis. The doctor expected a spontaneous miscarriage

Canonization painting of St. Stanislaus Papczyński on the pediment of St. Peter's Basilica in Rome.

resurrections. The first, in 1980, was experienced by a volunteer firefighter from Santiago de Chile, who was electrocuted (by a 380 volt current) and was in a state of clinical death. The second, in 1988, was experienced by an eleven-year-old girl who drowned in a swimming pool. After being pulled from the water, she showed no signs of life; she was not breathing, her heart was not beating, and her pupils did not react to light. Both came out of these accidents unharmed. (For more on both miracles, see pages 97–99.)

An even more spectacular miracle occurred in Germany, contributing to the canonization of Maria Crescentia Höss. In 1986, a thirteen-year-old girl named Margit was swimming in a river with a friend when she and her friend were pulled in by a

to occur soon. The patient was supposed to come back for a check-up in a few days. After three days she went to the same physician. He performed another ultrasound to see if a spontaneous miscarriage had occurred. If it had not occurred, he was to proceed with a procedure to remove the dead baby from the uterus. To his and the mother's surprise, he found that the fetus had a heartbeat. Given the earlier confirmed diagnosis, this seemed impossible. The doctor decided to repeat the test on another machine. The result confirmed that the baby was alive. Less than seven months later, the family celebrated the birth of the child, who was born healthy and is developing properly. As the postulator emphasized, a cousin, and at the same time the godfather of the child's mother, played a key role in obtaining this miracle. The man, who is a great venerator of Father Papczyński, had for many years entrusted all his problems, as well as those of his relatives and friends, to Papczyński, and had already obtained many graces through his intercession. It was no different when he learned of the problems of his goddaughter. Immediately, on March 28, he initiated a novena for the intercession of Father Papczyński to save the conceived baby. Other family members soon joined him. "The facts described above took place during this nine-day prayer," wrote Father Skóra.

The spectacular miracle of the resurrection of a child in the mother's womb was not the only resurrection performed through the intercession of the founder of Marians of the Immaculate Conception. Another miraculous resurrection took place while he was still alive. It happened at Góra Kalwaria in Poland. It involved the deceased daughter of Mrs. Raciborska—the owner of the nearby estate and forest in Cendrowice. Raciborska did not live on very good terms with the Marian fathers (she reportedly forbade them to gather brushwood in her forest) and first went to ask the Dominicans to pray for her daughter. When they were unsuccessful, the Dominicans instructed the woman to go to "miracle-worker Stanislaus, a Marian." Therefore, the deceased girl was brought to Calvary's cenacle and laid on a table, and Father Papczyński ordered her mother to go to Confession. Then he began to celebrate Mass at the altar of St. Raphael. It was then, during the elevation (or, according to another account, during the singing of the Gloria), that the child came back to life.

NOT ONLY PEOPLE

There is something else that needs to be mentioned. According to many biographies, the saints resurrected not only people but also animals. St. Martin de Porres famously resurrected and healed an old dog who had been killed. St. Joseph of Cupertino supposedly brought back to life a flock of sheep that had been killed by an avalanche. However, many more such animal resurrections were noted.

The president and first lady of Poland praying at the tomb of St. Stanislaus Papczyński.

Stained-glass window of St. Martin de Porres with the old dog he resurrected at his feet.

➤ *A statue of St. Patrick on the roof of the Milan Cathedral.*

➤ *Patrick's name was Maewyn Succat, and he came from a Roman Christian family residing in Britain.*

APOSTLE OF IRELAND

St. Patrick

Every March 17, the world turns green. Well, maybe not all of it, but certainly the parts where the Irish can be found. Citizens and emigrants from the Green Isle put on green hats and outfits, and green beer flows in streams. On this day, the memory of St. Patrick—the man who brought Christianity to Ireland—is celebrated in green.

Before that could happen, Patrick had to fight the all-powerful pagan cults spread by the Druids on the island. It wasn't an easy task, but when a humble man asks for help from God and trusts him completely, miracles happen.

Patrick's name was Maewyn Succat, and he came from a Roman Christian family residing in Great Britain. His father was a deacon and an official of the Roman administration. After an extraordinary life full of amazing events (at one point he was kidnapped by pirates and sold as a slave), Patrick became a bishop and, in 432, came to Ireland to preach the good news to its pagan residents and convert them to the Christian faith. The hierarch entered a completely pagan land, which was populated by Celtic tribes, divided into family clans and grouped around local rulers. The Druids and Filids were in charge of spiritual matters. Druids were pagan priests, basically sorcerers, who made sacrifices, practiced black magic, and drew their power from the forces of evil. According to the ancient philosopher Dio Chrysostom, "The kings were not permitted to do or plan anything without the assistance

of these wise men, so that in truth it was they who ruled, while the kings became servants and the ministers of their will."

Filids, on the other hand, were Celtic bards and soothsayers, "wise men," "poets," and "prophets," able to penetrate the mysteries of the future and conduct sacrificial rites. They were credited with the power to cast effective spells and curses, they were knowledgeable about herbs, they summoned and beseeched spirits, they were peculiar "historians" preserving in their memory myths, legends, and lineages of the kings of their tribe. Celtic religious beliefs and practices were by no means idyllic or angelic. The Celts worshiped deities who were usually personifications of the forces of nature. During the most important holidays, in addition to magical divination practices and licentious orgies, ritual murders took place—bloody human sacrifices were offered to the gods (although with time they were increasingly replaced with animal sacrifices). Most often, captives or criminals were killed, but sometimes innocent people and even children were the victims.

"It is believed that in Ireland, in the early Middle Ages, in the times of St. Patrick, in a place called Magh Slécht, the first-born and every third son were offered to the god Crom Cruach, meaning the Head of the Mound or the Bloody Head," Jerzy Gassowski writes in *Celtic Mythology*. The blood of the killed child was then sprinkled on the sacrificial altar, and its dismembered remains were buried in

Patrick entered a completely pagan land, which was populated by the Celtic tribes, made up of family clans. The Druids were in charge of spirituality. These were sorcerers who performed black magic and drew their power from the forces of evil.

Shamrock—a three-leaved clover, a symbol of Ireland. St. Patrick used it to illustrate the Holy Trinity.

various parts of the fields to ensure a plentiful harvest. The dead sacrificial victims were also burned. The Celts had a cult of human heads. Warriors used to cut off the heads of their enemies, then wear them around their waists and hang them on the walls of their houses. Such practices could not be accepted by Christians. Patrick's mission became to eradicate them.

The Druids and the Filids held great power. In order to have influence over the local kings and be able to evangelize and convert their people, Patrick had to overthrow these wizards and show that they were powerless against the will and power of the one and only God. He was well aware that he was undertaking an impossible mission. His social status was comparable to that of a criminal. His episcopate meant nothing to the Irish. What's more, from the moment he arrived on the Green Isle, he lived in constant danger. As he wrote, "For daily I expect to be murdered or betrayed or reduced to slavery if the occasion arises. But I fear nothing, because of the promises of Heaven; for I have cast myself into the hands of Almighty God, who reigns everywhere." Patrick was ready to suffer a martyr's death for Christ, and he could only count on God Himself. He trusted in God and he wasn't disappointed.

AN IMPORTANT CLASH

Surprisingly enough, Patrick had a relatively easy time with Druids' rivals, the Filids. It doesn't matter whether they read the stars and saw the acceptance of Christianity as a historical necessity, or whether they smelled an opportunity to finally become more important than their rivals. What matters is that Patrick managed to convince many of them, and it was from their group that the first converts and associates of the apostle were recruited, later forming the spiritual elite of Ireland. The apostle also managed to win over the Brehons—experts and interpreters of the law. It was a different case with the Druids. It wasn't that simple. Here, arguments and persuasion, most likely supported by subtle divine inspirations and signs, were no longer enough. Here, in order to help Patrick, God had to reach for the arsenal of really strong miracles and signs. And he did.

One of the most important clashes with the Druids, which took place on the plain of Brega near Tara—the royal residence,

Patrick is a saint of the Catholic, Old Catholic, Anglican, and Orthodox churches.

the largest town in Ireland at the time, the "capital of pagan worship"—had a truly miraculous nature. It was there that Patrick, inspired by God, decided to celebrate Easter. Muirchú, Patrick's biographer, writes:

> *It so happened in that year that a feast of pagan worship was being held, which the pagans used to celebrate with many incantations and magic rites and other superstitious acts of idolatry. There the kings, satraps, leaders, princes, and the nobles of the people assembled; furthermore, the Druids, the fortune-tellers, and the inventors and teachers of every craft and every skill were also summoned to King Loíguire at Tara, their Babylon, as they had been summoned at one time to Nebuchadnezzar. On the same night on which St. Patrick celebrated Easter, they also had a custom, which was announced to all publicly, that whosoever, in any district, whether far or near, should have lit a fire on that night before it was lit in the king's house, that is, in the palace of Tara, would have forfeited his life.*

Patrick—strong by the power of faith—didn't think much of this pagan custom. After the Easter prayers and the celebration of Holy Mass, he "kindled the divine fire with its bright light and blessed it, and it shone in the night and was seen by almost all the people who lived in the plain." In this case, however, the light of the fire symbolized a slightly different "rebirth" than the pagan one—the Resurrection of Jesus, His victory over death and Satan.

Outraged by the violation of pagan custom, the Druids then encouraged the king to immediately deal with the "wicked." Twenty-seven horse-drawn carts set off to fight Patrick. Each such cart consisted of two people—a charioteer and a warrior equipped with javelins, a sword, and a wooden shield bound with iron. Two Druids alleged to have the greatest demonic power also took part in the expedition led by the king.

The warriors and the Druids—leaving the king behind, away from the saint and his companions—did not attack or try to kill Patrick at once. They intended to question him first. They started talking to him.

A SHATTERED SKULL AND AN EARTHQUAKE

Muirchú writes:

> *Then they began their dispute, and one of the Druids named Lochru provoked the holy man and dared to revile the Catholic Faith with haughty words. Holy Patrick looked at him as he uttered such words and, as Peter had said concerning Simon, so with power and with a loud voice he confidently said to the Lord: "O Lord,*

St. Patrick's Day parade in Dublin, 2010. It's a St. Patrick's Day tradition to wear green clothes.

The Chicago River dyed green on St. Patrick's day, 2009.

⮝ St. Patrick's Cathedral in New York City.

⮟ Slemish Mountain, the first-known Irish home of St. Patrick. He worked as a shepherd for six years here.

who art all-powerful and in whose power is everything, who hast sent me here, may this impious man, who blasphemes thy name, now be cast out and quickly perish!" And at these words the Druid was lifted up into the air and fell down again; he hit his brain against a stone, and was smashed to pieces, and died in their presence, and the pagans stood in fear.

The king and his men tried to kill him. Patrick called on God Himself.

And at once darkness set in, and there was a dreadful uproar and the infidels fought among themselves, one rising up against the other, and there was a big earthquake which caused the axles of their chariots to collide with each other, and drove them violently forward so that chariots and horses rushed headlong over the plain until, in the end, a few of them escaped barely alive to Mons Monduirn, and by this disaster seven times seven men perished through the curse of Patrick before the eyes of the king as a punishment for his words, until there remained only he himself and three other survivors—that is, he and his queen, and two of the Irish.

Compelled by fear, the king bent his knee before God, but did not abandon his wicked intention to kill his servant. Patrick was well aware of this, but didn't treat the king as he did the Druid, Lochru. Once again he had to show his power to him to gain favor for his mission. So he did it in another, more peaceful way.

THE POWER OF DIVINE MIRACLES

Arriving at the royal palace, Patrick competed with the Druid, Lucet Máel (he was said to be the second most important Druid in Ireland at the time). They entered into a "dual of miracles."

During the feast, the Druid, in front of everyone, handed Patrick a cup into which he placed a drop of some sort of liquid. It's possible it was poison, or a drug. Those present in the hall looked curiously at the bishop to see what he would do. Patrick,

knowing that he had been put to the test, blessed the cup, and suddenly the liquid froze like ice. He then turned the cup upside down and the drop added by the Druid fell out. After blessing the cup again, the drink turned to liquid once more.

Astonished, Lucet Máel challenged Patrick to a test of strength. He proposed that they "show signs of their power" on the plain, bringing snow to the land. Patrick, however, refrained from such an act: "I will not bring down aught against the will of God," he said. The Druid considered this a ploy and boastfully declared that he would do it himself in front of everyone. He did as he said. After uttering the appropriate spells, he covered the plain waist-deep with snow. Patrick then demanded that he undo the "trick." The Druid then stated that he could only do it the next day, at the same time. "You can do evil, but not good. I act differently," Patrick said. He blessed the plain, and a miracle happened: "In no time, without rain or mist or wind, the snow vanished." The people who watched it couldn't help but be amazed. With this act, the bishop touched their hardened hearts. The Druid then performed another trick—he brought a thick darkness down over the plain. Unfortunately, he was unable to dissipate it. What the Druid couldn't do, Patrick did. Praying and blessing the place, he dispelled the darkness and "the sun shone again." Those gathered once again became convinced that Patrick's power was greater than the power of the Druid. "The people cheered and gave thanks." The king, who was watching this struggle, then proposed another test. "Dip your books in the water, and we will worship him whose books come out unspoiled." Patrick was ready to do so, but the Druid would not agree to such a test. He knew that water was used by Patrick during Baptism and he considered it to be his "god." Then the king proposed that they throw the books into the fire instead of water. The Druid refused again. He still probably had the blazing Paschal fire in front of his eyes.

Patrick then thought of another test. Lucet Máel and Benignus, who was accompanying the bishop, were to be locked in a hut built in the middle of

Mosaic of St. Patrick.

Patrick's attribute is the shamrock, a symbol of Ireland, held in his hand. Another one of his attributes is snakes, which, according to legend, he drove out of Ireland.

The Shrine of St. Patrick's Bell is on display at the National Museum of Ireland – Archaeology in Dublin. The inscription says, "Pray for Domnall Ua Lochlainn for whom this bell was made."

"The grave of St. Patrick in Downpatrick, Ireland."

nowhere. The Druid, wearing Patrick's garments, was sent to the part of the house made of fresh and wet wood, while the servant, clothed in the Druid's garments, was placed in the dry part. The hut was set on fire in front of the crowd.

> *And in that hour it so happened through the prayer of Patrick that the flame of the fire consumed the Druid together with the green half of the house, and nothing was left intact except the chasuble of holy Patrick, which the fire did not touch. On the other hand, happy Benignus, and the dry half of the house, experienced what has been said of the three young men: the fire did not even touch him, and brought him neither pain nor discomfort; only the garb of the Druid, which he had donned, was burnt, in accordance with God's will.*

THE BAPTIZED

Angered by the death of his second Druid, King Loíguire then threw himself at Patrick, wanting to kill him. But God held him back. For at the prayer and the word of Patrick the wrath of God descended upon the impious people, and many of them died. And holy Patrick said to the king: "If you do not believe now you shall die at once, for the wrath of God has come down upon your head." The pagan ruler—with reluctance—allowed himself to be baptized (although another biographer of Patrick, Tírechán, writes that he refused to receive this sacrament). A little while later, other members of his family received the Sacrament of Baptism, including two daughters of the king—fair-haired Ethne and redheaded Fedelm, who, right after this ceremony and having received the veils and the Eucharist, "fell asleep in death," going to the Lord.

A FRUITFUL VICTORY

What was the impact of St. Patrick's most important battle with paganism? It was substantial. Defeated and humiliated, the king granted him the freedom to preach the good news throughout his territory, ensuring that "he would not meet death in his kingdom." Thanks to this spectacular victory, with royal permission, Patrick could finally start the most important task before him—spreading the good news and Christianizing the country.

THE LAST CLASH

During his missionary journey through Ireland, Patrick stumbled upon the Druids several times. He repeatedly had to prove to them that it is not their demonic deities, but the Christian God, who is the true master of the universe. Tírechán describes two such encounters. One happened in Mag Aí. Two magicians of King Níall, Máel and Capitolauium, "fearing that people might make the ways of the holy man their own, grew very angry and brought the darkness of night and dense fogs." The darkness brought by magic lasted three days and three nights. Patrick dispersed it with a three-day fast and constant prayers to God.

Another encounter took place after Patrick crossed the River Moy, near the forest of Fochluth, where Patrick wanted to spend his second Easter. The Druids of the sons of Amolngid gathered before the chief Druid, named Recrad, and decided to kill the saint. Then they went to the bishop "with nine Druids clad in white garments with a host of other Druids." Patrick, in the company of Énde, son of Amolngid, and Conall, son of Énde, was baptizing a crowd of people. Only a fair-sized floodplain separated them. Patrick sent Conall toward the Druids and asked him to recognize the chief Druid; "for he did not want to kill someone else." When, at the agreed signal, Énde's son stood by the leader of the hostile group, Patrick "rose and raised his left hand to God in heaven, cursing the Druid" who dropped dead, and then burned as a "sign of punishment." "When everyone saw this miracle, the people scattered all over Mag Domnon, and Patrick baptized many people on that day," Tírechán wrote.

In this way, the Druids—great and powerful sorcerers—were defeated by Patrick, and shortly after his death, they passed into oblivion.

A stained-glass window from the cathedral in Oakland.

Statue of St. Patrick, Hill of Tara.

St. Patrick's Well.

Giant's Causeway in Ireland.

➤ *On the last Sunday in July, thousands of pilgrims climb Croagh Patrick in honor of St. Patrick. Some pilgrims climb the mountain barefoot as an act of penance.*

➤ *St. Patrick's Oratory at the peak.*

➤ *Croagh Patrick mountain. The name comes from the Irish* Cruach Phádraig, *meaning "St. Patrick's stack (pile)."*

STAFF AND ARMOR

The apostle of Ireland is also famous for many other miracles: he healed the sick, performed resurrections, conversed with the dead, met with angels many times (especially with an angel named Victor, whom he saw in a bush that was on fire but did not burn). When he prayed in the wilderness, he saw the "heavens open and the Son of God and His angels." He also

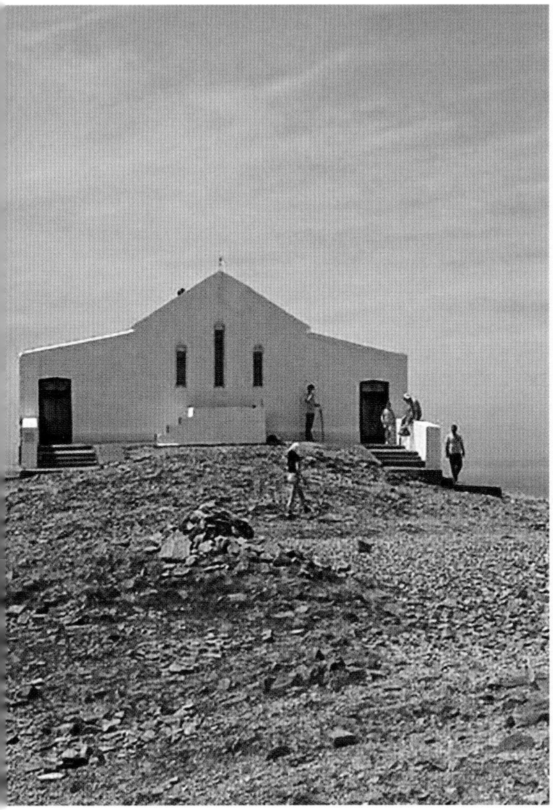

used miracles to punish those who didn't respect God's law. If the legends are to be believed, he worked many miracles using his "miraculous staff," the Baculus Jesu, a visible sign of God's help, received under miraculous circumstances on an island in the Tyrrhenian Sea before he arrived in Ireland. It was supposedly given to him by an eternally youthful couple "waiting for him since the time when God incarnate walked among the people." Jesus entrusted this young couple with the care of His staff and instructed them to hand it over to Patrick, at the same time telling him that he was to become the apostle of Ireland. This staff—wrapped in this poetic legend, and being perhaps a crosier or a processional cross—in the eyes of the pagans replaced the wands of the Filids and the Druids.

Apart from the staff, Patrick's greatest weapon was prayer. To protect himself from the attacks of pagans, witches, and Druids, as well as from the aggression of demons, Patrick prayed a special prayer of protection known today as Lorica, or St. Patrick's Breastplate. Thanks to it, he was able to get out of the worst oppression and, even today, this prayer has great power in defending against all the evil lurking for us.

THE NIGHTS BECAME DARKER

Ireland's most famous saint died on March 17. What year? It isn't known. It took place somewhere between 457 and 492 (typically the year 461 or 462 is used). It is said that he lived to the ripe old age of 120 years. Many miraculous legends are also connected with his death. Supposedly after the death of the bishop, there was no darkness in Ireland for 12 days, and after that time, the nights became darker than usual. Two clans fiercely competed for Patrick's remains (God, however, stopped them from spilling blood). Angels watched over his body, and fire gushed from his grave. Patrick's coffin—as commanded by his angel Victor—was placed on a cart drawn by two untamed oxen. The animals reached Dun Lethglaisse (now Downpatrick) where, according to legend, Patrick was buried.

A GREEN AND FLOURISHING ISLAND

Patrick's contributions to Christianity were enormous. Thanks to Patrick, Christianity prevailed in Ireland, and slavery, tribal warfare, and human sacrifice were forgotten. It was thanks to the apostle of Ireland that Irish Christianity began to flourish, and numerous monasteries and hermitages were founded. It was thanks to him that, over the next few centuries, Ireland became a flourishing island of saints and scholars; missionaries from this country saved European civilization after the fall of the Roman Empire.

Traditional Irish St. Patrick's rosettes.

1835–1907

SOLDIER AND FRIAR

Raphael of St. Joseph Kalinowski

St. Raphael Kalinowski

Born in the Polish city of Wilno (now Vilnius in Lithuania), the Discalced Carmelite Joseph Raphael Kalinowski represents, perhaps best of all the saints, the meanderings and dilemmas of the soul of a patriotic Pole—a member of a great and proud European nation.

▲ *Joseph Kalinowski, an officer in the Russian army.*

➤ *Joseph Kalinowski was arrested in March 1864 and sentenced to death, however, the sentence was changed to exile in Siberia. He ended up in Usolye-Sibirskoye, where he worked in a salt mine. In exile, he became certain of his religious vocation.*

On September 1, 1942, Poland was experiencing the bitter third anniversary of the German invasion and the start of World War II. On that very day, the Gestapo knocked on the door of the home of Father Władysław Miś—chancellor of the Krakow prince-bishop's curia and parish priest of All Saints Parish in Krakow. He was arrested most likely for helping Jews by writing them false baptismal certificates.

On December 13, the priest, who until then had been kept in a Krakow prison on Montelupi Street, was taken to Auschwitz.

MURDEROUS MARCH

In January 1945, despite a very harsh winter, Soviet troops relentlessly pushed westward. When only a few dozen kilometers separated them from the camp, the prisoners were evacuated. On January 18, the "death march" began. The Nazi German executioners rushed westward with a multitude of prisoners, most of whom resembled living skeletons. Among these unfortunates was Father Miś.

The 63-kilometer Gehenna, marked by the corpses of those who failed to make it or were bestially murdered along the way, ended at the station in Wodzisław

Śląski. The lucky ones who by some miracle managed to survive the march were crammed into open coal cars. It is estimated today that of the evacuated 56,000 people, between 9,000 and 15,000 died along the way. Along with other prisoners, Father Miś was first sent to the Mauthausen camp and then transferred to its subcamp, the Hunger and Death Camp in Ebensee, Austria. His "way of the cross" did not end until May 6, 1945, when American troops liberated the camp.

THANKS TO PROVIDENCE AND THE MOTHER OF GOD

In the chronicle of the All Saints Parish in Krakow, we find a record saying that it was only thanks to God's providence and the protection of the Blessed Mother that he returned from Ebensee.

He arrived in Krakow on July 10, 1945. Sick and debilitated, he merely managed to get home with the help of two walking sticks. His spine was in a tragic condition: some of his vertebrae had been destroyed by the heavy lifting he had been forced to do in the camps, and there was a purulent inflammation in his lumbar vertebrae. He moved with difficulty, as he had to pay for every step with severe pain.

Shortly after he returned to Krakow, an X-ray was taken which showed a significant bone defect in the spine in the area of the lumbar vertebrae. The medical prognosis was bad. According to the doctors, the bones couldn't rebuild themselves, and there was a serious concern that the damaged spine might break at the slightest strain, which in turn might result in leg paralysis. The priest was ordered to lie in bed, preferably in a cast. Father Miś was not too keen on this, not wanting to miss daily Mass and neglect his pastoral duties. According to the parish chronicle, "After two months of rest, having thanked the surgeons for their advice and trusting in God's help, he

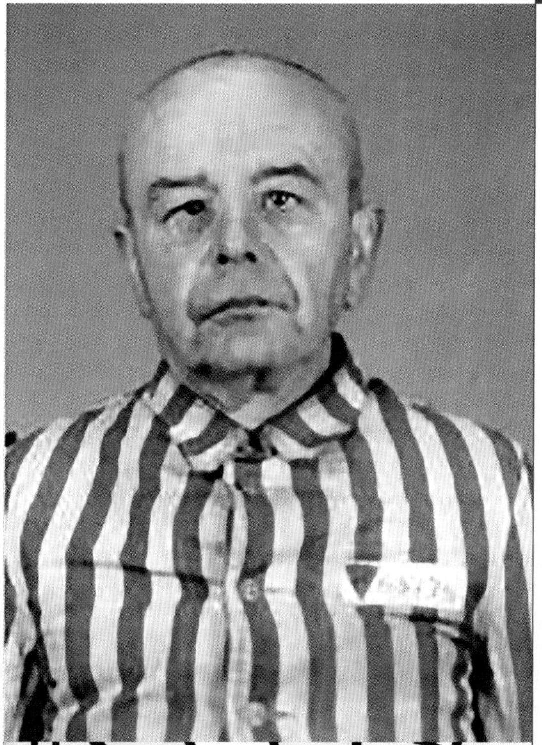

Father Władysław Miś in a prison-striped uniform, a photo from Auschwitz.

St. Raphael Kalinowski is depicted in a stained-glass window located in the Co-cathedral Basilica of the Assumption of the Blessed Virgin Mary in Kołobrzeg.

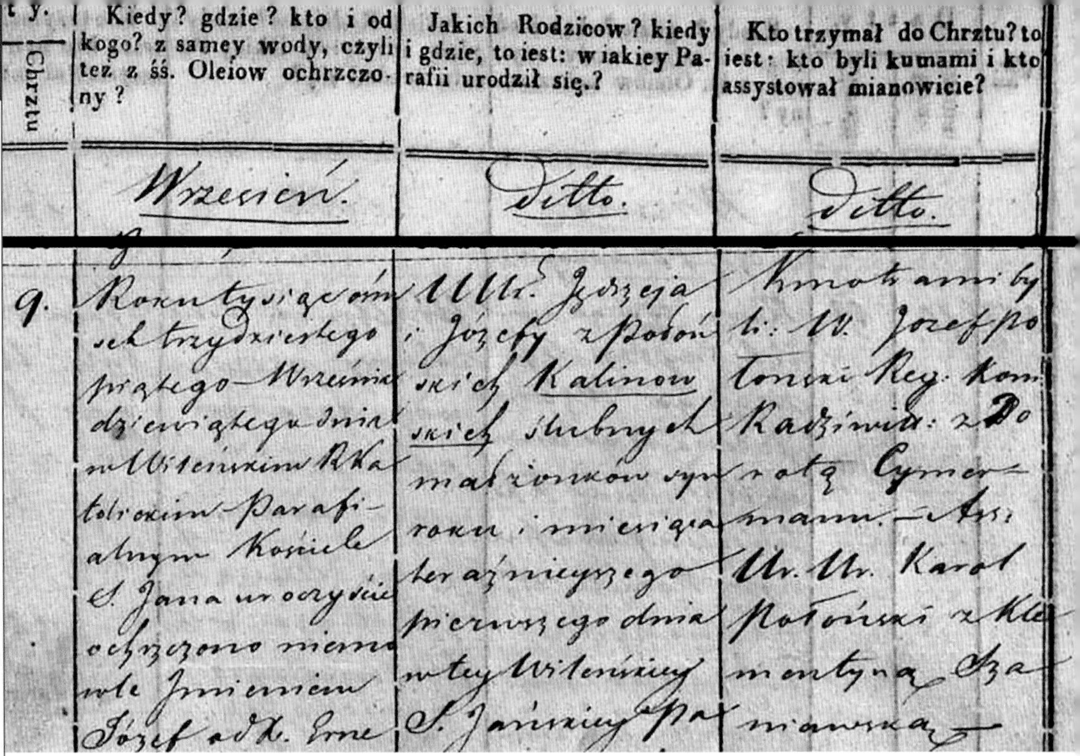
Kiedy? gdzie? kto i od kogo? z samey wody, czyli też z śś. Oleiow ochrzczony?

Jakich Rodzicow? kiedy i gdzie, to iest: w iakiey Parafii urodził się.?

Kto trzymał do Chrztu? to iest: kto byli kumami i kto assystował mianowicie?

Chrztu

Wrzesień. | Ditto. | Ditto.

9.

➤ *Joseph Kalinowski's birth certificate (St. John's in Wilno, 226/1835).*

resumed his pastoral duties in September 1945, temporarily relieving Father Franciszek Wojcik, a retired catechist from Lviv, who had been appointed parish administrator after the pastor's imprisonment." Father Miś discontinued any treatment.

THERE WERE NO DEFECTS!

On May 4, 1948, Father Miś, who moved about on crutches, was a guest of Bishop Stanisław Rospond. Hearing of his ailments, the Krakow auxiliary bishop encouraged him to pray for healing through the intercession of Father Raphael Kalinowski, a Discalced Carmelite who had died with the reputation of holiness. Father Miś listened to his advice, and, what's more, asked the Discalced Carmelite Fathers to pray a novena for his intention. While the Carmelites were praying, he felt relief from his suffering, and when the novena ended, he was healed.

The pains were gone, and the crutches proved no longer necessary. The well-known Krakow X-ray specialist Dr. Jerzy Chudyk then performed another X-ray, which showed no defects in the spine. The vertebrae and bones were fine. It was a miracle! The diagnosis of the radiologist was confirmed by another doctor, Dr. Stanisław Klosowski, who stated that the case was medically inexplicable.

Exhausted by both the toils of camp life and intense pastoral work, Father Władysław Miś did not enjoy his regained fitness for too long. A few years later, he was struck down by yet another illness. He died on October 30, 1954, at the age of 72. In 1980-1981, his inexplicable recovery from the first illness was once again investigated and declared a miracle. In June 1983, Father Raphael Kalinowski was beatified by the Holy Father.

WITH POLAND IN HIS HEART

Who was the mysterious friar who contributed to the healing of Father Władysław Miś? It was Joseph Kalinowski, who received the name Raphael later in his time in the monastery. He was born and grew up in a difficult time for Poles, when Poland did not exist on the map of Europe and its territory was seized and divided among three neighboring states—Russia,

Prussia, and Austria. The Polish nation, living under this yoke, was still healing from the wounds of the defeat of the anti-Russian November Uprising. Like Nazi Germany, the authorities of tsarist Russia (Joseph was born in the Russian partition) also bloodily suppressed every manifestation of patriotism. Particularly ruthless was the repression of the Church, which had always been a stronghold of Polishness in difficult times for the nation.

Joseph was born in Wilno into a Catholic family. His father was a math professor, and he had eight siblings. His mother died shortly after giving birth. Having no other choice, the young man graduated from the Engineering Academy in the Russian city of St. Petersburg. He became an engineer, an officer in the Russian army, and a captain in the tsarist army, but it was Poland, not Russia, that he had in his heart.

PATH TO GOD

During his studies in St. Petersburg, Joseph became indifferent to matters of religion and stopped receiving the sacraments. In his soul, however, he felt some indefinite restlessness—a longing, as he wrote himself, that consumed "his whole being." Seeking God, he reached for the following books: Chateaubriand's *The Genius of Christianity*, Maistre's *The Pope*, and Augustine's *Confessions*, so that toward the end of his studies he began to stop into churches. During one such visit to the Polish Church of St. Stanisław in St. Petersburg, he suddenly had a desire to confess. He even knelt in front of the lattice in the confessional, but soon realized that there was no confessor behind it. Then he burst into tears. After graduation, he went to work on the construction of the Kursk-Konotop railroad. Away from the hustle and bustle of the big world, he read the *Confessions* once more. He called them "a spring of new life." A prayer book also fell into his lap. As he later wrote in his memoir,

> *Reading this book had an immense effect on the soul, it particularly awakened a feeling of trust in the mediation of the Blessed Mother.*

Water from Elijah's spring, and a statue and bas-reliefs from the biblical story of Elijah.

Memorabilia of St. Raphael Kalinowski from the museum in Czerna.

Paintings by Jerzy Kumala depicting scenes from Kalinowski's life: participation in the January Uprising and the road to Siberia. Czerna Monastery.

The painting in the main altar of the St. Raphael Kalinowski Chapel in Czerna by Jerzy Kumala. Under the altar, there is a sarcophagus with relics of St. Raphael.

> *The remark on the importance of reciting the Angelic Salutation when in need stuck in my memory, and once, when I found myself in the gravest danger of losing my life, a fervent recitation of the Hail Mary saved me from doom.*[1]

"How benign and good for us are the means given to us by the Church of St. Peter, through devotional books, from which the truth of God shines through," he added. "I learned all the enormity of the need for established religious notions and finally turned to them. I look at life more calmly now and have become more indifferent to the pleasures of life." Soon he also reached for the New Testament. By then he was already among those who declared themselves "non-practicing believers," and he began to pray to the Mother of God.

The breakthrough came when he returned to Wilno and the anti-Russian January Uprising broke out in 1863. His cousin was then arrested and sent into exile by the Russians. Joseph decided to uplift him by bringing him a relic cross belonging to his teenage sister Marynia. However, Marynia gave it to Joseph on the condition that he would go to Confession. As he was a man of honor, he went to Confession and received Holy Communion on the Feast of the Assumption in 1863. It was a real breakthrough. "After ten years of dissent I have returned to the bosom of the Church: I have been to confession and I feel very good about it. I boast about it to you, because I consider this turn of mine in understanding of religion and faith to be an important event in my inner life."[2] A year later he added, "What God has done to my soul during those moments, which I have spent kneeling before a confessor, can only be comprehended by the ones who have experienced similar moments." From then on, he began to practice conscientiously: he attended Mass daily, received Holy Communion frequently, and went to Confession weekly. He decided to enter a Capuchin convent, but his plans were thwarted by his ardent love for his enslaved homeland.

EXILED TO SIBERIA

When the uprising was already declining, Joseph Kalinowski took up the post of head of the War Department in the Lithuanian insurrectionary government. Although he knew that he no longer had the slightest chance of victory, being an ardent patriot, he decided that he could not do otherwise. He did so despite himself, for he always claimed that the homeland needed not blood, but sweat.

In 1864, Kalinowski was arrested and sentenced to death. The death sentence was later commuted to ten years in Russian Siberia.

He served his punishment mainly in the salt mines of Usolye-Sibirskoye and Irkutsk, generously sharing money, material goods, and books, as well as faith and religious knowledge (which, as he wrote himself, "he found so late in life") with the poorer deportees and the impoverished indigenous population. He fought the prevailing despondency among the exiles, and the "physical and moral misery," earnestly longing for the conversion of Russia and the unity of Christians. It was then that his great pedagogical talent became apparent. He raised, educated, and catechized abandoned youth and orphaned children. He must have been a good pedagogue, because when he returned from exile, he was entrusted with the care of August Czartoryski—the oldest son of Prince Władysław Czartoryski. Had it not been for the partitions, the prince would have had a good chance of becoming king of Poland. Meanwhile, he stayed in exile in France, working persistently for the good of his beloved country. Kalinowski shaped the character of Gucio (as the prince was called),

Excerpt from the painting Morning *by Aleksander Sochaczewski, depicting the prisoners of Katorga camp on their way to work. St. Raphael Kalinowski was painted next to the guard.*

➢ *This painting by Jerzy Kumala depicts Kalinowski as a spiritual guide. It was inspired by the photograph shown next to it. (Czerna Monastery, St. Raphael Kalinowski Chapel built in 1981–1983.)*

Raphael Kalinowski was a valued confessor distinguished by extraordinary intuition and seeking to lead the penitent to repentance. Sometimes he heard confessions for more than a dozen hours at a time. He went to Confession himself a few times a week and prayed the Stations of the Cross every day.

strengthened his knowledge, and awakened his hunger for God. He must rejoice greatly in Heaven now, because ten years after their parting, the prince's son joined the Salesians of Don Bosco and in 2004 was beatified by Pope St. John Paul II.

Kalinowski, like his student, also took on a path of a religious vocation. In 1877, at the age of 42, he entered the Discalced Carmelites Order, beginning his novitiate at a monastery in Graz, Austria. He received the religious name Br. Raphael of St. Joseph.

PRIOR AND CONFESSOR

Entering the order, he was already fully formed in terms of his faith. After taking his monastic vows in 1882, he was ordained a priest and for many years was a prior of the monastery in Czerna near Krakow and later of the monastery he founded in Wadowice. He went down in the history of the congregation as a reformer who contributed to the revival of the entire Discalced Carmelites' province. The most important place of his pastoral ministry became the confessional, the place in which he experienced so many significant breakthroughs in his own spiritual life. He used to sit in what he called the "Tribunal of God's Mercy" for many hours a day, sometimes devoting even several hours to one penitent. He possessed a great gift of conversion. Many made a general Confession before him and changed their lives. He was patient, humble, and prudently gracious, and he restored the peace of mind of the scrupulous. No wonder there were long lines for him. It was in the cold and damp confessional of the Wadowice monastery that he contracted his last, fatal cold, dying in the reputation of holiness on November 15, 1907.

WADOWICE, THE YEAR 1989

It was a winter afternoon on January 18, 1989. Seven-year-old Olek Roman was crossing Zegadłowicza Street in Wadowice—the town where Father Raphael Kalinowski died and where John Paul II was born. Suddenly the screech of the tires and the dull sound of impact rang out. The speeding car ran into the boy, who hit his head on the asphalt with great force. Blood gushed from the child's mouth, nose, and ears. The boy lost consciousness. People immediately called an ambulance, which transported Olek to a nearby hospital. The boy's condition was serious—he had a fractured skull base and the shattered bones on the side of his head were bashed in. The boy's sister, who witnessed the accident, ran to get their parents. The father arrived first. His mother, who was at work at the time, reacted rather calmly. She said, "Well, it happened, and now it's all in God's hands."

Upon arriving at the hospital, Ms. Iwona met a Discalced Carmelite, Fr. Rudolf Warzęcha. It was Fr. Warzęcha who gave the boy the Sacrament of Anointing of the Sick. Today he is a candidate for the glory of the altars. The boy was under the care of medical experts, so the friar took the boy's mother to the hospital chapel to pray together for a happy outcome of the surgery. He also instructed the parents to start praying a novena to Bl. Fr. Raphael Kalinowski. As the mother later recounted, "Then he gave me the novena booklets and instructed me to distribute them in the family so that as many people as possible would pray for my son's intention, because the more people pray, the more powerful the prayer is." Father Warzęcha prayed the novena every day in a special place—Bl. Raphael's cell.

Wondering what to do next, doctors from Wadowice consulted specialists at one of Poland's most prestigious facilities

The monastery in Czerna, where Raphael Kalinowski held the dignity of abbot three times.

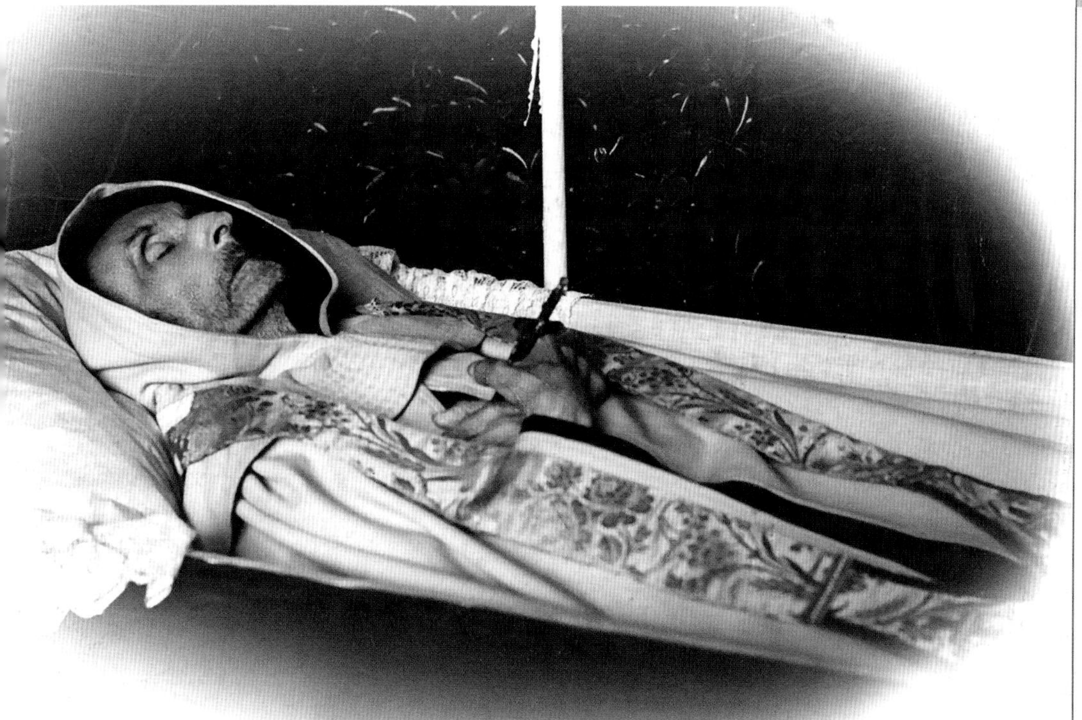

St. Raphael Kalinowski, last photo before being laid to rest. The photo was taken on November 15, 1907, at the monastery in Wadowice.

▼ *St. Joseph Church at the monastery of the Discalced Carmelite Fathers in Wadowice.*

providing treatment to children—the Children's Hospital in Krakow-Prokocim. However, Olek's condition did not allow for transport.

They decided to operate in the local hospital. The operation lasted more than two hours. After opening the skull, Dr. Stanisław Chmura noticed that the boy had cerebral contusion, the dura mater was damaged, and a section of his cortex and brain tissue were destroyed. Moreover, the surgeon had to remove several extensive hematomas.

There were complications. Twice, for a few minutes, the child's heart stopped beating. After the operation, Olek, with a vital signs monitor attached to him, was taken to the intensive care unit. There was nothing left for them to do but wait. "Will he survive?" None of the doctors were able to answer this question. Olek's mother was right—everything was in God's hands. However, Dr. Chmura, who had dealt with and heard about such cases before, thought the boy would die.

For ten days the little boy did not regain consciousness. His mother visited him every day and begged him to live. She did not think about the perpetrator of the accident. "I didn't focus on blaming him, but on praying and saving my child. On the eighth day of the novena, which everyone in the family prayed at that time, I put the relics of Bl. Raphael Kalinowski I had received from Father Rudolf to Olek's head." The next day, on the last day of the novena, the boy regained consciousness. What's more, although he suffered such great injuries and almost died during the operation, he was immediately able to communicate with the outside world. With his head bandaged, he was answering questions logically, reading, writing, drawing pictures, and singing songs that he had learned at school. The hospital

➤ *After returning to Poland from Siberia, St. Raphael Kalinowski was a tutor of Prince August Czartoryski, who later became a Salesian and a Blessed.*

Memorabilia of St. Raphael Kalinowski in the museum in Czerna.

staff were shocked. The nurses grabbed the phone to share the happy news with the child's mother, who was at work. They told her the story of how he woke up. "He said he wanted scrambled eggs," the boy's mother later recounted. When she came into the room, Olek asked her to bring him his favorite chocolate cake. It later turned out that the boy not only managed to survive the accident, but also had no further complications.

The child's mother later added, "After a month, Dr. Chmura told me that he never imagined that something like this could happen. He said that during the operation he felt as if someone was guiding his hand, as if someone was helping him." Doctors who examined the miracle for the canonization process of Bl. Raphael of St. Joseph also had no doubts. Thanks to their positive opinion, on November 17, 1991, John Paul II canonized him. Thus, the Polish Discalced Carmelite became the first representative of the order to be canonized after the famous Spaniard St. John of the Cross.[1] [2]

ENDNOTES

1 Quotes from Memoirs cit. per: Józef Kalinowski (O. Rafał od św. Józefa), Wspomnienia 1835-1877 [Memoirs 1835-1877], Lublin 1965, Seria: Materiały źródłowe do Dziejów Kościoła w Polsce [Series: Source Materials for the History of the Church in Poland], t. VII, TN KUL, Lublin 1965.

2 Cytaty z listów cit. per: Rafał Kalinowski, Listy [Raphael Kalinowski, Letters] wyd. Czesław. Gil OCD, TN KUL, Lublin 1978.

➤ *A unit of Cristeros before a battle.*

➤ *St. José Luis Sánchez del Río.*

➤ *A cartoon depicting members of Calles's government as torturers of Christ.*

LONG LIVE CHRIST THE KING!

St. José Luis Sánchez del Río

A teenager from Mexico, who would rather die than deny Christ, is a great hero of our faith, revered all over the world. He became recognized as a saint after he healed a little girl who was considered brain-dead.

In 1926, the Cristero Rebellion broke out in Mexico. Catholics rose up against the Masonic government of the atheist Plutarco Elías Calles. They fought to defend Christ and the Church, the Holy Mass, the possibility of receiving sacraments, and the free practice of their religion.

Plutarco Calles, who called himself the "personal enemy of God" and "antichrist," hated the Church and made every effort to destroy it: outlawing religious orders, exiling bishops, depriving the Church of property rights, and depriving the clergy of civil liberties, including the right to vote. Under a law he introduced, all Church property was confiscated and all Church orphanages, schools, and hospitals were closed. All religious processions were declared illegal. The possession of crosses and religious images was forbidden, even in private homes. Saying the word "God" called for punishment.

➤ *The leadership of the Cristeros.*

Priests—treated as criminals and madmen—were not allowed to celebrate the Holy Mass. Only government-approved priests were allowed to celebrate Mass, and they were also made to break the vow of celibacy. Many Catholics and activists were cruelly tortured and murdered (altogether, almost 100,000 Catholics were murdered in "free and socialist" Mexico from 1917 to 1937). They died with the words "Viva Cristo Rey" (Long Live Christ the King) on their lips. Among the victims was the thirty-nine-year-old father José Anacleto González Flores, leader of the Catholic Association of Mexican Youth from Guadajalara.

Calles's anti-Catholic dictatorship was supported not only by Soviet Russia, but also by the United States government, who wanted to gain access to Mexican oil deposits. Pope Pius XI strongly condemned the persecution of the Church in Mexico.

To instill fear, gallows with the corpses of the Cristeros were displayed along railroad tracks in Mexico.

MEXICAN TARCISIUS

Thirteen-year-old José Luis Sánchez del Río (1913–1928) lived in Sahuayo de Diaz, a town of about five thousand people. Anyone who has seen *For Greater Glory: The True Story of Cristiada* remembers the good, deeply religious boy. José Luis knew the murdered José Anacleto well and admired his courage. He saw others murdered. Despite opposition from his mother and General Prudencio Mendoza, the rebel general, the determined teenager, following in his brothers' footsteps, joined the ranks of the rebels.

Placed in one of the units under General Luis Guizar Morfin, he cleaned weapons, prepared meals, groomed horses, and carried the rebel flag. He was called Tarcisius, in honor of the ancient martyr who died in defense of the Eucharist.

DEATH? IT'S NOTHING!

The teenager was captured on February 5, 1928, during a clash between his unit and the Federales; the boy gave his horse to the general and helped him escape. The next day, he wrote a letter to his mother:

> *My dear mother: On this day, I was taken prisoner in combat. I think that I am going to die at the present time, but I do not care, mother. Surrender yourself to the will of God; I die happy, because I will bravely die next to our God. Do not worry about my death, which is what mortifies me. Tell my two brothers to follow the example of their youngest sibling, and to do the will of God. Have courage and give me your blessing along with my father's. Say hello to everyone for the last time and receive the heart of your son who loves you so much and longed to see you before he died.*

The next day, the teenager was taken to another prison established in his hometown—the parish church defiled by the federal military. Over the next few days, various attempts were made by soldiers to force him to deny his faith. To torment him mentally, he was ordered to watch the execution of another boy (the hanged Lorenzo later came back to life,

The beatification of José Luis Sánchez del Río in the stadium of Guadalajara, Mexico.

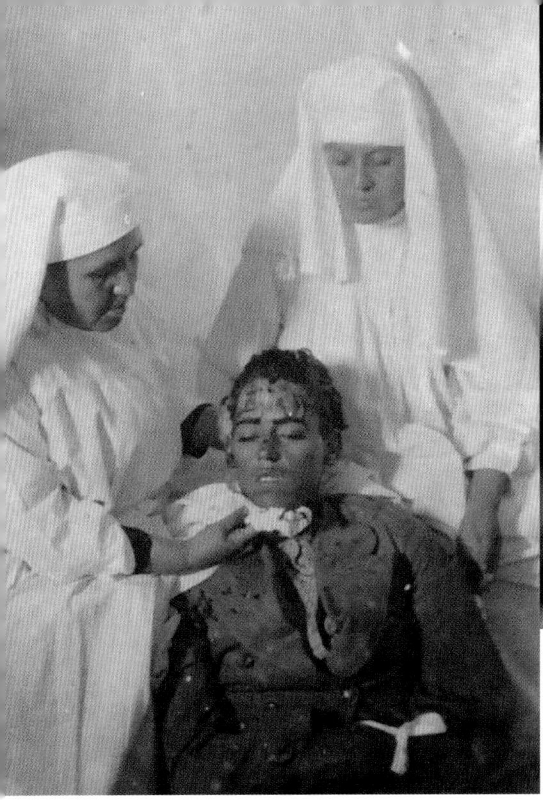

escaped, and re-entered the ranks of the Cristeros). The young Cristero did not give up. What's more, defending the dignity of the holy place, he killed three of Mayor Rafael Picazo's gamecock roosters that were kept inside the church.

He was then subjected to cruel torture—his teeth were knocked out and he was starved. "I'd rather die than betray Christ and my country," he told his executioners.

WE WILL SEE EACH OTHER IN HEAVEN!

February 10 came. Knowing he would soon die, the boy wrote his last letter. "I am sentenced to death; the moment which I've been waiting for so long, will come at 8 o'clock tonight," he wrote his aunt, asking her to pass on the news to his mother, as well as say goodbye to everyone for him, reassuring them of his love. "Christ lives, Christ reigns, Christ commands. Long live Christ the King and the Holy Mary of Guadalupe," he concluded. He managed to receive the Eucharist that was smuggled into the prison.

Around 11 o'clock, the federal soldiers took the boy to the army's headquarters church, located nearby. Then they cut the skin on his feet and tore it off. Dripping blood, with his hands tied behind his back, they rushed him to the cemetery. Along the way, he was ridiculed, stabbed with knives, and beaten with the end of a rifle. He was hit so hard that his jaw broke. José kept repeating: "Long live Christ the King! Long live Mother Mary of Guadalupe!" He was tempted for the last time: "If you say 'Death to Christ the King' we will set you free." He didn't say it. The boy was followed by his mother and a small group of friends, but they were stopped before the gate of the cemetery.

At the cemetery, the soldiers forced the boy to dig his own grave, then they submerged him several times in a well. "What should we tell your father?" they asked, torturing him mentally. (Macario Sanchez was in Guadalajara at the time, trying to collect the astronomical ransom proposed by the mayor for the release of his son.) "That we will see each other in Heaven," José declared. Moments later, one of the soldiers shot him in the temple. He was less than fifteen years old. José Luis was beatified November 20, 2005, along with thirteen other Mexican martyrs, by Benedict XVI. José Anacleto González, who was admired by the boy, was included in the group.

St. José Luis Sánchez del Río in the insurgent uniform.

Nuns preparing the martyr's body for burial.

The flag of the Cristeros, with an embroidered Our Lady of Guadalupe image.

➤ *Basilica of Our Lady of Health in Pátzcuaro, Michoacán, in Mexico.*

A HOMETOWN MIRACLE

To become a saint, José Luis needed a miracle. He waited for it less than three years. The miracle happened in Sahuayo, where José Luis was born and then martyred. Through Bl. José Luis's intercession, a young Mexican girl, Ximena Magallón Guadalupe Galvéz, was miraculously healed.

Paulina Galvéz Alvez, Ximena's mother, described her daughter's illness and her miraculous recovery in a post on her community's Facebook page on September 11, 2013.

The girl was born in the United States at the end of September in 2008. Less than a month old, she traveled with her family to Sahuayo, Mexico. During their stay in the city, the child unexpectedly developed a fever. Regular treatment didn't help. The doctor, suspecting that it could be something more serious than pneumonia, referred the family to Santa Maria, the city's hospital.

At the hospital, they had a difficult time diagnosing the febrile child. They admitted her, but three days later she was discharged. The child still had a fever and was taken to see Dr. Rosendo Sanchez in Aguascalientes. Dr. Sanchez was unsure what was wrong with Ximena—with a tentative diagnosis of atypical pneumonia, he sent her back to the hospital in Sahuayo. For two months, Mrs. Paulina lived in constant fear and uncertainty, and the child did not respond to any of the treatments used. Finally, one of the doctors concluded that the child was suffering from a bacterial infection—pneumococcus. The baby was taken once again to the doctor in Aguascalientes. The next test showed that fluid had accumulated in the child's right lung and she had to undergo a risky, life-threatening operation. It was suspected that the little one may have choked on her food. Ximena's family—left with no other choice—greed to the operation. They asked the doctor to do everything to save the baby. They entrusted the little one to God Himself, and they baptized the baby just before the surgery. This sacrament was

➤ *Relics of José Luis Sánchez del Río, the Blessed Martyr, in the San Bernardino de Siena Church in Xochimilco, Mexico.*

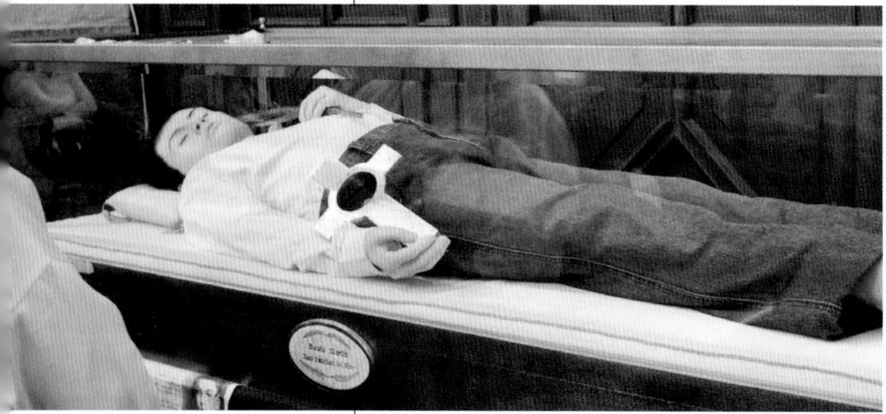

administered to the child by Fr. Agustíno Patiño. The operation was successful, but additional problems arose—it turned out that Ximena was suffering from tuberculosis. Mrs. Paulina reported that after the operation, the little one behaved differently than normal. She was placed in intensive care. The next day, they discovered the child had convulsions and suffered a stroke that, according to the doctors, had led to ninety percent brain death. Ximena found herself in a vegetative state, and from a medical point of view, even if she had survived, she would have been in a vegetative state. The parents once again asked for Dr. Rosendo's help. Ximena was placed in a coma from which she was to be awakened after seventy-two hours. After this time, it was to be seen if the little child would survive at all. Ximena's family began to flood Heaven with prayers. They attended Holy Mass daily, asking God for a miracle through the intercession of Bl. Joselito.

Mrs. Paulina was present when her daughter was to be woken up. When Ximena was taken off life support, her mother held the little one, still entrusting her to God and Bl. José Sánchez. Ximenita came out of her comatose state, opened her eyes, and smiled at the people around her. The doctors did not expect such a reaction. They were shocked. They recognized it as a miracle. The unexpected healing was later confirmed by tests—CT scan and EEG. The brain, which was thought to be dead, came back to life. What's more, the next day, it turned out that her brain was one hundred percent healthy. The doctors cautioned everyone not to be too joyful, because a stroke is a stroke, and although the brain started working again, it had been dead for some time. They predicted that, as a result of this, the child may have lost some vital functions. She may have lost the sucking reflex and have difficulty eating, or she might have trouble walking, seeing, hearing, or talking. Fortunately, their alarming predictions did not come true. As time went on, it became clear that the child didn't suffer the slightest damage from the stroke. Mrs. Paulina was happy and had no doubts about whom she owed this miracle to. It was God, through the intercession of Bl. José Luis, who showed them His power. Eight years after the miracle, it was officially approved. The canonization of the heroic young Cristero became a reality on October 16, 2016.

A unit of the Cristeros under the command of Manuel Michel surrendering under amnesty before the federal army in San Gabriel, Jalisco.

Cathedral of the Assumption of Our Lady in Guadalajara, Mexico.

Teresa in a Carmelite habit.

The grandfather of the future saint, Eulogio Solar, was a well-known person in Santiago.

Teresa in childhood photos.

SHE LOVED AND SUFFERED FOR THE SALVATION OF SOULS

St. Juana Fernández Solar Teresa of the Andes

Every year in October, tens of thousands of Chilean youths (around a million people a year) make a pilgrimage on foot to pray at the tomb of the country's first saint—the young Carmelite Teresa of Jesus, called Teresa of the Andes (1900–1920). Who was this extraordinary girl? What kind of life did she lead such that, dying before turning twenty, she deserved to be elevated to the glory of the altars? Who did she miraculously help?

"To young people who are being allured by the continuous messages and stimuli of an erotic culture, a society which mistakes the hedonistic exploitation of another for genuine love, which is self-giving, this young virgin of the Andes today proclaims the beauty and happiness that comes from a pure heart," wrote St. John Paul II.

JESUS WAS HER IDEAL

Juana Fernández de Solar was born in Santiago, the capital of Chile, as the fifth child of a very wealthy and deeply religious family. She was spoiled but also grounded. From her earliest days, she grew up in an atmosphere of real faith and healthy piety. She attended Holy Mass with her mother every day and, before

the age of seven, she prayed the Rosary daily with her brother. She forgot to do this once as a child, she admitted later in life! A spiritual milestone was her First Communion. She received the sacrament when she was ten years old. "Since that first embrace, Jesus did not let me go but took me for Himself," she recalled.

Indeed, from that moment on, her closeness with Jesus, as well as her friendship with the Virgin Mary, grew at a dizzying pace. "I live no longer, but He lives in me," she later said as a teenager, and these were by no means empty words. Do not think that she was a lay "nun" who was detached from the world, or a devotee full of complexes. Quite the opposite: she was an ordinary girl who was not without flaws or vices. Just like other children and teenagers, she went to school (and she disliked the boarding school to such an extent that she wanted to "let it go up in smoke"). Like other teens, she was happy to be in the company of her peers. She roamed the mountains and beaches with them, admiring the beauty of nature. She was passionate about horseback riding, and she liked playing tennis, swimming, diving, and driving fast. She played the piano and sang beautifully, she went to the theater, and she helped her mom at home and the priest in the parish. She was open to friendship, happiness, innocent fun, and jokes. She differed from her peers in one way: her continuous connection—full of joy and happiness—with God. She attended Holy Mass and received Holy Communion and, with God's help, she worked on herself, in an intense, remarkable way.

"My mind is taken up with Him alone. He is my ideal, an infinite ideal. I long for the day when I can go to Carmel to concern myself with Him alone, to abase myself in Him and so to live His life alone: To love and suffer to save souls," she confided to her sister Rebecca in 1916. She wanted to love Jesus without limits, to become

Teresa before entering the convent.

Teresa with her father, Miguel Fernández Jaraquemada.

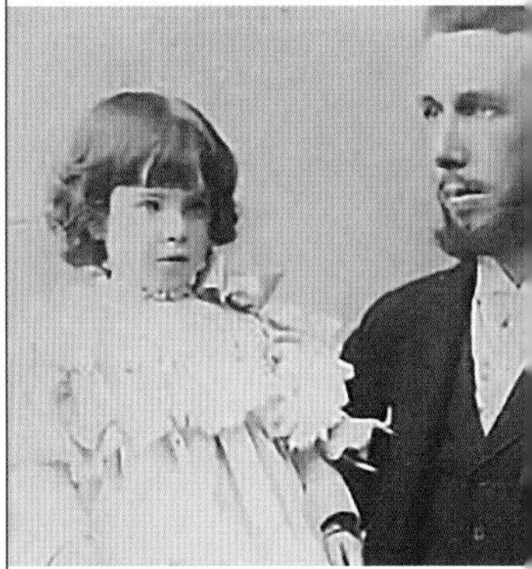

"My mind is taken up with Him alone. He is my ideal, an infinite ideal. I long for the day when I can go to Carmel to concern myself with Him alone, to abase myself in Him and so to live His life alone: to love and suffer to save souls."

a host like Him, a sacrificial victim for the sins of those who offended and saddened Him. She had already begun to experience the ecstasy of seeing Jesus with her mind. The Lord spoke to her, instructed her, and she listened. And although she wanted to "live only for Jesus," she later entered the Carmel of the Holy Spirit in the Andes—the poorest of monasteries. It seems as though she reached the height of her mystical development—close union with God—before this happened and before she fell asleep in the Lord from typhus. The rest—beatification in 1987 and canonization in 1993—were just formal confirmations of this.

Both spectacular miracles—the one that was approved for the beatification, as well as the one thanks to which Sr. Teresa of the Andes was canonized—occurred in Santiago de Chile. Almost six million people live in this great city—a third of the total population of Chile.

ELECTROCUTED

In 1980, Hector Ricardo Uribe Carrasco lived with his brothers and parents in one of the most beautiful neighborhoods in Santiago. The boy wanted to become a firefighter, but he was too young for that.

He applied to the Seventh Company of the capital's fire department, but was asked to join the Sixth Company, where the Youth Brigade had been formed only a year earlier. He did just that.

Based on lawsuits, numerous press reports, and maps of Santiago de Chile, I was able to determine that on the afternoon of December 4, 1983, a large fire broke out in a building located at the intersection of Maquinista Escobar and Bascuñán Guerrero. Eighteen-year-old Uribe—along with other young volunteers—quickly arrived at the scene. Around 4:45, he and the others went out onto the roof. In wet clothes, he tried to punch a hole in the roof to drag a hose

The simple Carmelite garment is the same for all the sisters scattered throughout the world.

The future saint with her brother.

St. Teresa's handwritten notes.

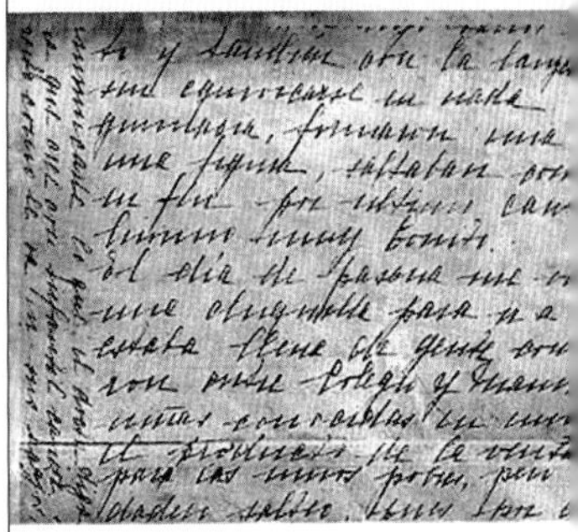

through so he could put out the fire more effectively. Sadly, he came across a 380-volt electric cable, accidentally damaged it, and got electrocuted by rubbing his wet pants against it. His limp body fell to the pavement. His heart stopped beating. Fortunately, there was a doctor nearby who immediately started resuscitation efforts. Uribe, however, showed no signs of life. He found himself in a state of clinical death. Finally, after being transported to the nearest medical facility, he was successfully resuscitated. Later that evening, his condition—despite two consecutive cardiac arrests and brain swelling—was finally stabilized. The doctors were under no illusions. In their opinion, the condition of the young man was so severe that even if he managed to survive, he would suffer from serious neurological complications for the rest of his life. The

St. Teresa of Ávila was a role model for the young nun.

next day—lying in the hospital, hooked up to life support—the young man was still unconscious. His family and friends decided

The monastic cell of St. Teresa of the Andes.

then that they would pray for his health through the intercession of the Handmaid of the Lord, Teresa of the Andes. Her relics were placed on the patient's chest. Three days later, on the eve of the Immaculate Conception of the Blessed Virgin Mary, the mother of the eighteen-year-old, Olga Carrasco de la Vega, his sister, and three firefighter volunteers with whom he was friends went on a pilgrimage to the grave of Teresa at the monastery in the Andes, located fifty miles from the capital. They prayed fervently for Hector's healing, and their prayers were answered!

Later that afternoon, Hector began to show the first signs of regaining consciousness. He began to move his eyelids. He was coming back to life, and his health improved minute by minute. The next day he was taken off the life support system. His bodily functions returned to normal. The boy was completely healthy.

The saint's grave is visited by pilgrims from all over South America.

Eight days later, a group of Hector's friends set out on foot again for the Andes, this time on a thanksgiving pilgrimage.

On December 20, Hector Ricardo Uribe Carrasco was discharged from the hospital "in very good health." The severe accident he suffered left no significant trace in the body. He was decorated with the Cruz de Hierro for his service in the fire brigade. Hector Uribe's healing was extensively studied in the coming years.

In 1987, the Vatican's medical and theological experts declared it a miracle. Pope John Paul II approved it the same year.

TRAGEDY AT THE POOL

Exactly five years later, on December 7, 1988, a group of twenty-three fifth-grade girls, under the care of six adults, went on a trip to the metropolitan swimming pool located within the Banco de Chile Stadium to celebrate the end of the school year.

Among them was a very talented and cheerful eleven-year-old named Marcela Antúnez Riveros. After dinner, the girl went into the water. Unable to swim, she jumped on an inflatable pool mattress, which carried her to the deep part of the pool (2.80 meters deep). She accidentally slipped, however, and found herself under water. She called for help but no one heard her. No one noticed that she was drowning. She couldn't breathe and lost consciousness. How long was she under water? No one knows. Maybe more than five minutes. The lifeguard, Juan Carlos, was only alerted after her friends, concerned about her absence, noticed there was a shadow in the water. The man jumped into the water, and after a moment he pulled the body of the child to the edge of the pool.

Unfortunately, Marcela showed no signs of life. She was unconscious and blue,

The majestic Andes from which the great saint takes her name.

Statue of St. Teresa in Santiago de Chile.

The Sanctuary of Auco-Rinconada in the Andes.

➤ *The Sanctuary of Auco-Rinconada in the Andes is the center of her cult. St. Teresa of Jesus is the first Chilean saint.*

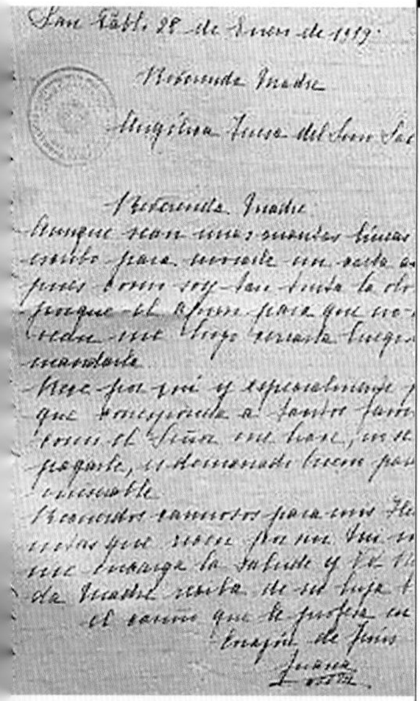

⮝ *Correspondence regarding St. Teresa of the Andes.*

➤ *St. Teresa of the Andes.*

her heart was not beating, she was not breathing, her pupils were unresponsive, her abdomen was bloated, and her tongue hung limply out of her mouth. Artificial ventilation and cardiac massage were started immediately. Chaos broke out. The girls screamed, cried, and whimpered that their friend was dead. The mother of one of the girls suggested then that it was necessary to call Bl. Teresa of the Andes for help. Most of them fell to their knees and began to pray fervently. How much time was spent in the efforts to resuscitate Marcela? This too is unknown, but it certainly lasted several more minutes. To make matters worse, in the confusion, no one called an ambulance. After a few moments, the girl made a guttural sound, but she was still unconscious. The ambulance was finally called, and when it arrived, the teenager was put on oxygen and transported to the hospital. She arrived in the emergency department at Clínica Alemana at 3:34 that afternoon. Dr. Gabriel Muñoz, an experienced doctor who had dealt with many such cases, received Marcela and expected not only damage and swelling of the brain, but also permanent damage to other organs—kidneys, heart, liver. That wasn't the case. Despite the very poor prognosis, just an hour after the unfortunate event, around 4:30, the girl began to breathe on her own, and soon after she was completely healthy. Even so, they still expected another health failure (as often happens in people who have drowned). She was discharged from the hospital after three days. To the surprise of doctors, despite many minutes spent under water, respiratory and cardiac arrest, and severe acidosis found after arrival at the hospital, which usually leads to multiple organ failure and death, the accident left her with no lasting damage—not even the smallest neurological disorders or psychological traumas. This event was analyzed and recognized as a miracle obtained through Teresa of the Andes.

She was called upon not only at the swimming pool, but also by the

girl's mother—Gladys Riveros de Antunez—during Marcela's four-day stay in the hospital. Many people prayed for her intercession to bring Marcela back to life. John Paul II approved this miracle on July 11, 1992.

Marcela Antúnez Riveros finished college as an outstanding student, and today she's an accomplished doctor.

A THOUSAND THANK-YOUS

The above-mentioned healings—which have been called resurrections—are only the tips of the iceberg. To this day, thousands of thank-yous have poured into the sanctuary in the Andes for graces received through the intercession of St. Teresa. As the sanctuary's website reads, the faithful thank her for saving their lives and health, for protecting children and families, for the grace of parenthood, and for help in obtaining employment.

1910–1997

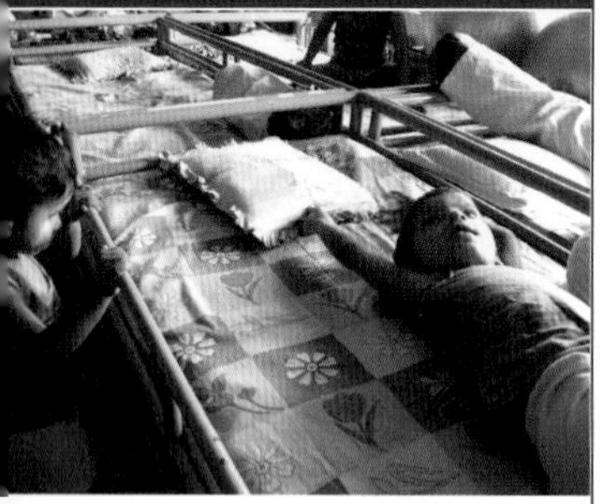

⮝ *Rescuing abandoned, sick, and homeless children, she founded the Shishu Bhavan orphanage. She fought against abortion, considering it the greatest threat to world peace.*

TEACHER OF MERCY FROM CALCUTTA

St. Mother Teresa

The founder of the Order of the Missionaries of Charity, she was able to see Christ in the poorest of the poor. She spread the message of mercy and joy to the world. Her life motto was the words of Jesus: "Whatever you did for one of the least of these brothers and sisters of mine, you did for me." She clung to Christ with all her heart, although for almost fifty years—until the end of her life—she "did not feel His presence." Living in the unholy twentieth century, she was already considered a saint during her lifetime.

Anjeze Gonxhe Bojaxhiu was born in Skopje (the capital of North Macedonia) in a devout and wealthy Catholic Albanian family. Her parents gave her—and the other two children—a wonderful example of Christian life: daily prayer together, performing numerous acts of mercy, and helping many poor and sick people. (The mother looked after an old, sick woman every day, and when a widow raising seven children died in the neighborhood, she took the orphans into her home without hesitation).

⮟ *Panorama of Darjeeling.*

ROAD TO CALCUTTA

Influenced by a Jesuit missionary and descriptions of his mission work, teenage Anjeze decided to become a missionary herself. In 1928 she left for Ireland, joined the convent of the Sisters of Our Lady of Loreto, adopted her religious name after St. Thérèse of Lisieux, and was sent to India. She became a teacher in schools run by Loreto nuns in Darjeeling and Calcutta.

In India, and especially in Calcutta, she was deeply impacted by the sight of horrific human misery—the crippled and the old, covered in wounds, living and dying in the streets, newborns thrown straight into the garbage, and homeless children. At thirty-six, Mother Teresa heard the voice of Jesus calling her to go out into the streets to serve the poor. She did so without any objections. She founded a new congregation—Missionaries of Charity, whose habit became the clothes of poor Hindu women: a white blue-rimmed sari.

Fighting for a dignified death for the sick and the weary poor dying in the streets, she set up the Home for the Dying, Nirmal Hriday—"Home of the Pure Heart."

Caring for the bodies, souls, and human dignity of lepers rejected by society, she organized mobile clinics and created a leper colony, Shanti Nagar (Place of Peace). Rescuing abandoned, sick, and homeless children, she founded the Shishu Bhaven orphanage. She fought with all her strength against abortion, considering it the greatest threat to world peace. She founded several hundred orders and charitable centers around the world.

POWER OF JOY

The caretaker of the poor encouraged others to love the Eucharist, to spend more time in adoration, to pray in order to help us recognize and fulfill God's will, and to draw inspiration from humble Mary, who was committed to the will of God. She talked about the need to love others and the importance of being sensitive to the needs of those around us. She called for liberation from selfishness and greed, defining wealth as "the ability to handle money for the good of others." She stressed the value of calm and silence, the saving power of forgiveness. She taught that "faith in action is love" and "love in action is service." To a world full of complaints, sadness, and fear, she preached not only a great message of love, but also of joy. "So often one smile can change another person's life, bring them joy, God, make suffering make sense. ... We shall never know all the good that a simple smile can do," she told Fr. Lush Gjergj. Our cheerfulness and happiness, according to Mother Teresa, is the "surest

Fighting for a dignified death for the sick and the weary poor dying in the streets, she set up the Home for the Dying, Nirmal Hriday—"Home of the Pure Heart." Caring for the bodies, souls, and human dignity of lepers rejected by society, she organized mobile clinics and created a leper colony, Shanti Nagar (Place of Peace).

The whole world admired the actions of this small, simple nun. She was seen as a "living saint," and she was honored with awards and titles, like the Nobel Peace Prize. Although she was Catholic, she was buried with the honors of an Indian national hero. In Calcutta alone, a million people bid her farewell.

way to preach Christianity to the pagan." She gave a simple but inspiring example from her own life.

> *Once a man came to Kalighat. I was there. After a little while he came back and said to me, "I came here with so much hate in my heart, hate for God and hate for man. I came here empty, faithless, embittered, and I saw a sister giving her wholehearted attention to a patient, and I realized that God still loves. I believe there is a God and that He loves us still.*

As Mother Teresa said, "God loves those who give with joy" and "the best way to show gratitude to God and people is to accept everything with joy."

> *In your environments, spread the joy of belonging to God, of living with Him and loving Him in others. ... To be happy and bursting with joy, you don't need much. It's enough to try to do God's will every day. ... Pray unceasingly, try to love and forgive. ... The modern world hungers for the joy that flows from a pure heart, because only those who are pure of heart will see God. ... A smile costs nothing but gives so much. ... Joy shines in the eyes, comes out in speech, shows up in facial expressions. When people see happiness in your eyes, they will see God in you.*

The whole world admired the actions of this small, simple nun. She was seen as a "living saint," and she was honored with awards and titles, including the Nobel Peace Prize. Although she was Catholic, she was buried with the honors of an Indian national hero. In Calcutta alone, a million people bid her farewell.

RELAXED REQUIREMENTS

John Paul II knew Mother Teresa personally and shared the common opinion about her holiness. The pope therefore decided to waive the five-year waiting period that is required after the death of a candidate for sainthood and the beginning of the process leading to canonization. The postulator was given the green light to start immediately. The other requirements, however, remained the same—specific miracles were needed.

During the beatification process, several miracles performed by God through the intercession of Mother Teresa were considered. Most of them, however, did not meet the strict Church criteria and could not be recognized as miracles. This is what happened with a French woman who, by touching a medallion from Mother Teresa, healed her ribs broken in a car accident. This was also the case with a young Palestinian girl who recovered from bone cancer after seeing Mother Teresa in a dream.

Only the healing of Monica Besra, a Hindu, was considered a miracle. This miracle happened in September 1998 in Patiram, India.

MEDALLION ON THE ABDOMEN

Thirty-two-year-old Monica Besra, mother of five, from the village of Dangram in West Bengal, had been receiving treatment for tubercular meningitis for a year when a tumor began to grow in her abdomen (specifically, on the ovary). In 1998, the woman was treated in several Indian hospitals. Her condition was getting worse and her belly was so distended that she looked as if she were six months pregnant. It was estimated that the tumor might have already weighed about eleven pounds. "The doctors were afraid to operate on me," Besra recalled. Seeing the woman's health deteriorate, the medics were convinced that she would soon die. With a fever, headache, vomiting, and a swollen stomach, the young mother ended up at the headquarters of the Missionaries of Charity in Patiram. "I had been in severe pain and was crying for two months. I was unable to sleep. I could only lie on my left side. The sisters gave me medicine but the pain didn't go away. I was praying to Mother Teresa, whose picture hung on the wall opposite of my bed," Besra said. It was decided that an

Missionaries of Charity in traditional saris on the street of an Indian city.

The Ambubasi festival is held annually during the monsoon season at the Kamakhya Devi Temple in Guwahati, in the Indian state of Assam.

1910–1997

➤ *Mother Teresa's orphanage in Calcutta.*

⮝ *An early photograph of Mother Teresa.*

operation would be necessary, but the woman was too weak and too sick to endure it. She couldn't sleep because of the pain.

On September 5—on the anniversary of Mother Teresa's death—Monica Besra prayed in the chapel of the Missionaries of Charity Sisters. She noticed that a strange light was coming out of the picture of the Handmaid of God. That day, the sisters placed a third-class relic on her abdomen—a medallion that had touched Mother Teresa's body—and said a prayer, asking her for help. The suffering woman fell asleep. When she awoke early the next morning, to her surprise, all the pain had stopped. Medical exams showed that the tumor had also disappeared—completely! The operation was no longer needed. And although some doctors suggested that it might have been the effect of the drugs taken, it was acknowledged that no drugs could have caused the huge tumor to disappear so suddenly and unexpectedly.

"I was cured thanks to the intercession of Mother Teresa," said Monica Besra, convinced of this fact. The miraculousness of this event was also confirmed by the Vatican commission in 2002. In 2003, John Paul II declared Mother Teresa blessed.

A MIRACLE IN BRAZIL

Five years after Mother Teresa's beatification, in December 2008, a second miracle happened, this time to Marcilio Haddad Andrino, a mechanical engineer from Santos in São Paulo. From the age of six he had kidney problems, which escalated to the point that at the age of eighteen he had to undergo a transplant, he later recounted during public appearances. At the beginning of the year 2000, Marcilio met his future wife Fernanda Nascimento Rocha. The couple decided to get married at the end of 2008. However, at the beginning of that year, the thirty-four-year-old man began to experience strange symptoms—he

➤ *Planting rice in Tamil Nadu, a state in southern India.*

began to have double vision and had convulsions. He was examined by many doctors, but none of them could tell what was wrong with him. Treatment attempts failed. His condition began to deteriorate: he stopped walking, and he had cognitive impairments. At that time, Fernanda's friend suggested to her that she turn to Mother Teresa for help. She herself had previously suffered from an aneurysm and—as she believed—was healed by her intercession. They began to pray, but the situation did not improve. The couple was also encouraged to pray through the intercession of Mother Teresa by a priest friend. With the wedding date coming up, Fernanda went to see him and received the relics of Mother Teresa. On the day of the wedding, the young husband was very weak, and the following days brought further deterioration of his health: memory problems and epileptic seizures.

On December 9, the sickly man woke up with a strong, throbbing headache. He had difficulty speaking. He asked his wife to pray for him. A priest was called to administer the anointing of the sick. The situation was very serious and the doctors were going to make a last attempt to save Marcilio's life. They planned to operate on him and drain the fluid that was building up in his skull, causing hydrocephalus and constricting his brain. He was given anesthesia and most likely lost consciousness. He was then taken to the operating room. During this time, Fernanda was praying for him— to God through the intercession of Mother Teresa. Before the surgery, in the operating room, to the surgeon's surprise, Marcilio woke up. "What am I doing here?" he asked, surprised, looking around the room. He felt great peace, and his head didn't hurt anymore. He told the doctor about it.

The doctor decided then that since the patient was no longer in pain, he would postpone the operation until the next day and would temporarily transfer him to the intensive care unit. That's what he did.

Ronald Reagan presented the Medal of Freedom to Mother Teresa in 1985.

➤ *Sarcophagus of St. Mother Teresa.*

⮝ *Headquarters of the Missionaries of Charity in Calcutta.*

⮝ *Mother Teresa of Calcutta received the Bharat Ratna, India's highest civilian award.*

Marcilio slept through the night without any problems, and in the morning—as he still felt no pain or discomfort—he was transferred to a general care floor. There he was reunited with his wife and his parents. He felt fine, and although he could not walk, he sat and talked to them normally. The operation turned out to be unnecessary because it was discovered that the abscesses, just as the hydrocephalus, shrunk by seventy percent. After three days and another CT scan, it turned out that everything was gone—not even scars from the abscesses were visible. The man spent Christmas at home.

"I was certain that Mother Teresa healed me," he said in 2016, during an August meeting in Rimini, Italy. His wife thought the same.

It turned out, however, that the man initially thought that the healing was due to an antibiotic taken the day before. The doctor himself led him away from that error, saying that "there is no antibiotic that would work immediately, the day after." "So what happened?" Marcilio's father asked. "Someone up there loves you very much," said the doctor, pointing to Heaven.

There was something else that could be considered a second miracle. The doctors predicted that the drugs taken by the man would make him sterile, and the couple would never have their own children. The married couple accepted it, recognizing that it would be as God wills. But God had other plans. Six months after his recovery, when the couple was already living in Rio de Janeiro, it turned out that Fernanda was pregnant. In 2012, the couple had their second child, and together with their children, they are now among the greatest devotees of Mother Teresa.

According to the postulator, Father Brian Kolodiejchuk, it was also a miracle that this case was discovered. "The miracle happened in 2008," he said, "but we didn't hear about it until 2013. The doctor wasn't a Catholic. After the pope's visit to Brazil, he was prompted to tell one of the Santos priests about it, and this news finally reached me and the Postulation Office. This set off a chain of events."

The healing was thoroughly investigated in 2015 and was considered Mother Teresa's second miracle. A year later, the caregiver of the poor was canonized.

THE LIGHT OF GOD'S LOVE

In the case of beatification and canonization, only posthumous physical healings are taken into account, but spiritual healings are important as well, and Mother Teresa had many that could be credited to her.

The most spectacular conversion to which she contributed—while still alive and in a rather miraculous way—involved one of the most eminent English journalists and a longtime BBC employee, Malcolm Muggeridge (1903–1990). The English journalist interviewed the most famous personalities of the century: Gandhi, Nixon, Eisenhower, Kennedy, De Gaulle, Khrushchev. Only one changed his life: Mother Teresa of Calcutta.

⮝ *Memorial House of Mother Teresa located in her hometown of Skopje.*

⮜ *Nirmal Hriday, Mother Teresa's hospice in Calcutta.*

In 1968, while preparing for a televised interview with the nun from Calcutta, the sixty-five-year-old journalist, who came from an atheistic and socialist family, was still a skeptical non-believer. He got involved in such a topic with great reluctance, and he suspected a flop. Meanwhile, the allegedly uninteresting and weak conversation with the future saint—to the surprise of television professionals—was very much liked by the viewers. He rode the wave. In 1969, English television viewers saw a documentary he made about Mother Teresa and the Missionaries of Charity. During its filming, something happened that Muggeridge took as a sign from God. Although it was very dark in the Home for the Dying in Calcutta and in theory the shots shouldn't have been useable, "it turned out that the part shot inside was bathed in a particularly beautiful soft light," while scenes shot in a sunny courtyard "were rather dim and blurry."

"How to account for this?" Muggeridge wondered in the book *Something Beautiful for God*. He continues:

> *Ken [the cameraman] has all along insisted that, technically speaking, the result is impossible. To prove*

Mother Teresa Cathedral in Pristina.

The most spectacular conversion to which she contributed—while still alive and in a rather miraculous way—involved one of the most eminent English journalists, the longtime BBC employee Malcolm Muggeridge (1903–1990). The English journalist interviewed the most famous personalities of the century: Gandhi, Nixon, Eisenhower, Kennedy, De Gaulle, Khrushchev. But only one changed his life: Mother Teresa of Calcutta.

A statue of Mother Teresa in Madrid.

> *the point, on his next filming expedition—to the Middle East—he used some of the same stock in a similarly poor light, with completely negative results. He offers no explanation, but just shrugs and agrees that it happened. I myself am absolutely convinced that the technically unaccountable light is, in fact, the Kindly Light Newman refers to in his well-known exquisite hymn. Mother Teresa's Home for the Dying is overflowing with love, as one senses immediately on entering it. This love is luminous, like the haloes artists have seen and made visible round the heads of the saints. I find it not at all surprising that the luminosity should register on a photographic film. ... So, the light conveys perfectly what the place is really like; an outward and visible luminosity manifesting God's inward and invisible omnipresent love.*

In his many years in the field, Muggeridge had learned all about the world's ideologies—imperialism, communism, socialism, National Socialism, social democracy, and liberalism. He came to the conclusion that all visions of creating an earthly paradise—based on the misconceptions of man—make life a "nightmare." But it was his friendship with Mother Teresa and his earlier trip to the Holy Land that made him interested in Jesus, completely changing him. Fascinated by them—and following in the example of Chesterton, Thomas Aquinas, and Augustine—Muggeridge began to write books loaded with Christian values. From an atheistic mocker, he became a Christian apologist; from a libertine he turned into an orthodox Christian, a harsh critic of moral permissiveness, an opponent of contraception and a defender of the sanctity of life. He recognized Marx and Freud as the greatest destroyers of Christian civilization, "the first replacing the gospel of love by the gospel of hate, the other undermining the essential concept of human responsibility." He greatly valued John Paul II. On November 27, 1982, in the chapel of Our Lady Help of Christians in the small village of Hurst Green, Malcom Muggeridge became a Catholic.

1591–1657

➤ *St. Andrew Bobola surrounded by angels.*

⮝ *St. Andrew Bobola with a palm of martyrdom, an image of Our Lady of Grace, Patron Saint of Warsaw, and a miniature coffin reminiscent of the great propitiatory processions of the saint during the Polish-Bolshevik war.*

DEVOTED MISSIONARY FOR JESUS CHRIST

St. Andrew Bobola

Many years after his cruel martyrdom, Fr. Andrew Bobola, a Jesuit missionary, confessed his deep desire to become the patron of his homeland, Poland. Today, his wish has been fulfilled. As one of Poland's patron saints, he has appeared to Poles several times and has helped to save Poland in difficult situations. He still helps those who turn to him.

"FIND MY BODY"

It was 1702. The turmoil of the third Northern War between Denmark, Russia, Saxony, Prussia, and Sweden threatened the Polish town of Pińsk.

Fr. Marcin Godebski, the benevolent rector of the Jesuit College of Pińsk, began a frantic search for a patron to whom to entrust the care of the school. One Sunday evening, April 16, an unknown Jesuit appeared to him. His luminous face showed sympathy. "Are you looking for a patron who will protect the college?" asked the vision. "You've got me. I'm your brother, Andrew Bobola. I was killed by the Cossacks in defense of the Faith. Find my body. For it is God's will that you separate me from the others."

Fr. Godebski ordered his juniors to find the man's coffin. The task wasn't easy. For two days they searched the damp depths of the church crypt, but Fr. Bobola's remains were not among the crumbling coffins. Where could he be?

On the second day of searching, Andrew Bobola appeared again, this time to the

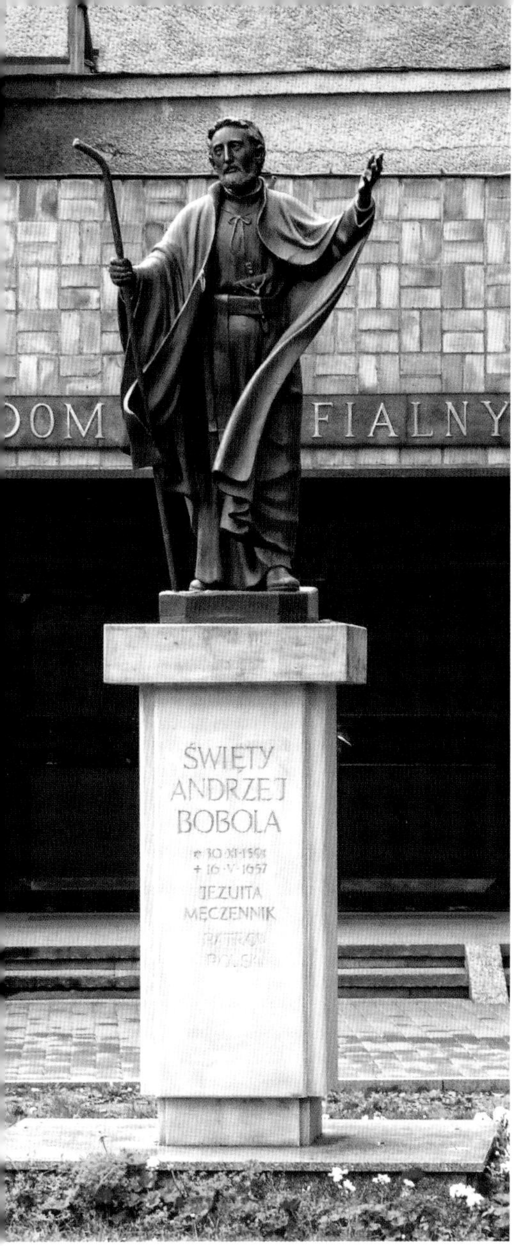

sacristan Prokop Łukaszewicz. Fr. Bobola told the sacristan exactly where his coffin was located. And so, on the third day, the search team went to the indicated place and, after only a few hits with a shovel, unveiled a plate on which was inscribed the last name Bobola. The coffin was dug up and cleaned. The group then opened the lid and saw the tortured body of the martyr.

Although almost half a century had passed since his death, Fr. Bobola looked as if he had been placed in the coffin only yesterday. His brutal wounds were perfectly visible. The flesh was intact, flexible, and odorless. His blood had clotted, but it had not lost its color. The incorrupt state of his body was a miracle. And as Fr. Godebski stared at the corpse, he recognized the face of the person who had visited him the previous Sunday night.

Since then, crowds of people have prayed in front of the new crypt in which the incorrupt corpse of Andrew Bobola was placed. The college—and the city—received its patron. The cult of Andrew Bobola grew, and many graces were obtained through his intercession.

In 1712, the General of the Jesuits began the official process to beatify Fr. Bobola. The martyr had grown so popular in Poland by this time that two Polish kings, Augustus II and Stanisław August Poniatowski, joined in his beatification efforts. The movement to beatify Fr. Bobola seemed to be heading toward success, as in 1755, Pope Benedict XIV officially recognized Andrew Bobola as a martyr for the faith. The official beatification, however, was hindered by the temporary official suppression of the Jesuit Order from 1773 to 1814, as well as the Partitions of Poland, which reduced Polish land to the point that by 1795, the state of Poland ceased to exist until after World War I.

"I WILL BE HER PATRON!"

The martyr, however, did not give up. He appeared for a third time in Wilno (now the Lithuanian city of Vilnius) in 1819, to a Dominican priest, physicist, and preacher, Alojzy Korzeniewski, who was being persecuted by the government of tsarist Russia. One evening, while Fr. Korzeniewski was staying in the monastery in Wilno, he turned to Fr. Andrew Bobola during evening prayer and asked him to pray for Polish independence. Fr. Korzeniewski was then about to retire to bed, when he suddenly saw a vision of Fr. Bobola!

Fr. Bobola told him to open the window. Fr. Korzeniewski did as he was told, but when he looked outside, he did not see

POLAND

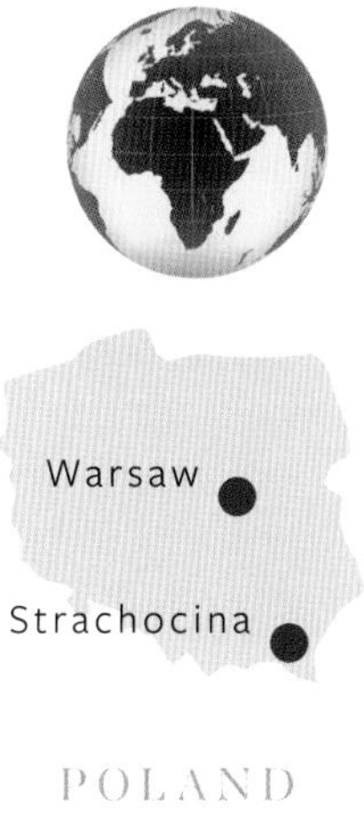

Statue of St. Andrew Bobola erected in front of his sanctuary.

Janów, Poleski. St. Andrew Bobola's place of death.

A painting of St. Andrew Bobola in the Church of the Holy Apostles Peter and Paul in Kamienna Góra, Poland.

the monastery courtyard but a vast plain. The mysterious visitor explained to him that he saw the land of Pińsk, where he had been martyred for his faith. The astonished Dominican then saw a great war in which many nations fought against each other with unprecedented ferocity. "When the war whose image you have in front of your eyes will end in peace, Poland will be rebuilt, and I will be her primary patron," the vision explained.

Two of these prophecies have been fulfilled. Poland regained its statehood in 1918, after World War I, and in 2002, Fr. Bobola became a patron of Poland. He is not yet the "primary patron" of the nation, but many still pray that he becomes so.

"I AM A CATHOLIC PRIEST"

Who was this Jesuit who so resolutely—with God's permission—sought to be a patron of Poland?

According to his biographers, Andrew Bobola was actually quite a difficult person. He was irritable, impatient, and lacking in self-control, but at the same time, he was an incredibly dedicated and zealous missionary with extraordinary courage.

Bobola came from a noble, deeply religious family. When he was fifteen, his parents sent him to study at an excellent Jesuit college in Braniewo. While he studied, Bobola felt a call to the priesthood, and so he became a Jesuit. He worked in many Jesuit communities in Poland and became known as a priest with great apostolic zeal. He was a moderator of the Sodality of Our Lady, and he was a great preacher and confessor with a gift of converting the lost.

In 1642, fifty-one-year-old Fr. Bobola was sent to the college in Pińsk, the capital of the district Polesia. Pińsk was located among impassible swamps and forests, yet it was only there—among superstitious Poleshuks and schismatic Orthodox Christians—that Fr. Bobola's gift of conversion would blossom in all its glory. His nine-year service in Pińsk, which was interrupted only once due to illness, was marked by numerous missionary trips that lasted several days. He fought widespread superstitions as he taught the true Faith, spiritually uplifting harassed Catholics and converting both pagan and Orthodox Poles. Fr. Bobola was open and kind, humble and selfless. His simple life—he often lived only on bread and water—drew many atheists to Christ and brought many Orthodox Christians back into communion with the Church. He even converted two entire villages in the region to Catholicism.

But the apostolic activity of this soul hunter, the "apostle of the Pińsk region," soon became a thorn in the side of the Orthodox, who called him a "disgusting Jesuit" and a "thief of souls." Soon, an opportunity came to confront him.

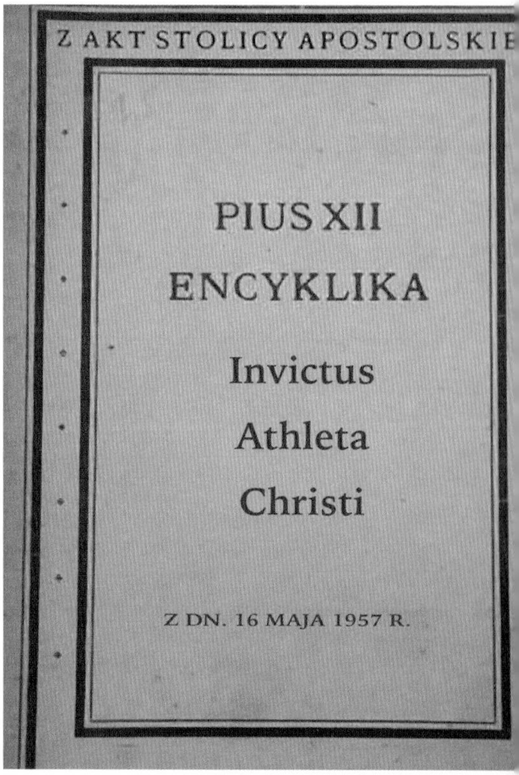
Z AKT STOLICY APOSTOLSKIE

PIUS XII

ENCYKLIKA

Invictus

Athleta

Christi

Z DN. 16 MAJA 1957 R.

Execution of St. Andrew Bobola.

His right eye was gouged out, strips of skin were torn off, his wounds were savagely scorched and rubbed with prickly bundles of straw. Nor was that enough: his ears, nose, and lips were cut off, his tongue torn out by the root, and finally, a weapon plunged into his heart. And, at long last, the valiant athlete, three hours after midday, displaying a truly marvelous example of fortitude, was pierced by a sword and achieved the glory of martyrdom. (Invicti Athletae Christi)

In 1655, Poland was invaded by the Swedes, and packs of Cossacks began to ravage its eastern borders. These Cossacks had a special hatred for Poles, Catholics, and Jesuits, and they looted and murdered wherever they went. By 1657, one Cossack force occupied Pińsk. Faced with mortal danger, Fr. Bobola left the city.

On May 16, the Cossacks reached Janów Poleski, a town in southeast Poland, and they murdered all Jews and Catholics living there. They were then informed that a dangerous Jesuit—a "thief of souls" —was hiding in a nearby town. The Cossacks found Fr. Bobola in a cart, captured him, and tried to force him to convert to Orthodoxy. He refused. They beat him, pulled out his nails, tied him to the horses, and took him more than two miles away to the market square in Janów. There, they hit him in the head with a saber, cut off three of his fingers, and cut his leg. They then dragged him to a shed where animals were slaughtered. The Cossacks asked Fr. Bobola if he was a Latin priest. He replied, "I am a Catholic priest; I was born in the Catholic Faith; in that Faith I wish to die. My faith is true; it leads to salvation. Repent and do penance, or else in your errors, you will be unable to receive salvation. By accepting my Faith, you will find the true God and save your souls."

These harsh words did not awaken any feelings of mercy in the Cossacks. Instead, the persecutors grew so furious that they started using even more severe forms of torment on the soldier of Christ:

> *Once again, "he was scourged, a crown like that of Jesus Christ was bound about his head, he was struck heavy blows and lay wounded by a scimitar. Next, his right eye was gouged out, strips of skin were torn off, his wounds were savagely scorched and rubbed with prickly bundles of straw. Nor was that*

On the three hundredth anniversary of the death of St. Andrew Bobola, Pius XII issued an encyclical Invicti Athletae Christi *("Christ's Unconquered Athlete"). He wanted to teach the world about the death of St. Andrew Bobola and hold him up as a great example of Christian courage.*

➤ *Janów Poleski. On the left, a part of the Orthodox Church of the Protection of the Holy Virgin is visible with the chapel of St. Andrew Bobola in the place of his martyrdom in the background. This chapel was destroyed by the Soviets after 1939.*

⮝ *St. Andrew Bobola with the palm of martyrdom and execution tools.*

enough: his ears, nose, and lips were cut off, his tongue torn out by the root, and finally, a weapon plunged into his heart. And, at long last, the valiant athlete, three hours after midday, displaying a truly marvelous example of fortitude, was pierced by a sword and achieved the glory of martyrdom."

These words come from Pope Pius XII, quoting Pius XI, in his encyclical *Invicti Athletae Christi* ("Christ's Unconquered Athlete"), which he wrote in 1957 on the three hundredth anniversary of the death of St. Andrew Bobola. This is how the future patron of Poland died on May 16, 1657. "Crimsoned in his own blood," he gave himself as his last sacrifice to God.

After killing the priest, the Cossacks heard a band of Polish knights approaching and fled, leaving the mangled corpse of the hated Pole lying in pools of blood.

Fr. Bobola's body was then transported to Pińsk and quickly—so as not to scare the young students of the college with the gruesome sight of the corpse—buried in the basement of the Pińsk church.

Fr. Bobola was one of about fifty Polish Jesuits murdered at this time, so initially, no one thought of him as an extraordinary candidate for the altars. What took place between him and the Cossacks—the purity of his heart, his self-sacrifice, his commitment to spreading the faith, his great courage, and his devotion—was known only to God. The martyr was forgotten for forty-five years.

But Providence had more in store for him.

AN ANSWERED PRAYER

The visions of Fr. Andrew Bobola and the fact that his body remained incorrupt are clear miracles. But in order to be a patron of Poland, Fr. Bobola had to prove his dedication to the people and demonstrate his intercession on their behalf.

In May of 1730, an epidemic of dysentery broke out in Wilno, Poland. Dysentery, which is most often caused by *Shigella* bacteria, attacks the digestive system and the intestines, and its most characteristic symptom is bloody diarrhea. The plague did not spare anyone, and most of its victims were children.

The Florkowski family was among the ill. The young parents, Regina and Franciszek, had already buried their son, and they were now fiercely fighting to save their second child, Marianna, who was not even two years old. The child had been tormented by bloody diarrhea for three months. No medication could help her. Anything the girl put in her mouth would pass undigested, covered in blood. Her body began to exude a strong stench that permeated the air in the house, as though she were already a rotting corpse. And poor Marianna developed such terrible swelling all over her body that she lay helpless and immobile. Life seemed to pass from her completely.

Anticipating the imminent death of her child, Regina went to the Church of St. John to pour out her sorrows and ask for advice from her regular confessor, Jesuit priest Aleksander Kaszyc. The priest advised her to pray with faith for the intercession of God's servant Andrew Bobola and to hear three holy Masses in honor of the Holy Trinity.

The mother, who had heard about the martyr, eagerly agreed and immediately fulfilled her priest's recommendation. With a trembling heart, she returned home and asked her husband at the door about the child. "She's still alive, but she's so weak that we shall not have her much longer," replied Franciszek. Regina then told her husband about where she was and what

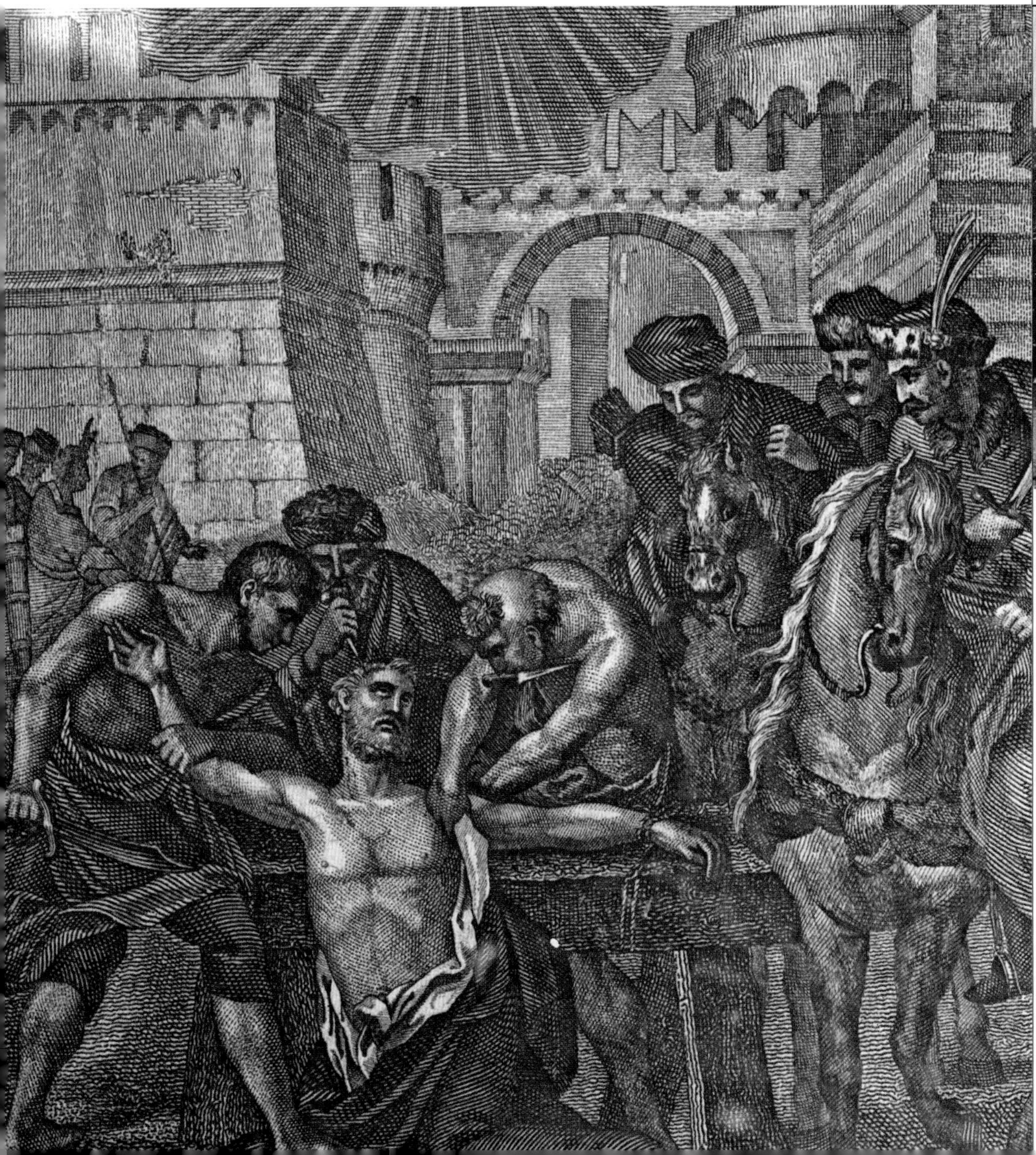

St. Andrew Bobola's shrine in Janów, Poleski. Photo from 1936.

The execution of St. Andrew Bobola.

St. Catherine of Alexandria Church and Sanctuary of St. Andrew Bobola in Strachocina, the hometown of the saint, where the saint requested to be venerated.

Pope Pius XI during the canonization ceremonies of Fr. Andrew Bobola.

she was doing and asked him to join her in entrusting their daughter to the servant of God. Franciszek was unfamiliar with Fr. Bobola, but he listened to his wife's plea and entrusted his little daughter to Bobola in his prayers.

Then, a miracle. As soon as the parents began praying, their child was able to keep food down for the first time in a while. The second day, the child was more lively, and by the third day, she was so healthy that it was as if she had never been sick. The girl had recovered, but the family was not yet free from distress.

Fr. Hieronym Kajsiewicz, a well-known priest of the time, described what happened next:

> *The mother ran to the confessor to tell him the happy news and to thank him for his advice. He obliged her to provide testimony before the commission responsible for the canonization of Blessed Martyr. She willingly promised to do so. But after a week, she heard from her husband that a certain father advised him not to speak under oath, as it was a dangerous thing to do. She herself was frightened and decided not to say anything in this respect and told her confessor about her decision. "Do what you want," he replied, "I will not force you, but fear that for this ingratitude God will punish you and take the girl from you." Caring very little about this threat, she returned home and found her daughter, who was perfectly healthy when she had left, moaning and tossing restlessly. Her stomach was hardened, her urine stopped, and medicine did not help.*
>
> *Seeing then, together with her husband and sister, who was present at the time, the clear punishment of God upon them, it struck all three of them with repentance and humility. They called the blessed one from their hearts and promised to tell the commission everything under oath, however difficult it would be. As soon as they had promised this, the girl was cured and lived without needing any medicine.*

LYING AS IF SHE HAD DIED

Six years earlier, in January 1724, another girl had struggled with dysentery: Katarzyna Brzozowska, the nearly three-year-old daughter of the noble Michał and

Joanna de Kalwedor of Pińsk. Fr. Kajsiewicz wrote that "within three months [the disease had] destroyed her.... The parents went to a pharmacy looking for medicine, but the pharmacist knew nothing could save her." The pharmacist refused to sell them anything.

Finally, when the girl had not eaten anything for three days and was "lying as if she had died," her desperate parents took her in their arms, got in a horse cart, and went to the grave of Andrew Bobola in Pińsk to ask his intercession. While their friends tried to dissuade them by saying that their daughter would die along the way, Michał and Joanna were stalwart in their faith. They ignored all remarks and made it to Pińsk, praying fervently all the while to their helper in Heaven.

At the grave, the Brzozowskas asked for the coffin of the servant of God to be opened. Then, according to Fr. Kajsiewicz, "the girl, who up to this point was almost lifeless, began to stretch out her hands, clearly wanting to walk and get closer to the coffin. As soon as her mother led her there, the little girl put her hands around the feet of the blessed one, kissed them piously and she immediately recovered, not the slightest trace of the past illness remained. She was healthy: eating and doing everything."

A SEVERE DISEASE DISAPPEARED WITHOUT A TRACE

Jan Chmielnicki was a nobleman in the nineteenth century who lived near Dubna, and his son suffered terribly from scurvy. According to Fr. Jan Popłatek in his biography *St. Andrew Bobola: Hunter of Souls*, which was published later in the 1930s, "The disease dragged on for many months. The child's body was covered with infected, festering wounds."

The child's condition was so dire that the father thought that it would be easier for a dead man to rise from the grave than for his son to recover. He had lost all hope, so he didn't call for a doctor or give the boy any medicine. The father ordered his son to be taken from Dubna to a nearby village where he ran a farm. Soon after, the boy became completely stiff, and all signs of life disappeared. His distraught mother burst into tears. One of the handmaids, Anna Ballaicha, tried to calm her down by saying that tears do not resurrect the dead, and she began to wash the child's body with water to prepare it for the coffin. At that moment, Mrs. Chmielnicki, filled with great trust, offered the child to God and immersed herself in prayer, invoking the intercession of Fr. Bobola. Immediately, all the symptoms of the disease disappeared, and after a week, the child was completely healthy.

News of this miracle was published in a June 1853 article in the newspaper *l'Univers* by Fr. Hieronim Kajsiewicz, who wrote of the "immediate and perfect healing of Chmielnicki's son." Soon after, that same year, Pius IX not only approved the miracle but declared Fr. Bobola among the Blessed.

THE MIRACLE ON THE VISTULA

After his beatification, Fr. Bobola's cult intensified again. In 1920, Poland was threatened with invasion by Soviet Russia, and so the relics of the hand of Bl. Andrew Bobola were carried in a procession as the people begged him, the Mother of God, and the patron of Warsaw, Bl. Władysław of Gielniów, for help.

Bishops at Andrew Bobola's canonization ceremony. In the first row, from the right, inter alia: Bishop of Tarnów Franciszek Lisowski, Bishop of Włocławek Karol Radoński; Bishop of Podlaskie Henryk Przeździecki; Metropolitan of Warsaw Cardinal-Priest Aleksander Kakowski; Metropolitan Archbishop of Lviv of the Latin Rite Bolesław Twardowski; Metropolitan of Wilno Romuald Jałbrzykowski; Bishop of Chełmno Stanisław Okoniewski; Bishop of Pińsk Kazimierz Bukraba.

➤ *Canonization of Andrew Bobola, St. Peter's Basilica.*

After the Miracle on the Vistula, efforts to canonize Bl. Andrew Bobola increased. He was finally canonized by Pius XI on April 17, 1938.

The people's prayers were answered! When the Soviet Russian army attacked Warsaw in August 1920, the Polish army miraculously defeated them. This victory was devastating to the Soviets; not only was their invasion halted, but the Red Army was never able to regain their forces, and they were forced to sign a peace treaty with Poland just a few months later. This Battle of Warsaw, otherwise known as the "Miracle on the Vistula," changed the fate of the Polish-Soviet War and saved all of Europe from the plague of Communism.

EXTRAORDINARY FATE OF AN UNDISTURBED BODY

At this time, Fr. Bobola's still-incorrupt body was in Połock (modern Polotsk, Belarus). It had been moved there after the Jesuit Church in Pińsk had fallen into the hands of the Orthodox in 1793. The Catholics feared that the Orthodox priests and monks would bury Fr. Bobola's coffin, and so they transported it to Połock, with the tsar's permission.

In Połock, the cult of Andrew Bobola began to spread even among Orthodox Christians! And so in 1886, in order to stop the veneration of what they considered to be a "false saint," tsarist authorities sent a special commission to Połock to remove Fr. Bobola's relics. But when one of the "commissioners" joked about "Polish methods of making saints," a brick fell on his head. The rest of the commissioners then decided it was best if the martyr's body were left alone.

Then, in 1922, the Soviet Russians sent another commission to Połock in order to investigate and confirm the body of the "religious fraud." The Soviets took the body out of the coffin and threw it on the ground. To their surprise, however, the corpse did not crumble. The investigation team falsely reported that "the corpse owes its good preservation to the properties of the earth in which it was found." A month later, armed Soviets seized the body and took it to Moscow, where they hid it in a warehouse.

In 1923, however, Pope Pius XI demanded Fr. Bobola's body as a form of payment for food and aid provided by the Vatican to the starving Soviet Union. The body of the Polish martyr was then placed in Rome, in the famous Jesuit Church of the Gesù.

NOT MAGIC BUT A MIRACLE

After the Miracle on the Vistula, the effort to canonize Bl. Andrew Bobola intensified. He was finally canonized by Pius XI on April 17, 1938. The Vatican considered two miraculous healings in the process of canonization: the first took place in Poland in 1922, and the other in Italy in 1933.

In the 1920s, Ida Kopecka from Krynica fell ill with osteomalacia, a serious weakening of the bones that causes chronic bone pain, muscle weakness, and difficulty walking. Today we know that osteomalacia is largely due to vitamin D deficiency, but at that time, this disease was treated with X-rays.

In the summer of 1922, at the end of the third week of therapy, Ida noticed a strange pink spot on the area of her skin being exposed to the radiation. Soon, this pink spot turned black. The doctor examining her determined that she had severe radiation burns and gave her a referral to see a specialist, Dr. Przybylski. "Who did this to you?" Dr. Przybylski asked, seeing the deep wound on the woman's body. After a thorough examination, he determined that he was unable to help her: "I have seen similar wounds, but I have never seen healed ones. I have, however, seen the skin fall off first, then the flesh and muscle down to the bone," he confessed, bandaging the wound and writing a prescription for an ointment.

His pessimistic predictions began to come true. The wound opened and a dark, foul-smelling pus oozed from it. Doctors predicted Ida's imminent death. And so Ida asked a Jesuit friend to hear her Confession and prepare her for death.

But Ida did not abandon all hope. Still searching for a medical remedy, she went to Kraków to seek the advice of another specialist. Yet, as she herself reported,

> *Meanwhile, the disease was progressing rapidly, the wound was growing. On Sunday morning, after returning from church and having breakfast, I went again with my sister to Dr. J. He left, and only his assistant, Dr. K, was there. He said he would like to see my wound. He looked at it, saying to himself: wound open, fifteen centimeters long, twelve centimeters wide, deep, thick pus, scraps of skin and flesh.*

After another consultation, which gave her no hope of recovering, Ida Kopecka went to the church again to pray. However, she could not immediately enter the church because Mass had not yet ended. She sat on a bench. After a moment, Fr. Hortynski approached her. The Jesuit priest asked her how she felt, consoled her, and advised her to pray for health through the intercession of Bl. Andrew Bobola. The Jesuit gave the

In Połock, the cult of Fr. Andrew Bobola was spreading among Orthodox believers, so in 1886, tsarist authorities sent a commission to remove his relics. But when a brick fell on one of the commissioner's heads, the martyr's body was left alone.

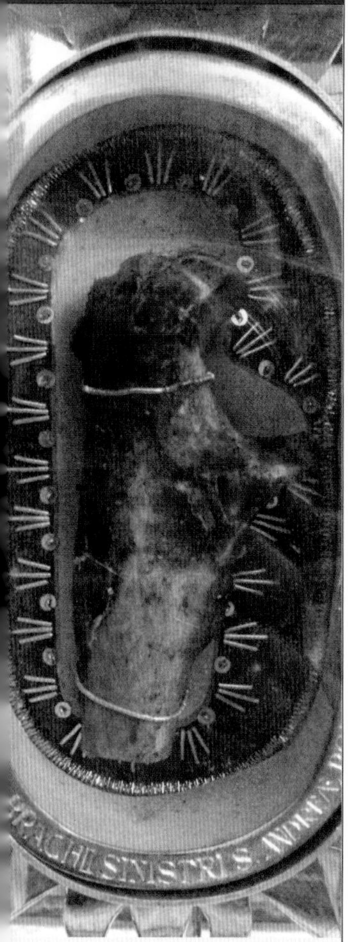

Wilno. A reliquary of St. Andrew Bobola.

woman relics of the blessed and promised to celebrate a Holy Mass the next day for her healing through his intercession.

Ida later wrote: "I placed the relics on my body next to the wound, knelt down, and prayed briefly: 'Bl. Andrew Bobola, ask for healing for me, if it is in accordance with God's will.'" That very evening, she felt much better. The next morning, she took off her bandage. It was clean. There were no pus stains on it. She ran her hand over the wound—the skin was dry and smooth. She looked in disbelief at the site of illness—there was no wound. "The skin grew back normally. On it were fully healed light brown spots!" she stated.

Ida Kopecka went to church that day, and then to see the doctor. She wanted to ask him if she could take a bath. The doctor didn't hide his anger. "A bath, with that wound? You're going to get an infection!" he shouted. Ida replied that the wound was gone. "How is it not there? Magic or something?" the doctor asked in disbelief. "Not magic, but a miracle," Ida said. The doctor looked at where the wound had been and became flustered. Gesturing vividly, he said, "It's gone—yes, it's gone, completely healed—and it was so big, black, smelly, deep! I just saw it two days ago!"

The healing was considered a miracle.

NO TRACE OF A DANGEROUS DISEASE

The second miraculously healed person who was considered for Bl. Andrew Bobola's canonization was Sr. Alojza Dobrzyńska, the superior of the Congregation of the Sisters of the Immaculate Conception of the Blessed Virgin Mary in Rome.

In October 1933, the fifty-six-year-old energetic and strong woman began to experience stomach ailments. In just a few days, she became incapacitated, and two months later, Sr. Alojza was no longer able

to leave her bed. The doctor examining her diagnosed her with a cancerous ulceration of the pancreas, which was confirmed by radiologic exams.

The disease was incurable, yet the woman was advised to undergo surgery in order to find some relief and comfort from her symptoms. Sr. Alojza decided she would go to Poland, to Pleszów.

The other sisters knew how serious her condition was, and they wanted to pray for her. Fr. Stanislaw Włudyga, a Jesuit priest who was staying in Rome, prompted them to pray to Bl. Andrew Bobola. He gave the sisters a novena to the martyr that he had composed. And so, on December 15, the sisters began to ask Bl. Andrew Bobola to pray for their superior. They prayed the novena in Sr. Alojza's room so she could join them in pleading. An altar with the relics of the blessed was placed on the

table, in front of which they lit a lamp. Prelate Tadeusz Zakrzewski also prayed fervently for the health of the sister, as did Fr. Włudyga, who prayed for three days in his room and then, on December 18, celebrated a Mass of Supplication in the Church of Il Gesù, where Bl. Andrew Bobola's body was being kept at the time.

When the first novena did not bring any improvement, the nuns, undaunted, began to say a second one. The sick woman's condition, however, remained unchanged. A subsequent radiologic exam, conducted on December 29, 1933, only confirmed the earlier diagnosis.

The next day, however, something changed. Sr. Alojza underwent a medical examination, and her doctor was surprised to see an improvement in her health. The sick woman, who had not been able to eat solid food for a long time and was taking in only fluids, ate a normal dinner. Her pale skin took on a normal color. Her fever subsided. And, what's more, she got up out of bed. From that moment on, she started walking around the house and attending Mass as if nothing had happened.

On January 7, 1934, Sr. Alojza traveled to Pleszów, Poland, in order to have her previously scheduled operation. When she reported for her pre-treatment medical examination, however, the doctors did not find even a trace of disease. Subsequent radiologic and clinical exams confirmed this finding. The sister was completely healed.

Later, Italian professors Philip Vercelli and Henry Pomponi, the representatives of the Sacred Congregation of Rites who were sent to investigate the miracle, reported that her healing simply "cannot be explained by natural forces."

St. Andrew Bobola Sanctuary in the Mokotów district of Warsaw, adjacent to the Jesuit Collegium Bobolanum.

⮝ *After his canonization in 1938, crowds of people greeted the train that carried the saint's remains from Rome to Poland. The relics were placed in a special reliquary casket in the Warsaw Jesuit shrine on Rakowiecka Street.*

During World War II, the relics of St. Andrew Bobola were successfully hidden in various churches and miraculously saved from bombing. After the war, they were returned to the Jesuit shrine in Warsaw, where they rest and are venerated to this day.

THE RETURN TO POLAND

After St. Andrew Bobola's canonization in 1938, the triumphal return of the martyr from Rome to Poland began. As the train holding his remains passed through Slovenia, Hungary, Czechoslovakia, and Poland, crowds of people greeted the saint with tears. The relics were placed in a special reliquary casket in the Jesuit shrine on Rakowiecka Street in Warsaw. When World War II broke out a year later, St. Andrew Bobola's remains were successfully hidden in various churches and were miraculously saved from bombing. After the war, the relics were returned to the Jesuit shrine, transported in secret from the Soviet authorities as "the corpse of a priest." To this day, St. Andrew Bobola's relics rest and are venerated in Warsaw.

APPARITION WITH A BLACK BEARD

The next, and most recent, apparition of St. Andrew Bobola took place in the Subcarpathian village of Strachocina near Sanok, Poland. Although the most important biographer of St. Andrew Bobola, Fr. Jan Poplatek, had already claimed in 1930 that Strachocina was the place where the saint was born, and locals had called the place of the former Bobola residence "Bobolowka" for ages, there was still some uncertainty about St. Andrew Bobola's birthplace. The saint decided to take care of this doubt himself.

Before World War II, in the rectory in Strachocina, something started happening. Successive pastors and people staying at the rectory heard strange noises and reported that a mysterious apparition would sit on their bed, pull off their covers, or pace outside their door. Lamps would fall, or a breviary. A stone fell from an empty choir; the chandelier in the church would swing. Priests were afraid to live in the rectory. One of them even ran up a tree at night.

The visits by the unknown spirit damaged Fr. Ryszard Mucha's health to the point that he ended up in the hospital. In 1983, he was replaced by Fr. Józef Niżnik. Fr. Niżnik knew nothing of the night hauntings when he moved into the rectory. Then, on the night of September 10, he was awakened by a blow to his hand. He saw a "slender, dressed in black" apparition "with a black beard." The priest thought it was an attack and rushed toward the intruder, shouting. The apparition moved away toward the window and disappeared.

The frightened priest couldn't go to sleep that night. In the morning, he learned the whole truth from the sacristan sister and

spent the next few nights in neighboring rectories. Yet after speaking to a sick pastor, the intrigued and courageous Fr. Niżnik sprang into action. He resigned from his studies at the John Paul II Catholic University and decided to stay in Strachocina longer. He took over the pastorate. In the next four years, the same spirit appeared many more times in the rectory, always at 2:10 in the morning. The priest soon associated the apparition with St. Andrew Bobola, as he learned that Padre Pio had told a particular Polish nun that St. Andrew had insisted on a cult in Strachocina.

On May 16, 1987, on the 330th anniversary of the martyr's death, Fr. Niżnik told his faithful that they should venerate St. Andrew Bobola. "We want you, Andrew Bobola!" he shouted. The next night, the apparition—after a characteristic knock—appeared for the last time. Fr. Niżnik was then convinced that the mysterious stranger from the afterlife had been St. Andrew Bobola himself.

In 1988, relics of the saint were brought with solemn celebration to the church built in his honor, and the small village of Strachocina became the second—after Warsaw—most important location of his cult.

Strachocina, Bobolówka, where St. Andrew Bobola was raised. In 1988, the relics of the saint were brought with solemn celebration to the church built in his honor. Strachocina is now the second most important location of the saint's cult after Warsaw.

1818–1894

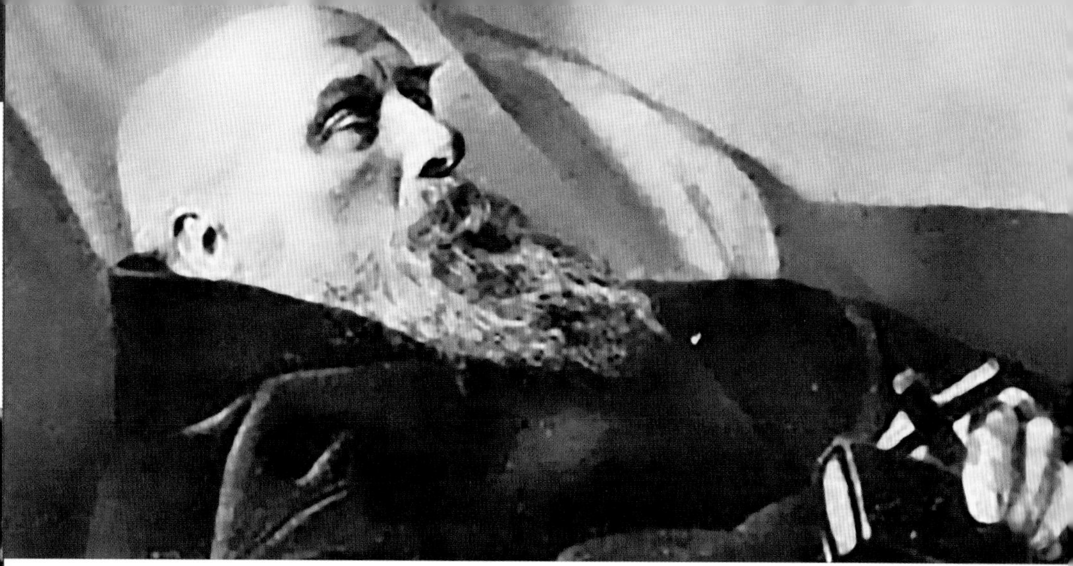

➤ *Posthumous photo of St. Conrad of Parzham.*

⮝ *The statue of Our Lady of Altötting, known for many graces, and the chapel with votive paintings illustrating miracles the faithful have received.*

KINDNESS, GENTLENESS, AND PATIENCE—ANTIDOTES TO EVIL

St. Conrad of Parzham

He was a Capuchin, a simple brother from Bavaria, Germany, who spent forty-one years in the most difficult place of monastic service: at the monastery gate. Benedict XVI counted him among the group of small saints "gifted with a gentleness that's often lacking in the wise and intelligent. … I think these small saints are the great sign of our times." Many people experienced his extraordinary help from Heaven.

"The Catholicism of my homeland, Bavaria, is based on an understanding that everything that's human should be given space: prayer, play, penance, but also joy." This is how Cardinal Joseph Ratzinger, the future Pope Benedict XVI, wrote about Bavarian Catholicism.

The heart of Bavaria and, at the same time, the most important place of worship in all of Germany is the Shrine of Our Lady of Altötting—a centuries-old pilgrimage site with a miraculous statue of the Blessed Virgin Mary. Praying before her in the Chapel of Grace, pilgrims have experienced numerous healings and miracles for centuries. In Altötting, however, not only is the Bavarian Black Madonna venerated, but so too is St. Conrad of Parzham, a humble brother who served in the local Capuchin friary of St. Ann. Br. Conrad—as a lay person—was called John Evangelist Birndorfer. He was born in Parzham (the town is known today as Bad Griesbach im Rottal) into a large but wealthy peasant family. He was still a teenager when he lost

both his parents within a span of two years. For the next fourteen years, together with his siblings, he farmed, combining hard work on the land with constant prayer.

At the age of thirty-one, following his vocation, Conrad left the farm, gave away his inheritance, and entered the Capuchin friary. He spent most of his time in Altötting. For forty-one years, he performed the most difficult and important job as porter. He received hundreds of thousands of pilgrims coming to the sanctuary. Showing angelic patience, he fulfilled their requests, answered questions, gave to those who asked, helped poor children, and fed a large group of people daily—sometimes as many as two thousand, for whom he always managed to scrounge up bread, soup, beer, and even a few coins. Sometimes he was called to the gate up to two hundred times a day, and—in spite of asthma and frequent unbearable stomach pains caused by gastritis—he patiently and humbly came to answer each time the bell was rung. Once, children rang the bell nine times in a row just for fun. He didn't get angry, but gently asked them to stop because he had to take care of other responsibilities. It's been said that, in a time when there were no telephones or even bells in cells and other monastic rooms, he had a special gift of finding friars summoned to the gate. Given the vast space of the monastery, this sometimes bordered on the miraculous. One day, one of the fathers, in order to prepare a sermon in peace, hid in the smallest church tower. He thought no one would find him here, but after some time he heard footsteps on the stairs and the porter calling: "Fr. Vincent, please come down! Someone wants to make a confession!"

Br. Conrad's kindness, gentleness, and patience was once tested by a beggar who came to the entrance of the shrine. The man asked for something to eat, and when Br. Conrad brought him soup, he tasted it

Statue of St. Conrad by the church in Parzham.

The family home of St. Conrad.

The main town square in Bad Griesbach.

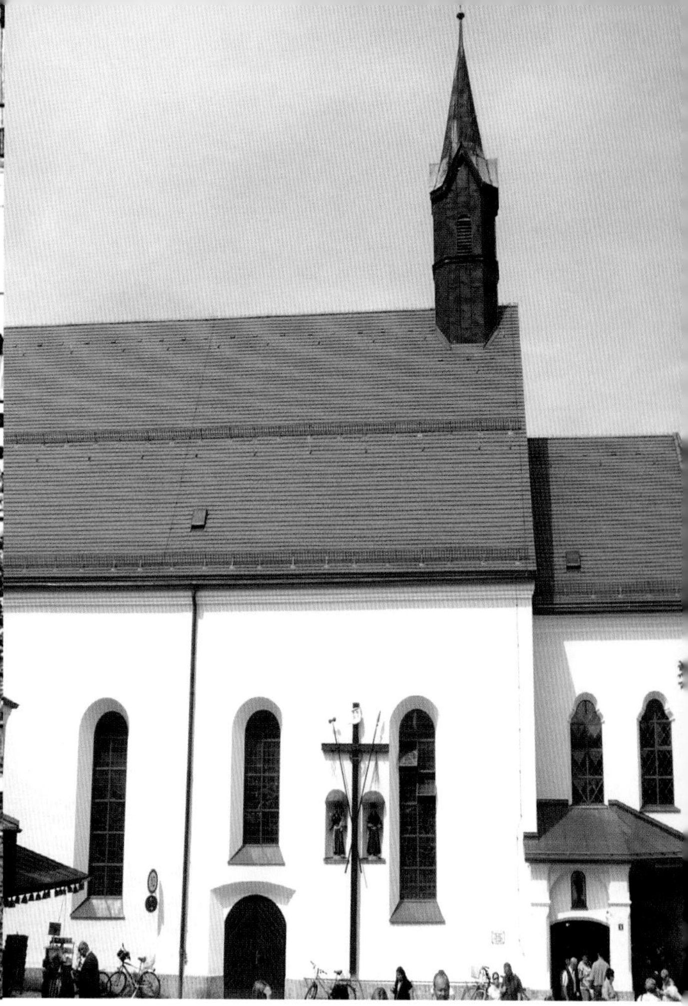

▲ *Altötting, Franciscan monastery.*

▲ *St. Conrad's Church in Altötting.*

and threw the bowl in the friar's face. "Am I a dog? Eat this yourself!" he shouted. Even a saint would have gotten angry, but Br. Conrad calmly wiped his face and replied: "You don't like this one? Wait just a bit, I'll bring you another one."

Br. Conrad also practiced the virtue of silence. He avoided saying unnecessary words. Already in the novitiate, as one of his vows, he wrote down that he wanted to always maintain strict silence and to speak only as much as was necessary "to have more time to talk to God." He stuck to this decision his entire life. Therefore, his few spoken words had great power and were able to transform people's hearts. Always seen with a Divine Mercy ring or a rosary in his hand, he remained in constant union with God. He spent his free time and entire nights adoring the Lord. He did this most often in a small chamber located under the stairs, near the porter's gate. The friars called it the St. Alexius Cell, in which there was a small window overlooking the tabernacle. He would also often pray in the crypt where his fellow Capuchin brothers were buried. Every day at 5 in the morning, he served in the Holy Mass in the Chapel of Grace with the miraculous statue of the Black Madonna. Some of the brothers and pilgrims claimed to have seen shining stars above his head, as well as fiery sparks or a beam of bright rays extending from his mouth toward the miraculous figure. His superiors gave him permission to receive Holy Communion daily, which was rare even in monasteries at that time.

He slept very little, no more than two or three hours, and at 3:30 he was up. He didn't eat much—mostly soup sprinkled with ashes. He became the embodiment of humility and purity, love for God and neighbor, faithfulness to duty. He had the gift of prophecy and reading people's hearts. He told many people that they would enter the convent and become nuns or priests. This often came to pass, despite the fact that Br. Conrad made these prophecies at a time when none of these people had even begun to discern a vocation.

In a letter to his sister, he wrote, "I'm always doing well. I'm always happy and content in God. I accept everything with gratitude from the Father in Heaven, be it suffering or joy. He knows very well what is best for me." The words "the cross is my book" became his life motto. He died in 1894, and his grave soon became a popular destination for pilgrims. In 1930, he was beatified, and he was canonized four years later.

Joseph Ratzinger, the Holy Father Benedict XVI, wrote the following about St. Conrad in his autobiography *Milestones: Memoirs, 1927–1977*: "In this humble and thoroughly kind man we saw what is best in our people embodied and led by faith to its most beautiful possibilities."

ANTIDOTE TO HITLER

Conrad of Parzham, whose canonization took place during the first years of the Third Reich, was a great sign for the era of Hitler's terror. During the canonization ceremony, which took place on the day of the descent of the Holy Spirit in 1934, Pope Pius XI thundered: "He should teach and remind everyone how far they have strayed from the right path of truth, renewing and glorifying pagan practices and customs, and rejecting and despising Christian teaching, which leads people to virtue and can bring true cultural progress."

Br. Conrad, as a man of great humility, became a specific antidote for Catholics to the dark ideology of pride and arrogance

hl. Br. Konrad, bitte für uns!

Holy Father Benedict XVI wrote the following about St. Conrad: "In this humble and thoroughly kind man we saw what is best in our people embodied and led by faith to its most beautiful possibilities."

The nave of the Church of St. Conrad of Parzham in Altötting.

⮝ *Town hall in Altötting, St. Conrad's hometown.*

⮟ *The interior of Conrad's family home on a postcard from the beginning of the twentieth century.*

that Nazism embodied. The one who welcomed and respected everyone and had a good word or a bowl of food for everyone was a sign of opposition to Nazism, which introduced a deadly division between superhumans and subhumans. Br. Conrad earnestly served the poor and devoted all his attention to them, especially those considered by National Socialists to be a "disgrace to humanity": former criminals, beggars, and the mentally ill. It's not surprising that Hitler's army of Brownshirts tried to torpedo German celebrations in honor of the new saint. Many of Conrad's devotees (including the owner of a printing company, Dr. Joseph Geiselberger, who was involved in the canonization) were terrorized and beaten. It didn't work: celebrations were held in Berlin and Altötting, where more than thirty-five thousand faithful participated in the celebrations related to the canonization in late August and September 1934.

HELP FROM HEAVEN

Br. Conrad was closely associated with the monastery and shrine in Altötting for nearly his entire life. And before he became known and loved all over the world, he mainly helped his Bavarian countrymen. Bavarians asked him for help in every time of need—when someone lost their job, when someone fell ill, when they suffered from family problems. The last emperor of Austria-Hungary, Bl. Charles I, who was dying in 1922 in exile on the Portuguese island of Madeira, also asked for his protection over his soul. And Br. Conrad—as long as it was in accordance with God's will—provided effective help.

RESTORING A HORSE'S HEALTH

Today, we can only imagine how important the horse used to be in the lives of country folk. In a time before tractors and

motorized farming equipment, a horse was more valuable than gold. People cared for these useful animals, and their illnesses were considered a real tragedy. Therefore, it's not surprising that, when an owner of a large farm near Wasserburg on the Inn River heard from his farmhand that the best horse in the stable had colic and was wallowing in pain, he was terribly worried. He immediately sent for a veterinarian. He didn't have good news for him. After examining the animal, the doctor said the horse would soon die, because he was already covered in cold sweat. The farmer remembered the sermon he had heard the previous Sunday. The priest spoke about how Br. Conrad helped villagers. "Br. Conrad, help me, my horse is dying and I have no money to buy a new one. I promise you that if the horse survives, I will go on a pilgrimage to your grave and give a small donation for the costs of your beatification process," the man declared. Just then, he saw the deathly ill horse suddenly jump. The next day, the veterinarian found a completely healthy animal in the stable. "It's a miracle," he said. The horse recovered, and the farmer kept his promise.

HE LOOKED AFTER HIS BEATIFICATION PROCESS

It also seems as if Br. Conrad contributed to his beatification in a rather unusual way. It was like this: Fr. Joseph Anton Kessler (1868–1947), guardian of the monastery in Altötting, undertook a great and difficult task: the construction of a new, larger church. In 1908, the difficulties seemed insurmountable. The obstacle was the Fendthof farm, which stood on the planned construction site. It had to be removed and rebuilt elsewhere.

An old woman then urged the guardian to call upon Br. Conrad for help. "You have someone downstairs in a crypt who will help you. It's Br. Conrad; you must go to him!" she insisted. The guardian obeyed. From that day on, he went down to the grave of the Servant of God every day and begged for help. And he obtained what he was asking for. Suddenly and unexpectedly, the problem was solved, and the construction of the basilica gained momentum. Another time Fr. Joseph Anton was in dire need of a thousand marks. On the morning of April 21, 1911, on the seventeenth anniversary of the death of Br. Conrad, Fr. Josef Anton went down to the crypt again. "Br. Conrad, if you are a saint, send me a thousand marks today, because I need them very much!" He only waited a few hours for a response. After dinner, the porter informed him that a man wanted to see him. A man from Munich, unknown

Conrad became the embodiment of humility and purity, love for God and neighbor, and faithfulness to duty. He had the gift of prophecy and reading people's hearts.

A sculpture of Br. Conrad in Altötting.

One of the most visited shrines in Europe. The Shrine of Our Lady of Altötting is visited by more than a million pilgrims per year.

The high altar at the Basilica of St. Ann.

to the guardian, handed him exactly one thousand marks for the construction of the church. The greatly astonished guardian went down to the crypt again to thank Br. Conrad and make a deal with him. "If you help me build the church, I will lead your beatification process" he promised. And so it happened. The Basilica of St. Ann—one of the largest churches in Germany—was consecrated on October 13, 1912, and Fr. Joseph Anton kept his promise: a day later, he initiated the beatification process of Br. Conrad.

MIRACLES UNDER THE MICROSCOPE

In the beatification process of the Capuchin porter, two miraculous healings, experienced by Elisa Erl and Kunigunde Aepfelbacher, were put under the microscope.

Elisa Erl was born January 16, 1917, in Wasserburg on the Inn River. After a difficult birth, it later turned out that the girl had serious problems with her legs: she was unable to walk or even stand. In addition to this, she was diagnosed with rickets. When she turned two, the doctors gave up all hope that she would ever be able to walk. George—Elisa's father—then remembered the promise made to him during one of his pilgrimages to Altötting by Br. Konrad, who died twenty-two years earlier. The friar—perhaps by means of his gift of prophecy, already foreseeing what was going to happen—told him that if he needed his advice in an emergency, he could always come to him. "And if I die, come to my grave, I will help you at any time," he added. And so George went. And with confidence—full of faith and trust—he knocked on his grave, as was common in those times. The first time nothing happened, so he went a second time, and then again and again. He completed his twenty-mile pilgrimages to Altötting on foot and by bicycle with fasting and prayers. The neighbors started to laugh at him, thinking that it was unnecessary toil. We can imagine their sarcastic smiles when he walked or rode past them. George, however, continued to plead for help. And it happened. On Sunday, October 29, 1922, his faith and perseverance were generously rewarded. On that day, George took the *Altöttinger Liebfrauenbote* (Messenger of Our Lady of Altötting) in his hand. He read—most likely aloud—about the extraordinary graces obtained through the intercession of the deceased friar. "Ah, if only he could help our Liserl, too. If only she could stand on her feet," sighed Maria, Elisa's mother. "Give him time. Br. Conrad will help. He promised me that," George replied. As he was speaking, five-year-old Elisa got up and walked around the table. Her crippled, curled feet and legs straightened. The child was healed suddenly and unexpectedly. George and Maria were overjoyed.

Until the end of her life, Elisa was a great devotee of Br. Conrad. And when, at the age of eighty-nine, she died, Conrad's image was placed on the funeral card along with a note saying she had been healed through his intercession.

Kunigunde Aepfelbacher from Kronach was a widow for forty years and, like Elisa, had problems with her legs, specifically with one of her feet. She suffered from bone decay and had an open wound on it for years. The doctors were helpless; they felt that she could no longer be healed. On May 29, 1919, the woman was admitted to Heiligkreuz Hospital in Munich. The treatment given there not only didn't help, but in fact worsened her condition. On the woman's left foot, above the ankle, there was a deep wound, and you could see the tendons and bones. The wound stank and secreted pus, and the pain continued to increase until it became unbearable. In 1924, after several years of suffering, Mrs. Aepfelbacher heard about Br. Conrad and the graces that people received because of his intercession. "Why shouldn't I receive it," she thought, and with confidence in her heart and prayer on her lips, she asked the Capuchin for help. She prayed continuously.

On the night of April 10, 1926, the pain was at its peak. The sick woman suffered tremendously. Once again she called out to Br. Conrad for help, and then, exhausted, she fell asleep. In the morning, the nurse caring for the woman was surprised that her patient was no longer moaning. "Mrs. Aepfelbacher, do you feel any pain today?" she asked. As she unwrapped the bandage, she was speechless: the open, pus-filled wound had

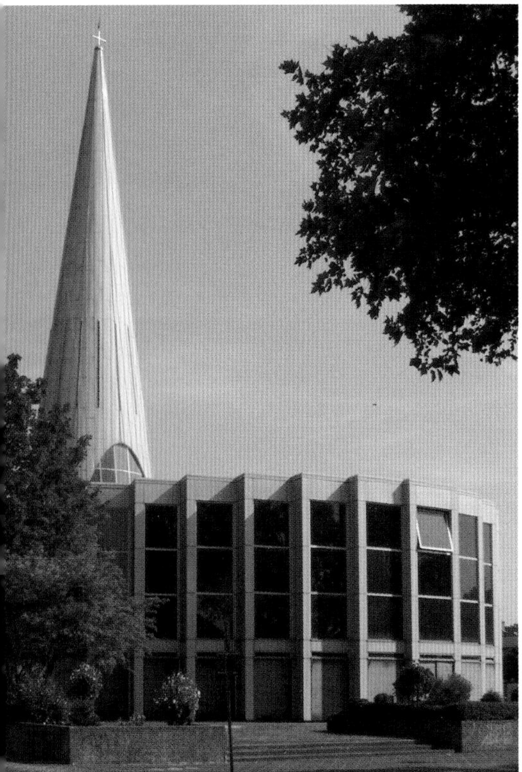

▲ *St. Conrad Church in Oker (Goslar), Germany*

▼ *St. Conrad Church in Herne, Germany.*

▲ *St. Conrad Church in Aschaffenburg, Germany.*

◄ *St. Conrad Church in Manheim, Germany.*

closed up, becoming covered with healthy pink tissue. The pain had also vanished. What was impossible became possible overnight. From that moment on, Mrs. Aepfelbacher stopped having problems with her foot, and she knew that she owed it to the merciful porter from Altötting.

ON THE WAY TO HOLINESS

Two subsequent medically inexplicable healings contributed to the canonization of Br. Conrad. In the case of Maria Zech from Bedernau in Swabia, Br. Conrad once again showed his extraordinary orthopedic abilities. After a huge wooden block fell on the woman's hand, she suffered from acute osteonecrosis. Her right hand was swollen and, over time, phlebitis and myositis set in. The sick woman's fingers curled up and tightened, so that no amount of force could bend them back. The patient was admitted to the Vincentinum Hospital in Augsburg. The disease, however, did not stop there. It covered other parts of the body: the other hand and both legs. The pain intensified. Doctors said that her right hand would have to be amputated. The operation was scheduled for August 4, 1930. The devastated woman was very afraid of it, and having learned about the extraordinary graces obtained through the intercession of Br. Conrad, she began to pray with faith and hope that he would come to her aid. She wasn't disappointed. On the night of August 12, 1930, Maria was suddenly and completely healed. The doctors couldn't believe it, but they had to finally admit that a miracle had occurred.

The second miraculously healed person was Auguste Scheidle from Lans. She was studying at the teachers' institute in Tyrol, Austria, when she contracted pneumonia, followed by tuberculosis, in 1928. The disease gradually began to destroy the sick girl's body. As Br. Konstanty Jaroń describes in his book on St. Conrad, "She took a break from her studies and her condition improved a bit." After returning to school, tuberculosis began to develop quickly. A mycobacterium was found in her sputum. Once again she stopped her studies. Despite the rest, blood poisoning set in. At the Hochzirl Hospital, where she was taken, everyone looked for the cause of her illness, but no diagnosis was forthcoming. What they observed was swelling and pus on the back, inflammation of the kidneys, and severe pain in the loins. To relieve her pain, she was transferred to a new hospital in Kettenbrücke, in the hopes that relief could be found in

Photo from the Vatican canonization celebrations of St. Conrad of Parzham.

Relics of St. Conrad are located in a glass coffin under the altar of the church in Parzham.

radiological therapy. Unfortunately, this attempt at a cure failed as well. Constant fever, night sweats, a vigorous cough, and blood appeared in the sputum. The sick woman was exhausted, pale, and was tormented by indescribable pain. Finally, the doctors surrendered, recognizing that they would no longer be able to help her. Her healing took place in 1930 in the chapel of the sanatorium in Hochzirl. During the Holy Mass, the patient begged Br. Conrad and the Blessed Virgin for the grace of healing. In an instant, Auguste felt that nothing was wrong with her anymore. She told her sisters about it, but they didn't want to believe her. They believed it only when the girl was examined by Dr. Kopf. "A hand from above intervened here," he said, surprised.

HE CONTINUES TO HELP

Br. Conrad was beatified in 1930. Four years later, the same pope—Pius XI—canonized him. To this day, thousands of believers pray in front of the sarcophagus of the holy Capuchin on Sundays, holidays, and during the pilgrimage season.

Petitions and messages of thanks are sent from all over the world. There have been times when even several thousand of them came in a single week. Simple people and great dignitaries venerate Br. Conrad because the humble porter and the great son of the German nation—a man of angelic patience, heroically fulfilling his ordinary, daily duties—remains what he was during his earthly pilgrimage: a friend and helper to all those in need.

HELPING HAND

St. Nicholas of Flüe Br. Klaus

Many Swiss are convinced that if it weren't for Br. Klaus—as the saint was called—there would be no Switzerland. The hermit and mystic was not only a spiritual guide and healer, but also a passionate Swiss patriot. He is considered the spiritual father of Switzerland, the architect of the old constitution of his country (effective from the Middle Ages to the time of the French Revolution), and the builder of the foundations of Swiss neutrality. He defended Switzerland not only during his lifetime, but to this day—as a patron—he takes care of this Alpine country and its residents.

On May 10, 1940, Germany attacked France and the Low Countries. The next day, the authorities of neutral Switzerland announced mobilization. The German army began to gather its forces at the country's border. It was feared that Hitler would invade Switzerland, bypassing the Maginot Line, to attack France from the Jura Mountains. Events were moving quickly. When Joseph Goebbels, the Third Reich's propaganda minister, announced on May 12 that within forty-eight hours there would be no more neutral countries on the map of Europe, the Swiss fell into a panic. Many of the wealthier residents of the northern cantons

The recently built Bruder Klaus Field Chapel.

Church in Schwarzsee (Plaffeien) dedicated to St. Klaus.

began a hasty escape to the south. The Swiss army, composed of half a million men and tens of thousands of women, was pushing the other way, stationing itself along the border with Germany. On the night of May 13, orders were issued to assume a state of the highest readiness. At two in the morning, the Swiss warned that the German invasion would take place in half an hour. In the event of an attack, it was planned to blow up tunnels and flood the valleys. However, the opposite happened, and the Germans didn't attack. Apparently, Hitler himself ordered a retreat. Why?

THEY WEREN'T CLOUDS

In these dramatic moments, the more religious Swiss—both soldiers and civilians—fell to their knees and called on Br. Klaus, their patron, for help. And then something strange happened: when the fate of Switzerland was still hanging in the balance, on the evening of May 13, 1940, in the night sky over Waldenburg, a huge shining hand appeared. The hand, or rather the palm, was surrounded by rays, and it was moving as if it were blessing the country. It was described as being "skeletal" at first, then "filling out" but still transparent. At the end of the transformation, it became skinny and bony again, dispersing completely. Thin fingers, pointing to the north, were also clearly visible. A strange phenomenon—lasting from ten minutes to half an hour, depending on the report—was observed by at least twenty residents of the city and many soldiers marching through it. It was even testified by residents of much more distant, and apparently even the Germans themselves saw it. Witnesses confirmed their accounts under oath. The miracle

Chapel in honor of St. Klaus on the Hannigalp, near Grächen in the canton of Valais, from 1971.

⮝ Home where St. Nichols of Flüe was born, Flüeli-Ranft.

was even written about in the local press. The Catholic newspaper *Basler Volksblatt* reported on May 17 of that year:

> *According to testimonies, on Monday, May 13, 1940, in the evening at 9:30 over Waldenburg in the direction of Fricktal, under the bright moonlight, a large, bright, silvery hand appeared. It was a clearly outlined, skeletal, bony hand with fingers slightly spread, lying flat, although slightly raised, defending Fricktal from the open border with the Germans.*

According to this description, the phenomenon disappeared after ten minutes. The majority of observers were certain this glowing bony hand belonged to Bl. Br. Klaus—Nicholas of Flüe. It was commonly claimed that in this way the saint assured the Swiss that he had them under his protection and nothing bad threatened them. The fact of the matter is that Waldenburg and the surrounding area is mainly inhabited by Protestants, so if it was only a "Catholic invention" and "all nonsense" they would strongly deny it. During that time, the occurrence of this strange phenomenon was also confirmed by many Protestants (although some of them saw in the strange limb not the hand of Br. Klaus, but the hand of God Himself!). They were ordinary clouds, skeptics later said. It was nothing like that. They weren't clouds. The sky over the town was cloudless that evening, which was unanimously confirmed by all the witnesses and meteorological institutes. It wasn't a flying object, either. The Swiss also claim the threat of German aggression was very real at that time. The next day, a Japanese radio broadcasted that at two in the morning the German army attacked Switzerland. Evidently, Hitler's decision to withdraw from the attack on this country had not yet reached his allies. Did St. Nicholas of Flüe miraculously help prevent this aggression? Perhaps there were more reasons that contributed to sparing Switzerland, but many Swiss people are still convinced that in those difficult times it was their patron saint who defended their country and saved them from war. To this day, the "Miracle of Waldenburg" is solemnly celebrated.

INTELLIGENT AND CAUTIOUS

Niklaus von Flüe (Latin: Nicolaus de Rupe, French: Nicholas de la Roche) was known as Br. Klaus. He lived in the late Middle Ages and was a typical Swiss, a quite wealthy peasant. He was born in the canton of Unterwalden, in the middle of Switzerland. As a young boy, he took part in several wars. While defending the country, he tried not to harm his enemies. He didn't kill or pillage. During one of the military campaigns, he prevented the destruction of the Dominican convent of St. Katharinental in Diessenhofen, and saved the residents of this town who took refuge there. He got married at the age of twenty-nine. He had a loving wife who was fifteen years younger than him and ten children—five boys and five girls. Although he never went to school, due to his intelligence, cautiousness, honesty, and strong character, he was entrusted with important social functions. He was a member of the council and judge of the canton of Obwalden. He was very concerned about injustices and wrongdoings, especially greed and bribery, which he had to deal with while performing public functions.

HE BECAME A HERMIT

However, there was something missing since his childhood. For a long time he had heard the voice of God echoing in his soul. Year after year, more and more, he desired to be alone with his Creator, to serve only Him.

After all the members of the household would go to bed, he would get up, kneel in the room near the stove, and pray for a long time. Almost every day he struggled with the devil, who tormented him. He experienced mystical visions and ecstasies, but he also went through depressive states and sadness. He often reflected on the words of Christ spoken in the Gospel: "In the same way, those of you who do not give up everything you have cannot be my disciples" (Luke 14:33). At fifty years old, following God's call, he finally decided to "give up everything" and devote himself only to God—to become a forest hermit and wander from one holy place to another.

ON THE WAY TO LIVING A HERMIT'S LIFE

At first, his wife, Dorothea Wyss, was undoubtedly opposed to his plans. Although she was financially secure, she couldn't imagine caring for so many children alone and living without her somewhat strange but loving husband.

Interior of a contemporary chapel dedicated to St. Nicholas in Switzerland.

Home of St. Nicholas of Flüe, where he lived for many years, Flüeli-Ranft.

A modern portrait of the saint.

Nicholas, however, constantly begged and pleaded with her. She finally gave in. She agreed to let him leave. She understood this wasn't another one of her husband's peculiar ideas, that it wasn't a simple and rash decision, that he didn't want to leave them out of selfishness and he wasn't looking for an easier life. She understood the driving force of his actions was God's call, to which he wanted to be faithful. She also knew he had consulted with his confessor on this matter.

The emotional final parting took place October 16, 1467. Dorothea said goodbye to her husband, holding the youngest fruit of their marital love in her arms—a tiny three-month-old baby. Nicholas, having entrusted the care of the family and the farm to his eldest son, was leaving penniless, in a long coarse robe sewn by his wife, girded with a rope. Dressed in a habit, barefoot, and with a shaved head, he set off with a rosary and staff in his hand. First he went abroad, to the Upper Rhine, where the mystics he admired—the "Friends of God"—were active. However, he never got a chance to stay there. God had other plans for him. He only got as far as Liestal, following the advice of a peasant. A divine order received in a vision led him to return to his homeland. He settled in a desolate and wild ravine called Ranft, located near his own home. He lived in a wooden hut, then moved to a tiny cell attached to a small chapel. The ceiling was so low that he could almost scrape his head on it. He slept on the floor; he didn't have a table. He spent time in meditation, contemplation, and prayer. Until he could fund a scholarship for his own chaplain from the alms given to the shrine, he attended Mass on Sundays in a nearby town. He initially ate dried pears, broad beans, herbs, and roots. He often fasted. His fasting soon took a more radical form.

Futuristic church dedicated to St. Br. Klaus in Spiez.

LIVING BY THE EUCHARIST ALONE

The most spectacular miracle associated with his mortal life was that for nineteen years he survived entirely on the Body of Christ. Of course, as is typical in such cases, this was suspected to be a fraud, and townspeople thought that the hermit ate in secret. Suspicions were dispelled by a special independent investigation conducted by authorities of the canton of Obwalden and authorities of the Church. Nicholas was constantly watched for a month to make sure he really ate nothing. This is what Michał Nowodworski wrote in 1874 about the Swiss hermit's inedia in his monumental *Church Encyclopedia*:

> *Only the Most Holy Body of Christ strengthened him in a supernatural way and sustained the life of the body. This miracle was investigated*

thoroughly and for a long time and recognized as genuine. When asked how he survived, he replied "God knows." At first, he himself was very surprised by this extraordinary gift of grace; any attempt to ingest food caused him, apart from disgust, great pain. This incredible way of life brought him much trouble from the authorities and especially from malicious people who suspected him of an association with the devil. His body was thin and withered, but he didn't feel his physical strength decline. His complexion was healthy. He could walk a lot and talk for a long time. He greeted his visitors with a handshake and a smile on his face.

This new way of life began painfully. Although he was tired from the journey, he wanted to spend the whole night in prayer under the open sky. But from great exhaustion, he fell asleep for a moment. When he awoke, he saw himself surrounded by a great light, like lightning, and he felt a violent pain, as if someone had cut out his insides with a knife. From that moment on, all feelings of hunger and thirst left him. He describes his condition best in the following words: "When I kneel by the priest and see how he receives the heavenly nourishment, or if I receive this grace myself, then my whole being is filled with heavenly consolation and bliss that I seem to swim in it, and its excess overflows into me. It is what nourishes me and makes me forget about all other food. The Body and Blood of Christ are my only food and drink. He dwells in me and I in Him. He is my food, my drink, my health, and my medicine.

ADVISER TO PRINCES AND BEGGARS

Thanks to this miracle, an extraordinary holy life, and great wisdom, Nicholas's fame spread throughout Switzerland and beyond its borders. He was considered a saint, and crowds of people from all over Europe began to flock to his tiny hermitage. Among them were ordinary onlookers, scholars, rulers and princes (including the duke of Milan and Archduke Sigismund of Austria), the sick who regained their health thanks to his prayers, the poor, city government officials, and people with various problems, to whom he always

Church on the site where the saint resided in Flüeli-Ranft.

Contemplation picture by Br. Klaus, depicting various stages of the Lord's life in the parish and pilgrimage church in Sachseln, Switzerland.

delivered accurate, prudent, and specific advice, often contained in just a few words. There were also suspicious theologians who harassed him and "investigated" his legitimacy with innumerable questions. Then the hermit—for his own spiritual good—was forced to limit the time he devoted to newcomers.

He had a prophetic spirit. He foretold the convulsions of the Reformation. "Be persistent in the faith of your fathers, because after my death there will be a major revolt in Christianity; then beware of the deceit of Satan, who will hunt with slyness and novelty," he warned his countrymen.

FATHER OF SWITZERLAND

Nicholas also made himself known as a passionate Swiss patriot and political adviser. He is considered the spiritual father of Switzerland, the architect of its ancient constitution, and the builder of the foundations of Swiss neutrality. His extremely wise, impartial advice contributed to the strengthening, reconciliation, and reunification of the country. After the victory over Burgundy, a major disagreement arose between the representatives of the rural and urban oligarchies, and civil war and disintegration threatened the Swiss Confederacy. The parish priest from Stans, Heini am Grund, came to the hermit at that time. Br. Klaus— already highly respected—relieved the tense situation. He gave the delegates simple and impartial advice: each of the cities and cantons must renounce its special privileges and rights. The hermit believed that only in this way could peace and unity be preserved. His advice turned out to be a success, and the delegates showed

A plate from the "official chronicle of Lucerne" of 1513 of Diebold Schilling the Younger, illustrating the events of the Tagsatzung at Stans in 1481. A priest named Heini am Grund visited Niklaus von Flüe to ask him for his advice to save the failing Tagsatzung at Stans, where the delegates of the rural and urban cantons of the Old Swiss Confederacy could not agree and threatened civil war.

common sense in agreeing to such terms. This led to the "Stans Agreement," which strengthened the federal union. Switzerland survived, and Br. Klaus was loved by all of the Swiss people.

It is worth mentioning that the youngest child of Nicholas and Dorothea became a theologian and priest. Among their descendants there were more than thirty priests, and Nicholas's grandson, Conrad Scheuber, became a hermit just like him.

MIRACLES AT THE GRAVE

From the moment of his death, the grave of the hermit became a major destination for many pilgrims and the site of a lively cult that became known for numerous miracles and extraordinary graces.

Already in 1488, a year after the death of Nicholas, twenty-three such miracles were recorded. In 1570, St. Charles Borromeo, cardinal and Archbishop of Milan, visited this place. The centuries-old cult of the saint was approved by Innocent X in 1649, which was equivalent to beatification. The Swiss hermit's canonization, however, had to wait until after World War II. Two spectacular miracles contributed to it. Through his intercession, two young village women from the canton of Solothurn were healed—Berta Schürmann from Egerkingen and Ida Jeker from Büsserach. Both women were present at the canonization ceremony in 1947 and told other pilgrims about their healings.

LOOK, I'M HEALED!

Coming from a poor peasant family with many children, Ida Jeker had a damaged left arm from early childhood. Her older sister accidentally pulled it out when she clumsily tried to get her out of bed. The limb was never professionally set and treated; Ida remained paralyzed, and her development was stunted. The girl couldn't work, which was a big problem for a poor, rural family. In addition, from the age of twelve, she began to get epileptic seizures. She had several attacks each week. The doctors were powerless. Both ailments were considered incurable. In the spring of 1937, her injured arm began to hurt badly. The pain was absolutely unbearable. She went to the doctor, who diagnosed her with neuritis and prescribed an ointment. Unfortunately, the liniment didn't help. What's more, after using it, the "whole arm became a pus-filled wound." That same year, on June 26, the local women's Sodality of Our Lady organized a pilgrimage to Sachseln. Nineteen-year-old Ida wanted to go, but the doctor was against it. In the end, however, it was agreed that she would go, but the arm would be bandaged thoroughly, and a special sling would be installed on the bus so that any vigorous shaking would not cause her additional pain. After arriving at the church in Sachseln, Ida, together with

Medallions from the main painting with scenes from the Gospel.

From the moment of his death, the grave of the hermit became the destination of many pilgrimages, a lively cult, which became known for numerous miracles and extraordinary graces. Already in 1488, a year after the death of Nicholas, twenty-three such miracles were recorded. In 1570, St. Charles Borromeo, cardinal and archbishop of Milan, visited this place. The centuries-old cult of the saint was approved by Innocent X in 1649, which was equivalent to beatification. The Swiss hermit's canonization, however, had to wait until after World War II.

⮝ *Nicholas as a mystic and visionary depicted on an engraving by Martini from 1892.*

other pilgrims, knelt near the reliquary in which the hermit's coarse robe was kept. When the priest placed the hermit's habit on her arm and gave her a blessing, something extraordinary happened. At that very moment, she felt as if she had been struck by lightning. The pulse went through her hands, feet, and head. She almost let out a scream. She realized that something had happened to her body, but she told no one. She discreetly left the church, drank her coffee, and got into the car. She was surprised to find that not only could she move the affected limb freely, but in addition she no longer felt any pain. She was happy in spirit, but she still couldn't believe it. Finally, when the pilgrims were passing by the Benedictine monastery of St. Andreas—Shrine of the Infant Jesus in Sarnen—she couldn't take it: "I'm healed! Look, I'm healed," she began to shout. The driver and the girls on the bus then began singing a hymn of praise to God. After reaching Büsserach, Ida wanted to cross the threshold of her home as quickly as possible to share the happy news with her parents and sisters. When she entered the house, her parents couldn't recognize her. She was bursting with joy. She then grabbed a heavy chair with her left hand, lifted it up five times, and began to carry it around the room. Her parents were speechless, unable to utter a word. During these joyous performances, the bandage slipped from the girl's arm and hung on her wrist. She took it off completely, and it turned out that the nasty wound on the arm had also disappeared. What's more, the epileptic seizures also stopped. Three days later, the girl went to the woodshed to split thick wooden logs with a heavy axe. She was perfectly healthy, and her left arm was no different from the right one. The news of this miracle spread throughout the area, and crowds of people began to flock to her home. Church authorities soon became interested in her healing.

YOU'RE DEAD!

In 1932, Berta Schürmann from Egerkingen caught severe tonsillitis that attacked the brain and spinal cord, leading to paralysis. She also developed pleurisy and inflammation of the bladder, which made her condition even worse. The paralyzed woman lay like Lazarus for two years, and doctors gave her no hope of recovery. Out of medical desperation, Berta was sent to the waters at the Rheinfelden health resort, but the treatment did not bring any improvement. After returning home, Berta was bedridden again. In addition, she developed a fever of over 102 degrees. According to doctors, the disease from which she suffered would soon lead to death. A "short time" turned into seven long years, but on May 4, 1939, the doctor examining her once again predicted her imminent death. The woman had already come to terms with it, but fearing the moment of death, she began praying to Bl. Br. Klaus for support and strength in the last moments of her life. Shortly afterwards came a memorable day for Berta—May 18, 1939, the Solemnity of the Ascension of Jesus Christ. The sick woman loved Jesus and liked this feast, so she asked Jesus to take her with Him on that very day. That day she began to feel pain, which from hour to hour grew worse and became unbearable. Loved ones kept watch at her bedside, expecting the worst, but when noon passed, Berta sent her loved ones to Vespers. She explained to them they had to go, and if it was God's will, she could die alone. When they left, she prayed again to Br. Klaus. "Brother Klaus, tell me a good word," she pleaded. When the clock struck half past one, she heard bells ringing from the nearby church. "Oh, they just started singing the Magnificat," she thought, and tried to join the prayer herself. "My soul proclaims the greatness of the Lord ... the Almighty has done great things for me, and holy is His name," she whispered. And that's when it happened. In one second, the pain suddenly and unexpectedly stopped. Completely. The woman felt that life had returned to her paralyzed body. "Br. Klaus!" she shouted. She sat on the bed, then got up, and without even getting dressed, in her "death shirt," she stood by the open window. She spread her arms in delight. She was still standing by the window when members of her family, returning from church, appeared on the road. They were surprised to see a figure in the window. "Ghost, not a ghost, surely a ghost," must have crossed their minds. "Berta, go back to bed, you're dead!" cried out her little sister. "She's already dead and that's how she wanted to say goodbye to us," moaned her mother, opening the door. After a moment, everyone rushed into the room, and we can only imagine their great amazement at the sight of Berta alive and healthy. "I am healed! I can run!" she shouted. There was a lot of joy and laughter. The next day, the doctor was needed only to confirm the sudden and complete healing.

Statue of St. Klaus of Flüe in Flüeli-Ranft.

ASCENSION DAY

In 1967, when Fr. Josef Konrad Scheuber described their cases, both healed women were still alive and enjoying good health. Berta Schürmann married, taking the last name Burkhardt, and Ida Jeker (later Schwarb) died in 2010. Note well: As Dr. M. Haesele wrote, Br. Klaus seems to particularly like Ascension Day. On that day he not only healed Berta Schürmann, but he was also canonized, simultaneously healing an Austrian woman from the area of Klagenfurt, who had been suffering from spinal tuberculosis for twelve years.

Church of St. Nicholas in Winkeln (St. Gallen).

Lily of the Mohawks, Kateri Tekakwitha. *Contemporary fresco by Marius Dubois in the Chapel of the Immaculate Conception, Auriesville Shrine.*

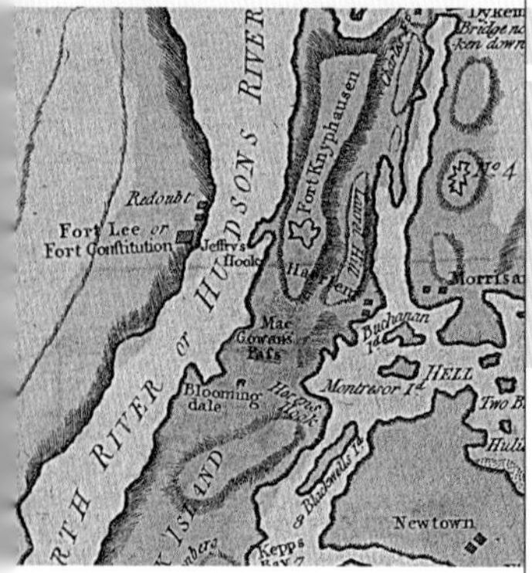

Map of Mohawk territory.

View of the Hudson River by Robert Havell, Jr.

THE LILY OF THE MOHAWKS

St. Kateri Tekakwitha

Kateri "Catherine" Tekakwitha became the first Native American saint. She was called the "lily of the Mohawks." One of the miraculous healings performed through her intercession was the rescue from the death of a young boy whose body was attacked by a flesh-eating bacteria.

On Saturday, February 11, 2006, five-year-old Jake Finkbonner from Ferndale, Washington, was playing basketball at the local Boys and Girls Club. The game was coming to an end.

Jake stopped and then jumped up to throw the ball into the basket when he was pushed from behind.

FATAL INFECTION

Unfortunately, the boy fell in such a way that he cut his lip on the base of a portable basketball hoop. The injury seemed harmless, like most injuries we often experience as children. Sadly, this was not the case. Although it happens extremely rarely, a minor

injury threatened the boy's life. It was because of the "carnivorous" bacteria *Streptococcus pyogenes*, which causes necrosis of connective tissue (*fasciitis necroticans*). After entering the human body, flesh-eating bacteria, with the help of secreted toxins, destroy the deeper layers of the skin.

The bacteria infected the wound and began to spread at lightning speed. The very next day, the previously healthy boy began a dramatic fight for his life (untreated, this disease has a mortality rate as high as seventy-one percent). His face turned red and swollen, he was in great pain, and he had a high fever. On Monday, the five-year-old was airlifted to Seattle Children's Hospital, located ninety miles from Ferndale. The very next day doctors informed his parents that their son was in critical condition. The boy, who was previously comely, now looked terrible, with a swollen, red-purple-black, bacteria-eaten face. Moreover, he felt and looked worse every day. He was intubated and bandaged, so that his face was almost completely covered. Every day, the bandages were unwound, more infected bits of tissue were cut out, and the boy was given fifteen different drugs before being placed in a hyperbaric chamber. For days, however, the fight was not so much for his health as for his life. During this time, Jake's parents heard many times that they should prepare for their son's death. Hearing such a bad prognosis, Elsa and Donny Finkbonner asked their friend, Fr. Tim Sauer, to prepare the boy for death: to give him last rites, or some alternative to it (the sacrament is usually administered to children aged seven and older).

The priest also ministered at the parish established for the Native Americans of the Pacific Northwest, and knew the life story

Mohawk warrior in hunting attire.

➤ *Mohawk tribe family.*

of Bl. Kateri Tekakwitha very well. Therefore, he advised the distraught parents to pray for their son's life and health through her intercession. They listened. They prayed for days and nights and asked family and friends to do the same. Fr. Sauer called on his parishioners to pray. Mr. and Mrs. Finkbonner froze when one day their son told them about his out-of-body experiences of being in Heaven and meeting Jesus there in the company of his recently deceased godfather.

He also told them that although he didn't want to leave, Jesus told him that he had to return to his parents and younger sisters. The boy later recounted during various interviews that, at one point during his illness, he was able to look down at his hospital bed, and at his parents sitting beside him. Then he also saw God, who was very tall and was sitting in a high chair, and even talked to Him, his deceased uncle, and his great-grandmother, as well as the angels.

After nine days of fighting for his life, Jake's aunt brought an unusual visitor to the hospital: her friend, Sr. Kateri Mitchell, executive director of the Tekakwitha Conference, and an Indian nun belonging to the Congregation of the Sisters of St. Anne of St. Regis Mission in Akwesasne, Canada. The boy's parents did not hide their amazement. They felt a thrill of excitement. After all, they had been praying for their child's life through the intercession of Bl. Kateri for days, and suddenly there was a person with the same

⮝ *Mohawks harpoon hunting.*

➤ *Detail of the statue of St. Tekakwitha from the doorway of St. Patrick's Cathedral in New York.*

name standing by their child's hospital bed. Not only that, but Sr. Kateri, who came from the East Coast, had with her a relic of the wrist bone of her blessed namesake (she always took it with her when she went to pray for someone). She placed it on the child's bed, on a pillow right next to his head, and together with his parents focused on fervent prayer, asking Bl. Kateri for a miraculous healing.

This was the turning point. Later that day, doctors performed a final surgery. After the operation, they found that the progression of the disease had been stopped and the boy would recover from it. From that day on, Jake's health began to improve. He eventually recovered completely and was able to return home from the hospital on Good Friday in April. The deadly bacteria had been defeated. Only the scars on his face today testify to the terrible moments he had to endure. Since then he has undergone a great many plastic and reconstructive surgeries, during which his skin was transplanted. The boy's recovery over time, after an in-depth examination, was considered a miracle. In an interview with *ABC News* in 2011, Jake, who was already a teenager, advised all those suffering from life-threatening illnesses by referring to his "heavenly" experiences. He said, "Don't be scared at all; either way, it will be a good way. If you go to Heaven, you'll be in a better place. If you live, you'll be back with your family." Obviously, being a good Catholic, he was well aware that some people might be afraid.[1]

Thanks to the recognition of this healing as a miracle, Pope Benedict XVI canonized Bl. Kateri Tekakwitha in 2012, thirty-two years after her beatification. Catherine Tekakwitha became the first saint among the indigenous peoples of North America. She has been called the "Lily of the Mohawks" and the "Genevieve of New France."

A Mohawk woman in a festive dress with a baby in a carrier.

INDIAN JOURNEY THROUGH TIME

Jake Finkbonner had two things in common with Kateri Tekakwitha. Both had Indian roots: the boy's father is a member of the Lummi tribe, and as a child, he had heard of Kateri Tekakwitha. Both also had similar problems (Kateri's face was scarred from smallpox, which had a very severe course and which killed members of her immediate family). They were only three centuries apart!

Is time any obstacle for us Catholics, believers in the communion of saints, in the never-ending union of those who are still on earth with those who are already in Heaven or Purgatory? The answer is obvious: *No.*

A longhouse of the Iroquois.

Statue of St. Kateri Tekakwitha at St. John Neumann Catholic Church in Sunbury, Ohio.

Kateri Tekakwitha was born in Ossernenon (now in upstate New York) in a settlement of Mohawks, one of the most belligerent and cruel Iroquois tribes, whose members ate the hearts and brains of their slain and stout-hearted enemies. She was just four years old when her parents and brother died of smallpox. The girl survived, but was left with marks on her face and severely damaged eyesight as a result of the disease.

She was adopted by her uncle, the village chief, who hated Christianity, even though the Mohawks' "war trophy," Kateri's mother from the Algonquin tribe, was a Christian.

Kateri did not follow in her footsteps for a long time. However, she became increasingly intrigued by the stories about God, the Great Spirit, His Son Jesus, and Mother Mary that were told by the "black gowns," the Jesuit missionaries who visited her village. The first visits of the missionaries ended in their martyrdom. At the same time, she knew that her new guardian would not allow her to receive Baptism. The girl led a modest life, rarely leaving the longhouse in which she lived with many members of her clan. She wove Indian ornaments, carried water, cooked meals, gathered brushwood, and helped in the corn fields.

She only asked to be baptized when she turned eighteen. She felt that she could no longer ignore God's call. She felt she had to and wanted to respond to His love with her own love. In honor of the famous mystic from Siena, she adopted the name Catherine. For a long time, she had to defend herself against marriage proposals. She always replied that her only fiancé was Jesus.

She faced a lot of pressure and harassment because of her conversion to Christianity. For example, because she refused to work on Sundays and holidays, she was not allowed to eat, was called a Christian dog, and endured many attempts to intimidate her.

Finally, she fled to the Kahnawake mission station on the St. Lawrence River (present-day Canada), established by the Jesuits, called the "fort of prayer," where only Indian Christians lived.

She worked there too: she taught children about prayer and religion, told stories about the saints, and cared for the sick and the elderly. On Christmas Day, 1677, she received her First Communion, and on the Feast of the Annunciation 1679, she took vows of lifelong chastity, which was revolutionary among the sexually lax Indians. Indians and missionaries admired her exceptional piety. Her favorite prayer was the Rosary, and she had many mystical experiences. Together with several other women, with whom she prayed fervently and fasted and mortified severely, she wanted to establish a conventual community, but her spiritual guardian did not agree.

A life full of extremely strict sacrifices and mortifications drove her into serious illness. She died during Holy Week at the age of twenty-four. The last words that came out of her mouth were "I love you, Jesus." Then something very strange happened. About fifteen minutes after her passing, the scars on her face healed completely.

SHINING LIKE THE SUN

Kateri appeared to several acquaintances shortly after her death. Just six days later, on Easter Monday, she was seen by Fr. Claude Chauchetiere, a priest at the mission. The priest saw her in a vision, shining like the sun with her eyes raised to Heaven. The monk also saw things that were about to happen, including the image of a destroyed church and an Indian being burned at the stake. She appeared to Father Chauchetiere again more than a year after her death. Shining with light, she instructed him to paint her portrait, which the priest did, refreshing his artistic skills. He painted many other images of her, which he then distributed among the faithful. Some of them contributed to miraculous healings when placed on the sick.

Anastasia, her spiritual mother, also saw her. Kateri woke her from a deep sleep and told her to look at herself. Surrounded by a bright light, she showed the Cross, urging everyone living in the mission to love it as she did. She also appeared twice to another Indian woman. The first time she came to tell her "goodbye," for she had already departed for Heaven. The other time she came after the girl when she had quarreled with her sister. At that time she urged her not to be angry and wrathful.

THE POWER OF THE CROSS

Since her death, however, Kateri has become known primarily as a great intercessor with God. As Emily Cavins writes in her book *Lily of the Mohawks*, "Through her intercession, Indians have received many graces. Among those healed were women experiencing difficult births, intestinal obstructions, respiratory ailments, rheumatic pains, smallpox, and incurable diseases."

Kateri cured not only bodies, but also souls, including those addicted to gambling or other sinful activities. Thanks to her, Indians began to engage in religious practices. For two years after the death of the pious girl, so many of these miracles happened that, eventually, the Jesuits stopped writing them down in detail.

The practice of mixing the dust from her robes or the dust and soil collected from her tomb with medicines was common, and a great healing power was ascribed to these relics.

St. Kateri Tekakwitha, St. Xavier del Bac Mission.

Many people were also healed through the cross that Kateri had in her hands when she passed away. One such story tells of a priest who wanted to write about Kateri's virtues but had some concerns because of certain rumors about her life. Not knowing whether or not to give them credence, he was once called to a dying man who was so weak that he could barely make a Confession. The priest suggested that they appeal together to Kateri. The dying man agreed, and then the clergyman handed him the aforementioned cross. Soon after, the man had to get out of bed so that his bedding could be changed. He got up and fell immediately. They thought it was his last moment. However, when he was laid back in bed, the man fell into a deep sleep, and when he woke up, he was healed.

In January 1681, a woman became gravely ill and was in critical condition. The same priest then gave her the Sacrament of Anointing of the Sick. He also handed her Kateri's crucifix, encouraging her to turn to God through her intercession. The woman placed the crucifix on her neck and immediately recovered. However, she refused to hand the crucifix back. The priest then gave her soil from the grave of the pious Indian woman as a substitute. The woman put it around her neck in place of the earlier relic. When she thought she was cured, she removed the dried soil and in an instant felt gravely ill again. Fortunately, the danger of death passed again as soon as she applied the said relic to herself.

Three years later, Kateri saved from death a three-year-old child who had choked on a seashell, and in the winter of 1693, Father Bruyas was healed from paralysis of his right hand through Kateri's intercession. These are just a few of the great many miracles interceded and still being interceded with God through the Indian saint.[2]

ENDNOTES

1 Bob Woodruff, Roxanna Sherwood, and Eric Johnson, "Washington Boy Says He Spoke to God After Flesh-Eating Bacteria Threatened Life," *ABC News*, July 28, 2011, https://abcnews.go.com/nightline/beyondbelief/washington-boy-spoke-god-flesh-eating-bacteria-threatened/story?id=14212228.

2 Emily Cavins, *Lily of the Mohawks: The Story of St. Kateri* (Cincinnati: Servant Books, 2013), 84.

Auriesville Shrine.

Statue of St. Kateri Tekakwitha at the Cathedral Basilica of St. Francis of Assisi, Santa Fe, New Mexico.

A holy medal of St. Kateri Tekakwitha.

1844–1879

THE SIMPLICITY OF THE REFINED SOUL

St. Bernadette Soubirous

It was February 11, 1858. The morning mist was fading over the small French town of Lourdes in the Pyrenees Mountains when, around noon, fourteen-year-old Bernadette Soubirous went to collect brushwood with two friends.

The girls walked along the banks of the Gave de Pau River and a stream called the Savy. When they reached the dirty and littered Grotto of Massabielle near the stream, something strange happened. Bernadette saw a Lady. It was the first of seventeen Marian apparitions, known today as the Apparitions of Our Lady of Lourdes, that the girl witnessed until July 16 of the same year.

Bernadette was a "simple" evangelist, the eldest of nine children of a poor miller. Her family lived together in one room, an "infested and dark hole" of a former "prison dungeon," and worked odd jobs. Nevertheless, they loved each other deeply and were very devout.

At the time of the apparitions, Bernadette could not read or write. She didn't know the *Catechism* or French (she spoke only

⮝ *Pilgrims entering the sanctuary head along a wide parvis toward the Basilica of the Immaculate Conception.*

➤ *Just after the first apparitions, people began to gather around the grotto, immersed in prayer.*

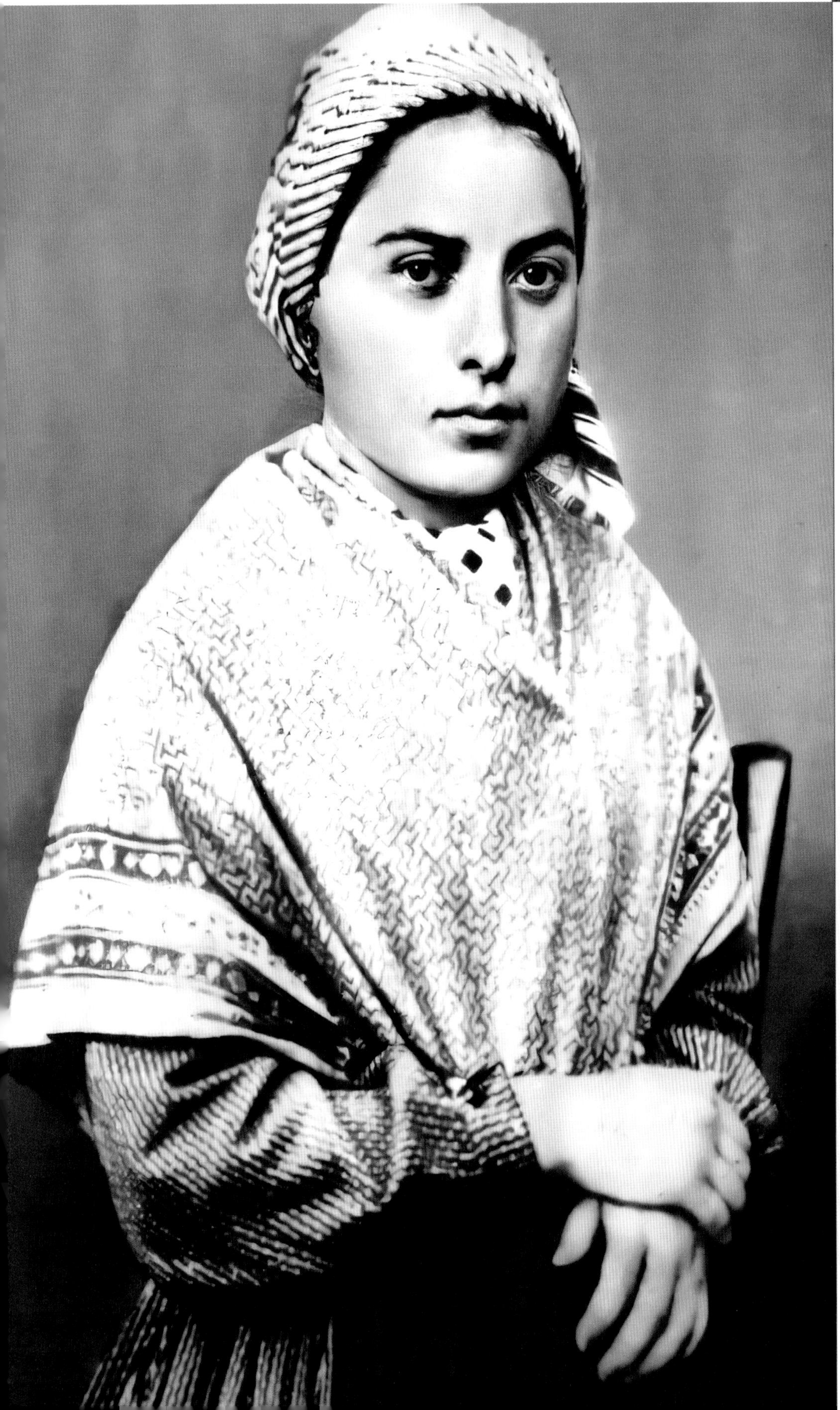

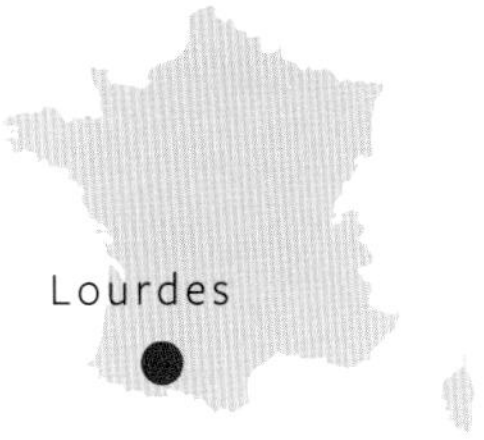

FRANCE

Bernadette was a "simple" evangelist, the eldest of nine children of a poor miller. At the time of the apparitions, her deeply loving and devout family lived together in one room in a former prison dungeon. She could not read or write, and she had not yet received Holy Communion.

▲ *Soubirous family home.*

➤ *Louise Soubirous, the mother of the visionary.*

▲ *Paul-Armand Cardon de Garsignies, Bishop of Soissons from 1847–1860. He was the first to meet with Bernadette Soubirous in Lourdes and took steps to allow the Grotto of Massabielle to be opened to the public.*

the Pyrenean dialect), and she hadn't yet received Holy Communion. She hardly ever went to school, and in addition, learning came with great difficulty to her. Instead of studying, she tended sheep and cared for her siblings.

Bernadette was also tiny and sickly. She had cholera as a child that caused her to suffer from severe asthma for the rest of her life. As a result, she always looked a few years younger than she really was, and at the time of her death, she was only four feet seven inches tall. Once, the Mother of God healed her of pneumonia through the miraculous waters of Lourdes, but she never received full healing from her other ailments. She had hemorrhages, spit blood, and complained of pains in her stomach and head. She was so sick that she received last rites four times, thinking that death was near. At the end of her life, she suffered from skeletal tuberculosis in her right knee.

APPARITIONS AND THEIR MIRACULOUS CONFIRMATION

After Bernadette's visions of Mary, she become famous. Whether she wanted it or not, crowds of people came to talk to her or just to touch her. Some loved her, and others slandered her. Satan himself "bent over backwards" to discredit the apparitions.

Many people claimed that the girl was mentally ill, that she was suffering from catalepsy, delusions, hallucinations, or hysteria, or that she was pretending or pointlessly lying. A nun at her school even asked her if she had stopped organizing "masquerade carnivals," while some saw the apparitions as an influence of occultism, the effect of religious fanaticism, or as a game. The doctors who examined her, however, did not diagnose her with any mental disorders. She was interrogated many times by Church and government representatives, and although some tried intimidating her and even threatening her with life in prison, she bravely stood firm by the truth, never letting anyone press her to say something that contradicted what she did indeed see or say. She was never found to have deviated from the truth in the slightest degree or to pretend for gain. She was truthful, completely genuine, and innocent.

Her parish priest, Fr. Peyramale, also approached the apparitions with great reserve and suspicion. He later, after learning the apparition called herself the Immaculate Conception, came to the conclusion that everything Bernadette said was true. He witnessed conversions and miraculous healings and became actively involved in fulfilling Mary's apparition requests. The priest asked

God for a sign to be sure the apparitions were true and received an answer one Sunday during Holy Mass. According to a nun to whom he recounted his tale, "I noticed a person with a bright halo around her head at the Master's table. I was greatly amazed by this sight. I gave her Holy Communion, not realizing who she was. I followed her with my eyes until she returned to her place. And there, as she turned to kneel, I recognized her as Bernadette. All my worries vanished. Since then I have had no more doubts about the apparitions."

In 1862, after a thorough examination of the apparitions by a commission appointed to verify their authenticity, Bertrand Sévère Laurence, Bishop of Tarbes, recognized them as true, supernatural, and divine.

BLINDED BY BRIGHTNESS

During the apparitions, Our Lady entrusted Bernadette with three secrets and taught her a special prayer. These were of a personal nature and were never disclosed by Bernadette. Mary also pointed to a place where, after Bernadette scraped at the muddy ground, an abundant spring gushed forth. Even during the time of the apparitions, the water from this spring, when received with prayer and faith in God's help, has led to many healings. To date, about seven thousand healings have been reported at the Sanctuary of Lourdes, of which seventy have been recognized as miracles.

One of the first miraculous healings is generally considered to be the extraordinary and unexpected recovery of a fifty-four-year-old quarryman, Louis Bouriette. Nineteen years earlier, Bouriette had been injured on the job in an explosion that had killed his brother. He himself was seriously injured and suffered from nerve damage in his right eye that eventually caused the eye to go blind.

◄ The police commissioner, Dominique Jacomet, tried to force Bernadette to retract what she had said about the visions, but she held to the truth.

▼ Fr. Peyramale didn't believe Bernadette's account, but he changed his mind when she brought a message from the Bright Lady: "I am the Immaculate Conception."

◄ Bernadette, a cheerful fourteen-year-old girl, was chosen by Mary.

➤ *Louis Veuillot, a well-known Catholic polemicist who fiercely opposed liberalism in the nineteenth century, went to Lourdes twice to talk to St. Bernadette.*

His physician, Dr. Dozous, found that "the right eye had suffered a deep wound in the lower part of the cornea … the pupil, being dilated as a result, had become almost completely unresponsive to light." Bouriette only saw "a hazy and pale light" with this eye and his doctor informed him that there was no cure.

Years later, Bouriette heard about the apparitions and the discovery of the spring in the Massabielle Grotto on February 25, 1858. He had great faith that water from this spring could heal him: "Holy Virgin, if it really is her, all she needs is a will to heal me," he said. He went to the grotto in early March, gathered muddy water from the stream into his hands, rubbed it in his eye, and asked Mary to be close to him and help him. He opened his eyes and was suddenly blinded by brightness. Astonished, he covered his left eye and, to his surprise, noticed that his right eye had regained full sight.

"I'm healed!" he exclaimed when he saw the doctor. "Impossible!" the doctor blurted out. The doctor took a notebook from his pocket and wrote a few words in it with a pencil. Covering his patient's left eye, he placed the paper in front of his right eye. "Bouriette has an incurable amaurosis of the eye and will never recover," read the man. Dr. Dozous, whether he liked it or not, had to admit that what he had written was not true after all, that the man had experienced a sudden and inexplicable healing. The doctor later described, "I examined Bouriette's eyes, which seemed no different from each other in the shape and organization of their many parts. Both pupils functioned regularly and correctly under the influence of light. There was still a scar on the right eye only." Professor Henri Vergez later confirmed Dr. Dozous's opinion. "This cure possesses a supernatural character," he stated.

After a special commission examined the details, on January 18, 1862, Bishop Laurence officially recognized this healing as a Church-confirmed miracle. After, a flood of miracles ensued. To this day, healing miracles are continuously reported at Lourdes.

➤ *Old Lourdes. Lithography. View of Cauterets (Hautes-Pyrénées). Published in 1835.*

BERNADETTE IN THE CONVENT

After the apparitions, sixteen-and-a-half-year-old Bernadette went to live with the Sisters of Charity, first in their hospice at Lourdes as a boarder and student and then, at the age of twenty-two, in the Convent of St. Gildard in Nevers. While she was welcomed as a novice with joy, Bernadette, now Sr. Marie Bernard, did not have an easy life in the congregation, as

Engravings showing the grotto of Bernadette's visions in Lourdes.

she suffered both spiritually and physically. Yet heroically humble, she saw "the love of the Lord Jesus" in her own crosses. She did penance, suffered, and prayed for sinners until the end of her life, just as Mary had requested.

Because Sr. Marie Bernard was sickly, she was considered unfit for most convent chores, but she could sew and embroider beautifully and therefore was tasked with embroidering vestments and altar cloths. Eventually, she was also able to work as a nurse in the convent infirmary and a sacristan assistant. She performed these duties with zeal.

While in the convent, Sr. Marie Bernard was kind and cheerful and had a wonderful sense of humor. One day, for instance, one of the sisters was boiling milk in the convent's infirmary, and suddenly it began to boil over. "Oh no! My milk is escaping!" the sister shouted as she ran to rescue the pot. "Hurry, sister, get the police!" Sr. Marie

Thanks to the Bishop of Nevers, Théodore-Augustin Forcade, Bernadette joined the Sisters of Charity.

➤ *Bernadette lived at the Convent of St. Gildard in Nevers.*

➤ *Family home of St. Bernadette.*

➤ *Esplanade before the Basilica of Lourdes. A postcard from the early twentieth century.*

Bernard cried out as she lay in her hospital bed. With such innocent jokes, she could entertain, defuse tension, and even teach.

One day, though, one of the sisters wanted the visionary to touch her rosary. She made up what she thought was a pretty good excuse. “Dear sister, look at my rosary—why is it rusting so much?” she said, extending her hand toward Sr. Marie Bernard. “Because, my dear, you don’t say it often,” she answered. The trick failed, and she did not take the rosary in her hand.

MIRACLES OF BERNADETTE

The above-mentioned plot is understandable, as later accounts of the nuns testify that while Sr. Marie Bernard was in the convent—and even earlier, in the hospice in Lourdes—many people she touched, or people who were touched by something that passed through her hands, experienced unexpected healings. What’s more, as testified in the episcopal process in Nevers, “according to the unanimous opinion of the entire convent community, Sr. Marie Bernard obtained several healings with her prayers during her lifetime.” Usually, these healings involved sick children who were brought to her to take care of them, even for a moment. One woman, who wanted to acquire anything that Sr. Marie Bernard had touched for her sick child, brought a knitted quilt that was "tangled and unfinished" and asked the sister to finish it. When she finished her work, the happy mother took her "quilt-relic" and covered the child with it. The baby recovered!

Sr. Marie Bernard also prophesied about the future of various people and had "supernatural premonitions about the date of her death."

MIRACULOUSLY PRESERVED

The visionary of Lourdes died at the age of thirty-five on April 16, 1879, after a long illness and much suffering. After her death, her body was exposed in an open coffin for two days. Throngs of people passed before her to pray by her, pay her last homage, and obtain relics by touching objects to her remains. The sisters themselves touched her hands with rosaries and other devotional items, work tools, and even officers' scabbards. On April 19, Sr. Marie Bernard's body was placed in an oak, then in an additional zinc coffin. The casket was sealed and transferred to the crypt of the convent's little Chapel of St. Joseph.

Thirty years later, when her body was exhumed, the examiners observed that it looked as if she had died not thirty years ago but just the previous day. Her corpse was perfectly preserved and flexible; it showed no signs of decay inside or out, and it had no smell.

The woman's beautiful face, tilted to the left and with slightly sunken eyes, showed an unearthly calmness. Her skin was smooth and retained its natural color. Her skin still clung to the muscles, and the muscles adhered to the bones. Her fingernails were

St. Bernadette's relics.

St. Bernadette's relics and a stone from the grotto in Lourdes.

During the exhumation of Bernadette's body in 1925, the examiners discovered that her corpse remained intact.

➤ *The interior of the grotto in Lourdes. Photos from the beginning of the twentieth century.*

in perfect condition, and her veins were visible under her skin. Her hair was still on her head, her teeth were preserved, and her ears were in perfect condition—but her nose seemed to be slightly damaged. Her body also looked a bit haggard, but this was not surprising given the visionary's poor health. Her left knee was also much smaller than the right, but this was due to the skeletal tuberculosis that she suffered from toward the end of her life. All in all, however, her body was intact.

The perfect condition of the sister's body was strange not only because of the time that had elapsed but also because the vault of the chapel was quite humid, and humidity usually accelerates decomposition. Indeed, the objects that

▼ In the middle of the nineteenth century, an old stone bridge was the only way to the place of the apparitions.

◄ Organized pilgrimages for the disabled visit Lourdes.

were placed in the coffin along with her body did succumb to the poor conditions of the tomb: her habit was damp and rotten, the rosary rusty, and the cross covered with patina.

Ten years later—on April 3, 1919—her coffin was exhumed for the second time. Little had changed since the first exhumation; once again, the corpse was still in perfect condition. It was even possible to carry her body to a table to examine it further. It didn't give off any unpleasant odors. Upon closer inspection, the examiners realized that some parts of the body were covered with patches of mildew and calcium salts, there was minor skin loss, and parts of the face were discolored. According to the doctors examining the corpse, however, these changes occurred as a result of the body having been washed in 1909.

The coffin was opened one final time before Bernadette's beatification in 1925—forty-six years after her death. Again, no major changes were found. Dr. Comte, who performed these procedures and examined the body, described what he saw in the *Bulletin of the Medical Association* at Our Lady of Lourdes. There, he expressed his astonishment that Bernadette's body, which had been lying in a coffin for forty-six years, was intact and practically "mummified," that it had a perfectly preserved skeleton, all ligaments, and perfectly preserved muscles. What surprised him the most was the elasticity of the liver, a very delicate organ that quickly disintegrates or calcifies and hardens after death. Yet in this case the liver was soft, as in a living person. The doctor considered such a fact to be a supernatural phenomenon—in other words, a miracle.

Bernadette's skin had suffered to a small extent because of the humidity of the tomb, and because the sister's face was slightly blackened, the eyes were sunken, and the nose was slightly damaged, a

⮝ *Basilica of the Immaculate Conception seen from the Gave de Pau River.*

➤ *Pope St. John Paul II was the first pope to make a pilgrimage to Lourdes. He went twice: on August 14, 1983, and August 14–15, 2004.*

sculptor was asked to make wax masks for her face and hands.

After her beatification, the incorrupt mortal remains of Bernadette Soubirous were clothed and put on public display in a coffin made of gold and glass. They can be seen to this day at the Chapel of St. Gildard at the Sisters of Charity in Nevers.

SANCTITY SUPPORTED BY MIRACLES

Pope Pius XI beatified Bernadette in 1925, and in 1933, she was canonized. She became a saint not only because she was a visionary but thanks to her holy life full of virtues, especially humility, purity, and poverty. Indeed, the wealth of this "uneducated daughter of common millers" was, as Pius XI said, the "simplicity of the refined soul." Her virtue was also proven by several miracles that occurred after her death.

In his excellent biography of St. Bernadette, Fr. Francis Trochu describes the miracles taken into account for Bernadette's beatification and canonization. He begins with the story of Henri Boisselet, a seventeen-year-old man who was suffering from tuberculous peritonitis in November 1913. Henri was close to death and received last rites. His loved ones, however, began praying a novena to Bernadette for him that was to end on December 8, the Feast of the Immaculate Conception. On that day, Henri was instantly and completely healed. At the start of World War I, he was even declared fit for military service and was drafted to the front. But Bernadette did not abandon him even then: while Henri was taken prisoner and spent thirty-two months in a prisoner-of-war camp, he was eventually released and came home healthy.

Sr. Marie Melanie Meyer of the Sisters of Divine Providence of Ribeauvillé worked in an infirmary in Moulins, France. In 1910, at the age of thirty, she began to experience severe abdominal pain and frequent vomiting, and she was diagnosed with stomach cancer. She was soon unable to eat any food. Close to death, Sr. Marie decided to make a pilgrimage to Bernadette's grave in Nevers. She suffered greatly the entire journey. Once inside the Chapel of St. Joseph, she forced herself to kneel down on the slab of the tomb. She prayed for an hour, either kneeling or sitting. Suddenly, her pain subsided. She felt great hunger and ate without difficulty. Her strength immediately began to return, and she returned to Moulins without any suffering or fatigue. The next day, she returned to her normal life and activities.

Another miracle occurred on August 3, 1925, only forty days after Bernadette's beatification. Alexis Lemaître, the Archbishop of Carthage and Primate of Africa, had suffered from a gastrointestinal disease for more than ten years. He received several treatments, but all were in vain. Eventually, the disease had become so advanced that, according to the doctors who cared for him, there was no hope of recovery, or at least immediate recovery. Nevertheless, he was determined to be a part of the solemn transfer of the relics of the newly Bl. Bernadette in Nevers. As he left for the ceremony, he experienced a serious surge in his symptoms, but he somehow found enough energy and made it to Nevers. Suddenly, as he watched the relics pass, he was instantly and completely healed. The archbishop returned to his position in Carthage and worked there until his death fourteen years later.

A view of the Fort in Lourdes by Charles Mercereau, around 1860.

1870–1957

BLESSED ARE THE MERCIFUL

St. Maria Elisabeth Hesselblad

She was Swedish, and throughout her life she deplored the divisions among Christians. Working toward Christ's one fold, she converted from Lutheranism to Catholicism and continued the legacy of St. Bridget of Sweden, who lived nearly six centuries earlier and Christianized the Scandinavian countries at a time when they were still pagan. St. Maria Elisabeth also renewed the Bridgettine order. God confirmed her holiness with two spectacular miracles. Equally miraculous was her own path to the Catholic faith.

Photo of Maria Elisabeth Hesselblad taken before she entered the Bridgettine Order.

She was born into a Swedish Lutheran family (Sweden's largest religion) and was the fifth of thirteen children. Her father was a sensitive shopkeeper with the soul of an artist, while her mother kept the family budget stable as a seamstress. The family was not wealthy, and they became even more impoverished when her father's business went bankrupt. The Hesselblad family moved frequently. Even as a child, Elisabeth Hesselblad wondered why the children in her school belonged to different churches, even though they were all Christians. After

The train station in Fåglavik (Västergötland, Sweden), the saint's hometown.

all, in the Bible, which she studied every day, it was written that there is only one shepherd and one fold. She prayed, asking God to show her the one fold in which He wants to gather all His sheep. One day, on a walk, when looking up into the sky, she once again asked God that question. She suddenly and unexpectedly felt some kind of wonderful peace in her soul and heard a voice saying: "Yes, my daughter, one day I will point it out to you."

She later experienced another extraordinary prophetic vision. She saw the "wide square" of the Roman house where St. Bridget lived in the fourteenth century, and through a window in one of the rooms she saw herself (twenty-eight years later this vision became a reality!). At sixteen, Maria Elisabeth became a maid and babysitter for the family of a military man from Karlsborg. Two years later, looking for work, she moved to the United States. There she started working as a nurse in New York's Roosevelt Hospital, and there her spiritual journey to the Catholic Church began.

TO THE CHURCH THROUGH THE HOSPITAL

Working in the hospital was quite a natural career path for Maria Elisabeth. As a child, she suffered severely from diphtheria and scarlet fever. Moreover, when she was twelve years old, painful, bleeding ulcers developed in her digestive tract. They caused her to suffer all her life. On top of that, shortly after arriving in New York, she became seriously ill and had to be hospitalized. At that time, she promised Jesus that if she recovered, she would devote herself to helping the sick and suffering.

She stayed at the hospital, no longer as a patient but as a member of the hospital staff. To become a nurse, however, she had to study for many years. In the New York hospital, she had the opportunity to meet Catholic immigrants from Ireland. She came into contact with many of those injured during the construction of New York's St. Patrick's Cathedral. Dying Irish people often asked her to summon a Catholic priest to help them on their last journey. She honored their requests, and she felt edified by their joyful and strong faith and their prayers. She was puzzled by the trust they put in the help of the Mother of God and her intercession, in Divine Providence, and in God's mercy. It was then that she saw the rosary for the first time. She also learned what role Confession played in the lives of Catholics and heard the truth about Purgatory.

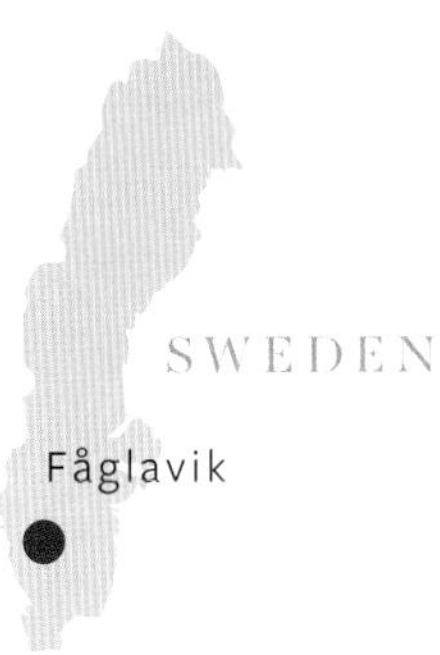

On June 5, 2016, during Mass in St. Peter's Square, Bl. Maria Elisabeth was canonized by Pope Francis together with Bl. Stanislaus Papczynski.

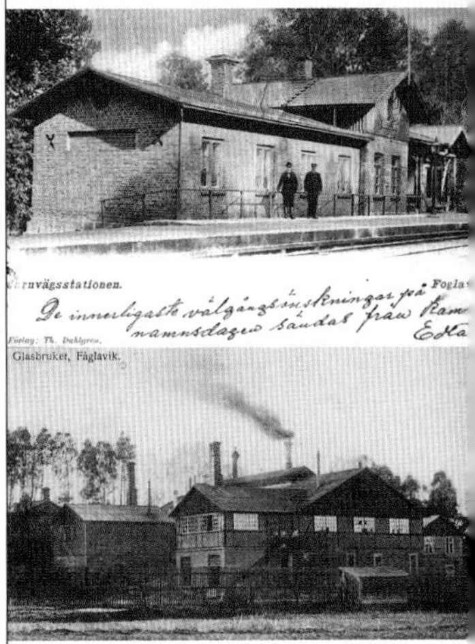

Fåglavik, the saint's hometown. The house where she was born and a small glassware factory.

▲ *Father Johann Georg Hagen, a famous astronomer, who was Maria Elisabeth's spiritual father.*

▼ *Bridgettines from all over the world came to the canonization of Maria Elisabeth Hesselblad.*

A LIVING CORPSE IN A NEW YORK MORGUE

One day Elisabeth experienced something very strange. While she was celebrating her birthday, one of the young doctors came up with a rather silly idea.

He decided to test the nurses' courage and invited them on a trip to the morgue. Elisabeth did not like this idea. She felt that they owed the deceased respect. Outvoted by the others, she went with them to intervene in case any of her colleagues felt sick, and then walked among the bodies, praying for the dead. When she decided to leave, the group was no longer there and the door to the morgue was closed. She was not frightened. She was not afraid of death nor of the dead. She also did not fear when she noticed that one of the dead men was breathing. It was a young man that was presumed dead after suffering a heart attack. She approached him and noticed not only his gentle breathing, but also that his body was warmer than the others. Without thinking too long, she dressed him in her own clothes and started artificial respiration. One can imagine the surprise of the hospital staff who opened the morgue door in the morning and found there a living young "dead man" and a nurse sitting by him half-dressed. "Don't ask me how it happened. I don't know. It was God's work," Elisabeth said, but in a bizarre and amazing way, she saved the young man's life.

IN THE ONE, TRUE…

Upon her return to the United States, Elisabeth, intrigued by Catholicism, continued to explore the mysteries of the Catholic Faith, spending many days at a Dominican convent in Saratoga Springs, caring for one of the sick Dominican nuns and using the library there. She also experienced another vision, during which she saw Catholic priests arguing about important topics and a pastor who came between them, "went gray like clay," and then broke into thousands of pieces.

Influenced by this vision, she first prayed to the saints—St. Ignatius of Loyola and St. Bridget, to be exact. Another day she noticed dust in the eyes of the statue of Mary located in the Dominican nuns' garden. She wiped them and then put the only green branch in the garden in the Madonna's hand. To the nuns' surprise, the branch remained fresh and green for several months. Shortly thereafter, Elisabeth prayed to the Mother of God for the first time, when she received a telegram informing her of her father's death.

Soon after, one of her friends informed her that she was joining the convent. Elisabeth was surprised and could not understand her decision. However, she accompanied her to the Visitandine convent in Washington. It was only after some time that she realized that joining a convent was by no means an escape from responsibility, but a response to a call, a vocation.

In 1902, thirty-year-old Elisabeth Hesselblad contacted the Jesuits in Washington and asked to be received into the Catholic Church. It so happened (it was certainly God's will) that there she met Fr. Johann Georg Hagen, who had Austrian roots and was a prominent astronomer. He later became her longtime spiritual guide and director of the Vatican's astronomical observatory. Certainly, Maria Elisabeth confided in him at the time about the pain she felt due to the divisions among Christians and her strenuous search for the "true fold," which, as God Himself once assured her, she would find. And she finally found it—in the one, true Catholic Church. In 1902, on the Solemnity of the Assumption of the Blessed Virgin Mary in the church of a Jesuit monastery in Washington, D.C., she received conditional Baptism (given when there is concern that a previous Baptism was invalid), and two days later received her first Holy Communion in the Catholic Church. A Christmas visit to her family home was a difficult experience for her. Her parents and siblings were astounded and embarrassed that she had become a Catholic. Maria Elisabeth patiently explained to them the contentious (and for them foreign) dogmas and practices of the Catholic Faith.

BRIDGETTINES 2.0

A year later, Elisabeth was already in Rome, following the footsteps of another Swedish woman, who lived in the pre-

St. Bridget writing down her visions, with an angel behind her prompting the mystic.

1870–1957

➤ *Fåglavik, the saint's hometown. Maria Elisabeth strenuously tried to restore the Swedes to their former faith. Unfortunately, her compatriots were not particularly interested in this.*

Maria came into contact with the last members of the Order of St. Bridget, which had been suppressed in the nineteenth century, living in Syon in the British Isles (and later with other Bridgettine convents in Spain, the Netherlands, and Germany). In 1906, she adopted the habit of the Bridgettines, and then, with the approval of Pope Pius X from 1911 to1913, formed its new branch, called the Order of the Most Holy Savior of St. Bridget, making it apostolic and ecumenical in character.

➤ *A beautiful page of Mother Maria Elisabeth Hesselblad's history was written during World War II. She bravely resisted a search of her Roman convent by the Germans, thus saving thirteen Jews from the holocaust.*

Reformation days of the undivided Church and was revered by both Catholics and Protestants. She wanted to take up and continue St. Bridget's work. She wished to devote herself to converting her compatriots and attracting them to the one true fold of Christ: the Catholic Church. She communicated this desire to the German bishop who was apostolic vicar of Sweden, but the hierarch, to her great disappointment, was not interested.

Maria Elisabeth then returned to New York with plans to become a doctor, but a severe illness, a stomach ulcer that had become active again, and malaria thwarted her plans. Doctors believed that she would not live very long, so she decided to spend her last moments in Rome, in the house where St. Bridget once lived—Casa di Santa Brigida. Given that the house was then home to a convent of Carmelite nuns, she stayed among them.

At the same time, she did not cease in her attempts to carry out her plans to convert the Swedes (and all Scandinavians) to the faith of their ancestors and continue the work of St. Bridget. She wanted to reactivate the Bridgettine Order, founded by the saint in 1344, and bring it back to Sweden. It wasn't easy, partly because the Catholics in Sweden were not at all interested in their spiritual roots, but her actions eventually had the desired effect.

Maria Elisabeth came into contact with the last members of the Order of St. Bridget, which had been suppressed in the nineteenth century, living in Syon in the British Isles (and later with other Bridgettine convents in Spain, the Netherlands, and Germany). In 1906, she adopted the habit of the Bridgettines, and then, with the approval of Pope Pius X, formed its new branch, the Order of the Most Holy Savior, making it apostolic and ecumenical in character. The convent in Rome, which frequently changed its address, received many pilgrims from Sweden and other Scandinavian countries. During World War I, Bridgettine nuns cared for orphans, children injured in war, and severely wounded soldiers.

ON SWEDISH SOIL

In the 1920s, despite the restrictive state regulations in place, to Elisabeth's great joy she managed to open convents in her homeland: in the suburbs of Djursholm, and a few years later a retreat center in Vadstena, where a convent founded by Bridget herself hundreds of years earlier was located (and where the saint's mortal remains were laid to rest).

More than the Catholics, she was helped by Lutherans, who, thanks to the renaissance of interest in the person of St. Bridget, got rid of their anti-Catholic prejudices by becoming members of the Society of St. Bridget. The house in Djursholm also hosted the greatest Scandinavian convert: the winner of the Nobel Prize for literature, Norwegian novelist Sigrid Undset. Still in the first half of the twentieth century, during Mother Hesselblad's lifetime, other monastic houses of the Bridgettines were established: one in the Swiss city of Lugano, one in Iver Heath near London, and one in India.

RIGHTEOUS AND "MOST EXTRAORDINARY"

A beautiful page of Mother Maria Elisabeth Hesselblad's history was written during World War II. She bravely resisted a search of her Roman convent by the Germans, thus saving thirteen Jews from the Holocaust. For this, she received the medal and the honorary title of Righteous Among the Nations. Until the end of her life, Mother Maria Elisabeth made numerous efforts to unite Christians (among other things, the Unitas association, which worked for the unity of Christians, found refuge in the Roman headquarters of the Bridgettines).

"The most extraordinary woman in Rome," as Cardinal Raphael Merry del Val called her, died at the ripe old age of eighty-six in the Roman house Casa di Santa Brigida in Piazza Farnese, which had been reclaimed by the order on April 24, 1957.

Maria Elisabeth died at the ripe old age of eighty-six in the Roman house Casa di Santa Brigida in Piazza Farnese, which had been reclaimed by the order on April 24, 1957.

⮝ *St. Bridget of Sweden, founder of the Bridgettines.*

RESTITUTIO AD INTEGRUM

In addition to her primary goal of converting Scandinavians to Catholicism and bringing about the unity of Christians, Maria Elisabeth Hesselblad remained sensitive to suffering and human poverty throughout her life. She also gave expression to this after her passing, contributing to two miracles that made her a blessed and later a saint. In 1999, the healing experienced by Bridgettine Sr. Martin Kochuvelikakate through the intercession of the Servant of God Mother Elisabeth Hesselblad was investigated. In 1985, the Indian nun, who was ministering in Mexico at the time, suffered from severe pain in her knee. Because of this, she had difficulty walking and had to undergo surgery two years later. At that time, it was discovered that the cause of her ailment was bone tuberculosis, and what's more, it turned out that the articular cartilage of her right knee was already completely destroyed. Neither the surgery nor the medications prescribed improved the nun's condition. She continued to experience severe pain, and even despite the use of crutches she was unable to walk, so she spent much of her time in bed.

As Aldo Maria Valli described in an interesting biography of the saint, in 1989, on the anniversary of her monastic vows, Sr. Martin, despite feeling very weak, decided nevertheless to walk to the chapel and pray to Mother Elisabeth for help in resolving her hard predicament. She certainly felt bad about being a burden rather than a help to others. She decided that it would be best and easiest to simply ask for the restoration of her health.

Despite the pain, she fell to her knees and prayed for a very long time. The next day she woke up at 5 o'clock, as she did every day. Right then the bell rang, calling all the sisters to prayer and Mass. Sr. Martin felt very bad that day; everything hurt and she was unable to get up on her own. She called out for someone to help her, but no one came. No wonder, as all the nuns of the convent were in the chapel. Suddenly she spotted a sister. She couldn't distinguish her face, but she heard a voice. The unknown nun called her "daughter" and instructed her to get up and come to her. "Mother, I feel very bad and can't get up," Sr. Martin replied, thinking she was speaking to a superior. "Yes, daughter, you are sick, lie down and sleep," she heard, after which the unknown sister fixed her pillows. Sr. Martin fell asleep again. She woke up three hours later, feeling somehow strange, different than usual.

She no longer felt any pain and was full of newly gained energy. She asked her superior if it was she who had visited her in the morning. It turned out, however, that it was neither she nor any other sister, as they had all gone to Mass in the chapel immediately after waking up. Could it be, then, that the visiting Bridgettine was the late Mother Elisabeth herself? Perhaps. From that morning on, Sr. Martin's leg was fully functional. She no longer had any mobility issues and was able to return to work. Two years later, in 1991, the sister, at the request of her superiors, underwent further examinations and X-rays. The results were amazing: the previously completely destroyed cartilage in the knee was now in good condition. It looked as if it had rebuilt itself—there had been a *restitutio ad integrum*, a complete recovery! It was something inexplicable from the scientific point of view. The immediate, complete, and permanent recovery, which was obtained through the intercession of the Servant of God Mother Elisabeth Hesselblad, was also confirmed by Vatican committees. In a word, it was clearly a miracle.

HE RECOVERED COMPLETELY

Another miracle, this time needed for canonization, was also linked to Sr. Kochuvelikakate. It happened in Cuba, where she came to work after her healing. The health problems of Carlos Miguel Valdés Rodriguez of Santa Clara, Cuba, began when he was two years old. The child suffered from headaches, vomiting, and insomnia. The diagnosis on May 25, 2005, was terrible. It was a tumor, specifically a medulloblastoma of the cerebellum of about three centimeters, and due to the pressure it placed on the spinal cord, the child was quadriplegic.

Carlos underwent two surgeries, which not only failed to improve his condition but made it even worse. Indeed, after the tumor was removed, additional neurological complications arose, and the prognosis was poor. Practically speaking, the child was already in a vegetative state. The suffering Carlos was transferred from one hospital in Havana to another for months, but the doctors were helpless.

Sr. Martin Kochuvelikakate, who at the time was the superior of a convent in Havana, learned of the child's disastrous

The vision of St. Bridget—the saint ascending to Heaven.

After an investigation, and interviews with numerous witnesses, doctors, and nurses, Pope Francis signed the decree on the miracle in December 2015. Carlos Miguel, along with his parents and those who helped him, was present at the canonization ceremony of the sister to whom he owed his health. This canonization took place on June 5, 2016, in St. Peter's Square, a day after Mother Elisabeth's birthday and a day before Sweden's national holiday.

health situation. On July 18, 2005, the boy, accompanied by his parents and Bishop Arturo González Amador, who was helping the family, left for Santa Clara. The Bridgettine sister grabbed the phone and called the hierarch, asking him to stop at least for a short while at their monastic house during his trip with Carlos and his parents. Bishop Amador began to explain that the child he was traveling with was very sick and they could not stop. However, the sister insisted, and he finally agreed. As Bishop Amador later told Catholic journalist Albert Carosa, "Once I arrived in the convent of the Bridgettines, I was the only one to get out of the car, whereas the parents of the child remained in the van with him, together with a seminarian and the driver, who kept the vehicle engine idling so that the poor child could remain cool under the air conditioner."

> *Sister Martin told me about the Blessed Mother Mary Elisabeth, whom I already knew of, and asked me if it was possible to beseech her intercession for the child and touch him with a bone relic of the blessed. However, I insisted that it should be short. We received the consent of his parents, and the sister and all recited the prayer of the blessed, the Our Father, the Hail Mary, and the Gloria, and rubbed the bone relic on the child's body, then giving it to his parents to repeat the gesture. We resumed the journey to Santa Clara immediately. His parents kept the bone relic that Sister Martin had handed over to them.*

The healing of little Carlos Miguel began immediately after the prayers and the imposition of the relic of Bl. Mary Elisabeth's finger. During the trip from the Bridgettine convent to the house of his maternal grandparents, he started to move his limbs in a way that was previously impossible for him. They already considered it a miracle. "On the return trip we prayed the Rosary and at a certain moment of the trip I could see that the child bent the elbow of his little arm. I had

the impression that everything was starting to change, and this increased our faith and our hope," said the boy's mother.

After the visit to the Bridgettine convent, the boy's condition began to improve every day. Soon the child could walk without assistance and was able to get up and down stairs. After a few days, Carlos regained full physical fitness, and all his neurological problems were also gone. He had no relapses.

He went to the Santa Clara hospital for a check-up on his own feet. The doctors and nurses who cared for him were astonished. Soon after, the child started running. Since then, Carlos Miguel has had no more health problems: there were no relapses or metastases. He was developing and growing up properly. As a teenager, he was a very good student and played sports. After an investigation, and interviews with numerous witnesses, doctors, and nurses, Pope Francis signed the decree on the miracle in December 2015. Carlos Miguel, along with his parents and those who helped him, was present at the canonization ceremony of the sister to whom he owed his health. This canonization took place on June 5, 2016, in St. Peter's Square, a day after Mother Elisabeth's birthday and a day before Sweden's national holiday.

A GUN THAT DID NOT FIRE

In 2007, the Vatican also investigated another supposed miracle through the intercession of Bl. Elisabeth Hesselblad and it too involved Sr. Martin Kochuvelikakate. In December 2001, while the nun was still in Mexico, she was attacked by three gang members. When the gangster pointed a gun at her, Sr. Martin called Bl. Elisabeth Hesselblad for help. Moments later, the gangster pulled the trigger, but the gun did not fire.[1]

ENDNOTES

1 Excerpts from statements by Bishop Amador and the mother of the healed Carlos Miguel: Alberto Carosa, "The new saint credited with healing a young boy with brain tumor," https://www.catholicworldreport.com/2016/06/04/new-saint-credited-with-healing-a-young-boy-with-a-brain-tumor.

Monastery in Grodno belonging to the Order of the Most Holy Savior of St. Bridget (Latin: Ordo Sanctissimi Salvatoris Sanctae Brigittae, abbreviated O.Ss.S.), or Bridgettines.

Large-Scale Miracles

Most of the miracles worked by Jesus affected individuals. However, some of them were experienced by a larger number of people at once. The multiplication of bread was one such miracle. Similarly, in the case of miracles of God's saints, there are many instances of group miracles. Here we describe a few of these events.

St. Agnes of Montepulciano *by Domenico Beccafumi.*

Large-scale miracles obtained through the intercession of the saints include miracles of food multiplication, similar to the Lord's own miracle at Cana.

God described two such miracles Himself when He appeared to St. Catherine of Siena. It was then that God revealed to her the methods He uses to help trusting believers in their bodily needs. One such method is the provision of food by multiplication.

One of these miracles happened at the Dominican monastery of St. Sixtus in Rome. Two friars received only one loaf of bread from donors, but they gave it to a poor man and returned to the monastery empty handed. That day, the Dominicans had nothing to eat. Nevertheless, in her *Dialogue*, quoting the words she heard from God, Catherine writes:

> *My beloved servant Dominic, enlightened by the light of faith and full of trust in My Providence, said: "Sons, sit at the table." The brothers, obeying his word, took their places at the table. Then I, who never fails one who trusts in Me, sent two angels with the whitest bread, which they had in abundance for several meals. This was an act of My Providence in which no man participated, but which was accomplished by the graciousness of the Holy Spirit.*

"Sometimes I multiply a small amount that is insufficient for the needs of my servants, as was the case with the sweet virgin, St. Agnes of Montepulciano," God continued. St. Agnes gathered eighteen young girls in the convent. "I allowed them to run out of bread once; three days they lived only on vegetables," God told St. Catherine.

> *I did it this way to fill Agnes with love for My Providence. As for those who were still imperfect, I prepared them for the miracle that would come later, which began to strengthen them in the light of the Most Holy Faith. After those three days of hunger, Agnes raised the eyes of her spirit to me and, bathed in the light of the Most Holy Faith, said, "Father and my Lord, my eternal betrothed, did you command me to take these virgins out of their parents' home for them to die of hunger? Help them, Lord, in their need." I inspired*

The Mystic Marriage of St. Catherine of Siena *by Clemente de Torres.*

A statue of St. Agnes by Girolamo Campagna, Frari.

her to make this prayerful request. I enjoyed witnessing her faith, and her humble prayer was pleasing to Me. My Providence heard the prayer brought before Me and I inspired a certain person to bring five small loaves to the monastery. Agnes, who had been told of this by Me, said to her sisters: "Go, my daughters, go to the gate and bring back the bread." When it was served, they sat down at the table and Agnes distributed the bread herself. I gave such power to this act that all of them were completely satiated, and such a quantity of leftovers was collected that they had them in abundance for a second meal.

MATTER GREW IN HAND

"There was only one loaf in the monastery, and it was already the hour of the meal, and all our stomachs were aching with

St. Agnes *by Domenico Zampieri.*

➤ *Bl. Maria Esperanza of Jesus.*

➤ *St. Germaine Cousin.*

➤ *St. André-Hubert Fournet.*

hunger." This is how Br. Thomas of Celano began his description of the miracle of the multiplication of bread, worked by God through St. Clare of Assisi. The saint summoned the cellarer sister and ordered her to distribute the bread, telling her to send one half to the brothers and keep the other half inside for the sisters. From this second reserved half, Clare ordered fifty portions to be sliced, based on the number of the poor ladies, and had it distributed to them. And when the pious daughter answered her that the old miracles of Christ would have to be repeated in order to get fifty portions from such a small piece of bread, Clare replied: "Daughter, do calmly what I tell you!" The daughter hastened to carry out her mother's order, and Clare hastened to pray to Jesus Christ for her daughters. And behold, by the grace of God, the crumbs grew in the hand of the cellarer until there was a generous portion to fill up all of the sisters.

God has also worked similar miracles through the aforementioned St. Catherine of Siena, St. John Bosco, St. Germain Cousin, St. André-Hubert Fournet, and St. Gaspare del Bufalo.

➤ *St. Gaspare del Bufalo.*

I PRAY, AND HE WORKS

Are similar miracles still happening today? By all means. Here's what an oblate confessed in his testimony about Maria Esperanza of Jesus (1893–1983) to Alfredo di Penta, later a pillar of the Sons of Merciful Love founded by her:

> *During the Jubilee Year, I participated in an event absolutely incomprehensible to me. A small amount of meat, bread, butter, or pasta was enough for mother to feed hundreds of people. While preparing the servings, she prayed in some unintelligible language. One afternoon, for unforeseen reasons, they ran out of wine for the guests who were to arrive the next day. In my presence, Mother Maria ordered the designated sister to wash the carboys and fill them with water. The next morning, she invited me to taste the contents of those carboys. To my surprise, I noticed, as did the other pilgrims, that it was perfect Frascati. At my request for an explanation, she replied simply: "I pray, and He works: after all, pilgrims too are truly His children."*[1]

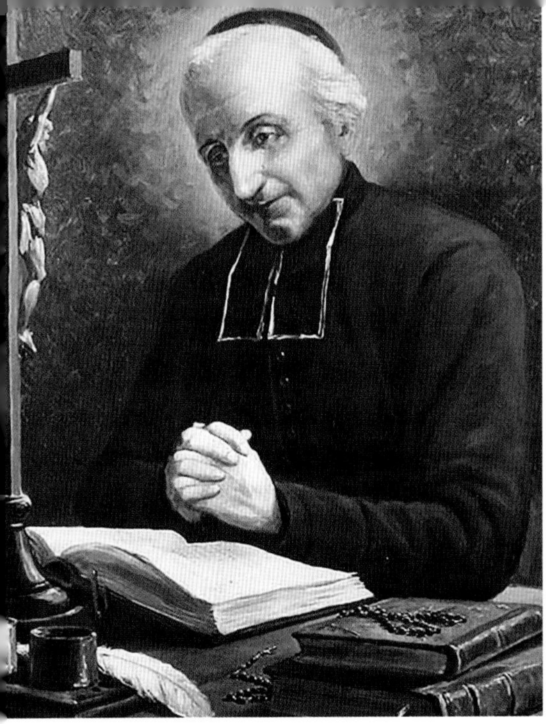

Mother Esperanza was also endowed with many other gifts: she experienced ecstasies, visions, and apparitions; she sweat blood; she was often beaten and tormented by Satan; miraculously the Host flew to rest on her lips by itself; she had the gift of bilocation and levitation; she received stigmata; her body emitted a pleasant fragrance; and God, during her lifetime and after her death, worked many healings and even resurrected people through her.

EUCHARISTIC MULTIPLICATIONS

Miraculous multiplications through the intercession of God's saints also took place after their deaths. Thanks to the miracle of the multiplication of rice, St. John Macías was canonized (for more on this miracle, see pp. 36–39), and an extraordinary multiplication of the Host occurred on January 15, 2007, at the Monastery of the Discalced Carmelite Sisters in Ragusa, during a Mass celebrated in front of the relics of Bl. Maria Candida of the Eucharist (this event was investigated during her canonization process). On the aforementioned day, the Mass was celebrated by a priest from the Oasis Movement, instead of one of the Discalced Carmelites, who were the monastery's chaplains.

The sacristan sister, however, had no idea that he would bring with him a large group of guests. The sister planned to prepare a new batch of Communion wafers for the next day, which was the anniversary of Maria Candida's birth.

The day before Mass on January 14, together with the convent's superior, the sacristan made sure that there were still about twenty wafers inside the tabernacle. She then added to them the four more intended for consecration. Knowing how many people usually take Holy Communion on a weekday, she was sure that this number was completely sufficient. She was wrong. The next day, while watching the church from the presbytery, she noticed with surprise and dismay that the number of faithful coming to Mass far exceeded the usual amount.

The sister informed the prioress, and then they both knelt down and immersed themselves in prayer. They asked Bl. Maria Candida to obtain for them a miracle so that everybody could receive Holy Communion. The extraordinary minister of the Eucharist, a fifty-seven-year-old man, who just before the distribution of the Holy Communion opened the tin and noticed that there were not enough wafers in it, also prayed for the same thing. It was finally time for Holy Communion. The priest, still praying, proceeded to give it. And then a miracle happened. Even though the priest had less than thirty consecrated Hosts at his disposal, he gave Holy Communion to more than forty people. What's more, there were still more than fifty wafers left in the tin! This was something incredible. Both the priest and the sisters were extremely surprised by this fact.

▲ *Bl. Maria Candida of the Eucharist.*

▼ *The bas-relief on the tomb of Bl. Ceslaus.*

Maria Crescentia Höss saved the town of Kaufbeuren from an air raid.

St. Nicholas of Flüe protected all of Switzerland from the Germans.

CESLAUS AND CLARE

However, these miraculous multiplications of both ordinary bread and Eucharistic bread are certainly less dramatic events than those miracles that saved people from death. Through the prayerful intercession of St. Clare of Assisi, the monastery of San Damiano in Assisi was saved from the Saracens, and the whole town of Assisi was saved from being ravaged by the soldiers of Vitalis of Aversa (see pp. 345–346).

In the same way that Clare protected Assisi's monastery, Dominican friar Bl. Ceslaus (1175–1242), who is believed to be a relative of St. Hyacinth of Poland, miraculously repelled the siege of Wroclaw's castle, saving from death many of the citizens of Wroclaw who took shelter there. Here's a brief background of what occurred: The thirteenth century, marked by two Mongol invasions in 1241 and 1260, was an extremely difficult time for Poland. The savage Mongols murdered and plundered without the slightest scruple, disregarding any and all principles. In 1241, they captured Sandomierz, ravaged and burned down Krakow, murdering approximately three thousand of the city's inhabitants and, after a stopover at Raciborz, headed on to Wroclaw. The armies of Boleslaus V and Vladislaus II were defeated.

Upon hearing the news of the approaching horde of Mongols, the citizens of Wroclaw panicked. They fled the city as quickly as possible, taking with them the most essential and valuable things they had. The rest of their precious items and most of their food was taken to the nearest castle, defended by the knights of Henry II the Pious. The abandoned houses were set on fire so that the Mongols could not boast of their destruction and could not set up shelters in them.

After invading the city, the aggressors completely destroyed its left bank and

laid siege to the castle, which was located near Cathedral Island. A remarkable thing happened then. Jan Długosz in his *Chronicles of the Kingdom of Poland* described it as follows:

> *But when they dragged out the siege for several days without attempting to capture the castle, Brother Ceslaus of the Order of Preachers, a Pole by descent, the first prior of St. Adalbert's in Wroclaw, who himself with the brothers of his order and other faithful took refuge in the Wroclaw castle, repelled the siege by praying to God with tears. For, while he was praying, a pillar of fire descended from the sky above his head and illuminated the whole city of Wroclaw with an ineffable, blinding light.*
>
> *Impacted by this unusual phenomenon, the hearts of the Tatars were overcome by fear and amazement to such an extent that they stopped the siege and fled rather than walked away.*[2]

Elsewhere, it was described in these terms:

> *Above Ceslaus floated a fireball, which, like a crown, encircled his head, and then fell into the middle of the invading army. It ignited with*

a loud bang, and like a grenade, it showered the enemies with a multitude of smaller fireballs, killing a great number of them, and filling others with fear and terror, making them flee and stopping the siege.

The event reportedly caused many conversions among the Mongols.

Ceslaus was considered a saint while he was still alive (he was credited with walking on and crossing the overflowing Oder River and with resurrection of the dead, including a boy who had drowned in the currents of the Oder). He probably died a year after the famous Mongol siege, and many miracles happened at his grave. In 1963, Pope Paul VI declared him the patron saint of Wroclaw, which he had saved.

KAUFBEUREN AND SWITZERLAND

The saint (then still a blessed) Maria Crescentia Höss was credited with miraculously saving her hometown Kaufbeuren from being bombed by the Allies during World War II.

Between 1944 and 1945, bombers appeared over the town several times. On April 12, 1945, the town was spared because the planes bombed Kempten; another time they were saved when the bombs dropped on the town missed their target, causing only minimal damage.

This took place at the end of World War II. At the beginning of the war, another saint, Nicholas of Flüe, protected all of Switzerland from the Germans.

On May 10, 1940, Germany attacked France and the Low Countries. People feared that the Germans would also invade Switzerland. On the night of May 13, orders were given and a state of emergency was put in place, and at 2 a.m., the Swiss warned that a German invasion would occur in less than half an hour. However, the Germans did not attack. It is said that Hitler himself ordered a retreat. Why? The Swiss believe that St. Nicolas of Flüe himself saved them from the invasion.

While the fate of Switzerland was still in the balance, on the evening of May 13, 1940, around 9 o'clock, a large, glowing hand appeared in the night sky above Waldenburg, a small town near Basel. The hand, or rather palm, was surrounded by beams and seemed to move, blessing the country. It is believed that it belonged to St. Nicolas of Flüe, and that in this way, he assured the Swiss that he was protecting them and that nothing bad would happen to them (for more about this miracle, see page 134).

HOW FR. SOPOĆKO SAVED BIALYSTOK

Fr. Michał Sopoćko (1888-1975) was the confessor of St. Faustina Kowalska and a great promoter of the devotion to the Divine Mercy. It was he who commissioned the painter Eugeniusz Kazimirowski to paint the image of the Divine Mercy in accordance with Sr. Faustina's instructions. He was also the spiritual father of a new religious community: the Congregation of the Sisters of Merciful Jesus. He spent the last years of his life in Białystok, a Polish city near the border with Belarus. He was beatified in 2008.

◄ *Bl. Michał Sopoćko saved Białystok from a catastrophic ecological disaster.*

▼ *A commemorative plaque in the Vilnius church that Michał Sopoćko was ministering.*

St. Gabriel saved a group of miners.

Before that happened, however, on the night of March 9, 1989, a freight train from the USSR arrived at the Białystok Fabryczny station. It was pulling twelve tank cars carrying pure liquid chlorine. Around 2:30 that morning, the transport headed toward the Białystok central station. Unfortunately, a moment later the train ran into a broken rail. The wagons overturned, and four tank cars, each containing about fifty tons of liquid chlorine, rolled to the side of the road. It was a disaster. If the tanks had leaked even a little, the city would have been instantly annihilated. The poisonous cloud of chlorine would have killed not only all the sleeping citizens, but every living creature in the area. The death zone would have covered an area of nearly two hundred square miles. Soon, teams of firefighters, railroad workers, and Civil Defense units arrived, and around 10 o'clock a chemical rescue unit from Płock arrived on the site of the disaster. According to the official report, "In a successful intervention, the derailed tank cars were lifted without being damaged. There was no chlorine leakage."

"The question remains how, in such a dangerous situation, there was no tragedy in Bialystok," the report continues. In the Białystok daily *Podlaski Courier*, these words were inserted next to the description of the incident: "Only a miracle, supported by the quick reaction of the railroad workers, saved Białystok from tragedy." The faithful were certain that it was indeed a miracle of Divine Providence or, even more likely, Divine Mercy.

In the general opinion of Białystok residents, it happened through the intercession of the Servant of God. The incident occurred near the place where he ministered and died, that is, near the chapel on Poleska Street. A few hundred meters away stands the building of the Church of the Divine Mercy Shrine, at which, a few months before the nearly tragic event, the mortal remains of the Servant of God were laid to rest after exhumation. Upon hearing of the danger threatening the city, people started praying fervently, asking for rescue through the intercession of the Servant of God Fr. Sopoćko. Prayers were held mainly in the chapel on Poleska Street and at the Shrine of the Divine Mercy.[3]

"As soon as Fr. Zbigniew Krupski, a disciple of Fr. Michał Sopoćko, heard about what had happened, he immediately ran to the chapel near the site of the accident, where Fr. Michał Sopoćko had ministered years ago, to celebrate Mass. He asked God to save the city through Fr. Sopoćko's intercession," recounted Genowefa Suchocka from Fr. Michał Sopoćko's Association of Venerators of the Divine Mercy of the Białystok Archdiocese.[4]

As early as 1989, a memorial signed by a group of people on behalf of the survivors was submitted to the local curia, expressing the opinion that Białystok had been particularly affected by Divine Mercy. The tank cars derailed in the neighborhood most closely associated with the Divine Mercy, in the place where Fr. Michał Sopoćko was seen praying the rosary during his lifetime. "We attribute our rescue to God's mercy. We trust that Fr. Michał Sopoćko himself interceded for us," Genowefa Stankiewicz emphasized. The thankful residents of Białystok erected a cross on the site in gratitude to the saint's miraculous intercession.

"ALL OF YOU, RUN! HURRY!"

In 1905 or 1906, a giant 330-pound candle arrived at the Italian shrine of St. Gabriel of Our Lady of Sorrows in Isola del Gran Sasso. It was a gift, a votive offering for the miracle of saving the lives of miners employed at one of the mines in Pittsburgh, Pennsylvania, sent by them.

It was a day like any other, an ordinary working day in 1905. The miners were just starting work, and among many international workers was a group of Italians from Abruzzo. Suddenly, from the depths of the pit, a voice reached their ears: "Go back! Go back! Get out! Get out! I am Gabriel from Our Lady of Sorrows," someone yelled. It startled them; they didn't know what to do. Stunned, they heard another call, "Quick, quick, go outside!" According to testimony given in 1963 by one of the miners, Domenic Mazzilli, St. Gabriel himself then appeared. He had a heart symbol on his chest and pushed them toward the exit. They listened and, terrified, began to flee. They got out of the mine, but as the shift was not over yet, they were turned back. They had almost made it to the entrance when suddenly the inside of the tunnel collapsed.

Many miners were then saved, including approximately forty Italians. All were venerators of St. Gabriel, and had entrusted themselves to him before starting work; after their miraculous rescue, they agreed to purchase the large votive candle as a sign of their gratitude.

St. Gabriel was also reportedly seen by the CEO of the company that employed these Italians. "He saw St. Gabriel, whom he then recognized in our house in one of the small pictures at the headboard of the bed," Mazzilli recounted.

ST. PHILIP WILL SAVE US

In 1688, thirty-eight-year-old Archbishop Vincenzo Maria Orsini de Gravina, who thirty-six years later became Pope Benedict XIII, gave extensive testimony to the miraculous rescue he experienced through the intercession of St. Philip Neri during the earthquake that had struck the Italian city of Benevento earlier that year, destroying the bishop's palace where he was staying at the time.

On January 14, 1703, the earth shook again in Nursia, Italy. This time St. Philip saved eight of his religious confreres: seven priests and one lay brother.

When a massive earthquake struck Nursia around 2 a.m. on Sunday, causing all the houses in the town to crumble to rubble, by God's Providence the six Oratorians and one lay brother stayed in one large room, keeping themselves warm by the fire.

In 2010, St. Gabriel's relic (a piece of his rib) was brought to St. Matthew's parish in Warsaw's Bialoleka district by the Passionists ministering there.

Photos of the derailed train taken the morning after.

⮝ *Handwritten notes of St. Philip Neri, his chair, and relics.*

Pietro Giacomo Bacci writes:

> *The superior, who had been caring for a sick man and was quite drenched, had just returned. Therefore, he stayed in the hall, instead of immediately going to his own room, as he was accustomed to, where he most likely would have died. ... The others also usually stayed in their own rooms, and Fr. Filippo Fusconi, feeling a little indisposed, asked the superior for permission to go to his room and lie down, but the superior asked him to stay a little longer, to which the father agreed.*
>
> *When the earthquake struck, Father wanted to run into the next room, thinking it would be safer than the one he was in, but although he tried several times to open the door, he was not able to get through. Finally, he managed to open the door halfway and was about to leave when he saw that not only the ceiling but also the roof and walls of the adjacent room were collapsing, so he immediately retreated.*

The other friars rushed under the arched passageway above another door in the same room and loudly begged St. Philip Neri to help them. Meanwhile, everything around them began to collapse. When the shaking stopped, the Oratorians tried to open the door, but it was blocked by the debris. They thought about tying their monastic belts together to exit through the window, but decided that such a rope would not be strong enough to sustain their combined weight. At that moment, aftershocks began. Without seeing any means of escape, they again called upon Philip for help, trusting that, just as he had saved them from greater danger, he would now provide them with the means to escape from the room in which they were trapped. "Do not be afraid, my brothers, St. Philip will save us," Fr. Filippo said.

Fr. Fusconi said that the only solution was to break a hole in the door. It was not safe, as the doorframe was rotten and at risk of cracking, but in the end, they managed to do it by using a piece of wood they picked up from the floor. The hole was small, but they managed to make it a little bigger, and eventually they all worked their way through. Miraculously, they also managed, despite the wind, to keep the candle flame burning while doing all of this. After climbing through the ruins in the dark, the Oratorians reached the city square safely. There they walked around all night in slippers, with only birettas on their heads, listening to the confessions of those who had fled the ruins of their homes. It rained heavily the whole time.

Fr. Benedetto Antonio Stefanelli, who just before the earthquake went to hear the Confession of a sick man, was also miraculously saved from death under the rubble of his house by invoking St. Philip. All the friars agreed that they were rescued thanks to the intercession of St. Philip.

Pietro Giacomo Bacci goes on to write:

> *There was another great miracle. Although the roof of the church had collapsed, the tabernacle was found intact under the ruins. On Tuesday morning Fr. Castellani (one of those rescued) went early to the church and found the entire ciborium intact, and after consuming the Most Holy Sacrament, he took it with him. It was also observed that, although the roof and parts of the walls of the church had been destroyed, neither the altar of St. Philip nor his image had been damaged. Moreover, in a small cabinet in the sacristy, the fathers kept a small part of the relic of the so-called præcordia of St. Philip enclosed in a gilded wooden bust, and although all the other buildings of the oratory were destroyed, the sacristy remained intact.*
>
> *In 1730, on the morning of May 12, there was a second earthquake in Nursia, no less terrible than the one in 1703; and this time too, the Oratorian fathers were evidently protected by St. Philip, for although the roof of the church and the house collapsed on them, and one of the fathers fell from the top of the house into the rubble, none of them died.*

St. Philip Neri listening to the Mother of God.

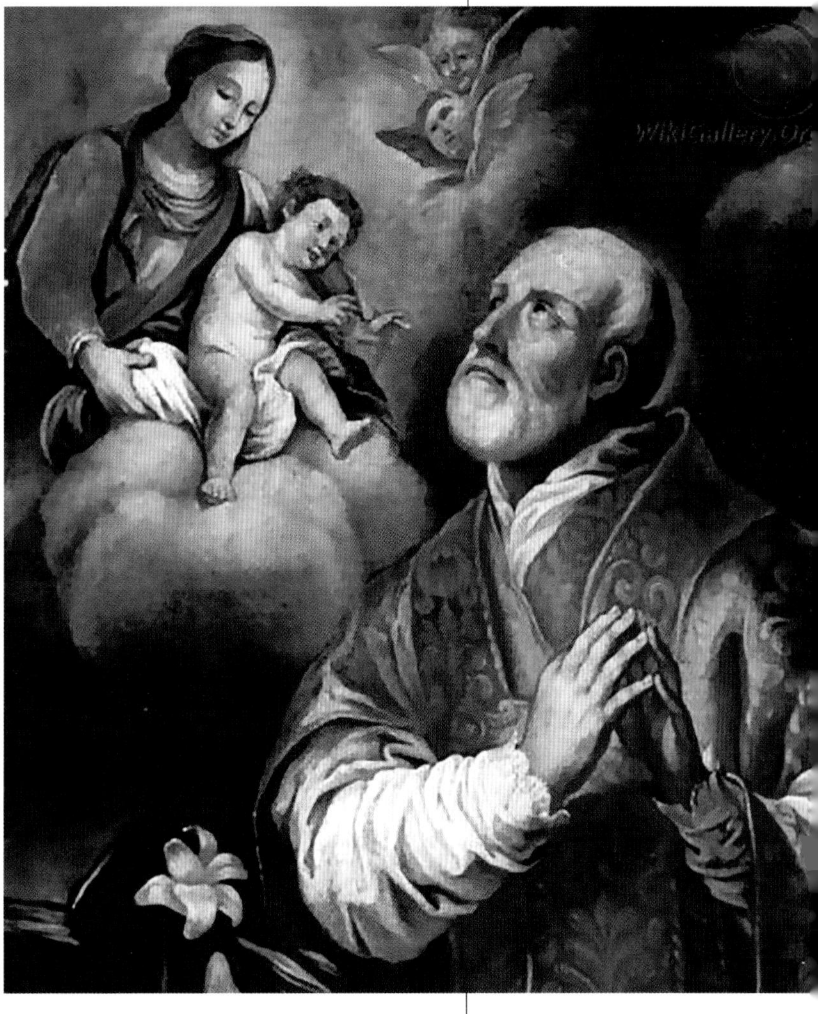

ENDNOTES

1 Świadectwo Alfredo di Penty na temat cudów bl. Matki Speranzy od Jezusa za [Testimony of Alfredo di Penta on the miracles of Mother Maria Esperanza of Jesus cit. por.]: Aldo Maria Valli, Matka Speranza. Świadek Miłości Miłosiernej, Wyd. Agape, Poznań 2014, s. [pp.] 70-71.

2 Cytat za: Legendy dominikańskie [cit. por. Legends of the Dominican Order/Dominican Legends], "W drodze" Poznań 1982, s. [pp.] 88.

3 Świadectwa o łaskach bł. MS, (doc) (opis lask z arch. postulatora). [Testimonies of graces of Blessed MS, (doc) (description of graces from postulator's archives).

4 Białystok ocalony [Bialystok saved], (Mieczysław Pabis, hb) w: "Miesięcznik Rodzin Katolickich. Cuda i Łaski Boże", 2/2013, s. [p.] 10.

1195–1231

➤ *Anthony's sermons, which he preached throughout Italy as well as in France, began to attract crowds of listeners. His extraordinary oratorical talent and phenomenal memory soon earned him a place as one of the most eminent preachers in the Church. He was also a humble and charismatic missionary with the gift of reaching the hearts not only of people, but also the hearts of other creatures, such as fish.*

THE FRANCISCAN MIRACLE WORKER

St. Anthony of Padua

Fernando Martins de Bulhões, better known today as St. Anthony of Padua, is one of the greatest miracle workers in the history of the Church. The number of miracles he performed is so impressive that one may often hear it said: "If you are looking for miracles, go to Anthony! You'll receive all the graces as evidence from him." Surely, there is not a Catholic in the world who, when looking for lost things, has not turned to him for help at least once.

Despite his title "Anthony of Padua," St. Anthony wasn't Italian; he was Portuguese. Anthony was born in Lisbon in 1195, and he joined the Canons Regular of St. Augustine at a young age. He lived in Lisbon at first, then in Coimbra. Anthony became a theologian, and he was ordained into the priesthood in 1219.

In 1220, Anthony witnessed the funeral of five Franciscans who had been martyred by Saracens in Morocco. Shocked by this event, he joined the Franciscans and—filled with missionary zeal—he tried going to Africa. God, however, had other plans for him.

After meeting with St. Francis, Anthony, who until then had led a hermit's life,

became the general preacher of the Order (and later also the provincial superior). Anthony preached throughout Italy as well as in France, and his sermons began to attract crowds of listeners. Anthony soon became the most eminent preacher of the Church. He had an extraordinary oratorical talent and a phenomenal memory, and he was a humble and charismatic missionary with the gift of reaching people's hearts. He was also a miracle worker.

A SURPRISING AUDIENCE

When Anthony visited a new place, everyone hurried to hear his sermons. In Padua, Italy, especially, huge crowds of tens of thousands of people would gather. Even knights and noblewomen, who were accustomed to nothing but comfort, nevertheless "rose at midnight to get ahead, and with lit torches, rushed to the place where he was to speak," according to a medieval chronicler.

St. Anthony is often depicted with a book and a white lily, as in Alvise Vivarini's painting.

The façade of the Basilica of St. Anthony in Padua, Italy.

➤ *Clock Tower in downtown Padua.*

➤ *Joseph Heintz the Younger,* St. Anthony of Padua: The Miracle of the Mule.

⮝ *Jean Bourdichon,* St. Anthony and the Mule, *from* The Grandes Heures of Anne of Brittany.

Anthony did not find an enthusiastic audience everywhere he went, however. One year, as the legend goes, the Franciscan friar came to Rimini, a city on the Adriatic coast of Italy. This fishing town was the center of Catharism, a then-flourishing heretical sect. Not only did no one there want to listen to Anthony's sermons, but he was also mocked. People didn't want to listen to him, so Anthony found other listeners. He went to the seashore and began to speak. "Listen to the Word of God, O ye fishes of the sea and of the river, seeing that the faithless heretics refuse to do so," he said, and suddenly the smooth surface of the sea began to ripple and bubble. A multitude of fish emerged from the Adriatic! The fish froze, seeming to catch eagerly every word uttered by the silver-tongued preacher. The fish went back into the water only after Anthony had finished speaking and had blessed them. The Cathars who witnessed this miracle couldn't believe it.

THE MULE AND ITS MAKER

One day, Anthony was challenged by a Cathar heretic, most likely a man named Bononillo, in Toulouse, France. Catharism, whose followers were also known as Albigensians, was a heresy that condemned the material world and human sexuality and which also rejected the sacraments of the Church and the Real Presence of Christ in the Eucharist.

The arrogant Bononillo insisted that the consecrated Host was simply ordinary bread, not the Body of Christ; in fact, he told the Franciscan, it was no different from ordinary food. Anthony realized that he could not convince the heretic through reason alone. And so the two agreed on a challenge: the matter would be decided, once and for all, by—a mule. "If the starving beast bypasses the fodder and hastens to bow down before its God, I will believe in the Catholic faith," the Cathar declared.

The animal was given nothing to eat for three days so that, as the heretic believed, it would dash toward the given manger with a great appetite, completely ignore the Blessed Sacrament, and consume its hay without hesitation. Anthony likewise fasted and prayed for three days. He hoped that God would allow the world to see that even an animal respects the Body of its Master and Creator.

The day of the trial arrived. The starving mule was taken out of the stable and placed between the manger full of hay and Anthony, who was holding the Body of Christ in his hands. "In the name and by the virtue of your Creator, who I, though unworthy, bring in my hands, I order you, poor animal, to come without delay to bow down humbly before the King of Kings. It is necessary for these men to recognize that every creature must submit to God the Creator, that every Catholic priest has the honor of making Him descend on the altar," Anthony said to the mule. The heretic urged the starved animal to eat the hay, but the mule ignored his encouragement, approached Anthony, looked at the most Holy Sacrament, bowed its head, and knelt down. Surprised by this turn of events, the heretic admitted defeat and converted.

Anthony performed many such miracles to convert and disprove heretics and apostates. Indeed, he managed to convert so many of them that chroniclers gave him the name "Hammer of the Heretics."

AN IMPULSIVE PENITENT

Anthony's sermons were not mere displays of eloquence. They led people to God—they converted them. He was an unsurpassed master in this respect.

After each of Anthony's sermons, he reaped a bountiful harvest of Confessions. He rejoiced over such conversion of heart in his listeners, but his joy came at great personal sacrifice. Sometimes Anthony would spend whole days in the confessional without eating or drinking. But he was a good confessor, and he could both read people's hearts and prophesy. Indeed, one of the oldest biographies of the saint, the *Benignitas*, tells us, "when the saint was still alive, some people came to the brethren and claimed with conviction that the blessed father appeared to them in the middle of the night, while they were sleeping in their beds, saying: 'Get up, Martin! Get up Agnes! And go to such and such brother or priest and confess to him this sin committed by you at such a time and in such a place,' which no one knew but God. Thus, many hidden sins were forgiven in the sacramental confession."

Sometimes, however, Anthony was a bit too forceful in the confessional. On one occasion, for example, Leonard of Padua confessed to him, "I kicked my mother and she fell to the ground." Anthony was blunt in his angry response: "The foot that hits

The Tempietto di Sant'Antonio in Rimini is dedicated to the memory of the Eucharistic miracle of the mule, which took place there, according to tradition.

Geoff Heggadon, St. Anthony and the Miracle of the Mule, *the Shrine of St. Anthony, Ellicott City, Maryland.*

one's father or mother deserves to be cut off!" he exclaimed. The young, impulsive man then returned home and cut off his foot as an act of penance! Anthony had, of course, not meant for the young man to take his words literally: he had only meant to shake Leonard's conscience and impress upon him the seriousness of his sin. And so, upon hearing what had happened, the Franciscan went to Leonard's house, placed the severed foot close to the stump of Leonard's leg, and made the sign of the cross. The foot immediately became attached to the stump!

Anthony likely understood after this event that he should approach his penitents a little more carefully.

WHERE YOUR TREASURE IS

In Anthony's time, the Church was actively speaking against usurers who lent money at high interest rates and so preyed upon the poor. Anthony, too, fiercely defended the poor: "Riches are thorns that sting and bleed; conniving moneylenders are ferocious beasts who rob and devour," he thundered during one of his sermons. One day, when the saint was preaching, word spread among the people that a notorious usurer had suddenly died. Anthony, seeing the commotion of the crowd and hearing whispers, asked what had happened. When he found out, he trembled and called out: "Look how the Word of God has come true, which warns: where your treasure is, there is also your heart. Open his chest and you will find his heart among his money!"

The body of the criminal was opened, and indeed, his heart was gone! The usurer's heart was instead found among the beloved coins in his trunk. And so the Lord made visual the teachings of His faithful servant.

"HE IS MY FATHER"

A man from Ferrara, Italy, refused to claim his wife's recently born baby as his own, as he suspected his wife of infidelity. Of course, in these days, there was no genetic testing and no way to prove the paternity of the child. The wife had no way to silence her husband's accusations.

And so she decided to call on Anthony for help. Anthony arrived, stood in front

⮝ *Marcantonio Bassetti,* St. Antony Reading, *seventeenth century.*

⮟ *View of Coimbra, Portugal.*

Basilica of St. Justina in Padua.

of the infant, and asked him to confess the truth. "I adjure you, in the name of Jesus Christ, tell me out loud so everyone can hear who your father is," he ordered.

And the baby spoke. "He is my father," the baby said, looking at the surprised man.

The husband burst into tears and took the infant in his arms. The family was at peace again.

A DEAD MAN SPEAKS

Anthony also helped his own family with his miracles.

One day, a young aristocrat was killed in front of the Lisbon Cathedral. His corpse was found in the garden of Anthony's father, Martin. Because Martin owned the property where the dead man was found, he was blamed for the murder. Martin was innocent, but he was nevertheless sent to prison. Anthony was living in Padua at that time, but he miraculously found out about his father's predicament and immediately set out to rescue him.

The Franciscan was to travel to Lisbon by foot. His route was nearly 1,400 miles—a distance that would have taken about twenty days without stopping. There was no way he could reach his father in time to save him, but Anthony trusted God and went anyway. He knew that nothing is impossible for God.

Anthony was right to hope and trust in God. After traveling only a couple miles, Anthony suddenly, and to his own surprise, found himself at the trial in Lisbon! Standing before the high court, Anthony made a statement saying his father was innocent. Unfortunately, even though Anthony was a clergyman, he was still the son of the accused, so he didn't have much persuasive power in court. No one believed

➤ *Guercino (Giovanni Francesco Barbieri),* St. Anthony of Padua with the Infant Christ.

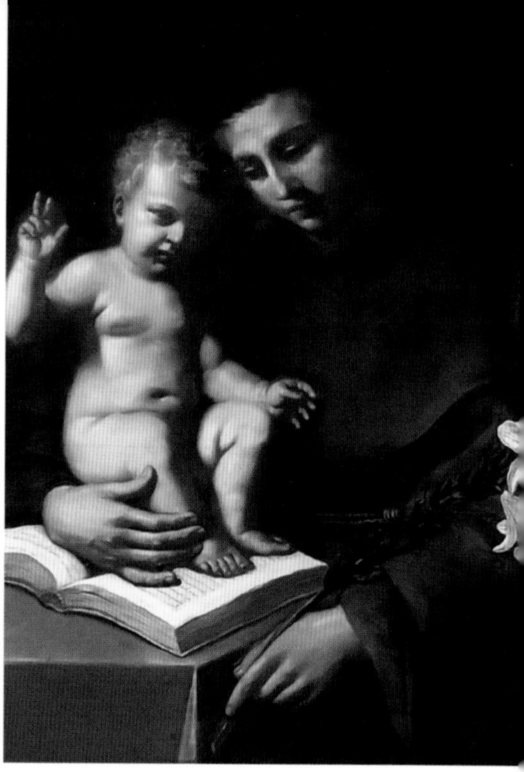

his statement, and the court demanded strong evidence to acquit Martin.

Anthony rose to the challenge: "The murdered man will testify to the truth of my words!" he said. The judge was intrigued; Anthony already had the reputation of a miracle worker. And so the judge—probably in the company of a large group of curious people—went to the cemetery. The tomb of the murdered man was opened, and Anthony summoned the deceased man to testify. Suddenly, the corpse rose, sat up, and testified to Martin's innocence! The corpse then turned to Anthony and asked him to release him from excommunication, and when he received such a pardon, he again fell into an eternal sleep.

The surprised judge then wanted Anthony to tell him who the murderer was. He was convinced that Anthony knew, and he awaited further explanations. But he was met with a firm refusal. "I have come to purify the innocent, not to expose the guilty," the friar said.

The miraculous events did not end there, however. Later, people discovered that Anthony was absent from Padua for only two nights and one day. Anthony had received from God the grace of bilocation, the extraordinary gift of being in two places at the same time.

TWO PLACES AT ONCE

The fact that Anthony received the gift of bilocation from God was also confirmed by another miracle. Anthony was preaching at the cathedral in Montpellier, France, for Easter Sunday when he suddenly remembered that he was meant to be singing the Alleluia with his fellow brothers at the Mass back at his convent. He was very upset because he had forgotten to ask anyone to replace him. Then, consciously or not, he interrupted the sermon for a moment, covered his head with a hood, bent over the lectern, and—in an instant found himself singing in the monastery. The friars also saw him singing in the choir.

When Anthony finished his obligation, he found himself back at the cathedral. He looked up as if nothing had happened and finished his sermon.

HEALINGS AND RESURRECTIONS

One of the most spectacular healings involved a three- or four-year-old girl named Padovana who suffered from paralysis and epilepsy. One day, Padovana's father approached Anthony carrying the girl in his arms. The child's father knew very well who he was dealing with, so with tears in his eyes, he begged the Franciscan to bless his little girl. Seeing that the man's faith was simple, strong, and full of hope, Anthony granted his request. The man came home with Padovana, placed her on the ground, and watched as she stood up and ran around the room. What's more, she didn't suffer a single epileptic attack after her meeting with Anthony.

⮝ *Italian school of painting,* St. Anthony of Padua with Baby Jesus, *ca. 1700.*

In addition to healings from bodily ailments, disabilities, and various diseases, Anthony, by the power of God, also performed resurrections. He resurrected a girl who drowned in a barrel and revived a child who had died in his sleep.

WITH THE INFANT JESUS

One of the last miracles performed by the Franciscan occurred near the end of his life, when he was staying in the home of his friend Count Tito Borghese in Campo San Pietro, near Padua. One day, the count was passing by Anthony's room and noticed a strange light emanating from the space. He looked inside and saw an extraordinary scene. Absorbed in ecstatic contemplation, the friar cradled in his arms "a Child of rare beauty, filled with joy and happiness." This Child, of course, was the Infant Jesus.

Once Anthony had recovered from his ecstasy, he forbade the count to speak of this event. Only after his death did the aristocrat feel released from his promise. This theme later became very popular in art.

MIRACLES AT THE TOMB

Anthony lived only thirty-six years. After his death, the wave of miracles intensified.

Basilica of St. Anthony in Padua.

Altar with a statue of St. Anthony of Padua in the Church of Our Lady of Sorrows in Teggiano.

Francisco de Zurbarán, The Apparition of the Child Jesus to St. Anthony of Padua.

The first miracle that occurred at Anthony's grave was the healing of a woman named Cunizza. For a year, Cunizza had been suffering from a tumor that had formed on her shoulder. In addition, she was shriveled up and could only walk with crutches. On the day of Anthony's funeral, she knelt at the grave of the deceased Franciscan and immersed herself in prayer. After a moment, she felt the tumor disappear. She then got up and straightened up, and she no longer needed the crutches. Crying out for joy, she went home, thanking God and Anthony.

Ever since, the practice of making pilgrimages to Anthony's grave has become widespread. Many have regained their health by touching his tombstone and praying fervently. In fact, within just a few months of Anthony's death, fifty-three miracles were reported to the pope. Taking all these miracles into account, on May 30, 1232, less than a year after Anthony's death, Pope Gregory IX canonized Anthony in Spoleto.

In 1263, the body of the saint was solemnly exhumed. His tongue was found intact. Bonaventure, himself a future saint, who was present at the time, ordered Anthony's tongue to be placed in a separate reliquary, where it has been kept to this day. In 1946, Pope Pius XII proclaimed Anthony a Doctor of the Church and granted him the title of "Evangelical Doctor."

More than eight hundred years have passed since Anthony's birth, yet the saint continues to support us and listen to our prayers. Each year, nearly five million people come to the tomb of "Il Santo" ("The Saint") in the basilica in Padua. Many of their prayers are answered.

➢ *Oratory of St. Anthony in the La Verna Sanctuary, where the saint lived for several months in 1230.*

➢ *Street procession with the statue of St. Anthony of Padua.*

THE RESURRECTION OF PARRISIO

One day, in Lisbon, a little boy named Parrisio went on a boat trip with his friends—without telling his parents. Unfortunately, a storm broke out shortly after their departure, and the boat capsized. The older boys managed to swim to shore, but Parrisio couldn't swim and went underwater.

When his mother heard, she ran to the shore and begged the fishermen to hurry and help rescue her son. The men managed to find the boy's body, but he was already dead. Parrisio's mother, however, did not give up. In that tragic moment, she began to pray to God through the intercession of St. Anthony. She promised that if the boy came back to life, she would persuade him to join the Franciscans. She trusted the saint so much that when it was time to bury

The Prato della Valle in Padua.

The reliquary of St. Anthony at the Shrine of St. Anthony in Ellicott City, Maryland.

the boy the next day, she wouldn't allow it. On the third day of continuous prayer, the boy suddenly and unexpectedly came back to life. He woke up as if he had only been sleeping.

When Parrisio grew up, he became a Franciscan, just as his mother had promised.

PATRON SAINT OF LOST ITEMS

Today, Anthony is often known as the patron saint of lost items. Catholics all over the world ask him for help when they lose things. But where did this belief come from?

There are two stories affiliated with this tradition. Some associate it with a miracle that happened in the French city of Montpellier. A young friar had run away from the monastery, and he had taken with him the book that Anthony used to teach. As he ran, the young friar encountered a hellish apparition blocking his way and preventing his wicked plans. The repentant Franciscan came back to the monastery and returned the book.

Others see the origin of this tradition in a miracle that happened in Portugal after the saint's death. A tired worker from the town of Alcácer do Sal who was a great devotee of St. Anthony wanted to refresh himself at a well. Before he submerged his hands in the cool water, he removed a gold ring from his finger and placed it on the rim of the well. After washing, the man went to put his ring back on, but it was gone! The man searched to no avail, so at last he turned in prayer to St. Anthony to help him find the lost item. A few months later, when the man was praying in church on the saint's feast day, one of his servants came up to him and handed him the lost ring, which the servant had found when he was pulling a bucket from the well.

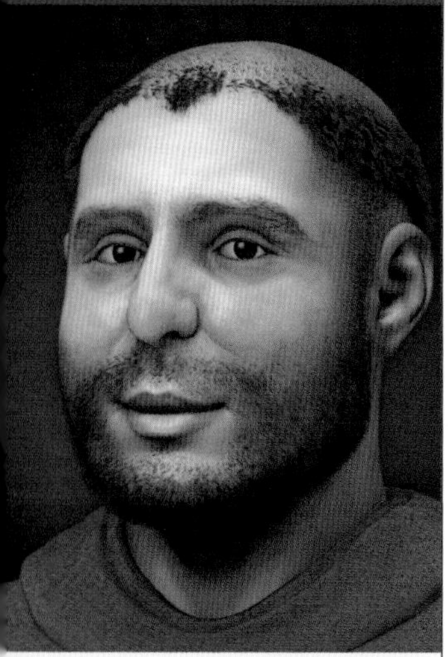

⮝ *A reconstruction of St. Anthony's face from his preserved skull. By Cícero Moraes.*

BREAD FOR THE POOR

St. Anthony is also a patron of the poor. In many churches even today, one can find a statue of St. Anthony next to a poor box. Today, money for the poor is offered as a form of gratitude for the graces received through the intercession of St. Anthony, and these donations are known as St. Anthony's Bread, this "bread" implying any sort of material help for the poor.

Legend has it that the tradition of St. Anthony's Bread is connected with a miracle that took place in Padua after Anthony's death. A small, twenty-month-old boy was playing in the kitchen and fell into a large pot of boiling water. His terrified mother immediately pulled him out, but the boy was already dead. The desperate mother begged St. Anthony for help. She promised that if he revived her son, she would offer to the poor as much bread as the child weighed. The child miraculously rose as though from a deep sleep, and the practice of giving bread to the poor was born.

AID OF VIRGINS

Anthony—like St. Nicholas—also has unmarried women under his care. For centuries, many women have asked St. Anthony for help in finding a good husband.

For example, there was once a young, unmarried Italian woman whose family had fallen into difficult times, and her mother urged her to find a wealthy lover who could help the entire family escape poverty. But the pious girl wasn't comfortable with her mother's immoral advice. She went to the statue of St. Anthony and asked God to help her through his intercession. Suddenly, the statue of St. Anthony came to life! The saint extended his hand to the girl and gave her a piece of paper with instructions written on it: "Go to the richest merchant in town and tell him to give you as much gold as this paper weighs."

The girl gladly complied. She found the merchant, who laughed yet assured her that he would grant this request. "After all, how much can such a piece of paper weigh," he confidently thought. He placed the sheet

⮞ *The altar and tomb of St. Anthony of Padua in his basilica in Padua.*

⮜ *A richly decorated balcony and colonnade in the Bo Palace in Padua.*

of paper on the scale and was speechless. The paper was as heavy as a block of lead! After weighing the piece of paper and determining the amount of gold that it was worth, the merchant remembered that he had promised St. Anthony exactly that much in gold for gilding his altar. He was ashamed that he had never fulfilled his promise and, without hesitation, gave the girl all the gold she was due.

And so the young woman obtained a dowry and could marry whomever her heart desired.

APPARITION IN POLAND

St. Anthony is also known for his many apparitions to the faithful, but the only apparition that has been approved by the Church happened in the small village of Radecznica, Poland, on May 8, 1664. There, St. Anthony appeared to a man named Szymon Tkacz and said, “I am St. Anthony; I have come by the will of the Supreme Lord to tell you that in this place the Most High will be praised.” The saint continued to tell Szymon to build a shrine in the village, and he promised that through his intercessions, “the sick, the blind, the lame, and those afflicted with various ailments will find and receive their consolation. The sick, health; the blind, sight; the lame, movement; all those who go to this place will not leave without gaining grace.”

During the apparition, the saint from Padua also blessed the water of a spring gushing from the hillside. Almost immediately after the apparition, the small village of Radecznica became famous for miracles and answered prayers. Today, pilgrims still flock to the church in the village and believe that the spring water there has miraculous properties.

⮝ *Anthony of Padua (left) and St. Francis. A cycle of frescoes with scenes from the life of St. Martin of Tours, in the chapel of the Lower Church of the Basilica of St. Francis in Assisi.*

➤ *Monument commemorating the victims of the German transit camp in Zwierzyniec.*

HE LED ME PAST THE BARBED WIRE

Anthony never leaves his devotees without help. One man, Władysław Wypych, who was from the village of Podborcze, less than five kilometers from Radecznica, witnessed his care firsthand.

During World War II, on the Feast of Sts. Peter and Paul, twenty-three-year-old Władysław went to Confession. The next day, he went to visit his father, who was working with five other men chopping wood. The laborers suddenly noticed German planes flying low, and they spotted an army coming up the road. The men knew they had to run. "It would be best to hide in the house, but we were afraid they would set it on fire," Władysław recounted. They decided they would hide in the field. "I ran into the wheat field, but they saw me. They chased me along the balks, firing machine guns. Bullets whistled over my head, ears of wheat were hit, falling to the ground."

Władysław escaped to a flax field, but he was soon captured and rushed to the village of Czarnystok together with four others. "We were escorted by three soldiers, pushing us with rifles," the man reported years later. "They took us to the field, where the fire station was. They told us to stand in a ditch. My eight-year-old sister came up to me. They didn't chase her away. She gave me a rosary. I took the rosary and began to pray. 'My life is over,' I thought."

The Germans prepared to execute the workers, but a man explained to them that they were not bandits but young workers who had simply run away because they were afraid.

"We were afraid we would go to the concentration camp in Majdanek; they took us to the camp in Zwierzyniec."

In Zwierzyniec, the Germans rushed the prisoners behind the barbed wire and then

into the barracks. Władysław remembered, "Everyone at home was very worried about me. My wife went to Radecznica to offer a Mass intention for me. I had a dream that night. I dreamed that St. Anthony came to me behind the barbed wire. He woke me up and said, 'Get up, get dressed, and come with me.' He led me past the barbed wire, through the gate, into the forest. He told me to go home and then disappeared. I got up in the morning and prayed. I started thinking about my dream." Władysław then decided that he would run away and, together with another boy, he approached the gate where a soldier was standing. "We saw a wagon-driver carrying a barrel on his way to the river for water. We clung to

⮝ *Relics of St. Anthony of Padua from the National Shrine of St. Anthony and Friary in Cincinnati, Ohio.*

In the spring of 1942, about a hundred French prisoners of war were imprisoned in the camp in Zwierzyniec.

To commemorate the tragedy of the civilian population, a church, dedicated to Our Lady Queen of Poland, was built in the location of where the main square of the camp was in Zwierzyniec. It was consecrated in May of 1980.

this barrel. When we got past the first set of barbed wire, the barrel went toward the river, and we went right. A soldier went after us. Shots rang out on the road. Another soldier came down from his observation post and went to see what was going on. I quickly approached the barbed wire. I jumped over it and ran into the woods, with my friend behind me. We ran about two hundred meters and stopped. We were weak and hungry, but free.

"I think it was St. Anthony who led me out. He helped me through this dream. St. Anthony came to me that night. I strongly believe this," he concluded.

THE POWER OF FORGIVENESS

St. Maria Goretti

Murdered for defending her virginity, the eleven-year-old Italian girl Maria Goretti (1890–1902) became a saint thanks to two miracles performed posthumously. But perhaps her greatest miracle was the sincere conversion of her killer.

➤ *Image of the saint from the beginning of the twentieth century showing Maria Goretti and the scene from her reconciliation with her murderer in his dream.*

Sentenced to thirty years in prison, he was serving his third year. And he was lucky. If he had been a little older at the time of the crime, he would have been sentenced to life imprisonment. Locked in solitary confinement—where he was to spend his first three years—in a tough prison in Noto, Sicily, he was experiencing a mental health crisis. He was surprised later that he didn't lose his sanity. Attempts to cheer himself up by humming songs about how much of a daredevil he was, and how, when he arrived back home, he would be greeted with cheers, was of no use. He knew that wouldn't happen—public opinion ripped him to shreds. He was one of the most hated men in all of Italy. He told a priest who once wanted to talk to him, maybe to help him confess, to go to Hell, almost beating him up. The prisoner lost his appetite, and was plunging into apathy and despair. And then, one night in December 1906, he had an extraordinary dream. In it he saw himself and his victim, a young girl. He was standing in front of a garden where white flowers grew. Beautiful, dressed all in white, she gathered them and then smiled at him like an angel, saying "take

➤ *A photo of a girl believed to be Maria Goretti, from 1902.*

➤ *Stained glass depicting St. Maria Goretti.*

ST. MARIA GORETTI

ITALY

them," and handed him fourteen white lilies, one by one. He accepted them and asked her for her forgiveness. When he received an armful, he hugged the flowers against himself. The lilies, symbolizing the virtue of purity, then burst into flames. The girl stood there and smiled at him, then disappeared.

"Maria ... Marietta smiled at me. She gave me lilies. She forgave me, she truly forgave me," he probably thought upon waking. He knew she had forgiven him when she was dying, but only now did he feel it, only now was he sure of it. He thought for a long time about the meaning of this dream. One thing is certain—it was this dream that turned his life upside down. It opened his eyes to goodness and truth. The victim's forgiveness, which only now occurred to him, had shown its powerful healing power. The man met with Bishop Giovanni Blandini of Noto soon after. Remorseful and wanting to redeem his sins, he asked the bishop for forgiveness in the name of God and—with his prompting—he wrote an "appeal to the world" in which, among other things, he urged others to stay away from immoral spectacles and anything that might lead them to sin. The prisoner was Alessandro Serenelli, and the girl he dreamed of was his victim—eleven-year-old Maria Goretti.

FATES INTERWINED

Maria Goretti was the eldest of seven children of Luigi and Assunta—virtuous, hardworking, and pious peasant farmers from Corinaldo, near Ancona. After a three-year stay in Colle Gianturco, in February 1900 the Goretti family—in search of a better livelihood—left for Ferriere di Conca, near Nettuno, and close to Rome. They performed hard and backbreaking work draining the Pontine Marshes. They also did farm work.

The family lived in one big house with Giovanni Serenelli and his son Alessandro, whom they had met in their previous place of residence. It wasn't an easy life, especially since only a few months after the move, Luigi Goretti died after a short illness contracted from the malaria-ridden swamps. Giovanni Serenelli and his son tried to take the helm of the merged families and exploit Assunta and her children.

MARIA

From an early age, Maria had to help her mother, and after her father's death, she took over most of her duties, looking after the animals, preparing meals, cleaning, and caring for the younger children. She was mature beyond her years, caring, gentle, self-sacrificing, obedient, and deeply pious. She prayed a lot (her favorite prayer was the Rosary), avoided impure conversations and immodest pictures, and set a good example for her brothers and sisters. She lifted everyone's spirit with a kind word and a smile. Everyone liked her. "The Lord

➤ *House of Maria Goretti, known as the Cascina Antica (on the right).*

⮝ *Alessandro Serenelli approached the Capuchin Friars in Ascoli Piceno, who welcomed him as a brother. He spent the rest of his days in Capuchin monasteries, working mainly as a gardener and living the life of a penitent.*

Jesus will protect us," she assured her mother when she was grieving the death of her husband.

Participating in Holy Mass and her first Holy Communion, which she received at age ten, were important experiences for her. The words spoken by the priest sank deep into her heart: "You must be willing to die rather than to sin."

LONER IN THE SWAMPLAND

When Maria was growing in virtue, Alessandro Serenelli, who lived in the same house and was treated by her like an older brother, became aggressive and vulgar. The boy had a very difficult childhood. He was the last of Giovanni's eight children, and he lost his mother when he was only a few months old. The woman died in a psychiatric hospital after trying to drown her child (most likely him) immediately after giving birth. His brother—a seminary student—also ended up in a psychiatric hospital and died there (some sources say he committed suicide). The rest of the brothers also died in dramatic circumstances. Constant moves didn't help his situation, either. On the contrary, they made things worse. Unable to warm up to a place, he couldn't establish lasting friendships with his peers.

At the age of five, Alessandro was already pasturing sheep. He briefly attended school, where he learned to read and write, a rare skill among Italian peasants at that time. His father preferred to get drunk rather than take care of him. He would go off on benders for days at a time. Alessandro was a shy, quiet loner. He spent most of his free time at home, reading the secular publications *Il Messaggero and Illustrata* and cheap crime novels. He hung up immodest pictures of women and actresses in provocative poses on his walls. Did he also look at pornography? It's hard to say, as access to it was very limited in those days. Spending a year working on fishing boats with his brother and older fishermen ruined him even more. He later spoke of the strong and uncontrollable bad habits he picked up during this work. He started drinking wine. Maria Assunta's mother, however, spoke highly of him. She presented him as a man who didn't drink, didn't cause trouble or cheat others, as someone who was religious, diligent at work, and treated his elders with respect. Was there another side of him? What was he really like?

PRELUDE TO THE CRIME

To her misfortune, he became obsessively lustful toward Maria. Mature and developed beyond her years, beautiful and serious, and at the same time pure and tough, she was different from most girls he knew, who could be bought for a small gift. Instead of trying to win her over with kindness and gentleness, Alessandro attacked her with crude, licentious words, even physically harassing her. Maria started hiding from him; she was afraid of his lustful glances and words. However, the boy was looking for an opportunity to be alone with her. He tried pleading and threatening her into submission. He would take on an unpleasant, commanding tone, wanting to show that he was in charge and that she was to obey him. Maria defended herself as best she could. What's more, every day she prayed for Alessandro, asking God to transform his soul. She twice rejected his persistent advances. The man was furious. He decided that if Maria rejected him again, he would kill her. He promised her that he would do this if she breathed a word to her mother about his solicitations. The girl became seriously afraid of him. She begged her mother not to leave her by herself.

FOR THE PRICE OF LIFE

On an ill-fated Saturday, July 5, 1902, Alessandro left for work with others. They were gathering fava beans and carrying the crops using two carts. Giovanni Serenelli was sick with malaria and Maria stayed home to mend his son's shirt. Two-year-old Teresina was sleeping on a blanket. It was around 3:30 in the afternoon. Under the pretext of leaving his knife, Alessandro stopped working and returned home. He had a plan. He took a long ten-inch awl used to make straw brooms and dragged the girl forcefully into the kitchen. He kicked the door shut. Threatening to kill her, he tried to rape her. She wouldn't give in. "What are you doing, Alessandro? You're going to go to Hell. It's a sin. It's a sin," she said, in an effort to make him stop. She defended herself. She screamed. Wanting to silence her, he stuffed a linen rag into her mouth. He tried to take off her clothes. He couldn't. Then he got furious. With

Basilica of Our Lady of Graces and St. Maria Goretti in Nettuno, bas-relief depicting the scene of mystical forgiveness of the murderer by Maria Goretti.

The scene of the mystical reconciliation of Maria with her murderer. Painting from the Shrine of Our Lady of Guadalupe.

➤ *Relics of St. Maria Goretti at St. Joseph Cathedral in Columbus, Ohio.*

It was around 8 p.m. when the girl, severely wounded and bleeding out, was taken to the hospital in Nettuno, and then immediately to the operating room. During the operation, which lasted more than two hours, the doctors tried to save her. They cut and sewed her up without anesthesia. In the end, they couldn't save her. Fourteen deep stab wounds resulted in her death.

the sharp awl in his hand, he stabbed her eleven times. "God, God, I'm dying. Mom, Mom!" cried Maria, losing consciousness. Alessandro, thinking the girl was already dead, left the room and threw himself on his bed. Maria then regained consciousness. She started screaming for help. Hearing this, Alessandro ran out from his room and stabbed her three more times, piercing her throat. After a moment, certain the girl was already dead, he returned to his room and tried to sleep, but Maria was still alive. With the last of her strength, she crawled out of the house and started screaming. She called for the sick Giovanni.

SHE WENT TO HEAVEN, HE WENT TO PRISON

It was around 8 o'clock that night when the girl, severely wounded and bleeding out, was taken to the hospital in Nettuno, and then immediately to the operating room. During the operation, which lasted more than two hours, the doctors tried to save her. They cut and sewed her up without anesthesia, admiring her courage and bravery to endure terrible suffering. In the end, they couldn't save her. Fourteen deep wounds resulted in her death.

Before dying the next day, she received last rites and forgave her killer. She begged those around her not to hurt him. "For the love of Jesus, I forgive him with all my heart! I forgive him and want him to be in Paradise with me!" she told the Archbishop of the Diocese of Nettuno who was at the hospital. "What a beautiful lady," she cried just before dying. "Look! She is so beautiful, full of light and flowers," she added.

She was immediately hailed as a saint and martyr. Large crowds attended her funeral. The largest Italian newspapers wrote about Maria and her martyrdom.

➤ *A photograph from the canonization Mass at St. Peter's Basilica in the Vatican.*

Two years after her death, her first statue was erected and her first biography was written. More and more pilgrims visited her grave each year. In 1929, the girl's body was exhumed and transferred to the sanctuary of the Madonna delle Grazie di Nettuno. Six years later, the process leading to her beatification was initiated.

A mob wanted to lynch Serenelli, but he was defended by the Carabinieri. Chained, he was taken to the barracks in Nettuno and then transported to the Regina Coeli prison in Rome.

The twenty-year-old confessed to everything, saying he had lost control. He tried to evade trial by using his alcoholic parents and family history of mental illness as an excuse. It was determined that he was sane, but it must be honestly admitted that he may indeed have had some psychological, perhaps even hereditary, defect or trauma from a difficult childhood. We already know what happened next.

TESTAMENT OF A REPENTANT MURDERER

Alessandro Serenelli spent fifteen years in the Sicilian prison in Noto. He was transferred to other places of detainment, where he had to work hard. He was released after twenty-seven years.

When he was released in 1929, Alessandro, tired of life, was a different man. At first, he was hired for various jobs as a peasant worker. On Christmas Day 1934, he met Assunta, Maria's mother, to ask her forgiveness. He received it! Assunta treated him like a returning prodigal son.

After some time, he approached the Capuchin Friars in Ascoli Piceno, who welcomed him as a brother. He became a Franciscan tertiary. He spent the rest of his days in Capuchin monasteries, working mainly as a gardener and living the life of a penitent.

Together with Assunta, Alessandro was present at the ceremony of her daughter's beatification in 1947 and—three years later—at her canonization. He died at the age of eighty-eight on May 6, 1970, in a Capuchin monastery in Macerata.

After his death, his spiritual testament was found. He wrote it in Macerata nine years earlier (this document is dated May 5, 1961):

> *I am almost eighty years old, and near the end of my days. Looking*

Maria Goretti's solemn funeral.

She was immediately hailed as a saint and martyr. Large crowds attended her funeral. The largest Italian newspapers wrote about Maria and her martyrdom. Two years after her death, her first statue was erected and her first biography was written. More and more pilgrims visited her grave each year.

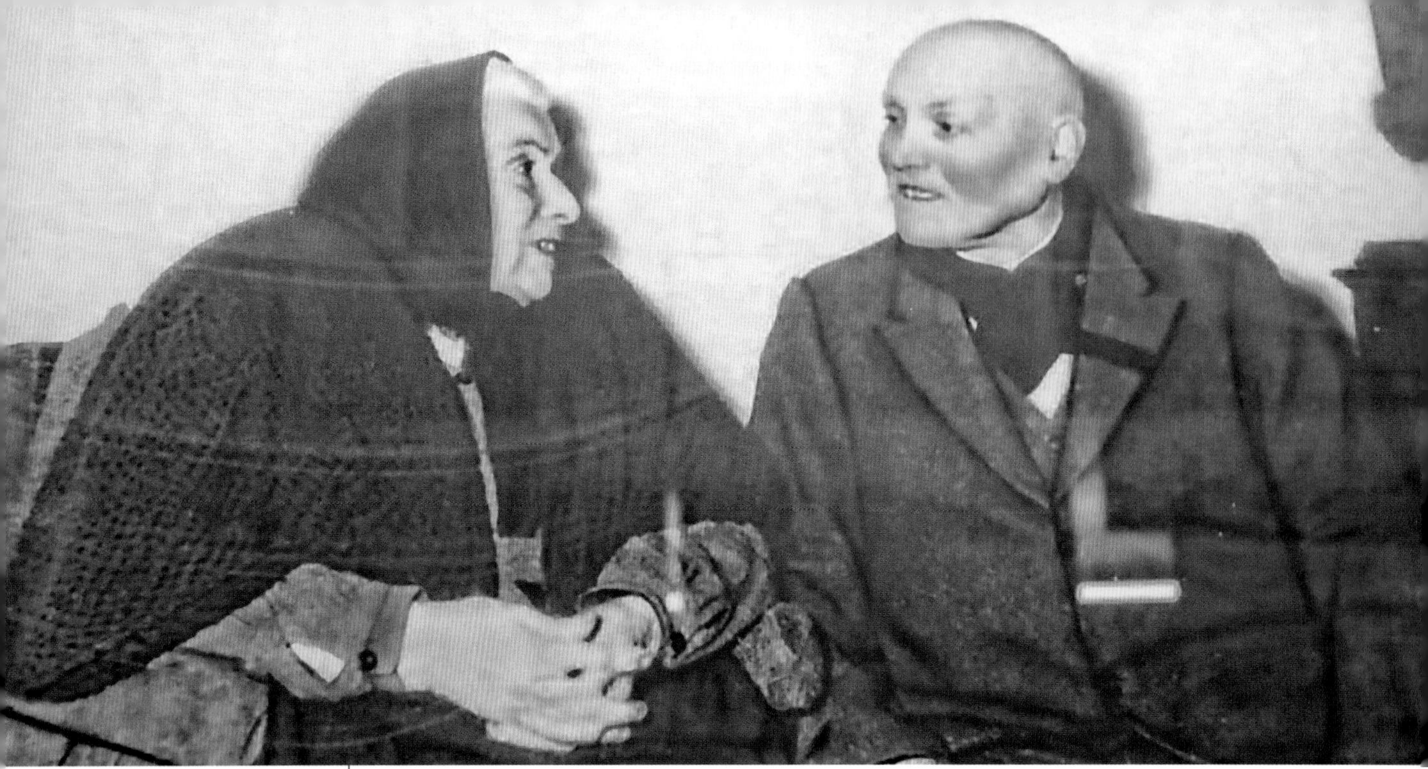

When he was released in 1929, Alessandro, tired of life, was a different man. At first, he was hired for various jobs as a peasant worker. On Christmas Day 1934, he met Assunta, Maria's mother, to ask her forgiveness. He received it! Assunta treated him like a returning prodigal son.

Wax statue of the saint.

back on the past, I recognize that, in my early youth, I went down a false path: the way of evil, which led me to ruin.

I saw the world through the lens of a corrupt culture, and was exposed to bad examples that most young people follow without giving them a thought; I didn't think about it either.

There were people of religious faith and practice near me, but I didn't pay them any mind, blinded as I was by a brute force that impelled me toward wickedness.

When I was twenty, I committed a crime of passion, the mere memory of which horrifies me today.

Maria Goretti, now a saint, was the angel that Providence sent to save me. Her words of reproach and forgiveness are still engraved on my heart. She prayed for me; she interceded for her own murderer.

Thirty years of prison followed. Had I not been underaged, I would have been condemned for life. I accepted the sentence I had earned with resignation: I understood that I was guilty. Little Maria was truly my light, my protector; with her help, I behaved well during those twenty-seven years of prison, and I sought to live honestly when society accepted me again among its members. The sons of St. Francis, the Capuchins Minor of Marche, welcomed me with seraphic charity, not as a servant, but as a brother.

I have been living with them for twenty-four years. And now, with serenity, I await the moment of being admitted to the vision of God, of embracing my loved ones again, of being near my protecting angel and her dear mother, Assunta.

May those who read this letter of mine learn the happy lesson of fleeing from evil and always following what is good and right from their childhood. Think of religion, with its precepts, not as something you can do without;

rather, it is true consolation, the only safe path in all circumstances—even the most sorrowful ones in our lives. Peace and goodness to you!

HIS BODY LIES BESIDE HIS VICTIM

Since 2007, the body of the repentant murderer rests in the shrine in Nettuno, near the relics of St. Maria Goretti, which are displayed in a crystal coffin. It is a beautiful symbol of the power of Christian forgiveness. Maria is the most well-known martyr for chastity in the Catholic Church and a wonderful role model for many young girls and boys of our time. As St. John Paul II said on the hundredth anniversary of her death:

> *St. Maria Goretti is an example for the new generations who are threatened by a non-commital attitude that finds it difficult to understand the importance of the values which admit of no compromise. … Her martyrdom reminds us that the human being is not fulfilled by following the impulses of pleasure but by living life with love and responsibility.*[1]

HELPING FAMILIES, THE SICK, AND THE INJURED

Recognized as a martyr who died in defense of her chastity, Maria Goretti didn't need miracles for her beatification. She had to be associated with two miracles, however, to be elevated to the status of a saint. Both happened, as if on cue, just a few days after the beatification. The first person to be healed was Anna Grossi Musumarra from Albano Laziale. The woman was suffering from exudative pleurisy. People suffering from this condition most often feel chest pain, have chills and a fever, sweat excessively, and cough.

At the time, such an illness could easily be fatal, especially since the sick woman had a very high fever and a large amount of fluid that had accumulated in her pleural

Relics of St. Maria Goretti.

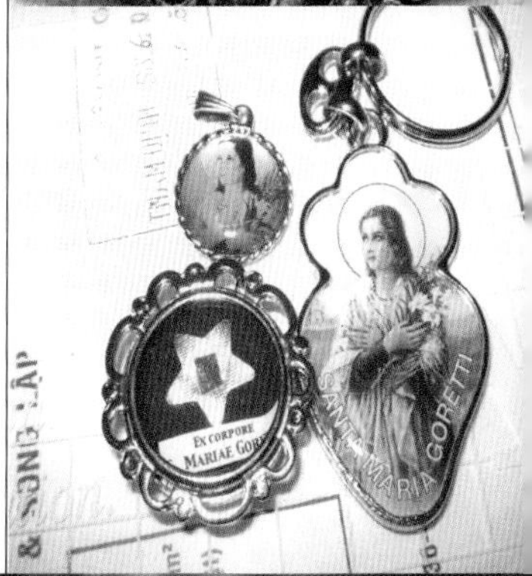

▼ *St. Maria Goretti is generally portrayed wearing a characteristic regional shawl and holding the palm of martyrdom.*

cavity. Many doctors thought nothing could be done medically, that only a miracle could save her. One of the doctors even made an inappropriate joke, saying that it would be a true miracle, except miracles are no longer in style. The sick woman was hospitalized, but she was not given any chance of survival. Anna then thought about her family. "What will happen to my family after my death? I can't die," she cried, calling upon Bl. Maria Goretti for help. When she finished praying, she felt strange. Her temperature was checked, and it had returned to normal. Not only that, but the illness also subsided. The doctors, who examined the woman before hospitalization, were called in. "It's impossible," they said, shaking their heads in surprise, recognizing that this healing had no scientific explanation. This miracle occurred May 4, 1947.

Giuseppe Cupo was also healed through the intercession of Bl. Maria Goretti. The Roman laborer worked on Monte Antenna. One day, a large boulder fell from the mountain, crushing his left foot. Those who saw it and the doctors called to the scene of the accident recognized there was no chance of saving the foot, and all said amputation would be necessary. This was tragic news for the man. He wondered who would support his family now. Wasting no time, he plunged into prayer to Maria Goretti, who had been recently raised to the altars. "Blessed Maria, show that you are a holy martyr. Heal me, let me return to work, and protect my family," he pleaded. And then, on May 8, 1947, a miracle happened. Almost immediately, the foot was whole and healthy again. The severe hematoma was only a faint memory. The doctors and his fellow workers were certain that a supernatural force must have contributed to the healing.

MIRACLES OF THE TWENTY-FIRST CENTURY

St. Maria Goretti performs miracles to this day. In June 2019, the publication *La Luce di Maria* wrote about the case of a seventy-year-old English woman. A few years earlier, the woman was making a pilgrimage to Borgo le Ferrier, the place of Maria Goretti's martyrdom, known in Italian as Casa del Martirio di Santa Maria Goretti. From childhood, the pious woman suffered from chronic arthritis. She said that sometimes her joints hurt so much that she prayed for death. She used crutches because of her knee pain, and she was on crutches when she entered the room where St. Maria was fatally wounded. She left the room without them. It was in the shrine that she discovered she was able to walk normally again. She no longer felt pain and could even kneel. The Englishwoman asked for official recognition of the miracle, but for this to happen, the road is extremely long. There

Basilica of Our Lady of Graces and St. Maria Goretti in Nettuno, where the relics of the saint are kept.

The only authenticated photo of Maria Goretti before her death.

would need to be a proper investigation and a lot of research involved.

In July 2013, the Zenit News Agency and the publication *Il Tempo* reported on another remarkable event. A young Canadian woman was sexually abused by her stepfather as a child. When the woman got married, she and her husband tried to have a child, but their efforts were fruitless. The woman went to a variety of specialists, but they all agreed that, due to the mental and physical traumas suffered from childhood, she would never be able to give birth. For the young couple, the information was devastating.

In June 2012, a reliquary containing the body of St. Maria Goretti arrived in Toronto, Canada, for public devotion. The young wife learned about it from television and decided to go to the saint with her husband. St. Maria was also a victim of violence, so who could help them if not her? The young couple knelt before the reliquary and prayed for the grace of parenthood. A few days later, the young woman saw the martyr in her dream. It strengthened her faith, and she knew the saint had her in her care and would certainly help her. She didn't have to wait long for these hopes to materialize. Soon after, she discovered she had become pregnant. That, however, was only half the battle. The doctors were confused, and some were terrified; they wondered how this could have happened, how they could have been so wrong in their medical predictions. Most of them probably thought that she wouldn't give birth. Nine months later, however, a girl was born.

On July 22, little Mercedes Maria was baptized in the shrine in Nettuno (it was extremely special because such ceremonies don't usually take place there). As *Il Tempo* records, St. Maria also gave the young woman the strength to face her stepfather during the trial against him.

ENDNOTES

1 Pope John Paul II, "Angelus, 7 July 2002," Vatican Website, https://www.vatican.va/content/john-paul-ii/en/angelus/2002/documents/hf_jp-ii_ang_20020707.html.

➤ *Jacinta and Francisco. A recently colorized photo of the little shepherds.*

CANDLES IN DARK HOURS

Sts. Francisco & Jacinta Marto

Not including the so-called Holy Innocents, the Fátima children became the Church's youngest saints as soon as the pope canonized them. They both passed away while they were still small children. "With this rite, the Church wishes to put on the candelabrum these two candles which God lit to illuminate humanity in its dark and anxious hours," said John Paul II on the day of their beatification on May 13, 2000. The official declaration of the siblings as saints was made possible thanks to the healing of a little boy only slightly younger than them.

A child over a precipice, trying to force its way over the windowsill or balcony railing? If you have children, you may have experienced this at some point too, or see it in your nightmares. On March 3, 2013, before 8 p.m., a little five-year-old boy named Lucas was playing with his little sister Eduarda in their grandfather's house in Juranda in northwestern Brazil.

Why did he get dangerously close to the window? No one knows. In his case, however, playing near the window ended in the worst possible way: he fell out.

➤ *The path of the little shepherds has not changed much since the apparitions.*

Olimpia and Manuel Marto, parents of Francisco and Jacinta.

PORTUGAL

Sculpture from Loca do Cabeço. The last meeting with the angel.

Unfortunately, the window was located twenty feet above the pavement.

After falling on the hard pavement, the boy's skull was crushed, and some of his brain tissue flew out. The unconscious boy was rushed to the hospital. His condition was critical and he fell into a coma. From the facility in Juranda, the child was sent on a nearly hour-long journey to a hospital in Campo Mourão. On the way, his heart stopped beating twice. They said his chances for survival were minimal.

However, doctors fought valiantly for the boy's life. They performed an emergency operation and took him to the intensive care unit. However, they informed his parents that even if Lucas survived, he would face a long and arduous rehabilitation, possibly remaining in a vegetative state for the rest of his life, or at best suffering from severe cognitive disorders. We can only imagine how such information must have shaken his parents. Not so long ago their son was completely healthy, and now all might be lost!

➤ *Kitchenware in the home of Francisco and Jacinta.*

➤ *Olimpia Marto was a simple woman, very pious and honest, while Manuel Marto was called "uncle" in the neighborhood because he was a serious, godly, and widely liked man. Jacinta and Francisco's mother used to say that her children's lives were a mystery, keeping in mind that Mary herself had chosen them to carry her message to the whole world.*

As people of faith, João and Lucilia fell to their knees and raised their hands to Jesus and Our Lady of Fátima. They knew that only a miracle could save their son. They also called the Carmelite convent of Campo Mourão to ask the sisters to pray for the boy.

Moved by their request, the nuns started a "prayer storm" before the relics of the Fátima shepherds. Soon the whole family, not only the parents but also other relatives, began to pray for the help of the shepherds.

After the operation, however, the child's condition was deteriorating, and they considered transferring him to an even more specialized facility.

However, on March 9—six days after the accident and two days after they started praying to God through the intercession of the little shepherds—something amazing happened. The boy suddenly woke up from his coma and, as if nothing happened, started interacting with the outside world!

Moreover, he spoke normally, was mentally, intellectually, and physically sound, and was showing no signs of any disability. The doctors were shocked, and the parents were joyful. During the following days, Lucas was examined many more times, observed, and finally allowed to go home on March 15. He was completely healthy, and the miracle was evident. Not only did the boy survive and remain fully agile, but the missing part of his brain *literally grew back*.

Almost exactly four years later, on March 23, 2017, the healing of little Lucas was officially approved by Pope Francis as a miracle for the canonization of Bl. Francisco and Jacinta Marto.

On the centenary of the famous Marian apparitions, the pope canonized the Marto siblings in Fátima on May 13, 2017. The healed boy and his parents could not miss the ceremony. Without hiding their tears, they shared what happened to them at a press conference held at the shrine.

They confessed at the time that the Carmelite nuns did not immediately start praying for their child's healing. When they called the convent the day after

Provisionally marked site of the apparitions. Photo from the early twentieth century.

Photograph of children taken after July 13, just after they were shown visions of Hell.

Jacinta and Francisco's parents in front of their home in Aljustrel.

the accident, the nun who answered the phone did not pass the message to the community as they were observing a period of silence. The Carmelite nuns had just had an hour of prayer, and the nun deduced from the caller's words that the child would die regardless and decided to pray not for the boy, but for the family. Community prayer in front of the relics of Bl. Francisco and Jacinta for the child's health did not begin until after another phone call on March 7.

One of them, after hearing about the family's tragedy, ran to the relics of Bl. Francisco and Bl. Jacinta, which were next to the tabernacle. She felt the impulse to pray the following prayer: "Shepherds, save this child, who is a child like you." She also convinced the other sisters to pray to the little shepherds to intercede for him.

CONSOLATION FOR SINS AND INSULTS

Francisco and Jacinta Marto were ordinary children, shepherds, from a poor, pious, numerous shepherd family. They liked to play, sing, and dance. They loved Jesus and Mary and listened to the stories of the Savior's Passion with a flushed face and fright. Francisco (1908–1919) was a quiet, serious boy, polite and compliant. He did not care or worry about anything. In terms of character, his sister Jacinta (1910–1920) was his opposite. She was a lively, stubborn, frolicky, and fussy girl. She often sulked, and she liked to pretend that she was a donkey. Both of them, however, shied away from lying, and their sins and misdeeds were generally limited to disobeying their parents and minor childish rascality.

The central event of their lives was their encounter with Our Lady during the apparitions experienced in Fátima in 1916 and 1917. At the time, they were accompanied by their cousin Lucia dos Santos. The apparitions completely changed them. Encouraged by the angel and Our Lady, they began to pray extremely fervently and make ascetic sacrifices. They changed. Jacinta became serious, modest, and kind, and Francisco finally began to care about

⮝ *Crowds from all over Portugal were flocking to the Cova da Iria valley in anticipation of the miracle.*

something. The girl admonished other children not to offend God by sinning. The boy often hid in the church to adore Jesus. Francisco's specialty became consoling the Lord Jesus for the insults He suffered from people, compensating Him for the sins of the world. He was ready to make any sacrifice for Jesus. Jacinta was especially worried about the vision of Hell and the fate of crowds of blinded sinners who head for eternal damnation because no one prays for them or practices self-mortification for them. She prayed and was tireless in coming up with smaller and larger offerings.

She did penance "as much as possible" to convert them and save them from Hell; she wanted to compensate for the insults inflicted on the Immaculate Heart of Mary and to suffer for the Heavenly Father.

All three mystics suffered as a result of being accused of lying. They were not spared by the secular authorities, their parents, and even their own parish priest. However, the children did not budge. What they saw and told was the truth, and despite requests and threats, they had not the slightest intention of saying otherwise. After all, to say otherwise would have been to lie. Mary also entrusted them with a secret that they were not allowed to reveal, and although there were various attempts to get the children to reveal it, they did not say a word.

Francisco and Jacinta did not live very long. They voluntarily agreed to accept the sufferings sent upon them by God, despite the fact that they were suffering from the effects of the Spanish flu epidemic that was then sweeping the world. Then, during one of the apparitions, Our Lady told them that they would soon die and go to Heaven. And so it happened. While they were still alive, many people received extraordinary graces thanks to their fervent prayers. It was no different after their deaths.

SIT UP! YOU CAN!

The healing that was taken under the microscope during the beatification process of the Fátima children was that of Maria Emilia Santos from Leiria, Portugal. In 1946, sixteen-year-old Maria Emilia was hospitalized with a high fever. At first glance, doctors thought it was the flu, but eventually, they determined that it was probably rheumatic fever. Although the girl was discharged from the hospital, she continued to feel unwell.

Two years later, she started to experience severe leg pains and stopped walking. She spent almost four long years in the hospital and sanatorium. Doctors suspected inflammation of the vertebrae and spinal

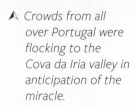

The crowd of skeptics and mockers became a crowd of believers in an instant. The sun began to spin intensely around its axis and seemed to rush toward the earth.

Cova da Iria valley. Jacinta in the arms of an automobile driver.

The crowd looking up at the sky on October 13.

cord, probably with a tubercular origin. They operated on the spine and knees. However, there were no results. She was finally discharged and sent home, but due to severe pain, the girl was still unable to walk. There was no improvement.

Ten years later, Maria Emilia could no longer even crawl. The pain she was experiencing was unbearable. Another orthopedist saw her and even wanted to treat her in Coimbra or Lisbon, but the woman had had enough doctors, which is hardly surprising. Unfortunately, eight days after that visit, she had to see them again.

Her condition worsened and she required another hospitalization. She ended up at the University Hospital in Coimbra, where she underwent a second spinal surgery with disastrous results. She became a paraplegic. Claiming that there was no cure for her condition, she was sent home.

On January 8, 1978, due to a fever, the woman was once again hospitalized in Leiria. This time she spent the next six years there. After that time, she was transferred to the St. Francis care facility. Fr. Fabrice Delestre describes her condition:

> *From then until 1987, she didn't consult any doctor, didn't take any special medication, only painkillers when the pain was very severe. She always laid on her side on the bed, completely numb from the waist down. She could only move her hands and head. She prayed, sang, and cried, but the discouragement, suffering, and great difficulty in accepting her situation led her, by her own admission, to become irritated and protest against those who served her and only wanted to do her good.*

One day a paramedic transported the woman to Fátima. It was from that time that Maria Emilia Santos began to have a special reverence for Francisco and Jacinta. Hoping for an improvement in her health, she began to pray novenas—one after another.

She prayed the Rosary and, starting another day of her novena, sighed reproachfully: "Jacinta, there is only one day left to finish another novena, and still nothing?" Just then she noticed that something strange was happening to her feet. She felt a strong warmth and tingling. She became frightened. The symptoms were getting stronger. "Sit up! You can!"—said a childish voice. When she heard these words for the third time, she finally gained courage—she threw back the quilt and sat down on the bed. She sat up! She could!

She immediately called for someone from the care facility staff, and when one finally came, she asked her to turn on the light. When it was on, the nurse was horrified and started screaming. She was frightened of the woman sitting on the bed. The director of the home and the rest of the staff and residents were summoned. They were amazed. After all, she had just been

➤ *Decoration over the tombs of Jacinta and Lucia.*

➤ *The tomb of Jacinta and Francisco in the Fátima cemetery. Photo from 1935.*

➤ *Canonization portrait of St. Jacinta Marto.*

screaming in pain while being washed. From then on, Maria Emilia began to ride in a wheelchair, in an upright position.

But that was not the end of the story. The woman continued to pray, this time asking the shepherds to help her stand up. February 20, 1989, was the sixty-ninth anniversary of Jacinta's death. "If you force me to walk today, I will be the happiest woman in the world," she said during prayer. And then she stood up from her wheelchair. She tried to bend her knees, and she felt no pain. She took her first steps, and moments later, supporting herself with a cane, she began to walk. After more than twenty years! When this healing was investigated at the Vatican ten years later, Maria Emilia was walking without difficulty.

The consultors from the Congregation for the Causes of Saints also declared it a miracle and naturally attributed it to the intercession of Francisco and Jacinta. On this basis, on May 13, 2000, John Paul II beatified Jacinta and Francisco at Fátima. The little shepherds of Fátima became the youngest blesseds in the history of the Church, surpassing Dominic Savio, who died shortly before his fifteenth birthday.

MIRACLES WORKED TOGETHER

It is interesting to note that a new procedural solution was used in the case of the Marto siblings. John Paul II decided that Jacinta and Francisco, because the most important events of their lives—the apparitions, the suffering they experienced from the authorities, the young age at which they were taken to Heaven—involved both of them, did not need for their beatification and canonization miracles worked separately, but together. The only condition was that they must be asked through the intercession of the siblings jointly. Special papal permission was also needed for such young children to be declared saints.

Canonization portrait of St. Francisco Marto.

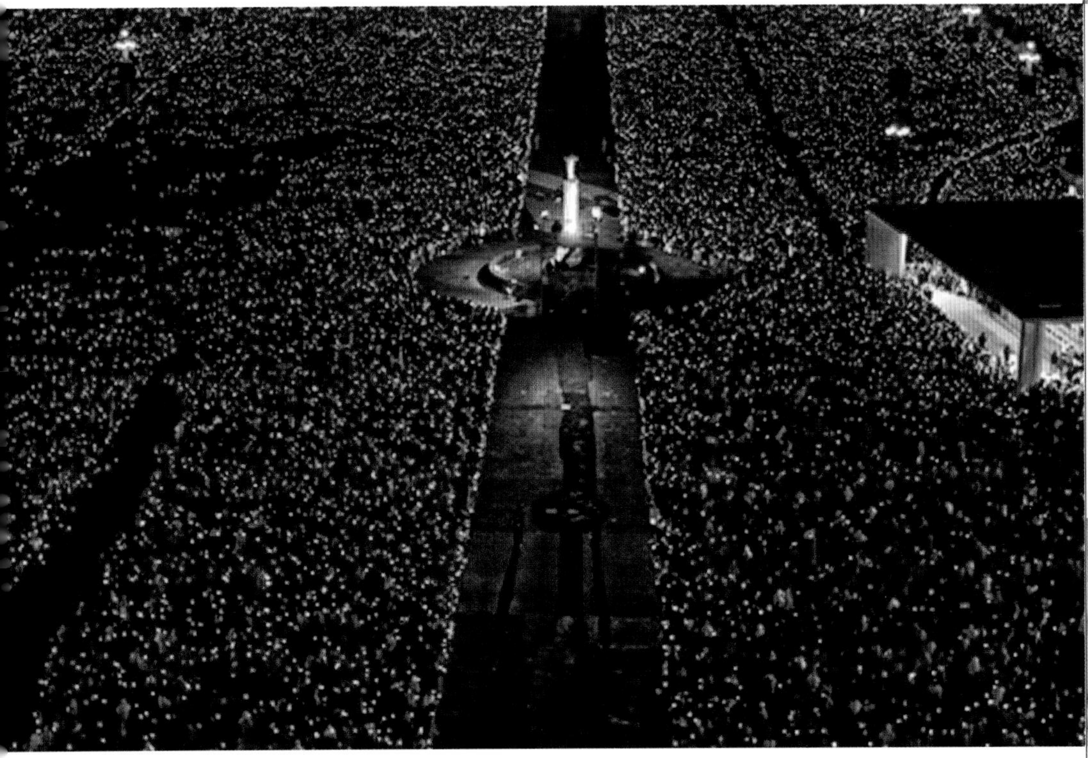

Night vigil with procession at Fátima.

The exhumation of Jacinta's incorrupt body fifteen years after her death, in 1935.

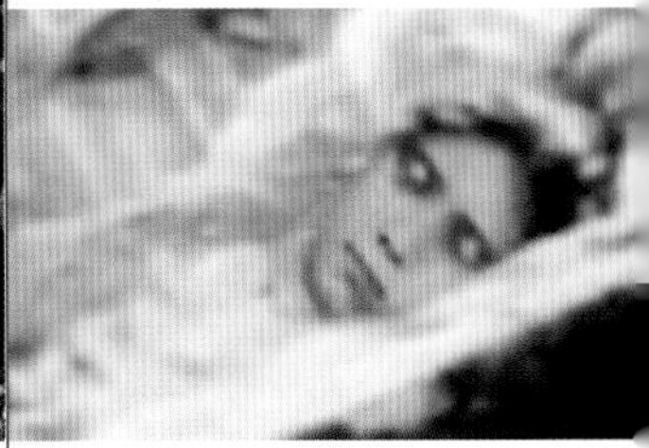

THEY FORGAVE THEIR OPPRESSORS

St. Christopher Magallanes Jara (24 Companions)

These brave men of the Mexican Revolution were martyrs and did not need a miracle to be beatified. They needed only one miracle to be canonized.

Cristóbal Magallanes is one of the twenty-five martyrs murdered and declared saints.

The condition from which María del Carmen Pulido Cortés, a pharmacist at a hospital in Guadalajara, suffered is called *Gravi mastopathia fibrocystica bilaterali cum praestantia sclerosis et adenosis* in Latin. In English, this condition is called bilateral fibrocystic mastopathy (degeneration of the mammary gland) with sclerosing adenosis. Although such lesions are benign tumors, they are extremely burdensome and painful.

It started with breast pain. In October 1991, the thirty-two-year-old woman had an exam that revealed cysts in both breasts. Some of the lumps were quite large. They were removed in November, but their histological analysis brought bad news. The lumps turned out to be the aforementioned disease.

Moreover, the prognosis was not good either. Doctors predicted that this condition, even if it could be cured temporarily, would essentially persist until menopause. As a result, the woman would also experience severe headaches, nausea, vomiting, and loss of appetite. At first, it was just as the doctors predicted: her ailments worsened and the young woman was forced to give up work and lie in bed. She then became depressed and stopped undergoing any treatment.

SHE ASKED AND IT WAS GIVEN TO HER

From the very beginning, as we read in the decree on the miracle, Mrs. Cortés asked God for healing through the intercession of Servants of God Fr. Cristóbal Magallanes and his twenty-four companions. As a

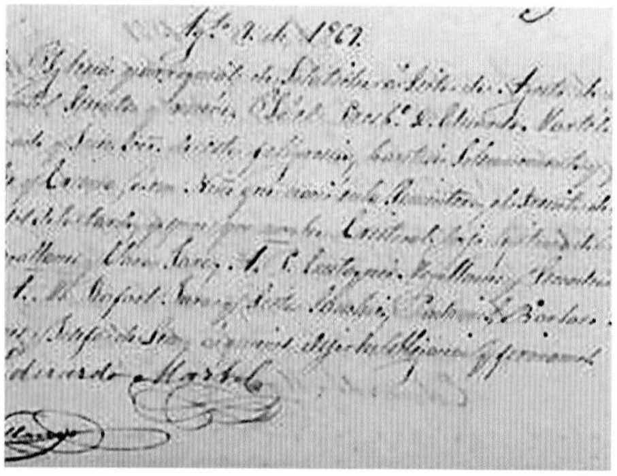

Baptismal certificate of Cristóbal Magallanes Jara dated August 7, 1869.

MEXICO

A statue of Cristóbal Magallanes Jara inside the Cathedral of the Assumption of Our Lady in Guadalajara.

Cristóbal Magallanes Jara was beatified on November 22, 1992, with a group of twenty-four companions, twenty-one of whom were priests and three were lay people. They were all victims of anti-Catholic persecution. They were canonized by Pope John Paul II on May 21, 2000, in St. Peter's Square.

➤ Fr. Miguel Agustín Pro, a Jesuit, was executed by firing squad on November 23, 1927, at a military shooting range, serving as a practice target for the execution squad.

➤ Fr. Francesco Vera was executed by firing squad after celebrating an illegal Mass in Mexico in 1927.

member of Catholic Action, she was a great venerator of these men.

In November 1992, she traveled to Rome for their beatification, although her doctors didn't want to let her go because of her poor health. Another check-up on January 7, 1993, revealed the presence of as many as fifty scattered cysts of various sizes. Upon her return, however, she continued to pray. After all, Jesus said, "Ask, and it will be given you; search, and you will find; knock, and the door will be opened for you" (Matt. 7:7).

At the time, a friend of hers who was a priest lent her a reliquary that contained relics of all twenty-five newly blessed martyrs. On January 30, 1993, the woman, praying fervently, placed the reliquary on her sick chest. A few moments later (two, maybe three minutes), she felt healthy and got out of bed.

It was not an illusion at all. All her ailments immediately vanished. All the cysts disappeared, which was confirmed by later tests. What's more, the cysts never returned. Doctors and theologians considered this to be a miracle brought about through the intercession of Bl. Cristóbal Magallanes and his twenty-four companions. The path to their canonization was opened, and John Paul II declared them saints on May 21, 2000.

LIFE FOR FAITH AND SERVICE TO GOD

Fr. Cristóbal Magallanes Jara and his twenty-four companions died for their faith after publicly forgiving their persecutors. During the anti-Catholic persecutions in Mexico in the early twentieth century (you can read more about this persecution and the Catholic uprising known as the Cristero War in the text dedicated to St. José Luis Sánchez del Río, see page 86), the martyrs shouted the words "Long live Christ the King" before they died.

Fr. Magallanes, who was a missionary, pastor, and founder of the underground seminary, and his former student Fr. Augustine Caloca Cortés were executed by the firing squad on May 25, 1927.

A year earlier, on the feast of the Assumption of the Blessed Virgin Mary, on

Fr. Magallanes, organizer of the underground seminary, and his former student, Fr. Agustín Caloca Cortés, were executed by firing squad on May 25, 1927.

August 15, 1926, the priest Luis Bátiz Ortega (Sainz) was executed by the firing squad together with lay members of the youth movement he founded: twenty-eight-year-old husband and father of three Emanuel Morales, twenty-year-old Salvador Lara Puente, and twenty-four-year-old laborer David Roldán Lara.

In 1928, the following priests died a martyr's death: Fr. Tranquilino Ubiarco Robles (a soldier who refused to hang him was also killed), twenty-seven-year-old Fr. Atilano Cruz Alvarado, Fr. Jesus Méndez Montoya (captured and shot while celebrating Mass), Fr. Justino Orona Madrigal, and twenty-seven-year-old Fr. Toribio Romo González.

The first priest who laid down his life for the Faith was Fr. David Galván Bermúdez. He died on January 31, 1915. On February 11, 1937, Fr. Pedro de Jesús Maldonado Lucero passed away as a result of torture and wounds inflicted on him. He was the last.

A photograph of St. Cristóbal Magallanes.

IT'S NOT ME, IT'S PHILOMENA

St. Jean Marie Vianney

St. Vianney was most often depicted praying.

St. Jean Marie Vianney (1786–1859) was a parish priest and is still a model for priests who are in charge of parishes. "The parish priest of Ars" was the pride of Catholic France. He was characterized by great practical wisdom. Although he wasn't one of the intellectuals, he certainly was no fool. Probably because he was extremely humble and modest, God gave him extraordinary powers of conversion and healing.

Jean Marie Vianney was the child of poor villagers from a village near Lyon, France, and lived in very difficult times. Three years after his birth, in 1789, the French Revolution broke out, which initiated a ruthless war against the Church. He had to take his First Communion in secret. As a young man, his education was hard going. He lacked the basics, as he only learned to read and write at the age of seventeen. He had serious problems with Latin, and other subjects taught in the seminary were beyond his mental capabilities. He flunked his seminary exam. "Dear Jean, you don't know a thing and you'll probably never learn. To whom can a donkey like you be useful?" sighed the professor. Vianney's reply was priceless: "Reverend professor, if Samson alone with the help of a donkey's jaw, still fresh, defeated a thousand Philistines, then just think what the Lord God could have accomplished with a whole donkey." Indeed, his answer was worthy of the greatest philosophers and theologians.

Fr. Vianney had his wits, and they were certainly healthier and more practical than many enlightened intellectuals, whose portrait he painted in one of his sermons, after—thanks be to God!—they took pity and ordained him at age twenty-nine:

> *Nothing affects him anymore, he despises everything. He knows that when he dies in this state, he will face eternal damnation. He doesn't care; he mocks salutary admonitions. He makes malicious remarks about sermons and priests. He says that priests are there to admonish, that it is their profession, that they tell lies. He speaks out against God and the Faith, against the clergy. He boldly transgresses God's commandments, drowns out his conscience, wallows in sins to the end, and wakes up only at the hour of death, when there is no longer any rescue for him, when escaping from the hounds of Hell is no longer possible.*[1]

FRANCE

Accustomed to the strictest self-sacrifices, pestered by swarms of penitents, this great mystic was characterized by inexhaustible patience and childlike simplicity.

Statue of St. Jean Marie Vianney.

He knew what he was talking about because, ever since he became parish priest in the shabby town of Ars in 1818, he had been converting such people day in, day out.

SAW HIMSELF IN TRUTH

One such ignoramus, a typical representative of the people of his time; who thought they had learned everything, was Maissiat. Fr. Francis Trochu wrote about him in his biography of St. John Marie Vianney, *The Curé d'Ars*:

He gladly called himself a philosopher, by which he meant that he believed only in reason. Having piously received his First Communion as a child, he abandoned the Catholic Faith during the worst era of the terror, later professing successively Islam, Judaism, Protestantism, Saint-Simonianism, Spiritualism, and finally succumbing to communism. His life resembled a fantastic novel.

In June 1841, Maissiat left Lyon with the intention of taking a trip to the Beaujolais mountains for a few days. However, in the vehicle he was traveling in, he met an old friend traveling to Ars. The friend began urging him to go to Ars with him. He promised that he would "see a priest who works miracles." Maissiat laughed derisively and replied that he did not believe in miracles, but eventually acquiesced to his companion's insistence.

The next day, out of curiosity, he went to the morning Mass celebrated by St. Vianney. He was very surprised when, after Mass, he saw the priest walking straight toward him. Moments later, Fr. Vianney put his hand on the man's shoulder, signaled Maissiat to follow him, and led him to the confessional. The man flinched at the mere sight of it.

The priest continued to stare at him; so overcome by his gaze, he obediently knelt before the latticed opening of the confessional. "After all, who cares?" he thought, and then coolly, without remorse or regret, he told the priest about his story and his misdeeds. The saint listened to him attentively, but, realizing the penitent's disposition, instructed him to come again the next day. "In the meantime, go to the altar of St. Philomena and tell her to obtain for you from the Lord Jesus the grace of conversion," he added. Maissiat went, and something extraordinary happened: he experienced God's grace. Weeping, he squeezed through the crowd and left the church. "Oh, how much happiness can be contained in tears!" he later recounted.

The next day, he did not go to the mountains, but, as requested, returned to the priest. His arrogance had vanished. He saw himself in truth. "Father, I don't believe in anything. Please help me!" he begged Fr. Vianney.

As Trochu writes, "The saint helped him so much that the geologist, having spent ten days by his side, full of faith, faced all human opinions and became one of the

Pilgrims flock to Ars every day. The pilgrims of the past are immortalized in a fresco in the basilica, while the new ones come in crowds from all over Europe.

A contemporary panorama of Ars.

Vianney, good to others and strict to himself, attracted people like a magnet. The church in Ars almost miraculously filled up with the faithful, and soon thousands of people began flocking to it.

most pious and zealous Catholics in the city. He died in the best disposition, which only Christian piety can inspire."

LIKE A MAGNET

Non-believers and open-minded atheists were just the tip of the iceberg. He also had problems with those who considered themselves believers, but decidedly did not want to take part in religious practices. When Fr. Vianney arrived in Ars, he found only a handful of faithful in a small, dilapidated church. In time, he got to know all the inhabitants of Ars inside and out and dealt with them admirably. For this they loved him, and in time, surprisingly, they even began to listen to him. The faithful admired the priest who prayed for hours before the Blessed Sacrament, slept and ate little, preached simple sermons, and spent many hours a day in the confessional. Fr. Vianney, good to others and strict to himself, attracted people like a magnet.

The church in Ars almost miraculously filled up with the faithful, and soon thousands of people began flocking to it from Paris and other parts of France. In his last year of ministry, he heard the confessions of approximately eighty thousand people!

He became known for his witticisms. He was once sent to preach the word of God in a parish where men had the unfortunate habit of leaving the church during the sermon. The saint stepped into the pulpit and said: "Pious listeners, today I am going to speak about cunning. Those of you who have it better leave the church now, for I would not wish to offend you, and the things I am going to say are rather unpleasant."

The faithful admired the priest who prayed for hours before the Blessed Sacrament, slept and ate little, preached simple sermons, and spent many hours a day in the confessional.

➤ *An old postcard showing the basilica in Ars. When Fr. Vianney arrived in Ars, he found only a handful of faithful in a small, dilapidated church. In time, he got to know all the inhabitants of Ars inside and out and dealt with them admirably. For this they loved him, and in time, surprisingly, they even began to ... listen to him.*

➤ *The presbytery in Ars was characterized by austerity and poverty. St. Jean Marie Vianney did not invest in comforts.*

Relics of St. Jean Marie Vianney and his austere kitchen in the presbytery of Ars.

He was once asked why, when he prays, he only mutters under his breath, but when he preaches, he almost shouts. "I think it's clear," he replied. "You see, when I preach, my words must reach the deaf or wake up those who are asleep, and when I pray ... Well, God has perfect hearing, after all."

He also had a way with habitual malcontents. "People are moving away from God because this world is bad; wars, famines, its just one thing after another," one of his parishioners complained over and over like a broken record. The good parish priest was getting sick of his complaining. "When one has an ugly face, it won't help to complain about the mirror," he told him finally.

IT'S NOT ME, IT'S PHILOMENA

God gave Fr. Vianney the gift of conversion, which none of the mortals could resist. But it was not just conversion. God also gave him the power to heal while he was still alive. Multitudes of sick and crippled people were flocking to him. In the many biographies of this saint, we can find a great number of descriptions of healings performed by him.

The parish priest of Ars, however, did not want people to attribute the power of working miracles to him. He had his way with those who tried to do so. He would refer them to St. Philomena, whom he revered, claiming that they owed the grace they had received not to him, but to her. In fact, he sometimes pouted at her for healing bodies more often than souls. Besides, some miracles happened precisely at the time when people asking St. Vianney for help, sent away by him, were praying before her image in the church.

It is possible that they worked some of the miracles together. Such was the case of a certain young girl from Charlieu, from the Loire department, who, as Fr. Trochu wrote, had one side of her body paralyzed, and

From 1878 to 1965, in addition to St. Sixtus, the basilica's patron saint was St. Philomena, whom St. Jean Marie Vianney especially venerated.

➤ *The saint's tattered shoes and modest utensils from the presbytery in Ars.*

although she could still drag her feet, her left arm was already completely dead.

> *When this poor sick girl wanted to tell the parish priest of Ars the long history of her misfortunes, the holy confessor interrupted her, saying: "Go, tell it to St. Philomena!" Then the poor girl squeezed her way through the tight crowd, to the altar of the young saint: "Give me back my arm or give me yours!" she begged. After saying these words, she was immediately healed, and she ran to the orphanage to share her happiness with her friends.*

WHITE TUMOR

In the case of miracles performed after death that were needed for beatification and canonization, however, Fr. Vianney could no longer shirk from performing them; he could no longer refer anyone to St. Philomena. What were these miracles, and whom did they involve?

In the case of the miracles needed for beatification, two were chosen from the seventeen examined. The first involved Adelaide Joly, a girl from an orphanage in Lyon, which was run by the Daughters of Charity. Eight-year-old Adelaide had been complaining of pain in her left arm

Mass at the Basilica of Ars, celebrated at the tomb of the great saint.

Pilgrims and religious congregating outside the Basilica of Ars.

for some time. "In September 1861, the teacher, who was reviewing our knitting, noticed that Adelaide was constantly idly resting her hand in her lap. She called her a little lazy," testified her older sister Leonida three years later. When it turned out that Adelaide was not lazy after all, the girl was taken to the surgeon of the city hospital. "White tumor," he pronounced, and predicted that Adelaide would have to wear a mechanical prosthesis for the rest of her life. However, the prosthesis was not ordered, as the girl's teachers wanted to try a different remedy first.

Leonida Joly recounts:

> *They told us to start praying a novena to the parish priest of Ars, and since they had a pair of old shoes that once belonged to the holy priest, they took out a shoelace from them, and tied it on my little sister's arm. After seven days, Adelaide told me: "Leonida, my arm doesn't hurt anymore." And from then on she could move her arm without any problem. However, the bandage was not removed until the ninth day of the novena. It turned out that the arm was already completely healed. Adelaide could move it at will in all directions and it had the same appearance as the other arm, without any trace of emaciation. The tumor was completely gone.*

CURED OF EPILEPSY

On January 1, 1862, six-year-old Leon Roussat, son of a baker from St. Laurent les Macoli, suffered nervous attacks. "At first they were slight. But later they became more severe and more frequent," his father recounted. The doctor they went to treated the child for worms, fever, and

Relics of St. Jean Marie Vianney in the minor basilica dedicated to St. Sixtus.

tapeworms successively, until he finally made the diagnosis that it was epilepsy. The local doctor's medications were not working, and the illness was getting worse. The parents took the boy to a doctor at Lyon's main hospital. They went out of the frying pan and into the fire. The doctor from Lyon recommended the boy take the waters; they tried this, but it only caused the seizures to worsen. "Leonek was falling on average five times a day." They soon returned to the same doctor, but again they were terribly disappointed by him. He stated that "the child is still young and he might recover from the illness on his own later," and added that they should not bring him anymore. Leon's parents were understandably very disappointed and saddened. On the way back, the baker decided that it was necessary to take the boy to Ars. Before they did so, however, they began praying a novena in honor of the parish priest. Did it help? Not yet. The boy's attacks only worsened, becoming both more frequent and more severe, until one day he fell and went cold for hours and afterward became paralyzed and speechless.

Mr. and Mrs. Roussat wanted to go to Ars as early as Easter Monday, but the parish priest with whom they were supposed to travel refused to go, fearing that the little one would not survive the trip.

They went on May 1. That was when the bishop of Belley, who had come to Ars to consecrate the cornerstone for the new church, was visiting. They met with him. He embraced and blessed the boy, instructing them to start another novena to the parish priest of Ars. Each day they were to pray just one decade of the Rosary. After the meeting with the bishop, the parents carried the child to the tomb of the holy priest and returned to the inn. By then they had already observed the first signs of improvement. The boy, who had been completely paralyzed until then, took a glass in his right hand, drank, and then began to play with matches, lighting them and throwing them far away.

On the way home, little Leon had only two mild attacks, but in the morning the paralysis returned. "Around ten o'clock," the child's father further reported, "we sat down at the table. Suddenly, to our joyful

A laddered two-wheeler standing under a shed in the courtyard of the presbytery in Ars.

amazement, Leon gave me a sign to move him, with the chair, away from the table, and when I did, he jumped down to the ground and started running, completely healed. He still had some trouble speaking, to say the least, but by the end of the novena, he had also completely recovered his speech. Since then, his health has been excellent." The doctors fully confirmed his words.

HEALED NUNS

Eleven years after the beatification of the most prominent parish priest of all time, two miracles were investigated and finally approved, confirming his sainthood. Sr. Eugenia (Antonia Buiricant of the Sisters of Mercy of St. Borromeo) had been suffering from varicose veins since early 1905. At first, they only bled, and then an ulcer measuring about two inches in diameter appeared. The sister could no longer walk. She was treated in Ranno, but to no avail. The parishioners there then gave her the idea of going on a pilgrimage to Ars. She was transported there, carried to the church, and seated in a chair next to the tomb. The sister remained there for an hour, praying and asking Fr. Vianney to allow her to return to her work in the kitchen. She was granted what she asked for. After praying, she felt well, got up, and walked to the inn. Upon returning to the convent, she went back to work in the kitchen.

The second healed was Mathilde Rougeol of Villers la Faye. At the age of twenty-eight, she was stricken with tubercular pharyngitis after a bout of the flu. She lost her voice, and when doctors declared that her illness was incurable she stopped all her treatments.

The distinctive body of the basilica towers over the sleepy little town that Ars is today.

During the 41 years of St. Jean Marie Vianney's ministry, the town of Ars was spiritually transformed, and crowds of the faithful from all over France were making pilgrimages there.

ENDNOTES

1 Święty J.M. Vianney, Kazania wybrane [St. J. M. Vianney, Selected Sermons], Oficyna Wydawnicza VIATOR, Warszawa 1999.5.58-59.

Miraculous Gifts, Charisms, and Other Phenomena

Each of us has some kind of charism, some gift given to us by God. Some of us are better than others at teaching, others are natural community workers, and so forth. According to St. Paul, a charism may also mean being a spouse or a superior, or living as a virgin. However, there were, and still are among us, people who have received extraordinary charisms and gifts from God: the gift of prophecy, speaking in tongues, healing the sick, the ability to know people's hearts, bilocation, stigmata, visions, and so on.

Bl. Alexandrina Maria da Costa fasted for more than thirteen years.

Angela of Foligno fasted for twelve years.

Marthe Robin lived on the Eucharist alone from age twenty-eight to seventy-nine.

Bl. Anne Catherine Emmerich.

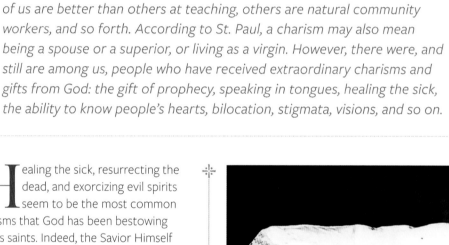

Healing the sick, resurrecting the dead, and exorcizing evil spirits seem to be the most common charisms that God has been bestowing on His saints. Indeed, the Savior Himself commanded His disciples to do so: "Cure the sick, raise the dead, cleanse the lepers, cast out demons. You received without payment; give without payment" (Matt. 10:8). Some of the saints also received from God the gift of food multiplication, or, more precisely, as in the case of other miracles, of interceding between God and people (for more on this, see "Large-Scale Miracles"). Here, too, one can see a clear connection to the miracles worked by Jesus Himself.

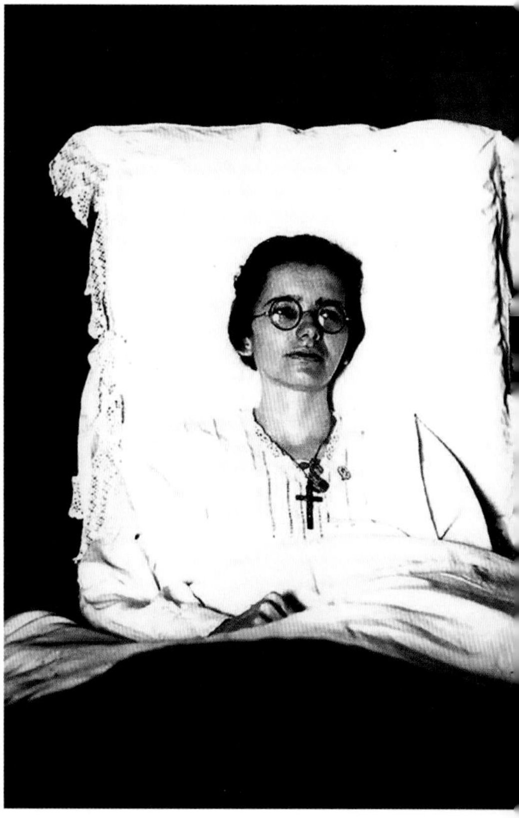

THE BREAD OF LIFE

Some saints received from God the extraordinary gift of inedia—for many years they lived on the Eucharist alone. This is because God wanted them to testify to the truth of the words spoken by Jesus: "I am the bread of life. Your

ancestors ate the manna in the wilderness, and they died. This is the bread that comes down from heaven, so that one may eat of it and not die. I am the living bread that came down from heaven. Whoever eats of this bread will live forever; and the bread that I will give for the life of the world is my flesh" (John 6:48–51). Of course, one can also see in this a reference to Jesus fasting for forty days in the desert. As Christ explained to Catherine of Siena in her *Dialogue*:

> *I grant ... a special power to plants and every other food, or I change the human body in such a way that it adapts to living on these few plants or to fasting better than it was before to living on bread and other foods that normally serve as nourishment for people. You know it is like this because you have experienced it yourself.*

Among the saints and blesseds of the Church who experienced inedia, we can name the following: St. Angela of Foligno (fasted for twelve years), St. Lidwina of Schiedam (thirty-eight years), St. Catherine of Genoa (twenty-three years), St. Nicholas of Flüe (nineteen years), Bl. Catherine of Racconigi (ten years), Bl. Alexandrina Maria da Costa (more than thirteen years), and Bl. Anne Catherine Emmerich.

Therese Neumann tried to eat liquid foods, but she was choking and vomiting, and then her heart hurt. When she stopped trying, she felt much better. As she confessed, from Christmas 1926 until the following September, she took only a teaspoonful of water along with Communion, and after that period, she no longer consumed even water. Swallowing the Host itself also caused her great difficulty. She claimed to be alive thanks to the Sacramental Savior inside her, until a short time before receiving the next Holy Communion. She added that whenever the substance of the Blessed Sacrament dissolves, she feels weak and "feels a great physical and spiritual longing for Holy Communion." Indeed, when the break between receiving the Body of Christ was longer than a day, Therese was close to fainting, her face turned gray, and her eyes became watery. After receiving the Eucharist, this condition would immediately pass.

The same thing happened to the completely paralyzed and bedridden French peasant Marthe Robin. From the age of twenty-eight to seventy-nine, she lived on the Eucharist alone, received every

Lidwina of Schiedam (below, top) did not eat for thirty-eight years, and St. Catherine of Genoa (above) did not eat for twenty-three years.

Inedia was also experienced by Therese Neumann (left) and Catherine of Racconig (below, bottom).

St. Catherine of Siena Receiving the Stigmata, *a painting by Domenico di Pace Beccafumi.*

St. Juliana Falconieri.

Thursday. During this time she felt thirsty, but was unable to swallow anything. She miraculously absorbed only the Body of Christ. In an interview with the French philosopher and writer Jean Guitton, Marthe Robin confessed that the Eucharist was her only food. She recounted that she couldn't swallow anything and only had her mouth dampened. She also said that the Eucharist was permeating into her, though she herself didn't know how this was happening. After each Holy Communion, the woman felt as if new life was being poured into her, as if she was melding into one with Jesus inside her body, as if she was being resurrected. Both of these cases were subjected to scientific observation, and any deception was ruled out.

FLYING HOSTS AND CHALICES

In the case of Marthe Robin, another extremely intriguing phenomenon was taking place: The host traveled to her mouth on its own, pulling itself out of the priest's fingers and traveling a distance of up eight inches. All the priests who had the opportunity to give communion to Marthe, and even one who, informed of this fact beforehand, held the Host more firmly, had the same impression—they clearly felt the Body of Christ pulling away from their hands.

However, the phenomenon of levitating eucharistic species was by no means new, having also been previously observed in the cases of St. Juliana Falconieri or St. Catherine of Siena.

Sometimes Hosts also miraculously permeated the body of the person receiving communion, and in the case of St. Mary Frances of the Five Wounds, it was even observed that the entire chalice with the Blood of Christ flew to her!

PARTIAL FASTING

So-called partial fasts were also a thought-provoking phenomenon. Many saints fasted so often or ate so little that, given the magnitude of the activities they undertook, other people doing the same would certainly pay for it with severe illness or outright death (this was the case with St. John Vianney, who lived on moldy potatoes). It was believed in such cases that God Himself miraculously kept them alive.

HYPERTHERMIA

In the case of some saints, their love for God was so great that they experienced the so-called "fire of love" (*incendium amoris*), manifesting itself as hyperthermia.

Hyperthermia is the phenomenon of a person reaching very high body temperatures that are normally lethal. In the medical literature, cases of the highest temperature (called "agonal" or "pre-agonal" because patients in whom they were recorded did not survive) are usually observed during attacks of epilepsy,

uremia, diseases of the central nervous system, tetanus infections, and sunstrokes. Medical hyperthermia has never been recorded above 111 degrees. But in the case of hyperthermia experienced by mystics, their body temperatures were sometimes much higher. Padre Pio had a fever of 118 degrees at one point. The fire of love was also experienced by other saints: Catherine of Genoa, John of the Cross, Teresa of Ávila, Stanislaus Kostka, Angela of Foligno, Margaret Mary Alacoque, Elizabeth of the Trinity, and Mary Magdalene de' Pazzi. The last one mentioned lived at the end of the sixteenth century, and burning with love for God, in order to cool her body at least a little, she reportedly had to frequently soak her hands in cold water and apply cold, wet handkerchiefs to her breasts.

Love for God could also manifest itself in anatomical changes, including expansion of the heart and displacement of the ribs, posthumously discovered marks, or wounds on the heart. Such phenomena were described in the lives of Philip Neri, Paul of the Cross, and Gemma Galgani. Sometimes it was associated with another gift from God: transverberation.

TRANSVERBERATION

Transverberation is a mystical piercing of the heart (manifesting itself often with a simple wound in the side and the heart) inflicted with a burning "spear of love." It is a reference to the wound inflicted on Christ on the Cross.

Padre Pio suffered a transverberation while hearing confessions of children. It was preceded by a vision of a "seraphic" attack, during which a "heavenly person" (Jesus) mystically pierced his soul with an invisible flaming dagger. Although the injury to his soul was invisible, Padre Pio suffered great pain for two days, and a wound appeared on his side. In his case, transverberation was a kind of spiritual preparation for receiving

St. Maria Maddalena de' Pazzi.

Ecstasy of St. Teresa.

St. Gemma Galgani.

stigmata. Transverberation was experienced by saints such as Francis of Assisi, Philip Neri, Catherine of Siena, Mary of Jesus Crucified, and many other mystics.

St. Teresa of Ávila wrote about a beautiful angel appearing to her imperceptibly, who, as it seemed to her, stabbed her several times in the heart with a long fiery lance. The Carmelite moaned with great pain, and yet she felt "excessive tenderness combined with it." She said, "No earthly joy can give such complete satisfaction," and that her "soul will not be content with anything less than God."

STIGMATA

Stigmata is one of the most frequently described gifts God has given His saints. It must be admitted that both visible (bleeding) and invisible (bloodless) stigmata are extremely painful gifts. Through the stigmata, mystics relive in their own bodies the painful Passion of Jesus, feeling the wounds of the Crucified One (wounds of the hands, legs, injuries caused by the thorns, and so on). Some mystics received stigmata only on Fridays, the day on which Jesus was crucified (in that case they usually lasted until Sunday), and some received them only during Holy Week. Painful wounds could persist for even longer periods, or they could spontaneously open and close for short periods of time. Although in many cases attempts have been made to argue that stigmata are the result of autosuggestion, hysteria, or simple deception, these accusations have mostly proven unfounded, and the phenomenon of stigmata is still without scientific explanation.

The first saint who received the stigmata in the history of the Church was St. Francis

▲ *The* Ecstasy of St. Teresa*—sculpture in white marble by Gianlorenzo Bernini (1652). Left transept of St. Mary of Victory in Rome.*

▼ *St. Padre Pio.*

of Assisi. He received them in 1224 when, two years before his death, he performed a forty-day fast and prayed on the slope of La Verna. He then experienced a vision of the seraph, who was hanging on the cross above him in the air. At one point, nail marks began to appear on his arms and legs, just as he had seen shortly before on the crucified Jesus.

His arms and legs looked as if they had been pierced with nails in the very center (the heads of the nails were visible on the inside of his hands and on the top of his feet, and their sharp ends were on the opposite side). The heads of the nails on the arms and legs were round and black, and their sharp ends were oblong and curved, protruding from the body. According to his brother and hagiographer Thomas of Celano, "The saint's right side was as if pierced by a lance. He had a red scar that often imbrued and splashed his tunic and pants with holy blood."

From then until now, the number of saints with stigmata is estimated at between three and four hundred. This noble group included great saints and blesseds, such as Catherine of Siena, Catherine of Genoa, Mary Magdalene de' Pazzi, Anne Catherine Emmerich, Gemma Galgani, and the Servants of God Teresa Neumann and Marthe Robin. Invisible stigmata were given to St. Mary Magdalene de' Pazzi, St. Teresa of Ávila, and St. Faustina Kowalska, among others.

The world's most famous stigmatist was, of course, St. Padre Pio. He first received the stigmata as a young priest in September 1910, at the age of 23. At the time, the Lord heard his plea and made them invisible. From that moment on, Padre Pio suffered pain in those places for eight years, and for several years he experienced the Passion by being crowned with thorns and scourged once a week. The visible stigmata

St. Francis receiving the Stigmata *by Giotto.*

appeared on his body on September 20, 1918, when he was praying in front of the cross in the presbytery of the church after celebrating Mass. The carving of the stigmata was the work of a mysterious person who, according to Padre Pio's account, "had his hands, feet, and side dripping with blood." All indications suggest that the person was Christ Himself. "The vision of the person moved away, and I noticed that his hands, feet, and side were pierced and blood was dripping from them," Padre Pio later recounted. The wounds were very painful and bled profusely—almost half a glass of blood flowed out of them daily. Padre Pio's stigmata were thoroughly examined and documented, ruling out any fraud. Equally intriguing was the fact that, two years before the Capuchin's death, the stigmata had begun to heal, and the last wound disappeared at the very moment of his death.

It is worth mentioning that Padre Pio had another very painful wound on his right shoulder ("the mystical mark of carrying the cross"). However, this wound was only discovered after his death (although Padre Pio told John Paul II of its existence). Indeed, a circular bloodstain about ten centimeters in diameter was found on Padre Pio's shirt.

In the case of Padre Pio, the stigmata, the piercing of the heart, and the wound on the shoulder were external signs of complete union with Christ, a transformative union, a mystical marriage, a mystical transformation into Christ crucified.

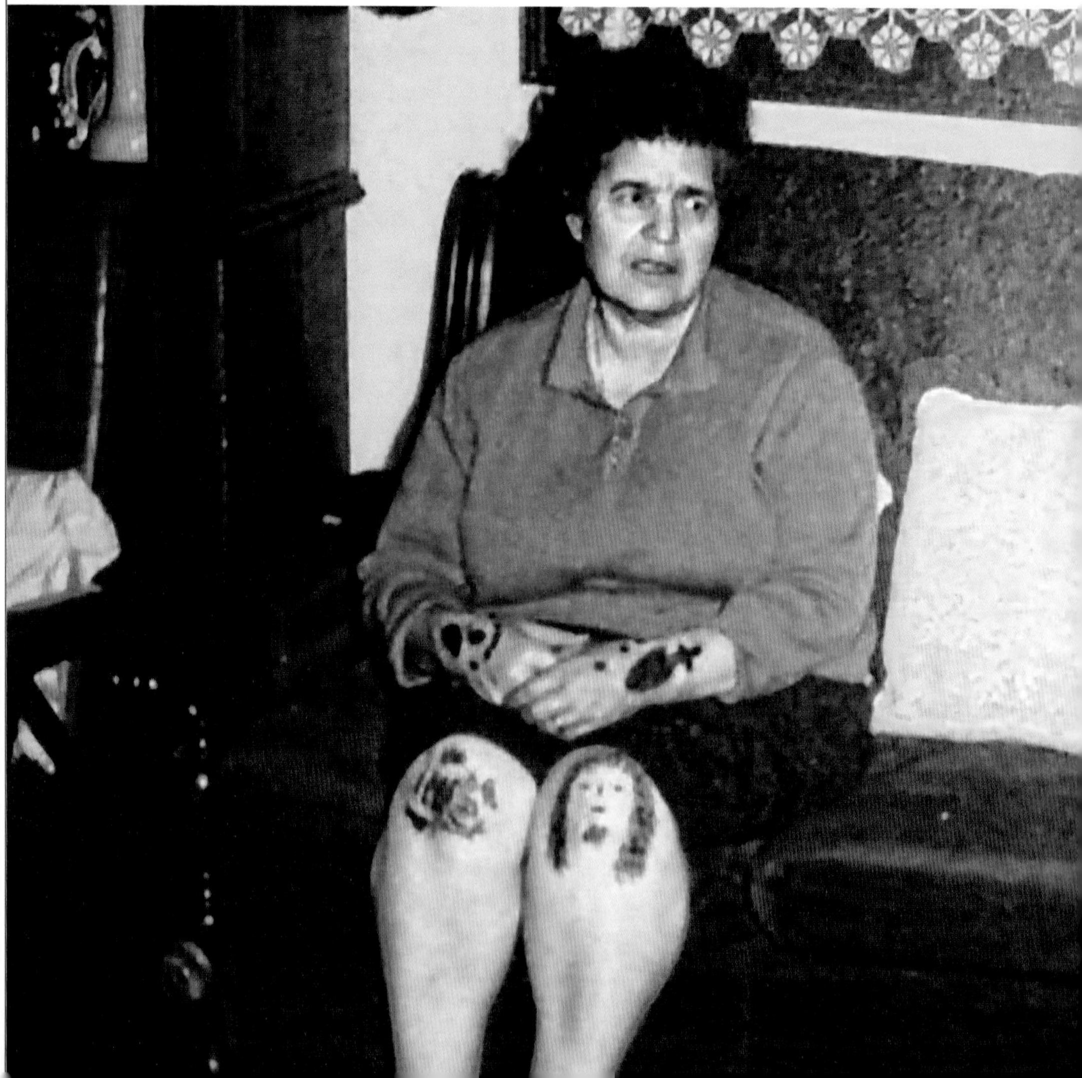

➢ *Images, Christian symbols, and inscriptions appeared on Natuzza Evolo's body, clothes, and sheets.*

An unusual phenomenon that repeated itself 182 times was observed in the case of a Portuguese mystic, paralyzed and bedridden Bl. Alexandrina Maria da Costa. From October 3, 1938, to March 24, 1942, every Friday, Alexandrina surprisingly regained power in her paralyzed limbs and got out of bed to experience with body and soul all the stages of the Passion except death from noon to three in the afternoon.

HEMOGRAPHY

Fortunata Natuzza Evolo from Italy, who died in 2009 with a reputation for holiness, was a stigmatic and also a good wife and mother of five children. In her case, one thing extremely peculiar was the so-called hemography (that is, images, Christian symbols, and inscriptions) that formed from her blood on her body, on her clothes, and on sheets and pillows on which she slept. On one such occasion, the phrase "Gloria del Sacro Cuore di Gesu" (Glory to the Sacred Heart of Jesus) appeared on a handkerchief that had been used to wipe her face.

Some saints received from God a mystical ring, that is, the visible sign of "mystical marriage" with God on their finger (Mary Magdalene de' Pazzi and Marthe Robin, among others, had such a mark).

LEVITATION

Levitation is another of God's gifts that has been observed in the lives of many saints. It is associated with love for God and usually happens in moments of mystical ecstasy. During such raptures, saints such as Teresa of Ávila, Francis of Assisi, Dominic de Guzmán, Ignatius of Loyola, Francis Xavier, Philip Neri, John of the Cross, Peter of Alcántara, Joseph Benedict Cottolengo, and Mary of Jesus Crucified, among others, floated above the earth.

However, the most studied and widely attested levitations were those experienced by St. Joseph of Cupertino, who lived in Italy in the seventeenth century.

His extraordinary flights began when he became a priest and settled at the monastery in Grotella. They almost always accompanied his ecstasies. About seventy instances of St. Joseph's levitations were observed in Grotella (and there were more than a hundred in total). One of the earliest "flights" was associated with him helping to raise a thirty-five-foot cross during the construction of the Stations of the Cross in Grotella. At the time, St. Joseph was about sixty yards from the place where a group of friars struggled with the cross's weight. As his biographers testified, at one point Joseph grabbed that heavy cross, flew into the air with it, placed it where it was supposed to be, and then started floating near one of the arms of the cross

An Italian who lived in the seventeenth century, Joseph of Cupertino was known for his mystical flights. Today he is the patron saint of pilots.

Sometimes the bodies of slender and small saints became remarkably heavy, as if they were made of lead. In the case of St. Bernadette Soubirous, this was observed during the apparitions in Lourdes.

to adore the Crucified One. The saint's flights were investigated by the Inquisition, and its members saw them with their own eyes: during the celebration of Mass, Joseph suddenly shouted, spread his arms, floated in the air, and then collapsed on the altar. After a moment of adoration, he shouted once again, began floating in the air, and then landed in the nave of the church. Then he began rotating on his knees. "Blessed Virgin Mary!" he repeated while spinning. The friar experienced ecstasy and also floated above the ground in front of Pope Urban VIII. "In the name of holy obedience, come down," the Holy Father then ordered him, and Joseph obediently descended to the floor. He also levitated in Assisi, where the friars wanted to hide him from the world. When he was there, he once ascended to a height of about fifty-six feet to kiss the image of the Mother of God placed over the loggia above the altar. The levitations of St. Joseph of Cupertino even contributed to the conversion of two Lutherans observing them: the Duke of Saxony J. F. Brunswick and nobleman Heinrich Blum.

BODIES HEAVY AS IF THEY WERE "MADE OF LEAD"

In the case of levitation, it was a matter of overcoming the force of gravity, but in the lives of the saints, the opposite phenomenon was also observed. Sometimes the bodies of slender and small saints became remarkably heavy, as if they were made of lead, and no force could move them. This happened, for example, in the case of Mary Magdalene de' Pazzi or St. Bernadette Soubirous (this was observed during the apparitions in Lourdes).

There were also saints showing, in moments of ecstasy, a strange insensitivity to fire (a kind of inflammability). This was experienced by St. Catherine of Siena, St. Francis of Paola, and the already mentioned Bernadette Soubirous.

FAST TRAVEL

Some saints received the gift of traveling extremely fast through space. One such "express journey" was experienced by St. Anthony of Padua, when he set out from Italy to Lisbon to rescue his father, who had been wrongly accused of murder. He had barely begun his journey on foot when he discovered that he already reached Portugal. Lightning-fast movement was also attributed to St. Mary Magdalene de' Pazzi.

HERE AND THERE

Bilocation was also connected to traveling through time and space, as some saints were seen in two (or more!) different places at the same time.

The bilocations of St. Alphonsus Liguori and St. Padre Pio are very famous and were frequently described. The gift of bilocation was also given to other saints: Anthony of Padua, Joseph of Cupertino, Lidwina of Schiedam, Marthe Robin, and Martin de Porres (although he never left Lima, he was seen in Africa, where he consoled slaves, in Mexico, and in China and Japan, where he supported missionaries serving there).

One especially remarkable case of bilocation was that of the Spanish nun and mystic, Mary of Jesus of Ágreda. She lived in the seventeenth century and was the author of the famous *Mystical City of God*, based on the apparitions she had experienced. While staying (physically) in Ágreda, Mary of Jesus at the same time was seen in North America. With the help of bilocation she was "transported by the aid of the angels" between 1622 and 1625 to evangelize in the New World. She was there at least five hundred times! The evangelization carried out by her among the Jumano Indians, an indigenous tribe living in what was then New Spain (today the state of New Mexico), prepared the foundation for the activities of later missionaries.

The Spanish friars were the first to arrive in the area to convert the local people. They were extremely surprised that the native people themselves were asking them to be baptized, that they already knew something about Jesus and had already been prepared to accept the Faith by the mysterious "lady in blue." During the missionaries' search for this "lady," it was found that she was Mary of Jesus, wearing a white habit with a blue mantle. She wrote about this unusual experience of being "carried by angels" herself. These bilocations were even investigated and authenticated by the Inquisition.

Unusual journeys in time and space were also made by Bl. Anne Catherine Emmerich. While always staying in her bed in Germany, the saint was mystically "transported" to biblical times, seeing and describing scenes from the Old and New Testament with extraordinary clearness and detail. Many other saints were mystically transported to other realms — to Purgatory, Heaven, or Hell.

SEEING THE FUTURE, KNOWLEDGE OF THE HEART, SPEAKING IN TONGUES

Among the extraordinary charisms and mystical gifts of God, we can also include supernatural knowledge of events happening at the same time in distant places (St. Albert the Great supposedly obtained information about the death of St. Thomas Aquinas in this way) and the gift of prophecy. Many saints had the

◄ *Bl. Anne Catherine Emmerich experienced unusual travels through time and space.*

▼ *While staying (physically) in Ágreda, at the same time Mary of Jesus was seen in North America.*

➤ *The angelic choirs seen by St. Hildegard. Hildegard conveyed to the Church the knowledge revealed to her by God concerning, among other things, the hidden truths and mysteries of the Faith, the sacraments, and the order of the cosmos.*

⮝ *St. Albert the Great had supernatural knowledge of events taking place in distant lands.*

latter ability: Hildegard of Bingen, Martin de Porres, Padre Pio, Catherine Labouré, and Joan of Arc, among others. St. John Bosco became famous for his so-called "prophetic dreams," which after some time came true in the real world.

Special forms of sight included the so-called "sense of holiness"—the supernatural ability to discern consecrated things, such as whether the Eucharist was consecrated or not (St. Lidwina of Schiedam, for example, had this ability), whether a person is a priest or only pretends to be one, and whether a particular relic is authentic. When a priest came to the Servant of God Marthe Robin one day, she sensed that he did not have the consecrated Host in his closed ciborium.

Such a gift might be related to the so-called discernment of spirits, and it must be admitted that a similar sense is also demonstrated by people possessed by an evil spirit, unerringly recognizing and avoiding objects that have been consecrated.

Equally intriguing is the extraordinary ability demonstrated by some saints to know the hearts, consciences, and even thoughts of people. This ability has been demonstrated by Philip Neri, Jean Marie Vianney, Padre Pio, and Martin de Porres, among others.

Some saints contacted other people through their guardian angels (Gemma Galgani, among others). To those who could not come to see him in person, Padre Pio suggested, "Send me your guardian angel," and then he gave them spiritual advice through their angels.

Remaining in special connection with spiritual reality, many saints contacted souls suffering in Purgatory (souls from Purgatory came to Padre Pio and St. Faustina Kowalska, among others). An unusual charism is glossolalia (speaking in unfamiliar tongues or, more generally, knowing languages one never learned).

Padre Pio spoke Mandarin, English, and various African languages, despite never formally learning any of these. Not only that, but people would say that a guardian angel helped Padre Pio read and write back letters in languages he didn't know.

PROFESSORS APPOINTED BY GOD

Some saints received the gift of knowledge—supernatural enlightenment of an intellectual, cognitive nature, received usually during revelations and ecstasies.

This is how German Benedictine nun and visionary St. Hildegard of Bingen (1098–1179) described what happened when she was forty-two years old:

> *The heavens opened and a blinding light of an extraordinary brightness poured into my mind. It also kindled a fire in my heart, which did not burn my breasts but warmed them ... and suddenly, I grasped the meaning of the books, that is, the Psalter, the Gospels, and the other books of the Old and New Testaments.*[1]

A little later, during successive visions, the Lord God ordered her three times to write down everything she saw and heard, which eventually resulted in many remarkable works in which Hildegard conveyed to the Church the knowledge revealed to her by God concerning, among other things, the hidden truths and mysteries of the Faith, the sacraments, and the order of the cosmos.

In the case of the Peruvian Dominican friar, St. Martin de Porres, the gift of knowledge manifested itself in a slightly different way: having no academic background at all, he was able to explain the most complicated theological issues clearly and simply to his young confreres, demonstrating his knowledge of St. Thomas Aquinas's *Summa Theologiae* and the Bible, although he had never actually read either of those works.

The gift of prophecy was given to St. Hildegard of Bingen.

God also gave both Hildegard of Bingen and Martin de Porres the gift of counsel. They advised the great hierarchs of the Church or dignitaries of the state on the most diverse matters, and their advice was always well considered.

MIRACULOUS LIGHT, BEAUTIFUL SCENT

In the case of some saints, the phenomenon of luminescence was observed—that is, an unusual heavenly light accompanied them. Sometimes it was so intense that it illuminated the entire cell in which the saint was praying or experiencing mystical ecstasy. Sometimes it took a more subtle shape of a halo around the head or an unusually illuminated face (one may see here a reference to the mystery of the

Transfiguration of the Lord and how our bodies will look after the resurrection).

Some saints emanated heavenly light while celebrating Mass or preaching. Luminescence was described in the case of saints such as Philip Neri, Ignatius of Loyola, Francis de Sales, Charles Borromeo, Angela of Foligno, Lidwina of Schiedam, and André Bessette of Montreal.

English journalist Malcolm Muggeridge reported on a strange, inexplicable, subtle light he had observed in a home for the destitute people run by Mother Teresa in Calcutta (see page 106 for more on this).

The phenomenon of miraculous scent is related to that of miraculous light. The odor of sanctity is, in many cases, a reality, not a metaphorical figure. Indeed, a wonderful, heavenly scent emanated from many of the saints. The odor of sanctity was sometimes a sign of the saint's supernatural presence. The scent of violets or, less often, lavender, roses, or incense was present in the farthest corners of the world and felt by those summoning St. Padre Pio, or even just looking at his image.

➢ *St. Polycarp.*

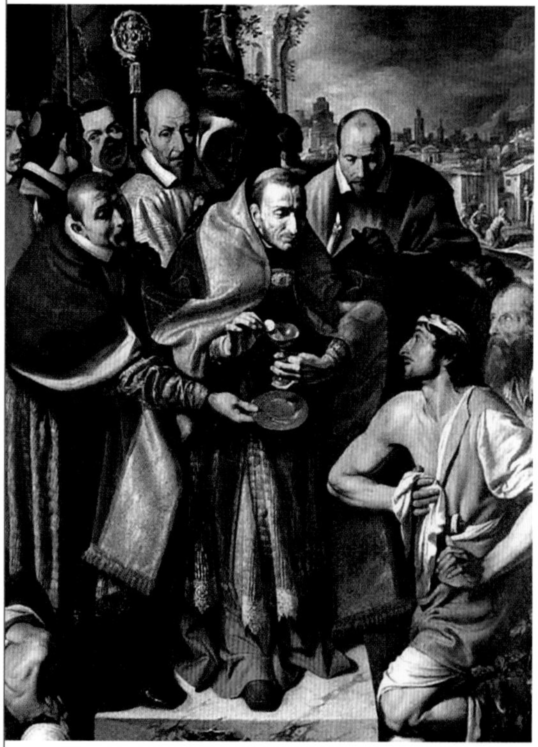

➢ *In the case of St. Charles Borromeo, people observed the phenomenon of luminescence, or the unusual heavenly light accompanying him.*

The Capuchin saint himself called this scent "the consolation of children," and with it, he communicated and still communicates to people that he is there for them and knows about their problems and troubles.

In the case of Padre Pio and several other saints, "fragrant blood" has also been noted. Blood, especially in a state of decomposition, does not emit a pleasant scent. However, it was different in the case of Padre Pio. A beautiful scent accompanied him from the moment he received the stigmata. His wounds, with fresh blood dripping from them, as well as old blood covering the bandages, smelled like sweet perfume.

One can read about the miraculous odor of sanctity in the descriptions of the life of St. Polycarp of Smyrna, St. Teresa of Ávila, St. Thomas Aquinas, and Mary of Jesus Crucified.

RESURRECTED BODIES

However, the odor of sanctity, or *odor sanctitatis*, usually appeared only after the saint's death and was related to his or her dead body (many bodies of saints, instead of emitting a smell of decay, even many days after death or after exhumation, emitted a pleasant scent).

Many other phenomena were observed after the saints' deaths; one of them was the lack of rigor mortis. Hundreds of cases like this, of bodies not decomposing for a long time or at all, have been described, including a few bodies stored in unfavorable conditions (St. Charbel and St. Bernadette are noteworthy here). Sometimes, only some of the body parts did not decompose (the tongue of St. Anthony of Padua, the heart of St. Bridget of Sweden, the hand of St. Stephen I of Hungary).

In some cases, even stranger phenomena were noted. Even many years after death, fresh blood flowed from the bodies of some saints (e.g., St. Catherine, St. Patricia, and St. Cyriacus of Rome), or other fluid oozed from them (St. Nicholas, St. Walburga, St. Felix of Cantalice, St. Mary Magdalene de' Pazzi, St. Charbel, and St. Gerard Majella).

VISIONS, REVELATIONS, LOCUTIONS

Some of the well-known mystical phenomena experienced by saints are, of course, ecstasies, visions, and revelations, and sometimes they even materialized in some way and became visible to others (e.g., many saints were seen holding the baby Jesus in their arms, drinking blood from the side of the body of Jesus, etc.). A great number of saints experienced locutions—that is, they heard voices coming from outside or in their heads, souls, and hearts (usually from God). Some also received the gift of tears.

St. Catherine of Bologna.

ENDNOTES

1 Flanagan, Sabina. *Hildegard of Bingen: A Visionary Life*. New York: Routledge, 1998.

▲ *Coronation ceremony during a wedding in the Syro-Malabar rite.*

▼ *The front and interior of St. Francis Church in Kochi, India.*

TO SUFFER WITH JOY

St. Alphonsa of the Immaculate Conception

This Sister of St. Clare from India was the first native Indian woman (the second ever person of that nationality) and the first representative of the Syro-Malabar Church to become a Catholic saint. As a young girl, she was miraculously healed, and after her death, she contributed to many different healings. The two miracles that made her a saint might be categorized as "orthopedic."

Her birth was provoked by a snake. Her mother delivered her prematurely after the trauma she experienced when a reptile wrapped itself around her abdomen while she was sleeping. This happened in Kudamaloor in India. Like her parents, Joseph and Maria Puthukari, members of an old, noble, but relatively poor family, Anna Muttathupadathu belonged to the Syro-Malabar Rite Catholic Church. Annakutty (as she was affectionately called) had four siblings and was the youngest in the family.

DETERMINATION REWARDED

Orphaned by her mother when she was just three months old, she was initially raised by her grandparents, before being taken in by her aunt—an affectionate, but domineering, strict, and exigent woman. Her methods of childrearing were more like animal taming. She cut the child off from the outside world, constantly yelled at her, and severely punished her for minor indiscretions (such as eating fruit, which her aunt considered harmful to her health). The girl endured this with humility and patience, out of love for Christ.

ST. ALPHONSA

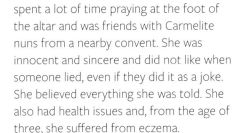

She was indeed very religious from a very young age. Even when she was just five years old, she led evening prayers at which the whole family gathered. Also later, she spent a lot of time praying at the foot of the altar and was friends with Carmelite nuns from a nearby convent. She was innocent and sincere and did not like when someone lied, even if they did it as a joke. She believed everything she was told. She also had health issues and, from the age of three, she suffered from eczema.

As a seven-year-old, after her First Communion, she offered herself to Christ and was already showing signs of a religious vocation. She was fascinated by St. Thérèse of Lisieux, whose biography she read. (Alphonsa was called the Little Flower of Kerala, just as Thérèse of the Child Jesus was called the Little Flower.) When they wanted to marry her off against her wishes, Annakutty prayed that she would be allowed to remain a virgin. Supposedly wishing that no one would want her, she put her foot in a container where the chaff was burned after the harvest and burned her foot (other sources suggest it was an unfortunate accident). She suffered immensely because of this. It took a long time for her to start walking normally, and she never regained complete mobility.

Finally recognizing the girl's determination, her aunt gave her permission to enter the Poor Clares' college in Bharananganam in 1927 (but even then she was pestered by suitors). In 1928 she became a postulant, taking the name Alphonsa of the Immaculate Conception in honor of St. Alphonsus Liguori. Two years later, she donned the habit.

MIRACULOUSLY HEALED

Between 1930 and 1935, Alphonsa was seriously ill and experienced much spiritual suffering. She taught in an elementary school for a year, but due to her poor health, she was "relegated" to the role of teacher's aide, parish catechist, and finally, because of her beautiful handwriting, secretary. On August 12, 1935, she became a novice. In August 1936 she took her solemn vows, and around this time she suffered, among other things, profuse bleeding from her nose and eyes and purulent wounds on her legs. Her health deteriorated so much that they expected the worst.

INDIA

Kuriakose Elias Chavara, a saint of the Syro-Malabar Catholic Church.

The Mar Thoma Sleeva (St. Thomas Cross) is a symbol associated with the Christians of Kerala, India.

Pilgrims from all over India visit St. Alphonsa's tomb, which is in the cemetery chapel of St. Mary's Forane Church, Bharananganam.

Had it not been for help from Heaven, the worst may have come. Alphonsa, along with the other Poor Clares, began praying a novena to the Indian Carmelite, Servant of God Kuriakose Elias Chavara (now a saint). The sisters asked for her healing, and soon their prayers were heard. After praying the novena in December 1936, Alphonsa returned to good health.

THE ROYAL WAY OF THE CROSS

However, she enjoyed her recovery only briefly. Her health suddenly began to deteriorate once more. One illness followed another. In mid-June 1939, Annakutty successively suffered from typhoid fever, pneumonia (twice), and nervous shock when, one October night in 1940, she saw a thief in her room (after this trauma, she had amnesia and was unable to read and write for a year). However, she fell in love with all her illnesses, for suffering made her more like Christ, her Betrothed, to whom she gave herself completely. She wanted these sufferings; she wanted to go through life along "the royal way of the cross." For her, suffering was love, and love was suffering. She offered herself to God out of love for Jesus. "I want to suffer with joy. It seems to me that my Divine Spouse wants to fulfill this desire," she claimed.

From 1945 onward, she experienced even more suffering. A cancerous tumor turned the last year of her life into a continuous agony.

She did not complain or lament, although health problems caused her to experience convulsions and vomit up to forty times a day. She then offered up her suffering to God and considered a day without suffering to be a day wasted. Despite her illnesses, she did not become antisocial or unpleasant to others; indeed, quite the opposite. She endured suffering with calmness, a smile on her face, and good humor. Full of humility, she considered herself to be worth less than a bug.

Urging the novices and sisters to accept suffering, she quoted Jesus' words about the seed that must die in order to bear abundant fruit; she spoke to them about the grapes that must be crushed in order to produce wine, which can later be turned into the Blood of Christ.

EFFECTIVE INTERCESSOR

When her health allowed her, she would go to the chapel to attend Mass. After Communion, she looked as if she was shining with an otherworldly light. People admired the way she prayed. The nuns testified that she looked as if she was in another world during prayer.

Her wonderful, sweet character and personal charisma made people turn to her for advice on all their problems, both physical and spiritual. She loved children very much and felt especially happy in their presence. Even during her lifetime, she was credited with extraordinary power to obtain miracles and graces from God. Children and teenagers asked her to pray for them before their exams and believed that she was extremely effective in helping them get good grades.

REVERED BY MANY

She died with a smile of innocence on her face just after midnight on July 28, 1946. She was thirty-six. Almost immediately, she began to be revered by many, mainly due to the students of the school run by the Poor Clares, on whom she made a great impression.

People who began to pray through her intercession experienced many miracles and received many graces. Not only Catholics, but also Hindus and Muslims began to make pilgrimages to her tomb at the monastery in Bharananganam near Kottayam, where she lived and died.

It is for this reason that India's first Syro-Malabar saint can today be an advocate of peace and reconciliation in a country where the persecution of Christians remains an ineradicable problem.

Indian postal stamp, which was issued in 1996.

The modest chapel in Bharananganam.

A SPECIALIST IN ORTHOPEDICS

The Indian Poor Clare, popularly known as Alphonsamma, was already healing people during her lifetime and continues to heal them after death. If we investigate the miracles that led to her canonization, it seems that, having a problem with her own foot, she became a kind of specialist in orthopedic healing.

The first such miracle approved by the Holy See was experienced by Thomas Abraham Athiyalil. He was born in 1947 with deformed feet, having a condition known as clubfoot. Clubfoot (*talipes equinovarus*) is a congenital defect, a deformity involving a fixed flexion of the sole of the foot and adduction of the forefoot. Both feet point inward, and it is impossible to walk on them. His parents drove him to doctors all over the state of Kerala and went to specialists in other Indian states, but to no avail.

Tomb of St. Alphonsa, Bharananganam, Kerala, India.

He was already eleven years old when his aunt advised his parents to let him go with relatives to the tomb of God's servant Sr. Alphonsa in Bharananganam. They listened. Upon reaching the tomb, they prayed fervently on their knees all day. The next day the boy's legs were already healthy. This fact was later confirmed by a famous Indian orthopedic specialist. A priest from the church in Ponkunnam, the family parish of the boy, held a thanksgiving service. The healed Athiyalil became a great venerator of his benefactress and an ardent promoter of her cult.

Little Ginil, the second son of a married couple, Shaji and Lissa, who reside in Mannarppara, also had serious orthopedic problems. The little boy was born in May 1998 in a hospital in Ettumanoor. After birth, it was discovered that both his legs were twisted from the knees down; he too had clubfoot. The doctors treating the boy said that in this case, it was necessary to use the Ponseti method and put both legs in a cast. It was to be removed after six days (according to this method, the cast is changed every week for a period of six to nine weeks; each time the gradually straightening feet are rearranged, and then, over the next few years, the results of this therapy are preserved with the use of special interconnected shoes).

The legs were put in plaster, but soon the child began to be very restless and cried constantly. The cast was removed and it turned out that it could not be put on again, as an infection had developed under it. Doctors then decided that there was nothing more they could do. Six months later, another orthopedist recommended surgery, the second method used for such cases. They decided not to do it, having heard of cases where such surgery had failed to produce the desired results.

Instead, the distraught couple went to their parish priest, and he advised them

Tomb of St. Alphonsa.

to seek help from Alphonsa. He said that they should start praying a novena and fast for their intention. They did so, and what's more, on November 13, 1999, they took the child to the tomb of the Indian Poor Clare in Bharananganam. Upon arrival, they laid him on the grave slab and, with tears in their eyes, prayed for two and a half hours, asking Bl. Alphonsa to take care of him. After praying, they returned to the relative's house.

As they were praying the Rosary in the evening at home, something unusual happened. Ginil, who had been lying by their side, and who until then had been moving around dragging his deformed and inert limbs behind him, suddenly stood up and, on straight, completely healed legs, holding his parents' hands, walked effortlessly across the room. What's more, he said "It's Annannamma (Alphonsa) that helped me walk," while pointing at a picture of the blessed. His parents shed tears of joy.

In mid-November, they told the vice postulator, Fr. Francis Vadakkel, about the miracle. Then the miracle was investigated and confirmed by five Indian doctors and in 2006 by five doctors who gathered at the Vatican. The fact of the matter is that many of the hundreds of described graces asked through the intercession of St. Alphonsa are specifically related to the straightening of orthopedic deformities.

Sr. Alphonsa's beatification (as well as that of Kuriakose Elias Chavara, a Carmelite through whose intercession she herself experienced healing) was celebrated by John Paul II on July 9, 1986, in Kottayam, during his apostolic journey to India. She was canonized on October 12, 2008, by Benedict XVI.

CHILDREN FIRST

Online one may find many miracles obtained through the intercession of St. Alphonsa written by people who prayed at her tomb on the day of her canonization or drank water with sand from her tomb. Many of these healings concern children.

Among others, there was a four-and-a-half-year-old boy who regained his sight after visiting her tomb, a toddler who suffered from encephalitis, a boy who had a congenital deformity of both lower limbs, a girl with epilepsy, and a teenager with asthma.

There have also been many healings from illnesses that were impossible to treat through medical means, such as leg ulcers, limb deformities, nodules, psoriasis, cardiomyopathy, spinal problems, and dengue fever. People often thank the saint for helping them pass difficult exams or conceive longed-for offspring, as well.

Chapel of the Tomb of St. Alphonsa.

POPE OF THE BLESSED SACRAMENT AND OF ORDINARY PEOPLE

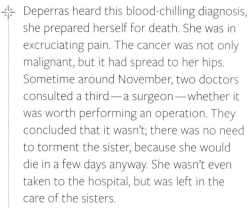

St. Pius X

The "Pope of the Blessed Sacrament," Pius X (1835–1914) was elevated to the canon of saints thanks to a Visitandine, a Poor Clare, a Grey Nun, and a lawyer from Naples. The last two cases of miraculous healings involved extraordinary visions.

Pius X has been called the "Pope of the Blessed Sacrament" because he was especially devoted to it. He promoted frequent reception of Holy Communion (at the same time urging frequent trips to the confessional, ensuring its worthy reception).

"Holy Father Pius X, heal her!" pleaded the Visitation Sisters from Dole, France, when, in July 1928, one of their sisters was diagnosed with cancer of the femur. From the moment sixty-nine-year-old Marie-Françoise Deperras heard this blood-chilling diagnosis, she prepared herself for death. She was in excruciating pain. The cancer was not only malignant, but it had spread to her hips. Sometime around November, two doctors consulted a third—a surgeon—whether it was worth performing an operation. They concluded that it wasn't; there was no need to torment the sister, because she would die in a few days anyway. She wasn't even taken to the hospital, but was left in the care of the sisters.

Sr. Germana, the infirmary nun who was caring for the sick sister, then grasped at one last resort. She brought *ex corporis* relics of Pius X, pinned them on the chest of Sr. Marie-Françoise, and encouraged the entire order to start a novena to Pius X for the nun's healing. At first, it didn't look good at all, and perhaps it was God's will that the sister die. On the other hand, Jesus encourages persistent praying: "Ask and it will be given to you," He said. And when the first novena didn't help, and the sister's condition deteriorated instead of improving, the Visitandines, not losing faith and trust that Christ's viceroy, who died in the opinion of holiness, would intercede with God for the desired grace, started the second novena.

Pius X ruled the entire Church from 1903 to 1914. Simple, humble, and poor, the great Vicar of Christ—still considering himself a simple country pastor—wanted to "renew everything in Christ" through the Immaculate Virgin.

Thanks to his humble origins, he always understood the needs of ordinary families and was always generous.

On the morning of December 7, Sr. Marie-Françoise, bedridden, felt a strange surge of strength; suddenly she was no longer in pain. She tried to sit up in the bed, and she found that she was able to move her sick leg without a problem. She was astonished. Only a few hours earlier, a doctor examined her and stated that death could come at any time. But instead of death, she experienced a new life.

It was incredible. It was a miracle. And what is more, it was medically unexplainable. This was confirmed by all three doctors, and then by eminent scientists from the hospital in Lyon, and—in 1950—by Vatican experts. What happed next with Sr. Marie-Françoise? Well, nothing out of the ordinary—she got out of bed as if nothing had occurred and, grateful to God and his servant Pius X for a miracle, returned to her normal communal activities.

A TUMOR THE SIZE OF AN ORANGE

Another healing took place in Italy. For years Sr. Benedetta de Maria—a Poor Clare from the convent in Boves—suffered from abdominal pain, even before she entered the order. Her condition deteriorated significantly when she was forty-three years old. She was in severe pain. A malignant tumor was found on the left side of her abdomen. It was big, very big—the size of an orange. The sister's imminent death was predicted. Given that the Servant of God Pius X was held in high regard in the monastery, it was he who was called on to save the sick woman. At the end of February 1938, the community began a novena for her healing. The doctor didn't believe in such methods and wanted to operate on Sr. Benedetta, but neither she nor her sisters would agree to it.

Relics of St. Pius X.

As pope, he reorganized the Roman Curia, initiated the writing of a new code of canon law, supported biblical studies, and focused on proper training of future clerics, the disciplining of clergy, catechesis, and sacred music.

The episcopal consecration of Giacomo della Chiesa (center)—the future Pope Benedict XV—by Pius X (left).

During the novena, in the early morning hours of February 27, Sr. Benedetta, with living faith, invoked Pius, took a piece of his relics *ex indumentis*, put it in her mouth, and swallowed it. And then something incredible happened: the pain was gone instantly, and the huge tumor disappeared. Sr. Benedetta, overjoyed, got up and went to the choir, where the other nuns were praying at that time. The sisters rubbed their eyes in astonishment, and she cried from joy. She fell to her knees and, lost in a prayer of gratitude, knelt for nearly an hour. Soon after, the doctor came. He was speechless when they told him what happened. But, after examining her, he found that the tumor had indeed disappeared. "Doctor," the mother of the community told him, "you still have such little faith." "There is no need to believe here," the doctor replied. "Here, we are faced with an undeniable, extraordinary fact." Sr. Benedetta, healed and happy, returned to her duties as portress, and the miracle itself was carefully examined and later approved as the second miracle needed for the beatification of Pius X.

➤ *He was most likely the last pope to travel by carriage.*

➤ *Giuseppe was the second of ten children, the son of simple parents from the village of Riese.*

SITTING NEXT TO THE BED DRESSED IN WHITE

Pius X was beatified in June 1951, and just a month later the first of the two miracles needed for his canonization occurred.

Sixty-nine-year-old Francesco Belsani, a lawyer from Naples, had serious lung problems. On July 7, 1951, he felt unwell and didn't know what was happening to him: his head started pounding, his muscles ached, and he developed a high fever that reached 102 degrees.

It looked like he had the flu, but it wasn't going away. In late July, a medical professor visited him and instructed him to thoroughly sweat it out and prescribed penicillin injections. This didn't help, so streptomycin injections were used. Once again, it was all in vain. The fever persisted and the sick man's condition only worsened.

In addition to the already-mentioned symptoms, he developed a cough with foul-smelling sputum that was difficult to expectorate, as well as hiccups, which were said to be dangerous for his heart. The fever rose to 104 degrees. The lawyer was barely alive. Perhaps it started with an infection, but the much more serious problem turned out to be an abscess in the right lung.

Seeing that all medical measures were ineffective, prayers began for the intercession of Pius X; at the same time, three important doctors conducted three case conferences. In the end, the medics decided to operate on Belsani, but the operation, due to his serious condition, proved impossible to carry out. It was thought that the man could die at any moment.

One night, at the end of August (most likely, as we read in the decree *super miraculo*, it was August 25) the lawyer's suffering—fever, cough, and hiccups—reached its apogee. The sick man again resorted to prayer, invoking Bl. Pius X for help, and his wife placed an image taken from the tomb of the newly beatified pope on his chest.

And then something very strange happened. The sick man suddenly saw him! He sat next to his bed, dressed in white, and then placed his hand on him and said, "Tomorrow you won't have any more hiccups." In an instant, the man felt much better—he stopped coughing, his fever went away, and his condition was improving hour by hour. On the morning of August 27, the patient who was expected to die was completely healthy, which—with great relief—was later confirmed by all the doctors examining him.

STAND UP AND WALK!

The figure dressed in white also appeared to a woman with meningitis. Thirty-three-year-old Sr. Maria Luisa, a Grey Sister from Palermo who worked at the local hospital, saw the figure dressed in white moments before being miraculously healed.

In December 1951, the sister became ill. Her head hurt. In early January, she had to stay in bed, and that's when it started: her fingers started to turn blue, her eyesight was blurry, and she felt her arms and legs becoming stiff as logs. She was completely unable to move them. A doctor then performed a lumbar puncture. The sister's condition, however, continued to deteriorate. Her head was exploding from the pain, her neck ached, and her entire spine had become stiff. She and the other sisters began to invoke Bl. Pius X for help. An image of the pope was placed on her head. A second picture was put on her nightstand. Next to it was a kerosene lamp. The first novena brought no improvement. The second one didn't, either. A third was started. The illness still didn't let up. It had been torturing the nun for almost two months. In mid-February, the sister's suffering intensified, and many thought she might die.

Relics of St. Pius in a glass coffin in the Vatican.

On February 14, the sister was suffering greatly, and in the afternoon she fell into a peaceful sleep. At four in the morning, she was awakened by a sister, who had come to give her another shot of streptomycin. Maria Luisa went back to sleep, and suddenly, on the wardrobe in front of her bed, she saw a monstrance with the Most Holy Eucharist; she asked the Lord to help her get up so that she could adore Him, when suddenly she heard a voice: "Stand up and walk." At the foot of the bed, she saw a figure dressed in white with a covered head, a figure she had seen on other sleepless nights.

Maria Luisa then got up and, bewildered and not knowing what was happening to her, went to the chapel. "I've been healed," she declared to the surprised nuns. She was telling the truth. Her superior, her sisters, the hospital chaplain, and her three doctors all agreed.

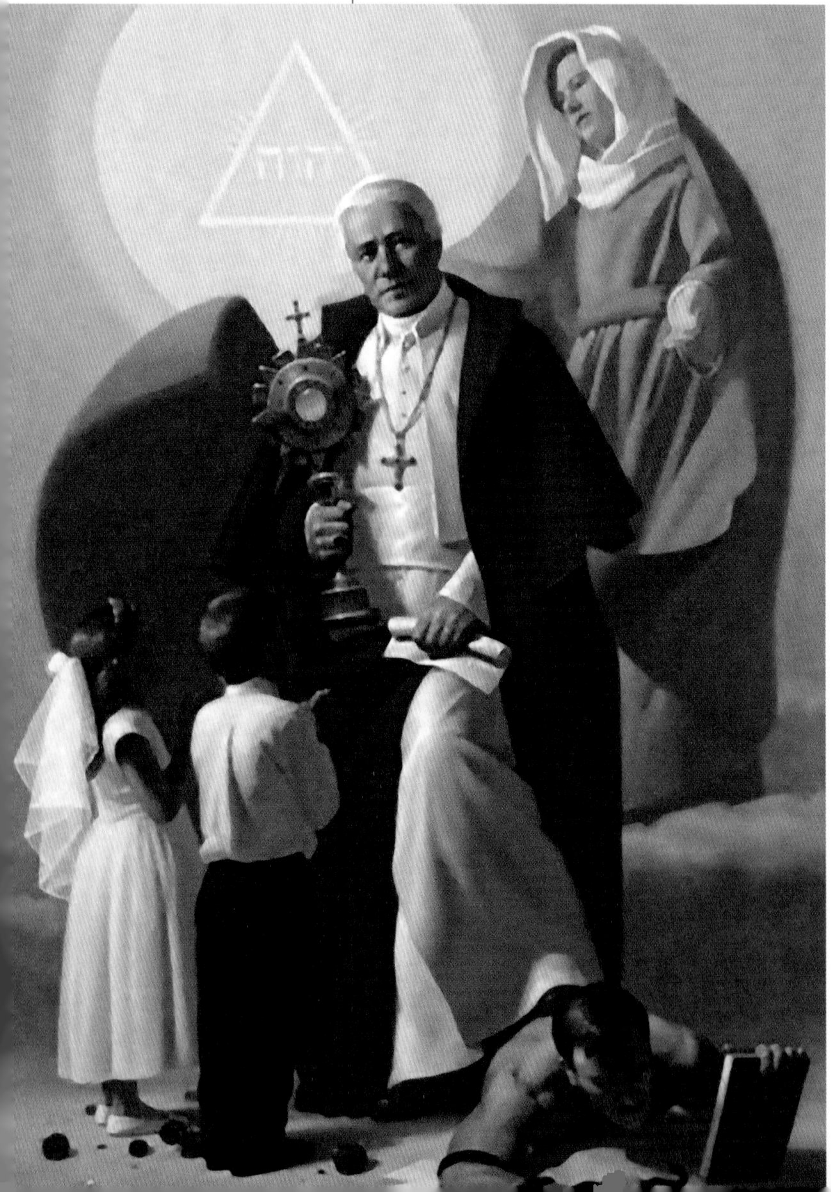

RESTORE ALL THINGS IN CHRIST

All four people mentioned above were healed thanks to the intervention of Pius X, born Giuseppe Melchiorre Sarto. The son of simple parents from Riese, Giuseppe was the second of ten children. His father was a postman and city courier, and his mother was a dressmaker. He had to walk six miles to school each day, often barefoot. Sometimes he would go hungry. Because of this, he understood the needs of ordinary families well, and he was always generous to the poor. He was able to study at the seminary in Padua thanks to a scholarship funded by the patriarchate of Venice. At the age of twenty-three, he was ordained. He was an extraordinarily pious, zealous priest and pastor, a protector of children and the poor, and a wonderful preacher. For these reasons, after staying in several small parishes, he was transferred to higher and higher positions in the local diocesan curia. Finally, Pope Leo XIII made him bishop of Mantua, and in 1892 cardinal and patriarch of Venice.

He ruled the entire Church from 1903 to 1914. Simple, humble, and poor, the great Vicar of Christ—still considering himself a simple country pastor—wanted to "renew everything in Christ" through the Immaculate Virgin.

As pope, he reorganized the Roman Curia, initiated the writing of a new code of canon law, supported biblical studies, and focused on proper training of future clerics, the disciplining of clergy, catechesis, and sacred music.

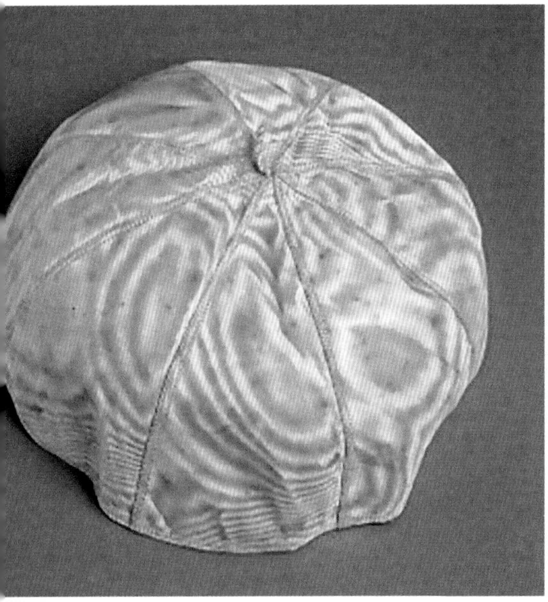

The Holy Father's *zucchetto.*

Pius X defended the Church against secular governments, socialism, Freemasonry, liberalism, and other dangerous trends that were causing it to rot from within. He condemned theological modernism, calling it "the synthesis of all heresies," and attacked relativism as well. He wrote an important encyclical *Pascendi Dominici Gregis* ("Feeding the Lord's Flock") on this subject, and members of the clergy were required to take a special oath against Modernism. Many criticized him for this, but it was good for the Church. He also wrote a simple, popular catechism, presented in a question-and-answer format, which is still valued to this day. Before his death, the pope tried to prevent the outbreak of World War I, but the secular authorities of the feuding countries didn't want to listen to him; he remained alone in his efforts in many of his other Church actions and reforms.

HOLY DURING HIS LIFETIME

Pius X has been called the "Pope of the Blessed Sacrament" because he was especially devoted to it. He promoted frequent reception of Holy Communion (at the same time urging frequent trips to the confessional, ensuring its worthy reception). He said that "Holy communion is the shortest and safest way to Heaven." He was also known as the "Pope of Children" because he liked them very much, understood them well, and introduced early Holy Communion for them, significantly lowering the age of admittance. Above all, people saw him as a pope of the common man. He showed this many times. Once, when he was a bishop, his secretary informed him that a countess, a pastor, and a poor woman were waiting for him. He, of course, met with the poor woman first. "She most likely has children at home and is in a rush," he explained.

During his lifetime, it was said that God gave him the power to perform miracles. Fr. W. Zaleski, in a biographical note about Pius X, writes the following:

> *"Please heal me!" pleaded a man with a paralyzed arm. "May God heal you, my son," the pope replied, touching his arm. The paralyzed man immediately regained control. A little Irish girl's head was completely covered with sores. The pope put his hand on the bandages, and the little girl cried out: "Mother, I'm healed!" A pilgrim from Germany, who was blind, wanted to reach the pope. The Holy Father touched him and he cried: "I see, I see again, Holy Father." A nun had cancer on her hand. "Please make a cross," she pleaded. The pope bent down, made the sign of the cross, and the sick woman recovered immediately. When enthusiastic crowds shouted, "Il Santo!" the pope corrected them with a smile: "My children, you pronounce my name wrong. My name is not Santo, but Sarto."*

These are but a few of the many cases of healing attributed to St. Pius X.

Pius X defended the Church against secular governments, socialism, Freemasonry, liberalism, and other dangerous trends that were causing it to rot from within. He condemned theological modernism, calling it "the synthesis of all heresies," and attacked relativism as well. He wrote an important encyclical Pascendi Dominici Gregis *("Feeding the Lord's Flock") on this subject, and members of the clergy were required to take a special oath against modernism.*

1739–1822

THE FIRST BRAZILIAN SAINT: PRESCRIBING PILLS OF FAITH

St. Frei Galvão

Anthony of St. Anne Galvão, a Franciscan commonly known in Brazil as Frei Galvão, was the first Brazilian-born saint of the Church. God blessed Frei Galvão with many gifts, and he treated the sick who came to him not only with medicine but also with special paper "pills."

▲ *The Marian shrine in Aparecida, halfway between the big Brazilian cities of Rio de Janeiro and São Paulo.*

➤ *Statue of Frei Galvão from the Mosteiro da Luz.*

A group of men once came to Frei Galvão and asked him to go to a remote farm where a young man had been suffering for days with severe kidney stones. The man's pain was so intense that his friends feared he would die. Frei Galvão, however, was unable to go with them due to his monastic obligations. So God inspired him with a rather original idea. He sat down at a table, took out a piece of paper and a pen, and began to write a sentence in Latin—a fragment from the Little Office of the Blessed Virgin Mary: *Post partum Virgo inviolata permansisti; Dei Genitrix, intercede pro nobis* ("After childbirth a pure Virgin thou didst remain; O Mother of God, intercede for us"). Then he rolled the paper so that it resembled a medicine pill, blessed it, gave it to the surprised men, and told them to bring it to the sick man. "Let the sick man receive it during prayer, and let him say the Rosary," he said. The men did as they were told.

Soon news of the suffering man's miraculous healing began to spread. The sick man had suddenly and unexpectedly recovered after saying the prayers and consuming the pill. His kidney stones

Wall portrait of Frei Galvão on azulejo ceramic tile.

passed, his pain disappeared, and he quickly returned to full health.

Shortly afterward, a distraught man came to Frei Galvão to ask for prayer and some medicine for his wife, who was having difficulty with childbirth. She had already been in labor for many hours, and both mother and child were in danger of dying. Frei Galvão made three of the same "pills" as before and gave them to the husband with the same instructions. They worked again. The woman said the prayers and swallowed the pills, her problems disappeared, and a healthy baby was born.

Thus was the birth of the famous "pills" of Frei Galvão.

The Franciscan later gave his "recipe" to the nuns under his care, and to this day, nuns, friars, and volunteers make and distribute them to the faithful. The people say a novena and swallow the pills on the first, fifth, and ninth days of their prayers, asking the whole time for the intercession of the saint. As a result, people still experience miracles that they credit to the prayers of Frei Galvão and to his holy medicine. Many have been healed from diseases, couples struggling with infertility have been able to conceive children, and women in high-risk pregnancies or with difficult childbirths have found relief. Of course, the pills themselves have no healing powers—the true healing power comes from God in accordance with His will—but like various blessed cords, medallions, and other sacramentals and relics, the pills help prepare us to receive God's grace, and they act in tandem with fervent prayer. Frei Galvão's pills have also played an important role in his beatification and canonization.

Relics of Frei Galvão from the parish of Guaratinguetá.

A FOUR-YEAR-OLD SAVED FROM DEATH

At the end of May 1990, four-year-old Daniella Cristina da Silva was admitted to the Emílio Ribas Hospital in São Paulo with late-stage Hepatitis A. The four-year-old immediately landed in the intensive care unit, and her condition continued to worsen. She had severe liver and kidney failure and was bleeding from her nose and gums, and her abdomen began to swell with fluid. The child also had to fight off bronchitis, pharyngitis, and two other infections.

Daniella was close to death, and no one thought she would survive. When she began having problems with circulation and breathing, her doctor recognized that only prayer could help—only a miracle could save her. And so the child's parents and Daniella's deeply religious aunt decided to entrust the girl to Frei Galvão. They procured his famous pills, gave them to her, and began the novena to the servant of God. The first water-soaked pill was given to the child in secret while she was still in intensive care. Meanwhile, family friends, neighbors, and nuns from the Mosteiro da Luz (Monastery of Light) prayed to God for a miracle.

Daniella's health improved almost immediately. Finally, on June 21, she was discharged from the hospital.

Her attending physician, who was questioned during Frei Galvão's beatification process, had no doubts that Daniella's recovery was due to divine intervention. Thanks to God and the intercession of Frei Galvão, the little girl could play, run, and live again.

HIGH-RISK PREGNANCY

Sandra Grossi De Almeida was a Chemistry teacher in Brazil who had suffered three spontaneous miscarriages due to a misshapen, bicornuate uterus with two very small and asymmetrical cavities. These anatomical defects meant that Sandra could not carry a pregnancy to full term, as her child would not have enough space to grow and develop.

Believing she would never give birth, Sandra and her husband adopted a girl, but in May 1999, she became pregnant again. Her obstetrician-gynecologist tried to save her baby by temporarily sewing her cervix closed (a standard procedure done in similar cases), but this procedure had no impact on Sandra's anatomical problems, and her doctors warned her that it was very unlikely she would carry the pregnancy to term.

A miscarriage was almost certain, and Sandra was warned that another miscarriage could also lead to a hemorrhage. And so not only the life of the child but also the mother's life was at risk.

Sandra, together with her family, called on Frei Galvão for help. From the second month of her pregnancy, Sandra prayed novena after novena and took Frei Galvão's famous pills. And her prayers were answered! While her doctors predicted that Sandra's pregnancy would not last beyond her fifth month, it instead progressed normally, without any bleeding or pain, until her third trimester.

In November 1999, Sandra was hospitalized at the Pro Matre Maternity

The canonization ceremony of Frei Galvão was celebrated by Benedict XVI in the Campo de Marte Airport in São Paulo, Brazil.

Altar of the Church of Frei Galvão in the Mosteiro da Luz.

Tomb of Brother Galvão inside the Mosteiro da Luz.

Hospital in São Paulo for observation. On December 11, when Sandra was thirty-two weeks pregnant, her amniotic sac ruptured. Her doctors performed a caesarean section immediately, and a little boy was born weighing about four pounds and measuring about seventeen inches long. Unfortunately, he had severe respiratory problems; his lungs were still undeveloped, and he needed to be intubated. But the family continued to pray, and Frei Galvão came to the rescue again. A day later, Sandra's son, Enzo, was disconnected from the ventilator: he was breathing on his own. To his doctors' surprise, a week later, he was completely healthy, and he and his mother were able to return home.

The obstetrician-gynecologist who took care of Sandra during her pregnancy and childbirth firmly believed that her successful pregnancy and birth was a miracle and that medicine and procedures alone could not have achieved such a successful outcome. Yet we probably never would have known about this miracle if Frei Galvão himself had not asked Sandra to share it. In early 2004, more than four years after Enzo's birth, Sandra began to suffer from insomnia. One night, she heard a voice that said, "You know how to ask, but you forget to reveal." She got out of bed and realized that Frei Galvão was asking her to spread the news of her miracle, as she owed him an unpaid debt of gratitude. And so that same night, Sandra wrote a letter in which she told the sisters of Mosteiro da Luz in São Paulo her story. Her insomnia passed, and her letter eventually reached the postulator for the canonization of Frei Galvão, Sr. Célia B. Cadorin. The miracle that had been innocently hidden under a bushel had finally seen the light of day. Her story was reviewed by seven doctors from Brazil and five from the Vatican, who confirmed it as a miracle.

PILLS OF FAITH

The website of Casa de Frei Galvão in Guaratinguetá features other testimonies of graces received through the intercession of Frei Galvão. Among many miracles attributed to the pills and intercession of Frei Galvão, the website tells of twins born in Chile as a result of the intercession of the saint, a young man from the village of Barra do Tatu who was healed from a heart murmur, and an eleven-year-old girl named Gabriela who recovered after a life-threatening appendectomy.

These pills—and their accompanying novena to Frei Galvão—have spread

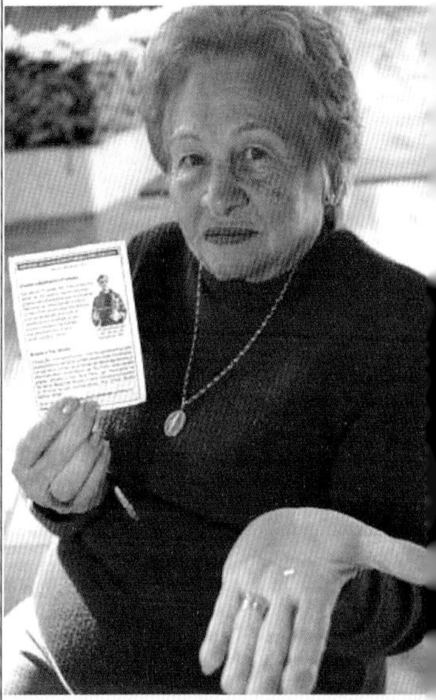

Frei Galvão's "pills"—with their accompanying novena to Frei Galvão—have spread around the world.

➤ *Bird's eye view of Guaratinguetá, in the state of São Paulo in Brazil.*

⮝ *Antonio Galvão de França, a boy from a good, Catholic family, was one of ten children. He was born in Guaratinguetá, near the prominent Shrine of Aparecida, halfway between the big Brazilian cities of Rio de Janeiro and São Paulo.*

⮝ *Mosteiro da Luz.*

around the world, even as far as New Zealand. A participant of World Youth Day brought Frei Galvão's pills to her friend who was suffering from sarcoma and whom the doctors had given only a year to live. Even though the woman wasn't Catholic, she agreed to take the pills and say the novena. A prayer group also prayed for her recovery, and her cancer disappeared.

CONFESSOR, BUILDER, CHARISMATIC

Who was this extraordinary Brazilian "divine apothecary" and "miracle worker"? Antonio Galvão de França, a boy from a good, Catholic, and wealthy merchant family, was one of ten children. He was born in Guaratinguetá, near the prominent Shrine of Aparecida, halfway between the big Brazilian cities of Rio de Janeiro and São Paulo. His parents, despite being wealthy, set him and his siblings a good example of generosity toward the poor.

Antonio and his brother attended a school run by the Jesuits, and Antonio thought he wanted to become a Jesuit. But at the age of twenty-one, and at the advice of his father, who was a Franciscan tertiary, he joined the order of the Discalced Franciscans, also known as Alcantarines. A year later, he was ordained a priest.

Antonio was greatly devoted to St. Anne, especially after the death of his young mother, and so he added her name to his religious name, Anthony of St. Anne. Yet he loved Mary above all, and he entrusted himself completely to her, consecrating himself as her son and eternal slave. On November 9, 1766, he recorded his fidelity to Mary in a special document signed in his own blood. He also vowed to defend her title of "Immaculate Conception," which was not yet an official dogma of the Church.

After his studies, Anthony became a preacher, porter, and, above all, valued confessor. He strictly observed the

monastic rule, and when he was called to the sick, he went on foot even to very remote places. The tall, strong, and handsome friar was practically associated with the St. Francis Friary in São Paulo his entire life, and the residents of this city, who lovingly referred to him simply as Frei Galvão, could not do without him.

From 1769–1770, he served as confessor to the Recollection of St. Teresa in São Paulo, a hermitage of women dedicated to St. Teresa of Ávila who lived in commune but not under religious vows. There he met the devout mystic and visionary Sr. Helena Maria of the Holy Spirit, who had had a vision of Jesus in which He asked her to establish a new Recollect house and a new congregation. Her vision was recognized as valid, and Frei Galvão got involved in her house's formation, despite prohibition from civil authorities. At last, the two officially established a new community of pious women under the patronage of Our Lady of the Conception of Divine Providence. Frei Galvão wrote the statutes for the community, looked after its development, and, after construction was completed and Sr. Helena had died, became its director and spiritual guardian.

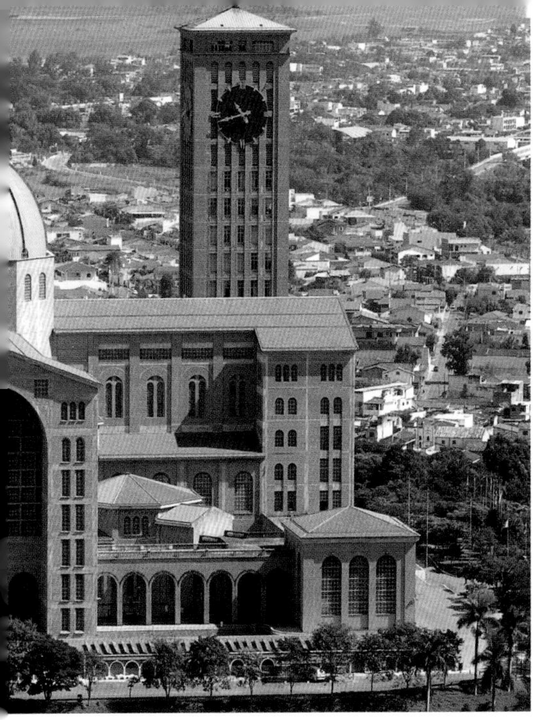

Pious girls who wanted to join the community kept coming, so the thirty-five-year-old Franciscan built another house over the next fourteen years. He then personally designed an adjoining church for the house and oversaw its construction over another fourteen years. The church was finally dedicated on the feast of the Assumption of the Blessed Virgin Mary in 1802. Eventually, the church along with the retreat house was transformed into a monastery, Mosteiro da Luz, and in 1929, the community founded by Frei Galvão was incorporated into the Congregation of the Immaculate Conception.

Frei Galvão was above all an extraordinary, devout friar who was full of love for God and others. In addition to caring for nuns, he took special care of the poor, the sick, the afflicted, and slaves (slavery was abolished in Brazil in 1888). He generously distributed the alms he received from the rich in order to help the poor and those in debt to moneylenders. But he was always very discreet in his generosity: his beneficiaries didn't find out who had helped them until much later.

God also blessed Frei Galvão with supernatural gifts and charismata such as telepathy, clairvoyance, prophecy, levitation, and bilocation. These miraculous phenomena usually occurred when he had to help the sick and the dying. He also seemed to have extraordinary healing powers, and he not only cared for the physical wellbeing of those who asked for his help but for their spiritual wellbeing as well.

At the end of his life, Frei Galvão was allowed to move to the Mosteiro da Luz, where he continued to serve the faithful by praying and giving spiritual lessons to the sisters. When he died at the age of eighty-three, crowds of faithful who considered him a saint and a miracle worker began to make pilgrimages to his resting place, Mosteiro da Luz. His holiness was of course officially confirmed by the Church through his beatification in 1997 by Pope St. John Paul II and canonization ten years later by Benedict XVI.

The home where Frei Galvão was born in the historic city of Guaratinguetá. A museum dedicated to him now operates there.

▼ *An image of St. Joseph Vaz (1720).*

▼ *Portrait depicting "Joseph Vaz, secular cleric from the Congregation of the Oratory of St. Philip Neri."*

MISSIONARY TO SRI LANKA

St. Joseph Vaz

Most countries today have their own saint. The small island of Sri Lanka (once known as Ceylon) has one: the missionary Joseph Vaz (1651–1711)—priest of the Oratory of St. Philip Neri. He is often called the Apostle of Ceylon. He was recognized as a saint after the miraculous healing of a woman who had difficulty with childbirth. The boy who was born then became a priest.

Compared to the massive size of nearby India, Sri Lanka is a tiny Asian country. The island has an area of twenty-five thousand square miles. Tradition says that Christianity was established here by St. Thomas the Apostle and, according to historical sources, a small group of Christians must have lived there as early as the fifth century (the first Christian artifacts found on the island date back to this time). We don't know what happened to the Christians there for the next thousand years, until the discovery of the island by Europeans. In 1505, Lourenço de Almeida's Portuguese fleet landed on the shores of the island. It was then—with the king's permission—that the first chapel was built and the first Holy Mass was celebrated. Soon after, the first Catholic missionaries began to arrive on the island. According to the Church's Statistical Yearbook from 2017, there are less than 1.6 million Catholics there today, representing less than eight percent of the total population, most of whom are Theravada Buddhists. Catholics are now the largest group of Christians on the island (eighty percent of Sri Lankan Christians are Catholics).

REVIVING THE CHURCH IN CEYLON

St. Joseph Vaz was born near Goa, a large city on the southwestern coast of India, which was then the capital of the Portuguese Empire in the East. His parents were of the Konkani Brahmin caste but were devout Catholics. He studied under the Jesuits and Dominicans, and in 1676 he became a priest. Being a great devotee of the Virgin Mary, a year after his ordination, he offered himself to her as a perpetual slave, which he confirmed when he wrote the "Letter of Captivity" (this happened even before this form of devotion began to be propagated by St. Louis-Marie de Montfort). In 1686 he founded the Oratory of St. Philip Neri in Goa, and a year later, he decided to go as a missionary to the Buddhist island of Ceylon. At that time, the situation for Catholics in Ceylon was worsening dramatically.

Fr. Vaz knew that after the Dutch, who were Reformed Protestants, took over part of the island and expelled the Portuguese living in Ceylon, Catholics faced

persecution, and for half a century, there were no priests who could serve them (residence on the island by Catholic clergy was forbidden under penalty of death).

MIRACLE OF THE RAIN

The priest wanted to save the local church. Pursued and persecuted by the Dutch, he miraculously managed to escape them, remaining in Ceylon for twenty-four years. He traveled, disguised as a beggar or as a regular worker, lived in poverty, and administered the sacraments in secret. What helped him hide so effectively was that he blended in with the residents of Ceylon with his dark complexion. He later established his base inland, in the Buddhist kingdom of Kandy, which was independent from Dutch rule and recognized the freedom of religion. But soon after arriving, in 1692, he was arrested. He was accused of being a spy and imprisoned. Four years later he miraculously regained his freedom. Literally!

It happened when his prayers were answered. After unsuccessful earlier attempts by Buddhist monks, at the request of the Buddhist king of Kandy Vimaladharmasurya II, Fr. Vaz prayed for a downpour and ended a severe drought (supposedly it had not rained for seven years). The king not only released him, but also gave him his personal protection. What's more, he allowed several other Oratorians from Goa to join Fr. Vaz in 1696, creating a Catholic mission in Ceylon.

SAMMANA SWAMI

People gave Fr. Vaz the name "Sammana Swami," meaning the angelic wiseman. He undertook long missionary journeys, baptized, served the sick selflessly and with great care during the smallpox epidemic, built places of worship, and translated the catechism and many prayers into Tamil, the local language.

Fr. Vaz died in Kandy at the age of fifty-nine, being a true caretaker of Catholics in Ceylon. Thanks to his heroic priestly ministry, they not only managed to survive the Protestant storm, but—after many conversions—they grew in strength. The apostle of Ceylon left a huge legacy: about seventy-five thousand Catholics, many catechists, fifteen churches, and four hundred chapels.

The Basilica of Bom Jesus built by the Jesuits in 1605.

Family home of St. Joseph Vaz, Sancoale, Goa.

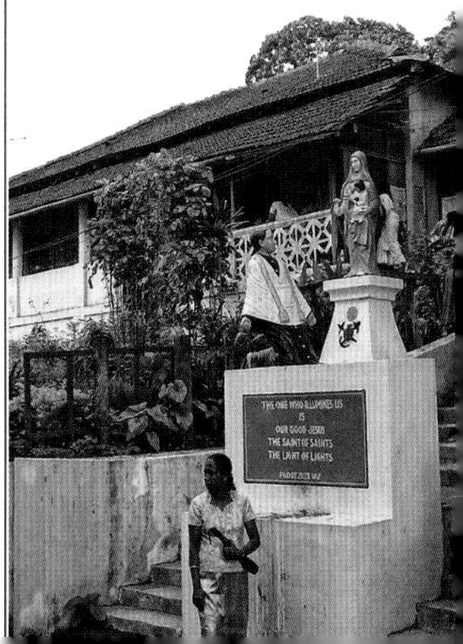

UNDER THE PROTECTION OF JESUS AND MARY

During his lifetime, he was credited with the ability to perform miracles. A woman saw Fr. Vaz with a child in his arms, and when she came closer, she noticed that the child was Jesus Himself.

There have been reports of the Mother of God appearing, protecting the missionary from soldiers searching for him in Colombo; of a miraculous crossing through a flooded river; and of an attack by a wild elephant that miraculously fell to the ground when Fr. Vaz, holding a rosary in his hand, began praying.

"MIRACLE SON"

One miracle was enough for Fr. Joseph Vaz to become a saint. This is because Pope Francis decided that for his canonization a second miracle would not be necessary (although since 1997, documentation of twenty-one alleged miracles were sent to the Vatican). Only one miraculous healing used in the beatification process was officially approved by the Church. It was the healing of Quiteria Carmela da Piedade Noronha e Costa from a hemorrhage during childbirth, which happened in 1938 in Panaji in the Indian state of Goa.

The sudden and complete cessation of a hemorrhage, followed by a premature birth, was considered to be an event that could not be scientifically explained. Fr. Cosma Jose Vaz Costa, Quiteria's son, described the event in detail in the *The Times of India* and in *The Catholic Register*. He said that his mother had serious problems related to subsequent pregnancies. Her first son was premature and lived only six hours. The next pregnancy was at risk due to hemorrhage, but this time the child—a girl—survived. Unfortunately, the next three pregnancies, during which there were hemorrhages, always ended in miscarriages in the fourth month of pregnancy. The Costas, however, dreamed of a having a son.

A young priest in the family who was serving in Cortalim and Sancoale suggested that the woman pray to God through the intercession of God's servant, Fr. Vaz.

In April 1938, Mrs. Costa became pregnant for the sixth time. The unpleasant scenario seemed to repeat itself; in the fourth month she suffered a massive hemorrhage. In spite of that, the pregnancy was maintained. Even so, the doctors at the hospital in Bangalore predicted another miscarriage. Mrs. Quiteria didn't even want to think about it. She placed all her trust in God and continued to ask for His help through the intercession of

View of the Temple of the Sacred Tooth Relic and the Queen's Bath in Kandy, Sri Lanka.

View of the Ella Gap overlooking the southern coast of Sri Lanka.

Fr. Joseph Vaz. She spent two weeks in the hospital. After that, she was sent home and recommended bed rest.

Lying down must have caused a great deal of pain for her because—reassured by the fact that nothing happened for a long time—she got up twice. Each time, she suffered from a massive hemorrhage. Luckily, she was able to avoid a miscarriage. The second time, Fr. Costa's mother was admitted to the hospital in Panaji. The head of the maternity ward, who examined her, stated that there was only a one percent chance that he would manage to keep either the mother or the baby alive. He was ninety-nine percent certain that both of them would die. On November 26, the woman, seven months pregnant, was unconscious and still bleeding, and doctors decided a caesarean section would be necessary. It was scheduled for November 28, but due to her condition, the woman was not expected to survive it. Devout friends placed an image of God's servant, Joseph Vaz, on her stomach and prayed for a miracle. A day later, the hemorrhage suddenly stopped, and on the same day, in the evening, the woman began to feel labor pains. She gave birth normally, by the forces of nature, although she lost consciousness again from the pain. Fr. Costa said that when his mother regained consciousness, the doctor told her that Fr. Joseph Vaz had performed a great miracle and saved her. And what's more, despite the complications, she gave birth to a healthy boy. The thirty-three-year-old mother survived, but what about the premature newborn? After the birth, this issue remained to be seen. The boy was as small as a frog. That's what was said about him. He weighed only two pounds and could fit in the palm of a hand. Incubators didn't yet exist. The baby's life was in danger, and he was quickly baptized in the hospital by a Catholic nurse. He survived, and even more remarkably, he didn't have any health problems related to his premature birth.

"I was brought up with the conviction that my mother and I should have died," wrote Fr. Cosma Jose Vaz Costa, history professor at the Pilar Seminary. "We both survived, thanks to Fr. Joseph Vaz. My mother accepted my vocation to the priesthood as a reward for her sufferings, though everyone else opposed it because I was the only son. When I left home in 1956 to enter the Pilar Seminary, my mother blessed me 'to be a missionary like Fr. Joseph Vaz.'" Fr. Cosma's mother lived to the ripe old age of ninety-four, and before her death she lived to see the beatification of her patron, Fr. Joseph Vaz. Her son, "thanks to God and Joseph Vaz," was ordained a priest in 1966. Fr. Cosma Jose Vaz Costa—the "miracle son," the "godson" of Fr. Vaz—was, among other things, a professor of Church history at the Pilar Seminary in Goa and founded a museum that catalogues nearly two millennia of Church history in India. He also made an important discovery. He found a cross of St. Thomas with Pahlavi script dating back to the seventh century in Agassaim, Goa, proving definitively that Christianity existed in Goa before the arrival of the Portuguese. The priest attended both the beatification ceremony of Fr. Vaz in January 1995 and his canonization in 2014.

Se Cathedral in Old Goa, a Roman Catholic cathedral dedicated to St. Catherine.

Joseph Vaz was appointed Vicar General of Ceylon and proceeded with organizing a missionary structure with a base in Kandy. From there, he set out on his missionary journeys in Ceylon.

A DUTCH PRIEST IN IRELAND

St. Charles of Mount Argus

Crowds of Irish people flocked to this Dutch Passionist priest in hopes of regaining their spiritual and physical health. Charles of Mount Argus spent most of his life in an Irish monastery, and he became a saint after he healed two Dutch compatriots.

➤ Fr. Charles loved to pray for people and bless them. Over time, many of the faithful began to seek his blessings.

➤ Memorial Cross at Harold's Cross Park in Harold's Cross, a suburb of Dublin, Ireland.

"I DO NOT ASK FOR MIRACLES"

Octavia Spaetgens Verheggen, a Dutchwoman, had known the life story of the Servant of God Fr. Charles of St. Andrew for many years. She had even visited his family home in Munstergeleen, but she had no special devotion to him.

Mrs. Verheggen had been widowed shortly after marriage, and she had learned how to manage on her own. She had a very sober view of the world, and—as Fr. Xavier, the vice postulator of the beatification process for Fr. Charles's cause, wrote—"she was given to action more than to contemplation." She didn't pray novenas, and she didn't recite any special prayers, but she zealously fulfilled every precept required by the Church.

Mrs. Verheggen also supported a charity under the patronage of St. Clement Hofbauer, and in 1951, at the age of seventy-one, she made a pilgrimage to Lourdes. It was there that she began to experience abdominal issues, including pain, nausea, and vomiting. A month later, she spiked a fever. When she returned to the

Netherlands on August 25, she underwent gallbladder removal surgery, but she experienced several complications after the surgery. She finally left the hospital in Maastricht on October 29.

In December, however, Mrs. Verheggen was hospitalized again. She had a high fever and still complained of severe abdominal pain. Her doctors examined her and discovered that she had a large tumor. Due to her age and physical condition, however, another operation was not an option, and there was nothing the doctors could do to remove the tumor. Mrs. Verheggen received morphine injections to ease her pain, but her condition continued to deteriorate. She felt unbearable pain and couldn't eat.

On January 19, 1952, Mrs. Verheggen returned home from the hospital and prepared herself to die. As she suffered from hunger and pain, one of her relatives, who was also related to Fr. Charles of St. Andrew, visited and suggested that she pray a novena to the Servant of God asking him for help in regaining her health. The sick woman had no intention of taking this advice at first, but one winter's night (either January 22 or February 15–16 of 1952), she began to pray.

As she prayed, Mrs. Verheggen heard "a voice from Heaven" urging her to call him for help. She said a prayer—not a prayer from the novena, but one in her own words. Her prayer was later recorded by the postulators of Fr. Charles's beatification process and then published in the biography *A Knight of the Crucified: Father Charles of Mount Argus*: "Fr. Charles, you still need to perform a miracle for your beatification. Help me in my distress. I do not ask for miracles, only stop this retching, as once it ceases I shall feel cured. But I am ready to die if the good Lord so desires."

She prayed fervently but with complete submission to God's will. She later stated that it was impossible to describe what she felt in those moments.

The next day, Mrs. Verheggen, who had had no appetite since the beginning of her illness and had even had difficulty looking at food, suddenly smelled food her daughter was cooking and, to her surprise, felt hungry! She asked her daughter for some food, and she was served a plate with a little purée, gravy, and apple jelly. She ate all of the food with a hearty appetite and without any nausea.

The next day, Mrs. Verheggen ate bacon, eggs, and sauerkraut. Two days later, she ate an exceptionally strong-smelling red herring

and an egg without any issue. Two weeks later, her doctors discovered that the tumor in her abdomen had shrunk significantly, and one week later, it was no longer even palpable.

In August 1952, Mrs. Verheggen underwent further examinations and had an X-ray taken. The results were absolutely amazing: the tumor had disappeared without a trace, and the woman was completely healed. Her surgeon, a Protestant, also confirmed that she was in perfect health. None of her doctors could explain how or why her tumor disappeared and her symptoms ceased. It was a miracle.

Mrs. Verheggen lived another twenty-two years. She died of natural causes at the venerable age of ninety-four.

PERSEVERANCE AND TRUST

On March 29, 1999, seventy-three-year-old Dolf Dormans from Munstergeleen, a village in the Netherlands that was also the birthplace of Bl. Charles, was admitted to the hospital in Sittard. He was diagnosed with a bowel obstruction, severe inflammation of the small intestine, and peritonitis (an infection of peritoneum, the membrane that covers the abdominal organs) caused by a ruptured appendix.

Market square in Sittard, in the Netherlands.

On March 29, 1999, seventy-three-year-old Dolf Dormans from Munstergeleen was admitted to the hospital in Sittard.

Half-timbered farmhouse in the center of Munstergeleen, where the miraculously healed Dolf Dormans came from.

The damage was severe, as his intestines and other internal organs were in very poor condition.

The surgeon excised the ruptured appendix and cleaned the abdominal cavity as best he could. The intestines and the inside of the patient's abdomen had to be rinsed out many times while Mr. Dormans was under general anesthesia, but the treatment didn't help much. Mr. Dormans was given parenteral nutrition (that is, via an I.V.) and antibiotics, but his condition only worsened. Even the slightest touch made his intestines leak further.

From the beginning of his illness, Mr. Dormans had turned to Bl. Charles of Mount Argus. He continuously asked him for help in overcoming his illness and to bless the doctors taking care of him. His local priest, the pastor of the parish of St. Pancras, even gave him relics of the blessed one. Mr. Dormans prayed ardently.

On April 11, Mr. Dormans's grandson made his First Holy Communion. After Mass, he visited his grandfather in the hospital and found the rest of the family by his bedside. The doctors thought that Mr. Dormans would die soon and had called the

Soon the sick man fell into a coma. He still, however, had a relic under his pillow—a bone of Bl. Charles. His family and many of the residents of Munstergeleen, where he was known and loved, continued to pray for him, and many other people were praying for him in the chapel in Bl. Charles's birthplace.

Yet just as the doctors had given up all hope, the Lord Himself took matters into His own hands. The very next day, Mr. Dormans suddenly woke up. As the days progressed, he began to recover from his illness without any further medical intervention. He showed no signs of infection and was no longer in pain.

Dr. Dormans's family doctor was convinced that Fr. Charles had performed this miracle. Dr. Dormans's surgeon also knew that he was not responsible for this sudden cure.

And so the man who was expected to die was discharged from the hospital on July 14, 1999. Later, in October, he underwent another operation to ensure that his intestines were working properly. The hospital reserved a full day for this operation, but when they opened the man's abdomen, they discovered that he was nearly in perfect health. The surgeons quickly connected the small intestines and closed a little hole; everything else had healed itself.

Joannes Andreas Houben was born in the Dutch village of Munstergeleen into a poor, Catholic family. He learned about the Congregation of the Passion of Jesus Christ, or the Passionists, while he was serving in the army.

Relics of St. Charles of Mount Argus.

family to pay their final respects. Another surgery had revealed that Mr. Dormans's intestines were completely destroyed, and the infection couldn't be stopped. He also started having problems with his lungs and heart. The doctors told the family that he would likely die within the next few hours, and they decided that if he did die, he would not be resuscitated.

The patient was given the Sacrament of the Anointing of the Sick, and his family said goodbye to him. They were still praying to Bl. Charles for help—not so much in terms of healing, but to peacefully help Mr. Dormans find "a good place in Heaven." They even began to discuss and make preparations for his funeral.

From then on, Mr. Dormans's digestive system functioned flawlessly, and he lived to a very old age. His healing miracle was approved by the Vatican, and as a result, Bl. Charles was canonized on June 3, 2007. Mr. Dormans, ever grateful to the man to whom he owed his miraculous recovery, was present for the canonization ceremony.

Mr. Dormans died in 2017, eighteen years after the dramatic fight for his life.

CLOSE TO GOD AND TO PEOPLE

The life story of this benefactor—St. Charles of Mount Argus, also known as Charles of St. Andrew—is not extraordinary at all. Joannes Andreas Houben was born in the Dutch village of Munstergeleen in the province of Limburg to a poor, Catholic family. He had ten siblings, and his father was a miller by trade. Joannes was a weak student in school, but he was very devout in his faith. In 1840, his studies were interrupted because he was drafted into the army, but he only spent three months in active duty because his parents paid someone to serve in his place. While he was in the army, Joannes heard about the Congregation of the Passion of Jesus Christ, or the Passionists, and after he completed his studies, he joined their order in Belgium. In 1850, he was ordained a priest. He was soon sent to England, and in 1857, he was transferred to the newly established monastery of Mount Argus on the outskirts of Dublin, Ireland. He spent most of the rest of his life in Ireland, and he never returned home to the Netherlands.

Fr. Charles of St. Andrew, as he was now known, had difficulties learning the Irish language. He was not a great preacher, and he never preached missions, yet his simplicity and piety, great devotion to the Lord's Passion and Mary (he supposedly saw her once in a vision), life of prayer, practice of religious virtues of poverty and humility, and devout celebration of Holy Mass impressed the Irish people. And he truly loved the Irish. He respected their struggle against oppression and their loyalty to the Catholic faith. When necessary, however, he took the time to correct and instruct them. Debauchery and drunkenness were rampant in Dublin at the time, and murders were commonplace.

Hundreds of thousands of people were drawn to him; they knew in their hearts he was close to God. He was also an excellent, compassionate confessor and spiritual director to whom crowds of penitents flocked. He devoted himself with all his heart to the service of the sick, including not only those suffering physically and mentally but also those who were broken in spirit and lost.

BLESS ME, FATHER!

Fr. Charles loved to serve and pray for people. Even when he was in the novitiate, Charles encouraged others to pray for Catholics who had turned away from the Church. As a priest and confessor, he added severe penance to prayer, yet he was also quick to pray for and bless those who asked him. While blessing others, he drew people's attention to prayer and encouraged them to unite their suffering to Christ's Passion and His Cross.

Over time, people began to seek out his blessings, as the Irish realized that many who went to Fr. Charles experienced healing and other miracles. At times, three hundred people would come to the monastery in one day asking for his blessing and for his prayers for physical

People were convinced that Fr. Charles of Mount Argus performed miracles with his blessings. There were times when in one day three hundred people would come to the monastery for his blessing.

or spiritual healing. Sometimes, he was taken outside the city to the sick who couldn't travel to Dublin. He himself would go to the hospital and to the homes of the sick. Many people he blessed regained their sight or hearing. Those who were crippled started to walk, the terminally ill recovered, and the mentally ill were cured. Sometimes Fr. Charles would sprinkle the suffering person with holy water and bless him or her with relics of St. Paul of the Cross, but other times he would simply touch someone while absorbed in prayer or put his hand on someone's head. Even some Protestants went to him for prayer and were healed. Some of these, such as a blind five-year-old boy from Dublin who regained his sight after three visits with Fr. Charles, later became Catholics.

In addition to healing, Fr. Charles was also known for his gift of prophecy. He predicted many people's futures without error, especially regarding their imminent death or their need to patiently carry their "cross" in union with Jesus.

And so already during his lifetime Fr. Charles was considered a miracle worker and a holy man.

STUBBORN MOTHER ARSENIUS

In his biography *Life of Blessed Charles of Mount Argus*, Fr. Oliver Kelly describes the healing of the Irish Sister of Charity Mary Joseph Arsenius, who suffered from incessant headaches as a young nun. When doctors could do nothing to help her, she told her troubles to Fr. Charles.

Fr. Charles's tomb, Church of St. Paul of the Cross, Mount Argus, Ireland.

He laid his hand upon her head and blessed her, and her pain disappeared.

Years later, when she was Mother Arsenius, she fell ill again, and her doctor said she needed an urgent operation. Mother Arsenius refused; she said she wanted to meet with Fr. Charles instead. Her doctor was both outraged and insistent, but Mother Arsenius persisted: "He will cure me," she declared.

The sisters were reluctant to fulfill her wish, and they delayed calling for Fr. Charles until Mother Arsenius collapsed from her illness. When they finally drove to Dublin from the Ballaghaderreen Convent, however, Fr. Charles refused meet with her! He believed Mother Arsenius had already done enough good in her life and deserved to go to her Father's house in Heaven. The sisters insisted, and he finally came to see her, but he found the sisters kneeling by their superior's bed and saying the *De profundis* for her soul. Mother Arsenius had died.

Fr. Charles, however, knelt by the bed and absorbed himself in fervent prayer. After a few minutes, Mother Arsenius began to show signs of life. Eventually, she completely recovered. She died more than forty years later at the age of ninety, thirty-nine years after her benefactor died.

LAST MOMENTS ON EARTH

At the end of his life, "poor old Charlie" —as he spoke of himself—suffered a great deal. Twelve years before his death, he was injured in a carriage collision that fractured his ankle and his leg. As a result, he walked with a limp for the rest of his life. He also began to suffer from intense headaches and toothaches.

In early December 1892, Fr. Charles grew increasingly ill, and he spent his last weeks unable to eat and in severe pain. According to those who were with him, however, he never uttered a word of complaint. He finally died on January 5, 1893.

After the Passionist's death, thousands of Dublin residents as well as pilgrims from all over Ireland journeyed to pay their respects in front of his coffin. The procession of mourners lasted for five snowy, winter days. His mortal remains were laid to rest in the cemetery behind the Church of St. Paul of the Cross in Mount Argus. Today, they lie inside the church in a special shrine.

Since Fr. Charles's death, many people—including Octavia Verheggen and Dolf Dormans—have turned to Fr. Charles for help. They pray for his intercession, make novenas, smear themselves with soil from his grave, and apply his relics to their bodies. And some still today experience sudden and miraculous healing.

Bust of St. Charles of Mount Argus from the church in Munstergeleen.

At the end of his life, "poor old Charlie"—as he spoke of himself—suffered a great deal. He walked with a limp and had intense headaches and toothaches for more than a decade, and his final illness left him in severe pain for weeks.

Relief, stained glass window, and relics of St. Thomas Becket.

Thomas Becket was credited with curing and saving from death several hawks, falcons, oxen, cows, pigs, and other livestock.

Very Unusual Miracles

Miracles, especially healings officially approved by the Church, usually have a fairly clear structure. A terminally ill person and often his relatives and acquaintances pray to God for his or her healing through the intercession of a saint and, after some time, the person suddenly, unexpectedly, and permanently regains full health. However, nothing is impossible for God, and sometimes, through His saints, he works much more extravagant miracles. And it must be said that sometimes in doing so, He reveals that He has a great sense of humor.

This was undoubtedly one of the strangest miracles in the history of the Church. A miracle, through the intercession of St. Thomas Becket (1118–1170), an English bishop and martyr, was obtained from God by ... a bird. The bird was domesticated and most likely belonged to one of the species that can learn human language. Parrots and bustards have such abilities, but so do European ravens, starlings, and jays. Reportedly, the bird had often heard others loudly calling St. Thomas Aquinas for help. It is possible that its owners were ailing pious people. As Jacobus de Voragine described in *The Golden Legend*, once upon a time this bird escaped from its cage and flew into a field. He was out of luck. Suddenly, out of the blue, a predatory sparrowhawk showed up and began to chase him. The sparrowhawk almost caught him, but the bird, using human speech, called out "St. Thomas! Help!" Immediately, the sparrowhawk dropped dead, and the little bird managed

to escape safely. The English saint was also credited with curing and saving from death several hawks, falcons, oxen, cows, pigs, and other livestock.

A LINGUISTIC MIRACLE

The healing of a deaf eight-year-old girl from Spanish Cantabria, a province in the north of Spain, was unusual. Her parents brought her to the famous and great miracle worker, Franciscan friar, and now saint, Salvador of Horta (1520–1567). Salvador blessed the child and asked the parents to stay in Horta for eight days, telling them to trustingly ask Our Lady for her healing. He assured them that their child would regain speech. And she did, just as the saint had said. After four days, the girl could speak. However, she was speaking *Catalan*, a language that her Cantabrian-speaking parents did not understand. Therefore, the couple again went to Fr. Salvador, begging him to make the girl speak the language of her ancestors. The friar instructed them to continue trustingly praying to Our Lady, and when eight days had passed, he said: "My friends, the Blessed Mother wants your daughter to speak Catalan for as long as she stays in Catalonia; when she returns to her homeland, she will speak in a language you can understand." The family set off. After crossing the border, Salvador's words came true and the girl began to speak Cantabrian. Many curious people accompanying the family witnessed this strange miracle.

SAINT WINDSURFER

Do you know the world's first windsurfer? Evidence would suggest that it was the Catalan Dominican St. Raymond of Penyafort (1175–1275). Raymond was a remarkable expert in canon law and theology. He converted Jews and Muslims in Spain. He was also a friend, confessor, and advisor to King James I of Aragon. A

St. Salvador and the Inquisitor of Aragon *by Bartolomé Esteban Murillo. Salvador was questioned by the Spanish Inquisition on account of his miracles. The Inquisition took no action against him after its investigation.*

The interior of Barcelona Cathedral—the chapel of St. Raymond of Penyafort.

St. Raymond of Penyafort, leaving the port of Soller in Mallorca, spread his cloak on the waves and tied one end of it to a pole, turning it into a sail. He made the Sign of the Cross over it and, as if on a windsurfing board, sailed to Barcelona, traveling more than 125 miles!

Port de Sóller, Mallorca.

fifteenth-century legend is related to the latter role. It is said that Raymond, enraged by the strenuous and unproductive attempts to exhort the immoral ruler (a chronic womanizer) to do better, had finally had enough of him. At the time, the two were on the island of Mallorca, so to separate himself from the ruler, the Dominican had to cross the sea.

James, however, refused to agree to this, threatening to kill anyone who helped Raymond leave the island. The Dominican, however, did not need help from any mortal, for he asked God Himself to help him. He went to the port of Soller in Mallorca, spread his cloak on the waves, and tied one end of it to a pole, turning it into a sail. He made the Sign of the Cross over it and, as if on a windsurfing board, sailed to Barcelona, traveling more than 125 miles. Such windsurfing with a "black cappa" seems to be a specialty of the Dominicans, as, according to legend, St. Hyacinth of Poland also traveled in this same way. In his case, however, it was only a short distance. He crossed a river.

UNUSUAL STIGMATA

Several peculiar miracles were associated with the person of St. Francis of Assisi. Two strange miracles involved paintings in which the saint was depicted with stigmata. Thomas of Celano wrote about a certain distinguished Roman lady who, having chosen St. Francis as her patron saint, hung a painted image of him in a prayer corner in her house. One day, while praying, she noticed that her painting had a serious flaw: St. Francis was portrayed without his stigmata. As Thomas of Celano records:

Several peculiar miracles were associated with the person of St. Francis of Assisi. Two strange miracles involved paintings in which the saint was depicted with stigmata.

Frescoes from Assisi.

With attentive eyes, she searched for the holy marks. Having not found them, she suddenly and with pain began to wonder at it. However, there was no use in wondering, as what was not in the painting had been simply left out by the painter. For many days the woman kept this in her heart and told no one, often looking at the painting and still in pain.

Suddenly something strange happened:

One day these wonderful marks appeared on the hands, just as they are usually depicted in other paintings; divine power added what human art had neglected. Terrified and immeasurably astonished, the woman hastily called her daughter and, pointing out to her what had happened, urgently inquired whether she had seen the image without stigmata until now. The girl confirmed and swore that formerly St. Francis had been depicted without stigmata, and now they appeared.

The woman then began to doubt "whether the image had not been marked in this way from the beginning," and only she was somehow unable to notice. "The power of God, having protected the first miracle from disdain, added a second one," Thomas of Celano further wrote. "Without delay the marks disappeared, and the image was stripped of its privileges so that the subsequent miracle proved the previous one true."

Another of the miraculous stories involving the poor man of Assisi recounts how one day the pope himself came to one of the French Franciscan monasteries, which housed the miraculous image of St. Francis. At the time, the monastery was also hosting two monks from another congregation. Not believing that St. Francis had received the stigmata, one of these monks committed a great infamy. He approached a painting depicting St. Francis, put a knife to it, and tried to scrape off the red marks of the Passion from the canvas. While he was scraping like this, suddenly St. Francis's arms and legs started bleeding. The culprit probably never felt stronger fear in his life. He discarded the knife and rushed to the confessional to confess his grave sin and seek God's forgiveness for his foolishness and unbelief.

His confessor then told him to go to the pope himself, tell him about what he had done and what had happened to him, and ask the Vicar of Christ to appoint an appropriate penance. Hearing the whole story, the pope rushed in front of the miraculous image that was still bleeding. "St. Francis, forgive this wretch," he pleaded on behalf of the culprit. "As satisfaction,

▲ St. Francis in Ecstasy *by Giovanni Bellini.*

▲ St. Francis of Assisi in Ecstasy *by Caravaggio.*

Franciscans from all three orders celebrate the Feast of the Stigmata of St. Francis of Assisi on September 17.

➤ *Sts. Cosmas and Damian performed transplantation surgery and, during the night, replaced the cancer-stricken limb of a certain man piously ministering in the Roman church of Sts. Cosmas and Damian with the leg of a deceased Ethiopian man.*

I will establish the feast of your stigmata. Your spiritual sons will celebrate it solemnly every year on September 17." After these words, the blood stopped flowing from the saint's image. Franciscans from all three orders still celebrate the Feast of the Stigmata of St. Francis of Assisi on September 17.

LOADED DICE FROM HEAVEN

Through another peculiar miracle, the Lord God attested the holiness of His faithful servant. In his *Treatise on Saints' Miracles*, Thomas of Celano wrote about a knight, named Gineldo, from Borgo San Sepolcro, in the province of Massa Trabaria, who "shamelessly insulted the deeds and miraculous marks of St. Francis. He greatly insulted the pilgrims coming to honor his memory, and said many foolishnesses against the friars in public." One day Gineldo was playing dice.

Full of madness and disbelief, he said to those present: "If Francis is a saint, then let the total value of this throw be eighteen dots!" We can only imagine how surprised he must have been when suddenly, "eighteen dots came up, and this result was repeated on nine more castings of the dice." But as it turned out, even that was not enough for the disbeliever to recognize Francis's holiness. He added sin to sin and added blasphemy to blasphemy. He said: "If it is true that this Francis is a saint, then may my body fall from the sword today, and if he is not a saint, then may I come out unscathed!" Well, he was in for it. "God's judgment," as Thomas of Celano further writes, "did not linger, since his speech had become a sin, condemning him to divine judgment! After the game was over, he insulted his nephew. His nephew grabbed a sword and sank it into his uncle's entrails. On that day the damnable man died, becoming a prey to Hell and a son of darkness."

The warning that the greatest biographer of St. Francis drew from this is, perhaps, worth remembering: "May the blasphemers be afraid, and know that their words are not an idle speech and that there is a God who delivers justice for the wrongdoing caused to saints."

AN OLD LADY BREASTFEEDING

And now we turn to a Franciscan miracle of a very different sort. An eighty-year-old woman from the Italian diocese of Sabino had two daughters, according to a description penned by the aforementioned Thomas of Celano.

One of them gave birth to a baby boy, and when she died, the baby was taken care of by her sister. However, when this second daughter became pregnant herself, her breasts suddenly stopped giving milk. This was a real problem, for "they could not find anyone to help the orphaned child, no one to give a drop of milk to the hungry infant." The little boy was getting paler and weaker, and the poverty-stricken grandmother was increasingly worried about him. She walked the streets, wailing and despairing that they would probably die together. The little one, however, was still screaming with hunger, so to calm him down a little at least, the old woman put her withered breast in his mouth. She then raised her tear-filled eyes to Heaven, begging for help and advice from St. Francis. And then she saw him! "Woman, I am Francis, whom you summoned while crying. Put your breast into the baby's mouth, for the Lord will give you milk in abundance," he said. The old woman did as she was told, and "immediately her eighty-year-old breasts filled with milk."

The news spread quickly and many came to see the breastfeeding old woman with their own eyes, including the provincial ruler himself, the count, who refused to believe the rumors. And they saw it with their own eyes! What is funny about this story is that, as Thomas of Celano wrote, the "wrinkled old woman" chased the curious count away and made him run a mile by shooting milk at him straight from her breast. The little boy grew very fast on this miraculous food, and soon no longer needed it.

MIRACULOUS TRANSPLANTATION

A man piously ministering at the Roman church of Sts. Cosmas and Damian was struggling with a huge problem. A widespread cancer had attacked and completely destroyed his entire thigh. One night, when the man fell asleep, he saw the two aforementioned holy doctors. They had various tools and ointments with them. "Where can we find the body to fill in the missing part once we cut off the rotten tissue?" asked one of them. The other replied, "An Ethiopian was buried today in the cemetery at St. Peter's Church. His body is still fresh, so let's take his leg and fill the space with it, and move this one to the cemetery."

They did exactly as they agreed upon. In the morning, the patient woke up and, surprisingly, no longer felt pain. He reached out and touched his leg. It was still in its place. It was still dark in the room, so he reached for a candle to get a better look at it, and what he saw left him speechless. It wasn't his leg! It was the leg of the Ethiopian from his dream. And when he had calmed down, he joyfully got out of bed and ran to tell others about his very unusual healing. A deputy was then sent to the grave of the Ethiopian who had just been buried.

In the tomb, next to a black man, there was a white, cancer-ridden leg.

This was the particular healing through which the most famous holy martyrs, brothers Cosmas and Damian, who lived at the turn of the third and fourth centuries, made history in the field of transplantation. Their most famous miracle, which is also depicted in many paintings, was described in *The Golden Legend* by Bl. Jacobus de Voragine.

The most famous holy doctors in the history of transplantation are brothers Cosmas and Damian, martyrs who lived at the turn of the third and fourth centuries.

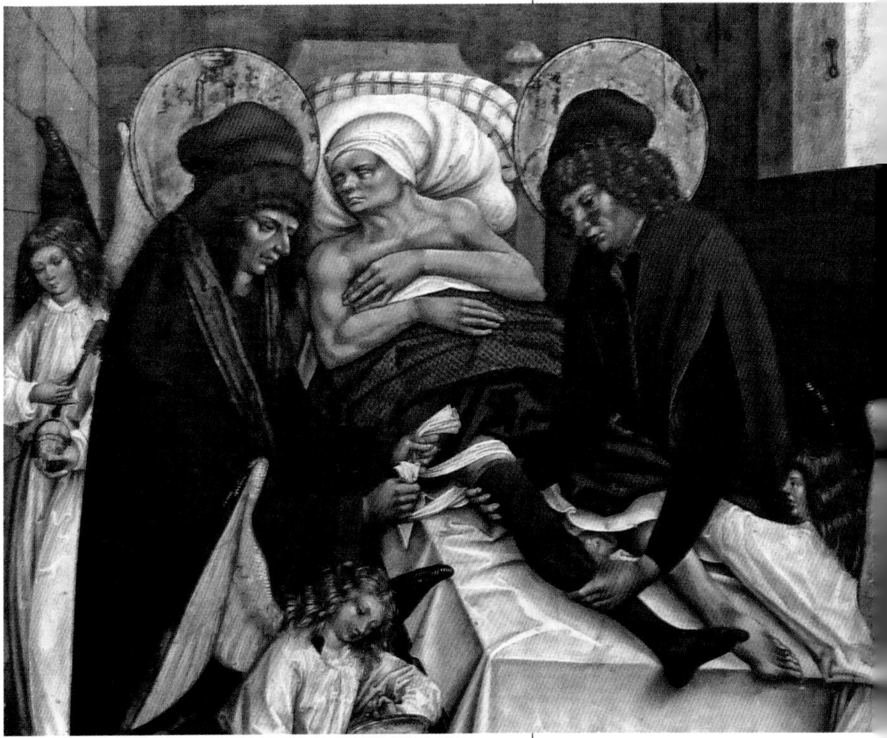

St. Thomas Aquinas traveled from Naples to Lyon for the council but fell ill on the way. It was the second half of February, during Lent. Exhausted, he stopped at a castle in Maenza.

ST. THOMAS AND THE BASKET OF HERRINGS

The Lord God cares about people who love Him and are faithful to Him. This was witnessed by the people who cared for St. Thomas Aquinas just before his death.

St. Thomas Aquinas traveled from Naples to Lyon for the council but fell ill on the way. It was the second half of February, during Lent. Exhausted, he stopped at a castle in Maenza, which belonged to Annibaldo of Ceccano, the husband of his niece. Aquinas had no appetite and did not want to eat anything. The physician accompanying him, John Guidon of Piperno, asked him if he would like something special. "Do you think you could bring me fresh herrings?" asked Thomas. He had taken a liking to them when he was staying in Paris, to where they were easily imported from the North Sea fisheries.

But there was a problem. In England or France, there was no problem with buying herring, but in Italy, there was—and a serious one at that! In the Tyrrhenian Sea, which was near Maenza, this species of fish did not exist. Fishermen there mainly caught sardines, tuna, and different types of crustaceans. Of course, in the thirteenth century, supermarket shopping was out of the question, and therefore there was not the slightest chance of fulfilling Thomas' wish. Just then a man named Bordonario, a fish supplier from nearby Terracina, arrived at the castle on a mule. He began opening baskets full of, as he claimed, salted sardines, but to the surprise of all the household members, after opening one of them, they found fresh herrings inside! And when the fishmonger swore that he had only brought sardines, Fr. Reginald of Piperno quickly ran to inform St. Thomas that God had given him everything he wanted—that he had provided him with herrings! It was so strange and amazing that people were sure that it was a miracle worked by God. They cooked some of the herrings, fried and ate the rest, but it is

During the canonization process of St. Thomas, the topic of the miracle of the herrings came up several times. It was examined with great care. Fr. Peter of Montesangiovanni, an old friar from Fossanova, who was present at the delivery of the fish, was asked how he knew that the fish found in the baskets were herrings.

St. Thomas Aquinas, Protector of the University of Cusco, *late seventeenth century.*

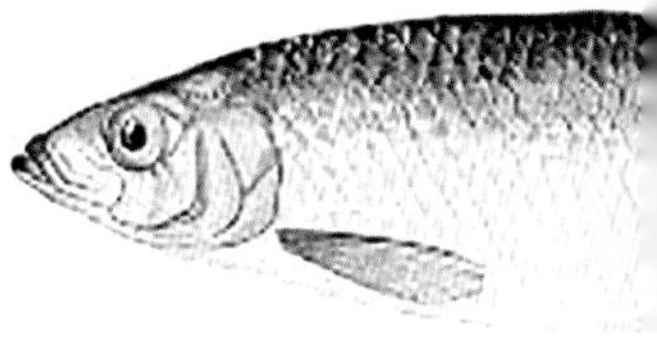

In a time without refrigerators, a fishmonger unexpectedly delivered ocean herring hundreds of miles inland.

The Vision of St. Philip Neri *by Giovanni Francesco Barbieri.*

not clear whether St. Thomas, having lost his appetite, ate even a little.

Probably not, unfortunately. Shortly thereafter, he was transported to a Cistercian monastery in nearby Fossanova, where he passed away.

During the canonization process of St. Thomas, the topic of these herrings came up several times. It was examined with great care. Fr. Peter of Montesangiovanni, an old friar from Fossanova who was present at the delivery of the fish, was asked how he knew that the fish found in the baskets were herrings. He replied that he had "seen salted herrings at the papal court in Viterbo," and besides, Brother Reginald, "who had eaten fresh herrings in the countries on the other side of the Alps," also stated that they were definitely herrings.

CONVERTED BY A "HOLY" PICTURE

Saints had all sorts of ways to convert sinners and disbelievers. They came to some even after their death. A peculiar miracle that God performed through the intercession of the Roman apostle St. Philip Neri was described by his biographer Pietro Giacomo Bacci.

This happened, as he writes,

> *shortly after the saint's death, when the first portraits of him became available. A man leading a bad life saw one such picture in the hands of his friend. He began to shake his head with contempt, mocking his companion, and at one point snatched the image from his hand, crumpled it into a ball, and hurled it to the ground. However, before it even reached the ground, the picture opened and unfolded, resuming its initial form. Moreover, it floated in the air just above the ground, as if held by an invisible hand.*

The wicked man, however, did not give up, and he stomped on it with his shoe. When he took the shoe off the picture, it started floating in the air again. Only then did he understand that this was a sign. Amazed by the miracle, the sinner knelt down and reverently lifted the image and then, "encouraged to repent," went to Confession. "From then on," Bacci testified, "he began to lead a good life."

During a great drought, a farmer refused to let Gerard or his companions drink from his well. "You will not give water to your neighbor, whom you should love as yourself? Then there will be no water in your well," Gerard said. The well immediately ran dry.

The mule became the instrument of a pedagogical miracle.

YOUR MULE WILL DIE! THERE WILL BE NO WATER IN YOUR WELL!

Similar miracles aimed at sobering up those who did evil were worked by the Lord God through other saints. Punishments sent by Him through the saints (some, I must admit, quite drastic) awaited blasphemers and those who insulted and mocked His faithful worshippers.

These miracles were undoubtedly educational, often leading these "criminals" to rapid, if not immediate, improvement. Several of them were related to the person of St. Gerard Majella and happened while he was still alive.

The Redemptorist friar once stayed overnight at an inn next to the Sanctuary of St. Michael on Mount Gargano. When he was about to leave, Gerard wanted to settle the bill for the night. The wicked man demanded a king's ransom. As Fr. Bernard Lubienski wrote in his biography of the saint,

> *Gerard was surprised and tried to convince the man that it was definitely too much, but the man did not want to accept a coin less. "If you don't stop persecuting me and tell me how much I should justly pay you, your mule will die," Gerard warned him. When he said that, the innkeeper's son rushed in and called out: "Father, come quickly! I don't know what happened to the mule, it's lying on the ground. Hurry, hurry!" The innkeeper turned pale, fell to his knees, and asked for forgiveness. "I forgive you," said the friar, "but do not forget that God*

remembers His poor. Woe betide you if you demand more than what is rightfully yours." Seeing that there was a saint in front of him, the innkeeper did not want to accept anything from him, but Gerard left what he thought was rightfully due on the table and left. On his way out, he entered the stable, blessed the mule, and restored it to health.[1]

And the innkeeper? "The innkeeper changed, and out of gratitude sent alms to the monastery in Deliceto."

Another time, during a great drought, a farmer refused to let Gerard or his companions drink from his well. "You will not give water to your neighbor, whom you should love as yourself? Then there will be no water in your well," Gerard said and walked away. When he had walked quite far from the well with the whole group, the farmer caught up with them, begging Gerard to take pity on him and the poor people in the neighborhood because his well had gone dry.

➤ *St. Gerard Majella.*

➤ *The Sanctuary of St. Michael the Archangel in Gargano.*

The interior of the Gargano grotto.

The water returned only when Brother Gerard went back and approached the well. And the farmer? Admonished once again by Gerard, he didn't forbid anyone from drinking water from his well ever again.

CAPON OR A FISH?

Let's go back to St. Francis for a moment. Bl. Jacobus de Voragine writes:

> *In the city of Alexandria, in Lombardy, St. Francis was a guest of a certain nobleman, who asked him, according to the words of the Gospel, to eat a little of whatever food was set before him. St. Francis agreed because of the piety of this man, and the man ran and brought the capon he had fattened for seven years. Once they were eating, a certain disbeliever came and asked for alms for the love of God.*

St. Francis talking to birds, *fresco from the Basilica of Assisi.*

Philip Neri and his relics in a special reliquary in Florence.

The man of God, having heard the holy name, sent the poor man a piece of the capon. In turn, the disbeliever kept the gift, and the next day, when the saint was teaching, he showed it to the people, saying: "Look what kind of meat this Francis of yours, whom you honor as a saint, eats! Yesterday evening he gave it to me!" However, instead of a piece of capon, everyone saw a fish in his hand, so they caught him and called him crazy. Hearing this, the man was ashamed and asked for forgiveness. When the vicious accuser came back to his senses, the meat also returned to its original shape.

SLIPPERS: APPLY DIRECTLY TO THE FOREHEAD

And now we will try to find the answer to the question of whether it is possible to heal a sick person by putting slippers on his forehead. The correct answer is: Absolutely, as long as they are not ordinary slippers, but second-degree relics belonging to a saint. This cure-all was discovered by the wife of an Italian merchant.

Ercole Cortesini, a merchant from Carpi, was deeply moved by the news of the mercy, virtues, and miracles of Philip Neri. When he arrived in Rome, he desperately wanted to see him and speak with him. When he was allowed to do so, he knelt before the saint, begged for his blessing, and asked the saint to pray for him. "I believe I saw the great saint, and at first glance my whole body began to shake," he said when he left.

Later, he absolutely wanted to get something that belonged to Philip as a relic. He managed to get a pair of slippers and a bit of the saint's hair, and he was given a rosary by St. Philip himself. In August, Ercole began his return journey from Rome to Carpi. He usually rode on horseback, but this time he decided to travel on foot. During the journey, he felt a severe headache and was nearly delirious. He then thought about the relics he had with him. As Bacci writes:

> *With no hesitation, Ercole instructed his wife to take the relics that were in his luggage and press them to his forehead. When his wife saw the old, worn-out slippers she started laughing. "And what is that? What are you going to do with those slippers?" she asked. "It doesn't matter, do what I tell you," he replied. "I know very well what I want." What did the*

poor wife do? Probably still laughing and mocking, she placed the old slippers on his forehead. Ercole then began to pray fervently, begging God to heal him of his pain, because of his devotion to Fr. Philip. He had barely finished this prayer when the headache and fever suddenly stopped. He then continued his journey in perfect health.

With the help of the slippers he acquired while St. Philip was still alive, Ercole also helped his nephew. The boy was running a high fever and was in severe pain due to a tumor that had formed on his body. They thought he was dying. That's when one of the slippers was placed on his tumor, and the tumor immediately broke off upon contact. The fever completely disappeared, and the nephew was cured.

WHERE IS THAT PASSAGE AGAIN?

Let's revisit St. Thomas Aquinas. How rich and extensive his legacy is, how monumental are the tomes he produced! Sometimes when someone is looking for something specific in his writings, he might go mad unless a miracle helps him. Here is an excerpt from a description of the testimony given by Bartholomew of Capua during the canonization process of St. Thomas Aquinas.

He added that he had the habit of reading the works of Thomas for several years. He once remembered reading somewhere in one of them that what is customary among Christians should be treated as legally binding. However, when he searched for this passage, he could not find it, although he searched diligently for several days whenever he had time to do so. Finally, he knelt down and asked Thomas himself to show him where it was. Then he opened Secunda Secundae, and the passage was directly in front of his eyes. He did not even have to turn the page.

Perhaps this seems like such a subtle little miracle, but similar little miracles, as I myself can testify, happen all the time.

MIRACLES BEYOND BELIEF

And now the miracles that, dear reader, I must warn you about. For these are the strangest of strange miracles. Living in a world full of skepticism, it is indeed difficult to resist the impression that these were not miracles, but some kind of strange jokes, works of unconfined religious imagination. However, such events, if they really happened, would after all most clearly illustrate the well-known and recognized truth that nothing is impossible for God.

St. Paul of the Cross (1694–1775) from Italy, founder of the Passionist Congregation, blessed a cooked hen with the Sign of the Cross, and when he finished saying "In the name of the Father," the bird came back to life and grew feathers. It then flew out of the window and scampered back to the house of a poor woman, from whom it had been stolen.

St. Francis of Paola threw the fried trout into the pond, crying out: "Antonello, in the name of Mercy, come back to life!" The trout came back to life and began splashing merrily in the pond.

In his book *Raised from the Dead*, Fr. Albert J. Hebert describes a legendary event that is said to have occurred in the home of the Goffredi family, at which St. Paul of the Cross (1694–1775), founder of the Passionist Congregation, was a guest. They served a hen for dinner.

> *"You did a bad thing by killing this poor animal, because its eggs were the only food that the poor woman to whom it belonged had. Let us therefore do a work of mercy. Open the window," the saint said to the host. Then he blessed the cooked hen with the sign of the cross, and when he finished saying "In the name of the Father," the bird came back to life and grew feathers. It then flew out of the window and scampered back to the house of the poor woman from whom it had been stolen. The miracle was reportedly written down under oath by an eyewitness but, for obvious reasons, it was not fully approved by the Church hierarchy.*[2]

There are, of course, also other similar resurrections and miracles without official approval from the Church, which, according to traditions and legends, were supposedly worked by another Italian saint, Francis of Paola (1416–1507), a hermit and founder of the Order of Minims of St. Francis of Assisi. Albert J. Herbert writes,

> *Francis of Paola had a domesticated trout named "Antonella" and a lamb named "Martinello." One day Antonella was swimming around in the pond, as befits a healthy fish. A priest ministering there spotted it, caught it, took it home, and began to fry it.*

The Passionist monastery in Monte Argentario.

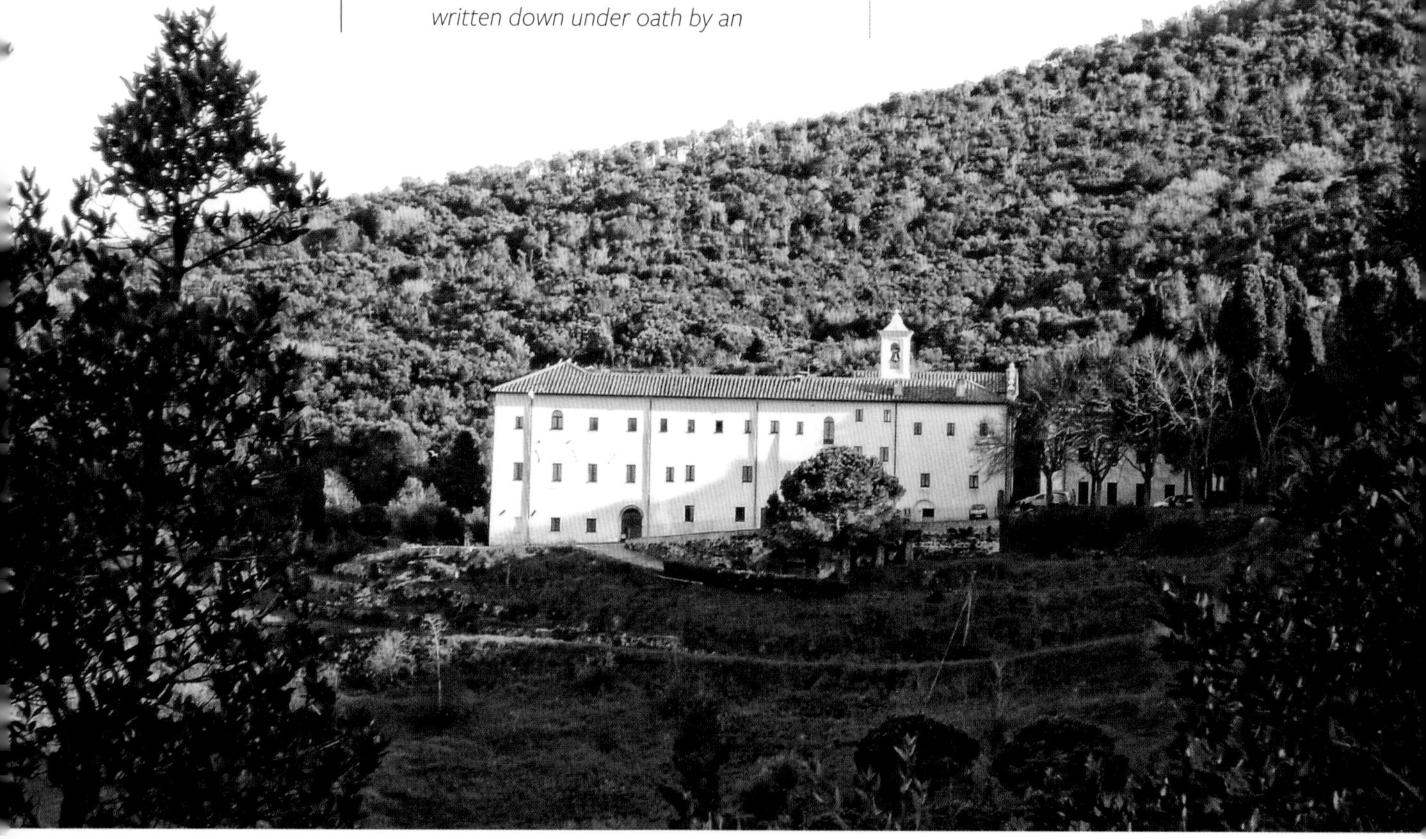

St. Francis noticed the absence of the fish and, either guessing what had happened to it or having discovered it through supernatural powers, ordered one of the friars to retrieve its remains. The culprit, having learned from the sent friar what Francis demanded, became very annoyed. He hurled the fried trout to the ground, crushing its remains. The Minim friar brought back everything he managed to retrieve to the saint. St. Francis of Paola threw the fried trout into the pond, crying out: "Antonello, in the name of mercy, come back to life!" The trout came back to life and began splashing merrily in the pond.

Later, while he was a guest at the home of the governor of Bormes, Francis brought back to life a cooked fish that the host served him, unaware that the saint had self-imposed an extremely strict diet.

On another occasion, with nothing but the bones and fleece of a lamb thrown into the oven, St. Francis of Paola brought his beloved Martinello back to life. The animal was already roasted and consumed by workers from a nearby construction site.

If you find these animal resurrections hard to believe, you certainly aren't alone.

St. Francis of Paola.

The main altar of the Church of Our Lady of the Rosary and the Chapel of St. Benedict with images of Our Lady of the Rosary (in the center recess), St. Francis of Paola (left) and St. Joseph (right), Cuiabá, Mato Grosso, Brazil.

ENDNOTES

1 Cytaty dot. cudownych "nauczek" dawanych przez św. Gerda Majellę za: [Quotes on miraculous "lessons" given by St. Gerard Majella cit.por.]: Bernard Lubieński CssR, Żywot świętego brata Gerarda Majelli ze Zgromadzenia Redemptorystów, Homo Dei, Kraków 2019, s. 141.

2 Albert J. Herbert, Raised from the Dead (Gasconia, NC: TAN Books, 1986).

▲ An illustration depicting the Siege of Orléans of 1429 by Martial d'Auvergne.

➤ An illustration by Albert Lynch depicting Joan of Arc, published in Figaro Illustré magazine in 1903.

THE VIRGIN OF ORLÉANS

St. Joan of Arc

Joan of Arc (1412–1431), known as the Virgin of Orléans, was burned at the stake when she was only nineteen years old. Before she was killed, the young shepherdess managed to save France and secured the coronation of Charles VII as the rightful ruler of her country. She experienced extraordinary visions and apparitions, and one of the posthumous miracles attributed to her pertains to fire.

On May 19, 1909, a great fire broke out in the village of L'hôtel És Bas in the north of France. The inhabitants of the nearby town of Tribehou came running to help, but they had nothing left to save. It hadn't rained for many weeks, and the straw-thatched roofs of the wooden houses, dry as bone, went up in flames in the blink of an eye. Because of the heat from the fire, most of the buildings couldn't even be approached. The metal door fittings and tin elements were red-hot. You could hear the glass windows breaking from the inferno. Only those buildings not yet on fire could be saved. And that's what was done.

Suddenly, word spread that in one of the burning houses, an elderly man, Jean Dumoitier—who was well-liked and called "father" by everyone—was left inside. Rescuers tried to make their way into the burning house, but the heat, fire, and smoke made it impossible; besides, as everyone was certain, the man must have been dead. Let us now look at the course of events from another view—from the perspective

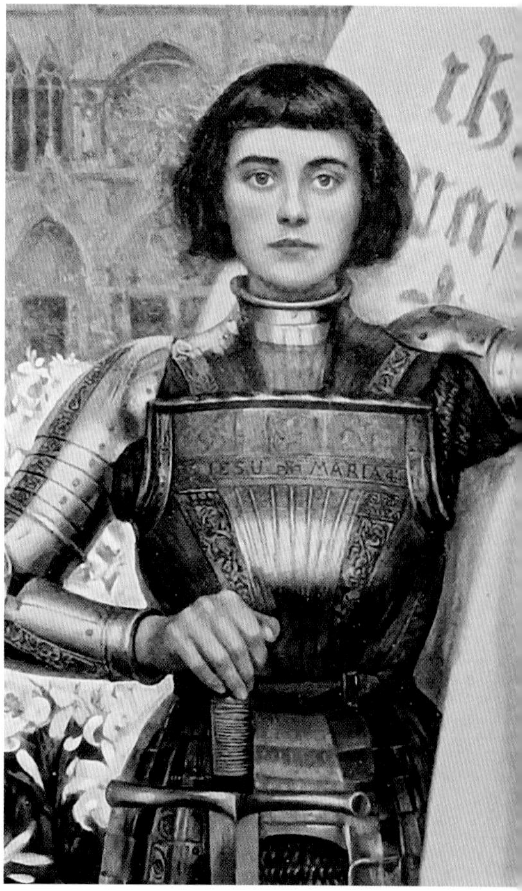

of the seventy-plus-year-old Jean Dumoitier, who made straw thatches. The man, “seeing the house opposite and his neighbor’s house on fire, realized his own house would immediately suffer the same fate,” we read in the *Annales du Mont-Saint-Michel* from 1912. He decided to save the furniture first. He took off the quilts from the bed and tried to take something else when, suddenly, “the thatched roof collapsed, surrounding the house on all sides with a large hedge of fire.” The old man was trapped.

Fortunately, the fire started from the roof and stopped momentarily on the ceiling, which, in accordance with local building tradition, was covered with a layer of compacted earth. However, it didn’t last long, and the fire, spreading down the stairs, reached the ground floor. “Flames engulfed the bedroom, then the kitchen. In the end, Dumoitier was forced to take refuge in a small room adjacent to the kitchen. The suffocating smoke choked him there; at the same time, excessive heat penetrated the window, shattering the glass.” What’s more: in front of the building thatch was burning, and a little farther down, on the opposite side of the road, a shed containing ten thousand bales of straw had ignited. It must have been hotter than Hell itself. Thick smoke billowed from the home. The seventy-year-old was suffering greatly and was being forced to stay “in his fiery prison” for more than an hour. He pushed flammable objects away as best he could and pressed his mouth against the mattress on the bed to breathe air without smoke. “It should be noted here that suffocation should have occurred. The thatched roof and the huge amount of straw that burned in front of Dumoitier’s window are more than enough to cause suffocation in an environment that’s absolutely unbreathable,” the *Annales* reported.

When the fire died down after more than an hour, people heard Dumoitier calling for help. They managed to enter the house and found him standing by the window. He was bewildered and frightened, but safe. Everyone saw it as a miracle. Who did he owe it to? The old man was certain: he had been saved by Joan of Arc. It was she who interceded on his behalf before God.

At a critical moment, when he had no hope of surviving, he thought of her and began calling upon her for help. He knew the blessed from a book he once read, and he knew she had been burned at the stake. This part of the girl’s biography was particularly touching. Therefore he concluded, not without reason, that it was she—and not the Blessed Virgin Mary from the nearby shrine in Délivrande—who would be the most appropriate intercessor in this misfortune.

“Blessed Joan of Arc, who went through the trial of fire, save me!” he shouted several times. “You were holy. You had no sins, and I am a sinner. Save me,” he begged. He promised if he lived, he would confess his sins. And he was heard.

Portrait of Joan of Arc by Clément de Fauquembergue.

Joan on a horse in an illustration from 1505.

➤ *Birthplace of Joan in Domrémy, where a museum is now located.*

⮟ *Medieval miniature,* Joan of Arc.

Those who later heard his story believed it was Bl. Joan who inspired him to use the mattress as a "filter" to breathe, which reduced the toxicity of the smoke, and it was she who saved him from the terrible fire.

FRAUDULENT PROCESS

The young nineteen-year-old warrior walked through fire almost six centuries ago. It happened on May 30, 1431, in Rouen. She died with the name "Jesus" on her lips. Her ashes were thrown into the Seine.

She was burned due to accusations of witchcraft and deviation from the Faith. None of the inquisitors from the church tribunal set up by the English, however, were able to prove any heresy. She provided extremely accurate, orthodox, and truly "God-inspired" answers, and her appeal to the pope, not in accordance with the obligatory procedure, was ignored. At that time, it was already obvious to many that she was convicted for purely political reasons. Defending France and leading the French to numerous victories, she exposed herself to danger by fighting against the English. Already twenty-five years after her death, the Church, with the authority of the Holy See itself, recognized that the trial was "filled with fraud, false charges, injustice, contradiction, and manifest errors concerning both fact and law," cleansing her from "any mark or stain."[1]

What's more, not only was she rehabilitated, but almost five hundred years later she was raised to the altars. In 1909, Joan of Arc was beatified, and in 1920 she was canonized. She quickly became the patron saint of France.

THE SHEPHERDESS SAVES FRANCE

Her life was absolutely extraordinary, full of mysterious events and apparitions. Joan was an ordinary, poor country girl from Domrémy, illiterate but very pious, to whom God—through His messengers—had given the extraordinary mission of liberating France from the Anglo-Burgundian occupation, which took place during the Hundred Years' War.

Joan learned about this extraordinary mission from the apparitions she began to

experience at the age of thirteen. During one of them she saw Michael the Archangel in the company of other angels. The prince of the heavenly army told her she had to go to France (that is, to the territory loyal to the Dauphin—the heir to the French throne). She heard this demand several more times. The girl also learned that she was to liberate Orléans, breaking the siege.

"The voice told me also that I should go to Robert de Baudricourt at the town of Vaucouleurs, who was the commander of the town garrison, and he would provide people to go with me. And I replied that I was a poor girl who knew neither how to ride nor lead in war," Joan recounted.[2]

During the first apparitions, Michael the Archangel also announced that two virgin martyrs—St. Catherine of Alexandria and St. Margaret of Antioch—would soon be appearing to her and would advise her on how to act and what to do, and Joan should believe their words because they were ordered by God Himself.

Joan waited four more years before she took action. During this time, she grew in virtue, attending Holy Mass as often as possible, confessing frequently, receiving Holy Communion, praying before the Blessed Sacrament, and giving up girlish games and fun. The voices of the angel and two saints instructed her to be good and to go to church regularly. She swore a vow of virginity.

When she turned sixteen, obeying the voices, she disguised herself as a man and set off for Vaucouleurs and then was escorted to Chinon, where the heir to the French throne, Charles VII, was residing. The Dauphin was surprised by her arrival and what she had to tell him. He was doubly surprised when he failed to deceive Joan by saying he wasn't the heir to the throne.

Joan, guided by voices from Heaven, didn't let herself be deceived. She disclosed several secrets, concerning only him, which were revealed to her by God. She told him, among other things, what he had been praying for on November 1, 1428: he had asked God to keep the kingdom of France

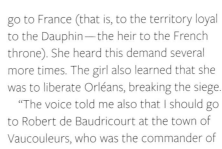

◀ *Miniature from the end of the fifteenth century.* Joan of Arc and the Dauphin Are Given the Keys to the City of Troyes.

▲ *Eugène Romain Thirion,* Joan of Arc Listening to the Voices.

During the first apparitions, Michael the Archangel also announced two virgin martyrs—St. Catherine of Alexandria and St. Margaret of Antioch—would soon be appearing to Joan to advise her.

◀ Joan of Arc at the Coronation of Charles VII, *Jean Auguste Dominique Ingres.*

➢ Joan Captured by the Burgundians at Compiègne. *Mural in the Panthéon in Paris.*

➢ Maid of Orléans at the Siege of Orléans, *Jules Eugène Lenepveu.*

for him if he was the true heir and the legitimate son of Charles VI; otherwise, he asked God to allow him to take refuge in Spain or Scotland.

While at the court in Chinon, Joan told Charles VII that, according to what the voices had told her, he was the rightful heir of France and should be crowned king. The heir to the throne put her to further tests and finally believed her. Suspecting a devilish trick, he ordered the theologians of Poitiers to examine the girl. After three weeks of interrogation, however, the scholars found no theological inaccuracies in what she was saying.

Joan also foretold four events—revealed to her by God—that would occur: first, the English would fail and abandon the siege of Orléans; second, the king would be anointed in Reims; third, Paris would submit to the French monarch; and fourth, the Duke of Orléans, who was in English captivity, would return to France.

At that time, voices informed Joan that behind the altar of the church of Sainte-Catherine-de-Fierbois there was a hidden sword, which she was to get out. It turned out to be true. The sword, dug up from the ground and marked with five crosses, supposedly belonged to Charles Martel. In addition, the voices told Joan to carry a banner—a white field with lilies, an image of God, angels, and the words *Jesus* and *Mary*.

Charles VII then sent her to Orléans as captain of a troop of men. Joan disciplined the morally fallen army of defenders and, leading them into battle, ensured the freedom of Orléans in May 1429. On the eve of victory, as the voices had told her, she had been wounded. Joan led the French to several more glorious victories.

On July 17, 1429, the second part of her mission was fulfilled: the coronation of Charles VII in the Cathedral of Reims. As Jules Michelet writes in his *Histoire de France*, Joan kneeled before the king and said, "Gentle king, now is fulfilled the will of God." Despite pressure from Joan, he delayed sending troops to conquer Paris for a long time. The charge failed, and Joan was wounded in the thigh.

During the next battle (at Compiègne), in accordance with what the voices told her, the Virgin of Orléans was captured, imprisoned, and then sold by the Burgundians to the English.

She was then transported to the castle of Rouen, where she was brought before the inquisitorial tribunal. We already know what happens next.

A MIRACLE IN LOURDES

The event we described at the beginning of this chapter, called by Pius X himself the "Miracle of Fire," was the third miracle considered during the process of canonization of the Virgin of Orléans. In the end, it was withdrawn because two others sufficed, in which miraculous events of a medical nature took place. One of these miracles connected in an extraordinary way the heroine of France with the most famous French site of Marian apparitions: the Shrine of Lourdes.

Thérèse Belin—suffering from peritoneal and pulmonary tuberculosis, complicated by an organic lesion of the mitral orifice—was healed. This miracle occurred on August 22, 1909, during a procession of the Blessed Sacrament, when a priest with a monstrance passed before the sick woman who was lying on a stretcher, most likely unconscious. Fr. Léon Cristiani, who desired Joan's canonization, secured authorization from the bishop of Orléans to call upon Joan of Arc's name during the blessing of the sick, with the hope of witnessing a potential miracle through Joan's intervention. Upon the initial appeal to the Bl. Joan of Arc, Thérèse regained consciousness; at the subsequent invocation, she elevated herself from her stretcher; and by the third plea, she found herself to have completely recovered. And it wasn't just a feeling. The seriously ill woman—as later research revealed—suddenly and unexpectedly returned to full health. Although this miracle happened in Lourdes, there was no doubt that it should be attributed to the intercession of Joan of Arc.

The second miracle used in the process of canonization was the immediate and complete healing of Maria Antonia Mirandelle from a disease perforating the sole of her foot. Specifically, it was most likely granulomatous osteomyelitis of the right sole, along with purulent embolism.

Paul Delaroche, Joan of Arc Being Interrogated in Her Cell by the Cardinal of Winchester.

➤ Joan of Arc's Death at the Stake *by Hermann Stilke.*

FAITH WAS REWARDED

Of course, before the canonization took place, eleven years earlier, the Virgin of Orléans was beatified. This was done by Pope Pius X. As part of the beatification process, three healings were recognized as miracles. The first was experienced by Sr. Teresa of St. Augustine, a Benedictine nun from Orléans, who had suffered from a chronic, incurable gastric ulcer since 1897. Some believed that the non-healing ulcer may have already turned into cancer. The bedridden nun, as described by Ford, had acute pains in the stomach, which increased continuously. She vomited blood almost daily, becoming weak and falling ill with other illnesses. She was presented with the dilemma of choking if she ate any food, or dying of starvation if she did not. The disease progressed, the pains grew worse, and the nun not only lost hope for healing, but was getting ready to receive the last rites because the doctor himself thought that she would not live long.

On July 30, 1900, the sister began a novena to Joan of Arc. She was constantly tormented by bloody vomiting, which intensified on August 6. On that same night, a crisis occurred. The sister became weak and fainted, and the next day she started vomiting again. That evening, Sr. Teresa asked the sisters to prepare her habit, saying that she would get out of bed the next day because she would be cured. The sisters, however, were not so sure. Rather, they believed the religious garment would be useful for a funeral.

The sick sister fell asleep and slept until two o'clock in the morning. She wanted to get up for Matins, but she stayed in bed until half-past five. She probably couldn't wait for morning because, when the hour came, she got dressed, went down to the chapel, prayed and received Holy Communion, and then went to eat. She ate feeling no more pain, and the vomiting of blood ceased. It became clear to everyone that her faith healed her and that on the last day of the novena she received a miracle, which was later—by the authority of the Holy See—officially confirmed.

ONE-DAY NOVENA

The second miracle occurred in 1893 in the town of Faverolles (Diocese of Évreux). Sr. Julie Gauthier of St. Norbert, of the Congregation of Divine Providence at Évreux, had a sudden and unexpected recovery. For years, she had suffered from a cancerous ulcer in her left breast, which caused her terrible pain. The sister, who was a teacher, had a group of girls under her care. One day, in the company of eight of her students, she went to the church and prayed with them for her healing through the intercession of Joan of Arc. Sr. Julie, as Ford described, wanted to make a novena, but she felt so bad that she was afraid she wouldn't be able to pray nine days in a row. Then she got an idea that she would make a novena in one day, during one single visit to the church. Each of the girls said the prayers for one day of the novena, and she herself completed the ninth day. And suddenly, their prayers were answered. The sister, who went to church with great difficulty, returned from it in full vigor. That same day she felt completely healthy, and—after medical examination—not without reason. She had fully recovered!

The third healing, in 1891, was experienced by Sr. Jean-Marie Sagnier of Fruges (Diocese of Arras), a nun of the congregation of the Holy Family, who had suffered for three months from ulcers and abscesses in both legs. Doctors diagnosed chronic osteoarthritis, which they believed to be caused by underlying tuberculosis. They were unable to cure it. Lacking help here on earth, the sister turned to Heaven for help. She began to make a novena through the intercession of the Servant of God, Joan of Arc, and on the fifth day—suddenly and unexpectedly—she regained her health. After removing the bandages, the inflammation disappeared, the ulcers and wounds healed, and there were no signs of disease on the bones. From then on, doctors and drugs were no longer needed.

Tower of Rouen Castle, the remains of the fortress, where Joan was imprisoned during the trial.

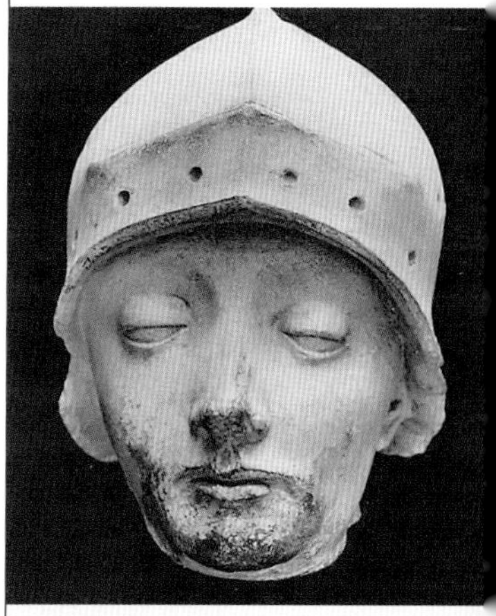

The head of a statue, long considered to have been modeled after the likeness of Joan of Arc.

ENDNOTES

1 Williamson, Allen. "Condemnation Trial–1456 July 7." *Joan of Arc Archive*. http://archive.joan-of-arc.org/joanofarc_1456_july_7.html.

2 Williamson, Allen. "Joan of Arc: A Life Summary Regarding Her Visions." *Joan of Arc Archive*. http://www.joan-of-arc.org/joanofarc_life_summary_visions.html.

272–305

➤ *Gerolamo Pesci's painting depicts the martyrdom of St. Januarius and the collection of his blood.*

⮝ *St. Januarius's tiara.*

⮟ *Domenico Gargiulo,* The Eruption of the Vesuvius and the Propitiatory Procession with the Relics of St. Januarius.

SIGN OF THE RESURRECTION

St. Januarius

You can see him everywhere in Naples. He is a true icon of this city. The Neapolitans call him "santo nuostro" and "yellow face," because of the golden hue of his face on his reliquary. San Gennaro, as he is called in Italy—a bishop and martyr closely associated with Naples and its surroundings—lived at the turn of the third and fourth centuries. He's famous for the miracle of the liquefaction of his blood, which is kept in a sealed ampoule. Every year, Italians excitedly follow the news from Naples: has it dissolved or not? If so, they believe that the saint still has them under his protection. If not, they fear that something bad will happen.

Although there is no agreement on this, this miracle was most likely first observed in 1389.

As a result of severe drought in Naples and the surrounding area, there was widespread famine and disease. It was then—during the public display of the relic—that the clotted blood of St. Januarius changed its state from solid to liquid. Since then, this phenomenon has taken place several times a year in the Cathedral of San Gennaro in Naples, where the relic is kept in a special reliquary, in two hermetically sealed ampoules (the first is about one-third filled with blood clots, and the second contains only a few lumps). This happens on September 19, the anniversary of the saint's martyrdom; the Saturday before the first Sunday in May, which commemorates the transfer of his remains

The blood reliquary of the saint.

Spire of San Gennaro.

St. Januarius, *by Caravaggio.*

to Naples; and sometimes on December 16, the anniversary of Naples's preservation from the eruption of Mount Vesuvius in 1631.

The blood—which, according to tradition, was collected immediately after the bishop's beheading—placed next to the reliquary with the saint's skull—turns into a liquid regardless of the ambient temperature and other external factors, regardless of the prayers offered by the faithful. It remains in the liquid state for about eight days. There were years, however, when the blood did not dissolve at all (for example, in 1976).

DEFYING NATURE

To this day, scientists have not been able to fully explain a phenomenon that not only contradicts common sense, but also breaks all the laws of physics. While the Church has accepted the cult of this extraordinary relic, it has never officially recognized the extraordinary transformation as a miracle. Professor Gastone Lambertini, a researcher of this phenomenon, said "it challenges every law of nature and every explanation that does not refer to the supernatural." For us believers it remains a "sign of eternal life and resurrection." Cardinal Prospero Lambertini—later Pope Benedict XIV—beautifully wrote about this relic: "There is blood in Naples that cannot wait for the resurrection." There's no doubt—though some people try to question it—that there's blood in the reliquary. Scientific research has proven it.

PROPHECY?

From the behavior of the blood, the Neapolitans draw conclusions about their future. The miracle is awaited in Naples like a prophecy. If the clotted blood dissolves quickly, that's a good sign. And

Good news for the residents of Naples: the blood of their city's patron has turned into a liquid and moves in the ampoule.

Cathedral of San Gennaro in Naples.

if it doesn't, people tremble with fear that something bad will happen, that some catastrophe will occur, or that hard times await them, not only locally but globally. There might be something to these prophecies, but one must keep a level head, because automatically linking episodes when the blood does not liquefy with various tragedies is quite far-fetched. What's more, some "prophecies" seem to be rather mere confirmations of facts that have already occurred. Neapolitan clergy fight against such an exaggerated approach to the blood relics. "People want to read into what happens to Januarius's blood. They wonder if there will be some kind of catastrophe when the blood doesn't liquefy," remarks Msgr. Vincenzo de Gregorio, custodian of the relics. "They still mention, for example, the famous eruption of Vesuvius in 1631, when the lava stopped in front of the relics. However, one cannot be guided by superstitions. I am trying to change this way of thinking." In addition, the Neapolitan clergy oppose turning the relics of the blood of St. Januarius into a fetish, a magical talisman that could obscure what is most important to people: faith in God.

NOT ONLY ST. JANUARIUS

The unusual changes to the state of blood sealed in the reliquary are by no means unique to the saint. The blood of other holy martyrs, enclosed in reliquaries, has similar properties. Its state—on certain days of the year—changes. This includes the blood of St. Pantaleon, St. Patricia, St. Lawrence (more specifically, a mixture of blood, fat, ash, and skin), and several other saints. In fact, during the Baroque period, Naples itself was called the city of blood, because as many as two hundred ampoules with the blood of saints were kept in its churches. Out of these two hundred, there are a dozen or so left today.

Jusepe de Ribera, St. Januarius Emerges Unscathed from the Furnace, *in Naples cathedral.*

The relics are taken in procession through the middle of street fairs.

DYING FOR THE FAITH

But let us get back to the most famous Neapolitan. St. Januarius most likely came from a noble, aristocratic family, and as a young man (supposedly at the age of twenty!) he became the bishop of Benevento. He served during the persecution of Christians, launched by Emperor Diocletian. Tradition says that he helped everyone without exception, and, for this reason, he was also valued by pagans. The most well-known version of this story goes like this: One day Januarius learned that his friend, Deacon Sossus of Miseno, who was about thirty years old, was in prison in Puteoli (known today as Pozzuoli). He was imprisoned there by the governor, Dracontius, who ruled on behalf of the emperor. For what reason? Perhaps only because he was a Christian, or perhaps because he opposed the cult of the Cumaean sibyl, to whom crowds and pilgrimages of pagans flocked (her cave was located near the ancient city of Cumae, a few kilometers from Puteoli). Januarius went to the prison with Deacon Festus and Lector Desiderius. He wanted to offer Sossus spiritual support, to confirm his faith. Upon arrival, all boldly and unanimously confessed that they were Christians, and—as might be expected—were imprisoned. The next day in the arena of the city amphitheater, they were thrown to the mercy of wild bears. They ultimately died elsewhere—all three (and three other people who stood up for them) were beheaded at the Solfatara—a volcanic crater and sulfur mine. It was then, according to tradition, that a pious woman named Eusebia collected Januarius's blood into two glass ampoules.

The woman did this in accordance with the Christian tradition of keeping relics and honoring people who died for their faith. In the days of the first martyrs, many Christians would secretly gather in the place where the martyrdom occurred. They would take the body to bury it. They also collected blood. The early Christians were convinced that when their fellow brothers

The martyrdom of Bishop Januarius in the amphitheatre at Pozzuoli.

272–305

➤ *The execution and collection of St. Januarius's blood.*

➤ *Traditional celebrations of the Festa di San Gennaro.*

in the Faith suffered a martyr's death, they were accepted by Christ as a reward for their faithfulness to Jesus, for their faithfulness to the Faith. The blood was intended for veneration, to preserve the memory of the martyr, and later it was used to accompany prayers for his intercession.

A FULFILLED PROMISE

Before strange things began to happen with the blood Eusebia collected, God authenticated Januarius's sanctity with more conventional miracles. One of them happened right after his death. On their way to the place of the execution, the condemned met a poor old man. He hoped that contact with the holy martyrs would obtain for him special graces from God. He fell to Januarius's feet and asked if he was worthy to receive a piece of his garment. "When my body is dead, know that I will personally give you a stole that I will be blindfolded with," the bishop assured him. And that's what happened. His body had not yet cooled down from the decapitation when he had fulfilled this promise. He appeared to the old man and handed him a stole. The overjoyed old man reverently hid it in his breast pocket. The executioner and the soldiers—not having seen it—made fun of the man. "So what? Did you receive what this convict we beheaded promised you?" they asked. "Of course," the old man answered, showing them his treasure. They looked at it and were greatly astonished. This and subsequent miracles obtained through the intercession of Januarius intensified the cult of the bishop and martyr executed in Pozzuoli.

PROTECTOR FROM DISASTERS

Crowds flocked to his relics (initially to the Neapolitan catacombs, and later to the Naples Cathedral), petitioning the saint for help in times of natural disasters—from the frequent threat from Mount Vesuvius, an active volcano erupting from time to time, from numerous epidemics, and from famine. Forty years after Januarius became the principal patron of the city, in 512, there was another eruption of Vesuvius, and the lava was stopped. This was thought to be a result of the intervention of the saint after the bishop of Naples, Stephen I, initiated the propitiatory prayer. "St. Januarius our protector, pray for us to our God," prayed the Parenti di San Gennaro, faithful devotees who form one of the oldest prayer groups for the saint.

FAMILY BOND

To this day, a close bond connects St. Januarius to Naples and to Neapolitans. It is unbreakable because, as the archbishop of Naples Cardinal Crescenzio Sepe says, "The history of the Neapolitan people can only be interpreted and understood in the light of the life and martyrdom of St. Januarius." Residents turn to St. Januarius because they consider him a part of themselves, a member of their family, someone to whom they can turn in any need, in sadness, pain, or in moments of joy. Despite the passage of years and centuries, St. Januarius has always been a point of reference for the residents of Naples, especially in times of hardship, volcanic eruptions, and natural disasters. Even today, every Neapolitan, regardless of their profession or social status, turns to the saint with every petition. And the fact that Januarius listens to them to this day is evidenced by the numerous votive offerings of thanksgiving that continuously flow into the Naples Cathedral: jewels, gold, silver hearts, engraved plaques with messages of thanks, baby pillows received as gifts to mark the occasion of childbirth, votive offerings in the shape of human figures or eyes, and even pacifiers.

GUARDIAN OF THE KING

The most valuable votive offerings are housed in the Museum of the Treasure of San Gennaro, adjacent to the Naples Cathedral. Among them is a royal gift: a diamond necklace. It has quite an interesting story behind it. When King Umberto I came to Naples for the first time with Queen Margherita, an attempt was made to assassinate them. They miraculously avoided death. The minister was wounded in the shoulder. The king and queen attributed their miraculous survival to St. Januarius and gave him a beautiful diamond necklace. Many people warned them then not to leave, lest they lose the protection of St. Januarius. However, they decided otherwise. Unfortunately, when Umberto traveled to Monza near Milan in July 1900, he died from an assassin's bullet.

St. Januarius's statue and jewels from the Treasure of San Gennaro.

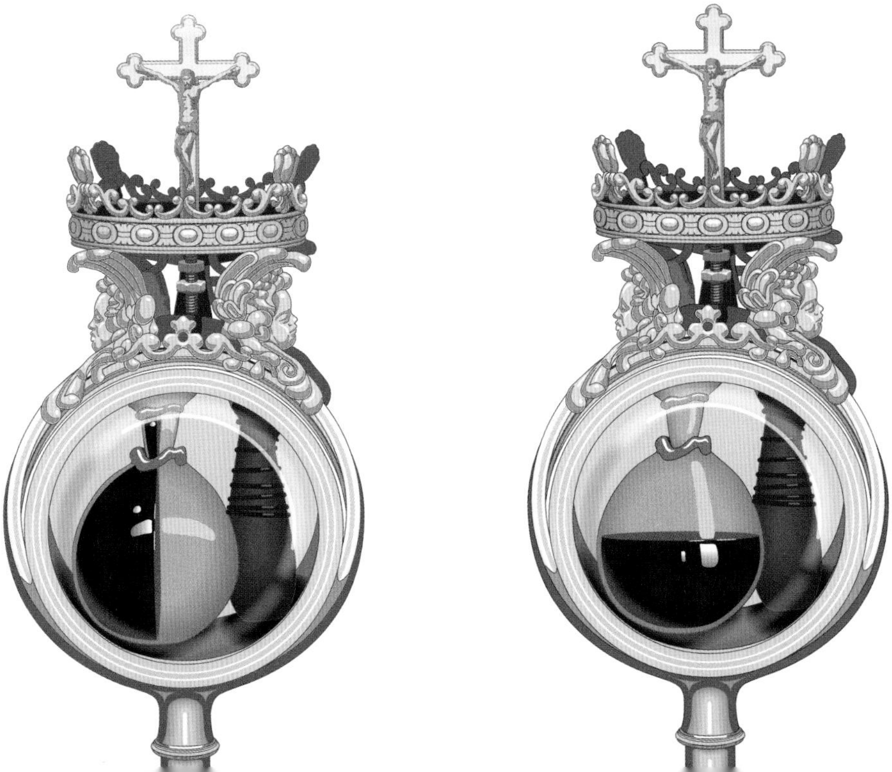

The congealed blood of St. Januarius turns to liquid and settles at the bottom of the vessel.

FILLED WITH THE POWER OF GOD

St. Gregory Thaumaturgus

St. Gregory, who was bishop of Neocaesarea in Pontus during the third century, is the only saint of the Catholic Church with the nickname "Miracle Worker." This is not without reason, as we shall see.

The bishop of Neocaesarea in the third century was St. Gregory the Miracle Worker. It was he who converted the inhabitants of the city from paganism and made them faithful disciples of Christ. He was born there, and there he called his countrymen to a new life in the Faith.

St. Gregory the Miracle Worker, according to tradition, was the first known person to whom the Virgin Mary and St. John the Apostle appeared.

It was the first half of the third century, and after studying at the school of the great theologian Origen, Gregory was preparing himself in seclusion to take over the bishopric of Neocaesarea in Pontus (today Niksar, in Turkey)—a city located on the coast of the Black Sea.

MARIAN APPARITION

Gregory was reading the Bible, meditating, turning the pages of the books, contemplating difficult theological problems, and asking God to reveal to him "hidden things." Just then, suddenly, the dimly lit room was brightened by a great light. He had a vision. He saw two figures: first an old man, then a woman. They were accompanied by an unearthly brightness. The scholarly theologian recognized the Virgin Mary and St. John the Evangelist in the apparition. The Mother of the Savior commanded her heavenly companion to explain to Gregory the most difficult truths of God—to reveal to him the mystery of piety. The result of the first recorded Marian apparition in Church history was the *Exposition of Faith*, which was dictated to Gregory by St. John himself. The "mystery of piety"—the doctrine of the Holy Trinity—was given to help the new bishop in the fight against all heresy.

SATAN ON A LEASH

Before Gregory could begin his bishopric ministry, he had to first reach Neocaesarea. St. Gregory of Nyssa, a bishop who lived about one hundred years later and wrote *The Life of St. Gregory the Wonderworker*, didn't hesitate to compare Gregory to Moses

TURKEY

The landscape of the Pontic Mountains. Pontus is the coastal part of Cappadocia.

St. Gregory of Nyssa, author of the Life of St. Gregory the Wonderworker.

St. Gregory treated the vision shown to him as if it were the manifestation of God Himself, who appears in light and cannot be seen by any human being. No one is pure enough not to be burned by the fire in their soul.

Gregory the Miracle Worker was born as Theodore and most likely came from a distinguished pagan family. Under the influence of Origen, Theodore was baptized and given the name Gregory.

Origen. For more than seven years, St. Gregory the Miracle Worker studied philosophy and theology under Origen.

St. Gregory of Nyssa, one of the Cappadocian Fathers, wrote about the life and miracles of Gregory the Miracle Worker.

himself. Gregory of Nyssa mentions an interesting legend about how during this journey, the newly appointed hierarch and several companions stopped in a pagan temple located near Neocaesarea due to nightfall and a raging downpour. Having no other choice, he decided to spend the night there. The evil spirits that resided there, however, could not tolerate his presence and fervent prayers. One of them froze at the invocation of the name of Christ, and the others fled at the mere sight of the Sign of the Cross. Gregory spent the whole night—as was his custom—praying and singing pious hymns in this temple.

At sunrise, a pagan priest came to the temple and noticed the place had lost its powers and he could no longer perform his pagan worship there. No miracles took place there anymore, and the oracle did not function. The demons were banished from there by the priest of Christ and could no longer be invoked. The enraged pagan then caught up to Gregory and began to threaten him for having the audacity to enter his temple. He threatened to make a complaint against him to the emperor and his state dignitaries. "The true God who commands devils has given me the power to cast out and summon evil spirits," Gregory explained to him. "If what you say is true, then tell the spirits to return," the priest said. Gregory then gave him a page torn out of a book, on which he wrote "Gregory to Satan: come back!" and ordered him to put it on the altar. The priest did as he was told. The demon came back. The astonished worshiper of evil spirits rushed back to the bishop, who was leaving, and begged Gregory to tell him about the God who had given him such authority and power. Gregory then introduced him to the truths of the Faith, but foreseeing that he would not understand the Incarnation, he said that God can only prove this truth by miracles. "If that is the case, tell the boulder to move to another place," the priest asked. Gregory, by the power of God, raised the boulder and began to move it. That was enough. The pagan priest gave up his previous life and became a Christian.

INVOLUNTARY HIERARCHY

The hero of these stories—St. Gregory the Miracle Worker—was born in Neocaesarea into a wealthy pagan family. He was originally named Theodore. At the

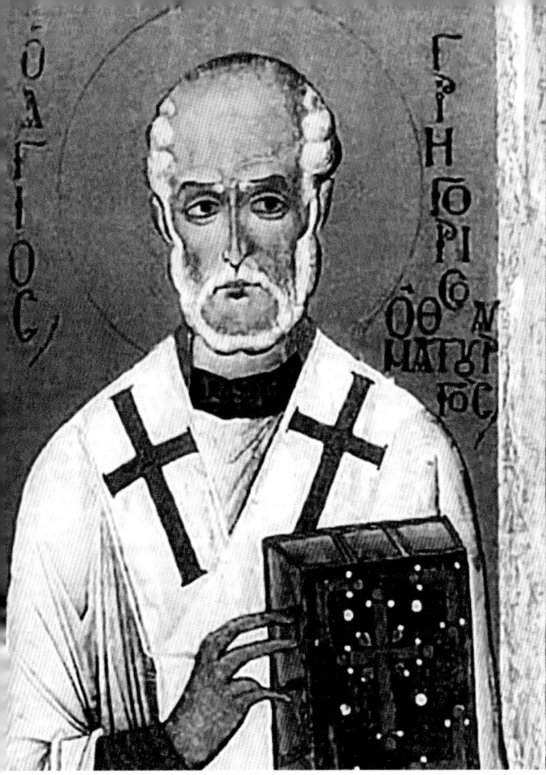

Traditional architecture in the rural parts of Pontus.

In Neocaesarea (now Niksar), Christianity was replaced by Islam.

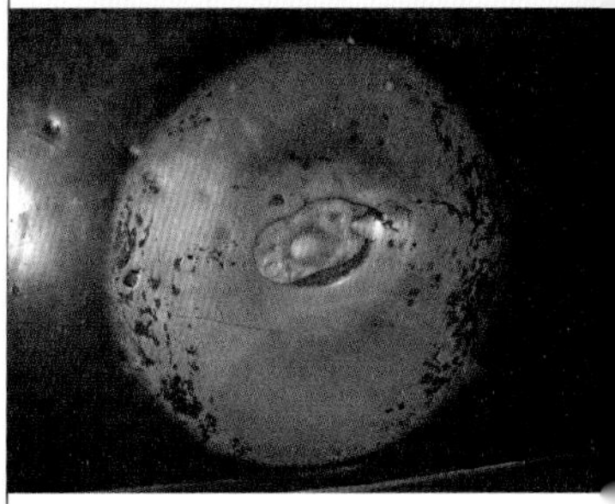

Column of St. Gregory in the Hagia Sophia, Istanbul. According to tradition, inserting a finger into the copper-covered hole and making a full clockwise rotation of the hand ensures the intercession of St. Gregory.

Neocaesarea at sunset.

age of fourteen, he lost his father and was raised by his mother. A few years later, Gregory intended to go with his brother, Athenodorus, to the Phoenician city of Berytus (today Beirut) to study law. At the same time, however, his brother-in-law was appointed assistant to the governor of Caesarea in Palestine and asked them to accompany his wife, who was to join him. They went. Gregory later recognized this as the work of Divine Providence and the care of his guardian angel, because it coincided with the arrival of the great Christian sage, Origen, from Alexandria to Caesarea. The brothers entered his school to study philosophy and theology instead of law. Gregory became Origen's favorite student, and Origen instilled in him a great love for Christ.

After his permanent conversion to Christianity, Baptism, and several years of study, ending with the delivery of his well-known public speech in honor of his master, he returned to his hometown of Pontus. It was expected at that time that the thirty-five-year-old man would share his knowledge with his compatriots and lead them. Instead, he retreated to a remote area, wanting to live the life of a hermit (although other sources say he intended to become a lawyer). In any case, his plans were interrupted by the pious Phedimus, archbishop of Amasea. He knew about Gregory's great abilities and extraordinary righteousness, and he decided to ordain him bishop of Neocaesarea. However, being unable to reach him (Gregory did not feel he was the right person to accept such a role and went into hiding), he did it "in spirit." Origen's student—whether he wanted to or not—accepted the office of bishop. However, he asked that before the official anointing he be allowed to study the truths of the Faith for some time and prepare himself better for such a responsible function. It was then that he experienced the aforementioned apparition.

BISHOPRIC MINISTRY

He was an extraordinary bishop. When he assumed this honorable position, there were only seventeen Christians living in Neocaesarea. When he died thirty years later, the numbers had reversed: now

⮝ *Trabzon. The Church of St. Sophia.*

there were only seventeen pagans in the city. It was he who converted and baptized St. Macrina the Elder, the grandmother of St. Gregory of Nyssa and St. Basil the Great. He also participated in the Synod in Antioch, where Paul of Samosata was condemned as a heretic. He mitigated the effects of the invasion of the Goths and Boranians in the 250s.

THAUMATURGUS, MEANING MIRACLE WORKER

People hailed him as a miracle worker, equal to the apostles, spreading the word about how he healed the sick with the help of his stole and his priestly vestments, expelled evil spirits from people and places, and stuck a crosier in the ground from which a tree grew, stopping the flooding of the River Lukos. He advised the inhabitants of the city of Koman to elect someone as bishop who wasn't from a wealthy family, but someone who was poor, though holy and understanding. They chose Alexander, the coal-heaver. Thanks to a miracle, together with his deacon he survived the persecution of Christians under Emperor Decius and protected his people from apostasy, and in a vision he saw the martyrdom of a young man. There was also talk of how he foretold a plague and then stopped it. Another time, while trying to build a church in Neocaesarea, Gregory couldn't find a good place for it. He turned to God Himself with this problem. He raised his hands to the sky, said a prayer, and ordered the mountain that was in his way to move to another spot. And that's what happened! Not only that: the church erected on this site miraculously survived an earthquake that reduced the entire city to rubble.

RECONCILED BROTHERS

An interesting story describes how Gregory miraculously reconciled brothers who were feuding over their father's inheritance. The men quarreled over the possession of a single lake. Neither one of them wanted to give it up and give it to the other. The well-respected Gregory, however, called them to live in harmony and peace. This was pleaded in vain. One of the brothers organized an army, as St. Gregory of Nyssa writes, "with many hands willing to commit murders" to appropriate the lake by force. The next day, when Gregory was to arrive at the lake, a battle was to take place. The man of God, however, could not allow this to happen. He prayed fervently all night, and at dawn he made the matter of dispute simply disappear: the lake dried up. The inundated basin turned into fertile soil that could be easily divided. The dispute was settled without bloodshed. When describing this, St. Gregory of Nyssa compared the bishop's act to the just judgment of King Solomon (when two women quarreled over a baby, the biblical ruler then ordered to cut the child in two, and the woman who shrieked and chose to give up any rights to the child rather than let it die was revealed as the true mother).

YOU MUSTN'T RIDICULE

From time to time, Gregory's mercy and kindness were abused. God, however, wouldn't allow His anointed one to be ridiculed.

Once, two Jews ambushed the bishop by the road. One of them pretended to be a corpse, while the other approached Gregory, lamenting that he had nothing to bury him in. The merciful bishop then threw his cloak over the supposedly dead man. When he was gone, amused by the successful ruse and naivety of the hierarch, the Jew began to poke his friend. "Get up!" he screamed, louder and louder. But it was in vain. The man who only pretended to be dead died under the holy weight of Gregory's cloak.

If the words of St. Gregory of Nyssa are to be believed, there were countless other miracles performed by Gregory the Miracle Worker.

Pontus, the coastal part of Cappadocia, was the homeland of Gregory the Miracle Worker. Cappadocia is primarily known for its characteristic tuff rock formations, in which houses and churches are carved in tuff stone. It was a center of Christian monasticism until the Ottoman conquest.

View of present-day Neocaesarea.

HE SAW SUFFERING JESUS IN HIS PATIENTS

St. Giuseppe Moscati

Before his death, he healed people as a physician. After his earthly pilgrimage, he continues to heal as a saint. St. Giuseppe Moscati is highly venerated in Naples and throughout southern Italy, but his example of sacrificial love for God and neighbor inspires people—especially doctors—all over the world. As a deeply religious person, he was well aware that human abilities are very limited and that the best doctor is God Himself.

Photo of Giuseppe Moscati as a child.

Giuseppe Moscati's office.

Pharmacy of the Incurables.

One day he was called to see a woman who had consulted him once before. He quickly realized she hadn't been taking the treatment prescribed by him. She was poor, and he understood that she had no money for it, but he didn't show it. He scolded the woman for disobeying him, and when he left, the sick woman's disheartened family found five hundred lire under her pillow. Another time, an acquaintance saw him in the most neglected, poorest

neighborhood of Naples. “What are you doing here?” the acquaintance asked. “Nothing special. I come here every day to work as a spittoon cleaner.” It turned out he was visiting a young man suffering from tuberculosis, who lived in a rented space. Every day he took the tissues with the coughed-up secretions from him, burned them, and brought him new ones. He did so out of concern for the fate of the young man, because he knew if the owners of the residence found out about his tuberculosis, even though he was no longer contagious, they would throw him out. He wrote an unusual prescription for another young man: “Treatment by Eucharist.”

DOCTOR OF THE POOR

The hero of these anecdotes, born in Benevento into a large aristocratic family, is Giuseppe Moscati, who was a well-known Neapolitan doctor and an outstanding scientist. He was called the doctor of the poor. He discovered his medical calling when one of his brothers—after falling off a horse—suffered a head injury. He had seizures as a result of it, and after a few years of suffering, he died. Giuseppe studied medicine at the University of Naples and was one of its most talented graduates. After completing his studies, he started working at the Hospital for the Incurables (the prominent *Incurabili*) in Naples, without giving up his scientific research activities at the Institute of Physiology. After some time he also became a university lecturer and director of the Institute of Anatomical Pathology. He had the chance to have a spectacular scientific career (he had more than thirty published scientific works, among other things), but he preferred to devote himself entirely to treating the sick, helping the poor, and training young doctors. “Love changed the world, not knowledge,” he said. He saw the suffering Christ in his patients. He treated many for free and even helped them financially. He preached the Christian Faith more by deeds than by words. Thanks to his efforts, cholera epidemics were brought under control. He was one of the pioneers of using insulin to treat diabetes, as well as a pioneer of using biochemical tests in diagnosis. He personally contributed to the rescue of the elderly and the sick from the hospital in Torre del Greco during the eruption of Mount Vesuvius on April 7, 1906. He was

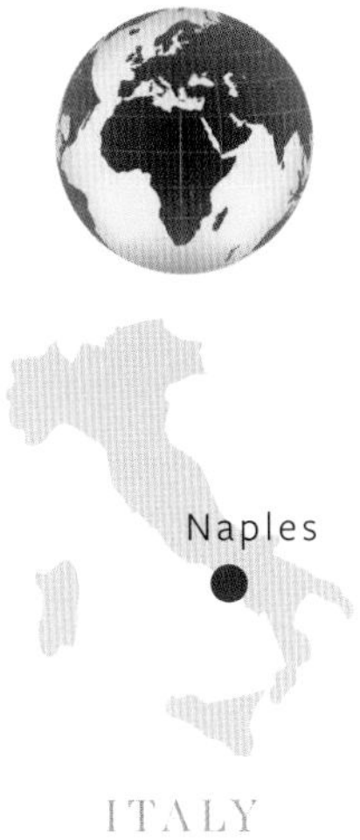

Panorama of Dormiente del Sannio.

➤ *Hospital of the Incurables in Naples.*

➤ *Bl. Caterina Volpicelli, Bartolo Longo's housekeeper, influenced the development of the spirituality of the future saint.*

impeccably honest and virtuous. He loved the truth and saw its source in God. He condemned the egotism of the "priests of science." In an era of raging secularization, he never hid his deep faith: he attended Holy Mass every day and received the Body of Christ at every opportunity. He died in the opinion of holiness, exhausted by extremely intense work, on Holy Tuesday, 1927. He was only forty-six years old.

DEATH TO INFECTION!

The first miracle that contributed to his beatification occurred on the night of February 7, 1941, in the province of Caserta in the Campania region of southern Italy, north of Naples. Five days earlier, twelve-year-old Raffaele Perrotta attended a Holy Mass celebrated in the chapel of the middle school of St. Thomas Aquinas in Piedimonte d'Alife (now called Piedimonte Matese). It was then that he began to feel the first symptoms emerging. His head started hurting. He became pale and started vomiting. He was placed in the bedroom of the dormitory where he lived, and a doctor was immediately called. The medic arrived in the late afternoon, and after examining him and seeing that the boy's neck was stiff and in pain, he concluded the boy was most likely suffering from meningitis. He then ordered ice placed on his head, isolated him from the other students, and insisted that he be taken to his family home in Calvi Risorta as soon as possible. And so it was done.

At home, he was taken care of by two other doctors, who confirmed and specified the initial diagnosis: meningococcal cerebrospinal meningitis. Raffaele's condition deteriorated significantly during this time—he lost consciousness, had a high fever, experienced convulsions, was delirious, and made inhuman sounds.

The doctors gave up, saying that there was no chance for recovery. The disease revealed itself in such a severe form that it would lead to death very quickly. Upon hearing this diagnosis, the family began preparations for the funeral. And then Fr. Giovanni Zumbolo, pastor of the local parish, stepped in. He gave the distressed family a picture of Giuseppe Moscati and instructed them to pray to him for help. The mother placed the image under the pillow on which Raffaele's head rested, and then she and the rest of the household all fell to their knees praying for his healing.

A few hours later, in the middle of the night, Raffaele suddenly and unexpectedly regained consciousness. He started speaking sensibly, and soon after he asked for something to eat. The doctors, when they arrived in the morning, were amazed. The boy showed no signs of illness and appeared to be in perfect health. Wanting to check it with a lumbar puncture, they collected cerebrospinal fluid for testing. Upon analysis, no meningococci or any other pathogenic microorganisms were detected. There was no trace of his illness.

In 1975, Raffaele and his large family attended the beatification of his benefactor. He was also present at his canonization ceremony. He passed away in 2015 at the age of eighty-six.

A DREAM ABOUT AN OPERATION

The second miraculously healed person was Constantino Nazzaro, a senior prison official in Avellino. In 1923, Constantino began complaining of back pain, and an abscess formed on the lower part of his right thigh. Doctors didn't know how to help him. They sent him to be treated at a hospital in Genoa, but long-term treatments proved ineffective. When his health deteriorated significantly, they finally found the cause. Addison's disease was to blame. People suffering from Addison's disease, due to the deficiency of hormones produced by the adrenal glands, are weak, and they have limited mobility and low blood pressure. With time, more and more ailments appeared: metabolic abnormalities, fever, insomnia, abdominal pain, nausea, and vomiting. Unfortunately, in those days, the disease was not treated properly, and the prognosis wasn't favorable. The administered drugs could only extend the life of the person suffering from it, but quite often an adrenal crisis would lead to death. There were no cases of complete recovery. One day, in 1954, saddened by his diagnosis, the man entered the Church of Gesù Nuovo in Naples. Seeing a group of people praying at the tomb of the doctor of the poor, Giuseppe Moscati, he approached it, knelt down, and began to ask the servant of God for help. He returned frequently for the next four

Relics of the holy doctor of the poor.

Bronze statue of Giuseppe Moscati by Pier Luigi Spolesa.

▲ *Images of the tireless doctor can be seen literally everywhere in Naples: in churches, in squares, and on cars.*

months, until, at last, his fervent prayers were answered. It happened that same year, in the summer, between the end of August and the beginning of September. Dr. Moscati came to him in a dream one night. The man dreamt that the doctor was operating on him, exchanging the diseased organs for healthy ones. What's more, he told him to stop taking his medicine. In the morning, after waking up, Constantino found that all his ailments had disappeared; nothing hurt him anymore. He was astonished. Even more astonished were the doctors examining him, who said he was completely healthy. There was no medical explanation for Constantino's miraculous healing.

WHY DON'T YOU COME TO ME?

Only one more miracle was needed for the canonization of Bl. Giuseppe Moscati. It occurred twenty-four years after Constantino Nazzaro was healed. Giuseppe Montefusco, from Somma Vesuviana, at the foot of Mount Vesuvius, experienced it. In 1978, the twenty-year-old man—who worked hard as a blacksmith—began to feel sick. He was pale and weak, often dizzy, and had no appetite. After some time, fever set in. His family doctor initially prescribed him antibiotics, but when they didn't help, he ordered a whole host of tests. The test results revealed severe anemia. He needed immediate hospitalization and a blood transfusion. After being admitted to the Cardarelli Hospital of Naples on April 13, 1978, it turned out that the young man had acute nonlymphocytic leukemia, also called acute myeloid leukemia. It is a very serious disease that usually ends in death in a short time. In Montefusco's case, however, the test results were so terrible that initially he was not given more than three days to live. But things did not play out in the grim way that doctors

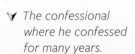

▼ *The confessional where he confessed for many years.*

anticipated. Although his test results were still poor, after several days in the intensive care unit, the patient was transferred to the hematology unit. His bones ached, he had an enlarged liver and spleen, and he was suffering from pancytopenia (a deficiency of all the morphotic elements of blood: erythrocytes, leukocytes and thrombocytes). He was given up to a month to live. And then something strange happened. First, there was a dream. The sick man's mother had a dream of a mysterious man who emanated an otherworldly kindness, a doctor in a white shirt, perhaps a lab coat. She realized she had to turn to him for help. "Why do you go to everyone and not to me?" he asked. She woke up. She didn't know who the man in the dream was. She told the pastor about it, and he directed her attention to Bl. Giuseppe Moscati, who was buried in the Church of Gesù Nuovo in Naples. The next day, the woman went to the church with her cousin and saw him there. Yes, it was him. The woman burst into tears, fell to her knees in front of his grave, and begged him for help. She acquired a picture to give to her son. Along with the image, she also took some water and soil from the room where the body of the blessed one had been to give to him. All the relatives began praying for the man's healing.

Montefusco took the picture and placed it in the hospital room, where three other patients were also lying. One of them was constantly blaspheming. The picture irritated him, so the sick man put it under a blanket. He began to pray. It was three in the morning when he suddenly woke up. His hospital companions were asleep in misery. Suddenly, he saw a doctor in a white shirt enter through the open door. "Don't worry, you will be healthy," he said, and walked out. The man also noticed a wooden cart for delivering medicine.

The saint's relics.

The tomb of the doctor of the poor.

DEUS ABSCONDITUS

Church of St. Giuseppe Moscati.

Image of Moscati in the altar of the Church of Gesù Nuovo.

The next day, Montefusco told his mother and the doctors everything. The medics laughed at him because no doctors were around at three in the morning; what's more, wooden carts had been long outmoded by metal and plastic. Giuseppe, however, was convinced that his namesake, Bl. Giuseppe Moscati, visited him that night at three in the morning. It didn't take long for his words to come true. The leukemia disappeared soon after. It was something absolutely incredible because everyone was convinced treatment could not lead to this! The medically inexplicable healing was later unanimously confirmed by doctors of the Vatican medical commission. On this basis, on October 25, 1987, Pope John Paul II canonized the Neapolitan physician. The healed Giuseppe Montefusco was in attendance at the ceremony.

GRACES ARE STILL FLOWING

The Neapolitan doctor contributes to many healings to this very day. Every day he listens to people who, praying at his sarcophagus, ask him to intercede with God. There are many testimonies of the graces received today. You can read about them in every issue of the periodical *Il Gesù Nuovo*. The saint continues to help with all kinds of medical needs, something that is most clearly evidenced by the various votive offerings made to him, which can be seen in huge numbers on the walls of the museum dedicated to this extraordinary man of God at the Basilica of Gesù Nuovo.

Modest furnishings of the selfless doctor's bedroom.

▼ *The church of the Salesians in Turin, which was built in the late nineteenth century.*

➤ *Already devoted to Mary as a child, St. John brought from his family home a fervent religiousness and veneration for the Blessed Mother.*

HEALINGS, RESURRECTIONS, AND PROPHETIC DREAMS

St. John Bosco

The miraculous healings of four Italian women contributed to the beatification and canonization of Don John Bosco. However, many extraordinary healings took place even before his death. In fact, he is still helping today. To this day, Salesian bulletins are full of thanksgiving for the graces asked through his intercession. The founder of the Salesians also received from God other charisms, among which the most striking was the gift of prophetic dreams.

"The first healing took place in Rimini," one can read in Pius XI's decree *Geminata Laetitia*, with which the pope approved miracles prayed for through the intercession of Bl. John Bosco. Anna Maccolini fell ill in October 1930 with bronchopneumonia and influenza, which lasted until the following February. Around the middle of December 1930, vein inflammation appeared on the left leg and near the left thigh, so that the entire leg was covered to such an extent that making any movement was impossible. At the same time, the leg was swollen to twice its thickness. It should be noted that if phlebitis is a severe disease for the young, it is much more dangerous for the old due to arteriosclerosis. This was the opinion of the two doctors treating the patient, who agreed on the diagnosis. Taking into account the serious age of the woman, as she was seventy-four years old, and even more the accompanying flu infection, they thought it was unlikely for her to recover from the disease. Moreover, as all doctors

know, sudden recovery from phlebitis is impossible. The aforementioned Anna, one night, at the end of the same year, after

The main altar of the Basilica of Mary Help of the Faithful in Turin, with an image of the Mother of God, painted at St. John's request.

➤ *Statue of Mary Help of Christians.*

⮝ *The oratory founded by Don Bosco served poor and abandoned youth as a place to meet, play, and study.*

⮝ *St. John Bosco was canonized by Pius XI on Easter 1934.*

a three-day devotion to Bl. John Bosco, having touched a diseased vein with a relic, suddenly felt completely healed from phlebitis. The pain and swelling disappeared, and the freedom of movement and bending returned. The complete recovery is attested to not only by the doctors who treated the patient, but also by the experts who visited Anna months after her recovery. The three experts, appointed by the Holy Congregation, unanimously agree with the doctors treating the patient in the diagnosis and in the recognition of the miracle.

The case of the second miracle is similarly clear. Catherine Pilenga, born in Lanfranchi, suffered from an arthritic condition, primarily affecting her legs and knees, causing significant damage to her veins, although not life-threatening. Despite undergoing various treatments since early 1903, none proved effective.

She journeyed to Lourdes twice, yet on neither occasion did she experience any healing, including her visit in May 1931. Before departing Lourdes, she beseeched the Blessed Virgin: "Since I did not receive the grace of healing here, may my devotion to Bl. Don Bosco bring about my healing in Turin." Thus, her appeal to John Bosco and the universal intercession of the Virgin Mary became apparent. Upon returning from France and finding herself in the same dire situation, she visited the Basilica of Our Lady Help of Christians in Turin on May 6. Assisted by her sister and the coachman, she alighted from the carriage, entered the basilica, took a seat, and prayed before the tomb containing the body of Bl. John Bosco. Approximately twenty minutes later, she knelt down. Upon rising, she walked to the altar of the Virgin Mary and knelt once more. It was then, as if awakening from a dream, that she realized she had been healed. Without assistance, she walked freely, to the amazement of all those who knew she had been unable to move before.

She stepped into the coach, climbed the stairs, and descended without any difficulty. Her healing was lasting, according to the doctors and experts who examined her, and the miracle was soon recognized by the Church.

ULCER AND ARTHRITIS

However, two other healings, involving a nun named Provina Negro and a young woman named Teresa Callegari from the Emilia-Romagna region, were instrumental in Don Bosco's beatification.

In 1905, Sister Provina Negro of Giaveno, belonging to the Congregation of the Daughters of Mary Help of Christians founded by Don Bosco, was afflicted with an advanced stomach ulcer. She endured excruciating pain, weakness, and loss of appetite. Treatment by Dr. Farini in nearby Turin proved futile, and her condition worsened. Encouraged by her fellow sisters, she embarked on a novena to the Servant of God Don John Bosco. On Sunday, July 29, 1906, Sr. Provina prayed alone. In a spontaneous act, she crumpled a picture of Don Bosco, which she had kept by her bedside, and swallowed it. Almost immediately, she felt completely healed, and she didn't feel ill any longer. She never complained of stomach problems again.

Twelve years later, in November 1918, twenty-year-old Teresa Callegari from Castel San Giovanni contracted post-infectious pneumonia. Although she overcame this illness, she developed acute post-infectious arthritis as a complication, affecting multiple joints. Medical interventions proved ineffective, and her health continued to decline, rendering her unable to eat by 1921. Doctors predicted her imminent demise. Persuaded by a parish priest and a nun, Teresa embarked on a novena to John Bosco. After one novena, she commenced another, but unfortunately, her health continued to deteriorate.

One January day at four in the morning, on the last day of the novena, Teresa woke up, started talking to another arthritis patient, and suddenly experienced an unusual vision. She noticed that a priest was standing on the right side of her bed, next to a table. "*Bogia le gambe*" he spoke to her in the Piedmontese dialect. The girl did not know this dialect, but she concluded that he told her to move her legs. She did so, and then she immediately stood up and started walking. She was very surprised that she no longer felt any discomfort. The priest, whom she recognized as Don Bosco, with a smile on his face, withdrew step by step until he completely disappeared. She was healed, and the doctors had nothing left to do except confirm it.

A BEACON OF THE CHURCH

The heavenly benefactor of these four women, John Bosco, came from a poor family. He was born in northern Italy and lost his father at the age of two. He was a farmhand, a tailor's apprentice, a cobbler, and a waiter, but eventually he succeeded in realizing his dream

In addition to the Salesian Congregation, St. John Bosco founded the Order of the Daughters of Mary Help of Christians and the Salesian Family.

The relics of St. John Bosco are displayed for public veneration.

A plaque that commemorates Don Bosco's stay at the seminary in Chieri, where the saint studied from 1835 to 1841.

The shrine founded by St. John Bosco is a spiritual center of the Salesian ministry.

of becoming a priest. From then on, he devoted himself wholeheartedly to helping poor, abandoned boys wandering the streets, first in Turin and later in other cities throughout Italy. Loving them unconditionally, St. John Bosco did everything he could to make them into respectable citizens and save their souls. He helped them materially and spiritually and organized decent entertainment for them. He opened oratories, schools, and workshops for them, wrote books and edited magazines with them in mind, and founded thriving congregations of Salesian brothers and sisters. He also built churches. In his activities and in his educational model, he combined the sober spirituality of Francis de Sales with the cheerful approach of Philip Neri. He was a great venerator of Our Lady Help of Christians. Through the Salesian congregation he founded, he spread his educational system to the farthest corners of the world.

Thanks to his Salesian schools and institutes, many boys and girls who were in danger of going down the wrong path or becoming poor have gained a solid spiritual foundation and moral backbone, and what's more, acquired a good profession that allows them to make a decent living. Papal decrees called him, among other things, a beacon in the extremely difficult times of the nineteenth century, a priest according to the Heart of Jesus, an incomparable educator, and a propagator of faith and holiness.

MIRACULOUS INTERVENTIONS

Even during his lifetime, Don Bosco was credited with the gift of healing the sick (he healed, among others, a blind girl, six smallpox-stricken boys, a paralyzed ten-year-old girl, and a woman moving on crutches), multiplying food, and even raising the dead. In a rather strange way, Don Bosco healed a pyrexial man. First, he recommended that the sick man confess and receive Holy Communion. After the man did so, Don Bosco handed him a box of pills and instructed him to take them for the next few days. The man followed this instructions, and although no doctor had been able to help him before, he felt better. His fever stopped and he completely recovered. When local pharmacists examined the pills in hopes of finding a new cure for high fevers, they were astonished to find that they contained nothing more than plain bread. One day Don Bosco began distributing Holy Communion. However,

he noticed that the Hosts were scarce, and the faithful were very numerous. And then, in a bizarre way, the Hosts began to multiply. As a result, there was enough for everyone! On another occasion, Don Bosco promised the boys that they would be given edible chestnuts when they returned from a walk. Mother Margaret, who ran the kitchen for the boys, cooked half a large bag of chestnuts, thinking that it would be enough.

When the hungry boys returned, Don Bosco began handing out chestnuts. His charges lined up, and everyone was receiving a full beret of chestnuts. Mother Margaret realized that with such a distribution, there would not be enough for everyone. However, the priest did not give up and continued to generously give out chestnuts to his young charges, who approached one by one. When all the boys got their portions, there were still two portions of chestnuts left at the bottom of the basket—enough for Don Bosco's mother and himself.

One evening there was a shortage of bread for dinner for his charges. It was pointless to send the boys to the bakery, as its owner demanded payment for previous bread deliveries. Don Bosco himself began distributing dinner. This was not an easy task, as there were fifteen slices of bread left for three hundred boys. The pupils lined up. The priest handed each of them one slice of bread from the basket. When all the boys received bread, there were fifteen slices left at the bottom of the basket—precisely as many as there were at the beginning!

Margaret, mother of St. John Bosco.

The house in Becchi, near Turin, where John Bosco was born in 1815.

The façade of the Basilica of Mary Help of Christians in Turin, which was consecrated in 1868.

In 1870, while Don Bosco was in Florence, he was approached by the Marquise Girolama Uguccioni. The woman begged him to go with her to her villa, to her dying godson. When they arrived, they found that the boy had already died. The priest and those present then said a prayer to Our Lady Help of Christians. Then Don Bosco gave the deceased a blessing. Suddenly, something unexpected happened.

As soon as he finished reciting the appropriate formula, the boy yawned and began to breathe. He returned to the world of the living, and news of this miracle spread through the neighborhood.

Aloysius Orione, founder of the Orionine Fathers and a saint himself, can also be counted among those healed by Don Bosco.

Here's his story: when St. John Bosco died, the multitude of the faithful went to visit his coffin, which was on display in the church. Many wanted to take small relics. Some handed various objects, such as pictures or rosaries, to Don Bosco's pupils, who then touched his body with them. Aloysius Orione hung around among Don Bosco's charges.

He came up with the idea that he would make balls of bread, touch Don Bosco with them, and then distribute them to anyone willing. Unfortunately, while cutting the loaf, he very severely and deeply cut the index finger of his own right hand. He fell into a panic because it occurred to him that with a damaged finger he would not be able to fulfill his dream of becoming a priest (in those days this was a very real obstacle!). He quickly wrapped the bloody finger in a handkerchief, ran to the chapel where the deceased was laid, and touched Don Bosco's hand with this finger. When he removed his makeshift bandage, only a small scar remained from the deep wound.

WONDROUS DREAMS

Yet it wasn't through healings (although there would certainly be numerous such accounts today, as they have been and continue to be published in every Salesian bulletin since Don Bosco's passing), miraculous food multiplications, raising the dead, or even bilocation that the Salesian founder gained renown. What was most extraordinary in his life were his prophetic dreams. He experienced more than a hundred of them. Through these dreams, St. John Bosco received insights about his own life (he had his first such dream at the age of nine, in which he witnessed the transformation of mischievous boys into virtuous ones!), the fate of the Church, the Salesians, and the oratory he established. Through his dreams, he glimpsed into the future and even perceived the state of conscience of his students.

The most renowned dream remains the one concerning the two columns from May 30, 1862 (immortalized in Turin's Basilica of Our Lady Help of Christians).

In the dream, the priest witnessed a great battle at sea. A multitude of small and large vessels were engaged in combat against one majestic ship. Behind the grand vessel, smaller boats received orders from it and endeavored to defend themselves from enemy assaults through myriad maneuvers. The large ship was assailed by a wide array of weapons (cannons, firearms, explosives, and even books). The adversaries appeared to benefit from the opposing wind and turbulent sea.

Amidst the waters rose two sturdy and towering columns. Atop the first column shone a luminous Host, accompanied by a plaque bearing the inscription *Salus credentium* ("Salvation of believers"). On the second, lower column, bearing the inscription *Auxilium Christianorum* ("Help of Christians"), stood a statue of the Immaculate Virgin.

The grand ship was steered by the Holy Father. Despite enemy attacks, the pope convened the captains of the smaller vessels twice and valiantly endeavored to position the ship between the two columns, securing it with ropes and anchors. The holes inflicted by the enemy on the ship's side were sealed by the wind blowing from the columns. The assailants lost their cannons and other weaponry and resorted to hand-to-hand combat. Although the pope was slain, his successor promptly assumed his position and successfully guided the ship between the two columns, anchoring it. At this moment, the enemy vessels suddenly ceased or sank, and the smaller boats likewise docked near the columns.

Don Bosco's collaborator, Bl. Fr. Michael Rua, was the first to interpret this dream. According to him, the pope's ship symbolizes the Church, the vessels represent individuals, and the sea signifies the world. Those defending the Church are virtuous individuals, while adversaries seek to undermine it. The two salvific columns represent devotion to the Most Holy Virgin and frequent reception of Holy Communion. St. John Bosco further elucidated that the enemy ships symbolize persecution, and there are two means to safeguard oneself from great confusion: devotion to the Most Holy Virgin and frequent reception of Holy Communion.

His exceptional care and devotion to the young have made St. John Bosco the patron saint of young people, pupils, and students.

This bronze statue depicts St. John Bosco surrounded by his charges. Today, it stands in front of the basilica.

▲ *François Joseph Navez,* The Massacre of the Innocents.

▲ *The youngest saint we know by name is a three-year-old named Cyricus, also known as Quiricus.*

➤ *Pieter Brueghel the Younger,* The Massacre of the Innocents.

Miraculous Children

Among the saints, blesseds, and servants of God, one can find many children. Among them are believers who died at a young age, great lovers of the Eucharist, girls who died defending chastity, and little great martyrs who preferred to lose their lives rather than renounce their Christian faith. Today, the young witnesses of the faith still obtain many graces for their faithful venerators.

Have you ever wondered who is the youngest saint of the Catholic Church? Without a doubt, it is the Holy Innocents—about fifty boys up to the age of two, murdered in the early years of the first century on the order of Herod the Great, who, fearing the loss of power, wanted to kill the Messiah—the newborn Jesus. As *flores martyrum*, these children have been venerated in the Church since the first century.

A THREE-YEAR-OLD SAINT

And who is the youngest saint known to us by name? Most likely, it's the three-year-old Cyricus, also known as Cyriacus, Quiriac, Quiricus, or Cyr. Cyricus, especially venerated in France as St. Cyr, was the son of a wealthy Christian noblewoman, Julitta of Iconium (today Konya, in central Turkey). During the persecution of Christians in 304, Julitta fled with her son to Tarsus, where she was captured and tortured. They

attempted to coerce her into making an offering to pagan deities.

Cyricus, held and entertained at the time in the arms of the governor, Alexander, broke into tears, pushed him away, and bit and scratched his persecutor. Infuriated, Alexander angrily threw him against the stairs, shattering his skull. Alongside her son, Julitta was also slain—she was skinned, drenched in burning tar, and finally beheaded.

APOSTLE OF THE DIGITAL AGE

Two thousand years after the Holy Innocents, a young Italian named Carlo Acutis (1991–2006) began to be venerated by the faithful. Carlo was a devoted

⮝ *William Holman Hunt,* The Triumph of the Innocents.

⮜ The Virgin and Child surrounded by the Holy Innocents *by Peter Paul Rubens.*

Carlo was a great lover of the Eucharist, the Mother of God, and computers. Considered a computer science prodigy, he wrote programs and created websites (including websites about the Eucharistic miracles).

Relics of St. Imelda.

admirer of the Eucharist, the Mother of God, and computers. Regarded as a computer science prodigy, he authored programs and developed websites (including ones dedicated to Eucharistic miracles). He enjoyed anime, action and detective films, television game shows, and video games.

He kept dogs, cats, and goldfish, and he even created humorous videos with his pets. Despite coming from a privileged background, he remained humble. Carlo displayed interest in nearly every aspect of the Catholic Faith. From the day of his First Communion, the Eucharist held a central place in his life; he considered it his "highway to Heaven." He frequently dedicated himself to the Mother of God and faithfully prayed the Rosary daily. He found inspiration in St. Francis of Assisi, striving to emulate his example. Carlo seized every opportunity to evangelize and catechize others, seeking to save souls both among the living and those in Purgatory, as well as aiding those in need. He successfully converted a Hindu named Rajesh, who served in their home, along with several relatives and friends. Unconcerned by mockery of his piety, Carlo fearlessly defended and taught the Faith, and he was willing to challenge established opinions and customs, even if he was the only one to stand up.

Tragically, Carlo fell ill suddenly and unexpectedly at the age of fifteen and was diagnosed with leukemia. Despite his illness, he offered his suffering to God for the intentions of the pope and the Church, aspiring to bypass Purgatory and enter Heaven directly. He endured his illness for only ten days before passing away.

The miracle required for his beatification occurred in Campo Grande, Brazil, in October 2013. After Mass and a prayer service at a local parish, a priest blessed the faithful with an image and relic of Carlo Acutis. A grandfather approached the priest with four-year-old Matthew in his arms. Matthew suffered from an annular pancreas, a rare congenital anomaly causing severe emaciation, abdominal pain, and constant vomiting. Prior to approaching for the blessing, Matthew asked his relatives what he should request. "Ask to stop vomiting so much," he heard. He followed their advice. Subsequently, he began to eat normally and ceased vomiting. Tests later revealed that he had been healed completely.

THEIR GREAT LOVE FOR THE EUCHARIST

Carlo Acutis is one among many of the children who had a profound love for the Eucharist; perhaps the most remarkable testament of devotion to Jesus in the Most Holy Sacrament was demonstrated by eleven-year-old Imelda Lambertini (1322–1333).

It was the morning of May 12, 1333, the eve of the Ascension of the Lord. Dominican nuns from a convent in Bologna

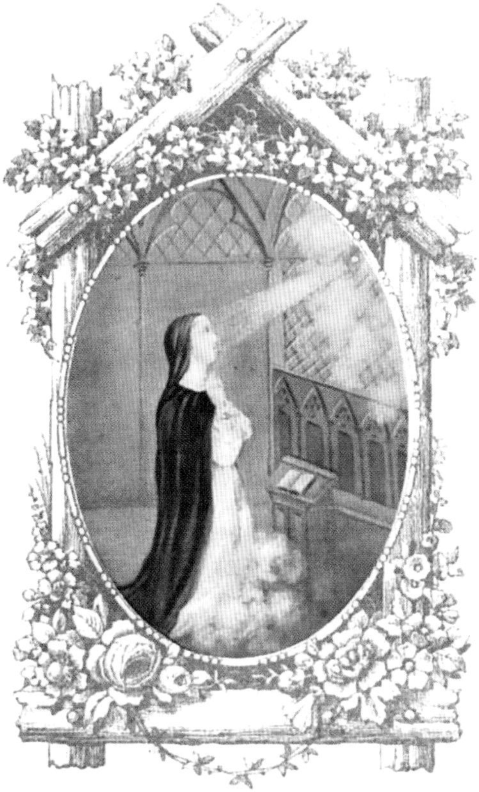

were in the midst of celebrating the third day of prayers of the cross. The Mass had commenced. "From his temple, he heard my voice; my cry came before him, into his ears," they recited in the Introit. Equally significant words were found in the Gospel: "Ask, and it will be given you; search, and you will find; knock, and the door will be opened for you." Among the nuns was Imelda, an eleven-year-old novice hailing from Count Lambertini's family. Despite her fervent desire to receive Jesus in Holy Communion, she had been advised to wait a little longer due to her young age. Following the Eucharist, while the sisters proceeded to breakfast, Imelda returned to the chapel. Moved by the words she had just heard, she knelt down and prayed.

Suddenly, she sensed an unusual fragrance and saw a radiant light illuminating the chapel. She looked up to discern its source and beheld it: above the chapel's vault floated the Host, gleaming brightly. Imelda stood and reached out her hands toward it, and at that moment, the Host began to hover above her head. Imelda's absence was noted in the refectory, prompting one of the nuns to fetch her. However, the extraordinary light and enchanting scent drew all the other nuns to the chapel. A priest was summoned,

The glass coffin of St. Imelda.

The most remarkable testimony of love for Jesus in the Most Holy Sacrament was given by eleven-year-old Imelda Lambertini.

Devotional picture depicting the miracle that happened to the young Imelda.

Thirteen-year-old Tarcisius did not hesitate to lay his life in defense of the Eucharist. The boy was sent with Holy Communion to the imprisoned Christians and was attacked by pagans. Protecting the Body of Christ from desecration, he died a martyr's death, most likely by stoning. Today he is the patron saint of altar boys.

and upon witnessing the miraculous sight, still clad in his liturgical garments, he brought forth the paten he held before him. Slowly, the Host began to descend, and when it landed on the paten, the priest took it in his hand and approached Imelda. "*Agnus Dei, qui tollis peccata mundi*," he proclaimed. Imelda opened her mouth and received the Body of Christ. Following Communion, she bowed low, enveloped in gratitude. Moved by the miracle, the sisters chose not to disturb her and exited the chapel. Upon their return about a dozen minutes later, Imelda remained kneeling. One of the sisters gently touched her, and Imelda collapsed to the floor.

She was found lifeless, her heart unable to contain such overwhelming joy—it had burst from her immense love for the Lord. Imelda's tomb became a site of pilgrimage for countless faithful, where many experienced extraordinary graces. Today, having been declared blessed, Imelda Lambertini is revered as the patron saint of children preparing to receive First Communion.

LITTLE LI AND THE GREAT ARCHBISHOP

Among the devoted lovers of the Eucharist, we must also mention a young Chinese girl whose unwavering faith deeply moved Archbishop Fulton Sheen, a candidate for sainthood himself. Her story greatly inspired him to initiate his daily practice of hour-long adoration of the Blessed Sacrament.

According to an account from one of the missionaries, this event took place in China around 1949, amidst the rise of the Chinese Communist Party. One day, Communist soldiers stormed into a church, openly mocking the gathered faithful, and proceeded to vandalize, destroy, and desecrate the sacred space before them. They desecrated the tabernacle, scattered the consecrated Hosts onto the floor, and trampled them underfoot with their boots. As evening fell, they departed, locking up the priest, who was serving in the parish and teaching at the local school, in a coal locker adjacent to the church. From his confinement, the priest had a vantage point

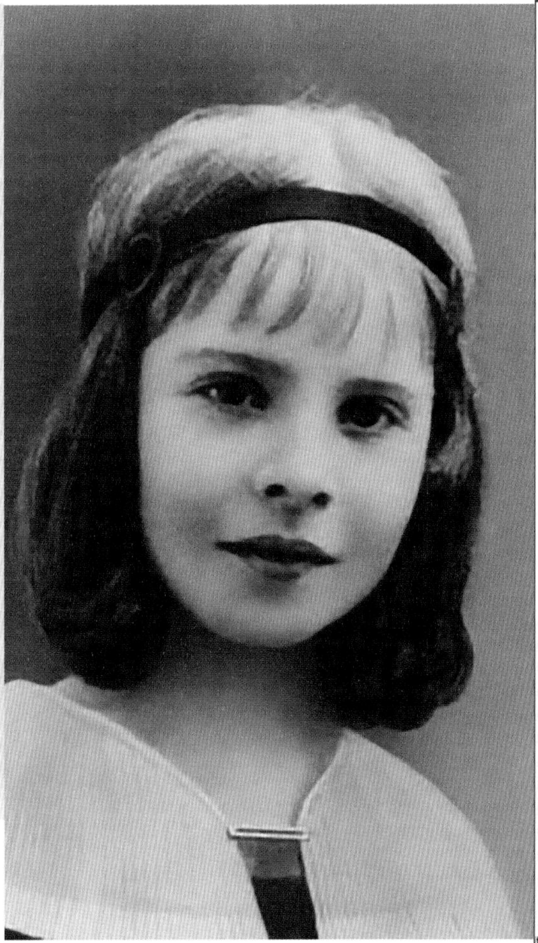

The girl in the photos, who converted the gravedigger, Gustin of Annecy-le-Vieux, was called Anne de Guigne (1911–1921).

overlooking the church and witnessed an extraordinary sight each dawn. For many consecutive days, a young girl would sneak into the church through a window. She would kneel, reverently take one of the Hosts from the ground with her tongue, and then engage in adoration. This ritual continued until, one day, a soldier spotted her. He pursued the girl into the church and shot her. It's reported that by that time, she had already received the last of the thirty Hosts scattered across the church—her sacred viaticum. Known by some as Li, the identity of this young Chinese girl remains shrouded in mystery, and she may never receive official canonization. Nevertheless, it's widely believed that she resides in Heaven, rejoicing in the presence of her beloved God.

Centuries earlier, at the time of Emperors Valerian and Galen's persecution of Christians, thirteen-year-old Tarcisius fearlessly defended the Eucharist. According to a sixth-century document titled *Passio Stephani Papae*, he served as an acolyte under Pope Stephen. Tarcisius was entrusted with delivering Holy Communion to imprisoned Christians and was assaulted by pagans on his journey.

Protecting the Body of Christ from desecration, Tarcisius met a martyr's end, likely by stoning, around August 257—the same day as Pope Stephen. Today, he is revered as the patron saint of altar boys.

YOUNG BELIEVERS

In the early twentieth century, an elderly man named Gustin lay on his deathbed in a French hospital. Gustin, a gravedigger in Annecy-le-Vieux, had long ceased attending church. Despite a visit from a priest, Gustin rebuffed him with insults

Many young saints became patron saints of children and young people around the world or in their home countries.

➤ *Anne de Guigné (center), pictured with her mother and siblings.*

⮝ *Among the young saints is Stanislaus Kostka, a Pole who became a novice in the Jesuit order and a role model of determination.*

and ejected him. However, someone discreetly slipped a small photograph into his hand. As he gazed at the solemn face of the young girl depicted in the photo, he was captivated by her eyes, which he said were "full of God." In that moment, something within him shifted. He requested a priest and departed this world reconciled with God.

The girl in the photograph was Anne de Guigné (1911–1921), hailing from a devout, aristocratic family in Annecy. From birth, she was described as "a little tyrant—spoiled, prideful, temperamental, and disobedient; she tormented both people and animals." However, after her beloved father's death in World War I, when she was four, she underwent a transformation. Witnessing her mother's anguish, she resolved to be good and obedient, undertaking the arduous task of self-improvement. By the age of five, she received First Communion and Confirmation, thereafter becoming a little soldier of Jesus Christ. Embracing a life of unconditional obedience, good deeds, and sacrifices, she relinquished her own desires and preferences, striving to please others.

Moved by the plight of a young mother whose home had been ravaged by fire, Anne organized a fair, raising a sum of thirty francs for her. She fervently prayed for sinners, dedicating her prayers, sacrifices, and minor sufferings to their conversion. Devoutly living out the sacraments of the Church, she aspired to enter a convent and emulate her beloved St. Thérèse of Lisieux. Anne passed away at nearly ten years old after a month-long battle with what was likely meningitis.

She bore the pain of her illness with patience, offering it to the Heart of Jesus in reparation for His suffering and for the salvation of sinners. Even after her passing, she continued to aid her neighbors through her intercession, showering the earth with a torrent of extraordinary graces. Similarly, the venerable Servant of God, fourteen-year-old Bernhard Lehner (1930–1944) only lacked a miracle for canonization. Bernhard, aspiring to become a priest, succumbed to diphtheria. Living in Nazi Germany, he exemplified Christian virtues throughout his life and met his end in the same spirit.

Among the ranks of young saints is Stanislaus Kostka, a seventeen-year-old Pole who persevered as a novice in the Jesuit order despite numerous obstacles. He stands as a model of determination (more on page 386). Additionally, Dominic Savio, who passed away at nearly fifteen years old, and the young mystics from Fátima, Francisco and Jacinta Marto, have also been recognized as great saints of the Catholic Church (more on pp. 208–215).

ON THE WAY OF THE CROSS

A great testimony of faith and love for God was given by those children who, before their deaths, battled a particularly severe and painful illness.

A Roman girl, the venerable servant of God Antonina Meo, nicknamed "Nennolina" (1930–1937), was just five years old when her parents noticed a lump on her left knee. It was cancer—osteosarcoma. The sick leg was amputated, and the girl returned to school, received her First Communion, and at the age of seven and a half (on May 19, 1937) received the Sacrament of Confirmation. Seven days later, it turned out that the cancer had spread to the lungs, and then metastasized to the head, limbs, mouth, and throat. The pain became stabbing and nagging. They drained fluid from her left lung and, using only local anesthesia, removed three of her ribs. In mid-June, then six-year-old Nennolina received the Sacrament of the Anointing of the Sick. She died on July 3, 1937. She suffered greatly because of her illness but did not show it. She was experiencing agonizing pain, but she always kept a smile on her face.

She united her pain with Christ's suffering, feeling a vocation to participate in His Passion. Aware of the value of suffering, she offered it to God for the conversion of sinners and the salvation of souls. "There is also the apostolate of suffering," she once said during a religion class. "It is fulfilled when a sick person does not complain or fall into despair, but offers his or her suffering to God." She became such an apostle herself. She left behind a bundle of letters written to Jesus, God the Father, the Holy Spirit, the entire Holy Trinity, the Mother of God, and her guardian angel, which are a testament to her immense spiritual maturity.

Venerable Servant of God Alexia González-Barros y González (1971–1985), from Madrid,

An Italian teenager, the venerable servant of God Angiolino Bonetta was also battling cancer.

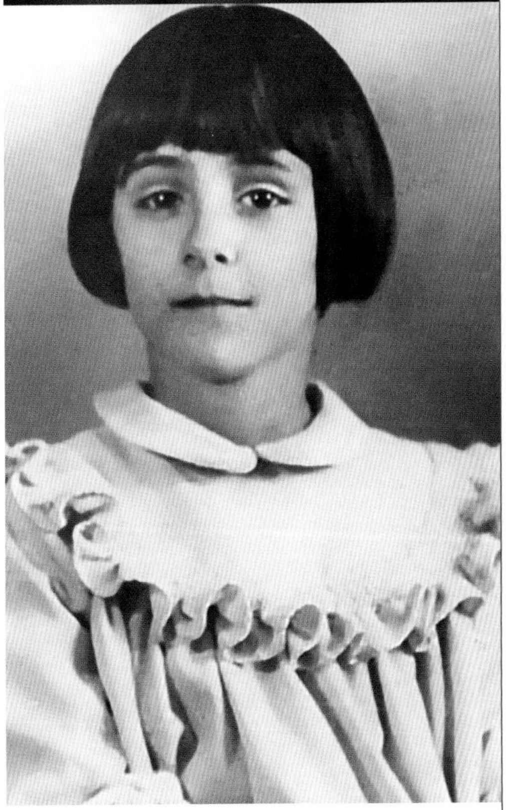

Servant of God Antonina Meo, nicknamed Nennolina. She left behind a bundle of letters written to Jesus, God the Father, the Holy Spirit, the entire Holy Trinity, the Mother of God, and her guardian angel, which are a testament to her immense spiritual maturity.

whose spiritual mentor was Fr. Josemaría Escrivá de Balaguer, was diagnosed with a malignant tumor at the age of fourteen, which soon left her body paralyzed. Over the course of ten months, she bravely battled cancer, enduring four major surgeries and a multitude of treatments. Despite the limited effectiveness of medical interventions and the intense pain they caused her, in her final moments, Alexia was confined to her bed, where she bore her cross with acceptance, admirable patience, and joyful heroism. She offered her suffering for the Church, the pope, and her neighbors, passing away peacefully with dignity and joy, eager to embrace the Mother of God. Her unusual, joyful attitude, guided by her life motto since the age of six, "Jesus, that I may always do what You want!" astonished the hospital staff.

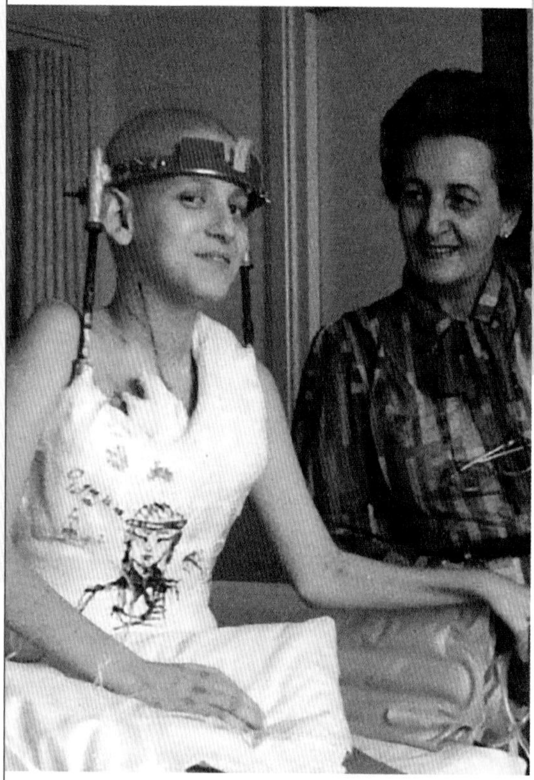

➤ *Venerable Servant of God Alexia González-Barros y González (1971–1985) from Madrid, whose spiritual mentor was Fr. Josemaría Escrivá de Balaguer, was fourteen years old when she was diagnosed with a malignant tumor that soon paralyzed her body.*

Similarly, Angiolino Bonetta, a simple country boy from the Po Plain in Italy and the venerable Servant of God, also battled cancer. Despite his physical suffering, Angiolino maintained his inner joy and cheerfulness throughout his ordeal. When his leg was amputated and he returned home, many of his friends inquired about what had happened to his leg. Some were told it was eaten by rats, while others heard that the sisters had an appetite for good beefsteak. Determined to continue collecting offerings for the church, Angiolino convinced the parish priest that people would be more generous toward a crippled boy. Despite his declining health, he continued to grow spiritually, offering his sufferings for the conversion of sinners and joining the Silent Workers of the Cross, a Catholic association founded by Luigi Novarese. This association aimed to make sick and suffering individuals aware of their role as soldiers in the Church, testifying to Christian truth through suffering with a smile.

As Angiolino's illness progressed, confining him to his bed, he endured great suffering with a joyful spirit. As he approached death, he assured his mother, who kept vigil at his bedside, that he had made a pact with the Mother of God. He believed that when his time came, she would come for him, and he would fly straight to Heaven, having asked her to purify him in this world. Four hours later, he peacefully drew his last breath. Over fifteen hundred people attended his funeral, and the inscription on his tombstone reads: "Angiolino Bonetta, Silent Worker of the Cross, suffered in joy to atone for sins and save souls."

A nine-year-old Spanish girl, the venerable Servant of God María del Carmen González Valerio y Sáenz de Heredia (1930–1939), succumbed to scarlet fever after enduring great suffering. Despite her own pain, she fervently prayed for the conversion of the murderers of her father, who was killed while fighting for God and Spain during the Spanish Civil War. It is believed that she obtained from God the conversion and salvation of Spanish president and Freemason Manuel Azaña.

According to the diocese's bishop, His Excellency Bishop Théas, who provided spiritual assistance to Azaña at the time, the former president received the Sacrament of Penance with full consciousness on November 3, 1940, in Montauban, a city in southeastern France near Toulouse. Azaña passed away with the love of God and the hope of seeing Him.

BLESSED ARE THE PURE IN HEART

A significant number of saintly and blessed children include girls who sacrificed their lives in defense of chastity and virginity, *in defensum castitatis.*

> *Girls of her age cannot bear even their parents' frowns and, pricked by a needle, weep as for a serious wound. Yet she shows no fear of the bloodstained hands of her*

An inscription was engraved on the slab of the tomb of the candidate for beatification: "Angiolino Bonetta, Silent Worker of the Cross, suffered in joy to atone for sins and save souls."

The venerable Servant of God María del Carmen González Valerio y Sáenz de Heredia (1930–1939) prayed for the conversion of the murderers of her father, who was killed while he was fighting for God and Spain during the Spanish Civil War. She is credited with obtaining from God the conversion and salvation of Spanish president and Freemason Manuel Azaña.

executioners. She stands undaunted by heavy, clanking chains. She offers her whole body to be put to the sword by fierce soldiers. She is too young to know of death, yet is ready to face it. As a bride, she would not be hastening to join her husband with the same joy she shows as a virgin on her way to punishment, crowned not with flowers but with holiness of life, adorned not with braided hair but with Christ Himself.

This poignant description by St. Ambrose in his work *On Virgins* portrays St. Agnes (291–304), one of the most revered saints of Christian antiquity.

According to Ambrose's *Passion*, Agnes hailed from a distinguished family and was renowned for her beauty. At the age of twelve, the son of the governor of Rome began to court her. Agnes, however, declared to him that she "had already been betrothed for a long time to someone far more noble and mighty, in whose embrace she would keep her virginity."

When the governor learned that Agnes spoke of Christ, he ordered her capture and, using both entreaties and threats, attempted to compel her to renounce her vow of chastity and offer homage to pagan idols.

When these initial threats failed, the governor resorted to a more extreme threat, promising to deliver Agnes to a brothel, where she would endure the fate of a prostitute. Trusting in God's aid, Agnes steadfastly refused to prostrate herself before the governor's "stone goddess" or succumb to "another man's immoral obscenity." Subsequently, she was taken to the brothel, where "an angel appeared to her and clothed her in a radiant robe, shielding her from defilement." The surrounding light deterred anyone from approaching her, and those who dared risk it lost their sight. Despite this, the governor's son, bolder than the others, attempted to satisfy his lust and met his demise.

Distraught, the governor accused Agnes of witchcraft and declared that he would reconsider if she could bring his son back to life. Miraculously, the young man was resurrected and testified to the truth, affirming the supremacy of the Christian God. Enraged pagan priests, viewing Agnes as a threat, incited the populace to demand her death.

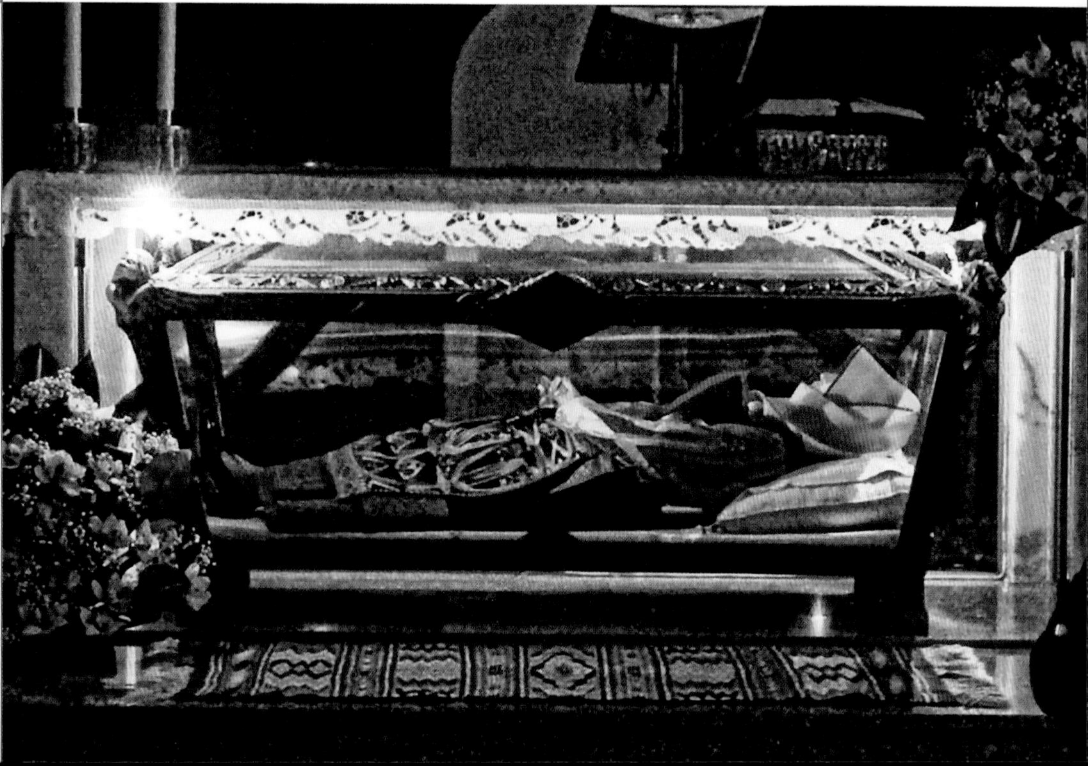

Bl. Antonia Mesina.

Italian Bl. Antonia Mesina (1919–1935) was laid to rest in her tomb in regional dress.

figures such as the Virgin Mary and Maria Goretti.

On May 17, 1935, sixteen-year-old Antonia attended Mass and received Holy Communion. After the Mass was over, she went to a nearby forest to gather firewood. There, a young boy attacked her and tried to rape her. When she resisted him, enraged and blinded by lust, he furiously began hitting her on the face and head with a stone that he held in his hand. With the final blow, delivered with a larger stone, he crushed her skull. Upon later examination, it was discovered that there were seventy-four wounds on Antonia head, which was mutilated beyond recognition. She died, but, as it turned out, she managed to preserve her virginity.

The locals, who attended her funeral in large numbers, declared her an exceptional holy child "educated in the school of Maria Goretti." Pope John Paul II beatified her.

St. Agnes depicted in a stained-glass window with a martyr's palm.

Skull of St. Agnes.

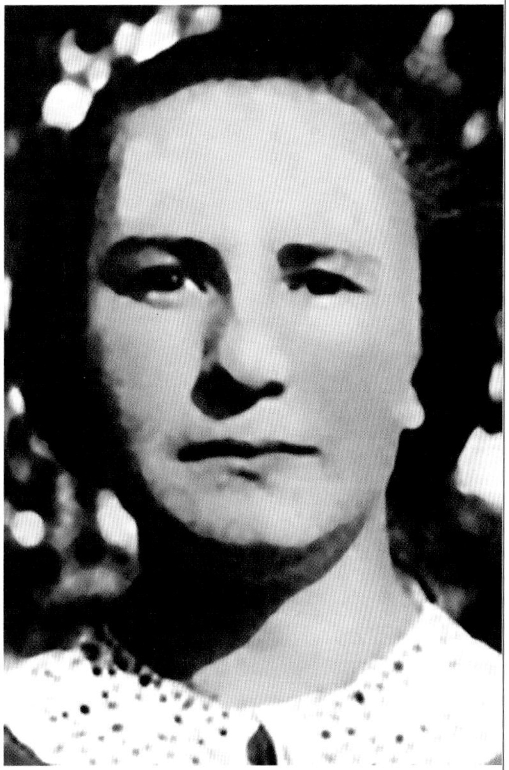

Bl. Anna (Anka) Kolesárová.

Despite the governor's inclination to spare her, fearing his own exile, his successor ordered Agnes to be burned at the stake. However, the fire miraculously failed to harm her. Ultimately, she was martyred by having her throat pierced with a sword at the tender age of thirteen. Her tomb became a site of Christian pilgrimage, renowned for miracles, including the healing of Constance, daughter of Constantine the Great.

Today, St. Maria Goretti (see more on pp. 198–207), known as the "Agnes of the Twentieth Century," is celebrated for numerous miracles. Additionally, Bl. Antonia Mesina (1919–1935), an Italian girl from Sardinia, sacrificed her life for chastity and innocence. Raised in a devout household, Antonia dedicated herself to household duties and caring for her siblings after her mother's illness. Despite her young age, she actively participated in the "purity crusade" within her parish, drawing inspiration from

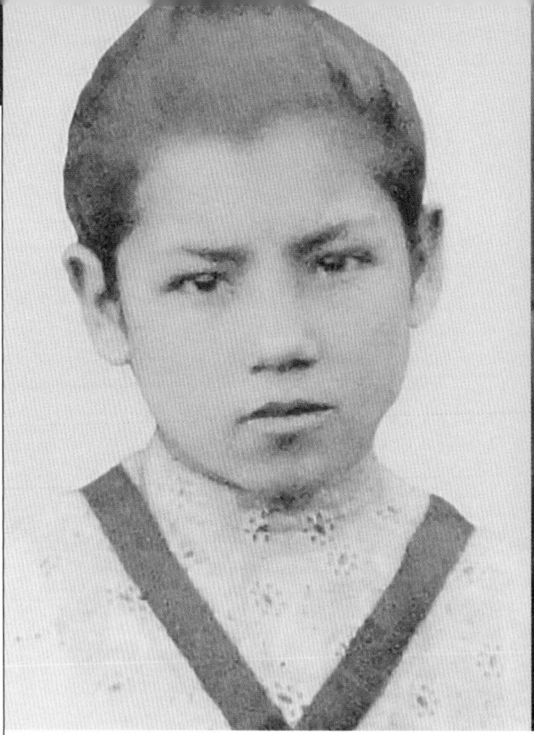

➢ *Thirteen-year-old Chilean Bl. Laura Vicuna, patroness of broken and feuding marriages.*

➢ *Bl. Karolina Kózka.*

Many graces had already been obtained through the intercession of a Polish woman, Bl. Karolina Kózkówna (1898–1914). She was a profoundly believing, good, obedient, hard-working, and dutiful sixteen-year-old girl from a peasant family, wholeheartedly devoted to God and to her neighbor. During World War I she was killed in the forest by a Russian soldier, enraged because she fought in defense of her virginity and dignity.

As Bl. Karolina Kózkówna is to Poles, so Bl. Anna (Anka) Kolesárová is to Slovaks. A devout sixteen-year-old Slovak girl from Vysoká nad Uhom, she was killed on November 22, 1944, while defending herself from being raped by a Soviet soldier.

The Americas also has its "martyrs of chastity." One of them is the twelve-year-old Chilean Laura Vicuna, patroness of broken and feuding marriages, who sacrificed her life so that her mother would return to the path of faith and sacramental life, and the twelve-year-old Brazilian Bl. Albertina Berkenbrock of São Luís, who was cruelly murdered on June 15, 1931, during an attempted rape by one of the young workers employed at her father's factory.

SEMANARIO DE SUCESOS
Ha muerto Josefina Vilaseca, la María Goretti catalana
Pereció a consecuencia del bárbaro atropello, por defender su pureza

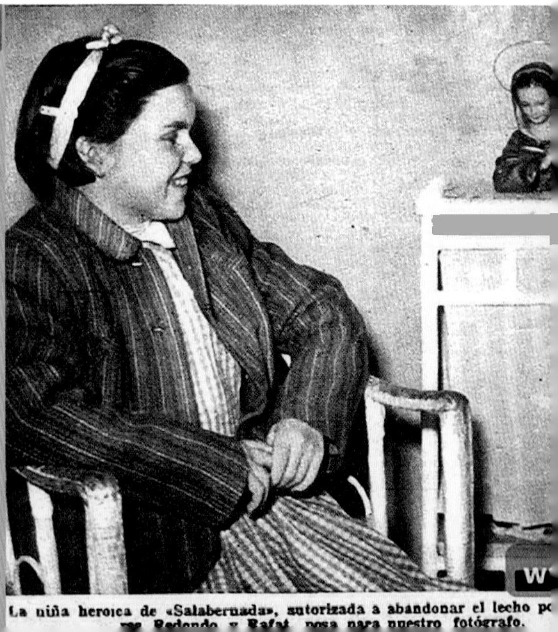

La niña heroica de «Salabernada», autorizada a abandonar el lecho po

➢ *Josefina Vilaseca Alsina.*

THEY DIDN'T RENOUNCE THE FAITH

The miraculous healing of a young girl played a pivotal role in the eventual canonization of Bl. José Luis Sánchez del Río. His martyrdom occurred during the Cristero War, a period marked by resistance against the oppressive, anti-Christian regime of the Freemasons (for further details, see pages 86–91).

Echoing the courage of early Church martyrs, Bl. José sacrificed his life for the Christian Faith. Similarly, St. Pancras of Rome, who lived in the late third and early fourth centuries, and St. Pelagius, a Spaniard from the tenth century, both exemplified unwavering devotion to their religion, even in the face of persecution and forced conversion attempts to Islam.

St. Pelagius, a Spaniard who resisted forced conversion to Islam.

ON THE WAY TO SAINTHOOD

There are, of course, many more children who are saints, blesseds, and venerables than I managed to list here, and many more are still waiting to be discovered and formally declared.

Perhaps other teenage "martyrs of chastity" will also be honored someday, such as the Italian fifteen-year-old Arcangela Filippelli (killed on February 7, 1869, in Russo, Italy, by a man who attempted to rape her), thirteen-year-old Marisa Morini from Ferrara (murdered in March 1964), Marisa Porcellana from Turin (murdered on July 4, 1964), thirteen-year-old Portuguese girl Maria Vieira da Silva (murdered on June 4, 1940, in Vila de São Sebastião), and twelve-year-old Spanish girl Josefina Vilaseca Alsina (killed on December 25, 1952, by a twenty-four-year-old mentally disabled shepherd in Manresa, near Barcelona).

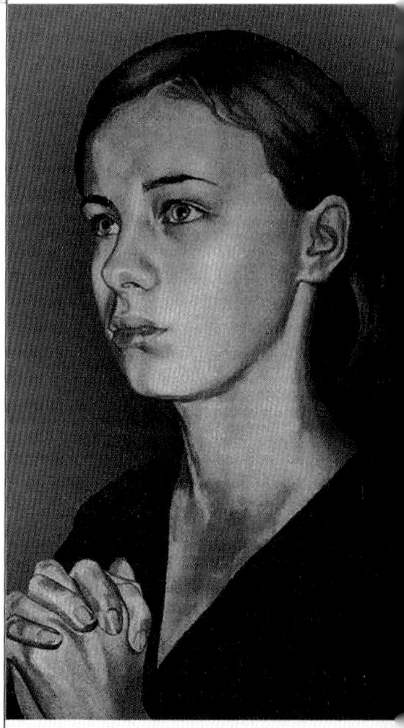

Arcangela Filippelli.

Among the candidates for beatification is an eight-year-old French girl, Anne-Gabrielle Caron (2002–2010), from Toulon. In February 2009, she was diagnosed with Ewing's sarcoma, a highly malignant bone cancer. To give meaning to her suffering, she dutifully offered it up for various intentions. She feared death and suffered greatly, and yet with a radiant smile she asked God to place upon her the collective suffering of all the other children in the hospital. She also offered her suffering for poor sinners and other unfortunates. She was worried about her distressed parents. Together they asked God for a miracle, and she even stayed at Lourdes, but a miracle never came to pass. She had been dying for a long time and was in immense pain. She passed away at just before midnight on Friday, July 23, 2010. Despite her young age, she was a paladin of Catholic Faith, and her determination in the face of suffering is an example for us all.

The group of candidates for sainthood also includes an eight-year-old French girl, Anne-Gabrielle Caron from Toulon.

➤ *The interior of the Basilica of St. Clare in Assisi.*

ON THE WAY TO JESUS WITH ST. FRANCIS

St. Clare of Assisi

To this day, St. Clare (1193–1253), imitator and close collaborator of St. Francis, teaches us that true strength does not lie in wealth but in poverty, that it's worth more to be happy with what you have than to have more, and that true happiness rests in forgetting about ourselves and giving ourselves to others as we help them on their journey to Heaven. God has blessed and still blesses His people through her intercession.

St. Clare, from a fresco by Simone Martini in the Lower Basilica of St. Francis in Assisi (ca. 1320).

Clare came from a noble, pious family living in Assisi, Italy. Her parents cared for her deeply and gave her a thorough education.

She felt a vocation to religious life from a young age and rejected all marriage proposals. Even as a child, she was extremely empathetic to the needs of the poor, and she shared with them everything she could get her hands on. Then, when she was eighteen, she met a young man named Francis, the son of a rich merchant, who had renounced all his possessions to follow Christ and live the gospel. She was impressed by his life and sought to emulate him in his poverty and humility. He became not only her spiritual father and teacher but also her brother.

Clare decided to give herself entirely to Christ and to live His gospel. On the night of Palm Sunday, 1212, she and another girl ran away from home and went to the chapel of Porziuncula to meet with Francis. With the consent of the bishop, she took a coarse, penitential habit and a religious veil

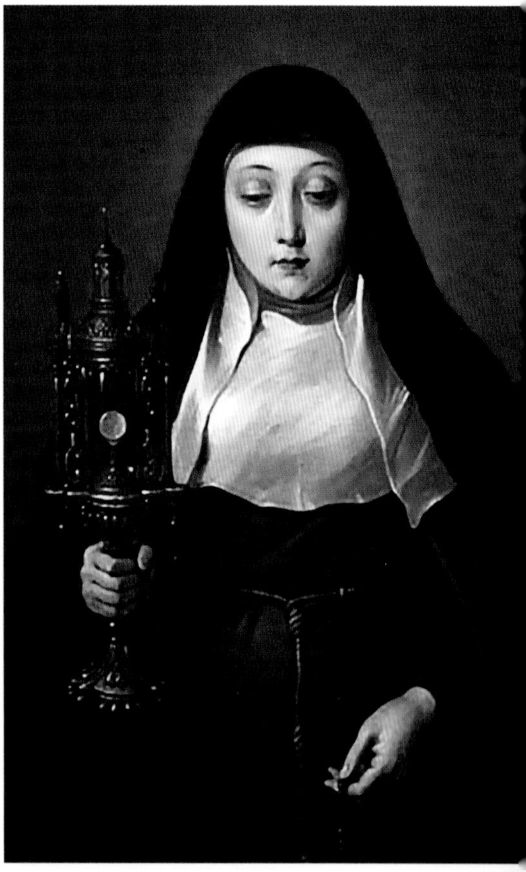

from Francis's hands and began a new life. While her family tried to persuade her to return home and to marry, she vehemently refused. Soon, she made her home in a building next to the Church of San Damiano.

Shortly thereafter, other girls and women (including one of her own sisters and, eventually, her mother) joined Clare in the cloistered community, and the Order of Poor Ladies, the Second (female) Order of St. Francis, was born. Today, this community is most often referred to as the Poor Clares, or the Order of St. Clare, because Clare was not only their first superior but also wrote their religious Rule, which stresses, in addition to obedience and chastity, radical poverty: not owning anything at all. This vow of poverty was so novel that the pope himself had to sanction the Rule.

As she grew older, Clare became sick; yet before she left for her Father's house in Heaven at the age of sixty, she managed to become known not only for her extraordinary life of humility, penance, mortification, visions, and ecstasies, but also for her many miraculous intercessions. These miracles only continued after her death. As a result, her canonization process was remarkably fast: just two years after her death, Pope Alexander IV officially declared Clare to be among the saints.

THE MIRACLE OF THE MULTIPLICATION OF LOAVES

As to the miracles performed by Clare during her earthly life, it's worth reading the original words from the testimonies given just three months after her death

Fresco depicting St. Clare and the Sisters of her Order in the Church of San Damiano, Assisi.

Gothic altar of the Poor Clares in the Cologne Cathedral.

St. Clare receives the formula vitae *("little rule of life") from St. Francis.*

by her fellow nuns—eyewitnesses of her life and deeds—as well as testimonies of lay persons that were compiled by a Franciscan friar, Br. Thomas of Celano, at the request of the pope.

Br. Thomas tells us of a certain miracle:

> *There was once only a single loaf in the monastery, and the time of hunger and the hour of eating had come. Having called the refectorian, the saint bade her divide the loaf and send half of it to the friars and keep the rest for the sisters. Of this remaining half, she ordered fifty pieces to be made, according to the number of the ladies, and placed before them at the table of poverty. When the devout daughter made answer that in this case the ancient miracles of Christ would be necessary in order that such a small piece of bread might be divided into fifty parts, the mother replied, "Do what I tell thee, daughter, and trust what I say." When the daughter hastened to fulfill the mother's commands, the mother hastened to direct her pious sighs to her Christ for her daughters. By the divine favor, the little piece of bread increased in the hands of her who broke it, and an abundant portion was provided for each one of the community.*

THE MIRACLE OF THE OIL

One day, Clare and the other sisters realized that the monastery had run out of oil. The cloistered sisters could not simply go out and ask around for more oil, so Clare called Br. Bentevenga, and he agreed to go begging in the community on their behalf, though he did ask the sisters to provide him with a container to hold any oil he might be given. Clare took a jar, washed it with her own hands, and left it for the brother on a wall near the door of the house. When Br. Bentevenga came for the jar, however, he found it completely filled with oil. He tried to discover the identity of the sisters' mysterious benefactor, but absolutely no one could tell him how the jar had come to be filled.

Br. Thomas of Celano continues the tale:

> *For through the intervention of God alone that vessel was found filled with oil, the prayer of St. Clare having anticipated the solicitude of the friar for the succor of the poor*

daughters. The aforesaid brother, however, having seemingly been called in vain, murmuring a little said: "These women have called me in jest, for behold the vessel is full!"

ENEMIES REPELLED

The most well-known miracle attributed to St. Clare's prayer and fervent love for the Most Blessed Sacrament is the saving of San Damiano and Assisi from Muslim mercenaries ("Saracens") who were fighting for the Holy Roman Emperor Frederick II against Pope Innocent IV. Br. Thomas of Celano beautifully describes the event as told by the many sisters who accompanied Clare at this time:

By reason of the calamities that the Church suffered in different parts of the world under Emperor Frederick [II], the valley of Spoleto very often drank of the chalice of wrath. Bands of soldiers and of Saracen archers numerous as bees were stationed by the imperial command to lay waste to fortified castles and to besiege cities. And when at one time their hostile fury was directed against Assisi ... and the army was already close to the gates, the Saracens ... rushed into the confines of San Damiano, even into the cloister of the virgins.

The hearts of the ladies sank within them from fear, their voices trembled with terror, and they went in tears to the mother. Although she was ill, Clare with a stout heart directed that she be led to the door and placed before the enemy with a silver casket, enclosed in ivory and in which the Body of the Holy of Holies was most devoutly kept, preceding her.

And as she wholly prostrated herself before the Lord in prayer she said to her Christ amid tears: "Doth it please Thee, my Lord, to deliver Thy defenseless handmaids, whom I have nourished with Thy love, into the hands of the pagans? Defend, O Lord, I beseech Thee, these Thy servants whom I in this hour am unable to defend." Presently He sent her of His special grace a voice as if of a little child that sounded in her ears: "I will always defend thee." "My Lord," she said, "and if it please Thee protect the city, for it supporteth us for love of Thee." And the Lord answered: "It will be troubled, but it shall be defended by My protection."

▲ *The motif of St. Clare adoring the Holy Sacrament is constantly repeated in sacred art.*

▲ The Death of St. Clare, *by the Master of Heiligenkreuz.*

Then the virgin, raising her tearful face, comforted the weeping, saying: "Rest assured, I bid you, little daughters, that ye shall suffer no harm; only trust in Christ." Nor had an instant elapsed before, the boldness of these dogs being changed into fear, they quickly descended the walls they had scaled, being overthrown by the power of her prayers.

Another time, when Vitalis of Aversa, a man "desirous of renown and valiant in battle," attacked and surrounded Assisi with his army, Clare ordered the sisters to bring ashes. After sprinkling the ashes on their heads as an act of penance, the Poor Clares immersed themselves in prayer and asked God to save the city. The next day, God performed another miracle: "The entire army was broken up and the proud man departed, contrary to his vows; neither did he harass that land any further. For the leader of the war himself perished by the sword soon afterward."

PATRON OF TELEVISION

One of the sisters of the convent, Sr. Philippa, tells that on the night of Clare's last Christmas on earth, she was so ill that she could not leave her bed and attend Mass in the chapel with her sisters. She was left alone in her room, grieving the opportunity to worship Christ on the eve of His birth.

But God decided to grant His servant a special blessing. As Br. Thomas of Celano continues,

Clare then began to think on the little Jesus and to grieve sorely that she might not be present at His praises, and said with a sigh, "Lord God, behold I am left alone with Thee in this place."

And lo! Suddenly the wonderful music that was being sung in the Church of S. Francesco began to resound in her ears; she heard the voices of the friars chanting the psalter, she listened to the harmonies of the singers; she even perceived the sound of the organ. She was by no means so near to the place that all this could happen in the natural order unless either the solemnity was brought nearer to her by divine influence or her hearing was endowed with superhuman power. But what surpasses even this marvel is the fact that Clare was worthy to see the manger of the Lord. In the morning, when her daughters came to her, the Blessed Clare said: "Blessed be the Lord Jesus Christ, who when ye left me did not abandon me. By the grace of Christ I have indeed heard all the solemnities that were celebrated last night in the Church of S. Francesco."

Sr. Philippa testified during Clare's canonization process that Clare had heard not only the organ of the chapel but even the brothers' responsories and the entire Office, and that it had all been just as clear as if she had actually been there.

Because of this rather unusual miracle—a mystical grace granted by God to console Clare during her illness—the saint was proclaimed by Pope Pius XII as the patron of television in 1958.

CASTING OUT SATAN

Throughout her monastic life, Clare struggled with Satan (sometimes he even physically tormented her), but she always emerged victorious from these battles. The evil one often tempted her, but he always received a firm dismissal. As Br. Thomas of Celano reports:

Once in the dead of night, as she was weeping, the angel of darkness stood by her in the form of a black boy and admonished her, saying: "Weep not so much, for though shalt become blind."

"He will not be blind who shall see God," straightway replied Clare, whereupon he departed in confusion.

The same night after Matins, while Clare was praying as usual bathed in tears, the deceitful counselor approached. "Weep not so much," he said, "lest in the end thy brain, becoming softened, should flow out through thy nose: in any case thou wilt have a twisted nose."

"He suffereth no injury," replied Clare quickly, "who serveth the Lord," and the devil at once making off, vanished.

Clare also freed many possessed people from Satan's clutches. Among them was a

The façade of the Church of St. Clare in Assisi.

St. Clare praying with St. Francis.

The Basilica of St. Clare in Assisi, view of the building complex.

devout woman from the diocese of Pisa who "through the merits of the saint ... had been freed from five demons. For the demons at their expulsion confessed that the prayers of St. Clare had enraged them and cast them out of the body of the possessed" (Br. Thomas of Celano).

THE POWER OF THE CROSS

Clare also received from God the gift of healing various diseases by making the Sign of the Cross over the sick. In this way she healed many sisters as well as other people who came to her asking for help.

One day, Francis of Assisi himself sent a mentally ill friar named Stephen to Clare. Knowing her "great sanctity" and revering "the greatness of her power," he asked her to make the Sign of the Cross over him. "This daughter of obedience," wrote Br. Thomas of Celano, "at the command of the father, signed Stephen with the sign of the cross and made him sleep for a little while in the place where she was wont to pray. After a short sleep, the brother rose up sound and returned to the father, delivered from his insanity."

Before they were healed, the sick would sometimes see Clare in visions or dreams. Sr. Benvenuta, born in Perugia, had been suffering from voice loss for two years and could only speak in a whisper. As she testified later, as recorded by Br. Thomas of Celano, "On the night of the Assumption of Our Lady, it was shown to [me] in a vision that the Lady Clare would heal [me]. [I] awaited the day with longing. No sooner had it dawned than [I] hastened to the mother and asked for the sign of the cross, and being signed, [I] speedily recovered [my] voice."

There were also group healings. Another sister testified that "there was a great multitude of sick sisters in the monastery afflicted with diverse ills. Clare as usual entered the place with her wonted medicine and, having made the sign of the cross five times, five were immediately cured of their infirmities." Indeed, many times, whenever one of the sisters had pain, either in the head or in any other part of the body, the blessed mother, with the Sign of the Cross, relieved them of it.

Br. Thomas of Celano summed up Clare's healing charisma very beautifully: "From these facts, it is surely clear that the tree of the Cross was deeply rooted in the heart of the virgin and that, while its fruit refreshed the soul, its leaves yielded medicine for the body."

MIRACLES FROM BEYOND THE GRAVE

The river of grace and miracles didn't stop after Clare's death. In the *Golden Legend* of Bl. Jacobus de Voragine, we read about a child from Perugia who "had in his body the devil," although he may have suffered from a disease rather than a possession. The boy would throw himself into fire, hurl himself against the ground, and gnaw on stones, and he also showed many other bizarre and disturbing behaviors. He would often have such fits about twice a day, and not even two people could stop him. Meanwhile, the most enlightened, wisest doctors were wringing their hands over his case. Finally, the boy's distraught father called upon St. Clare with tears in his eyes. He asked her to send his child health. He went to her grave, laid his sick son on it, and began to pray with faith and hope. And his prayers were answered—the boy was freed from the disease, and the disturbing behaviors and symptoms never returned.

The same hagiographer also wrote about a man named Jacob who had been blind for two years. Once, a child who was leading him let him go unattended. Jacob fell, broke his arm, and seriously injured his head. Afterward, one night, as Jacob slept by the bridge, he saw a lady in his dream who said to him, "Jacob, wherefore comest thou not to me for to be whole?" In the morning, Jacob told the other blind men about the dream. They told him about a recently deceased woman in Assisi through whom God had worked many miracles, and they said that the sick who came to her tomb left healthy. Jacob first went to Spoleto, and he had the same dream. So he immediately set out for Assisi. When he got there, he encountered a huge crowd. He had no chances of entering the monastery, much less reaching Clare's grave! Greatly saddened, he fell asleep near the monastery with a stone under his head. That night, he heard the words, "Jacob, if thou mayst come and enter herein, God shall do well to thee." In the morning, Jacob began to pray, and he begged the crowd to let him through. Surprisingly, the crowd parted and let him pass. When he finally reached Clare's tomb, the tired man fell asleep. Then he saw St. Clare again. "Arise up, for thou art all whole!" she said. He woke up, got up, and "saw the clearness of the day." The healed man praised the Lord who had bestowed such a grace on him through the merits of St. Clare, and he urged others to join him in thanking God for the blessings he was sending.

Many people with disabilities or broken arms and legs have been healed at the saint's grave. Lame children have walked, and a servant whose swollen neck appeared bigger than her head was healed. And after the mother of a small child who had been snatched away by a wolf called on St. Clare to help, her child was miraculously saved.

There have been many more similar cases. In each miracle attributed to her intercession, St. Clare continues to show the faithful Christian her constant love, attention, and care.

Wax figure of St. Clare of Assisi at the Basilica dedicated to her.

St. Clare saving a child mauled by a wolf.

Cura Gaucho was a tireless apostle, preaching the gospel, teaching the truths of the Faith, and converting those who had strayed from God. He encountered many outcasts, bandits, and fugitives hiding from justice in the mountainous area of his parish.

Photo from 1866.

PARISH PRIEST OF ARGENTINA

St. José Gabriel del Rosario Brochero

He was simply called Cura Brochero (meaning Fr. Brochero) or Cura Gaucho, which refers to the name of the farmers and ranchers who had homesteads on the Argentine pampas. He was an embodiment of missionary zeal and a great community worker, a humble and modest priest, wholeheartedly devoted to those who were most in need. Today, he is Argentina's most famous saint and the patron saint of the Argentine clergy. He brought God, His immeasurable love, and His mercy to all. What contributed to St. Jose's canonization were the healings of two children interceded through him.

Fr. José Gabriel del Rosario Brochero (1840–1914) was not a priest behind a desk but, in the words of his countryman Pope Francis, a true "shepherd with the smell of sheep." He was an extremely active apostle of Christ. He traveled in a colorful poncho, drinking his yerba mate in a calabash gourd, on a mule named Malacar. He would go out to the people and catch them like a fisherman catching fish.

He was born into a large Argentine family. He had nine siblings. When he was almost sixteen, he entered the seminary in Córdoba, becoming a priest ten years later. While studying at the university, he befriended, among others, the future president of Argentina Miguel Juárez Celman, and became a Dominican tertiary. After his ordination, he lived and ministered in and around Córdoba. From 1869 until nearly the end of his life, he was the parish priest of the very large parish of San

Wearing a warm poncho and a distinctive hat, Cura Brochero would seamlessly find his future penitents in the farthest corners of the Argentine pampas.

The Argentine pampas, which Cura Brochero constantly traversed in his missionary journeys.

Alberto, with more than ten thousand poor parishoners. While ministering there, he lived in the nearby Villa del Tránsito. As a community worker, he was active in local communities, encouraging people to fight poverty and work for the common welfare: to build roads, bridges, a railroad, water mains, schools, churches, chapels—in a nutshell, all the infrastructure that did not exist at the time of his arrival.

When needed, he would grab a pickaxe or shovel without hesitation. He was tireless in his apostolate, preaching the gospel, teaching the truths of the Faith, and converting those who had strayed from God (and he encountered many outcasts, bandits, and fugitives hiding from justice in the mountainous area of his parish).

In loving his neighbor, he always went beyond his limits. He connected with people with ease and was with his faithful

Capuchin church in Córdoba, Argentina.

The urn containing Cura Brochero's remains.

in good times as well as bad. As a newly ordained priest, he sacrificially ministered to them during the cholera epidemic in Córdoba (more than four thousand people died during this time). He consoled people and administered the sacraments without concern for his own health. For the sake of souls, desiring to win them to the Lord, he traversed vast deserts and high mountains day after day.

Toward the end of his life, he contracted leprosy. As a result of the disease, he lost his hearing and eyesight around 1906. He died in the reputation of holiness on January 26, 1914, in Villa del Tránsito, a town that was renamed Villa Cura Brochero just two years after he died, in recognition of his countless spiritual and material contributions.

HE MIRACULOUSLY SURVIVED

This tragic accident happened near Córdoba, on the road near Falda del Cañete. There are several overpasses at the site, and also a lookout point named after Cura Brochero. On September 28, 2000, on this road, a van suddenly veered into the opposite lane of the road and collided head-on with a car carrying an Argentine family and their infant child.

Nicolás Flores, eleven months old, who was in the back seat with his mother Sandra, suffered very serious injuries. He was drenched in blood, his skull was crushed, and the left side of his brain was completely destroyed. His grandfather, who was driving the vehicle, died on the spot. His grandmother and mother were seriously injured. Only Osvaldo, the child's father, was unaffected by the accident and he was the first to resuscitate Nicolás. At that moment, feeling that he was losing his son, he asked God's servant Fr. Brochero to save him. Why exactly that priest? The explanation is simple: he and his wife are both from the Traslasierra region, where Fr. Brochero once ministered. Whom was he supposed to summon, if not a well-known countryman who died in the reputation of holiness and was locally revered?

After fifteen minutes, the fire department, police, and ambulance arrived at the scene

Statue of José Gabriel Brochero in Villa Cura Brochero, Córdoba province, Argentina.

of the disaster, and Nicolás was taken to Holy Trinity Hospital in Córdoba. He was in an extremely poor condition.

The boy stopped breathing three times, and three times his little heart stopped beating: twice while in the ambulance, and once while in the hospital. The third time he was resuscitated for ten minutes and they already wanted to declare him dead. However, one of the doctors insisted that they not stop, and five minutes later the little boy came back to life. Nevertheless, the doctors still did not give him the slightest chance of survival.

Shivers run down the spine when one reads an excerpt from the Vatican's *Decretum super miraculo*, the decree from December 20, 2012, containing a long list of all the severe injuries suffered by the infant:

> *Very severe craniocerebral trauma, coma, subarachnoid hemorrhage, intraventricular hemorrhage, left hemisphere subdural hematoma, right-sided hydrops and subdural hematoma, exposed occipital craniocerebral wound, intracranial hypertension, severe ischemic hypoxia with three prolonged and consecutive cardiopulmonary arrests.*

As you can see, from a human perspective, the case appeared absolutely hopeless.

Based on the tests conducted, it was predicted that, even if they managed to keep Nicolás alive, he would remain in a vegetative state. He would not see, hear, speak, or walk. At first, this seemed to be the case, as the infant did not respond to stimuli for a long time.

The child's family and friends, however, persevered in storming Heaven with prayers. They pestered Fr. Brochero, never losing faith or hope that he would obtain for them from God the miracle of Nicolás's life and recovery. And it worked! The boy miraculously survived. Not only that, but the bones of his skull also grew back, and his brain began to work normally again.

The remarkable recovery of the young Argentine was put under the microscope in 2009, and the doctors who reviewed the case finally ruled that the healing was complete, permanent, and scientifically inexplicable. In a word, they considered it a *miracle*. On September 13, 2013, Cura Brochero was beatified.

In 2016, Nicolás was still suffering from hemiparesis on the right side of his body, but he no longer had difficulty moving,

A crowd of the faithful at the beatification ceremony of St. José Brochero.

and he even played soccer. His miraculous recovery was reported on by almost all of Argentina's secular and Catholic newspapers.

He functioned completely normally, which amazed the doctors. He went to school, he could speak, and he had no problems with his hearing—a remarkable fact, given the total destruction of the left hemisphere of his brain. The holy priest Brochero was, and probably still is, a close friend of his.

A FORTY-FIVE-DAY COMA

The second miracle necessary for Fr. Brochero to become a saint occurred in December 2013 and involved Camila Brusotti of San Juan, an eight-year-old girl who was a victim of domestic violence. On October 28, 2013, the girl's mother brought the unconscious Camila to a local center for women and children. Although she claimed that her daughter had fallen off a horse, the court, which soon took up the case, sentenced both her and the child's stepfather for beating her. The girl suffered many injuries (including old wounds and bruises, there were more than forty). The worst was a skull injury and very severe brain damage caused by a massive stroke and hematoma in the right hemisphere. She fell into a coma. In this case, too, doctors predicted that it would be impossible to keep the child alive, and even if they succeeded, she would remain in a vegetative state.

When the child's mother and stepfather argued over who was to blame, the girl's maternal grandmother cared for her and fervently prayed for Camila's healing through the intercession of Fr. Brochero. Her biological father, who was informed of Camila's critical condition by doctors, also prayed for his daughter's health. They prayed the novena, and Camila made it through the first, most difficult hours. After forty-five days in a coma in the intensive care unit, in early December, she finally began to respond, move her limbs, and speak. She finally recovered enough to leave the hospital on December 25.

The doctors who treated her could not hide their surprise. The fact that she came out of it was something utterly extraordinary in their eyes.

Today Camila is living a normal life, although she is still struggling with the trauma caused by the abuse of her mother and stepfather.

Fr. Brochero, photo from 1910.

THE SAINT WHO COMES IN A DREAM

St. Gabriel Possenti

In Italy, he is considered the patron saint of youth and a great miracle worker. He has contributed to obtaining numerous graces and has helped a vast number of people. His shrine in the village of Isola del Gran Sasso d'Italia at the foot of Monte Corvo, the highest peak in the Apennines, is a votive museum that is completely covered in offerings made in gratitude for received graces. New votive offerings are still being made! The young, beautiful, and always smiling Passionist saint also has a rather peculiar trait: he often appears to people before healing them, whether in dreams or even in waking life.

Holy medal of St. Gabriel Possenti.

Gabriel of Our Lady of Sorrows intervened on behalf of a future saint, Gemma Galgani (1878-1903), an esteemed Italian mystic and stigmatist. Despite his passing thirty-seven years prior, the young Passionist had not yet received official recognition as blessed or saint.

Gemma endured numerous ailments from childhood, with the most severe affliction striking her in late 1898 and early 1899, when she was confined to her bed. She suffered from meningitis, which caused her to experience paralysis of her arms and legs, spinal curvature, and total deafness.

The excruciating procedures performed without anesthesia—the excision of the ulcer and the searing cauterization of her lower back with scalding cauters—proved futile. Despite fervent prayers from her family members, who conducted three-day devotions and numerous novenas, Gemma's condition showed no signs of improvement.

Relics of St. Gabriel Possenti.

◄ St. Gabriel of Our Lady of Sorrows, *a painting in the parish hall of Völs am Schlern.*

From 1841 to 1856, St. Gabriel Possenti studied in Spoleto, first at the Institute of the Brothers of the Christian Schools, then at a Jesuit college.

St. Gabriel's resolutions from his monastic notebook: "To abide in the presence of God with the help of repeated acts of prayer.
Not to act under the influence of human affections in order to be seen or for my benefit, advantage, or pleasure, but only for God.
I will check my desire to talk."

It was only when she received a biography of a revered Passionist who had died at a young age that a turning point occurred. Initially dismissive, Gemma placed the book under her pillow, only to turn to it when assailed by a "terrible temptation" instigated by Satan. In a moment of desperation, she beseeched Gabriel twice in spirit, first for the salvation of her soul and then for the healing of her body.

Upon finally reading the biography that evening, Gemma found solace and inspiration in its pages, revisiting it multiple times out of admiration. She wept upon returning the book, holding Gabriel in high esteem and keeping his picture beneath her pillow. From that moment on, she began to sense his presence and even perceived his apparitions. In their initial nocturnal encounter, occurring in a dream, Gemma immediately recognized Gabriel, who praised her disillusionment, sacrificial spirit, and tears shed over his biography. He expressed affection for her and promised to visit again before disappearing, leaving Gemma to kiss his habit and rosary.

During their subsequent encounter, he addressed her as his sister and encouraged her to take a monastic vow. However, Gemma's ailment progressed, leaving her completely paralyzed and afflicted with excruciating headaches. Debilitated and confined to bed, Gemma's greatest distress stemmed not from her illness itself, but from her inability to receive the sacraments—Confession, daily Mass, and Holy Communion. On February 2, 1899, a priest arrived to administer the last rites.

In her dire state, Gemma was advised to pray a novena to Bl. Margaret Mary Alacoque, though she undertook this with wavering conviction. On the third attempt, as she commenced the novena, she felt a hand rest upon her forehead just before midnight. A male voice gently rebuked her for her forgetfulness and instructed her to pray the novena to the Heart of Jesus with unwavering faith, along with separate prayers honoring St. Margaret. It was later revealed that this mysterious visitor was once again her celestial companion, Gabriel.

From that point forward, Gabriel visited Gemma daily during the novena, joining her in prayer. As the novena drew to a close on the first Friday of the month dedicated to the Sacred Heart of Jesus, Gemma availed herself of the Sacrament of Confession and received Holy Communion. It was during this sacred encounter that she not only conversed with Gabriel but also heard the voice of Jesus Himself. Overwhelmed by emotion, Gemma was rendered speechless as the Savior assured her of His complete self-giving and asked if she, too, would belong entirely to Him. He affirmed her as His and Mary's daughter, promising that she would lack nothing, even if stripped of all earthly comforts and support. In that moment, she was healed, rising from her bed just two hours later. Gemma recounted that her family wept tears of joy upon witnessing this miraculous transformation.

Following her miraculous healing, Gemma received further extraordinary graces, as foretold by Jesus. Gabriel continued to appear to her on numerous occasions, strengthening her faith and guiding her on her journey to holiness. He also prophesied the establishment of a cloistered Passionist convent in her hometown of Lucca. Gemma affectionately referred to him as her confrere, deepening her connection with the Passionists and finding spiritual guidance from one of their members, who became her spiritual father.

A FLIRT ON HIS WAY TO GOD

The heavenly helper of St. Gemma Galgani was born Francesco Possenti. Born into a wealthy family in Assisi, Francesco was the eleventh of twelve children, with his father Sante serving as the mayor of Assisi and a functionary of the Papal States. At the tender age of four, Francesco experienced the loss of his mother. Despite attending religious schools, he led a life filled with worldly pursuits and entertainment. Known for his skill in dancing, horsemanship, and marksmanship, he was also fond of the company of girls, earning

The old streets of Isola that the young friar walked.

The famous icon from Spoleto Cathedral.

Panorama of Macerata. In this city, St. Gabriel Possenti entered the Congregation of the Passion of Jesus Christ.

➢ *The townspeople of Isola del Gran Sasso are convinced that it was young Possenti who saved their homes from being burned down by the occupying army under the command of Giuseppe Garibaldi.*

⮝ *Sanctuary of Our Lady of Loreto in Spoleto.*

him the nickname "damerino," meaning that he was a flirt. Additionally, he engaged in vices such as smoking cigarettes and playing cards.

However, Francesco's life took a transformative turn when he experienced a conversion during a procession aimed at invoking grace to avert a cholera epidemic in Spoleto. It was during this procession that he felt a profound encounter with Our Lady, represented in the image known as the icon of Spoleto. Sensing her gaze upon him, Francesco heard a voice within his heart declaring, "Francesco, the world is no longer for you." This divine intervention marked the beginning of his journey towards a life of holiness and devotion to God.

Despite his father's initial reluctance, the eighteen-year-old Francesco entered the Passionist order in 1856, filled with joy and a profound commitment to practicing the virtues of humility and obedience. Throughout his life, he maintained a special devotion to the Mother of God, the Passion of the Lord, and the Blessed Sacrament. Francesco's compassionate nature led him to be particularly sensitive to the plight of the poor, and he was known for his generosity towards beggars.

At the age of twenty-two, as a young cleric, Francesco found himself confronting a band of twenty Italian republican rebels under the command of Giuseppe Garibaldi who had invaded the village of Isola del Gran Sasso in central Italy. In a remarkable display of courage, he intervened to protect a young girl by disarming one of the bandits, and astonishingly showcased his marksmanship by shooting a small lizard that crossed their path. This demonstration of skill and bravery prompted the republicans to flee the village, leaving the residents deeply grateful. In a gesture of appreciation, they escorted Francesco back to the monastery in a celebratory procession.

Francesco's life was not without hardship, as he battled tuberculosis from a young age, a disease that ultimately claimed his life shortly after his ordination to the priesthood at the tender age of twenty-four. Despite his short life, Possenti's unwavering faith, courage, and compassion left an indelible mark on all who knew him.

FOUR MIRACLES

Maria Mazzarelli, a twenty-one-year-old resident of Isola del Gran Sasso, suffered from advanced pulmonary tuberculosis, pleuritis, and multiple suppurative abscesses. The miraculous event occurred on October 23, 1892. Maria, appearing like a living corpse due to her grave illness, had a dream of Our Lady, who instructed her to visit the grave of a "penitent saint residing in a nearby convent." Recognizing this saint as Gabriel, Maria was instructed to take something belonging to him, form a cross, and place this relic near her wounds while kneeling over his grave, asking for grace.

Maria shared her dream with a Passionist father, who encouraged her to undertake

Isola del Gran Sasso, the village where St. Gabriel died and where the miracle of Maria Mazzarella's healing occurred.

On February 27, 1862, the day he was "born for Heaven," he received a vision of the Blessed Virgin Mary, which prepared him to pass through the "gate of death."

a three-day devotional at Gabriel's tomb in Isola del Gran Sasso. Following Mary's instructions, Maria pressed a cross formed from a belt belonging to St. Gabriel to her wounds, leading to a miraculous healing. On the third day of the devotional, her illness inexplicably vanished, leading to her complete recovery.

Approximately two years later, Mary's prophetic words were fulfilled. In early February 1894, Maria fell ill again, this time with severe pneumonia, which tragically led to her passing on February 13 of the same year. Despite her eventual death, Maria's initial miraculous healing remains a testament to the power of faith and divine intervention.

On the path to sainthood for Gabriel, three additional healings were recognized as miracles. The second beatification

Panorama of Isola. On the day of Gabriel's funeral, the townspeople were already praying not for the soul of the deceased, but for his intercession, because the young friar died in the reputation of holiness.

miracle involved the immediate and complete healing of Dominic, who was relieved from a "complicated inguinal hernia." The other miracles leading to Bl. Gabriel's canonization concerned Giovanni Battista Cerra from Pontecorvo and Luigi Parisi from Gallipoli.

Giovanni Battista Cerra, a farmer from Pontecorvo, experienced a miraculous healing in 1909 from progressive ankylosing spondylitis, which had afflicted him for fifteen years. After praying to Bl. Gabriel at the Passionist church in Pontecorvo, he felt a sudden relief from his ailment and was able to straighten his spine, returning home unaided.

Luigi Parisi, a carpenter who had suffered from a right-sided inguinal hernia since he was sixteen, lived with sharp pains, swelling, and intestinal dysfunction for many years. Despite doctors recommending surgery, Parisi resisted and prayed daily for healing through the intercession of St. Joseph. Upon receiving the biography of Bl. Gabriel as a gift, he learned about the saint's miracles, including the healing of hernias. During a severe episode of pain, Parisi requested a statue of the Blessed and embarked on a three-day Devotional for healing. By the second day, his pain and swelling vanished, and he felt healthy enough to resume his normal life and work. Doctors confirmed his inexplicable and complete healing from the chronic hernia in February 1912. This miracle led to the establishment of the parish of St. Gabriel in Gallipoli in 1986 and the construction of a church in the saint's honor in 1998.

A DREAM BECAME REALITY

Another grace, one of the most famous healings attributed to the intercession of this young Passionist, was also associated with St. Gabriel.

Lorella Colangelo, originally from the Teramo area but residing in Montesilvano near Pescara, fell ill the day after Easter, March 30, 1975. The ten-year-old girl, who had been experiencing minor ailments, including minor epileptic episodes, since she was six years old, reported to her mother that while at school, she could neither sit nor stand. What's more, she couldn't walk either. When she tried, she fell.

At first, it was thought to be some temporary physical weakness, so medications and strengthening treatments were prescribed. Due to a lack of improvement, her family consulted an orthopedist, who detected a slight curvature of the spine. The treatments he prescribed were discontinued, as they only worsened the girl's condition. Lorella was referred to a hospital in Pescara, from where, recognizing the seriousness of the situation, doctors transferred her to a hospital in Ancona. She stayed there for almost a month until it was finally determined that the problem was neurological rather than orthopedic. Eventually, she was diagnosed with leukoencephalopathy.

People with this illness experience damage to the white matter of the brain and the insulation around nerves. The disease is characterized by progressive motor, visual, cognitive, and behavioral impairments. They also suffer from epilepsy, and their condition gradually deteriorates.

This was also the case for this girl. Lorella's condition worsened by the day, and eventually, she could no longer even get out of bed. She sat there motionless and had to be transported in a wheelchair or carried.

On the night of June 20, Lorella suffered a very severe epileptic attack that lasted about twelve hours. The following morning, her mother returned from home and found her depressed after the aforementioned crisis. As soon as she recovered a little, she turned to her mother to reveal to her the secret she had been hiding from her aunt for the last few days. She said, "Mom, for about a week, St. Gabriel has been appearing to me and telling me to go to his shrine, so he can make me walk."

From a testimony later written down by Lorella herself, we can see how the first of these apparitions occurred and what happened during the following ones. It first happened on a Sunday, when both the aunt and the patients who were lying with Lorella in the same room went to Mass.

The parish of St. Matthew the Apostle and Evangelist in Warsaw.

On September 20, 2014, the cornerstone was consecrated and the new church was named the Shrine of St. Gabriel of Our Lady of Sorrows and Young Saints.

The historic church of San Gabriele dell'Addolorata in Isola del Gran Sasso d'Italia. In 1959, St. Gabriel was declared the patron saint of the entire Abruzzo region.

The girl then saw an intense light, from which emerged a friar dressed in a black habit, cloak, and sandals. On his chest was a heart-shaped emblem—the sign of the Passionists. She immediately knew it was St. Gabriel. Smiling, he invited her to his shrine for the first time, assuring her that she would experience healing there. Then he turned around and disappeared. She would then see him in her dreams throughout the week. He always told her the same thing. On the third day, however, he began to feel sad that she wasn't listening to him. He asked why she wasn't coming to him and finally urged her to come to him "before she runs out of time." That's why she told her mother about everything.

Lorella's mother had absolutely no reason to doubt her daughter's words and promised to take her there. Later that afternoon, the woman went to see the chief physician, Franco Angeleri. She told him that she intended to accompany the girl to the shrine of St. Gabriel since Lorella said that this saint had appeared to her. The doctor then asked her to come to him with her daughter. Only then would he decide. They came back moments later. After the checkup, the doctor asked if the girl had really seen the saint, and what he had told her. Lorella communicated that Gabriel had instructed her to visit his shrine. The doctor asked Lorella to write down an account of this and handed her paper and a pen. She promptly did so. The physician read this remarkable confession and ordered it to be included in her files. He gave his approval for the trip. Then both ladies waited for official permission to leave the hospital, to no avail. They finally left the hospital

Panorama of Spoleto, the town where Gabriel Possenti lived until he turned eighteen.

without the usual formalities. They took the afternoon train and, after a journey of more than four hours, they arrived in Pescara and from there embarked on a journey to their home in Montesilvano.

The following day, accompanied by her parents and a group of relatives, Lorella journeyed to the shrine in Isola del Gran Sasso d'Italia. A little after ten in the morning, their two cars arrived at the shrine square, where some observers noticed a woman, Aunt Lilla, carrying in her arms a sick girl who was evidently paralyzed. Upon reaching the church, Aunt Lilla gently placed Lorella on the saint's tomb, as recounted in a testimony. Shortly afterward, Lorella felt a "sweet drowsiness" and drifted into sleep. Filled with hope and trust, Lorella's father and grandmother remained at her side, while her mother ventured to a nearby store to purchase a shirt for her husband, whose emotions had caused his current attire to be drenched in sweat. Meanwhile, the rest of the family mingled with the gathering of pilgrims from the parish of Saint Gabriel in Terni, who were also present at the shrine.

After approximately fifteen minutes, Lorella beheld an intense light from which St. Gabriel emerged, bearing a warm smile and holding a wooden crucifix in his hand. Addressing her, he asked, "Lorella, do you recognize me?" "Yes, you are Gabriel!" she eagerly responded. "In that case, rise and go!" he instructed. At that moment, Lorella regained consciousness, her smile illuminating the surroundings. With determination, she placed her hands on the glass slab, rose to her feet, and gracefully climbed over the railing of the tomb.

Accompanied by her father and grandmother, Lorella proceeded to the saint's chapel, where they were joyfully reunited with their astonished family members. Meanwhile, Lorella's mother returned to the church, only to find the tomb deserted. Seeking answers, she inquired of those present how Lorella had come to the chapel. To her amazement, they informed her that Lorella had walked there unassisted. Overwhelmed with emotion, she exclaimed, "My God, she is healed! A miracle has occurred!" Lorella was now completely restored!

He used to say: "Love for love, blood for blood, suffering for suffering. The Lord does not look at quantity, but quality. One must serve God with a big heart and an ardent soul." He ignited people's zeal, acting in consonance with the saying: "To kindle others, one must be burning oneself."

MINERS RESCUED

Among a veritable sea of other graces, St. Gabriel was also credited with miraculously saving miners (mostly Italians from Abruzzo) from death in an American mine. (There is more written about this event in the chapter "Large-Scale Miracles," p. 181.)

1579–1639

Relics of St. Martin de Porres.

MARTIN, APOSTLE OF MERCY WITH BROOM IN HIS HAND

St. Martin de Porres

Brother Martin de Porres (1579–1639) a Dominican friar from Lima, Peru, today is one of Latin America's most famous and popular saints. He was of mixed race and is unquestionably among the greatest South American miracle workers. He became famous for his miraculous healings and other graces obtained from God during his lifetime.

This accident happened on August 25, 1956. It was summer vacation. Five-year-old Antonio was spending it in Garachico, a small village in Tenerife, part of the Canary Islands. He was an exceptionally naughty boy, as he stated years later, describing the incident in an interview with Humberto Gonar of the newspaper *El Día* and a reporter from the Peruvian newspaper *El Comercio*. That day he met another boy on his way. The kid, who came from a poor family in Garachico, had with him a bar of Legano soap (Legano is a popular brand in Spain). Antonio took

One of the many schools in the Martin de Porres network.

it from him and, without thinking about what he was doing, threw it into a building that was still under construction. The little boy cried. "He told me his father would kill him. Times were hard and such soap must have had great value at the time," Antonio recounted.[1] Only then did the little rascal realize what foolishness he had committed. He decided to fix it. He calmed the little boy down and promised him that he would find the soap for him.

He did as he said. Climbing up the façade of the building, he was already about to stand on the roof when the stone block he had grabbed fell off. Antonio fell to the pavement. The piece of the wall that weighed about sixty-six pounds, almost twice as much as he did, unluckily fell on the boy's leg. You can imagine the outcome. The left leg and the foot were completely crushed.

The injured boy was immediately transported to the St. Eulalia Clinic in Santa Cruz de Tenerife. However, his foot was in terrible condition. It was becoming more and more purple overnight, until it finally began to blacken and stink. The boy was given antibiotics and vasodilators, but they were not expected to help much. The diagnosis was unambiguous: the leg was being destroyed by gangrene. When the boy's general condition also deteriorated, with rapid pulse, fever, and symptoms of hepatitis, on August 31 the three doctors decided that amputation would be necessary.

They did everything to avoid it, but in the end, they had to surrender. If they didn't amputate, the boy would be at risk of sepsis, and that meant almost certain death. The doctors gave up, but Antonio's mother did not. On the night of September 1, the woman placed a picture with a relic of Bl. Martin de Porres on his leg. The relic was brought from Madrid by a relative. Throughout the night she cried and prayed.

The amputation was planned to be performed on the afternoon of September 2. However, during the preparations, after

PERU

The holy medal of St. Martin de Porres

Altar in the Cathedral of Lima. In the middle, St. Rose of Lima. On the right, St. Martin de Porres.

➤ *The parish church of St. Philip and St. Martin de Porres in Boyacá.*

the bandage was removed, they noticed that the foot was hot and pink again (this was a sign that blood was circulating in it again), and the black scabs of gangrenous flesh peeled away when moved, showing fresh, bleeding tissue. After a further examination, it turned out that the boy's general condition had also improved, including a drop in his pulse rate and temperature. Doctors were shocked by this discovery. This couldn't have happened, and if it could, it wouldn't have happened overnight. The surgery was canceled, and from that day on, the doctors observed a gradual growth of new skin. Moreover, the boy stopped running a fever altogether. By September 10, Antonio was almost completely healed.

The Dominican friars became interested in the case. On February 9, 1957, doctors also became aware of the woman's prayer and the relic. Comparing the facts, they then issued a certificate that such an inexplicably rapid healing of the wound could have had supernatural cause. A few years later, the case was also investigated by other doctors, who considered the healing a miracle. The full name of Antonio—who, as the healed boy from Spanish Tenerife, was called the "child of the miracle"—was Antonio Cabrera Pérez-Camacho. Today he is a well-known dentist in Santa Cruz. He sees St. Martin's influence today not only in the healing that he experienced, but also in his choice of profession, because the Peruvian saint is, after all, the patron saint of barbers, and in his time barbers and dentists were the same thing. Another miracle happened as a result of this healing. The previously non-believing doctor Angel Capote, who treated the boy, became a Christian after what he witnessed.

Relics of Martin de Porres at his shrine in Lima, and a statue prepared to be dressed in vestments.

The first canonization miracle was the healing of a seriously ill eighty-seven-year-old woman from the Paraguayan city of Asunción. The elderly lady, who had enjoyed good health up to that point, felt severe abdominal pains on the evening of September 7, 1948. She began to vomit intensely, and she complained about her heart. Doctors decided that surgical intervention was necessary, but the family, due to the woman's age, did not want to consent to it. Instead, on September 13, they began to storm Heaven with prayers, and after two days, in the morning, the woman was completely healed. On May 6, 1962, Pope John XXIII canonized Bl. Martin de Porres.

THREE OUT OF TWELVE

Before this happened, Martin de Porres had to become blessed. This happened in 1837 during the pontificate of Pope Gregory XVI. Among the twelve healings that were considered in preparation for his beatification process were the

Peruvian postal stamp dedicated to the great saint.

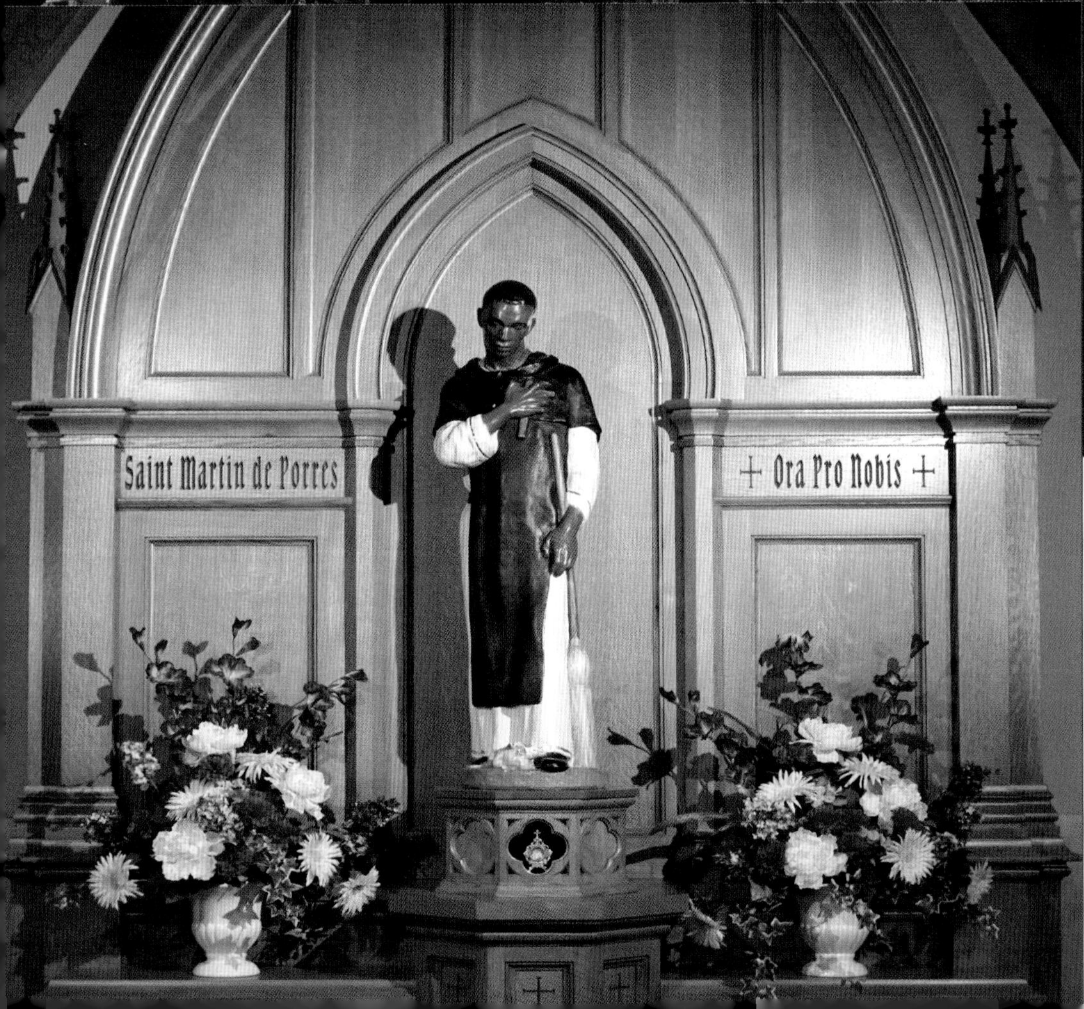

The statue of St. Martin de Porres in the Dominican church in Washington, D.C.

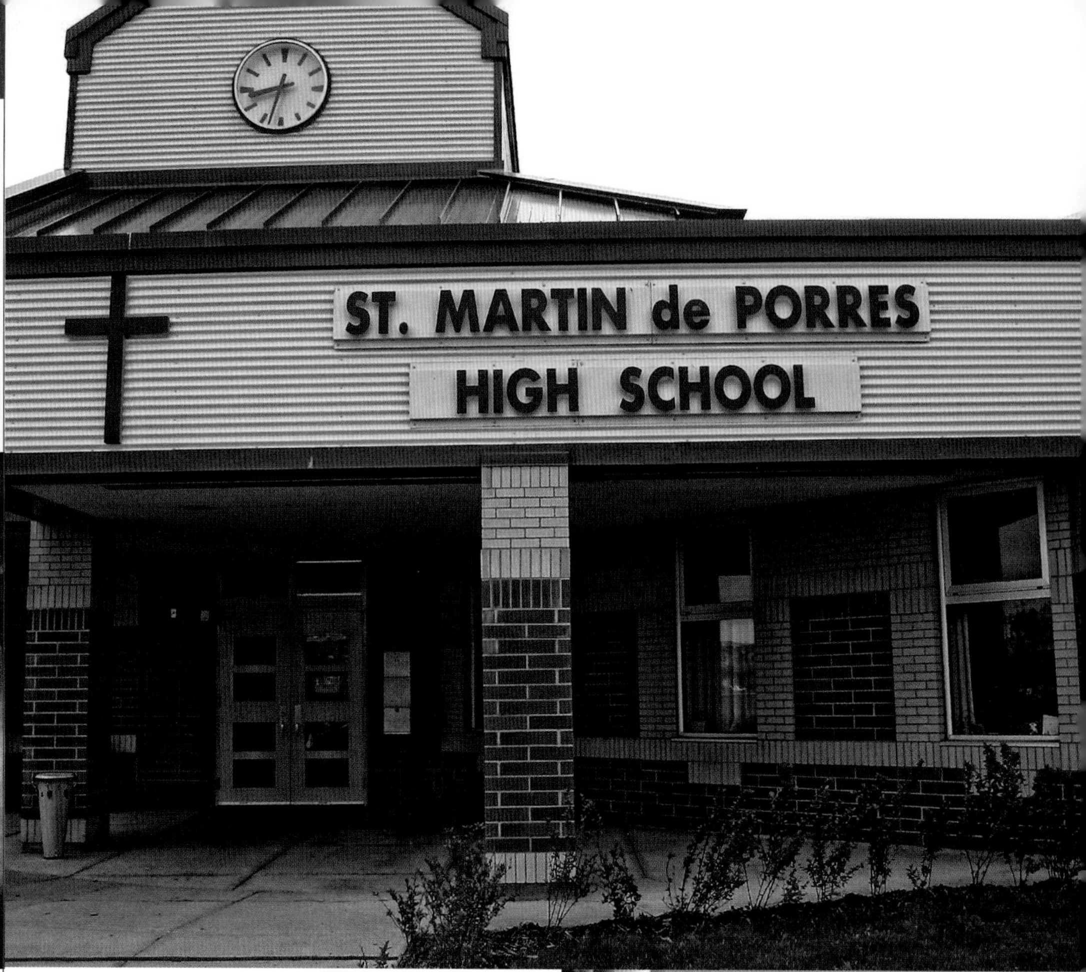

The tomb of St. Martin de Porres in the Basilica and Maximus Convent of Nuestra Señora del Rosario, Lima.

immediate healing of an apoplectic, the resetting of the previously impossible-to-reset dislocated jaw of a woman who had been thrown from her saddle by a mule, a bizarre solution to urological problems, relieving pain in the side of the body, and bringing back to life a boy who was believed to be already dead from a malignant fever (most likely malignant hyperthermia). In some cases, they used an image of St. Martin or soil collected from his grave.

An eminent Peruvian physician, José Manuel Valdés, author of a nineteenth-century biography of Martin de Porres (*The Admirable Life of the Blessed Friar Martin de Porres*), considered two of these twelve healings to be " clearly extraordinary," neither of which anyone would deny the miraculous nature of.

Statue of St. Martin de Porres, St. Dominic's Church.

"The first," the doctor wrote, "was the healing of Elvira Moriano, who, carrying a clay pot full of milk, fell on a window. The pot broke, and a shard lodged in Mrs. Moriano's eye, piercing the eyeball. The humors contained in it spilled out." The injury was extremely painful; the woman screamed in agony, and the eye swelled up and seemed to flow out of the eye socket. The surgeon who was called did not bring good news. He thought he could only alleviate the symptoms. He believed that the eye was no longer salvageable. At this tragic moment, a Dominican friar gave the woman a relic of Friar Martin, instructing her to confidently entrust her trouble to him. Mrs. Moriano put it to her eye and fell asleep. When she woke up, her pain had gone. What's more, she felt that her eye was also fine. The doctor, who arrived in the morning, took off the bandage and noticed that the eyeball of the injured eye had stuck to it, and in its place in the eye socket there was already another eye, quite healthy, crystal clear, and beautiful. He examined it and found that the woman could easily see with it all the objects that were presented to her.

As many as twenty-one witnesses were interviewed in this case, and none of them had the slightest doubt that it was a miracle. Mrs. Moriano herself later used to show everyone her carefully stored old eye.

The second undeniable miracle was the healing of Melchior Varanda. The boy, who was about two years old, fell from the roof of a house that was thirty-six feet high. The infant sustained a fractured skull and lost consciousness. Blood gushed profusely from his eyes, mouth, and nose.

The surgeon was unable to do much at this point, so the family began praying to God through Friar Martin's intercession.

Stained-glass window depicting St. Martin de Porres, St. Pancras Church, Ipswich.

⮝ *One of the Peruvian saint's many works of mercy: a hospital.*

And what happened? "The broken bone was firmly solidified, and the next day he was declared healthy. Five witnesses verified the event," Valdez described.

Dr. Valdez also considered the healing of Antonia de Lamos to be unquestionably miraculous. She was dying and was tormented by fever and persistent diarrhea. When no one on earth could help her anymore, the woman, praying fervently, asked Friar Martin for help. She then experienced a "great consolation." St. Martin de Porres appeared to her, and during his heavenly visit, he immediately healed her.

FATHER OF MERCY

Although he was the son of Spanish grandee Juan de Porres, he was born of a liaison with Anna Velazquez, a freed slave of African (and perhaps also Native American) descent. Martin de Porres was a dark-skinned man. He was raised in poverty and bore the stigmas of both his illegitimate birth and his mixed race. However, his father gave him financial support, thanks to which Martin became a barber-surgeon, which means that he practiced barbering, surgery (treating wounds, bloodletting), and herbalism. Martin was very pious and charitable from childhood onward. As a teenager, at the invitation of a friar, he joined the Dominicans, where for a long time he was a servant, a tertiary, and eventually, after being allowed to take vows, a lay brother or "conversus."

At first, he performed the most mundane services: sweeping, mopping floors, cleaning toilets, laundry, and cooking, but over time he was entrusted with the role of infirmarian, or monastery medic.

In a monastery in Lima, he became known for his many unconventional behaviors. God endowed him with unusual charisms. He sometimes fell into a religious ecstasy during fervent prayer, and even levitated.

⮞ *The great saints of Peru: St. Martin de Porres, St. Rose of Lima, and St. John Macias.*

He miraculously knew the innermost secrets of human hearts and consciences, and had the gift of prophecy, clairvoyance, and bilocation. Although he never left Lima, he was seen in Africa (where he is said to have comforted slaves), in Mexico, and even in China and Japan, where he was said to have supported the missionaries. He was seen at the bedsides of the sick

He saw the suffering Christ in each of the poor, caring for the well-being of their bodies and souls.

(often appearing despite locked doors). Thanks to the gift of profound knowledge given to him by God, without any studies, he was able to flawlessly explain the most complicated theological problems to his young confreres. He provided legal advice to the archbishop (Martin cured him of severe pneumonia), as well as to the viceroy. He became famous for his extremely strict asceticism (like St. Dominic, he lashed his body three times each night with a whip, and slept only three or four hours a night). Even during his lifetime, he was already considered a miracle worker blessed with the gift of healing. The friar from Lima was admired for his great heart and his humble ministry of mercy. The father of mercy helped everyone without the slightest exception, filling the shelters he created—and even his sister's house—with the poor and the sick. He saw the suffering Christ in each of the poor, and he cared for the well-being of their bodies as well as their souls.

Full of humility, he lived in great friendship with animals. He cured, fed, and took in not only dogs and cats, but even mice and rats, and they obeyed him unconditionally. He was friends with many people who were later declared saints: Rose of Lima, Francisco Solano, Turibius of Mongrovejo, and John Macías.

When he died of severe malaria, he was escorted to his burial site by crowds of Lima residents, both great dignitaries and the poorest of beggars. His iconography today include a broom, a dog, a cat, and even mice.

The friar from Lima was admired for his great heart and his humble ministry of mercy. The father of mercy helped everyone without the slightest exception, filling the shelters he created with the poor and sick.

Martin was very pious and charitable since childhood. As a teenager, at the invitation of a friar, he joined the Dominicans, where for a long time he was a servant, a tertiary, and eventually after being allowed to take vows, a lay brother "conversus."

ENDNOTES

1 "El niño que hizo santo a Martín de Porres," *El Día*, May 6, 2012, https://www.eldia.es/2012-05-06/sociedad/2-nino-hizo-santo-Martin-Porres.htm.

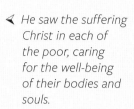

1887–1968

Padre Pio's stigmata appeared during his first years of priesthood.

Panorama of Pietrelcina.

WONDERWORKER OF PIETRELCINA

St. Padre Pio

Few Catholics worldwide remain unaware of the remarkable figure of St. Padre Pio Francesco Forgione. At the dawn of the twentieth century, this Italian Capuchin friar was blessed with an extraordinary array of gifts and charisms from God, contributing to numerous remarkable healings and conversions. He is widely acclaimed, and rightly so, as one of the preeminent saints of the twentieth century. During Padre Pio's canonization in 2002, Pope John Paul II lauded him as "a living embodiment of the goodness of God the Father" and "a generous conduit of divine mercy."

Francesco Forgione, later known as Padre Pio, hailed from a humble rural family in the Italian village of Pietrelcina. Entering the Capuchin order at the age of sixteen, he was ordained a priest seven years later. The majority of his life was spent within the confines of the monastery in San Giovanni Rotondo.

Gifted by God with extraordinary charisms, Padre Pio possessed the ability to heal physical and spiritual maladies, discern the secrets of individuals' hearts, and

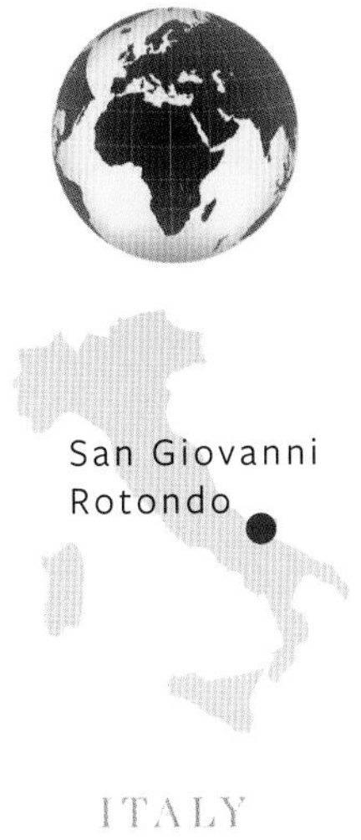

Wonderworker of Pietrelcina.

Pietrelcina, the charming town where Francesco Forgione, the future Padre Pio, was born and raised.

perceive their thoughts. He demonstrated the gifts of prophecy, bilocation, and levitation. Astonishingly, he communicated in languages he had never formally studied. His body temperature regularly soared to 118.4 degrees and, at times, even reached 125 degrees, likely attributable to the mystical fire of love that consumed his soul. During ecstasies and visions, Padre Pio experienced the tangible presence of Jesus Christ and the Virgin Mary, as well as contact with souls undergoing purification in Purgatory.

The first manifestation of the stigmata occurred when Padre Pio was a young priest in September 1910, at the age of twenty-three. Initially desiring for the stigmata to remain invisible, his prayers were answered by God. Visible stigmata appeared on September 20, 1918, while he was in prayer before the cross following Mass. The wounds, agonizingly painful and exuding copious blood, produced nearly half a glass of blood each day. Prior to this, Padre Pio had undergone a transverberation—a mystical experience wherein a celestial entity pierced his soul with an invisible, burning dagger—more than a month earlier.

Padre Pio endured intense pain for two days, during which a physical wound appeared on his side. Two years before the Capuchin's passing, his wounds began to heal, with the final wound vanishing at the moment of his death.

A set of bells in the square in front of the basilica.

From the first instance of his stigmatization, Padre Pio was always accompanied by a delightful fragrance of violet, rose, or incense. This fragrance, detectable during his lifetime and even after his passing in the farthest reaches of the globe, continues to signify his spiritual presence and compassionate care. He himself referred to it as a "consolation of children."

Throughout his earthly journey, Padre Pio grappled with torment from the devil. Manifesting in grotesque forms, the devil assailed him, presenting temptations, disrupting his interactions with others, and even assuming the guise of a refined gentleman to confess to him. At times, he appeared disguised as Christ, the Virgin Mary, or one of Padre Pio's fellow friars.

In his battle against the forces of darkness, Padre Pio found support from St. Michael the Archangel, whom he deeply revered, and particularly from his guardian angel. This celestial companion aided him in comprehending, reading, and writing in foreign languages. Through this divine assistance, Padre Pio extended spiritual guidance to those unable to seek him out in person. As potent weapons in the struggle against evil, the revered Capuchin advocated for vigilant prayer, spiritual mentorship, humility, and the cultivation of virtues such as faith, hope, and love. He urged trust in God, devotion to St. Michael the Archangel and the guardian angel, reverence for the Mother of God, and the devout recitation of the Rosary.

Padre Pio's extraordinary piety and God-given charisms led many to regard him as a saint and a profound miracle worker during his lifetime. In humility, he would often remark, "I am but a humble Franciscan who prays." Faithful adherents flocked to the Masses he celebrated, crowded around the confessional where he offered absolution, and sought his guidance, solace, and spiritual direction.

Gifted with the grace of healing from God, Padre Pio facilitated the spiritual transformation of numerous hardened sinners and disbelievers, igniting within them a fervent faith. There were days when he received more than two hundred letters soliciting spiritual aid or expressing gratitude for his intercessions.

In the 1950s, a modern basilica dedicated to Our Lady of Grace was erected next to the former monastic church.

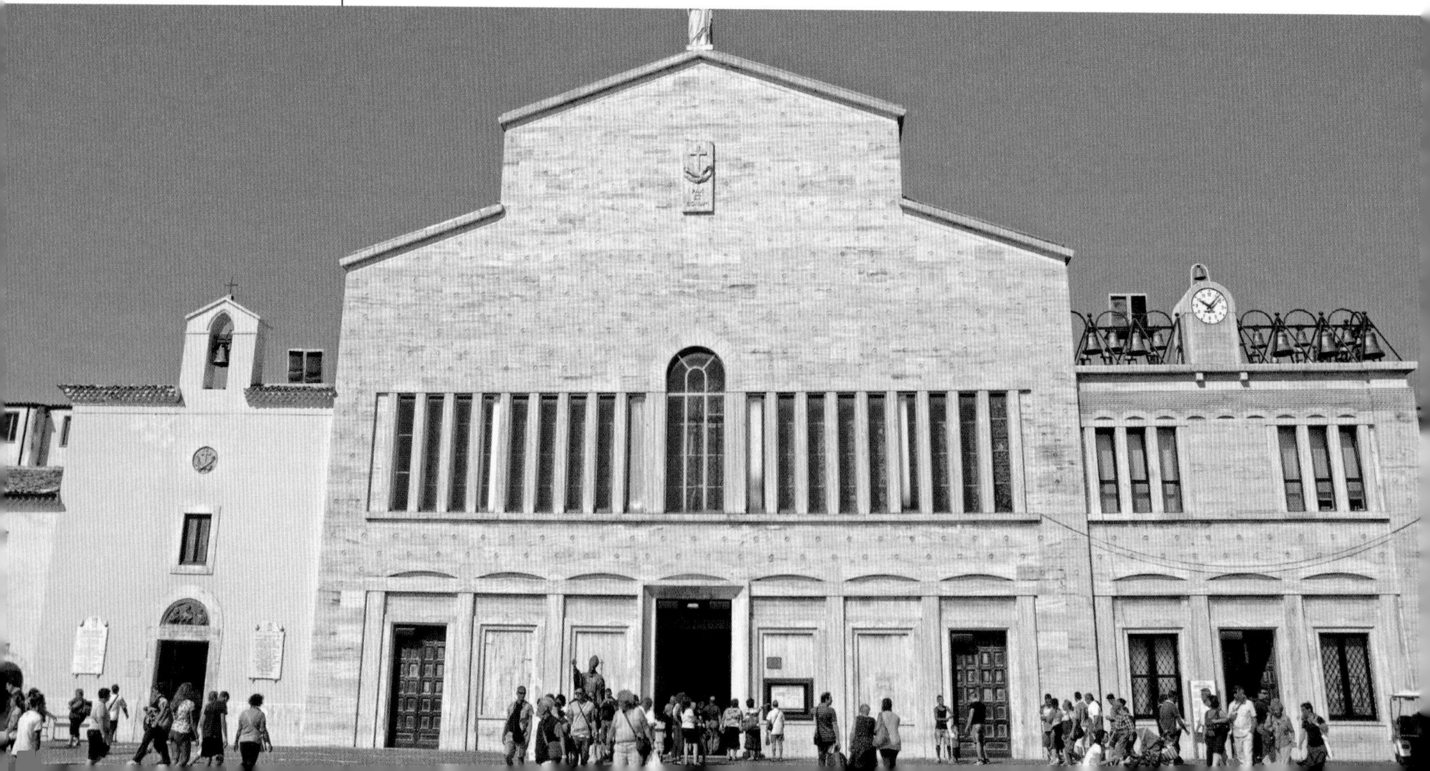

Today, more than seven million pilgrims visit San Giovanni Rotondo every year. In this aspect, the Shrine of Padre Pio is second only to the Shrine of Our Lady of Guadalupe, which is visited by ten million faithful annually.

Padre Pio devoted himself to the ministry of the confessional. Sometimes, he heard confessions for more than a dozen hours a day.

In 1959, Padre Pio fell gravely ill, confined to his bed for several months, and doctors had little hope for his recovery. However, through the intercession of Our Lady of Fátima, God granted him healing. He peacefully passed away on September 23, 1968, yet his intercessory influence persisted even beyond his earthly life. To this day, through his intercession, countless individuals experience God's grace, undergoing physical and spiritual healings and conversions. His enduring legacy includes the establishment of the Home for the Relief of Suffering (a hospital) and the formation of many prayer groups.

Accounts of Padre Pio's life consistently underscore the miraculous nature of his existence, challenging conventional understanding and transcending the laws of this earthly realm. While his surroundings bore witness to many miracles and extraordinary phenomena, these occurrences merely served as signs pointing toward a greater truth—or rather, to Someone greater.

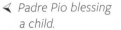

Padre Pio blessing a child.

The cell of the holy Capuchin in San Giovanni Rotondo.

▲ Above the entrance to the monastery's small church, one can see the window from which Padre Pio used to bless local residents and pilgrims.

▲ The House for the Relief of Suffering operating in San Giovanni Rotondo.

▼ The church in San Giovanni Rotondo is impressive in its architecture.

In the closing paragraph of his book *Mysterious Powers of Faith*, Jean Guitton poignantly remarked, "The remarkable aspect of mystics lies not solely in their exuberant phenomena, but in the profound ideas they exemplified, etching upon the world the visage of the Holy Spirit, His vibrant essence. It is through love alone that such preparation is made. Love!"[1]

SURGEON FROM HEAVEN

According to the criteria established by Pope John Paul II, Padre Pio required only two miracles for his canonization. As expected, the discovery of these miracles posed no significant challenge.

The beatification of Padre Pio in 1999 was facilitated by the miraculous recovery of an Italian woman named Consiglia de Martino. Her health tribulations commenced on October 31, although they truly manifested on All Saints' Day in 1995. While preparing to attend Mass, the forty-five-year-old mother of three suddenly experienced excruciating pain and breathlessness, accompanied by a swelling approximately the size of an orange around her collarbone.

At a hospital in Salerno, following extensive examinations, including a CT scan, Consiglia de Martino received a diagnosis of a ruptured lymphatic channel in the throat, likely stemming from trauma, leading to a profuse leakage of approximately half a gallon of lymph into her body. The severity of her condition escalated rapidly, necessitating urgent surgery.

A devoted follower of Padre Pio, Consiglia appealed to him for assistance while still at home. Upon learning of the imminent surgery at the hospital, she fervently implored for healing through Padre Pio's intercession. Relatives, friends, and Capuchin friars from San Giovanni Rotondo, whom she had enlisted for prayer via phone, also petitioned for a miraculous intervention. The scheduled operation was slated for November 2, with plans to remove the excess lymph and repair the ruptured channel.

Overwhelmed with fear, Consiglia persisted in beseeching Padre Pio for aid. "Please guide my hand as if you were the surgeon. Please, operate on me," she silently prayed. Within hours, she experienced a peculiar sensation: an unseen force seemed to unfasten the buttons of her shirt. Sensations akin to gentle surgical incisions and sutures in her neck followed, accompanied by the sudden disappearance of swelling and discomfort. To her astonishment, Consiglia also detected the unmistakable scent associated with Padre Pio's miraculous presence.

Feeling remarkably improved, Consiglia requested that she be discharged from the hospital. Intrigued by her unexpected recovery, doctors postponed the scheduled surgery and conducted further examinations. Remarkably, it was revealed that the fluid leakage into her lungs had resolved spontaneously, and the lymphatic channel showed no signs of rupture. Medically inexplicable and achieved within less than twenty-four hours, this spontaneous healing defied conventional understanding. Following a rigorous medical and theological inquiry, it was affirmed that the organ's affliction was genuine, no medical intervention had occurred, and the healing was immediate, complete, and enduring. Piecing together the evidence, it was concluded that the enigmatic "surgeon" behind this miraculous intervention could be none other than Padre Pio. Five years later, a second miracle occurred.

PADRE PIO WITH ANGELS

On January 20, 2000, Matteo Pio Collela, an eight-year-old boy, fell suddenly ill. While still at school, he began feeling tired and complained of a headache. Shortly thereafter, he developed a high fever, accompanied by convulsions and vomiting. As his condition deteriorated, Matteo began to lose consciousness, and petechiae, tiny red or purple spots, appeared all over his body. His father, a physician, promptly took him to the hospital where he worked, the House for the Relief of Suffering in San Giovanni Rotondo. Tragically, Matteo exhibited symptoms consistent with hyperacute meningitis, compounded by meningococcal sepsis.

Matteo was admitted to the intensive care unit, where his condition rapidly deteriorated. Despite the medical team's diligent efforts, his blood pressure plummeted, and his creatinine and bilirubin levels spiked dramatically. Manifestations of septic shock and acute bradycardia ensued, with each of his organs progressively ceasing to function. By morning, eight of his vital organs, including his kidneys and lungs, had failed.

⮝ *Padre Pio surrounded by children.*

⮟ *A building in Orta San Giulio, northern Italy, where an image of the Capuchin saint appeared on a wall in 1997.*

⮝ *Padre Pio celebrated every liturgy with great veneration. Mass was for him a real participation in the events of the Lord's Passion. He was focused, serious, immersed in prayer, and moved by the miracle taking place.*

➤ *A statue of St. Padre Pio standing in the alley of the shrine.*

Physicians, confronted with the dire prognosis, expressed grim certainty that Matteo's survival was improbable. Even if, by some miraculous intervention, he were to survive, severe brain damage would be inevitable.

Yet, amidst the despair, Matteo's mother, Maria Lucia Ippolito, refused to relinquish hope. A devotee of Padre Pio, she wasted no time in petitioning for divine help. Organizing an extensive prayer campaign, she fervently beseeched for a miracle through the intercession of the revered Capuchin, as well as Jesus the Merciful. Each day, she devoutly recited both the chaplet prayed by Padre Pio and the Divine Mercy chaplet. Rallying others to join her in prayer and to receive Holy Communion for her son's intention, she maintained a vigil of prayer, kneeling before Padre Pio's tomb, in his cell, or in the monastery's presbytery before the crucifix where the Capuchin received the stigmata. Maria Lucia's dedication extended to the point of being willing to sacrifice her own life for her son's.

Even as Matteo's heartbeat faltered and her husband, also a physician, suggested that survival was improbable, Maria Lucia continued to have hope. With their son on the brink of death, she persevered in her prayers, steadfast in her belief that miracles were possible, even in the face of seemingly insurmountable odds.

The relentless and seemingly futile struggle to save Matteo's life teetered on the brink of despair, with the specter of death looming ominously at every turn.

In a desperate bid to stave off death, one of the doctors, driven by sheer desperation, administered an unprecedented dose of epinephrine to the child: five ampoules, an amount five times greater than the standard dosage for an adult. Despite this drastic intervention, coupled with other medications and treatments, medical experts remained pessimistic about the overall prognosis.

However, a remarkable turn of events occurred in the early afternoon of January 21. Unexpectedly and inexplicably, the boy's heart began to beat with increasing strength and regularity. Miraculously, all of his organs gradually resumed normal function, and his vital signs steadily normalized. Subsequent examinations of the boy's brain revealed no discernible damage, confounding medical professionals who were unable to provide a scientific explanation. It was undeniably a miracle.

Yet the battle for the child's health and life was far from over. Although Matteo emerged from the coma on January 31, 2000, he remained unconscious for several more days. However, upon awakening, he displayed remarkable lucidity, exhibiting full awareness and control of his body and demonstrating comprehension and recognition of his surroundings. In a surprising moment of normalcy, he even expressed mundane desires, requesting chocolate and a PlayStation.

Following his awakening, Matteo inquired about Padre Pio, expressing a desire for his presence by his side. He recounted vivid experiences from his time in the coma, recalling visions of himself, angels standing vigil by his bedside, and a bearded old gentleman clad in long brown robes holding his hand. Matteo had experienced the palpable presence of Padre Pio himself.

On February 26, Matteo was discharged from the hospital, now fully restored to health. The sole remnants of his harrowing ordeal were the scars left behind by the disease.

Medical literature worldwide fails to document a case where an individual with more than five failing organs has survived. Remarkably, Matteo's condition was even more dire, with a staggering *nine* organs and systems rendered dysfunctional: the nervous system, respiratory system, cardiovascular system, gastrointestinal system, kidneys, liver, blood clotting, adrenal glands, and skin. Despite the overwhelming odds against him, Matteo defied medical expectations and emerged victorious. "His case astonished the scientific world," remarked Dr. Pietro Violi, who conducted investigations into Matteo's recovery. Subsequently, Matteo's illness was meticulously classified as meningococcal hyperacute sepsis with extensive intravascular coagulation connected to multiple organ failure.

San Giovanni Rotondo, once a small Italian town, is today a place of worship visited by millions of pilgrims.

A new, mosaic-lined church in San Giovanni Rotondo glitters with gold.

1887–1968

The body of the great mystic was laid to rest in a crystal coffin and put on public display.

Padre Pio's sandals.

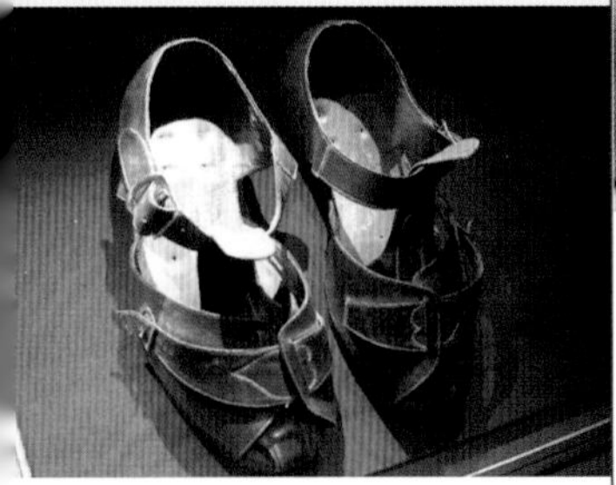

Relics of Padre Pio.

EYES WITHOUT PUPILS

A particularly extraordinary miracle occurred during Padre Pio's lifetime involving Anna-Gemma di Giorgi, who was born without pupils, leading doctors to conclude that she would never be able to see. Devastated by this prognosis, her family turned to prayer, clinging to the hope of a divine intervention.

When Anna-Gemma was seven years old, a nun who was a relative visited the family and suggested seeking Padre Pio's intercession. Anna-Gemma's grandmother, deeply moved by this suggestion, redirected all her prayers to God through Padre Pio's intercession. She implored the nun to send a letter to Padre Pio on their behalf. Although no response was received, the nun experienced a remarkable dream wherein Padre Pio appeared and inquired about the girl for whom she had been offering prayers. Astonishingly, the following day, a letter from Padre Pio arrived in the nun's mailbox, assuring her of his prayers for the blind child.

Inspired by this "coincidence," the nun encouraged the family to bring Anna-Gemma to Padre Pio in San Giovanni Rotondo. Accompanied by her grandmother, Anna-Gemma embarked on the journey. It was during this visit that the miraculous occurred. Suddenly, Anna-Gemma began to perceive shadows and shapes, including what appeared to be a boat, despite no physical change in her eyes. She had gained the gift of sight!

Upon their arrival in San Giovanni Rotondo, both the woman and the girl proceeded to Confession. Anna-Gemma, under her grandmother's guidance, was to request grace from Padre Pio. However, in the midst of the moment, she forgot to make the request. Nonetheless, she recalled feeling Padre Pio's touch upon her eyes with his stigmatized hand and the Sign of the Cross being made. Tearfully, her grandmother made the request in her own Confession, fervently pleading for her granddaughter's healing.

Subsequently, during Holy Communion, Padre Pio once again bestowed his blessing upon Anna-Gemma's eyes with the Sign of the Cross.

On their journey back home, Anna-Gemma began to perceive shapes and eventually gained the ability to see clearly, despite her eyes lacking pupils. The physician who later examined her was

astounded, unable to comprehend the inexplicable restoration of her sight. Others were equally bewildered by the miraculous turn of events.

With her newfound sight, Anna-Gemma resumed her studies, learned to read and write, and embraced a life of normalcy. By the time of Padre Pio's canonization, she had matured into a woman and was invited as a guest to an Italian television studio.

A COMEDIAN AT THE FOOT OF THE ALTAR

Padre Pio's influence extended beyond miraculous healings to encompass numerous conversions, including those of prominent figures from the entertainment industry. Among them was Carlo Campanini, one of Italy's most renowned actors and comedians, who appeared in 127 films from 1939 to 1969. Campanini's initial encounter with Padre Pio occurred in 1939, when he himself was still a relatively unknown comedic actor.

Accompanied by fellow actors from the touring theater, Campanini journeyed to the Capuchin during Holy Week. In a candid interview with Italian journalist Renz Allegri, Campanini confessed that he initially regarded Padre Pio as a mere "magician" and harbored hopes of financial gain from their encounter.

At the time, Campanini grappled with the demands of a nomadic lifestyle, constantly traveling with his wife while leaving their three children under the care of his sister. He yearned for stability and a profession that would allow him to settle down permanently. Spiritually, although he was baptized, he had drifted away from regular church attendance since his childhood.

Upon arrival, the actors faced initial challenges in meeting Padre Pio, as he was enduring heightened suffering during Holy Week. Eventually, they were informed that Padre Pio would hear their confessions the following morning after Mass. True to the arrangement, after enduring a lengthy Mass, during which Campanini struggled with the duration and the requirement to kneel continuously, he knelt before the confessional lattice. It quickly became apparent that there was no need for Campanini to vocalize his concerns, as Padre Pio already possessed knowledge of his innermost thoughts and struggles. "He compelled me to commit to changing my

The modern exterior of the church dedicated to Padre Pio in San Giovanni Rotondo.

Relics of Padre Pio.

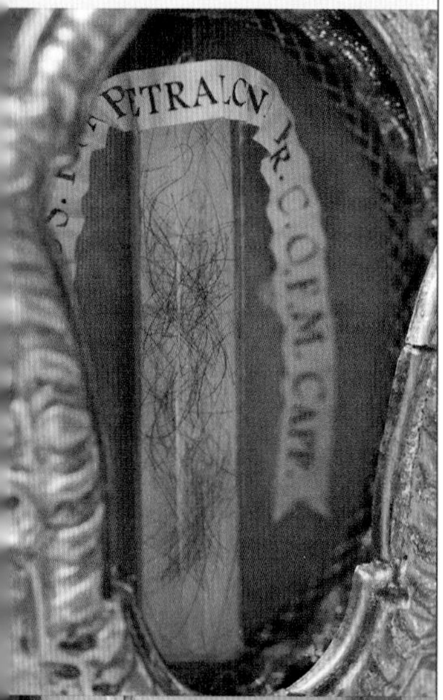

life, after which he granted me absolution," recounted the comedian.[2]

Inwardly, Campanini also petitioned Padre Pio for assistance in securing permanent employment closer to home.

The actor's unspoken desire was swiftly granted, almost miraculously, as Campanini secured the role that catapulted him into stardom. With fame came wealth, and he soon acquired his own residence. However, despite Padre Pio's silent intercession, Campanini failed to heed the Capuchin's guidance. Despite his newfound success, he descended into a pattern of frequent and grave sin. Nonetheless, the encounter with Padre Pio and his words continued to haunt Campanini like a persistent thorn, revealing an emptiness and discontent that fame and fortune could not assuage.

"Internally, I felt shattered, drained, despondent, weary, and profoundly sorrowful. I even envied those who possessed the resolve to end their own lives." A turning point arrived when the Campanini family received a visit from a local parish priest, who encouraged them to consecrate their home to the Sacred Heart of Jesus and partake in Holy Communion.

On Epiphany Day, January 6, 1950, Campanini found himself wandering aimlessly through the streets of Rome, consumed by restlessness and sadness. Eventually, he found himself drawn to

the Church of St. Anthony. Despite initial hesitations, he felt compelled to approach the confessional lattice. "After half an hour," he recounted, "I emerged with tears streaming down my face. I felt reborn, and a profound sense of joy permeated our home as I participated in the celebration and received Holy Communion with my family."

Campanini wasted no time in informing Padre Pio of his life-altering transformation. Returning to the confessional, he underwent a profound spiritual renewal that redirected the course of his life. From that moment onward, he embraced his faith wholeheartedly, never again neglecting Sunday Mass and

Luminous angels lead pilgrims to the tomb of the Capuchin saint.

A modern chapel with the crystal coffin of Padre Pio.

attending daily Mass whenever possible. He devoted every available moment to Padre Pio, emerging as one of his staunchest apostles. Upon his death on November 20, 1984, in Rome, Campanini was laid to rest in the cemetery of San Giovanni Rotondo.

A SAINT WITH A SAINT

Padre Pio and John Paul II shared a remarkable and somewhat unconventional relationship. The young priest Karol Wojtyła first encountered the Italian stigmatist in 1947 during his studies in Rome. It was reported that during this meeting, the Capuchin revealed to Wojtyła glimpses of his future.

Fifteen years later, now a bishop, Karol wrote a letter to Padre Pio, entreating him to pray for the recovery of Wanda Półtawska, a renowned pro-life advocate from Krakow, who was battling cancer. Just eleven days later, another letter was dispatched, expressing gratitude for Padre Pio's intercession, which had resulted in Wanda's miraculous healing.

In 1974, six years after Padre Pio's passing, Cardinal Wojtyła journeyed to the friar's tomb in San Giovanni Rotondo to commemorate the twenty-eighth anniversary of his ordination to the priesthood. Little did he know that one day he would ascend to the papacy, and it would be under his pontificate that Padre Pio would be beatified and later canonized as a saint of the Catholic Church.

ENDNOTES

1 Jean Guitton, Jean-Jacques Antier, Tajemne moce wiary [Mysterious Powers of Faith by Guitton Jean, Antier Jean-Jacque]. Znaki i cuda, Oficyna Wydawniczo-Poligraficzna Adam, Warszawa 1997, s. 276.

2 Fragmenty wypowiedzi C. Campaniniego za: Renzo Allegri, Cuda Ojca Pio [Excerpts from statements by C. Campanini cit. por. : Miracles of Padre Pio / I miracoli di padre Pio by Renzo Allegri], WAM, Kraków 1999, s. 180, 183 i 184.

LIVING FOR GREATER THINGS

St. Stanislaus Kostka

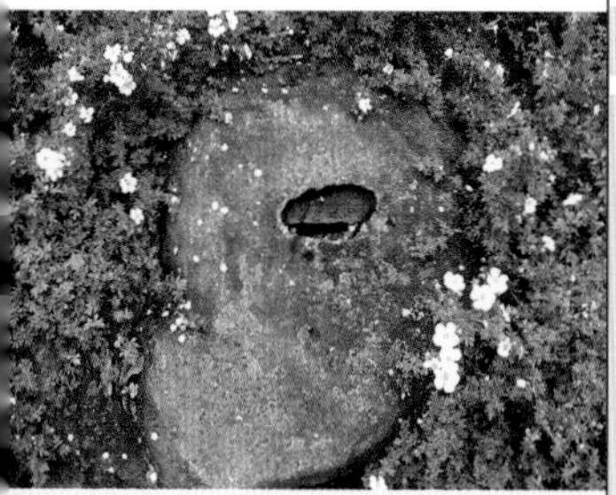

⮝ *According to tradition, this is the footprint of St. Stanislaus Kostka in stone in Rostkowo.*

⮟ *St. Stanislaus Kostka's linden in the church garden in Rostkowo.*

St. Robert Bellarmine venerated him. St. Francis de Sales and St. Alphonsus Liguori wrote about him. St. John Bosco set him as an example to his charges. St. John Paul II sought spiritual light and help from him. For all of us, he can be an example of determination in the realization of a vocation. The intercession of the holy young man, a miracle worker of the seventeenth century, contributed to a huge number of miracles and graces obtained on all continents. The three most important, thanks to which he was declared a saint, happened in France, Poland, and Peru.

The first of the three miracles, approved in 1713 by Pope Clement XI, was the healing of a French woman, Anna Theodora de Ligniville. Hailing from the aristocratic Ligniville family of Lorraine, France, the young girl fell ill in early October 1601. Some accounts of this miracle suggest that her suffering stemmed from an attempt on her life, as a man allegedly tried to poison her by giving her a poisoned drink.

The severity of her illness brought Anna Theodora unspeakable suffering. For fourteen months, she endured violent convulsions, some lasting an entire day. Her health deteriorated to such an extent that she received the Sacrament of the Anointing of the Sick, as her family expected her to pass away imminently.

In addition to the relentless convulsions, Anna Theodora suffered from muscular atrophy in her legs and feet during this period. Jesuits, as described in an eighteenth-century Italian biography of St. Stanislaus, recounted the distressing state of her limbs. Her legs had become

⮞ *Church of St. Stanislaus Kostka, Rostkowo, former family seat of the Kostka family.*

A stained-glass window of St. Stanislaus Kostka in the church dedicated to him in Pittsburgh, Pennsylvania.

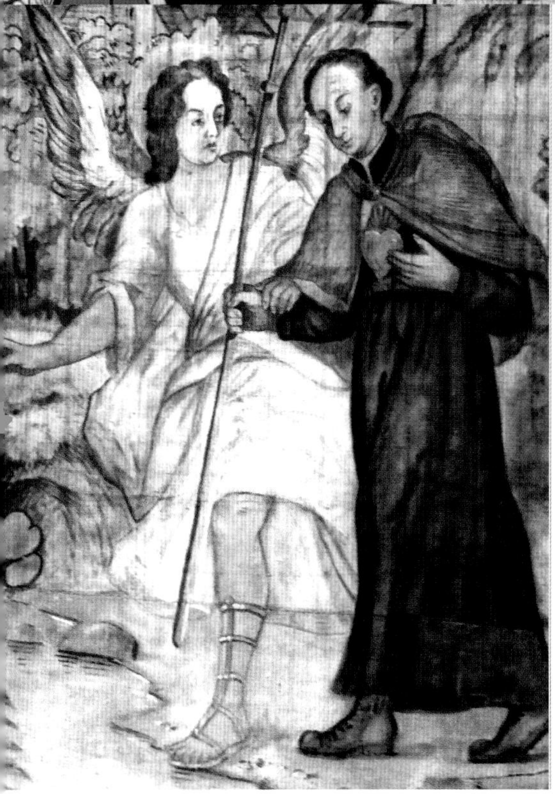

St. Stanislaus Kostka on pilgrimage to Rome.

so emaciated that only bones and skin remained visible. In some areas, the bones seemed poised to pierce through the skin, while in others, the skin appeared detached from the bone, movable and foldable like a veil. She had lost the ability to stand, walk, or even move her legs, feet, or toes.

Despite extensive medical efforts over the fourteen-month period, Anna Theodora's condition showed no signs of improvement. Her family spared no expense in seeking treatment, consulting not only local physicians but also the foremost medical experts from across France. Yet all concurred on the diagnosis: the disease was deemed incurable, with no prospect of amelioration.

At that time, Philip Emanuel de Ligniville, the brother of the sick girl, returned from Rome bearing a relic of Stanislaus Kostka. He encouraged his sister to choose this young man as an intercessor with God.

Front of the Gregorian University in Rome.

Church of St. Andrew on the Quirinal in Rome.

Around November 18, 1602, Philip presented the relic, along with a paper portrait of the saint, to his ailing sister before departing for Nancy.

Anna Theodora harbored a profound and ardent affection for the young man from Poland, and as her brother had advised, she selected him as her special intercessor. With great trust and hope, she began beseeching him to intercede for her restoration to health.

On Sunday, November 24, in an attempt to provide solace to the patient, she was placed on a portable chair and conveyed to Mass at the parish church in Houécourt. Despite her efforts to move her legs or even her feet, she found herself unsuccessful.

Seated in the church, she fervently reiterated her appeals to the saint for the grace of health. She particularly implored him for assistance during the elevation of the Eucharist.

"O Lord, if it is your will to honor your servant Stanislaus Kostka, please grant me, through his merits, the grace of health," she pleaded to the God concealed within the Eucharistic species. It was precisely at that moment, between the elevation of the Host and the elevation of the chalice, that she experienced a profound and inexplicable relief from her suffering. The patient sensed a surge of vitality coursing through her body, ultimately reaching all her limbs, particularly her legs, which had hitherto felt lifeless. Briefly losing consciousness, she awoke to find herself completely free of infirmity.

As the Mass concluded, she rose to her feet and, reveling in the newfound strength in her legs, swiftly and gracefully made her way back to her home, located a mere two hundred steps from the church. One can only imagine the shock and astonishment of those who witnessed this miraculous transformation. Equally swiftly, accompanied by her mother, servants, and numerous faithful, Anna Theodora returned to the church to offer solemn thanks to God and St. Stanislaus for the miraculous gift she had received. Subsequently, she embarked on a pilgrimage, on foot, to the shrine of Our Lady of Castel Nuovo.

During a hearing held in Toulon in 1621 as part of the canonization process, Anna Theodora testified that since her miraculous healing, she had never again experienced pain or suffered from any ailment.

MALIGNANT FEVER

The second miracle took place in Poland at the Benedictine monastery in Koscielna Wies near Kalisz. The parish priest and abbot, Fr. Andrzej Faust Unikowski, a devout venerator of Stanislaus Kostka, fell gravely ill in July 1640 with a malignant fever that afflicted him for seven weeks, leaving him in a state of extreme exhaustion. "I couldn't even move my arms or legs," he recounted in his testimony.

Ecstasy of St. Stanislaus Kostka *by Giovanni Odazzi.*

Despite exhaustive efforts by medical professionals, no cure seemed effective. By August 28, his condition was deemed to be beyond hope, and preparations for his death were made. Fr. Andrzej lay on a rug on the ground as his confreres anointed him with holy oils and recited prayers. In the dead of night, he summoned Fr. Sylwester Lampartowicz and requested that if he were to survive until morning, Mass be celebrated for him at the Jesuit church in Kalisz, specifically at the altar of Bl. Stanislaus. He also sent Roman Krośnowski, not yet ordained, to accompany him.

Placing his trust entirely in the intercession of the saint, Fr. Andrzej awaited the outcome. The designated friars reached Kalisz at five in the morning. Meanwhile, feeling the extreme cold numb his entire body, Fr. Andrzej rolled off the floor onto his bed, where an image of Stanislaus watched over him. Closing his eyes, he sensed a presence at the foot of the bed. Despite his initial terror, he raised his hand and was surprised to feel no pain. Testing his limbs, he found himself able to move freely. Soon, he rose from the bed, feeling revitalized and strong, as if he had never been ill. Summoning his astonished servants, he requested his clothes and soon stood before his brethren, who initially mistook his vigor for the delirium preceding death.

Afterward, however, he managed to persuade them otherwise. "It was God and Blessed Stanislaus Kostka who restored my health, and it happened precisely at the moment when Fr. Sylwester celebrated Mass for my intention at the altar of the blessed in Kalisz," he later recounted.

The next morning, the abbot proceeded to the church as if nothing extraordinary had occurred. At the cemetery, he encountered the two physicians who had attended to him during his illness. Upon seeing him, they made the Sign of the Cross

The chapel of St. Stanislaus Kostka at the Church of St. Andrew on the Quirinal in Rome.

In 1621, by the decision of Pope Gregory XV, his skull was transported from this tomb to Poland. There, by the decree of King Wladyslaw IV Vasa, it rested in the Church of the Holy Apostles Peter and Paul in Krakow. At the end of the eighteenth century, due to the suppression of the Jesuit order, his skull disappeared.

➤ *St. Stanislaus Kostka was often depicted as a priest embracing the baby Jesus.*

➤ *The tomb in the chapel of St. Stanislaus Kostka at the Church of St. Andrew on the Quirinal in Rome.*

in disbelief. The abbot then informed them of the miraculous healing and invited them to join him for a Mass of thanksgiving.

Upon returning to the monastery, the abbot enjoyed a hearty meal and a sip of wine, with no lingering trace of the fever or illness that had afflicted him. As the friars dispatched to Kalisz returned, the timing of the Mass was compared with the time of the mysterious vision experienced by the abbot, revealing an astonishing correspondence between the two events.

PARALYSIS

In 1673, within the novitiate of the Society of Jesus in Lima, Peru, resided a young novice named Francis Xavier Salduendo, afflicted by paralysis. At fourteen, Francis suffered from paralysis that affected the entire right side of his body, from shoulder to foot. His right arm and leg were immobile, devoid of sensation, and his entire right side felt numb and rigid. Despite the efforts of Lima's foremost physicians, employing advanced treatments and medications, there was no improvement in his condition.

For twenty days, Francis endured this affliction, until November 13, coinciding with the commemoration of Bl. Stanislaus Kostka. On this day, a test was conducted to verify the sensation in his paralyzed side, using a long, thick needle. The result was disheartening, as Francis felt no sensation whatsoever, as if he were an inert corpse.

Around noon, two fellow novices, John Blanc and John de Alera, were sent by the superior to console Francis and engage in meditative discussion on matters of holiness. The feast day of Bl. Stanislaus provided a fitting topic for their conversation.

During their discussion, John Blanc expressed a conviction that Stanislaus would miraculously heal Francis. Encouraged by this assertion, Francis tearfully beseeched the saint for his health

swiftly and effortlessly, devoid of any pain. The entire community later convened to offer solemn gratitude to God and Stanislaus Kostka for this extraordinary grace.

Twenty-six years later, during the canonization process of St. Stanislaus, Francis testified that he had remained in robust health ever since, never again afflicted by sickness. The miraculous healing of the novice ignited fervent veneration of the young Polish Jesuit in Lima, triggering a cascade of graces and miracles attributed to his intercession.

Upon recognizing these three miracles, Pope Benedict XIII canonized Stanislaus Kostka as a saint in 1726.

LITTLE KNIGHT OF CHRIST

St. Stanislaus Kostka hailed from an affluent Catholic noble family and was born in December 1550 in Rostkowo, within Poland's Mazovia region. At the age of fourteen, accompanied by his elder brother Paul and a tutor, he embarked on a journey to the esteemed Imperial Jesuit College in Vienna.

There, he applied himself diligently to his studies while fervently practicing his faith. Amidst the backdrop of the Protestant Reformation, he nurtured a profound devotion to the Eucharist and held a deep reverence for the Virgin Mary. Stanislaus attended Mass daily, adored the Blessed Sacrament, and adhered to the religious customs of his time, partaking in Holy Communion once a week. He engaged in fervent prayer, often entering into contemplation of Christ's Passion, experiencing occasional ecstasies. He recited the Rosary, prayed the Little Hours, and immersed himself in devotional literature. He actively participated in the Sodality of the Blessed Virgin Mary and the Confraternity of St. Barbara. Notably, he upheld the virtue of chastity, detesting vulgarity, indecency, and frivolous pursuits,

St. Stanislaus Kostka in the altar of the Poznań Parish Church.

St. Stanislaus holding the baby Jesus.

and made a solemn promise: to recite the Our Father and Hail Mary daily in his honor, fast on the eve of his feast day, and offer flower bouquets at his chapel. Seeking an image of the saint, John Blanc promptly procured a paper picture, which Francis reverently kissed and placed on his paralyzed arm. In an instant, the paralysis vanished, and sensation returned. Francis could freely move his once-immobile arm and leg. Astonished and elated, he repeated the process with his leg, experiencing the same swift recovery.

The superior, upon hearing the news, hurried to the infirmary and found Francis already moving his formerly paralyzed limbs with ease.

Instructed by the superior, Francis rose and dressed himself, a task he accomplished

➢ *St. Stanislaus Kostka being lashed by his brother Paul while in Vienna.*

⮝ Communion of St. Stanislaus Kostka *by Ludovico Mazzanti.*

➢ Our Lady with Sts. Stanislaus Kostka, Aloysius Gonzaga, and Ignatius of Loyola *by Simon Czechowicz.*

similar to his Italian counterpart, St. Aloysius Gonzaga. Despite facing ridicule and persecution for his devoutness, Stanislaus remained steadfast in his dedication to God, striving to please Him and minimize discord with his brother, guided by his motto, "I was born for greater things."

His burgeoning desire to join a religious order, particularly the Jesuits, intensified over time, leading him to make a vow to God pledging his future affiliation. In December 1565, he fell seriously ill. Unable to receive the sacraments due to his condition, he implored St. Barbara for assistance. In a vision, he beheld her bringing him Holy Communion. On another occasion, he encountered the Virgin Mary, who placed the infant Jesus in his arms and urged him to join the Jesuits. Miraculously, Stanislaus experienced a swift recovery thereafter.

After enduring a lengthy and arduous journey, overcoming numerous obstacles with unwavering resolve, Stanislaus finally reached the General of the Order, Francis Borgia, who admitted him to the novitiate on October 28, 1567. Despite facing resistance from his father, who vehemently opposed his decision to join the order, Stanislaus impressed everyone with his fervent faith, deep piety, rigorous mortifications, humility, obedience, and exemplary fulfillment of his novice duties.

In the early months of 1568, Stanislaus solemnly took his vows. However, in August of the same year, he fell ill unexpectedly. While his illness surprised others, Stanislaus himself had prayed for the grace to depart from this world on the Feast of the Assumption of the Blessed Virgin Mary. His prayer was answered, as he peacefully passed away shortly after midnight on August 15, 1568, accompanied by the Mother of God.

Stanislaus's cause of death was likely malaria, although doctors were perplexed by the suddenness of his demise, given his prior good health. Revered by many as a saint, his relics were sought after, and devotion to the Polish youngster, hailed as a true knight of Christ, swiftly spread around the world following his death.

HOMELAND UNDER PROTECTION

As an "unofficial citizen of Heaven," Stanislaus Kostka, revered as the patron saint of Poland since 1674, was believed to have repeatedly intervened to safeguard his homeland from the perils of frequent wars and invasions. His intercession was credited with securing victories against the Ottomans and their Cossack vassals at Chocim in 1621 and Beresteczko in 1651 (both then part of Poland-Lithuania, but today in western Ukraine).

Regarding the pivotal battle of Chocim fought against the Turks, a remarkable vision experienced by a Jesuit in Kalisz, more than six hundred miles away, added to the saint's lore. Fr. Nicolaus Oborski witnessed a celestial spectacle during which the Mother of God, cradling the infant Jesus, appeared in a chariot drawn by two fiery steeds. Alongside them was St. Stanislaus Kostka, fervently praying and directing his gaze toward the Polish knights engaged in battle. This divine apparition was interpreted as a sign of divine intervention, and shortly thereafter, news of a favorable treaty for Poland reached Kalisz.

Moreover, St. Stanislaus's influence extended beyond the battlefield. He reportedly appeared twice to the Italian Jesuit Julius Mancinelli, alongside the Virgin Mary, contributing to the official recognition of the Most Holy Virgin Mary as Queen of Poland in 1656, a momentous event in Poland's religious history.

Accounts of miraculous occurrences associated with images of the saint further enhanced his reputation. Images of Stanislaus Kostka, particularly those in Lublin and Krakow, were said to exhibit unusual phenomena, such as sweating. This phenomenon was documented by Peter Hyacynt Pruszcz in 1745, who described how the image in Krakow remained wet despite frequent wiping. A commission was formed to investigate this miraculous occurrence, and a handkerchief used to wipe the miraculous sweat was preserved as a relic. To this day, the image and the handkerchief remain objects of veneration in the church dedicated to St. Stanislaus Kostka.

1846–1878

➤ In a grotto near Alexandria, Mariam received one of the most extraordinary apparitions: The Virgin Mary's constant presence and care for several weeks.

THE LITTLE ARAB

St. Mary of Jesus Crucified (Mariam Baouardy)

She was twenty years old when the stigmata appeared on her body. She experienced numerous ecstasies and apparitions in her life, during which she talked with Christ, the Virgin Mary, St. Joseph, and various other saints and angels. Her heart was mystically pierced; she received the gifts of prophecy, reading people's hearts, and performing bilocation and levitation. It has been said that she received more charisms from God than St. Padre Pio himself. The miraculous healings of two small children contributed to her being raised to the glory of the altars.

▲ Mariam's story begins in Bethlehem, where her parents' prayers were answered.

In 1867, Mariam received the habit and the name Sr. Mary of Jesus Crucified.

Mariam was from I'billin, a village in Galilee. Her parents prayed for a healthy child (in the Grotto of the Nativity in Bethlehem!) since all their previous children (twelve sons) died shortly after birth. Their prayers were answered by God through the intercession of Mary. Two years after Mariam, her brother Boulous was born. Unfortunately, a year later their parents died, and Mariam was taken to her rich uncle's house in Alexandria, Egypt. When she turned thirteen, her uncle decided to marry her off. She refused. As punishment, she was treated like a servant. The girl then decided to ask her brother for help. She wrote a letter to him and asked a Muslim acquaintance to deliver it. He agreed, but he demanded she convert to Islam in exchange for the favor.

When she refused, the enraged man slit her throat and threw her out onto the street. She woke up in a cave, where she was taken care of by an unfamiliar nun (Mariam remained convinced until the end of her life that it was the Virgin Mary herself!). After four weeks, the mysterious nurse took her to the Church of St. Catherine, served by Franciscan friars. Mariam never returned to her uncle's house.

She earned a living as a servant. From Alexandria, she moved to Jerusalem, then to Beirut, and finally to Marseille, where she became cook for a family of Arab immigrants.

Feeling called to religious life, she entered the convent of the Congregation of the Sisters of St. Joseph, but when she began to experience ecstasies and stigmata appeared on her body, the head nuns decided the postulant wasn't suited for their congregation. Thanks to her novice mistress, Mariam entered the cloister of the Discalced Carmelites in Pau. She was uneducated and illiterate, so the sisters entrusted her with work in the kitchen. In 1867, she received the habit, taking the name Sr. Mary of Jesus Crucified. In the novitiate in Pau, she experienced supernatural events more frequently, including a possession. "Little Nothing," as she called herself, was gifted

Thanks to her novice mistress, Mariam entered the cloister of the Discalced Carmelites in Pau. She was uneducated and illiterate, so the sisters entrusted her with work in the kitchen.

Tomb of Sr. Mary of Jesus Crucified in the monastery in Bethlehem.

➤ *In the novitiate in Pau, she experienced supernatural events more frequently, including a possession. "Little Nothing," as she called herself, was gifted by God with the knowledge of a wiseman and an incredible panoply of charisms.*

➤ *Relics of the holy Little Arab.*

by God with the knowledge of a wiseman and an incredible panoply of charisms. From France, Sr. Mary and a group of sisters set out to India to establish a monastery in Mangalore. There—on Indian soil—she made her profession of perpetual vows. In Mangalore, she experienced more difficult moments. Some of the supernatural events occurring in her life were considered to be the work of Satan. Sr. Mary was sent to Pau, and a few years later she embarked on another journey—to Bethlehem and Nazareth, where, following orders from Jesus Himself, she initiated the construction of monasteries. Following the apparitions, the Little Arab also became a great propagator of the devotion to the Holy Spirit.

She died in the Holy Land on August 26, 1878, after a brief illness, at thirty-three, the same age as our Lord when he was crucified.

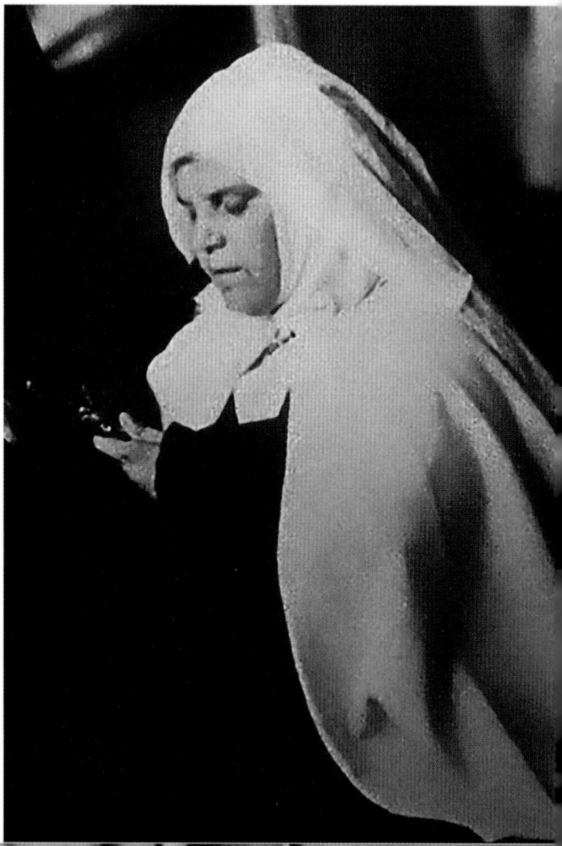

The most well-known photo of Mariam Baouardy and the relics of the Little Arab.

SHE JUMPED TO HER FEET

General muscular hypotonia in a person with severe rickets—this is how the official Vatican decree regarding the miracle, authorized by Pope John Paul II, describes the disease from which Khaznech Jubaran Abbdoud was miraculously healed in 1929. She was a three-year-old girl from the Galilean village of Shefa-Amr. The baby was born with rickets and was frail and weak. Her condition did not improve with time. The family was poor and couldn't afford the child's treatment. No form of therapy was undertaken. The girl's future was dim. Her parents and relatives began to pray for her healing through the intercession of Sr. Mary of Jesus Crucified, a Galilean from the nearby village of I'billin, whose glory of holiness was very much alive among them. On December 20, 1929, on the seventh day of the novena, Khaznech, the girl who had been lying motionless on the bed all her life, bolted out of bed and began running, jumping, and rejoicing. She was completely healed, and her problems never returned. This healing was investigated first in 1931 via a diocesan process in Jerusalem, but the appropriate Vatican consultants would only deal with it fifty years later. Because the girl's parents could not afford a doctor, there was no medical testimony to refer to. Given this fact, and the reports of eyewitnesses and relatives that the girl's healing was sudden and complete, it could be concluded that no pharmaceutical or surgical interventions occurred which could explain away the miraculous. On the basis of this miracle, the beatification of the Little Arab was made possible, and it took place in St. Peter's Basilica on November 14, 1983.

Mariam encountered saints at least three times during her life, including St. Joseph with the Child Jesus.

➤ *The relics of the Little Arab on display in the Carmel Monastery in Bethlehem.*

⮝ *The Little Arab's road to holiness is marked by suffering and humility.*

A COMPLICATED HEART DEFECT

Another small child was the beneficiary of the second miracle obtained through the intercession of Sr. Mary of Jesus. His name was Emanuel, the son of Biagia and Luigi Lo Zito from the town of Augusta in Sicily. The couple wanted children very much, and for years they prayed to God to give them one. Their prayers were finally answered, but there were complications. When Biagia was almost ready to deliver the baby, doctors discovered that the child's umbilical cord was wrapped around its neck twice over, and if the boy was to be saved, a caesarean section would have to be performed immediately.

The baby—weighing less than six pounds—was born at noon on April 16, 2009. Despite his low birth weight, there was no indication that anything was wrong with him at first.

Later that afternoon, however, when the newborn was brought to the mother to be fed, Biagia noticed her son's hands and feet were blue, and he was crying softly. It made her think something was wrong.

The following day, the boy was transferred to a more advanced hospital, at the family's request. Upon examining the child, the doctors had horrible news for the parents. They diagnosed him with pulmonary hypertension, and said that his condition was critical. It turned out that the newborn, apart from problems with his lungs, also suffered from an incurable congenital heart defect (a complex congenital heart defect in which the pulmonary veins do not go toward the heart, but instead turn into the hepatic system).

The boy's odds of surviving were slim. The only solution was surgery, but fearing the toddler would not survive it, it was considered whether it would be possible to perform it at all. The child was then taken to yet another hospital, this one St. Vincent in Taormina. On April 20, Luigi Lo Zito made sure the child was baptized and then went home to get clothes for the dying child. On his way, he encountered his friend Luigi Ingaliso, a great devotee of Bl. Mary of Jesus Crucified. This encounter turned out to be very significant. Sr. Maria Lucyna of the Cross quoted the words contained in Mr. Ingaliso's written statement:

> *Mr. Zito told me the chances of saving little Emanuel were very slim, and only a miracle could save him. Returning home, I remembered a gift from our trip to the Holy Land from Christmas 2008, when we visited the Caramel in Bethlehem to pay homage to the relics of Blessed Mary of Jesus Crucified. There, along with three other pilgrims, I had the honor of bringing the urn containing the mortal remains of Mariam to the altar during the Eucharist. We received her relics. When my wife was pregnant, she kept them beside her bed to protect our baby. In this moment of despair and pain the Zitos were experiencing, I decided to give them these relics, which I did so immediately.*

Mr. Ingaliso also initiated prayers for the healing of little Emanuel. He was joined by the family, residents of Augusta, and Carmelite sisters from Bethlehem and other Carmels of the Holy Land, as well as from Carmels in Sicily.

Meanwhile, in the hospital in Taormina, doctors decided that an operation on the child would be too risky. The boy was dying. His mother begged to be transported by ambulance from Augusta, where she was recovering after giving birth, to the hospital in Taormina, so that she could be with her son in his final hour. She prayed to the Little Arab with all her might and rubbed her relics on the boy. What happened next can only be called a miracle. The child made it through the crisis without surgery and today is a perfectly healthy young man. Physicians were unable to explain Emanuel's sudden and complete healing. The healing of the newborn was authenticated by Pope Francis on the feast day of St. Nicholas, December 6, 2014.

The Carmel in Bethlehem. Photo from the early twentieth century.

The canonization portrait of Mariam displayed on the façade of St. Peter's Basilica during the solemn Holy Mass raising the Little Arab to the glory of the altars.

"Away from me, Satan!" Powerful Exorcists

▲ *When confronting malevolent forces, all exorcists inevitably invoke the power of God, particularly through the name of Jesus.*

The Lord Jesus cast out a great number of evil spirits from the possessed. By His command and by the power of His name, His apostles and disciples did the same. Evil spirits were also cast out by a number of saints. Today, often calling upon saints for help, hundreds of exorcists around the world cast out demons every day, because, as the Apostle Peter reminds us, "Like a roaring lion your adversary the devil prowls around, looking for someone to devour." (1 Pet. 5:8)

When confronting malevolent forces, all exorcists inevitably invoke the power of God, particularly through the name of Jesus. Yet, in the ceaseless struggle against Satan, they also beseech assistance from other heavenly figures entrenched in the battle against evil. Foremost among these is the Virgin Mary. Additionally, they call upon St. Michael the Archangel, leader of the heavenly army, along with the other archangels, guardian angels, and the saints who dwell in the presence of God.

The saints, in their unwavering dedication to liberating humanity from the clutches of darkness, proved to be formidable exorcists. Living in close communion with God and enduring the torments inflicted by Satan, their efficacy in this spiritual warfare was profound. During the nascent spread of Christianity, they often engaged in exorcisms as part of their daily endeavors, as documented in the accounts of their lives. Satan typically recoiled most from those who embodied humility and practiced rigorous prayer and mortification. Notable among this group are St. Anthony the Abbot, St. Nicholas, St. Patrick, St. Martin, and numerous other saints from antiquity to the present, all of whom demonstrated remarkable success in combatting malevolent spirits.[1]

Satan typically recoiled most from those who embodied humility and practiced rigorous prayer and mortification. Notable among this group are St. Anthony the Abbot, St. Nicholas, St. Patrick, St. Martin, and numerous other saints from antiquity to the present, all of whom demonstrated remarkable success in combatting malevolent spirits.

➤ *Continuing their mission of freeing mankind from the power of the prince of darkness, the saints, living close to God and tormented by Satan (to no avail), were very effective exorcists. In the past, at a time when Christianity was just starting to spread around the world, exorcism was almost a daily activity for the faithful.*

CASTING OUT BY A SLAP IN THE FACE

The patron saint of exorcists is St. Benedict of Nursia, who lived at the turn of the fifth century. He effectively fought the devil, although he was not an exorcist.

We can find descriptions of two such instances from the life of St. Benedict contained in the second book of St. Gregory's *Dialogues*. There we can read about a certain unordained clergyman from the church of Aquinum.

> *His bishop, the venerable Constantius sent him ... on a pilgrimage to many graves of the martyrs in the hope that he would regain his health through their intercession. However, the holy martyrs did not answer his prayer, so the greatness of the grace bestowed on Benedict could become more evident. Finally, he was brought to the servant of almighty God, Benedict, who prayed from the bottom of his heart to the Lord Jesus Christ and immediately cast out the enemy from the possessed man. He then gave this command to the healed man: "Go and from now on do not eat meat. Also never dare to be ordained a priest. On the day you dare to receive ordination, you will immediately fall back under the power of Satan." Unfortunately, it soon happened just as Benedict had predicted. This clergyman walked away healed, and since recent suffering usually leaves anxiety in the soul, he obeyed the*

> *commands of the man of God for a while. But when, after long years, he saw many older than him already departing from this world, and that he was being overtaken by younger ones who had been ordained, he disregarded the words of the man of God, as if he had already managed to forget, and received ordination himself. The devil, who had once left him, soon possessed him again and tormented him for so long that he finally took the man's life.*

Fortunately, the second story, in which Pope Gregory the Great shows us Benedict casting out Satan with a simple slap, ended much better:

> *One day, when Benedict was walking to the chapel of St. John, located at the very top of the mountain, he met Satan on the way, who, taking the form of a vet, was carrying a horn and a trivet. "Where are you going?" the man of God asked him. "I am going to my brothers," replied the devil, "to give them medicine." The venerable father then went to pray, and after he finished praying, he hurried back. Meanwhile, an evil spirit came upon an elderly monk who was just drawing water. He immediately possessed him, threw him to the ground, and tormented him cruelly. When the man of God, returning from prayer, saw him so severely tormented, he simply slapped him. And this slap instantly cast out the evil spirit, who from that point on never dared to harass this monk again.*

To this day, many exorcists, like the world's most famous exorcist, Fr. Gabriele Amorth, who died in 2016, use the so-called St. Benedict's Cross when performing the rite of exorcism. It is a crucifix with St. Benedict's holy medal inscribed in it, and it is considered an extremely effective weapon in the fight against Satan.

➤ *St. Catherine of Siena also became famous for her great power to cast out evil spirits that she received from God.*

STABBED WITH THE ARROW OF HUMILITY

St. Catherine of Siena also became famous for her great power to cast out evil spirits that she received from God. Gabriele Amorth recounts, in his book *Memoirs of an Exorcist: My Life Fighting Satan*, that exorcists would often refer the faithful to St. Catherine for help.

Living in the fourteenth century, the Italian Dominican tertiary Catherine of Siena was one of the Church's greatest mystics, and today she is a Doctor of the Church and patron saint of Europe. Catherine was renowned for her unwavering connection to the divine, often found immersed in heavenly contemplation and engaging in deep conversations about God with fellow intellectuals. Her life was dedicated to prayer and acts of mercy, punctuated by moments of profound spiritual experiences.

Catherine's spiritual journey was marked by frequent dialogues with the Lord, ecstatic states, and encounters with celestial beings, including Jesus, Mary, and

⮟ Exorcism of the Possessed, *a fresco from Trecento (below);* Stories from the Legend of St. Benedict *by Spinello Aretino (right).*

various saints. She experienced mystical phenomena such as levitation, visions, and even mystical unions with Christ, along with bearing the invisible stigmata. Despite her divine encounters, Catherine was not immune to the trials of spiritual warfare, enduring torment from demons. However, her encounters with darkness only strengthened her resolve, emerging unscathed each time.

Her biographer, Bl. Raymond of Capua, recounted instances where Catherine's intercession led to miraculous deliverance from possession. One such case involved an eight-year-old girl named Laurence, whose family was deeply devoted to God. Despite their efforts to seek relief through relics and prayers, Laurence remained afflicted by a malevolent spirit, speaking Latin fluently despite lacking knowledge of the language. Desperate for help, Laurence's parents turned to Catherine, who initially hesitated due to her own ongoing spiritual battles. However, guided by divine intervention, Catherine ultimately helped to liberate Laurence from the grip of darkness.

Despite Catherine's initial reluctance, her confessor, moved by sympathy for Laurence's parents, clandestinely brought the afflicted girl into Catherine's cell. Bound by the dictates of obedience, Catherine had no choice but to comply with the confessor's directive to allow Laurence to stay overnight. Faced with this unexpected confrontation with evil, Catherine found solace in her tried and tested refuge: prayer. Throughout the night, she engaged in fervent spiritual warfare, guiding Laurence in prayer and confronting the demonic forces that assailed them. As dawn approached, the demon, albeit with fierce resistance, succumbed to Catherine's unwavering faith, and Laurence was restored to her normal state, the darkness vanquished by the power of prayer.

Upon sensing the resurgence of the demonic assault on Laurence, Catherine wasted no time and hastened to the residence where the girl was staying, accompanied by her female companion. Upon their arrival, they were greeted by a distressing sight: Laurence's countenance was markedly altered, her face flushed with anger, a clear sign of the demonic presence within her.

Summoning her unwavering faith, Catherine boldly addressed the malevolent entity, referring to it as an "infernal dragon" and invoking the name of the Lord Jesus Christ. With steadfast determination, she led Laurence to the altar, where she fervently prayed for the girl's deliverance. After a period of intense spiritual battle, Catherine emerged victorious, leading Laurence out, completely liberated from the clutches of evil.

Possessed people were often brought to Padre Pio. He prayed for them, suffered, and was repeatedly lashed by the evil spirit. There is a well-known photo of Padre Pio's swollen and bruised face. The day before this photo was taken, he had taken in a person who was possessed, and during the night the evil spirit took revenge by hitting his head on the floor several times. The friars, who heard the noise coming from his cell, came to his aid. Padre Pio needed medical attention; he needed as many as five stitches on his brow.

Assuring Laurence's parents of her daughter's safety, Catherine proclaimed with confidence that such affliction would never befall the girl again. True to her word, Laurence remained free from demonic influence, returning to the monastery, where she continued her faithful service to God, her unwavering devotion standing as a testament to Catherine's miraculous intervention.

Catherine herself later admitted that the demonic presence she confronted in Laurence proved to be stubborn, as their spiritual battle persisted until just before dawn. Despite Catherine's fervent pleas in the name of the Savior, the demon adamantly refused to relinquish its hold on the girl. Only after a protracted struggle did the demon relent, issuing a chilling ultimatum: if forced to depart from Laurence, it would possess Catherine instead.

In response, Catherine, fortified by her unwavering trust in Divine Providence, resolved to submit herself to God's will. Recognizing that without God's permission the demon held no power, she bravely surrendered herself to whatever fate God deemed fit. In this moment of true humility, the demon's arrogance was pierced, and its influence over Laurence waned, leaving her with only minor afflictions, such as garbled speech and a swollen throat.

Undeterred, Catherine invoked the power of faith and compassion, laying her hand upon Laurence's neck and tracing the Sign of the Cross, thereby restoring her to full health.

In another instance recounted by Raymond of Capua, Catherine's divine authority over evil spirits was further affirmed through the miraculous healing of a woman possessed by a demon in Rocca Castle, where Catherine had been residing. This testimony emphatically attested to Catherine's divine mandate to expel demons and heal the afflicted, underscoring her profound connection to the divine realm.

"BY HIS VERY PRESENCE"

Even in more recent times, St. John Bosco (1815–1888), the founder of the Salesians, demonstrated remarkable prowess as an exorcist. Fr. Amorth hailed him as a singular figure, both for the severe assaults he endured from Satan and for his extraordinary effectiveness in liberating individuals merely through his presence.

One notable incident, occurring on June 4, 1885, toward the end of his life, stands as a testament to his power. The superior of a religious community in Caen sought Don Bosco's aid for a woman possessed by an evil spirit. Despite Don Bosco's frail health, there was uncertainty whether he would be able to attend Mass that morning. Yet, to the astonishment of many, he did. Almost immediately upon the commencement of Mass, the woman sensed the departure of the malevolent presence that had plagued her, a tangible manifestation of Don Bosco's divine efficacy.

"HE SNATCHED MANY SOULS FROM THE CLUTCHES OF SATAN"

St. Padre Pio stands as one of the most formidable allies in the ongoing battle against evil spirits. Throughout his life, Satan relentlessly assailed him, subjecting him to temptations and inflicting physical and mental torment upon him. Yet, despite these trials, Padre Pio remained steadfast in his faith and unyielding in his devotion to God. His close bond with the divine shielded him from harm, ensuring that Satan's attacks could not weaken his resolve.

From his youth, Padre Pio was fortified by the assurance of St. Michael the Archangel's unwavering support in spiritual battles, a promise that sustained him throughout his life. Padre Pio's mere presence was often sufficient to liberate the possessed from demonic influence, echoing the efficacy witnessed in the case of St. John Bosco.

Fr. Amorth, who had the privilege of personally meeting Padre Pio and regarded himself as his spiritual son, affirmed Padre Pio's remarkable ability to rescue souls from the clutches of Satan. Through his unwavering faith, profound spiritual insight, and unfaltering commitment to God's will, Padre Pio emerged as a beacon of light in the darkness, tirelessly combating the forces of evil and leading countless souls to salvation.

In addition to engaging in clandestine battles with Satan, possessed individuals were often brought to Padre Pio for deliverance. For them, he offered prayers, endured suffering, and bore the lashings of evil spirits. A well-known photograph captures Padre Pio's swollen and bruised face. The day before the photo was taken, Padre Pio had attended to a possessed individual, and during the night, the demon exacted revenge by violently striking his head against the floor. The noise prompted the friars to rush to his aid, and Padre Pio required medical attention, receiving as many as five stitches on his brow bone.

In September 1964, an eighteen-year-old girl from Bergamo, long under the grip of a demonic entity, was brought to Padre Pio for help. Despite being gravely ill, Padre Pio delegated other priests to address the case. However, the possessed girl, instead of subsiding, unleashed a torrent of screams directed at the friars. The demon adamantly refused to depart, declaring that only Padre Pio had the authority to cast it out. As Padre Pio prepared for the exorcism through prayer and fasting, he was attacked in his cell, thrown to the floor, and brutally assaulted. The commotion and Padre Pio's cries of pain drew the attention of fellow friars, who rushed to his aid, finding him battered and bruised. Despite his injuries, Padre Pio continued his ministry, eventually celebrating Mass in the presence of the girl from Bergamo. During the Mass, the girl suddenly screamed and fainted, only to awaken free from the grip of evil. While Padre Pio healed from the ordeal, he continued to suffer the lingering effects of the attack.

Fr. Amorth, reflecting on his experiences as an exorcist, attests to the constant aid of Padre Pio. He recounted instances where individuals under his care felt Padre Pio's presence and assistance, even if they were unaware of it. Some experienced dreams of Padre Pio standing by their side, providing solace in their affliction. During exorcisms, evil spirits trembled in terror at the mention of Padre Pio, acknowledging his involvement in the spiritual warfare.

Exorcising the Blind and Mute Man *by James Tissot.*

Three Miracles of St. Zenobius *by Sandro Boticelli, at the National Gallery in London.*

"HIS HUMILITY SCARES US THE MOST"

Another of Padre Pio's "spiritual sons," the Italian Capuchin exorcist Fr. Cipriano de Meo, who passed away in 2019, received assistance from an exorcist from the seventeenth century—Capuchin Fr. Matteo da Agnone. Fr. Cipriano served as the vice-postulator of Fr. Matteo's beatification process and successfully concluded its diocesan stage. He carried out his ministry as an exorcist in Serracapriola near Foggia, within the Capuchin monastery and the Church of Our Lady of Grace, where Matteo's mortal remains are interred.

Who was Fr. Matteo? His name was originally Prospero Lolli, and he was born in Agnone, a small town in central Italy. In 1674, an event occurred that had a profound impact on his life. While on his way to school, the eleven-year-old Prospero encountered a classmate carrying a gun. Out of curiosity, he took the gun and accidentally fired it, fatally injuring his classmate. Though Prospero escaped punishment, the memory of his dying classmate and his grieving mother haunted him for the rest of his life. He spent years repenting for his actions and eventually received forgiveness and even the love of the deceased classmate's mother. After years of study, he joined the Capuchins, where his exemplary humility earned him the reputation of a demon slayer.

They discerned a gift for exorcism in him even during his time as a cleric. One day, a wretched woman, tormented by an evil spirit for thirteen long years, arrived at the monastery in Castel Bolognese where Don Matteo was residing. The friars spared no effort to assist her: they performed exorcisms, observed fasting, and offered fervent prayers. Yet their efforts yielded no results. The devil remained unmoved. Under persistent pressure, Satan eventually disclosed the condition for his departure: he insisted that only Br. Matteo of Agnone, whose humility posed the greatest threat, could compel them to leave. He emphasized Matteo's ability to subdue and chastise them, underscoring the importance of his presence.

The friars were astounded. Hastily, they sought out Matteo, who initially resisted their pleas, dismissing the devil's words as untrue. It was only through the insistence of obedience that he relented. Descending to the church, Matteo prostrated himself before the Blessed Sacrament, remaining in prayer for an extended period. His profound humility further provoked the evil spirit, which contorted the body of the possessed woman. She gnashed her teeth and foamed at the mouth, yet Matteo, immersed in fervent supplication, remained steadfast. His unwavering resolve eventually compelled the devil to cry out, "What does this Brother Matteo seek from me? I can no longer endure his presence!" With those words, the evil spirit departed from the woman, who was liberated after enduring years of torment.

Although surprised by the turn of events, Br. Matteo promptly retreated to his cell to engage in study. Later ordained as a priest, he pursued theological studies and obtained a doctorate. Revered for his holy life and profound theological insights, Matteo became a highly sought-after preacher and held numerous influential positions within the order. He was renowned as a devout Mariologist, fervently venerating the Immaculate Virgin Mary and her Assumption. Blessed with various gifts and charisms, including prophecy and healing, Matteo passed away in Serracapriola on All Hallows' Eve in 1616. Miracles began to transpire at his gravesite, attesting to his sanctity and intercessory power.

More than three centuries later, Fr. Cipriano assumed the role of parish priest in Serracapriola. Throughout his eighteen-year tenure, while seeking allies in the battle against evil, he observed a peculiar phenomenon involving the possessed individuals in contact with Fr. Matteo's tomb in the local church, as well as with the shroud that once enveloped his mortal remains. Those afflicted by possession, who typically exhibited composure upon entering the modest Capuchin church, suddenly displayed a range of violent behaviors at Fr. Matteo's tomb.

They convulsed, had diarrhea, threw up (occasionally expelling various objects: talismans, nails, shards of glass, and the like), wept or lost consciousness, lashed out, bit, and pounded their fists against the tomb's covering slab. They groaned, shrieked, uttered blasphemies, and vehemently cursed the friar interred therein. Some afflicted individuals collapsed inertly to the ground mere meters away from Fr. Matteo's tomb, while others weakened and found themselves unable to approach it.

Many vehemently resisted being led to Fr. Matteo's tomb, behaving as if they were in the midst of an exorcism. Behind these reactions lay the influence of Satan, who had taken possession of their bodies.

Panorama of Serracapriola, the town where the famous exorcist Don Matteo passed away.

Matteo of Agnone was a sought-after preacher, a great Mariologist, and a venerator of the Immaculate Virgin Mary and her Assumption. God endowed him with various gifts and charisms, including the gift of prophecy and healing. He died in Serracapriola, All Hallows' Eve in 1616, and miracles began to occur at his grave.

⮝ *St. Francis Borgia frees a possessed person.*

St. Cyriacus was a deacon and ministered in Rome in the late third and early fourth centuries. He converted and healed many people and became famous for being a great exorcist.

Fr. Matteo to release them from these invisible bonds. Such poignant scenes occurred frequently during exorcisms, bolstering my faith in Fr. Matteo's power to combat the devil. I recall the case of a boy from the province of Venice who, out of curiosity, engaged in satanic rituals at school. He spiraled into self-destruction and became incapable of studying. His parents brought him to me. At Fr. Matteo's tomb, the boy experienced a violent reaction but was swiftly liberated.

This testimony was corroborated by numerous eyewitnesses.

Another peculiar phenomenon occurs at Fr. Matteo's tomb. Pilgrims visiting the church in Serracapriola bring photos of their afflicted relatives and friends. Some of these photos, when pressed against the vertical and impeccably smooth marble tombstone that seals the niche, inexplicably adhere to it, defying gravity. According to Fr. Cipriano de Meo, these are typically images of individuals enduring severe demonic torment and in dire need of prayers for alleviation.

During his ministry, Fr. Cipriano, with the assistance of Fr. Matteo, succeeded in freeing more than thirty individuals from the clutches of an evil spirit.

"During exorcisms, invoking Fr. Matteo brings considerable trouble to the devil," Fr. Cipriano remarked in an interview with Patrizia Cattaneo, author of *How to Defend Yourself Against the Devil.*

> *When I command, "Fr. Matteo, cast down your enemy," even the most resistant individuals collapse instantly and writhe on the ground. When I add, "Bind their hands and feet," an unseen force restrains them. Finally, I beseech*

FLAME OF FIRE AND STENCH OF SULFUR

St. Cyriacus of Rome, a revered member of the Fourteen Holy Helpers, serves as an aide to another esteemed Italian exorcist, Fr. Michele Bianco.

St. Cyriacus, a deacon, ministered in Rome during the late third and early fourth centuries. Renowned for his conversions and miraculous healings, he gained widespread acclaim as a formidable exorcist. According to tradition, he expelled an evil spirit from the daughter of Emperor

Diocletian himself, as well as from Joba, the daughter of a Persian king. Even today, he continues his exorcistic work by assisting Fr. Bianco at the shrine in Torre Le Nocelle, where an ampulla containing his blood is venerated.

Miraculous liberations have been occurring at Torre Le Nocelle for more than three hundred years, with one of the earliest documented accounts dating back to May 20, 1709. On that day, Francesca Variano di Vinchiaturo, aged twenty-five, was liberated from prolonged harassment by rebellious spirits. Fr. Penna, who was ministering at the shrine at the time, recounted how a flame of fire mixed with smoke emerged from Francesca's mouth as soon as the exorcism began, filling the church with a sulfurous stench and prompting distress among the gathered congregation.

Another notable incident occurred on August 15, 1714, the Feast of the Assumption of Our Lady, when thirteen women possessed by demons were freed during an exorcism witnessed by several priests and a multitude of people. Similarly, on August 8, 1710, the Feast of St. Cyriacus, brothers Antonio and Domenico di Rienzo of Rocca di San Felice were delivered from the torment of evil spirits, with Antonio having been possessed for thirteen years and his brother for twelve.

On August 7, 1712, Giovanna di Montefalcione, a married woman possessed for twenty-five years, was also liberated after visiting numerous holy places without success. Contemporary accounts, as detailed by Patrizia Cattaneo in her book *St. Cyriacus*, include the testimony of a Swiss man who visited Torre Le Nocelle in May 2015. Witnessing the liberation of a French man exhibiting terrifying diabolical manifestations, the Swiss visitor was astonished by the transformation, as the once-possessed individual, previously unable to tolerate sacred surroundings, returned to the church "meek as a lamb" after just five minutes of prayer from Fr. Michele Bianco. This powerful experience left the witness with strengthened faith.

THE GREAT POWER OF INTERCESSION

The intercession of saints is of profound importance in the battle against evil spirits, and often possession is overcome through the intervention of saints who were not specifically invoked. During exorcisms, the presence of a saint becomes palpable, leading to the saint's invocation for assistance in subsequent liberations.

Fr. Amorth emphasized the frequency and efficacy with which saints liberated the possessed, a phenomenon documented extensively throughout history in the lives of numerous saints. He suggests that the exorcist's personal relationship with the saint plays a significant role, akin to a spiritual affinity.

Fr. Amorth acknowledged the significant role of heavenly helpers in his own exorcism ministry, including Fr. Cipriano de Meo, whom he witnessed invoking Fr. Matteo with palpable effect. Despite attempting to invoke Fr. Matteo himself, he did not experience success. Alongside Mary and Padre Pio, he also relied on the intercession of Pope John Paul II, whose strong advocacy was evident to him, as the devil confessed to hating the late pontiff for thwarting his plans, likely referring to communism.

Fr. Amorth also held Fr. Candido Amantini and Bl. Francisco Palau y Quer in high regard. The latter, a Carmelite during an era marked by rationalism and atheism, conducted exorcisms and ministered to the mentally ill, utilizing both spiritual and medical approaches.

Rome has witnessed many victories of St. Cyriacus over Satan.

On the feast of St. Cyriacus, brothers Antonio and Domenico di Rienzo of Rocca di San Felice were freed from the torment of the evil spirit.

Similarly, Polish exorcist Fr. Jan Pęzioł attests to one demon's fear of various saints, particularly Old Testament figures like Elijah, as well as St. Martin, St. John Paul II, St. John Vianney, St. Catherine of Siena, and St. Teresa of Jesus. However, the demon's strongest reaction was reserved for St. Padre Pio. Additionally, the demon reacted vehemently to invocations of the Litany of the Saints, protesting and screaming when certain saints were called upon. Notably, the demon exhibited intense fear in the presence of the Virgin Mary, regarding her as the most formidable adversary.

WITH THE DEVIL ON A CHAIN

The saints invoked by exorcists are a truly international group, but it is also true that many countries have their own domestic saintly exorcists.

St. Procopius of Sázava, revered in the Czech Republic, remains an icon of spiritual warfare. Living in the tenth and eleventh centuries, St. Procopius is celebrated for his valiant struggles against demonic forces. Depicted in art alongside St. Michael the Archangel, he is portrayed subduing the devil with a chain or strap, symbolic of his frequent confrontations with malevolent entities.

St. Procopius's legend is rich with tales of miraculous feats and spiritual battles. Stories tell of his expulsion of a thousand evil spirits from a nearby cave, testifying to his formidable spiritual prowess. One particularly iconic tale recounts how he harnessed the devil to a plow, compelling him to till the earth under the watchful gaze of a cross. This resulted in the Devil's Furrow, a prominent geological feature that stretches from Sázava to Chotouň, a tangible reminder of St. Procopius's divine authority over darkness.

His reputation for miracles and prophetic gifts preceded him during his lifetime, and his legacy continued to inspire awe and deliverance from demonic influences for generations after his passing. The Sázava monastery, where he resided, became a beacon of hope for those seeking liberation from spiritual oppression, a testament to the enduring impact of his divine intervention.

Among the many records, one stands out. A possessed man, who was full of anger, screamed in a terrifying manner, and thrashed in such a way that several strong men were barely able to hold him down. The scene was fraught with tension as the possessed man's eyes fell upon St. Procopius, his screams reverberating through the air with an eerie intensity. In a voice twisted by torment, he lashed out with accusations, his words dripping with malice and defiance.

"Why do you seek to cast me out?" he cried, his voice a harrowing symphony of desperation and anguish. "What violence do you want to inflict on me? This place is *my* sanctuary. Why do you wish to banish me?"

Despite the torrent of accusations hurled his way, St. Procopius remained resolute, his heart heavy with compassion for the tormented soul before him. Sensing that the demon would not yield easily, he made a solemn decision.

Turning to one of his trusted disciples, St. Procopius entrusted the task of performing the exorcism to him, knowing that the battle ahead would require both spiritual strength and unwavering faith. Meanwhile, he embarked on a journey of prayer and fasting, dedicating himself wholly to the plight of the possessed man.

Several days turned into a week, and as St. Procopius continued his vigil of supplication, a remarkable transformation began to unfold. The grip of the evil spirit tightened, sending violent tremors coursing through the afflicted man's body. Then, in a startling twist, a black bird emerged from his mouth, a sinister manifestation of the darkness within.

Undeterred by this ominous sight, St. Procopius pressed on, his prayers a steadfast beacon of hope amidst the gathering shadows. In a moment of divine intervention, the bird plummeted to the ground and shattered into fragments, a poignant symbol of the triumph of light over darkness.

With the specter of evil vanquished, the freed man offered heartfelt thanks to God and St. Procopius, his soul liberated from the chains of torment.

Another time, Satan possessed a girl who had been tempted and attacked for a long time.

In the dead of night, a girl besieged by the forces of darkness found herself cast out from her home by the devil's relentless grip. Following a desperate search, she was discovered in the desolate wilderness, her spirit broken, her voice silenced by the sinister presence that held her captive. Seeking refuge in the sanctuary of the church, her mother's prayers echoed through the halls, pleading for deliverance from the malevolent forces that plagued her daughter. But as days passed and despair deepened, hope seemed fleeting.

Then, the mother heard of miracles at the tomb of St. Procopius, which offered a glimmer of hope amidst the darkness. With faith as their guide, they embarked on a pilgrimage, placing their trust in the saint's intercession. At the hallowed site, surrounded by the echoes of prayers, divine grace descended, banishing the shadows that had ensnared the girl. In a moment of miraculous transformation, the darkness fled, and the girl's spirit was set free.

◄ Prince Oldřich Meets with Hermit Procopius, *by Josef Mathauser.*

Exorcists often call upon saints from their own homelands to aid them in their battles against evil spirits. In the Czech Republic, for instance, they honor St. Procopius of Sázava, a monk who lived during the tenth and eleventh centuries. Renowned for his confrontations with demons, St. Procopius is depicted in artwork alongside St. Michael the Archangel, both figures restraining the devil with chains or straps.

ENDNOTES

1 Please see the following works as the source material for this chapter: Gabriele Amorth, *Memoirs of an Exorcist: My Life Fighting Satan* (Częstochowa: Edycja Świętego Pawła, 2010); Gabriele Amorth, *Exorcists and Psychiatrists* (Częstochowa: Edycja Świętego Pawła, 1999); O. Cipriano de Meo, *Matteo: The Fate of the Friar from Agnone* (Kondrat-Media, 2015); Patrizia Cattaneo, *How to Defend Yourself Against the Devil* (Częstochowa, 2013); Rafal Olchawski, "By the Power of the Name of Jesus: Protonotary Apostolic Jan Pęzioł, Interviewed by Rafal Olchawski," in *Gaudium* (Lublin, 2017).

DNIEPER, MARY, AND THE BLESSED SACRAMENT

St. Hyacinth

In Latin he's called Iacchonis and Hyacinthus, and around the world he is also known as Hyacinth of Poland. In Poland, he is known as St. Jacek. Next to Stanisław Kostka, Maximilian Kolbe, Sr. Faustina, and John Paul II, he is one of the most popular Polish saints today. He is considered a great thaumaturge, or miracle-worker. To the moment of his canonization on April 17, 1594, nine hundred miracles had been reported thanks to his intercession. Descriptions [of these miracles] fill thirty pages of the most important publication in the Catholic Church about saints—the voluminous Acta Sanctorum*—and make an electrifying impression.*

➤ *El Greco,* The Apparition of the Virgin to St. Hyacinth *(1614).*

St. Hyacinth's canonization process, already started in the thirteenth century, was an uphill battle; something always got in the way. Official documents, part of an extensive correspondence, circulated between Poland and the Vatican. Petitions were sent by kings, nobles, and hierarchs of the Church. The documents from the first information process were lost during the Sack of Rome,

➤ *Marcin Zaleski,* Church of the Dominicans in Krakow *(before the fire in 1850).*

the ravaging and pillaging of the Eternal City by German and Spanish mercenaries in 1527. Finally, in 1592, the Vatican managed to handle the matter. There were more than thirty sessions at which Hyacinth was recognized as being worthy of canonization. Eight out of the huge number of miracles attributed to him were officially approved (nine hundred were already mentioned then, including more than fifty resurrections!).

PETER AND JUDKA

At the very end of the canonization process on March 17, 1594, at the publicum consistorium held in the presence of the pope, many cardinals, legates, and Christian lords, Bl. Hyacinth's advocate—after outlining his life—described some of the following miracles.

When St. Hyacinth was headed to the Skałka in Kraków for the feast of St. Stanislaus, patron of Poland, he found a great number of people standing on the bank of the Vistula. One of the women, Flawisława, who was aware of St. Hyacinth's sanctity and the love he had toward the afflicted, fell down at his feet crying and asked that her son, Peter, who drowned the day before and was now lying on the shore, be brought back to life by his prayer.

The blessed man, moved by mercy, weeping in private, humbly asked God to listen to him, and having returned to his body, taking the dead man by the hand, in front of all, said this: "Peter, may Our Lord Jesus Christ, whose glory I preach, restore you to life through the intercession of the Blessed Virgin." He instantly arose and gave thanks to the Lord God, to the Blessed Virgin Mary, and to St. Hyacinth.

He performed a similar miracle with the son of a noble widow named Przybysława, the lady of Syrnik Castle.

The aforementioned son was sent by his mother, together with a boy, to Krakow to invite St. Hyacinth to preach on the Feast of St. James, the patron of that village. On his way home he drowned in the river Raba, and his body, after searching for a long time, could not be found. St. Hyacinth, in the presence of many people and invoking the name of Christ, ordered the water

Holy Trinity Church in Krakow. St. Hyacinth's Chapel—there, in the late-baroque tomb located on the altar, are the remains of the saint. The altar was made by Baltazar Fontana between 1695 and 1703.

⮝ *St. Hyacinth's Blessed Mother—according to a legend, the statue of the Madonna was saved by St. Hyacinth during the Tartar invasion in 1240, when he moved it from the besieged Kiev to Halych.*

to place the body of the young man on the bank, to whom the saint spoke these words: "Wislaus, my son, may Our Lord Jesus Christ, who gives life to all things, resuscitate you. Wislaus arose full of life."[1] The crowd of people who were gathered at the site joined in praise to God.

When a noble lady, whose name was Judka, was so severely paralyzed that she could not utter a single word, her son, named Prandot, losing money and time on medicine, brought his mother to St. Hyacinth, humbly asking that his prayer to the Lord God save her. The holy man turned to the infirm and said, "Let the Lord Jesus Christ save you from this infirmity and restore health to your tongue." The disease left her instantly, and she, having been healed, praised the Lord God earnestly.

LIKE ST. PETER

St. Peter, the Prince of the Apostles, was of such great faith that when the Lord asked him to walk on water, he immediately got out of the boat and came toward the Lord. Just like Peter, St. Hyacinth also walked on water. When he was to preach the word of God, the Vistula overflowed in Wyszogród in the Masovia region. Having not found a vessel or boat, he said to his brothers, Florian, Bobin, and Benedykt: "Let us ask the Lord God, to whom the heavens, earth, sea, and all springs are obedient, to let us cross these swift waters for His holy glory." After having finished praying and making the Sign of the Cross over the river, he started walking on it. He looked back at his companions who, frightened by the rapidity of the water, did not dare to follow. He took off his cloak and spread it over the water, saying to them: "Beloved brethren, this is the bridge of Christ, in His name follow me, and do not be afraid." Floating on this cloak, they arrived at the city, and people who saw this praised the Lord God with their hearts and mouths.

The holy man performed a similar miracle a second time: When the Tartars stormed Kiev as he was standing at the altar still in his priestly robes, he took the ciborium containing the Blessed Sacrament and the alabaster image of the Blessed Virgin through the Dnieper, a swift and deep river that divides Asia from Europe, and he safely crossed with his people. Describing this famous legendary miracle in more detail, Seweryn of Luboml wrote that Hyacinth "was already in the middle of the church, when the statue of the Glorious Virgin ... loudly called after him: "Hyacinth, my son, wilt though leave me behind to be trampled underfoot by the Tartars? Take me with thee!" St. Hyacinth, amazed upon hearing this voice, said, "Holy Virgin, how can I, thy image is too heavy." The Virgin responded: "Take me nevertheless, my Son will lighten the burden." Then the holy man, holding the ciborium in one hand and carrying the statue in the other, which seemed lighter than cane, left safely with his brothers amid the infidels who were ravaging the monastery and killing everyone. Over the Dnieper, he spread his cloak for his brothers and led them to the other bank of the river dry-shod.

BLIND CHILDREN AND DAMAGED CROPS

On the feast day of St. Stanislaus, Reverend Hyacinth visited the church of the saint in Krakow, and a noble woman named Witosława, who gave birth to two blind children, approached him. Weeping, she begged the holy man to heal her children with his pleasing prayers to God. The blessed man, moved by mercy, prayed and made the Sign of the Cross over their eyes, restoring their sight.

A second noblewoman of the village of Kościelec called Reverend Hyacinth to her home. On that day, dark clouds arose and rained down large hail across the region, destroying crops and leaving nothing harvestable in the fields. When St. Hyacinth arrived, the aforementioned lady, with all the people of that land, came crying and lamenting to him, asking him to save them in their distress. Moved by love, the holy man asked them to keep vigil that night and to ask God, who Himself performs great miracles, for mercy. The next day, when the sun had risen, their crops had returned to their former state of perfection and were as beautiful as before. They all praised Almighty God, and they sang about His greatness everywhere.

Until then, people talked about the miracles he performed during his lifetime. Soon the Lord deigned to glorify His servant with this great miracle on the day of his funeral: a noble young man named Żegota, behind the Church of St. Florian, fell off a fast horse and broke his neck, badly bruising himself, and died.

St. Hyacinth saving the Blessed Sacrament and a statue of the Virgin Mary from the Tartar invasion.

St. Hyacinth in the main altar of the Dominican Church in Friesach, Austria.

Ventura Salimbeni, St. Hyacinth Odrowąż Healing the Blind Twins (1590–1610).

Reliquary of St. Hyacinth made by Sigismund III Vasa, circa 1611, and kept in the Holy Trinity Church in Krakow.

Stained-glass window depicting St. Hyacinth and Bl. Ceslaus receiving habits from the hands of St. Dominic.

St. Hyacinth Basilica located in the Jackowo neighborhood in Chicago.

His grief-stricken parents, mourning the death of their son, brought his body to the grave of St. Hyacinth. They prayed for a long time, begging the holy man for his intercession with Lord God, to see him alive and well.

MIRACLES FROM THE SIXTEENTH CENTURY

Due to a lack of time, the Church's advocate left out three miracles, which had been approved during earlier trial assemblies (the above-mentioned miracles by him, such as the resurrection of the son of Przybysława, events on the Dnieper, and the healing of the blind twins, were not examined in Rome, and were not officially approved or included in a later papal brief).

The three miracles which were clearly missing from that statement pertained to the resurrection of a child and the healing of two women. In the Bull of Canonization issued by Pope Clement VIII, they were described as follows:

> *There was a child, who was born a stillborn, whose father carried him to the grave of the blessed, and as soon as he offered himself to God as a pious votive, to the astonishment of all, the child immediately came to life. A miraculous event also happened to Urszula Adamowej. She had been suffering from an incurable disease for two years and experienced great pain. Finally, her condition deteriorated so much that for two months she ate nothing; only water sustained her. She regained the health she wanted after all when her daughter Agnieszka most humbly called Blessed Hyacinth for help.*
>
> *Lastly, it wasn't human medicine at all, but the piety and merits of Blessed Hyacinth himself that restored the health of Barbara Pasternak from Krakow who, after giving birth, fell ill with dropsy, so much so that everyone doubted her recovery. Thus the extraordinary sanctity of the servant of God was clearly confirmed.*

HELP WITHOUT LIMITS

St. Hyacinth healed the sick, resurrected children and the drowned, helped pregnant mothers, and among the great number of graces obtained through his intercession, there were also peculiar events, such as the resurrection of a dead heifer and chickens and liberations from evil spirits. Sometimes, before St. Hyacinth would grant grace, he would appear to the petitioner. The saint's hagiography also describes miracles that happened not only in Poland, but also in numerous cities in Italy, in Spain, and even in distant Peru. Of course, many extraordinary graces were also obtained after the canonization of the Dominican.

MIRACLE-WORKER

Who was he? Now well-known throughout the world, the Polish thaumaturgus was one of the pillars of the newly established Order of Preachers (the Dominicans). Called the "Light from Silesia" because he came from the wealthy Silesian Odrowąż family, he was born in Kamień Śląski, near Opole. After years of studying in Krakow and at European universities, he became a canon of the Krakow chapter. His relative, Bishop Iwo Odrowąż, persuaded him to travel to Italy and join the newly formed mendicant order, the Dominicans. Together with Ceslaus (now Blessed) and Herman of Germany, St. Hyacinth personally met St. Dominic. From 1221, already as a Dominican, St. Hyacinth devoted himself to apostolic work. Returning from Rome to Poland, he evangelized in Austria, in Czechia, and in Moravia. In 1222, he co-founded the monastery of the Holy Trinity in Krakow, which became a sanctuary for Polish Dominicans. From there, he embarked on longer missionary journeys, organizing monasteries in the dioceses of Poland and Czechia. From the monastery in Gdansk, which he founded, he Christianized pagan Prussia and Yotvingia, and later journeyed to Kievan Rus'.

Bl. Bronislava praying to Christ.

Two years before his death, Bl. Bronislava had another special spiritual vision, in which she learned about the death of St. Hyacinth.

In 1243, Hyacinth, exhausted by this work, returned to Krakow. Beloved by the people, he preached and heard Confessions in Krakow and in the surrounding villages. He was a great devotee of the Eucharist and of the Virgin Mary and tirelessly spread their cults. He went to the Lord on the day of the Assumption of the Blessed Virgin Mary, August 15, 1257, and was buried in the Dominican church in Krakow. Bishop Jan Prandota and Hyacinth's sister, Bl. Bronislava, a Norbertine nun, had extraordinary visions then: they both saw St. Hyacinth being led into Heaven. According to legend, the fact that he would be a great miracle-worker was assured by the Blessed Mother herself. Appearing to him in a vision during personal prayer, she assured him that he would obtain whatever he asked of Jesus through her.

Ludovico Carracci, Apparition of the Virgin and Child to St. Hyacinth.

It is believed that it was Hyacinth who brought an extremely popular dish to Poland from Kievan Rus': pierogi. Supposedly, after the Tartar invasion, when there was famine in the Polish lands, St. Hyacinth fed the poor with pierogi made by him.

Seal of the University of Bologna, where St. Hyacinth completed his studies.

ENDNOTES

1 Albert J. Herbert, *Raised from the Dead* (Gasconia, NC: TAN Books, 1986).

➤ Sanctuary of St. Rita in Roccaporena.

⮝ Roccaporena. The chapel is the matrimonial home of St. Rita.

A SPECIALIST FOR THE MOST DIFFICULT CASE

St. Rita of Cascia

The entire life of St. Rita (1381–1457), wife, mother, widow, and nun, is shrouded in the miraculous. The Italian woman, who in a life full of suffering and humiliation never lost her faith and trust in God's love, goodness, and justice, is recognized today as a particularly effective intercessor in cases considered the most difficult and even hopeless in the eyes of the world. John Paul II once said that she was an "expert in suffering." She learned to understand the sorrows of the human heart.

Rita, also known as Margherita Lotti, was born to Amata Ferri and Antonio Lotti, a respected couple from Roccaporena in Umbria, central Italy. The couple had struggled with infertility for twelve years until Amata received assurance from a heavenly voice that she would bear a daughter. The voice instructed them to name the child Rita in honor of St. Margaret (Margherita), and their daughter was born as foretold.

Legend surrounds Rita's infancy, with tales recounting a miraculous incident. While Rita's parents worked in the fields, the infant lay in a basket, surrounded by a swarm of bees. These bees allegedly landed on the child and entered her mouth. A passerby, noticing this, intervened despite having a severe hand injury. As he chased away the bees, his wound inexplicably healed. This event became part of the lore surrounding Rita's extraordinary life.

The oldest depiction of St. Rita in a fresco in the Church of St. Francis in Cascia.

A statue of St. Rita in the votive chapel.

DEATH BETTER THAN SIN

Despite feeling a calling to the monastic life, Rita obediently followed her parents' wishes and married Paolo di Ferdinando di Mancino. Their union bore fruit in the form of two sons. Rita's devoutness and constant prayers deeply influenced her husband, Paolo, who underwent a significant transformation, becoming more responsible and devout himself after witnessing Rita's exemplary behavior, especially following the birth of their children.

Rita's happiness was short-lived, as her husband fell victim to the feuds between families and was gravely injured. Despite the reconciliation he achieved with both people and God before his passing, their sons, following the tradition of vendetta, sought vengeance for their father's death. In response, Rita fervently prayed that her sons would not succumb to the cycle of hatred and commit mortal sin; instead, she pleaded for their forgiveness toward their father's killers. Rita's prayers were answered, albeit in a manner both unexpected and deeply painful: within a few months of their father's death, both of Rita's sons fell ill and passed away. However, on their deathbeds, they found it in their hearts to forgive their father's murderers.

SAINTS AND A DRY STICK

After the tragic losses of her husband and sons, Rita, then around thirty-six years old, sought solace in the religious

➤ *A courtyard of the monastery: the grapevine planted by St. Rita and the well from which she used to draw water to water the grapes.*

⮟ *Portrait of St. Rita, detail of the chest that contained the body, Sanctuary of Cascia.*

life and attempted to enter a convent of Augustinian nuns in the nearby town of Cascia. However, she faced rejection from the superior, who declined to accept her. Yet, Rita found assistance from her patron saints. One day, St. John the Baptist, St. Augustine, and St. Nicholas of Tolentino appeared to her and miraculously guided her into the convent, despite the closed doors. With their intervention, Rita was granted admission.

Within the convent, Rita demonstrated exceptional obedience and humility. Among her trials was the task of watering a dry stick twice daily, as instructed by her superior. Although her fellow sisters viewed this task as futile, over the years, the stick miraculously transformed into a flourishing grapevine, a testament to Rita's steadfast faith and the power of divine intervention. This miraculous transformation was revered as a sign of Rita's sanctity.

WOUNDING THORN

As a nun, Rita embraced a life of prayer, asceticism, and rigorous penance. She selflessly devoted herself to aiding the sick and the impoverished, following the example set by her parents. Additionally, she acted as a peacemaker, working to reconcile feuding parties in her community. Known for experiencing ecstatic visions, Rita is believed to have subsisted solely on the Eucharist for a period of time.

In a profound moment of prayer and meditation, Rita fervently asked God to allow her to share in the sufferings of Christ's Passion, even if only in a small way. In response to her supplication, a thorn from the crown of thorns adorning the crucifix before her miraculously detached and deeply pierced her forehead. This divine manifestation granted Rita her desired participation in Christ's suffering, marking her with a sacred wound reminiscent of the stigmata.

The wound inflicted upon Rita, akin to the stigmata, bore a significant mark and emitted a foul odor, necessitating her seclusion from society. However, at Rita's impassioned plea during prayer, the wound

briefly healed, though the pain persisted. This temporary reprieve allowed Rita and her fellow Augustinian sisters to undertake a pilgrimage to Rome, likely for the canonization of St. Nicholas of Tolentino in 1446 or during the Jubilee year festivities four years later.

ROSES AND FIGS

During her lifetime, Rita was already revered as a saint and was sought after for intercessory prayers. Through her supplications, the Lord performed miracles, including the restoration of health to a paralyzed girl and the liberation of a woman from demonic possession. As she lay on her deathbed, a remarkable event occurred: Rita requested her cousin bring roses and figs from her former garden in Roccaporena. Despite the wintry conditions, her cousin discovered a beautiful red rose and figs beneath the snow. Rita interpreted this as a divine sign that her prayers had been answered and that her deceased husband and sons were in Heaven with God.

FIRST MIRACLES

Rita passed away during the night of May 21, 1457. Following her death, her forehead wound healed, and her body emitted a sweet fragrance—a sign of her sanctity.

The surroundings of Roccaporena.

Garden of the Miracle. Figures of St. Rita and her relative bringing her roses in winter, which the dying saint asked for.

A wooden coffin of St. Rita is displayed in the saint's cell. On the wall, a painting depicting the scene of St. Rita's death.

➤ *Portrait of St. Rita at the monastery in Cascia.*

⮟ Santa Rita de Casia *by Miguel Cabrera.*

In reverence of her, Rita's remains were not interred in a traditional tomb, but were instead placed in a specially crafted coffin. Cecco Barbaro, who had lost the use of his hands, miraculously regained their function after touching Rita's body on the bier.

The healing of Cecco's hands was among the first of several miracles witnessed on the day of Rita's passing. Another notable event occurred three days later, on May 25, when Battista D'Angelo of Col Giacone, who was blind, regained his sight—an extraordinary testament to Rita's sanctity and intercessory power.

The healing of Lucia di Sante Lalli of Castello di Santa Maria on June 8, 1457, stands out among the miracles attributed to St. Rita. Completely blind in one eye for fifteen years and with severely impaired vision in the other, Lucia was led by her mother to the body of Bl. Rita. After fervently praying for fifteen days, she experienced a miraculous healing of both eyes, leading to tears of gratitude and awe.

By June 8, 1457, a total of eleven similar healings had been officially recorded, meticulously documented by notary Domenico Angeli of Cascia in the *Codex Miraculorum*. This book, compiled at the behest of Cascia's authorities, chronicled miraculous healings and graces attributed to St. Rita. Over time, numerous extraordinary healings and other favors were reported, many of which may not have been officially recorded.

According to Fr. Augustine Cavallucci, author of a biography of St. Rita published in 1610, a wide range of physical healings and spiritual interventions were attributed to her intercession. These included recovery from serious illnesses, restoration of sight, hearing, and speech, healing of wounds and ulcers, relief from incurable conditions, and liberation from possession by evil spirits. St. Rita's intercession was also sought in situations of imminent danger and spiritual distress.

One particularly remarkable miracle recounted in the beatification records involved Francis of Monferrato, a nobleman afflicted with a severe throat ailment around 1510. After three successive visions of a nun with a wound on her forehead, Francis, prompted by the nun in his dreams, sought out her grave for healing. Despite initially mistaking the location, his faith led him to the tomb of St. Rita, where he experienced a miraculous cure after her intervention.

The journey of Francis of Monferrato to Cascia exemplifies the profound impact of St. Rita's intercession on individuals seeking healing and divine intervention. Despite initial confusion about the location, his perseverance led him to the correct destination, guided by providential encounters with fellow travelers from Nursia.

Upon reaching Cascia, Francis expressed his gratitude by making a significant donation and participating in a thanksgiving procession to honor the miracle he experienced. His journey culminated in a moment of spiritual reflection as he listened to a sermon delivered by the Franciscan friar Lodovic of Cascia, deepening his connection to the faith and the miraculous intervention of St. Rita.

The official recognition of St. Rita's miracles continued with the inspection of her tomb on October 20, 1626, by a delegation appointed for this purpose. This inspection revealed a remarkable display of votive offerings and testimonies to the graces obtained through St. Rita's intercession. The numerous votive images and offerings bore witness to the widespread veneration of St. Rita and the countless favors attributed to her heavenly aid.

Considering the veneration and all the miracles mentioned, in 1628, Urban VIII declared her blessed.

A WONDERFUL SCENT AND TWO HEALINGS

The canonization process of St. Rita spanned centuries, reflecting the enduring reverence and widespread recognition of her holiness. Despite initial setbacks in 1737, the official acknowledgment of her heroic virtues in 1896 paved the way for her eventual canonization. Three miraculous events, including the continuous exuding of a pleasant scent from her incorruptible body, further affirmed her sanctity.

The fragrance emanating from St. Rita's body, a phenomenon documented by tradition and numerous witnesses, served as a tangible sign of her spiritual presence and intercession. This heavenly scent persisted after her death, regardless of whether her coffin was open or closed, and its intensity seemed to amplify with each reported instance of divine grace attributed to her intervention. Fr. Cavallucci's observations in 1610 underscored the enduring nature of this miraculous fragrance, linking its manifestation to the ongoing miracles wrought through St. Rita's intercession.

Among the documented miracles, the healing of Elisabetta Bergamini from smallpox stands out. Facing the threat of

Scenes from the life of St. Rita engraved on the portal of the basilica.

⮝ *The wedding ring of St. Rita.*

⮝ *The coffin of St. Rita in the basilica in Roccaporena.*

blindness due to her condition, Elisabetta's parents sought the intercession of St. Rita, clothing their daughter in a special votive habit. Four months later, Elisabetta experienced an unexpected restoration of her eyesight, defying medical expectations.

Similarly, Cosma Pellegrini's recovery from severe chronic ailments after an encounter with St. Rita highlights the saint's intercessory power. Confronted with a near-death experience, Cosma saw Rita, whose greeting coincided with the sudden disappearance of his illness. His subsequent return to health and vigor astonished those around him, attesting to the miraculous nature of his healing.

The use of oil from a lamp burning over St. Rita's body, as well as the distribution of small loaves of bread baked by Augustinian nuns, also yielded remarkable results. These practices, accompanied by fervent prayers, were associated with calming storms and obtaining favorable weather conditions, illustrating the widespread belief in St. Rita's intercessory role in both physical and environmental matters.

St. Rita's reputation as a protector against the plague stems from her compassionate care for plague victims during her lifetime. This legacy endows her with a special relevance in times of epidemic crisis, offering hope and solace to those afflicted by disease. Additionally, her role as a peacemaker and mediator in familial and social conflicts underscores her enduring significance as an intercessor for reconciliation and harmony.

Through these diverse miracles and intercessions, St. Rita continues to inspire devotion and offer assistance to those in need, embodying the timeless values of faith, compassion, and healing.

MIRACLES OF FORGIVENESS

St. Rita helps us to this day with the most difficult problems, but by looking at her life, we can also learn something

else that has a special significance in our Christian lives and, of course, in the eyes of God: the difficult art of forgiving. Every year since 1988, the municipality and convent of Cascia have awarded a special international prize: a medal, the Riconoscimento Santa Rita.

The award is given to women who emulate the virtues that Rita heroically cultivated (including her suffering and love toward her family), but for years the most important group of award winners have been women who, like Rita, were able to forgive the killers of their loved ones.

In 1999, the award winner was Eleni Tzoka, a popular Polish singer with Greek roots. The woman experienced great trauma when her only daughter died. On January 20, 1994, the dead body of the seventeen-year-old girl was found in a forest near Gniezno.

She had been murdered by a vengeful ex-boyfriend. A month after the breakup, he drove her to the woods and shot her, consumed by his selfish and possessive obsession. Although the death of her beloved Aphrodite was an unimaginable blow to Eleni and she still relives it every day, the woman was able to forgive the young murderer. As she confessed in a May 2006 interview for the monthly magazine *Miracles and Graces from God*:

> *I didn't blame him, but first of all, I looked for the causes of this tragedy—the tragedy of two families, my relatives and the family of this boy. It was very important to me that he showed remorse and apologized. Everyone should learn to forgive during their life. If we say that we believe and that we are Christians, then we must learn to forgive. When we forgive, we free ourselves from very bad emotions that kill us from within and do not allow us to go on living. If we do not forgive, in a sense we stop in time and stand still, we do not move forward. All the time we only think about how we could get revenge. We then nurture very destructive emotions within ourselves. Forgiveness gives us freedom. It is thanks to forgiveness that I can work today, I can sing, I am a cheerful person, I smile, I just live.*

Marianna Popiełuszko, the mother of Bl. Jerzy Popiełuszko, is also a recipient of the Riconoscimento Santa Rita award. Her son was bestially murdered by functionaries of the Communist Security Service. She too was able to forgive the murderers.

The main altar of the Basilica of St. Rita in Cascia.

Relic of St. Rita, her mantle in the Sanctuary of St. Rita in Roccaporena.

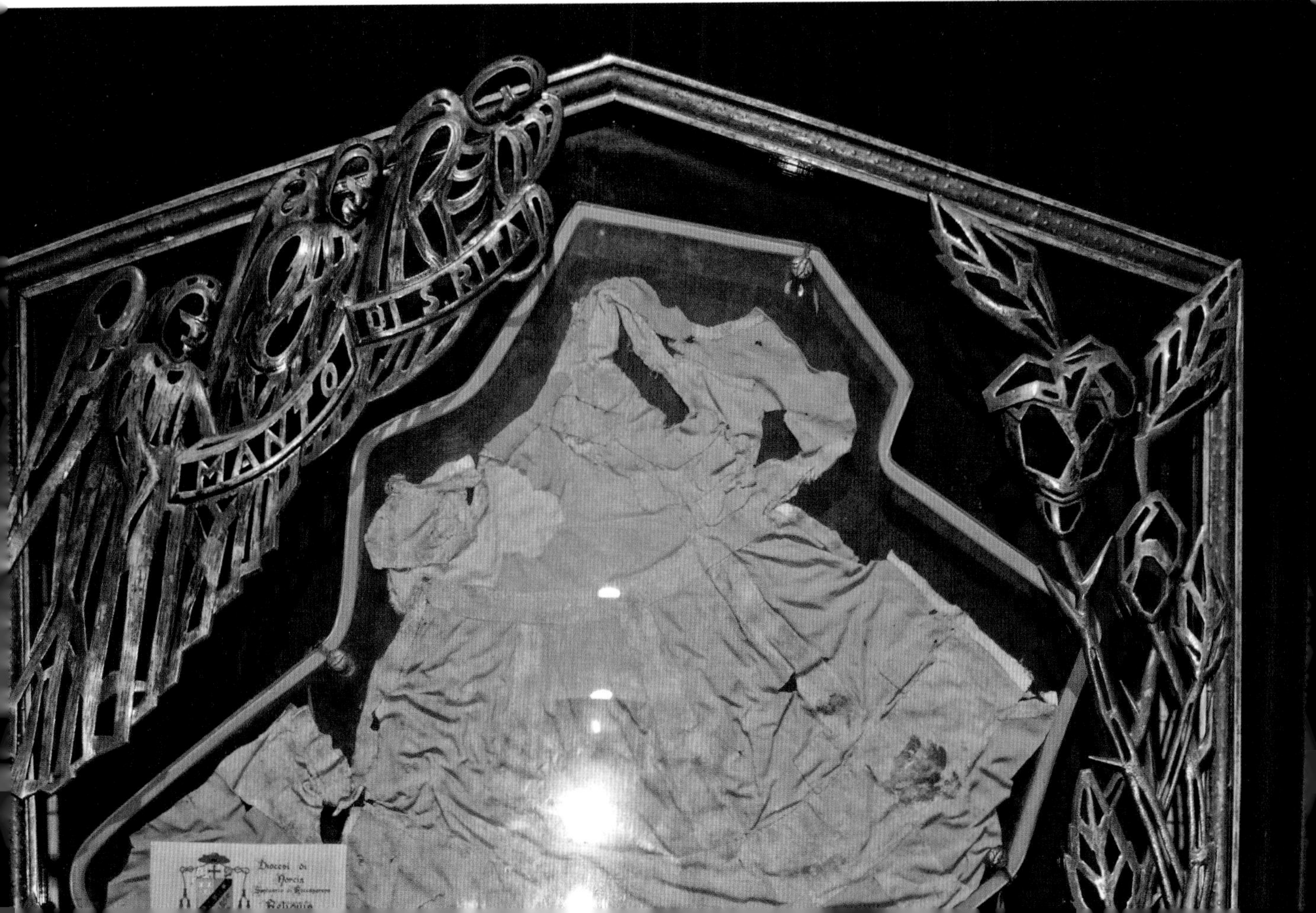

1182–1226

POOR MAN RICH IN GRACE

St. Francis of Assisi

Benozzo di Lese di Sandro Alessio, Scenes from the Life of St. Francis.

St. Francis of Assisi is one of the most well-known and recognizable saints of the Catholic Church. Indeed, there probably isn't a Catholic in the world who hasn't heard of "God's madman." People have loved him for his great simplicity and poverty, his capacity for joy, faith, and love, his respect for all God's creatures, and his radical evangelization. Yet few Catholics are familiar with the many miracles that have occurred as a result of his intercession.

Baptized as Giovanni di Pietro di Bernardone but called Francesco (Francis) by his father, St. Francis was the son of a wealthy cloth merchant from Assisi. His childhood was similar to that of other wealthy children in Assisi: he played, participated in feasts, and dressed up, and he was incredibly popular. At the age of twenty, he joined the local military and fought in a battle against the Italian city of Perugia, during which he was captured and spent a year in a dungeon. He then suffered a long illness, but after he recovered, he tried again to join the military. Yet on his way to war, in Spoleto, Italy, he heard God calling him to return to Assisi. When he returned home, Francis exchanged clothes with a beggar, began to beg, and prayerfully awaited God's further instruction in solitude. As a sign of his complete devotion to prayer, penance, and the will of God, Francis kissed a leper.

One day, while he was praying near the run-down church of San Damiano, Francis heard Christ speaking from the Cross: "Francis, go and repair My house, which, as you see, is falling into ruins." At first, he took these words literally and began to plan how he could rebuild the church building. In order to get money for renovations, Francis took several bolts of valuable fabrics from his father's house and sold them. When his

Francis's family home.

Carlo Giovanni Crivelli, Francis with the Blood of Christ (*1490–1500*), *Museo Poldi Pezzoli.*

Panorama of Assisi.

1182–1226

➤ The Christmas Celebration in the Forest of Greccio.

➤ *Francis before the Sultan. Francis met Sultan Al-Malik al-Kamil in Egypt and tried to convince him to renounce Muhammad and accept the Christian Faith. Francis also suggested a test: Francis and the sultan's dervishes would each walk through a fire. God would show who would withstand the test.*

father discovered the theft of his property, he took Francis to the bishop's court and publicly disinherited Francis. In response, Francis returned all the money back to his father, then he stripped off his fine clothes, handed them to his father, and declared that since his parent had disowned him, he would from now on call only God his Father.

Francis then not only repaired the destroyed church of San Damiano but also two more churches, including his beloved little chapel of Porziuncola, near Assisi. It was only later that Francis understood that God was actually asking him to "repair" the entire, universal Church!

On February 24, 1208, during a Mass celebrated in the Porziuncola, Francis was moved by the words of the Gospel about the sending of the apostles: "Take no gold, or silver, or copper in your belts, no bag for your journey, or two tunics, or sandals, or a staff" (Matt. 10:9–10). He saw the extraordinary value of rejecting all property and fell in love with what he called "Lady Poverty." He removed his shoes, cast aside his staff, put on a rough tunic, and began to preach repentance to the nearby towns. Soon others joined him, forsaking material comforts and following Francis's simple life of prayer and extreme poverty. When Francis realized that he was gaining followers, he went to Rome to seek approval from the pope. And so was born the new Franciscan order, the Friars Minor.

Francis and his friars wandered from city to city living and preaching the gospel and calling for conversion and repentance. But Francis's activity was not limited to preaching in Italy. He attended the Fourth Lateran Council in 1215, where he met, among others, St. Dominic, the founder of the Dominican Order. Then, in 1219, Francis traveled to Egypt and preached the truth of Jesus to the sultan himself. A year later, Francis returned to Italy, and in 1223, he famously built the first Christmas Nativity scene in Europe and inaugurated the first Nativity play. And in mid-September 1224, while making a forty-day fast in honor of St. Michael in La Verna, Italy, *il Poverello*, "the little poor man" of Assisi, became the first person who, by the will of God, received stigmata, the wounds of Christ's Passion.

The strict life and the suffering he endured, however, strained the health of

St. Francis, and eventually he became almost completely blind. He died in 1226, at the age of forty-five, naked, arms outstretched, and lying on the floor of the Porziuncola. Less than two years later, on July 16, 1228, Pope Gregory IX proclaimed him a saint.

VISIONS OF THE CROSS

Through the stigmata, St. Francis was—as Br. Thomas of Celano wrote in *The Treatise on the Miracles of Saint Francis*—"conformed" to the Body of Christ.

Francis's relationship with the Crucified Christ was evident to his followers much earlier, however. His first companions experienced several extraordinary visions of Francis and the Cross of Christ. Br. Silvester, for example, according to the *Little Flowers of St. Francis*, saw "a cross of gold proceeding out of the mouth of St. Francis, which went lengthwise as far as Heaven and the arms of which extended to the extremities of the world." Another friar, Br. Monaldo, witnessed Francis floating in the air with his arms spread out as though on a cross. Br. Pacifico beheld a great, multicolored Tau symbol on Francis's forehead, shining with a golden light.

MIRACULOUS POWERS

Many other miracles occurred during Francis's lifetime, as God blessed him with the gifts of healing (sometimes only with the help of the Sign of the Cross) and casting out demons. Once, for example, in the town of Rieti, Italy, Francis took the

◄ *José Benlliure y Gil,* St. Francis Appears on a Chariot of Fire.

▲ *St. Francis giving his mantle to a poor man.*

▼ *Jan van Eyck,* St. Francis Receiving the Stigmata.

➤ *A fresco by Giotto depicting the dream of Innocent III.*

⮝ *Henry Justice Ford,* St. Francis Brings the Wolf to the City [of Gubbio], The Book of Saints and Heroes (*1912*).

➤ *Dream of the palace.*

water he had used to wash his own hands and feet and used it to heal oxen who were severely ill with plague.

God also miraculously fulfilled and satisfied all of Francis's needs and desires. Francis multiplied and supplied food and clothing, and many experienced miraculous powers from bread and other food he had blessed. Br. Thomas of Celano tells that food blessed by Francis not only was preserved from spoiling but also seemed to be able to keep away violent storms! Others said that they were cured of illnesses after touching his clothes or his cord. One especially powerful source of healing was hay from the Nativity manger, which was given to women to aid in childbearing and to cure animals of various infections.

THE WOLF BECAME AS GENTLE AS A LAMB

Even though some saints had special friendships with various animals, there's no doubt that the greatest friend of God's creatures was St. Francis. Francis loved all animals, and he received from God a supernatural power over them. All sorts of animals flocked to him and obeyed him.

The famous *The Little Flowers of St. Francis*, a literary masterpiece of the Middle Ages, tells of one such miraculous "conversion" of an animal. The story goes that the town of Gubbio, Italy, was terrorized by a fierce and wild wolf that was stealing and attacking not only animals but also people. St. Francis took pity on the residents of Gubbio and went to the lair of the terrifying wolf. When the wolf saw Francis, he opened his horrific maw and snarled his teeth, yet he suddenly closed his mouth and stopped as St. Francis made the Sign of the Cross. "Brother wolf, come here," Francis calmly said. "On behalf of Christ, I command you to do no harm to me or to anyone else."

The fearsome wolf became as gentle as a lamb and laid himself at the saint's feet. Francis then scolded the wolf for destroying and killing God's creatures, especially people, and stated that "as a thief and the worst of murderers," he deserved to be hanged. Francis promised,

The miracle of the crucifix.

Exorcism of the Demons at Arezzo.

however, to make peace between the beast and the people, provided that the wolf would not hurt them again. When the wolf gave a sign that he agreed, Francis also promised him that on the same condition, he would persuade the inhabitants of the city to feed him until his death, since Francis knew that the wolf had only attacked and harmed because of his hunger. The wolf nodded his head, gave the saint his paw as a sign that he agreed to these conditions, and, tame as a lamb, went with Francis back to the city.

Francis then preached to the crowd in the main piazza. He called for repentance and reminded the people that God only allows such horrors to fall on His people because of sin, and he warned them that the eternal flames of Hell are much more fearsome and dangerous than a simple wolf that can harm only the body. When he finished his sermon, he told the residents about the deal he had made with the animal. From then on, the wolf, fed by the inhabitants of Gubbio, lived with the people in friendship and died of old age two years later.

The Ecstasy of St. Francis *by Giotto.*

The vision of the thrones.

➢ *Ludovico Carracci,* St. Francis in Meditation, *Dulwich Picture Gallery, London.*

➤ *Giotto's frescoes in Assisi.*

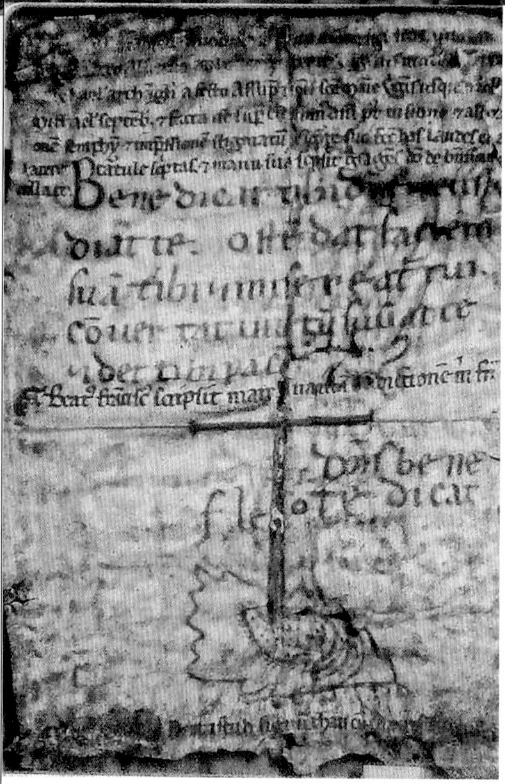

➢ *Autographed blessing given by St. Francis to Br. Leo.*

➢ *Lower Church of the Basiica of St. Francis in Assisi.*

THE ANIMALS REMAIN IN HIS POWER

Br. Thomas of Celano described many similar cases of the saint's extraordinary power over animals. When Francis walked among flocks of birds and touched their heads with his tunic, they, contrary to their nature, would not fly away, and when he called them to listen to the Word of God, they seemed to express a sort of contentment. Indeed, Br. Thomas writes, "Then the birds began to arch their necks, to spread out their wings, to open their beaks, to look at him, as if to thank him, while he went up and down in their midst stroking them with the border of his tunic, sending them away at last with his blessing." At his command, to the amazement of the people watching, the swallows would stop chirping so that he could deliver his sermon undisturbed.

Once, he received a large, live fish as a gift and released it. The fish kept playing in the water in front of the saint and did not swim away until it was commanded by the saint. Another time, a pheasant refused to depart from his side. Francis tried twice to release it, but it always came back; the second time it returned to the door of Francis's cell and entered under the tunics of the brothers who were in the doorway! When the pheasant finally separated from the saint, it seemed hurt and refused to eat.

A hare and a rabbit that had been given to Francis jumped on his lap despite their innate flightiness. Sheep flocked to him, bees constructed a honeycomb in a clay cup from which he drank, and when Francis died, a swarm of larks flew to mourn him with their little voices and to celebrate his entry into Heaven.

Br. Thomas of Celano also tells of one particularly moving story of Francis and a cricket. This cricket lived in a fig tree near the Porziuncula chapel and was known for its sweet chirping. Once, Francis called to it to come, and it climbed into his hand. He then asked "sister cricket" to sing and praise God. The cricket immediately obeyed. It chirped and sang, and Francis joined in, singing in praise of their Creator. At last, Francis told the cricket it could stop and return to its tree. The cricket obeyed and stayed in its tree for eight days, awaiting Francis's further command. Whenever Francis would leave his cell, he would come to the cricket, touch it, and ask it to sing, and the cricket would always happily comply. At last, Francis gave the cricket permission to leave its tree and go where it wanted. The cricket left and was never seen in the area again.

In the hermitage in Alvernia, Francis made friends with a falcon that would wake him in time to say the Divine Office at night. And while it is of course common for birds to start singing at certain hours of the day, the falcon would remain silent whenever Francis was ill so that he could sleep during the night, but it would resume its birdsong at dawn to wake him for the day.

Indeed, it seemed that all of nature had respect for Francis. He even seemed to have power to rule over inanimate nature. For example, Francis would pray, and water would gush out of rocks and openings in the earth or turn into wine. His respect for nature was also great. Bl. Jacobus de Voragine writes in his *The Golden Legend*, "He spared to touch lights, lamps, and candles, because he would not defile them with his hands. He went honorably upon the stones for the worship of him that was called Stone.... He was replenished of marvelous joy for the love of his Creator. He beheld the sun, the moon, and the stars, and summoned them to the love of their Maker."

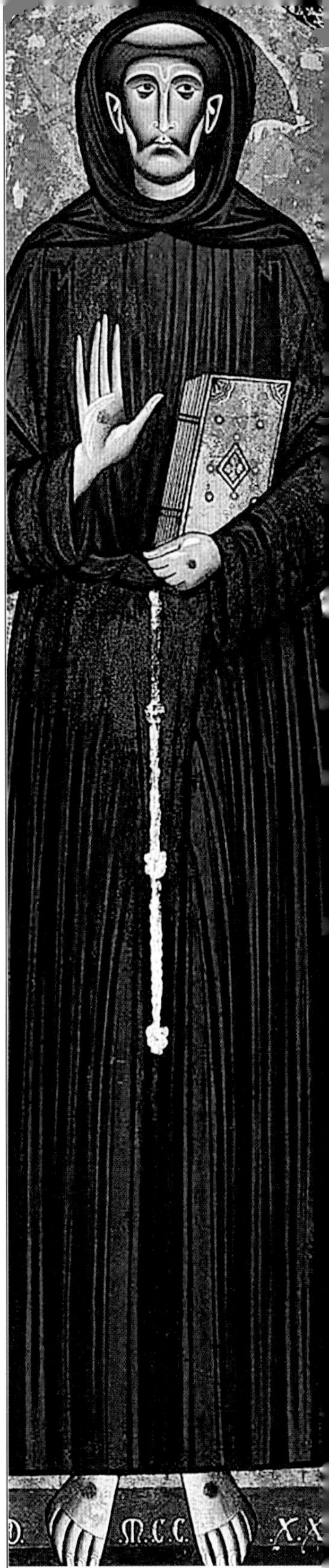

Giotto di Bondone, Confirmation of the Rule, *Assisi.*

➤ *Choir room in San Damiano Church, Assisi.*

⮝ *Jusepe de Ribera,* St. Francis of Assisi.

➤ *Tomb of St. Francis in Assisi.*

MIRACLES AFTER FRANCIS'S DEATH

Spectacular miracles didn't stop happening even after the death of the "Poor Man of Assisi." For the sake of "the merits of St. Francis," God has resurrected people from the dead (you can read about two of these resurrections in the "Miraculous Resurrectors" section, page 56), and many people have been healed, including a seriously injured guard who fell from a tower, a boy who was crushed by a heavy gate, people on whom heavy boulders fell, a priest who fell under a mill wheel, drowning sailors, a little boy who choked on a clasp, a beaten resident of Ceprano, a man who fell from a cliff, and people who were injured in accidents while building churches dedicated to St. Francis.

The prayers of St. Francis have healed people sick with typhus, dropsy, severe cases of hernia, and leprosy, as well as those suffering from hemorrhage, women with childbirth problems, the blind and those with eye diseases, the deaf, epileptics,

< *Habit Francis wore around 1215.*

Relics of St. Francis in Assisi.

people with arthritis, the paralyzed, the insane, the possessed, and the disabled. Many times, before he healed the sick, he appeared to them in dreams or visions.

One of the more compelling healings St. Francis was miraculously involved in occurred at the Franciscan monastery in Naples. Br. Thomas of Celano writes:

> *A brother named Roberto of the residence of the brothers in Naples had been blind for many years. Excess flesh grew in his eyes and impeded the movement and use of his eyelids. Many brothers from other places had gathered there on their way to different parts of the world. The blessed father Francis, that mirror and exemplar of holy obedience, in order to encourage them on their journey with a new miracle, healed the aforesaid brother in their presence in this way.*
>
> *One night Brother Roberto lay deathly ill and his soul had already been commended, when suddenly the blessed father appeared to him along with three brothers, perfect in holiness, Saint Anthony, Brother Agostino, and Brother Giacomo of Assisi. Just as these three had followed him perfectly in their lives, so they readily accompanied him after death. Saint Francis took a knife and cut away the excess flesh, restored his sight, and snatched him from the jaws of death, saying, "Roberto, my son, the favor I have done for you is a sign to the brothers on their way to distant countries that I go before them and guide their steps."*[1]

St. Francis has also rescued troubled sailors who were unable to lift jammed anchors on their own or who were in danger of shipwreck. He has saved farmers whose crops were affected by various plagues, destroyed an infestation of worms devastating vineyards, eliminated wheat weevils in a priest's storehouse, and stopped a plague of

➤ *Cloister of Sixtus IV.*

➤ *Side entrance to the basilica.*

⮟ *Church of San Damiano.*

⮝ *Monastery cloister of San Damiano.*

⮝ *Window in San Damiano.*

locusts. He has broken shackles and freed those unjustly imprisoned, and he has helped those being tortured endure their suffering.

COMPASSION FOR A MOURNING MOTHER

One beautiful story shows how Francis poured hope and comfort into the heart of a mourning pregnant woman. Giuliana was the wife of a nobleman from Calvi, and all of her children had died soon after they were born. Four months into one pregnancy, after many of her children had died, she didn't quite know whether to be happy or to cry, as she continued to mourn her lost children and feared for the one she was carrying. But one night, as she slept, a woman appeared to Giuliana in a dream. The woman carried a beautiful infant in her hands and joyfully offered him to her. "Take this child confidently, the one that Holy Francis sends to you," she said, handing the baby to Giuliana. But Giuliana refused. "Why would I want this baby," she said, "when I know it will soon die like all the others?" The woman responded, "Take this child confidently. Holy Francis sends him to you out of compassion for your grief. He shall surely live and enjoy good health."

These words were repeated three times before Giuliana finally took the baby. Upon waking, the woman told her husband about her dream. They were both overjoyed. When it was time for Giuliana to give birth, she delivered a healthy baby boy. The boy not only lived, but he grew beautifully, soothing the pain of his parents after the loss of his older siblings.

HE EXTRACTED THE SWORD AND HEALED WOUNDS THROUGH HIS STIGMATA

After his death, Francis also healed people through his stigmata. Bl. Jacobus de Voragine writes in *The Golden Legend*:

> *In the realm of Castile* [*in Spain*] *there was a man devout to St. Francis who went on a time to*

compline to the church of St. Francis. And men lay in await for to slay him, and instead of another man he was taken by error and ignorance, and was wounded and left as half dead; and after, the cruel murderer stuck his sword in his throat, and left it therein, and might not draw it out, but went his way. And then men cried and ran hither and thither, and the man was bewailed like as he had been dead.

Details of what happened next are found in Br. Thomas of Celano's *Treatise on the Miracles of Saint Francis*:

Because the living spirit was still in the man, the advice of doctors prevailed: that the sword not be removed from his throat. (Perhaps they did this for the sake of confession, so that he might be able to confess at least by some sign.) The doctors worked the whole night until the hour of matins to wipe away the blood and close the wounds, but because of the multiple, deep stab wounds, they could do nothing and ceased treatment. Some Lesser Brothers stood by the bed with the doctors, filled with grief, awaiting the departure of their friend.

Then the brothers' bell rang for matins. The man's wife heard the bell and, groaning, ran to the bed and cried: "My Lord, rise quickly, go to matins, your bell is calling you!" Immediately, the one believed to be dying, with a groaning rumble of the chest, struggled to stammer some wheezing words. And raising his hand toward the sword stuck in his throat, he seemed to be motioning for someone to remove it. A miracle! The sword immediately sprang from its place, and in the sight of them all it flew over to the door of the house as if launched by the hand of a very strong man. The man got up, unharmed and in perfect health, as if

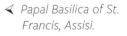

▲ *Interior of the Upper Church in Assisi.*

◀ *Papal Basilica of St. Francis, Assisi.*

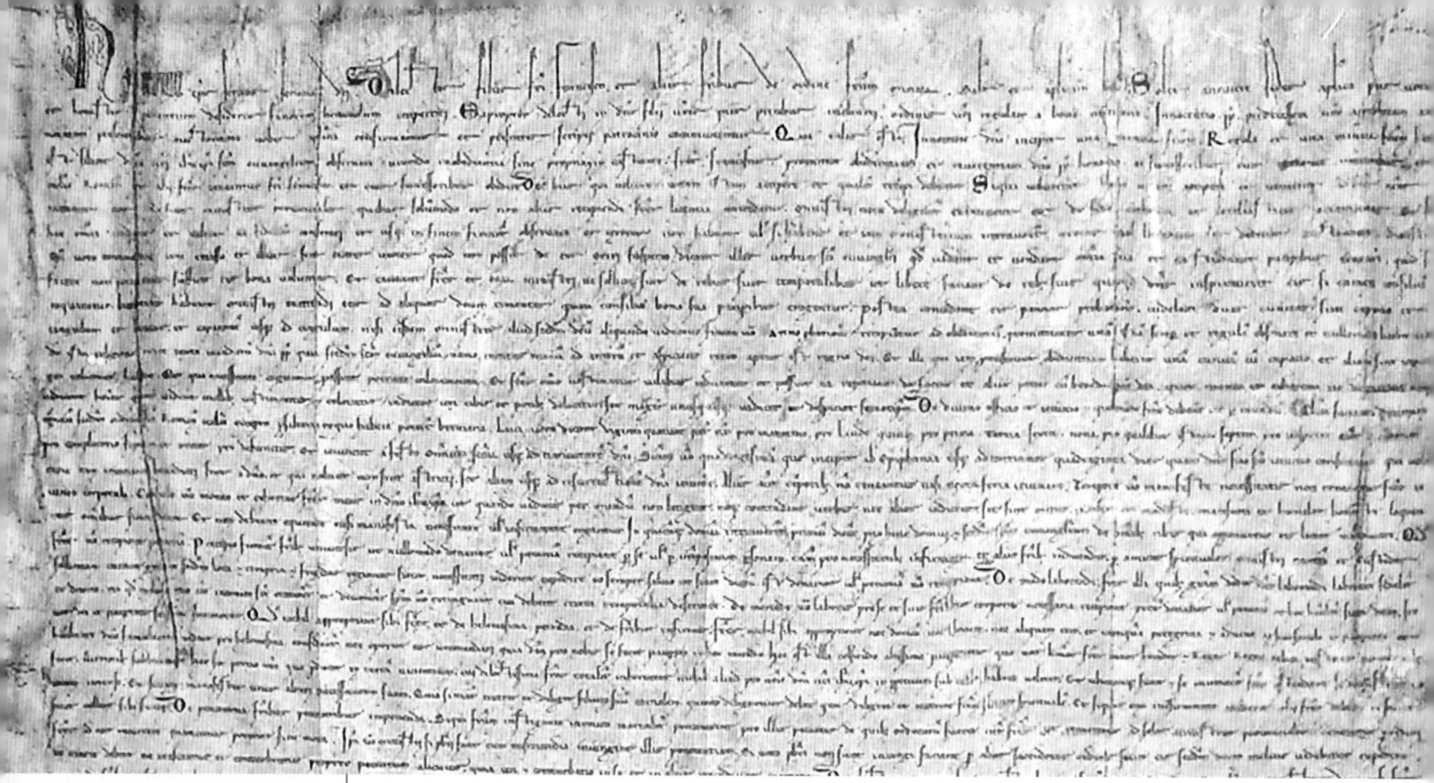

The Franciscan Rule.

Lodovico Cardi (*Cigoli*), St. Francis of Assisi.

rising from sleep, and recounted the wonderful deeds of the Lord.

Such great amazement seized the hearts of all that they all seemed out of their minds. They thought they were seeing a fantastic vision. But the one who was healed said, "Do not be afraid! Do not believe that what you see is false, because Saint Francis, to whom I was always devoted, has just left this place and has cured me completely of every wound. He placed those most holy stigmata of his over each of my wounds, and he rubbed all of my wounds with their gentleness. By their touch, as you see, he wondrously knit together everything that was broken. When you heard the rattle of my rumbling chest, the other wounds were already healed with great gentleness. Then the most holy father seemed to be leaving, with the sword left in my throat. Since I could not speak, I signaled to him with my weak hand to extract the sword, the one threat of imminent death. Immediately he took hold of it, as you all saw, and threw it with a powerful hand. And thus, as before, with the sacred stigmata he stroked and rubbed my throat. He so perfectly healed it that the flesh that was cut and what was still intact both appear the same."[2]

THE ORDERS, THE GREATEST MIRACLES!

And yet it wasn't the strange miracle with the sword, nor the miraculous resurrections, nor the power over animals that Francis's greatest biographer, Br. Thomas of Celano, considered the most important of his miracles. According to him, St. Francis's greatest miracle was—and it's hard not to agree with him—the "mission of the two Orders," the Franciscans and the Poor Clares. For while the world was "growing filthy with a mange of vices," while "orders were slipping away from the footprints of the apostles," and while "the night of sinners had reached mid-course in its journey, and silence had been imposed on sacred studies," the "sacred miracle," the orders of St. Francis, "warned,... roused, and ... frightened" the world so that "quickly there came to light the long-buried perfection of the primitive Church."[3]

And indeed, "never since the time of the apostles was there such an outstanding, such an amazing warning to the world," such a vineyard of God, that "in the briefest time, [extended] its fruitful branches from sea to sea," bearing fruit in the form of many saints and martyrs.[4]

Cenni di Pepo, Madonna Enthroned with the Child, St. Francis, and Four Angels, *Assisi.*

St. Francis and Scenes from His Life, *Pescia, Italy.*

ENDNOTES

1 "Treatise on the Miracles of Saint Francis by Thomas of Celano," in *Francis of Assisi: Early Documents*, vol. 2, *The Founder*, ed. Regis J. Armstrong, J.A. Wayne Hellmann, William J. Short (New York: New City Press, 2000), 447–448.
2 Ibid., 407–408.
3 Ibid., 399.
4 Ibid., 400.

APOSTLE OF HEAVENLY JOY

St. Philip Neri

The coat of arms of Confederation of Oratories of Saint Philip Neri or Oratorians. It was founded in 1551 by St. Philip Neri in Rome.

Philip Neri was a great Italian priest, "Apostle of Rome," founder of the Oratorians, a mystic who experienced numerous ecstasies, and the greatest prankster among all the saints. He was considered a saint during his lifetime, and people were already telling stories about the miracles he worked, so it's no wonder that he was canonized just twenty-seven years after his death.

One day Pope Clement VIII suffered an acute attack of gout. The disease attacked his hands. Having learned about this, the aged "Apostle of Rome," Fr. Philip Neri, began to pray for his healing and went to see him in person. The ailing Holy Father was lying in bed and protected himself from the lightest touch. Any touch or even movement of the bed itself caused him acute pain, so he told Philip to stay away and not touch him under any circumstances. Philip, however, could not be so easily dismissed. "Your Holiness need not be afraid," he said, then he came up and grabbed the pope's hand. Trembling all over his body, Philip squeezed it with great love and fervor, and suddenly the pain stopped. "Now you may continue to touch

San Pier Gattolino in Florence: the parish where Philip Neri lived with his family.

Church of San Tommaso in Parione, where Philip Neri was ordained a priest.

me, for I am greatly relieved," said Clement VIII, who recounted what happened to him that day many times, presenting it as one of the proofs of Philip's holiness. "From then on, even after the saint's death, whenever His Holiness found himself stricken by the illness, if he only entrusted himself to Philip, the pain was always alleviated," wrote Philip Neri's biographer Fr. Pietro Giacomo Bacci.

A FLORENTINE IN ROME

Philip Neri was born in Florence as the son of a notary. He was supposed to become a merchant like his uncle from the Monte Cassino region, but not feeling a vocation for it, he went to Gaeta and then to Rome, where he became a tutor to the children of a wealthy Florentine. There he began to study philosophy and theology. Being a young man of ardent faith, he spent whole nights praying in the catacombs. There, on Pentecost 1544, he experienced mystical ecstasy. His heart was ignited by the fire of the Holy Spirit, the heat of heavenly love and joy. He saw a sphere of fire that went into his mouth and reached his heart. For the rest of his life, a trace of this event remained on his body—an enlarged heart, a deformation of the ribs forming a bulge, a constant feeling of heat, and frequent, extremely strong heart palpitations that made his whole body tremble. Soon after this event, burning with apostolic zeal, Philip became one of the founders of the Confraternity of the Holy Trinity for the care of pilgrims and the sick who came to the Eternal City. Even back then, he was already called the "Apostle of Rome." At the age of thirty-six, encouraged by his confessor, he became a priest and soon established a great evangelization and pastoral work: the Oratory. The Roman elite, artists, merchants, bourgeoisie, clergy, youth, and anyone else seeking answers to their spiritual questions and wishing to deepen their religious knowledge began to flock

The Pontifical Polish College in Rome (Pontificio Collegio Polacco) was founded on September 1, 1582, thanks to the efforts of Philip Neri.

The Virgin appearing to St. Philip Neri, *by Giovanni Battista Tiepolo.*

Santa Maria in Vallicella, home of the Congregation of the Oratories.

to this place. Among other things, they met there to spend time talking, praying together, discussing, reflecting on the Scriptures, and participating in artistic events. The priest's first disciples and associates recruited future members of the Oratorian congregation, which the pope approved in 1575.

St. Philip was a respected spiritual guide and confessor (although he often gave his flock very extravagant penances). He was gifted with a natural charm, unaffectedness, and a great sense of humor. Even during his lifetime, many people considered him a saint, which he tried to counteract by pulling off various jokes. There were times, for example, when he paraded around Rome in a turban made of pillowcases, or with a beard shaved on one side of his face only. He was also famous for his pranks, and he used them to cure people of pride and teach them the virtue of humility, which he particularly valued.

He used to say that abiding in holy joyfulness is a way to make progress in the most holy virtues.

HE COMMANDED THE FEVER

The Apostle of Rome had the gift of healing and even raising from the dead. Many people were healed by God when Philip Neri made the Sign of the Cross over them or on their bodies. Sometimes it was enough for him to place his hand on the sick place (as in the case of Pope Clement VIII), to say a prayer beside the sick person, or even to "tell the disease to cease in the name of God," or express a wish that a person would recover. He ordered his most prominent disciple, Cesare Baronio, to banish the fever in his name. "Then Baronio," according to Bacci, "full of the holy faith, said: 'Fever, I command you in the name of Father Philip to leave me,' and in just a moment he was able to get dressed and go to the Vatican Basilica, which was a mile and a half away." Philip also had a special grace from Almighty God to liberate women from the dangers they usually endure in childbirth.

NOT ONLY THE GIFT OF HEALING

The Lord God also endowed Philip Neri with other extraordinary charisms. According to Bacci, "He saw in the spirit—that is, he had the gift of seeing things happening in various places where he was not present, but which in some way concerned him." This was the case, for example, with dying people. There were many occasions when he sent his disciples to people who, although he could not know it, were facing death and urgently needed Confession and Anointing.

St. Philip Neri *by Sebastiano Conca, a painting from the eighteenth century.*

Vision of St. Filippo Neri *by Charles de la Haye, National Gallery of Scotland.*

In a miraculous, supernatural way, God revealed to him the secrets of people's hearts and the state of their consciences. No secret or grave sin (kept in secret and unconfessed) and no fall or temptation could be hidden from him. Not only that, but he could also read people's thoughts.

He had the gift of prophecy and the gift of counsel. He advised not only ordinary people, but also popes, the king of France, superiors of religious orders, and even saints.

People experiencing ecstasies or manifesting supernatural abilities were also sent to him, and he flawlessly detected whether these phenomena came from God or an evil spirit. He knew whether someone was a saint or a mere impostor. He was also an effective exorcist. Although he performed exorcisms reluctantly and took great care to properly distinguish whether mental illness was involved, he freed many people from the power of evil spirits. In retaliation for the humiliation and insults he suffered, the devil troubled him nightly, lurking and lying in wait for his life and his health.

▼ Federico Borromeo, *a portrait of a friend of St. Philip Neri by Giulio Cesare Procaccini.*

▼ The Communion of St. Philip Neri *by Giuseppe Angeli (painting from the Museo del Settecento Veneziano).*

"Another of the extraordinary gifts Philip received from God," Bacci writes, "was the ability to appear in several places at once, especially to help those who entrusted themselves to him when their souls or bodies were in danger."

He experienced visions and many ecstasies during his life, especially during Mass. He was seen levitating, and shortly before his death, he was freed from illness and pain by Our Lady, whom he saw in a vision.

SHINING LIKE THE SUN

The wave of extraordinary events and graces related to Philip Neri did not stop after his death. What's more, there were even more of them than during his lifetime.

Shortly after his death, Philip appeared to many people (mostly nuns). Bacci describes six such cases. The strangest involved Sr. Caterina Paluzzi, a Dominican tertiary from Morlupo near Rome. The woman had just received Holy Communion when "a venerable old man" in a priestly robe "dressed in white and shining like the sun" appeared to her. Caterina saw his virtues inscribed in golden letters and encountered the souls of people who had made it to Heaven thanks to him surrounding St. Philip.

The first miraculous healings happened even before Philip's body was placed in the tomb. As the Office for the Dead was being recited beside the body resting on the bier, Antonio Carrari, a clergyman and penitent of Philip who was experiencing profound mental anguish, entered the room. In his fervent intention to participate in the recitation, he wholeheartedly commended himself to the saint and promptly found deliverance.

Among the first healed people was an eleven-year-old boy named Agostino, who upon leaving the church noticed that an

ulcer that he had in his mouth disappeared without a trace.

Many healings occurred through the rose petals with which the body of St. Philip was covered. As Bacci writes, "Maria Giustoniani, a girl from a noble family, got rid of severe headaches when her mother rubbed her head with a strand of St. Philip's hair."

Another time, a three-year-old boy whose legs were bent and maimed so much that he could not walk regained power in them when he touched the body of the late Philip. Later, many people smelled a very sweet fragrance ("similar to the smell of roses and other flowers that were not in bloom at the time") emanating from the burial site of the deceased priest.

RELICS LIKE ... A HAMMER

In his biography of St. Philip Neri, Pietro Giacomo Bacci carefully divides miracles and graces according to the type of relics through which they were obtained: the so-called praecordia (a fragment of the body near the heart), the particles taken from it (some drank it with wine), the hair (which was cut and sometimes swallowed with water), the fragments of the rosaries that the saint used during his lifetime, and also rosaries that touched his body after his death.

A strand of the priest's hair and a piece of cloth stained with his blood kept Stefano Calcinardi from succumbing to temptation. The man was walking toward Trinità dei Monti one day in August when he was accosted by an immodest woman. "He was already close to succumbing to temptation," Bacci wrote, but then he clearly felt the weight of the relics hanging on his chest, as if a hammer of some kind began to strike him. "He was overtaken by weakness, so that he almost fell to the ground, and heard a voice, which seemed to be the voice of the saint, saying 'Be careful of what you do; depart from here and flee from sin!' As soon as he came to his senses, he got away and did not fall into sin."

Neri's priestly biretta, together with his shirts, slippers, socks, handkerchiefs, and pillows, also proved to be full of graces.

Those who only read about the life and miracles worked by him, those who promised the saint to make a thanksgiving votive offering, made some other pious vow, devoutly visited his tomb, or touched sick places with an image depicting him were also healed and protected from sins and temptations.

YOU WILL NOT DIE THIS TIME!

The saint appeared to some people before they were healed. Two months

⮝ *Ecstasy of St. Philip Neri by Matteo Rosselli.*

⮝ Philip Neri and St. Camillus de Lellis, *his spiritual son, by Antonio Friz.*

St. Felix of Cantalice, a great friend of Philip Neri.

The Massimo alle Colonne—a palace that witnessed the miracle of the resurrection of fourteen-year-old Paolo, son of Fabrizio of the Massimo family. *(See chapter on Miraculous Resurrectors, page 56.)*

after the death of Philip Neri, Drusilla, the wife of hairdresser Antonio Fantini, fell from a balcony into the yard of a house, hitting her head on pieces of iron lying on a table. She sustained very serious injuries: her nose was crushed, her teeth broken, her lip cut in three places, her left hand deeply wounded, and her knee shattered; her right eye protruded from the eye socket, and her other eye was injured so badly that she lost her sight completely; blood gushed from her mouth, and she looked like a corpse. When she was found and carried to bed, she showed no signs of life. Neighbors and relatives thought she was already dead.

Her husband was not at home at the time, and as soon as he became aware of the accident, he ran to St. Philip's tomb to plead for his intercession. In the meantime, surgeon Antonio Franco arrived. When he examined the wounds and injuries, he judged her survival to be an impossibility. For this reason, he did not suture the wounds of either her hand or her lip, but applied a little protein to the wound on her palm and rubbed her eyes with white ointment, thinking that she would die in a very short time. But the woman did not die. As Bacci records, she spent the next fifteen days in a coma, unresponsive to all stimuli.

She was living entirely on fluids. After fifteen days had passed, when everyone thought that her recovery was impossible, Antonio, who had a habit of visiting the saint's tomb every day, entrusted his wife to him with especial fervor. He added to his prayers a vow that if she recovered, he would have this miracle painted and carry the finished piece to St. Philip's tomb. His prayers were soon answered. One morning, as Antonio departed for Mass at St. Philip's Church, leaving the sick woman alone at home, she confided her innermost thoughts to St. Philip, her spiritual mentor. While in prayer, she experienced a sudden heaviness upon her chest, as if someone were pressing a handkerchief into her throat and then gently removing it. It was at this moment that her vision was restored. Before her appeared a saintly figure resembling a priest, adorned with a halo, clutching a blood-stained handkerchief. "Do not be afraid, you will not die this time," he said.

Instantly, all the wounds of her head, ear, lip, nose, and hand were healed, as perfectly as if she had never been wounded. At that time, Drusilla's husband returned from Mass and entered her room. "May God forgive you for this intrusion, because as soon as you opened the door, St. Philip disappeared," Drusilla said as he walked in. "He appeared to me and healed me," she added. Although the head wounds were healed, the woman's right knee was still swollen and inflamed. The surgeon decided that an amputation was necessary. Drusilla, however, begged him to wait until the next morning and asked her husband to bring her an image of the saint. In the evening, she placed the image she received on her knee, and at night she again entrusted herself to the saintly father. And so it happened. Around midnight, the priest appeared to her for a second time in the same glory. He unwound the bandages from her knee and touched it, and she was completely healed. She called out to her husband so he could see the saint too, but before she could wake him, Philip had already disappeared. The surgeon who arrived in the morning was shocked to see a completely healthy knee, and it never caused Drusilla any inconvenience.

However, the woman was still lethargic, sore, and weakened from the fall. Unable to get out of bed and attend to her household chores, she prayed to the saint for a third time, so that this time he would heal her completely. Her prayer was answered, and for the third time, he appeared to her as beautiful and radiant as at the beginning. At the sight of him, her entire body was reinvigorated. The priest grabbed her head, shoulders, and feet, and restored her to her former strength and health through stretching. Later that morning, the injured woman went to the market and went about her work as energetically as before her accident. All people who knew about her terrible fall marveled that she was not only alive but indeed had returned to full and perfect health.

A SAINTLY FISHERMAN

Philip Neri helped people not only in cases of illness or injury, but also freed people from prisons, rescued people who had recourse to him for help during earthquakes, AND provided livelihoods for those who needed help.

Pasquale Pinelli received help from him in his tuna fishery. The fisherman was falling into greater and greater poverty; for several years, he had caught very few fish. As Bacci records, "Hearing much about the holiness of St. Philip and the miracles he worked, he placed a small image of the saint in a reed, and when he went out for another catch, he threw it into the sea."

He hoped it would help him catch many fish. His companions thought that bad weather and rough seas would guarantee another poor season, but Pasquale encouraged them to have faith in Bl. Philip, because, as he stated, "he will be the patron and protector of this year's fishing." And he was! In addition, the Roman priest proved to be an extremely generous patron: that year, to his great surprise, Pasquale and his companions reportedly caught more than two hundred tons of tuna, an incredibly valuable fish at the time.

Relics of St. Philip Neri.

Relics of St. Philip Neri.

St. Philip Neri *by Carlo Dolci.*

A DAGGER IN THE NECK

The extraordinary healings that happened through the intercession of Philip Neri were so numerous that there was no difficulty in declaring him blessed and then canonizing him just as quickly.

In his biography of St. Philip, Bacci described more than two hundred extraordinary miracles and graces. But, as he himself mentions, there were many, many more. One of the most spectacular and best-documented miracles, however, happened a few months after the canonization of the Apostle of Rome. Paolo d'Alessandro de Bernardis served at the home of nobleman Rinaldo Rinaldi. Paolo once argued with another servant working in the same house. "Today is November 7, 1622, and I will give you a reason to remember this day well," the other servant announced.

The same morning, Paolo went to the Chiesa Nuova church and, after hearing Mass, went with faith to the chapel and altar of St. Philip. He prayed the Lord's prayer and Hail Mary several times and entrusted himself wholeheartedly to St. Philip begging him to save him from the persecution of his enemies, and especially from the threats he had heard that morning from his fellow servant. When he returned home, his fellow servant seemed quite calm.

Later that evening, Paolo went out as usual to attend to his master's business, and since he didn't suspect anything, he left home unarmed. He had not gone more than ten steps away from the door when he was suddenly attacked by the enemy in front of the Church of St. Catherine of Siena near Monte Magnanapoli.

The man stabbed him in the neck with a dagger. The weapon pierced the esophagus and came out on the other side of the neck. The aggressor left the weapon in the body of the attacked man and fled from the scene. Stunned by the blow, Paolo didn't quite know what was going on. He didn't know he was injured, thinking he had received a blow with a stick. However, sensing that something was wrong, he called upon St. Philip for help. He seemed to hear St. Philip's voice saying, "Do not be afraid, you will not be harmed at all."

Only after he made it home did he see that a dagger was sticking out of his throat. He pulled it out and threw it away. He then felt a searing pain. "Jesus!" he called out. He again entrusted himself to St. Philip, and, entering the house, he began to call out to his master. Rinaldo came running, accompanied by a visitor to the house. "Don't be afraid, God will help you!" They comforted the wounded man. Yielding to the pleas of Paolo, who felt he was dying, they summoned his priest friend as quickly as possible. The priest, seeing that Paolo was passing away and any moment could be his last, gave him absolution before the end of Confession. In the meantime, three surgeons arrived, and after carefully examining the wound, they each ruled that it was undoubtedly fatal. The wound was treated, but Paolo grew weaker and weaker every minute. His master then sent for Fr. Ottavio, the pastor of the Church of Santi Apostoli. When he arrived, he listened to the entire Confession, but, not knowing whether the wounded man was able to swallow, refrained from giving him viaticum.

Paolo, unable to sleep, spent the night entrusting himself to St. Philip. He did not fall asleep until about four in the morning. About an hour and a half after waking up, he discovered that he was miraculously cured. He tried moving and turning his head; he was successful. What's more, he didn't feel the slightest pain in the process. The next day he tried to spit, and he easily did so, as if nothing had happened. "St. Philip of the Chiesa Nuova miraculously cured me," he proclaimed.

Again, surgeons were summoned, and once again they examined the wound and the patient. They noticed that the wound was neither swollen nor inflamed and that there was no longer any blood in the saliva; the patient spoke, moved his head with ease, and showed no worrying symptoms. With astonishment, and to the indescribable joy of all people concerned, they had to admit that the injured man was doing fine. They all proclaimed it a miracle, and declared that even pulling a thin silk thread (let alone a dagger) through the patient's neck would not have been possible without causing his death.

It was therefore concluded that the healing that occurred in just a few hours was clearly the result of a heavenly intervention.

Later that morning, Paolo wanted to go to the Chiesa Nuova to thank the saint, but the doctors advised him to rest for three or four more days. By that time, the wound had completely healed, leaving behind just two small scars as a memento.

After five days, Paolo got up and went to the Chiesa Nuova. As an expression of gratitude for saving his life, he made a votive offering in the form of a plaque with a depiction of the miracle painted on it. When news about the miracle spread around Rome, many people came to see Paolo and touch his scars.

Guercino's painting at the State Museum of San Marino.

Bibliography

All of the links listed in the bibliography below were active when the first edition of the book in Polish was submitted for publication.

ST. GEMMA GALGANI

SPECIAL THANKS TO: MARIONITE FATHERS FROM POLSKA MISJA MARONICKA

Bejda, H. *Ilustrowana księga świętych* [Illustrated book of saints]. Kraków: Dom Wydawniczy Rafael, 2014.

———. *Księga 100 wielkich cudów* [Book of 100 great miracles]. Kraków: Dom Wydawniczy Rafael, 2005.

———. *Św. Gemma Galgani: Mała biografia* [St. Gemma Galgani: A small biography]. Kraków: Dom Wydawniczy Rafael, 2014.

"Decretum super dubio [Miracles for beatification]." *Acta Apostolicae Sedis* [Acts of the Apostolic See] 25 (1933): pp. 212–214.

"Decretum super dubio [Miracles for canonization]." *Acta Apostolicae Sedis* [Acts of the Apostolic See] 31 (1939): pp. 186–188.

Galgani, G., St. *The Diary of Saint Gemma Galgani.* Warszawa: Fundacja Żywe Słowo, 2013.

Gesualda, S. *Święta Gemma Galgani: Kwiat Męki Pańskiej.* Rzym-Częstochowa-Paryż: Wydawnictwo Zgromadzenie Świętego Pawła, 1938.

Grygiel, L. "Gemma Jezusem wypełniona." *Życie Duchowe*, no. 40 (2004).

Miesięcznik Rodzin Katolickich Cuda i łaski Boże [Catholic families monthly magazine God's miracles and graces] no. 2 (2017).

Ruoppolo, G. *Głębie duszy czyli Święta Gemma Galgani* [Depths of the soul or Saint Gemma Galgani]. Wrocław: Wydawnictwo Maria Vincit, 2010.

Święta Gemma Galgani, Dziewica z Lukki bł. Gemma Galgani. Warszawa-Struga-Kraków: Michalineum, 1988.

Villepeele, J.F. *Der Torheit des Kreuzep: Die heilige Gemma Galgani 1878–1903.* Hauteville: Parvis Verlag, 1978.

Zoffoli, E., C.P. *Święta Gemma Galgani: Życiorys i modlitwy* [Saint Gemma Galgani: Biography and prayers]. Warszawa: Wydawnictwo Księży Werbistów Verbinum, 2012.

ST. PEREGRINE LAZIOSI

Bejda, H. *Święty Peregryn: Patron chorych na raka* [Saint Peregrine: Patron saint of cancer patients]. Kraków: Dom Wydawniczy Rafael, 2016.

Benassi, V. *San Pellegriono da Forli: Una speranza par i mallati inguaribili, Edizioni Santuario S. Pellegrino.* Forli: Petry, 1996.

Erthler, fra Paolo M., O.S.M., ed. *S. Pellegrino Laziosi dell' Ordine dei Servi di Maria patrono della cita e diocesi di Forli, Vita e preghiera: Guida del santuario.* Edizioni Santuario S. Pellegrino, 1995.

The Grotto. Order of Friar Servants of Mary. www.thegrotto.org.

Mroczkowska, J. *Święty Peregryn, Patron chorych: Rzecz o nadziei, cudach i gibelinach* [Saint Peregrine, Patron saint of the sick: A tale of hope, miracles and Ghibellines]. Kraków: Wydawnictwo WAM Księża Jezuici, 2015.

Ordo Servorum Mariae. www.servidimaria.net.

Serra, A. *Pellegrino Laziosi da Forli dei Servi di Maria (1265 c.–1345 c.): Storia, culto, attualità.* Forli: Santuario di S. Pellegrino, 1995.

stperegrine.org/national-shrine/

ST. TERESA BENEDICTA OF THE CROSS

SPECIAL THANKS TO: FR. EMMANUEL CHARLES MCCARTHY

Adamska, J.I., O.C.D. *Błogosławiona Edyta Stein.* Kraków: Wydawnictwo OO. Karmelitów Bosych, 1988.

Baldwin, R.F. "Miracle: Did Auschwitz Victim's Intercession Save Benedicta's Life?" *The Church World*, May 14, 1987.

Bejda, H. *Ilustrowana księga świętych* [Illustrated book of saints]. Kraków: Dom Wydawniczy Rafael, 2014.

———. *Nawróceni* [Converts]. Kraków: Dom Wydawniczy Rafael, 2008.

"Decretum super miraculo [Miracle for canonization]." *Acta Apostolicae Sedis* [Acts of the Apostolic See] 89 (1997): pp. 808-809.

Herbstrith, W. *Edyta Stein: Ofiara naszego czasu* [Edith Stein: A victim of our times]. Warszawa: Verbinum, 1998.

McCarthy, E. Ch. "Pondering a Miracle and the Living Mystery behind It: The Canonization of Edith Stein," *Vocations and Prayer Today* 7, no. 2 (April/June 1999): p. 36.

Miesięcznik Rodzin Katolickich Cuda i łaski Boże [Catholic families monthly magazine God's miracles and graces] 8 (2009).

Neyer M.A., O.C.D., *Edyta Stein: Dokumenty i fotografie* [Edith Stein: Documents and photographs]. Kraków: Wydawnictwo OO. Karmelitów Bosych, 1987.

Praśkiewicz, S., O.C.D. "Cud do kanonizacji siostry Teresy Benedykty od Krzyża" [Miracle for the canonization of Sister Teresa Benedicta of the Cross]. Karmelici Bosi. www.karmel.pl/cud-do-kanonizacji-siostry-teresy-benedykty-od-krzyza/.

Stein, E. *Autoportret z listów: Część pierwsza 1916–1933* [Self-Portrait in letters, 1916–1933 (Collected works of Edith Stein)]. Kraków: Wydawnictwo OO. Karmelitów Bosych, 2003.

———. *Dzieje pewnej rodziny żydowskiej* [Life in a Jewish Family]. In *Pisma*, vol. 1. Kraków: Wydawnictwo OO. Karmelitów Bosych, 2000.

Teresa Benedicta of the Cross, St. *Mądrość Krzyża* [Wisdom of the Cross]. Wrocław: TUM Wydawnictwo Wrocławskiej Księgarni Archidiecezjalnej, 1988.

———. *Rozważania o Eucharystii* [Reflections on the Eucharist]. Wrocław: TUM Wydawnictwo Wrocławskiej Księgarni Archidiecezjalnej, 1997.

ST. HEDWIG, QUEEN OF POLAND

Bejda, H. *Wielka księga polskich świętych* [The great book of Polish saints]. Kraków: Dom Wydawniczy Rafael, 2015.

"Decretum super miraculo [Miracle for canonization]." *Acta Apostolicae Sedis* [Acts of the Apostolic See] 89 (1997): pp. 810–811.

Jagosz, M. *Beatyfikacja i kanonizacja świętej Jadwigi królowej* [Beatification and canonization of Saint Hedwig the Queen]. Kraków: Wydawnictwo Naukowe Uniwersytetu Papieskiego, 2003.

Miesięcznik Rodzin Katolickich Cuda i łaski Boże [Catholic families monthly magazine God's miracles and graces] 2 (2009), 18 (2011).

Przybyszewski, B. *Błogosławiona Jadwiga Królowa zdobna wcnoty*. Kraków: Wydawnictwo św. Stanisława BM, 1996.

Stabińska, J., O.S.B. *Błogosławiona Jadwiga Królowa* [Blessed Queen Hedwig]. Kraków: Wydawnictwo Archidiecezji Krakowskiej, 1987.

Święch, Zbigniew. "Ostatni cud Królowej Jadwigi [The last miracle of Queen Hedwig]." *Alma Mater* 4 (Spring 1997). Accessed September 30, 2020. https://www.sodalicja.org/modlitwy/wezwania-generala-hallera/.

ST. JOHN OF RICE (MACÍAS)

SPECIAL THANKS TO: EDITORIAL OFFICE OF ALMA MATER

Bertaina, M.C. *San Giovanni Macias* [Saint John Macias]. Ordine dei Predicatori
Provincia San Tommaso d'Aquino in Italia. http://www.domenicani.net/page.php?id_cat=21&id_sottocat1=195&id_sottocat2=211&id_sottocat3=0&titolo=San%20Giovanni%20Macias.

Gaeta, S. "Riso e acqua per tutti." *Il Timone* 186 (July 2019): pp. 62–63.

Krupińska, Dominika. "Rewolucjonista." Motyw Prosty. September 17, 2012. http://myslispodchustki.blogspot.com/2012/09/rewolucjonista.html.

Messori, V. *Przemyśleć historię. Katolicka interpretacja ludzkiego losu* [Thinking about history: A Catholic interpretation of human fate], vol. 2. Kraków: Wydawnictwo M, 1999.

Paul VI. Canonization Homily. https://imelda.swieccy.dominikanie.pl/index.php?p=sw_Jan_Macias.

Praśkiewicz, S., O.C.D. *Cuda przedłożone Stolicy Apostolskiej i kanonicznie zatwierdzone do gloryfikacji najnowszych świętych i błogosławionych Karmelu Terezjańskiego* [Miracles submitted to the Holy See and canonically approved for the glorification of the latest saints and blesseds from the Order of Discalced Carmelites]. Kraków: Kuria Krakowskiej Prowincji Karmelitów Bosych, 2002.

"Super dubio, cud rozmnożenia ryżu." *Acta Apostolicae Sedis* [Acts of the Apostolic See] 67 (1975): pp. 129–132.

"*Św. Jan Macias OP.*" *Święci Pańscy*. September 18, 2012. http://martyrologium.blogspot.com/2012/09/sw-jan-macias.html.

"Un risotto miracoloso." Una Penna Spuntata. July 26, 2014. https://unapennaspuntata.com/2014/07/26/miracolo-riso-juan-macias/.

Wikipedia. "Miracolo del riso di Olivenza." https://it.wikipedia.org/wiki/Miracolo_del_riso_di_Olivenza.

ST. LAURA MONTOYA

SPECIAL THANKS TO: BOB GUTHERMAN

Castiblanco, S. "Jocosidad, humildad, virtudes y milagros en la vida de una santa." Gaudium Press. March 12, 2014. https://es.gaudiumpress.org/content/56749-jocosidad-humildad-virtudes-y-milagros-en-la-vida-de-una-santa/.

"Conozca el milagro que permitiría canonización de primera santa de Colombia." Redacción ACI Prensa/EWTN Noticias. November 14, 2012. https://www.aciprensa.com/noticias/conozca-el-milagro-que-permitiria-canonizacion-de-primera-santa-de-colombia-94799.

"Decretum super miraculo [Miracle for beatification]." *Acta Apostolicae Sedis* [Acts of the Apostolic See] 96, no. 1 (2004): pp. 61–62.

"Decretum super miraculo [Miracle for canonization]." *Acta Apostolicae Sedis* [Acts of the Apostolic See] 105, no. 10 (2013): pp. 938–940.

"El milagro que volvió santa a Laura Montoya." May 8, 2013. *El Espectador*. https://www.elespectador.com/noticias/actualidad/vivir/el-milagro-volvio-santa-laura-montoya-articulo-421012.

John Paul II. Homily. April 25, 2004. https://www.vatican.va/content/john-paul-ii/en/homilies/2004/documents/hf_jp-ii_hom_20040425_beatifications.html.

Jose Ricardo Navarro. "Carlos Restrepo, el 'Laurito' rescatado de la muerte." *InfoSCARE* 6, no. 3 (August–October 2016).

"Laura Montoya Upegui (1874–1949)." Vatican.va. https://www.vatican.va/news_services/liturgy/saints/ns_lit_doc_20040425_montoya_en.html.

"Milagros para la canonización de hoy de los mártires de Otranto, Laura Montoya y Madre Lupita [13-05-12]." Foros de la Virgen María. May 13, 2012. https://www.forosdelavirgen.org/articulos/milagros-para-la-canonizacion-de-hoy-de-los-martires-de-otranto-laura-montoya-y-madre-lupita-13-05-12.

Misioneras de María Inmaculada y Santa Catalina de Sena. https://madrelaura.org.

———. https://web.archive.org/web/20130822161816/http://www.madrelaura.org/sitio/images/stories/biografia/madralaurabio.pdf.

ST. MAXIMILIAN MARIA KOLBE

Bartoszewski, G., O.F.M. Cap., S. Budzyński, and C. Ryszka. *Życie i cuda polskich świętych kanonizowanych i beatyfikowanych za pontyfikatu Jana Pawła II* [Lives and miracles of Polish saints canonized and beatified during the pontificate of John Paul II]. Warszawa: Oficyna Wydawniczo-Poligraficzna Adam, 2001.

Bejda, H. *Księga 100 wielkich cudów* [Book of 100 great miracles]. Kraków: Dom Wydawniczy Rafael, 2005.

———. *Wielka księga polskich świętych* [The great book of Polish saints]. Kraków: Dom Wydawniczy Rafael, 2015.

Błogosławiony Maksymilian Maria Kolbe: Dokumenty, artykuły, opracowania [Blessed Maximilian Maria Kolbe: Documents, articles, studies]. Niepokalanów: Franciszkanie, 1974.

Domański, J., O.F.M. Conv. *Ojciec Maksymilian Kolbe*. Warszawa: Akademia Teologii Katolickiej, 1971.

Kijas, Z.J., O.F.M. Conv. *Św. Maksymilian Kolbe*. Kraków: WAM, 2011.

"Litterae Decretales: Beato Maximiliano Mariae Kolbe, Sacerdoti professo Ordinis Fratrum Minorum Conventualium, Sanctorum honores decernuntur." *Acta Apostolicae Sedis* [Acts of the Apostolic See] 76 (1984): pp. 5–12.

Miesięcznik Rodzin Katolickich Nasza Arka [Catholic families monthly magazine our ark] 7 (2004), 1 (2008).

Strzelecka, K., O.S.U. *Maksymilian Maria Kolbe*. Kraków: WAM, 1982.

"Super dubio." *Acta Apostolicae Sedis* [Acts of the Apostolic See] 63 (1971): pp. 786–787.

Winowska, M. *Szaleniec Niepokalanej: Święty Maksymilian Maria Kolbe* [Madman of the Immaculate: Saint Maximilian Maria Kolbe]. Niepokalanów: Wydawnictwo Ojców Franciszkanów, 1999.

Wojtczak, A., O.F.M. Conv. *Ojciec Maksymilian Maria Kolbe*, vol. 1–2, Niepokalanów: Franciszkanie, 1982.

MIRACULOUS RESURRECTORS

Hagiographic articles by the author published between 2000 and 2021 in the Catholic families weekly *Źródło* [Spring], Catholic families monthly magazine *Cuda i łaski Boże* [God's miracles and graces], and evangelization newspaper *Dobre Nowiny* [Good news].

Bacci, P.G. *The Life of Saint Philip Neri, Apostle of Rome, and Founder of the Congregation of the Oratory*. Vol. 2. London, Dublin and Derby: Richardson, 1847.

Bejda, H. *Księga 100 wielkich cudów* [Book of 100 great miracles]. Kraków: Dom Wydawniczy Rafael, 2005.

List Postulatora Generalnego do współbraci. https://www.stanislawpapczynski.org/pl/news/article.php?NID=4157.

Skarga, P. *Żywoty świętych Pańskich na każdy dzień przez cały rok, Ż* vol. 4. Kraków: Wydawnictwo Księży Jezuitów, 1936.

Thomas of Celano. *Traktat o cudach św. Franciszka z Asyżu* [The treatise on the miracles of Saint Francis]. Translated by C. Niezgoda, O.F.M. Conv. fzs.radom.pl.

ST. PATRICK

Bejda, H. *Pancerz św. Patryka: Słowa mocy, które dają ochronę*. Kraków: Gloria24.pl, 2014.

Borsje, J. "Druids, Deer and 'Words of Power': Coming to Terms with Evil in Medieval Ireland." *Approaches to Religion and Mythology in Celtic Studies* (2008). https://www.academia.edu/50074807/Druids_deer_and_words_of_power.

Bulas, R.M. "Lorica *świętego Patryka uzupełniona i poprawiona wersja artykułu zamieszczonego w*" [Faeth Fiadha: Saint Patrick's Lorica]. *Vox Patri* 46–47, no. 24 (2004): 547–559.

Cahill, T. *Jak Irlandczycy ocalili cywilizację: Nieznana historia heroicznej roli Irlandii w dziejach Europy po upadku Cesarstwa Rzymskiego* [How the Irish saved civilization: The untold story of Ireland's heroic role from the fall of Rome to the rise of medieval Europe]. Poznań: Media Rodzina, 1999.

Czarnowski, S. *Kult bohaterów i jego społeczne podłoże: Święty Patryk bohater narodowy Irlandii.* Warszawa: PWN, 1956.

Dillon, M., and N.K. *Ze świata Celtów* [Celtic realms]. Warszawa: PIW, 1975.

Gąssowski, J. *Mitologia Celtów.* Warszawa: WaiF, 1978.

Grzybowski, S. *Historia Irlandii.* Wrocław-Warszawa-Kraków: Wydawnictwo Ossolineum, 1998.

Królikowski, A. *Epopeja Celtów.* Częstochowa: Wydawnictwo WSP, 1999.

Krajewska, A., ed. *Modlitwa Celtów* [Prayer of Celts]. Translated by A. Krajewska. Kraków: Wydawnictwo M., 2002.

Panuś, K. *Święty Patryk.* Kraków: Wydawnictwo WAM, 2004.

Schlette, F. *Celtowie. Łódź:* Wydawnictwo Łódzkie, 1987.

Św. Patryk: Pisma i najstarsze żywoty. Kraków: Wydawnictwo Benedyktynów Tyniec, 2007.

Van Doorn-Harder, N. and L. Minnema, eds. *Coping with Evil in Religion and Culture: Case Studies.* UK: Cambridge Scholars, 2008, pp. 122–149.

ST. RAPHAEL KALINOWSKI

Bejda, H. *Wielka księga polskich świętych* [The great book of Polish saints]. Kraków: Dom Wydawniczy Rafael, 2015.

Chronicle of Wszystkich Świętych [All Saints] Parish in Krakow.

"Decretum super dubio." *Acta Apostolicae Sedis* [Acts of the Apostolic See] 82 (1990): pp. 1573–1576.

Gil, C., O.C.D. *Rafał Kalinowski karmelita bosy 1835–1907.* Kraków: Karmelici Bosi, 1983.

Gulgowski, M. *Jestem własnością innych: Święty Rafał Kalinowski 1835–1907.* Kraków: OO. Karmelici Bosi, 1990.

Józef Kalinowski (O. Rafał od św. Józefa): Wspomnienia 1835–1877 [Joseph Kalinowski (Fr. Raphael of St. Joseph): Memoirs 1835–1877]. Materiały Źródłowe do Dziejów Kościoła w Polsce, vol. 7. Lublin: TN KUL, 1965.

Kalinowski, R. *Listy.* Wydawnictwo Czesław. Gil OCD, TN KUL, Lublin 1978.

———. *Myśli i słowa* [Thoughts and words]. Kraków: Wydawnictwo Karmelitów Bosych, 2001.

"Litterae Apostolica E: I Venerabili Servo Dei Raphaeli Kalinowski a S. Ioseph Beatorum honores decernuntu." *Acta Apostolicae Sedis* [Acts of the Apostolic See] 76 (1984): pp. 1045–1047.

Maliński, M. *Święci na nasze dni* [Saint for our times]. Wrocław: TUM Wydawnictwo Wrocławskiej Księgarni Archidiecezjalnej, 1987.

Miesięcznik Rodzin Katolickich Cuda i łaski Boże [Catholic families monthly magazine God's miracles and graces] 3 (2004), 7 (2011).

Prokop, K.R. *Św. Rafal Kalinowski.* Kraków: Wydawnictwo WAM, 2007.

Stabińska, J., O.S.B. *W nawróceniu i w ciszy: Święty Rafał Kalinowski.* Kraków: Wydawnictwo Karmelitów Bosych, 2001.

"Święty Rafał od św. Józefa (Józef Kalinowski) 1835–1907." Karmelici Bosi. https://www.karmel.pl/swiety-rafal-od-sw-jozefa-jozef-kalinowski-1835-1907/.

Praśkiewicz, S., O.C.D. *Cuda przedłożone Stolicy Apostolskiej i kanonicznie zatwierdzone do gloryfikacji najnowszych świętych i błogosławionych Karmelu Terezjańskiego* [Miracles submitted to the Holy See and canonically approved for the glorification of the latest saints and blesseds from the Order of Discalced Carmelites]. Kraków: Kuria Krakowskiej Prowincji Karmelitów Bosych, 2002.

Wider, D., O.C.D. *Będziesz miłował.* Kraków: OO. Karmelici Bosi, 1983.

ST. JOSÉ LUIS SÁNCHEZ DEL RÍO

Ciborowska, A. *Josélito ją uzdrowił* [Josélito healed her]. October 16, 2016. https://naszdziennik.pl/mysl/168457,joselito-ja-uzdrowil.html.

"Documenta Vaticano 'Milagro' en el Hidalgo." *La Contra Portada.* January 27, 2014. http://lacontraportada.com.mx/documenta-vaticano-milagro-en-el-hidalgo/. Facebook, September 11, 2013. https://www.facebook.com/SAHUAYOSHYphoto s/a.126495620703927.15217.107335072619982/632823823404435/.

Ferreira, C.R. *Młody męczennik Blogoslawiony José Luis Sánchez del Río.* Kraków: Wydawnictwo św. Stanisława, 2013.

Rondon, M.X. "Conozca el milagro que permitió la canonización de José Sánchez del Río, el niño cristero." Aciprensa. January 25, 2016. https://www.aciprensa.com/noticias/conozca-el-milagro-que-permitira-canonizacion-de-nino-cristero-de-mexico-87720.

———. "Desconectaron a la bebé, la consideraban en vida vegetal, la dieron a la mama ... y la niña sonrió." Religión en Libertad. January 26, 2016. https://www.religionenlibertad.com/ciencia_y_fe/47398/desconectaron-a-la-bebe-la-consideraban-en-vida-vegetal-la-dieron.html

"Storia della piccola Ximena, salvata dal miracolo del "cristero" 14enne José Sanchez del Río." *Tempi.* January 29, 2016. https://www.tempi.it/storia-della-piccola-ximena-salvata-dal-miracolo-del-cristero-14enne-jose-sanchez-del-rio/.

Ximena, la niña milagro del beato José Sánchez. https://noticieros.televisa.com/mexico-estados/ximena-nina-milagro-beato-jose-sanchez/.

ST. TERESA OF JESUS OF THE ANDES

Acta Apostolicae Sedis [Acts of the Apostolic See] 79 (1987): pp. 1007–1008.

Acta Apostolicae Sedis [Acts of the Apostolic See] 85 (1993): pp. 201–203.

A.P.S. "El Bombero Resucitado." Cuerpo de Bomberos de Satiago. https://www.sexta.cl/actos-de-servicio/696-el-bombero-resucitado.

Santa Teresa de Jesús de Los Andes: Juanita Fernández Solar. http://www.santateresadelosandes.cl/.

Santuario Teresa de Los Andes. https://www.santuarioteresadelosandes.cl/.

Portaluz, E. *Cuando su hija estaba a punto de morir, por mediación de Santa Teresa de los Andes, Dios la salvo.* https://www.portaluz.cl/articulo_imprimir.asp?idarticulo=327.

Praśkiewicz, S., O.C.D. "Cud zatwierdzony do beatyfikacji siostry Teresy z Los Andes (Juanity Fernández Solar)" [Miracle approved for beatification of Sister Teresa of Los Andes (Juanita Fernández Solar)]. https://www.karmel.pl/swieta-teresa-od-jezusa-z-los-andes-juana-fernandez-solar-1900-1920/.

Teresa of Los Andes, St. *Dziennik* [The diary]. Kraków: Wydawnictwo Karmelitów Bosych, 2000.

ST. MOTHER TERESA

Bejda, H. *Księga 100 wielkich cudów* [Book of 100 great miracles]. Kraków: Dom Wydawniczy Rafael, 2005.

———. *Nawróceni* [Converted]. Kraków: Dom Wydawniczy Rafael, 2014.

Briefing on the Canonization of Mother Teresa—02.09.2016. https://www.youtube.com/watch?v=7inU9qTjamI&list= PL7-SwoRvgby4K-JdNIuVZ5jH9EKqcBu9Mo.

Bunson, M. "The Miracles That Made Mother Teresa a Saint." *National Catholic Register*. August 29, 2016. https://www.ncregister.com/daily-news/the-miracles-that-made-mother-teresa.

"Decretum super miraculo [Miracle for beatification]." *Acta Apostolicae Sedis* [Acts of the Apostolic See] 95, no. 7 (2003): pp. 485–487.

Facciotto, P. "Marcilio, storia di una guarigione miracolosa." *La Nuovo Bussola Quotidiana*. September 4, 2016. https://lanuovabq.it/it/marcilio-storia-di-una-guarigione-miracolosa.

Fazzini, G. "Marcilio Haddad Andrino: Non solo una vita ma tre." *Famiglia Cristiana*. January 9, 2016. https://www.famigliacristiana.it/articolo/marcilio-haddad-andrino-non-solo-una-vita-ma-tre.aspx.

Gjergji, L. *Ukochać, Żyć, Świadczyć: Duchowość Matki Teresy* [Mother Teresa: To live, to love, to witness: Her spiritual way]. Gorle: Wydawnictwo Velar, 1999.

Harris, E. "I Was Sure That It Was Mother Teresa Who Healed Me." Catholic News Agency. September 5, 2017. https://www.catholicnewsagency.com/news/i-was-sure-that-it-was-mother-teresa-who-healed-me-12981.

Kettler, S. "Mother Teresa: The Miracles That Made Her a Saint." Biography. October 14, 2020. https://www.biography.com/news/mother-teresa-miracles-saint.

Muggeridge, M. *Matka Teresa z Kalkuty* [Something beautiful for God]. Warszawa: Instytut Wydawniczy PAX, 1975.

Nasza, A. *Miesięcznik Rodzin Katolickich* [Catholic families monthly magazine our ark] 9 (2003).

"Santa Teresa de Calcutá—Fernanda e Marcilio." Facebook. https://www.facebook.com/MarcilioeFernanda

"Santa Teresa de Calcutá: O Milagre Brasileiro. Documentário [CC]." YouTube video. https://www.youtube.com/watch?v=SYY6FX-ZqWE0&list=PL7-SwoRvgby4KJdNIuVZ5jH9EKqcBu9Mo&index=2

ST. ANDREW BOBOLA

Bejda, H. *Wielka księga polskich świętych* [The great book of Polish saints]. Kraków: Dom Wydawniczy Rafael, 2015.

"Decretum super dubio [Miracles for canonization]." *Acta Apostolicae Sedis* [Acts of the Apostolic See] 29 (1937): pp. 347–349.

Kajsiewicz, H. *Życiorys błogosławionego ojca Andrzeja Boboli kaplana profesa Towarzystwa Jezusowego za wiarę katolicką od schyzmatyków okrutnie zamęczonego 1657 roku*. In *Pisma x. Hieronima Kajsiewicza ze zgromadzenia Zmartwychwstania Pańskiego, tom II: Mowy przygodne, nekrologi, życiorys bl. Andrzeja Boboli*. Berlin: W. Księgarni B. Behra, 1870.

Kuźnar, S., S.I. *Święty Andrzej Bobola męczennik i patron Polski*. Kraków: Wydawnictwo WAM, 1998.

Miesięcznik Rodzin Katolickich Cuda i łaski Boże [Catholic families monthly magazine God's miracles and graces] no. 7/2005.

Nižnik J. *Święty Andrzej Bobola niestrudzony wyznawca Chrystusa*. Strachocina: n.p., 2001.

Paciuszkiewicz M., S.I. *Andrzej Bobola*. Kraków: Wydawnictwo WAM, 2000.

Paciuszkiewicz, M., S.I., M. Topczewska-Metelska, and W. Wasilewski, eds. *Będę jej głównym patronem: O świętym Andrzeju Boboli* [I will be her main patron saint: About Saint Andrew Bobola]. Warszawa: Wydawnictwo WAM, 1995.

Poplatek, J., S.I. *Św. Andrzej Bobola: łowca dusz*. Sandomierz: Wydawnictwo Diecezjalne i Drukarnia, 2007.

Wieliczka-Szarkowa, J., and J. Szarek. *Jestem święty Andrzej Bobola: Zacznijcie mnie czcić*. Kraków: Wydawnictwo AA, 2016.

Źródło [Catholic families weekly spring] 33, numer specjalny: Św. Andrzej Bobola (2007).

ST. CONRAD OF PARZHAM

Altötting Herz Bayerns. https://www.altoetting.de.

Bruder Konrad. *Der heilige Pförtner von Altötting, Bayerischer Rundfunk, Deutscher Kapuzinerprovinz*. DVD. Deutschland, 1999.

"Decretum super dubio [Miracles for beatification]." *Acta Apostolicae Sedis* [Acts of the Apostolic See] 22 (1930): pp. 289–291.

"Decretum super dubio [Miracles for canonization]." *Acta Apostolicae Sedis* [Acts of the Apostolic See] 26 (1934): pp. 237–239.

http://bruder-konrad.de.

Jakob, M. "Pfarrer von Amberg-St. Konrad, Predigt zum 96. Todestag von Schwester Maria Fidelis Weiß am 11. Februar 2019, 18.00 Uhr, Kloster Reutberg." www.schwester-fidelis-weiss.de.

Jaroń, K. *Brat Konrad z Parzham, kapucyn, Święty furtian*. Kraków: Wydawnictwo Serafin, 2018.

Kessler, J.A. *Im Dienste Gottes und der Mensche: Ein Lebensbild des Dieners Gottes Konrad Birndorfer von Parzham, Laienbruder aus dem Kapuzinerorden*. Altötting: im Rufe der Heiligkeit, 1894. München: Verlag Josef Kösel und Friedrich Pustet, 1928.

Kuster, N. *Konrad z Parzham. Menschenfreund und Gottesmann*. Kevelaer: Verlagsgemeinschaft topos plus, 2018.

ST. NICHOLAS OF FLÜE (BR. KLAUS)

SPECIAL THANKS TO: BR. MARINUS PARZINGER, ROLAND KAUTH, AND AGNIESZKA RZEMIENIEC

SPECIAL THANKS TO: SR. DIANA PAPA OSC

Bruder Klaus. https://bruderklaus.com.

Burkhard Feuerstein, P., F.S.O. "Der heilige Bruder Klaus und das 'Wunder von Waldenburg'" Das Werk. http://www.daswerk-fso.org/glaube-und-leben/der-heilige-bruder-klaus-und-das-wunder-von-waldenburg.

"Das Wunder von Sachseln, part 1." https://www.youtube.com/watch?v=ortzbdbEk6Q&list=PLRrCH5eE9wFN_KmzRfSv6eV-3bV-so_noV&index=2&t=0s.

"Das Wunder von Sachseln, part 2." https://www.youtube.com/watch?v=2jRIYaWgsXo&list=PLRrCH5eE9wFN_KmzRfSv6eV-3bV-so_noV&index=3&t=0s.

Das Wunder von Waldenburg. https://www.hand-waldenburg.ch/de/home.

"Eine leuchtende Hand am Himmel! Bruder Klaus Gedenktag am 13. Mai 2010." Kath.ch. https://web.archive.org/web/20140814011626/http://www.kath.ch/47921.

Encyklopedja Kościelna [Encyclopedia of church],vol. 5. Warszawa: Michał Nowodworski, Czerwiński i Spółka, 1874, Hasło: Flue Mikołaj.

Ernst Meier. "Die Hand über der Schweiz." eManSwitz. December 19, 2017. Youtube video, 26:56, https://www.youtube.com/watch?v=k-fxdsqFc350&feature=emb_title.

"Es war keine Wolke und kein Flugobjekt!" Zukunft CH. https://www.zukunft-ch.ch/es-war-keine-wolke-und-kein-flugobjekt/.

Fink-Wagner, U. "Nikalus von Flue." https://kirchenblatt.ch/links/archiv/ausgabe-14/niklaus-von-fluee.

Haesele, M. "Wie Bruder Klaus zwei Solothurnerinnen heilte." *Santa Rita* 17, no. 2 (October 1967). Helvetia Catholica. http://helvetia-catholica.blogspot.com/2007/04/wie-bruder-klaus-zwei-solothurnerinnen.html.

"Hl. Bruder Klaus—Niklaus von der Flüe." http://kath-zdw.ch/maria/bruder.klaus.html.

Lawrence-Vögtli, E. "Wunder von Busserach: Als Ida Jeker plötzlich Holz spalten konnte." bz. June 26, 2017. https://www.bzbasel.ch/solothurn/weitere-regionen/als-ida-jeker-ploetzlich-holz-spalten-konnte-131462796.

"Niklaus von Flüe." Heilige der Schweiz. https://www.heiligederschweiz.ch/niklaus-von-fluee/.

Scheuber, J.K. *Ein Urschweitzer erzählt*. Luzern: Räber Verlag, 1965.

Summus Pontifex illustrat virtutes domesticas, civiles et sociales Sancti Nicolai de Flüe, adstantibus christifidelibus ob sollemnia eius canonizationis Romae coadunatis. Acta Apostolicae Sedis [Acts of the Apostolic See] 39 (1947): pp. 364–372.

"Zeit: 13. Mai 1940, Pfingstsonntag Abend; Ort: Waldenburg im Baselbieter Jura." http://www.kwicfinder.com/KWiCFinder_Queries/01-108-18-Apr-S003.D0007-waldenb.html.

ST. KATERI TEKAKWITHA

Acta Apostolicae Sedis [Acts of the Apostolic See] 104 (2012): pp. 1095–1097.

Anishinabe Spiritual Centre. www.anishinabespiritualcentre.ca.

Armstrong, P. "St. Kateri Affirms Indigenous Catholics and All the Faithful." *National Catholic Register*. July 14, 2013. https://www.ncregister.com/news/st-kateri-affirms-indigenous-catholics-and-all-the-faithful.

Cavins, E. *Lily of the Mohawks: The Story of St. Kateri*. Cincinnatio, OH: Servant Books, 2013.

Crowley, C.F. "Kateri Gets Miracle She Needed." *Times Union*. December 19, 2011. https://www.timesunion.com/local/article/Kateri-gets-miracle-she-needed-2412929.php.

"Eleven-year-old Boy's Survival of Flesh-Eating Bacteria Declared a Miracle by Pope as American Indian Woman Credited with Saving Him Is Approved for Sainthood." *Daily Mail*. December 21, 2011. https://www.dailymail.co.uk/news/article-2076891/Jake-Finkbonners-survival-flesh-eating-bacteria-declared-miracle-pope.html.

Mauser, E.W. "Boy's Recovery a Kateri Miracle." *Catholic Register*. October 20, 2012. https://www.catholicregister.org/features/item/15267-boy-s-recovery-a-kateri-miracle.

Parietti, J. "The Miracle Boy." *Northwest Catholic*. http://nwcatholic.org/features/nw-stories/the-miracle-boy.html.

Woodruff, B., R. Sherwood, and E. Johnson. "Washington Boy Says He Spoke to God after Flesh-Eating Bacteria Threatened Life." ABC News. August 2, 2011. https://abcnews.go.com/Nightline/beyondbelief/washington-boy-spoke-god-flesh-eating-bacteria-threatened/story?id=14212228.

ST. BERNADETTE SOUBIROUS

"Decretum super dubio [Miracles for beatification]." *Acta Apostolicae Sedis* [Acts of the Apostolic See] 17 (1925): pp. 254–257.

"Decretum super dubio [Miracles for beatification]." *Acta Apostolicae Sedis* [Acts of the Apostolic See] 25 (1933): pp. 318–321.

Bejda, H. *Księga 100 wielkich cudów* [Book of 100 great miracles]. Kraków: Wydawnictwo Rafael, 2005.

Messori, V. *Tajemnica Lourdes: Czy Bernadeta nas oszukała?* [Lourdes mystery: Did Bernadette deceive us?]. Kraków: Wydawnictwo Znak, 2014.

Objawienie się i cuda Najświętszej Maryi Panny Niepokalanie Poczętej w Lourdes, na podstawie dzieł Dr. Boissarie—naczelnego lekarza kliniki w Lurd opracowal [Apparition and miracles of the Blessed Virgin Mary Immaculately Conceived in Lourdes, based on the works of Dr. Boissarie—the chief physician of the clinic in Lourdes]. Kraków: X.NN, 1904.

Trochu, F. *Święta Bernadetta Soubirous* [Saint Bernadette Soubirous]. Niepokalanów: Wydawnictwo OO. Franciszkanów, 1983.

Tygodnik Rodzin Katolickich Źródło [Catholic families weekly spring] 1, special edition about St. Bernadette Soubirous (2010).

Werfel, F. *Pieśń o Bernadetcie* [The Song of Bernadette]. Translated by M. Klos. Warszawa: Wydawnictwo Promic, 2016.

ST. MARIA ELISABETH HESSELBLAD

"Carlos Miguel Valdés, Niño cubano, sanado milagrosamente de tumor en el cerebelo permitió la canonización de Mary Elizabeth Hesselblad." Camino Católico. June 7, 2016. https://caminocatolico.com/carlos-miguel-valdes-nino-cubano-sanado-milagrosamente-de-tumor-en-el-cerebelo-permitio-la-canonizacion-de-mary-elizabeth-hesselblad/.

Carosa, A. "New Saint Credited with Healing a Young Boy with a Brain Tumor." *Catholic World Report*. June 4, 2016. https://www.catholicworldreport.com/2016/06/04/new-saint-credited-with-healing-a-young-boy-with-a-brain-tumor/.

"Decretum super miraculo [Miracle for beatification]." *Acta Apostolicae Sedis* [Acts of the Apostolic See] 92 (2000): pp. 540–542.

Odden, P.E.. "Den hellige Elisabeth Hesselblad (1870–1957)." Den katolske Kirke. http://www.katolsk.no/biografier/historisk/ehesselb.

Valli, A.M. *La ragazza che cercava Dio. Vita di Maria Elisabetta*. Hesselblad: Ancora libri, 2016.

LARGE-SCALE MIRACLES

Bacci, P.G. *The Life of Saint Philip Neri, Apostle of Rome, and Founder of the Congregation of the Oratory*, vol. 2. London, Dublin and Derby: Richardson, 1847.

Catherine of Siena, St. *Św. Katarzyna ze Sieny, Dialog o Bożej Opatrzności* [Dialogue of Saint Catherine of Siena by St. Catherine of Siena]. Poznań: Wydawnictwo W drodze, 2001.

D'Anastasio, F. *San Gabriele dell'Addolorata: Il grande operatore di miracoli*. San Gabriele Edizioni, 2006.

Die Wunder der Heiligen Crescentia. https://www.all-in.de/kempten/c-lokales/die-wunder-der-heiligen-crescentiaa902523.

Legendy dominikańskie [Dominican legends/legends of the Dominican order]. Poznań: Wydawnictwo W drodze, 1982.

Pabis, M., and H. Bejda. *Białystok ocalony* [Białystok saved]. *Miesięcznik Rodzin Katolickich Cuda i łaski Boże* [Catholic families monthly magazine God's miracles and graces] 2 (2013): S. 10.

Praśkiewicz, S. O.C.D. *Cuda przedłożone Stolicy Apostolskiej i kanonicznie zatwierdzone do gloryfikacji najnowszych świętych i błogosławionych Karmelu Terezjańskiego* [Miracles submitted to the Holy See and canonically approved for the glorification of the latest saints and blesseds from the Order of Discalced Carmelites]. Karmelici Bosi. https://www.karmel.pl/domniemany-cud-eucharystyczny-badany-do-kanonizacji-siostry-marii-kandydy-od-eucharystii/.

Sikorski, M. *Błogosławiony Czesław: Patron Wrocławia*. Nowa Ruda: Wydawnictwo Ziemia Kłodzka, 1993.

Skutsch, H. *Żywot błogosławionego Czesława z rozmyślaniami i modlitwami*. Wrocław, 1863.

Świadectwa o łaskach bł. MS. Opis lask z arch. postulatora. [Testimonies of graces of Blessed MS. Description of graces from postulator's archives.]

Świadectwo Alfredo di Penty na temat cudów bl. Matki Speranzy od Jezusa za. [Testimony of Alfredo di Penta on the miracles of Mother Maria Esperanza of Jesus cit. por.]

Thomas of Celano. *Żywot św. Klary z Asyżu br. Tomasza z Celano* [Life of St. Clare of Assisi by Thomas of Celano]. Translated by C.T. Niezgoda, O.F.M. Conv. http://kety.klaryski.org/czytelnia/wczesne-zrodla-klarianskie/133-zywot-sw-klary-z-asyzu-br-tomasza-z-celano.

Valli, A.M. *Matka Speranza: Świadek Miłości Miłosiernej* [Mother Speranza: Witness of merciful love]. Poznań: Wydawnictwo Agape, 2014.

Woroniecki, J. *Błogosławiony Czesław—dominikanin 1175(?)–1242*. Opole: 1947.

ST. ANTHONY OF PADUA

Gamboso, V., O.F.M. Conv. *Życie świętego Antoniego* [Life of Saint Anthony]. Wrocław: Wydawnictwo św. Antoniego, 1995.

Miesięcznik Rodzin Katolickich Cuda i łaski Boże [Catholic families monthly magazine God's miracles and graces] 6 (2006).

Nauczyciel Ewangelii: Św. Antoni z Padwy [Teacher of the gospel: St. Anthony of Padua]. Kraków-Asyż: Wydawnictwo Franciszkanie, 1998.

Niezgoda, C., O.F.M. Conv. *Cudotwórca z Padwy: Żywoty św. Antoniego Assidua, Benignitas i Raymundina*. Kraków: Wydawnictwo Bratni Zew, 1995.

———. *Św. Antoni Padewski. Życie i nauczanie*. Warszawa: Akademia Teologii Katolickiej, 1984.

ST. MARIA GORETTI

"Allucutione ad christifideles qui Romam convenerant ad beatificationem Mariae Goretti celebrandam." *Acta Apostolicae Sedis* [Acts of the Apostolic See] 39 (1947): pp. 352–358.

Cenci, F. "Diventa mamma per intercessione di Maria Goretti." Zenit. July 11, 2013. https://it.zenit.org/articles/diventa-mamma-per-intercessione-di-maria-goretti/.

"Decretum super dubio [Miracle for canonization]." *Acta Apostolicae Sedis* [Acts of the Apostolic See] 42 (1950): pp. 312–314.

Du Parc, J. *Niebo nad moczarami*. Warszawa: Wydawnictwo Sióstr Loretanek, 2002.

http://mariagoretti.altervista.org.

John Paul II. Angelus. July 7, 2002. https://www.vatican.va/content/john-paul-ii/en/angelus/2002/documents/hf_jp-ii_ang_20020707.html.

Lindenman, M. "Alessandro Serenelli: Sinner for Our Time?" Diary of a Wimpy Catholic. Patheos. https://www.patheos.com/blogs/diaryofawimpycatholic/2015/07/alessandro-serenelli-sinner-for-our-time/.

Sanicanti, A. "Santa Maria Goretti: il suo ultimo miracolo al vaglio." https://www.lalucedimaria.it/borgo-le-ferriere-miracolo-maria-goretti/.

Santa Maria Goretti—Corinaldo. http://www.santamariagoretti.it.

Santi Beati. "Santa Maria Goretti." http://www.santiebeati.it/dettaglio/28150.

Święta Maria Goretti. http://www.mariagoretti.pl.

www.mariagoretti.org

STS. JACINTA & FRANCISCO MARTO

"Beatificación de Francisco y Jacinta." http://www.angelfire.com/extreme/neostars/fatima/beatificacion.htm.

Bejda, H. *Ilustrowana księga świętych* [Illustrated book of saints]. Kraków: Dom Wydawniczy Rafael, 2014.

De Juana, A. "Este es el milagro de la canonización de Francisco y Jacinta, los pastorcitos de Fátima." ACI Prensa. May 11, 2017. https://www.aciprensa.com/noticias/este-es-el-milagro-para-la-canonizacion-de-los-pastorcitos-de-fatima-76594.

De Louvencourt, J.F., O.C.S.O. *Rekolekcje fatimskie z Franciszkiem i Hiacyntą*. Warszawa: Wydawnictwo Księży Marianów, 2005. http://pastorinhos.com.

"Decretum super miraculo [Miracle for beatification]." *Acta Apostolicae Sedis* [Acts of the Apostolic See] 92 (2000): pp. 74–75.

"Decretum super miraculo [Miracle for canonization]." *Acta Apostolicae Sedis* [Acts of the Apostolic See] 110, no. 5 (2018): pp. 648–650.

Delestre, F. "El milagro que posibilitó la beatificación de los Pastorcitos de Fátima." http://corazones.org/maria/fatima/milagro_beatificacion.htm.

Praśkiewicz, S., O.C.D. *Cuda przedłożone Stolicy Apostolskiej i kanonicznie zatwierdzone do gloryfikacji najnowszych świętych i błogosławionych Karmelu Terezjańskiego* [Miracles submitted to the Holy See and canonically approved for the glorification of the latest saints and blesseds from the Order of Discalced Carmelites].

Rocha, A. *Cud w Fatimie, Stella Maris, czerwiec 1997* [Miracle at Fatima, Stella Maris, June 1997]. Translated by E.B. Vox Domini. https://voxdomini.pl/prorocy/fatima/cudownie-uzdrowiona/.

Z błogosławionymi Hiacyntą i Franciszkiem w XXI w. [With Blessed Jacinta and Francisco in the 21st century]. Marki: Michalineum, 2000.

ST. CHRISTOPHER MAGALLANES JARA (24 COMPANIONS)

"Decretum super miraculo [Miracle for canonization]." *Acta Apostolicae Sedis* [Acts of the Apostolic See] 92 (2000): pp. 69–70.

Godoy, L.S. "San Cristóbal Magallanes." https://lsgsancristobalmagallanes.wordpress.com/.

Gonzalez, F.F., M.C.C.J. *28 męczenników meksykańskich, Męczennicy XX wieku*, vol. 14. Poznań: Pallotinum, 2001.

"Litterae Decretales quibus Christophoro Magallanes et XXIV Sociis Sanctorum honores decernuntur." *Acta Apostolicae Sedis* [Acts of the Apostolic See] 93, no. 7 (2001): pp. 417–421.

"Un solo milagro logra 25 santos y beato." Portaluz. May 22, 2015. https://www.portaluz.org/un-solo-milagro-logra-25-santos-y-beatos-1175.htm.

ST. JEAN MARIE VIANNEY

SPECIAL THANKS TO: JOLANTA ZAKRZEWSKA

Darche, J. *Vie nouvelle du curé d'Ars et de Sainte Philomène vierge et martyre*. Palmé, 1865.

de Montrond, M. *Le curé d'Ars*. Lefort, 1860.

Le cure d'arp: Notice biographique sur Jean-Baptiste-Marie Viannay, mort en odeur de Sainteté le 4 Aout 1859. 5th ed. 1859.

John Vianney, St. *Kazania wybrane, Oficyna Wydawnicza*. Warszawa: VIATOR, 1999.

Joulin, M. *Jan Maria Vianney: Ciche życie proboszcza z Ars* [St. John Mary Vianney: The quiet life of the parish priest of Ars]. Poznań: Wydawnictwo Święty Wojciech, 2009.

Mahieu, P., O.S.B. *Kwiatki proboszcza z Ars*. Kraków: Esprit, 2011.

Monnin, A., and C. Douniol. *Esprit du Curé d'Ars: M. Vianney dans ses catéchismes, ses homélies et sa conversation*. 1868.

Pélagaud, J.B. *Vie merveilleuse de M. J.-M.-B. Vianey, curé d'Ars*. 1861.

"Pius XI Litterae Apostolicae 'Christi nomen,' beato Ioanni Baptistae Mariae Vianney, confessori, parocho vici «Ars», honores sanctorum decernuntur." *Acta Apostolicae Sedis* [Acts of the Apostolic See] 17 (1925): pp. 465–481.

Trochu, F. *Proboszcz z Ars, Święty Jan Maria Vianney 1786–1859*. Poznań: Uniwersytet im. Adama Mickiewicza, Wydział Teologiczny, Redakcja Wydawnictw, 2004.

MIRACULOUS GIFTS, CHARISMS, AND OTHER PHENOMENA

Hagiographic articles by the author published between 2000 and 2021 in the Catholic families weekly *Źródło* [Spring], families monthly magazine *Cuda i łaski Boże* [God's miracles and graces], and evangelization newspaper *Dobre Nowiny* [Good news].

Bejda, H. *Ilustrowana księga świętych* [Illustrated book of saints]. Kraków: Dom Wydawniczy Rafael, 2014.

———. *Księga 100 wielkich cudów* [Book of 100 great miracles]. Kraków: Dom Wydawniczy Rafael, 2005.

Catherine of Siena, St. *Św. Katarzyna ze Sieny, Dialog o Bożej Opatrzności* [Dialogue of Saint Catherine of Siena by St. Catherine of Siena]. Poznań: Wydawnictwo W drodze, 2001.

Fiejdasz, L. "Zjawiska paranaturalne w sprawach beatyfikacyjnych." *Roczniki Nauk Prawnych*, 16, no. 2 (2006): pp. 287–301.

Flanagan, S. *Hildegard of Bingen: A Visionary Life*. New York: Routledge, 1998.

Guitton, J., and J.J. Antier. *Tajemne moce wiary: Znaki i cuda* [The mysterious power of faith: Signs and miracles]. Warszawa: Oficyna Wydawniczo-Poligraficzna Adam, 1997.

Katechizm Kościoła Katolickiego [Catechism of the Catholic Church]. Poznań: Pallotinum, 1994.

Sbalchiero, P. *Niezwykłe zjawiska wiary*. Kraków: Wydawnictwo M., 2007.

Thomas of Celano. *Tomasz z Celano, Traktat o cudach św. Franciszka z Asyżu* [The treatise on the miracles of Saint Francis]. Translated and edited by C. Niezgoda, O.F.M. Conv.

Treece, P., *Ciala uświęcone*. Gdańsk: Wydawnictwo Exter, 1994.

ST. ALPHONSA OF THE IMMACULATE CONCEPTION

"Decretum super dubio [Miracle for beatification]." *Acta Apostolicae Sedis* [Acts of the Apostolic See] (1985): pp. 665–669.

"Decretum super miraculo [Miracle for canonization]." *Acta Apostolicae Sedis* [Acts of the Apostolic See] 99, no. 7 (2007): pp. 613–614.

http://www.saintalphonsamma.org

Radhakrishnan, M.G. "God's Chosen One." *India Today*. October 27, 2008. https://www.indiatoday.in/magazine/nation/story/20081027-gods-chosen-one-737975-2008-10-17.

Saint Alphonsa Syro Malabar Cathedral Preston. https://www.stalphonsacathedralpreston.com/.

www.alphonsa.net

ST. PIUS X

Bazin, R. *Papież Pius X*. Kraków: Wydawnictwo Księży Jezuitów, 1935.

Benedict XVI. "Saint Pius X." *Niedziela Ogólnopolska*.

Borrelli, A. "San Pio X (Giuseppe Sarto) Papa." Santi Beati. http://www.santiebeati.it/dettaglio/24100.

Dal-Gal, R.G. *S. PIO X. Papa: Edizioni Il Messagero di San Antonio*. Padova: Basilica del Santo, 1954.

"Decretum super dubio [Miracles for beatification]." *Acta Apostolicae Sedis* [Acts of the Apostolic See] 43 (1951): pp. 138–140.

"Litterae Decretales Beato Pio X Pont. Max. Confessori, Sanctorum Honores Decernuntur [Miracles for canonization]." *Acta Apostolicae Sedis* [Acts of the Apostolic See] 47 (1955): pp. 113–128.

Parrochia di Riese Pio X. https://parrocchiariesepiox.it.

Parrochia San Pio X. http://www.sanpioxlipunti.it.

Zaleski, W. S.D.B. *Święci na każdy dzień*. Warszawa: Wydawnictwo Salezjańskie, 1997.

ST. FREI GALVÃO

SPECIAL THANKS TO: ABBE LAURENT BISELX, F.S.S.P.X.

Arautos do evangelho. https://www.arautos.org/.

Casa de Frei Galvão. https://www.casadefreigalvao.com.br/.

Cavalheiro, E. "Milagres de Frei Galvão são exemplos concretos de Fé." Jornal Santuário. https://www.a12.com/jornalsantuario/noticias/conheca-historias-de-fe-em-frei-galvao

Codorin, L.C.B. "Postuladora do Beato Frei Galvão revela o milagre aprovado para a canonização." Notícias. December 22, 2006. http://noticias.cancaonova.com/brasil/postuladora-do-beato-frei-galvao-revela-o-milagre-aprovado-para-a-canonizacao/

de França, F. *Frei Galvão: A vida do primeiro santo nascido no Brasil*. Lebooks Editora, 2014.

de Sousa Araujo, A. "Santo António de Sant'Ana Galvão, OFM (1739–1822): Primeiro Santo natural do Brasil." *Lusitania Sacra* 23 (January–June 2011): pp. 243–262.

"Decretum super miraculo [Miracle for beatification]." *Acta Apostolicae Sedis* [Acts of the Apostolic See] 91 (1999): pp. 119–121.

"Decretum super miraculo [Miracle for canonization]." *Acta Apostolicae Sedis* [Acts of the Apostolic See] 99, no. 5 (2007): pp. 384–386.

Ezabella, F. "Brasileiras que receberam milagre de frei aguardam missa do papa." April 27, 2007. https://noticias.uol.com.br/ultnot/reuters/2007/04/27/ult27u61075.jhtm.

Frei Galvão, http://gshow.globo.com/programas/mais-voce/v2011/Mais-Voce/0,MUL481194-10345,00-FREI+GALVAO.html.

"Jovem de 1º milagre pensou em ser freira (entrevista), 'Folha de S. Paulo.'" Folha de S. Paulo. https://www.folha.uol.com.br/fsp/brasil/fc1105200720.htm.

"Milagre de são Frei Galvão—comprovado para sua beatificação." Breviário. March 13, 2011. https://rezairezairezai.blogspot.com/2011/03/milagre-de-sao-frei-galvao-comprovado.html.

"Novo milagre de Frei Galvão foi salvar vida de mãe e filho." Globo.com. December 12, 2006. http://g1.globo.com/Noticias/SaoPaulo/0,,AA1397723-5605,00-NOVO+MILAGRE+DE+FREI+GALVAO+FOI+SALVAR+VIDA+DE+MAE+E+FILHO.html.

Santuário Frei Galvão. https://www.santuariofreigalvao.com/.

"Vaticano reconhece 2º milagre e deve canonizar Frei Galvão." http://gi.globo.com/noticias/saopaulo/0..aa1391283-5605,00.html.

"Vaticano reconhece milagre de Frei Galvão." http://gi.globo.com/Noticias/Brasil/0,,AA1391665-5598,00-VATICANO+RECONHECE+MILAGRE-DE-FREI-GALVAO.html.

Vlahou, A. "Milagre duplo confirma santidade de frei Galvão." BBC Brasil. December 22, 2006. https://www.bbc.com/portuguese/reporterbbc/story/2006/12/printable/061222_santobrasileirorc.

ST. JOSEPH VAZ

"Acta Francisci Pp. Litterae Decretales quibus Beato Iosepho Vaz sanctorum honores decernuntur." *Acta Apostolicae Sedis* [Acts of the Apostolic See] no. 7 (2016): pp. 711–714.

Akkara, A. "Indian Priest, 'Miracle Son,' Are Eager for Blessed Vaz Canonization." *Catholic Register*. January 10. 2015. https://www.catholicregister.org/home/international/item/19505-indian-priest-miracle-son-are-eager-for-blessed-vaz-canonization.

"Blessed Joseph Vaz." http://www.oxfordoratory.org.uk/bl-joseph-vaz.php.

Costa, C. "Apostolic Christianity in Goa, a Talk with Fr. Cosme Costa." Mar Alvares Media. June 21, 2015. YouTube video, 50:32. https://www.youtube.com/watch?v=P8y-YxHKhHw.

"Decretum super dubio [Miracle for beatification]." *Acta Apostolicae Sedis* [Acts of the Apostolic See] 86 (1994): pp. 175–176.

Gasbarri, C. *Przemytnik Chrystusa. Św. Józef Vaz Cor—Apostol Cejlonu. Życie. Cuda. Dzieła*. Kraków: Wydawnictwo AA, 2015.

"My Birth, a Miracle of Bl. Joseph Vaz." *Times of India*. September 19, 2014. https://timesofindia.indiatimes.com/city/goa/My-birth-a-miracle-of-Bl-Joseph-Vaz/articleshow/42834021.cms.

Pereira, V. "Pilar-Goa: Close Encounters with 'Miracle Child' Fr Cosme Costa at Fr Agnel Monastery-Pilar." https://www.mangalorean.com/pilar-goa-close-encounters-with-miracle-child-fr-cosme-costa-at-fr-agnel-monastery-pilar/.

Rocznik statystyczny Kościoła 2017 r. Watykan: Libreria Editrice Vaticana, 2019.

"Saint Joseph Vaz." OMI. https://www.omiworld.org/our-charism/our-saints/non-oblate-causes/saint-joseph-vaz-1651-1711/biography/.

"Saint Joseph Vaz." Oratory of Saint Philip Neri. https://www.birminghamoratory.org.uk/saint-joseph-vaz/.

Schmalz, M. "Who Are Sri Lanka's Christians?" *The Conversation*. April 21, 2019. https://theconversation.com/who-are-sri-lankas-christians-115799.

ST. CHARLES OF MOUNT ARGUS

Carroll, D., C.P. *A Knight of the Crucified. Blessed Charles of Mount Argus 1821–1893*. Dublin, Ireland: Elo Press.

D'Arcy, B., C.P. *Saint Charles of Mount Argus*. Enniskillen: Print Factory, 2007. http://homepage.eircom.net/-mountargus/charles/pen_pictures.htm.

"Decretum super dubio [Miracle for beatification]." *Acta Apostolicae Sedis* [Acts of the Apostolic See] 80 (1988): pp. 1800–1802.

Heilige Pater Karel. https://paterkarelkapel.nl/.

"Jan 5—Saint Charles of St Andrew of Mount Argus (1821–1893)." CatholicIreland.net. January 5, 2012. https://www.catholicireland.net/saintoftheday/saint-charles-of-mount-argus/.

Kelly, O., C.P. *Blessed Charles of Mount Argus: An Apostolic Mystic 1821–1893*. Dublin: Elo Press, 1989.

———. *Life of Blessed Charles of Mount Argup: Passionist Priest 1821–1893*.

"Litterae Decretales—Beato Carolus a S. Andrea Houben Sanctus fit." *Acta Apostolicae Sedis* [Acts of the Apostolic See] 100, no. 4 (2008): pp. 209–212.

Mount Argus Parish. https://www.mountargusparish.ie/about-saint-charles-of-mount-argus/.

Nevin, E., C.P. *St. Charles of Mount Argup: The Man I Knew.* http://homepage.eircom.net/~mountargus/charles/downloads/charles_life_nevin.pdf

Pekelder, W. "Voor het volk wás pater Karel al Heilig." https://www.trouw.nl/nieuws/voor-het-volk-was-pater-karel-al-heilig-baa23b-4c/?referer=https%3A%2F%2Fwww.google.com%2F.

VERY UNUSUAL MIRACLES

Hagiographic articles by the author published between 2000 and 2021 in the Catholic families weekly *Źródło* [Spring], families monthly magazine *Cuda i łaski Boże* [God's miracles and graces], and evangelization newspaper *Dobre Nowiny* [Good news].

Acta Sanctorum Marti, vol. 2, p. 672. 1735.

Bacci, P.G. *The Life of Saint Philip Neri, Apostle of Rome, and Founder of the Congregation of the Oratory.* Vol. 2. T. Richardson, 1847.

de Voragine, J. *The Golden Legend.* https://catholicsaints.info/golden-legend-lives-of-saints-cosmo-and-damian.

———. *The Golden Legend.* https://catholicsaints.info/golden-legend-translation-of-saint-thomas-of-canterbury/.

———. *Zlota legenda.* Translated by J. Pleziowa. Warszawa: Prószyński i S-ka, 2000.

Fontes vitae S. Thomae Aquinatip: Notis historicis et criticis illustrati, curis et labore dr. Prümmer OP ... Apud ed. Privat Bibliopolam, Tolosae. N.p., n.d.

Hebert, A.J. *Raised from the Dead.* Gastonia, NC: TAN Books, 1986.

Jagla, J. "*Święci Kosma i Damian Cudowni lekarze i chirurdzy w kulcie i w ikonografii.*" *Panacea* 3, no. 28 (July–September 2009): pp. 30–31.

Łubieński, B., C.S.S.R. *Żywot świętego brata Gerarda Majelli ze Zgromadzenia Redemptorystów.* Kraków: Homo Dei, 2019.

Thomas of Celano. *Traktat o cudach Świętego Franciszka z Asyżu* [The treatise on the miracles of Saint Francis]. Translated and edited by C.T. Niezgoda, O.F.M. Conv. www.fzs.radom.pl. "Prawdziwy znak." *Nasza Arka* [Our ark], no. 10 (2004).

———. *The Treatise on the Miracles of Saint Francis.* https://franciscantradition.org/francis-of-assisi-early-documents/the-founder/the-treatise-on-the-miracles-of-saint-francis/1552-fa-ed-2-page-464.

ST. JOAN OF ARC

"Beata Ioanna De Arc, Virgo, In Sanctorum Caelitum Album Refertur Benedictus Episcopus Servus Servorum Dei Ad Perpetuam Rei Memoriam." *Acta Apostolicae Sedis* [Acts of the Apostolic See] 12 (1920): pp. 514–529.

Bejda, H. *Ilustrowana księga świętych* [Illustrated book of saints]. Kraków: Dom Wydawniczy Rafael, 2014.

———. *Księga 100 wielkich cudów* [Book of 100 great miracles]. Kraków: Dom Wydawniczy Rafael, 2005.

"Decretum super dubio [Miracles for beatification]." *Acta Apostolicae Sedis* [Acts of the Apostolic See] 1 (1909): pp. 167–169.

"Decretum super dubio [Miracles for canonization]." *Acta Apostolicae Sedis* [Acts of the Apostolic See] 11 (1919): pp. 187–189.

Górka, J. *Dziewica Orleańska. Błogosławiona Joanna d'Arc,* Tarnów: nakl. aut., 1911.

Górka, J. *Św. Joanna d'Arc* Dziewica Orleańska: 1429–1929, Kraków: Wydaw. Księży Jezuitów, 1930.

Lepetit, J. *Sauvé des flammes par la Bienheureuse Jeanne d'Arc.* In *"Annales du Mont-Saint-Michel," Revue Mensuelle Illustrée, Chronique du Pèlerinage du Mont-Saint-Michel.* Organe de l'Archiconfrérie Universelle de Saint Michel, 38e Année. 11e Livraison. Février, 1912. https://www.pelerin-montsaintmichel.org/bibliotheque-numerique; 38_1_1911%20(2).

Pabis, M. and H. Bejda. *Gdy przychodzą dusze.* Kraków: Dom Wydawniczy Rafael, 2014.

Prokop, K.R. *Joanna d'Arc.* Kraków: Wydaw. WAM, 2009.

Saint Joan of Arc Center. http://www.stjoan-center.com/.

Ste Jeanne D'Arc. http://www.stejeannedarc.net.

Williamson, A. "Condemnation Trial—1456 July 7." Joan of Arc Archive. http://archive.joan-of-arc.org/joanofarc_1456_july_7.html.

———. "Joan of Arc: A Life Summary regarding Her Visions." Joan of Arc Archive. http://www.joan-of-arc.org/joanofarc_life_summary_visions.html.

ST. JANUARIUS

Bejda, H. *Krew świętych.* Kraków: Dom Wydawniczy Rafael, 2019.

"The Blood of St. Januarius." *Chemistry in Britain* 30, no. 2 (1994): p. 123. www.cicap.org.

De Ceglia, F.P. *Il segreto di san Gennaro. Storia naturale di un miracolo napoletano.* Torino: Giulio Euinaudi editore, 2016.

Malafronte, L., and C. Maturo. *Urbs sanguinum: Itineraria alla ricerca dei prodigi di sangue a Napoli.* Napoli: Edizioni Intra Moenia, 2012.

Ponticello, M. *Un giorno a Napoli con San Gennaro: Misteri, segreti, storie insolite e tesori.* Roma: Newton Compton Editori, 2016.

Reino, B. *Krew wiecznie żywa. Życie, śmierć i cuda św. Januarego.* Warszawa: Oficyna Wydawniczo-Poligraficzna Adam, 2007.

ST. GREGORY THAUMATURGUS

Leclercq, H. "St. Gregory of Neocaesarea." *The Catholic Encyclopedia*, vol. 7. New York: Robert Appleton, 1910. http://www.newadvent.org/cathen/07015a.htm.

The Life of Gregory the Wonderworker by Gregory of Nyssa. https://web.archive.org/web/20080513192134/http://www.sage.edu/faculty/salomd/nyssa/index.html.

Skarga, P. *Żywoty świętych Starego i Nowego Zakonu* [The Lives of the Saints from the Old and New Testaments]. Vol. 2. Edited by M. Kozielski. Kraków: Wydawnictwo PSB & PERFEKT, 1995.

Starowieyski, M. "Najstarszy opis mariofanii." *Warszawskie Studia Teologiczne*, numer specjalny (2017): pp. 308–317.

ST. GIUSEPPE MOSCATI

Ausilio, C. "San Giuseppe Moscati, i 3 miracoli del medico dei poveri." Vesuviolive.it. November 16, 2017. https://www.vesuviolive.it/cultura-napoletana/225106-san-giuseppe-moscati-i-3-miracoli-del-medico-dei-poveri/.

Bejda, H. *Ilustrowana księga świętych* [Illustrated book of saints]. Kraków: Dom Wydawniczy Rafael, 2014.

"Decretum super dubio [Miracles for beatification]." *Acta Apostolicae Sedis* [Acts of the Apostolic See] 67 (1975): pp. 745–746.

"Decretum super dubio [Miracle for canonization]." *Acta Apostolicae Sedis* [Acts of the Apostolic See] 79 (1987): pp. 1114–1116.

del Guercio, "G. Parla il medico che ha studiato i miracoli di San Giuseppe Moscati e di Papa Giovanni XXIII." *Aleteia.* September 4, 2018. https://it.aleteia.org/2018/09/04/parla-il-medico-che-ha-studiato-i-miracoli-di-san-giuseppe-moscati-e-di-papa-giovanni-xxiii/

del Grosso, A. "San Giuseppe Moscati tra vita e miracoli." April 15, 2014. https://www.positanonews.it/2014/04/san-giuseppe-moscati-tra-vita-e-miracoli/134751/.

Dynowska, M. *Józef Moscati, lekarz ciała i duszy* [Giuseppe Moscati, healing souls and bodies]. Katowice: Księgarnia i Drukarnia Katolicka S.A.

Ferraro, M. "Giuseppe Moscati, ecco i tre miracoli del medico santo." Fanpage.it. https://napoli.fanpage.it/giuseppe-moscati-ecco-i-tre-miracoli-del-medico-santo/.

Immediata, B. *Św. Józef Moscati: Historia świętego lekarza.* Kraków: Esprit, 2018.

Kaczmarek, L. *Światło wśród mroków: Święty lekarz Moscati* [Light amidst the darkness: Saint physician Moscati]. Poznań-Warszawa: Księgarnia św. Wojciecha, 1948.

Miesięcznik Rodzin Katolickich Cuda i łaski Boże [Catholic families monthly magazine God's miracles and graces] no. 3 (2018).

Papasogli, G. *Giuseppe Moscati 1880–1927: Leben eines heiligen Arztes.* Stein: Christiana-Verl., 1982.

ST. JOHN BOSCO

Bejda, H. *Księga 100 wielkich cudów* [Book of 100 great miracles]. Kraków:]. Dom Wydawniczy Rafael, 2005.

Bolletino Salesiano 18, no. 4–5 (Aprile–Maggio, 1934). http://digital.biblioteca.unisal.it.

"Decretum super dubio [Miracles for beatification]." *Acta Apostolicae Sedis* [Acts of the Apostolic See] 21 (1929): pp. 165–167.

"Decretum super dubio [Miracles for canonization]." *Acta Apostolicae Sedis* [Acts of the Apostolic See] 26 (1934): pp. 31–34.

Frigida, F. "I sorprendenti miracoli di Don Bosco." Papaboys. July 6, 2016. https://www.papaboys.org/i-sorprendenti-miracoli-di-don-bosco.

Lettera Decretale di Sua Santità Pio XI Geminata Laetitia Che Proclama Santo Don Giovanni Bosco. http://www.vaticana contentB/pius-xi/it/letters/documents/hf_p-xilett_19340401_geminata-laetitia.html.

Miesięcznik Rodzin Katolickich Nasza Arka [Catholic families monthly magazine our ark], no. 2 (2002).

Pokłosie Salezjańskie 17, no. 12 (December 1933).

Stella, P. *Don Bosco: Nella storia della religiosità cattolica, volume terzo, La Canonizzazione (1888–1934), Ottobre 1988—Libreria Ateneo Salesiano, Roma, AR. Aprile 2012, Libro dell'Istituto di Scienze dell'Educazione dell'Università di Verona.* https://www.donboscoland.it/uploads/07d7a0bd4ae4220bfce7e6133a6b8ff9Br.pdf.

Ukleja, R. *Triumf Kościoła według wizji św. Jana Bosko* [Triumph of the Church according to the vision of St. John Bosco]. Wrocław: Wydawnictwo Arka, 2005.

Von Matt, L. and H. Bosco. *Ksiądz Bosko.* Warszawa: Wydawnictwo Salezjańskie, 2000.

MIRACULOUS CHILDREN

SPECIAL THANKS TO: FR. ARTUR ŚWIEŻY

Hagiographic articles by the author published between 2000 and 2021 in the Catholic families weekly *Źródło* [Spring], families monthly magazine *Cuda i łaski Boże* [God's miracles and graces], and evangelization newspaper *Dobre Nowiny* [Good news].

Alexia González-Barros y González. www.alexiagb.pl.

Ambrose, St. *De virginibus.* http://www.konsekrowane.org/dokumenty/ambrozy.pdf.

———. *De virginibus.* Translated by J. Drzewowska.

America Needs Fatima. https://www.americaneedsfatima.org/Conversions/the-little-girl-who-inspired-archbishop-fulton-sheen-s-vow.html.

Anne-Gabrielle Caron. www.anne-gabrielle.com.

Berdejo, E. "Carlo Acutis: Este es el milagro que lo hará beato." ACI Prensa. https://www.aciprensa.com/noticias/carlo-acutis-este-es-el-milagro-que-lo-hara-beato-21587.

Borriello, L. *Prostota serca, Antonina Meo-Nennolina, Ksiagarnia św.* Katowice: Jacka, 2006.

Carlo Acutis. www.carloacutis.com.

De Troyon-Montalambert, R. *Mała uczennica Jezusa Anna de Guigne* [Little disciple of Jesus Anna de Guigne]. Poznań: Wydawnictwo Hlondianum, 2005.

Gori, N. *Eucharystia: Moja autostrada do Nieba: Historia niezwykłego nastolatka* [Eucharist. My highway to heaven: The story of an extraordinary teenager]. Kraków: ESPe, 2010.

Hanter, E. *Mali przyjaciele Jezusa Eucharystycznego* [Little friends of the eucharistic Jesus]. Szczecinek: Fundacja Nasza Przyszłość, 2007.

Les Amis d'Anne de Guigne. https://www.annedeguigne.fr.

Meo, M. *Nennolina—sześcioletnia mistyczka: Świadectwo matki* [Nennolina—a six-year-old mystic: Her mother's testimony]. Kraków: eSPe, 2008.

Miesięcznik Rodzin Katolickich Cuda i łaski Boże [Catholic families monthly magazine God's miracles and graces], no. 2 (2015).

Mondrone, D. *Angiolino: Chłopiec, który umiał cierpieć.* Roma: Edizioni Centro Volontari della Sofferenza, 1986.

Moscone, F. *Siewcy nadziei, Cisi Pracownicy Krzyża* [Sowers of hope, silent workers of the Cross]. Głogów: 2003.

Occhetta, F. *Carlo Acutip: La vita oltre il confine*, Gorle: Editrice Velar, 2013.

Pabis, M. and H. Bejda. *Nastoletni cudotwórcy* [Teenager miracle-workers]. Kraków: Dom Wydawniczy Rafael, 2016.

Venerable Mariacarmen. www.maricarmengv.info.

ST. CLARE OF ASSISI

Canonization Process of Saint Clare. Part I – Gloriosus Deus. https://kapucynki.pl/proces-kanonizacyjny-swietej-klary-cz-i-gloriosus-deus/

Life of Saint Clare of Assisi, transl. Br. Thomas of Celano. http://kety.klaryski.org/czytelnia/wezesne-zrodla-klarianskie/133-zywot-sw-klary-z-asyzu-br-tomasza-z-celano

"Miracles and graces of God," *Monthly Magazine of Catholic Families* No. 6 (2012).

Voragine J. de, *The Golden Legend: Or, Lives of the Saints*, vol. 6. London: J M Dent and Co., 1900.

ST. JOSÉ GABRIEL DEL ROSARIO BROCHERO

"Camila, la chiquita que casi muere a golpes, el segundo milagro del padre Brochero." TN. September 10. 2015. https://tn.com.ar/sociedad/camila-la-chiquita-que-casi-muere-a-golpes-el-segundo-milagro-del-padre-brochero_618025/.

"Decretum super miraculo [Miracle for beatification]." *Acta Apostolicae Sedis* [Acts of the Apostolic See] 105, no. 8 (2013): pp. 806–808.

"Decretum super miraculo [Miracle for canonization]." *Acta Apostolicae Sedis* [Acts of the Apostolic See] 109, no. 12 (2017): pp. 1391–1393.

Francini, M. "Per Redazione Papaboys, Il 'Cura Gaucho (Brochero): riconosciuto il miracolo: Verso la canonizzazionee festa in Argentina." Papaboys. https://www.papaboys.org/il-cura-gaucho-brochero-riconosciuto-il-miracolo-verso-la-canonizzazione-e-festa-in-argentina/.

Frigida, F. "Confermato il secondo miracolo attribuito all'intercessione del Cura Brochero." Papaboys. https://www.papaboys.org/confermato-il-secondo-miracolo-attribuito-allintercessione-del-cura-brochero/.

http://www.curabrochero.org.ar.

Jara, F. "Camila, la niña del milagro que convirtió a Brochero en Santo." https://www.infobae.com/sociedad/2016/10/16/camila-la-nina-del-milagro-que-convirtio-a-brochero-en-santo/.

"La conmovedora historia de Nicolás Flores, el joven del milagro de Brochero." Infobae. October 11, 2016. https://www.infobae.com/sociedad/2016/10/11/la-conmovedora-historia-de-nicolas-flores-el-joven-del-milagro-de-brochero/.

"La Otra Mirada-Primer Milagro José Gabriel Brochero Nicolas Flores, Guillermo Calvar." YouTube video. https://www.youtube.com/watch?v=TdRyoWiS4xU Floresa.

Montero, M. "Camila, la niña que llevó a Brochero a lo más alto." https://www.valoresreligiosos.com.ar/Noticias/camila-la- nina-que-llevo-a-brochero-a-lo-mas-alto-8268.

"Nicolás Flores, el milagro del cura brochero." Canal 21 San Rafael. Facebook video, 3:00. https://ms-my.facebook.com/Canal-21SanRafael/videos/nicolas-flores-el-milagro-del-cura-brochero/589029695175978/?_so__=p ermalink&_rv=related_videos.

"Nicolás Flores, el niño del milagro del cura Brochero." https://www.lavoz.com.ar/ciudadanos/nicolas-flores-el-nino-del-milagro-del-cura-brochero.

"Nicolás y Camila, los nenes de los milagros del santo Cura Brochero." TN. https://tn.com.ar/politica/nicolas-y-camila-los-nenes-de-los-milagros-del-santo-cura-brochero_745884.

"Nunca dejen de pedir Nico Flores, el niño del milagro de Brochero." https://radiomaria.org.ar/nunca-dejen-pedir-nico-flores-nino-del-milagro-brochero/.

Premat, S. "Camila Brusotti: Brochero hizo un milagro por mí." https://www.lanacion.com.ar/sociedad/camila-cuando-estaba-internada-brochero-hizo-un-milagro-por-midesde-la-llegada-del-chavismo-al-poder-eeuu-tuvo-varios-cruces-con-venezuela-una-relacion-conflictiva-nid1865374/.

"Qué hizo el cura Brochero para ser canonizado." Infobae. https://www.infobae.com/2016/01/22/1784775-que-hizo-el-cura- brochero-ser-canonizado/.

ST. GABRIEL POSSENTI

SPECIAL THANKS TO: DAMIEN CASH

Bątkiewicz-Brożek, J. "Gabriel skuteczny." *Gość Niedzielny*, no. 1 (2016).

Bejda, H. *Ilustrowana księga świętych* [Illustrated book of saints]. Kraków: Dom Wydawniczy Rafael, 2014.

———. *Św. Gemma Galgani: Mała biografia* [St. Gemma Galgani: A small biography]. Kraków: Dom Wydawniczy Rafael, 2014.

D'Anastasio, F. *San Gabriele dell'Addolorata: Il grande operatore di miracoli*. San Gabriele Edizioni, 2006.

Decree of Benedict XV, all miracles with extended descriptions of miracles for canonization. *Acta Apostolicae Sedis* [Acts of the Apostolic See] 12 (1920): pp. 474–485.

di Eugenio, P. *San Gabriele dell'Addolorata*. San Paolo Edizioni, 1997.

https://www.nondisolopane.it/Il-santo-del-giorno-27-febbraio-san-gabriele-delladdolorata/.

https://www.parrocchiasangabrielegallipoli.it/il-miracolo/.

"Il Santo del giorno—27 febbraio—San Gabriele dell'Addolorata."

Kostrzewa, C., S.S.P. *Święty Gabriel*. Częstochowa: Edycja Świętego Pawła, 2016.

Michael, S.S. *Portrait of Saint Gemma: A Stigmatic*. Kenedy, 1950.

Pabis, M. and H. Bejda. *Gdy przychodzą dusze ... Tajemnica świętych obcowania*. Kraków: Dom Wydawniczy Rafael, 2014.

ST. MARTIN DE PORRES

"Acta Ioannis Pp. XXIII, In Sollemni Canonizatione Beati Martini de Porres, Confessoris, laici professi ex Ordine Praedicatorum, in Basilica Vaticana die VI mensis Maii a. MCMLXII, dominica secunda post Pascha, peracta." *Acta Apostolicae Sedis* [Acts of the Apostolic See] 54 (1962): pp. 305–309.

Bejda, H. *Ilustrowana księga świętych* [Illustrated book of saints]. Kraków: Dom Wydawniczy Rafael, 2014.

"Decretum super dubio [Miracles for canonization]." *Acta Apostolicae Sedis* [Acts of the Apostolic See] 54 (1962): pp. 227–230.

Gonar, H. "El niño que hizo santo a Martín de Porres." https://www.eldia.es/2012-05-06/sociedad/2-nino-hizo-santo-Martin-Porres.htm.

Iraburu, J.M. "San Martín de Porres, humilde mulato peruano." http://traditio-op.org/santos/San%20Martin%20de%20Porres/San%20Mart%C3%ADn%20de%20Porres%20humilde%20mulato%20peruano%20Jos%C3%A9%20 Mar%C3%ADa%20Iraburu.pdf.

La corona del Rosario con San Martino de Porres per le intenzioni del Papa. Roma: Postulazione Generale O.P., 1962.

Legendy dominikańskie [Dominican legends]. Translated and compiled by J. Salij. O.P. Poznań: Wydawnictwo W drodze, 1982.

Mariategui, J. "Un Santo Mulato en la Lima seicentista." *Revista peruana de epidemiologia* 8, no. 2, (December 1995): pp. 43–50, https://sisbib.unmsm.edu.pe/bVrevistas/epidemiologia/v08_n2/Un%20Santo%20Mulato.htm.

"Protagonista recuerda milagro de canonización de San Martín de Porres." https://www.aciprensa.com/noticias/protagonista-recuerda-milagro-de-canonizacion-de-san-martin-de-porres.

"Revelan detalles de milagros que llevaron a los altares a San Martín de Porres." https://www.aciprensa.com/noticias/revelan-detalles-de-milagros-que-llevaron-a-los-altares-a-san-martin-de-porres#.URF53vKGmSo.

Valdez, J.M. *Vida admirabile del bienventurado fray Martin de Porres, Huerta y Campresores-Editores*. Lima, 1863.

ST. PADRE PIO

Alimenti, D. *Ojciec Pio*. Gorle: Velar, 1988.

Allegri, R. *Cuda Ojca Pio* [Miracles of Padre Pio]. Kraków: Wydawnictwo WAM, 1999.

———. *I miracoli di padre Pio*. Kraków: WAM, 1999.

Bejda, H. *Księga 100 wielkich cudów* [Book of 100 great miracles]. Kraków: Dom Wydawniczy Rafael, 2005.

———. *Nawróceni* [Converted]. Kraków: Dom Wydawniczy Rafael, 2008.

Błogosławiony Ojciec Pio z Pietrelciny: Żywy obraz Chrystusa Ukrzyżowanego i Zmartwychwstałego [Blessed Padre Pio of Pietrelcina: A living image of the crucified and risen Christ]. Edited by G. Majka, O.F.M. Cap. Kraków: Wydaw. M, 2000.

Camillieri, R. *Błogosławiony Ojciec Pio: Droga do świętości* [Blessed Padre Pio: The path to holiness]. Wrocław: Wydaw. SEMEN, 1999.

"Carlo Campanini." http://www.mymovies.it/dizionario/biblio.asp?a=1009.

Contald, T. "Historia uzdrowienia Consiglii de Martino." Translated by R. Cielicki, O.F.M. Cap. *Głos Ojca Pio* 115, no. 1 (2019). https://glosojcapio.pl/swietosc/item/202-historia-uzdrowienia-consiglii-de-martino.

"Decretum super miraculo [Miracle for beatification]." *Acta Apostolicae Sedis* [Acts of the Apostolic See] 91 (1999): pp. 587–589.

"Decretum super miraculo [Miracle for canonization]." *Acta Apostolicae Sedis* [Acts of the Apostolic See] 94 (2002) pp. 491–493.

Fragmenty wypowiedzi C. Campaniniego za: Renzo Allegri, Cuda Ojca Pio [Excerpts from statements by C. Campanini cit. por.: Miracles of Padre Pio].

Gaeta, S. *Błogosławiony Ojciec Pio: Stygmaty wiary*. Kraków: Wydawnictwo WAM, 1999.

Guitton, J. and J.-J. Antier. *Tajemne moce wiary: Znaki i cuda* [The mysterious power of faith: Signs and miracles]. Warszawa: Oficyna Wydawniczo-Poligraficzna Adam, 1997.

http://www.teleradiopadrepio.it/interviste_record_long.php?Rif=589. [Interview with Benvenuto Campaninim.]

Ippolito. M.L. *Cud kanonizacyjny Ojca Pio: Uzdrowienie Matteo—relacja matki*. Warszawa: Wydawnictwo Marianów, 2003.

Ippolito. M.L. *Cud kanonizacyjny Ojca Pio: Uzdrowienie Matteo—relacja matki*. Warszawa: Wydawnictwo Marianów, 2003.

Majka, G.F., O.F.M. Cap. *Na drodze do Boga: Życie i wybrane pisma O. Pio kapucyna stygmatyka* [On the path to God: The life and selected writings of Fr. Pio the Capuchin Stigmatist]. Kraków: Kapucyni, 1984.

Miesięcznik Rodzin Katolickich Cuda i łaski Boże [Catholic families monthly magazine God's miracles and graces], no. 6 (2004).

———, no. 9 (2008).

Ojciec, P. *Osobowość i posługa w relacjach współczesnych*. Edited by Irena Burchacka. Warszawa: Instytut Prasy i Wydawnictw Novum, 1988.

Peroni, L. *Ojciec Pio* 1, no. 2 (2008).

Sbalchiero, P. *Ojciec Pio: Święty stygmatyk z Pietrelciny* [Padre Pio: The stigmatic saint of Pietrelcina]. Poznań: Święty Wojciech, 2010.

Schug, J.A., O.F.M. Cap. *Kocham wszystkich jednakowo: Ojciec Pio. Łódź: Archidiecezjalne Wydawnictwo Łódzkie, 1997.*

Winowska, M. *Prawdziwe oblicze Ojca Pio OFM Cap. Kaplan i apostoł*. London-Warszawa: Veritas Foundation Publication Centre, Wydawnictwo Michalineum, 1999.

ST. STANISLAUS KOSTKA

Badeni, J., S.I. *Św. Stanisław Kostka*. Kraków: Wydaw. OO. Jezuitów, 1921.

Bejda, H. *Wielka księga polskich świętych* [The great book of Polish saints]. Kraków: Dom Wydawniczy Rafael, 2015.

Bońkowski, S. "Święty Stanisław Kostka." In *Polscy święci*, edited by Joachim Roman Bar, vol. 8. Warszawa: Akademia Teologii Katolickiej, 1987.

Bońkowski, S. and J. Majkowski, S.J. "Stanisław Kostka." In *Nasi święci: Polski słownik hagiograficzny*, edited by Aleksandra Witkowska, O.S.U. Poznań: Księgarnia św. Wojciecha, 1999.

Jestem stworzony do rzeczy wyższych: Święty Stanisław Kostka—patron Polski, patron młodzieży. Kraków: Wydawnictwo Św. Stanisława, 2018.

"ŁASKI I CUDA ŚW. STANISŁAWA KOSTKI—1." http://skostka.blogspot.com/2010/09/aski-i-cuda-1.html.

Majkowski, J., S.J. "Stanisław Kostka." In *Hagiografia polska: Słownik bio-bibliograficzny*, vol. 2, edited by Romuald Gustaw, O.F.M. Poznań-Warszawa-Lublin: Księgarnia św. Wojciecha, 1972.

Miesięcznik Rodzin Katolickich Nasza Arka [Catholic families monthly magazine our ark], no. 9 (2008).

Pruszcz, P.H. *Kleynoty stołecznego miasta Krakowa* [Gemstones of the city of Craow]. Kraków: KAW, 1983.

Relacya albo krotkie opisanie Cudow niektorych y dobrodzieystw przednieyssych, B. Stanislawa Kostki Soc: Iesu. Piotrkowczyk Andrzej, w drukarniey Andrz. Piotrk. typogr. K.I.M. Roku Panskiego, 1630.

Strojnowski, J. *Anioł ziemski z Rostkowa: Opowieść na historycznych danych oparta*. Plock: Bracia Detrych, 1936.

Święty Stanisław Kostka, Płock: n.p., 1995.

Tamburinus, M.A. *Vita di S. Stanislao Kostka della Compagnia di Gesù*, Nella stamperia di Antonio de' Rossi, nella Strada del Seminario Romano, 1727.

Tygodnik Rodzin Katolickich Źródło [Catholic families weekly spring] 33, numer specjalny poświęcony św. Stanisławowi Kostce, oprac. H. Bejda (2018).

Warszawski, J., S.I. *Największy z międzynarodowych Polaków Św. Stanisław Kostka: Opowieść—rozprawka o świętej woli, wzruszającym nabożeństwie—i wielkich cudach* [The greatest of international Poles St. Stanislaus Kostka: A story—a treatise on holy will, moving devotion—and great miracles]. Rzym-Chicago: Sacred Heart Mission House, 1961.

Żywoty Świętych Patronów polskich, napisal X. Piotr Pękalski Ś. T. Dr. Kan. Stróż Ś. Grobu Chrystusowego: Z ośmią rycinami [Lives of the holy patron saints of Poland, written by Fr. Piotr Pękalski St. T. Dr. Kan. Guardian of the Holy Sepulchre of Christ: With eight illustrations]. Kraków: 1862.

ST. MARY OF JESUS CRUCIFIED (MARIAM BAOUARDY)

Brunot, A. *Miriam: Mała Arabka. Siostra Maria od Jezusa Ukrzyżowanego*. Gdańsk: Exter, 2006.

"Canonization of blessed Mariam Baouardy 1846–1878 sister Mary of Jesus Crucified, Carmelite of Bethlehem." carmeliteinstitute.net.

"Decretum super dubio [Biography]." *Acta Apostolicae Sedis* [Acts of the Apostolic See] 74 (1982): pp. 355–360.

"Decretum super dubio [Miracle for beatification]." *Acta Apostolicae Sedis* [Acts of the Apostolic See] 76 (1984): pp. 61–63.

"Decretum super miraculo [Miracle for canonization]." *Acta Apostolicae Sedis* [Acts of the Apostolic See] 108, no. 12 (2016): pp. 1439–1441.

Miesięcznik Rodzin Katolickich Cuda i łaski Boże [Catholic families monthly magazine God's miracles and graces], no. 12 (2011).

p. Maria Lucyna od, K., O.C.D. "Droga do kanonizacji Małej Arabki otwarta." *Głos Karmelu* 2 (2015).

Praśkiewicz, S., O.C.D. "Cud do kanonizacji siostry Marii od Jezusa Ukrzyżowanego." Karmel.pl. https://www.karmel.pl/cud-do-kanonizacji-sw-marii-od-jezusa-ukrzyzowanego/.

———. *Cuda przedłożone Stolicy Apostolskiej i kanonicznie zatwierdzone do gloryfikacji najnowszych świętych i błogosławionych Karmelu Terezjańskiego* [Miracles submitted to the Holy See and canonically approved for the glorification of the latest saints and blesseds from the Order of Discalced Carmelites].

———. "Cud do beatyfikacji siostry Marii od Jezusa Ukrzyżowanego." Karmel.pl. https://www.karmel.pl/cud-do-beatyfikacji-siostry-marii-od-jezusa-ukrzyzowanego.

"AWAY FROM ME, SATAN!" POWERFUL EXORCISTS

Allegri, R. *Cuda Ojca Pio* [Padre Pio's miracles]. Kraków: Wydawnictwo WAM, 2003.

Amorth, G. *Egzorcyści i psychiatrzy* [Esorcisti e psichiatri or Exorcists and psychiatrists]. Częstochowa: Edycja Świętego Pawła, 1999.

———. *Wspomnienia egzorcysty: Moje życie w walce z szatanem* [Memoirs of an exorcist: My life fighting Satan]. Edited by Marco Tosatti. Częstochowa: Edycja Świętego Pawła, 2010.

Cattaneo, P. *Jak bronić się przed diabłem* [How to defend yourself against the devil]. Częstochowa: Edycja św. Pawła, 2013.

———. *San Ciriaco: Diacono e martire: Culto, miracoli, escorcismi dai tempi antichi a oggi*. 2nd ed. Feletto Umberto, Tavagnacco: 2016.

de Meo, C. *Matteo: Losy zakonnika z Agnone* [Matteo: The fate of the friar from Agnone]. Kondrat-Media, 2015.

Life of Saint Benedict, 2nd Book of the Dialogues of Saint Gregory the Great. https://www.benedyktynki-sakramentki.org/mediateka/czytelnia/zywot-sw-benedykta/.

Pęzioł, J. *Mocą imienia Jezusa: Z Fr.infułatem Janem Pęziołem, egzorcystą rozmawia Fr.Rafał Olchawski* [By the power of the name of Jesus: Protonotary apostolic Jan Pęzioł, interviewed by Rafal Olchawski]. Lublin: Wydawnictwo Gaudium, 2017.

Raymond of Capua. *Rajmund z Kapui, Żywot świętej Katarzyny ze Sieny* [Saint Catherine of Siena by Raymond of Capua]. Translated by K. Suszyło, O.P. Poznań: Wydawnictwo W drodze, 2010.

Royt, J., P. Sommer, and M. Stecker. *Sazavsky Klašter, Narodni pamatkovy ustav*. Praha, 2013.

Ryszka, C. *Spotkania z egzorcystami* [Meeting with exorcists]. Bytom: Oficyna Wydawnicza 4K, 2004.

Svatý Prokop divotvůrce, Z dobovych pramenů zpracovali otcove OSBM v Sazavskem klaštere. Olomouc: Vydal Řad sv. Basila Velikeho v CR v Sazave, 2003.

ST. HYACINTH

Herbert, A.J. *Raised from the Dead*. Gasconia, NC: TAN Books, 1986.

Jacek, St.. *Życie i cuda*. Poznań: Wydawnictwo W drodze, 2019.

———. *Życiorys-modlitwy, pieśni*. Warszawa: Akademia Teologii Katolickiej, 1989.

O Żywocie Cudach, Y Postępku Kanonizaciey Błogosławionego Jacinkta, fundatora pierwszego w Polszcze: braciej Zakonu Kaznodzieyskiego Dominika świętego. Kraków: Czworo Ksiąg, 1595, https://www.wbc.poznan.pl/dlibra/publication/5410.

"Sancti Hyacintho." *Acta sanctorum augusti* 3, no. 37 (1737): pp. 344–379.

Salij, J., O.P., ed. *Legendy dominikańskie* [Dominican legends/Legends of the Dominican order]. Translated by J. Salij, O.P. Poznań: Wydawnictwo W drodze, 1982.

Spież, J.A., O.P. *Św. Jacek Odrowąż*. Kraków: Wydaw WAM, 2007.

Woroniecki, J., O.P. *Św. Jacek Odrowąż i sprowadzenie Zakonu Kaznodziejskiego do Polski* [St. Hyacinth of Poland and the introduction of the Order of Preachers in Poland]. Kraków-Katowice: Esprit, 2007.

ST. RITA OF CASCIA

SPECIAL THANKS TO: ROLAND KAUTH I AGNIESZKA RZEMIENIEC—FOR YOUR HELP IN GATHERING SOURCES

"4 Fragmenty wypowiedzi E. Tzoka za" [Excerpts from E. Tzok's statement cit. por.]. *Miesięcznik Rodzin Katolickich Cuda i łaski Boże* [Catholic families monthly magazine God's miracles and graces], no. 5 (2006).

"Breve racconto della vita e dei miracoli della beata Rita: Dipinti del XVII Secolo del Monastero di Santa Rita da Cascia, Testi di Pietro Amato, Mario Bergamo, Toti Carpentieri." Cascia, Chiesa di S. Francesco d'Assisi, 21 maggio–18 luglio 1993.

Carpentieri, T. "Per Grazia Ricevuta: Ex-voto artistici conservati nel Monastero di Santa Rita da Cascia." Cascia, Chiesa di S. Francesco d'Assisi, 21 maggio-30 giugno 1992.

Dawidowski, W., O.S.A. *Święta Rita*. Kraków: Wydawnictwo WAM, 2008.

Giovetti, P. *Rita z Cascii: Święta od spraw niemożliwych*. Częstochowa: Edycja Św. Pawła, 2010.

Kosloski, P. "I miracoli straordinari che hanno portato alla canonizzazione di Santa Rita." Aleteia. May 22, 2018. https://it.aleteia.org/2018/05/22/miracoli-che-hanno-portato-canonizzazione-santa-rita/.

Lemoine, J. *Rita: Święta od spraw trudnych i beznadziejnych*. Kraków: WITKM, 1994.

Miesięcznik Rodzin Katolickich Cuda i łaski Boże [Catholic families monthly magazine God's miracles and graces], no. 5 (2006) and no. 5 (2014).

Miracoli Santa Rita da Cascia. https://digilander.libero.it/raxdi/miracoli.htm.

Monastero Santa Rita da Cascia. https://santaritadacascia.org.

Odorisio, M.L. "La narrazione 'miracolosa.' I miracoli di S.Rita da Cascia (XV–XVII sec.)." http://dprs.uniroma1.it/sites/default/files/22.html.

Pabis, M. *Cuda świętej Rity, patronki w sprawach najtrudniejszych*. Kraków: Dom Wydawniczy Rafael, 2012.

"Potwierdzone cuda świętej Rity! Głusi słyszą, niemówiący mówią, a niewidomi odzyskują wzrok!" Fronda.pl. May 22, 2016. https://www.fronda.pl/a/potwierdzone-cuda-swietej-rity-glusi-slysza-niemowiacy-mowia-a-niewidomi-odzyskuja-wzrok,72048.html.

Vida y milagros de la gloriosa Santa Rita de Cassia del orden de los ermitaños de San Agustin, Tomás (O.S.A.) Dávila, José Badarán (O.S.A.), en la imprenta de Francisco Sanz, 1705. Breve racconto della vita, e miracoli della b. Rita da Cascia. Nella Stamperia della R.C. Apost., 1628.

Vite della B. Chiara di Montefalco e della B. Rita da Cascia dell'ordine degli eremiti di S. Agostino scritte dal R.mo P. maestro Lorenzo Tardy. Lorenzo Tardy, dalla tipografia Manfredi, 1841.

ST. FRANCIS OF ASSISI

Chesterton, G.K. *Święty Franciszek z Asyżu* [Saint Francis of Assisi]. Warszawa: PAX, 1976.

de Voragine, J. "Legenda na dzień św. Franciszka 4 października" [Legend for St. Francis feast on Oct. 4]. In *The Golden Legend*, translated by J. Pleziowa, pp. 465–477. Warszawa: Prószyński i S-ka, 2000.

Franciszek z Asyżu, św., Pisma św. Franciszka i św. Klary. Warszawa: . OO. Kapucyni, 1992.

Kwiatki świętego Franciszka z Asyżu [Little flowers of St. Francis]. Translated by L. Staff.

Warszawa: Wydawnictwo Sara, 2000.

Le Goff, J. *Święty Franciszek z Asyżu*. Warszawa: Czytelnik, 2001.

Niewiadomy, S., O.F.M. *Obrazki z życia Świętego Franciszka z Asyżu*. Kalwaria Zebrzydowska: Calvarianum, 1989.

Ryś, G. *Franciszek: Życie—miejsca—słowa*. Kraków: Wydawnictwo św. Stanisława BM, 2013.

Thomas of Celano. *The Treatise on the Miracles of Saint Francis*. https://franciscantradition.org.

———. "Treatise on the Miracles of Saint Francis by Thomas of Celano." In *Francis of Assisi: Early Documents, vol. 2: The Founder*, edited by R.J. Armstrong, J.A. Wayne Hellmann, and W.J. Short. New York: New City Press, 2000.

Żywczyński, M. *Franciszek największy święty, jakiego zna historia*. Niepokalanów: Bratni Zew, 2000.

ST. PHILIP NERI

Bacci, P.G. *The Life of Saint Philip Neri, Apostle of Rome, and Founder of the Congregation of the Oratory*. Vol. 2. London, Dublin, and Derby: T. Richardson, 1847.

Bombardier, J., C.O.R. "*Św. Filip prorok radości*." *Oratoriana* 49 (August 2004): pp. 56–79.

Pabis, J., Fr., ed. *Life of St. Philip Neri*. Vol. 20. Translated by Fr. J. Pabis. Tarnów: Filipinów, 1931.

Turks, P., C.O.R. *Filip Neri, czyli ogień radości*. Oficyna Współczesna, 2001.

List of Illustration Sources

All photos are as given in the original Polish edition.

FRONT MATTER

Wikimedia/© Alvesgaspar/ CC BY-SA 4.0, 5© Karl Agre/Flickr.com courtesy of Fr. Krzysztofa Jędrzejewskiego MIC, Sanktuarium w Licheniu [Licheń Sanctuary]. © Caffe_Paradiso/Flickr.com, © Marta Bejda 20-21 Fra Angelico/ © EastNews

Photos from the table of contents are included in the descriptions of the ones from chapters dedicated to each saint

1. ST. GEMMA GALGANI

Wikimedia public domain © Elena Korn/Fotolia.com © Fistra/Fotolia.com, Wikimedia public domain, /Flickr.com, Wikiedia/ Opusdei28/Creative Commons Attribution-Share Alike 4.0 International license, ©Toshiki/ Flickr.com,© Bluemoonart/Cathy/Flickr.com, ©Bluemoonart/Cathy/Flickr. com, Wikimedia/© José Luiz Bernardes Ribeiro / CC BY-SA 3.0,© Erwin/Flickr.com, 632 Wikimedia/Manuelarosi/ Creative Commons Attribution-Share Alike 3.0 Unported license, Wikimedia/© Abraham Sobkowski OFM/ Creative Commons Attribution-Share Alike 4.0 International, 3.0 Unported, 2.5

2. ST. PEREGRINE LAZIOSI

Wikimedia/public domain, ©Alexander Szep/Flickr.com, ©Thank You/Flickr.com, ©Alexander Szep/Flickr.com, Wikimedia/ ©Mx. Granger/Creative Commons CCO 1.0 Universal Public

Domain Dedication; ©Tim Buss/Flickr.com, Wikimedia/© Krzysztof Wysocki/ GNU Free Documentation License

3. ST. TERESA BENEDICTA OF THE CROSS

Wikimedia/ © Gerd Eichmann/Creative Commons Attribution-ShareAlike 4.0 International, Wikimedia/© Julo/public domain, Wikimedia/©Tanzania/ Creative Commons Attribution-Share Alike 3.0 Unported, Wikimedia/© Andreas Praefcke/public domain, Wikimedia/© Kaos pl / GNU Free Documentation License/Creative Commons Attribution-ShareAlike 3.0, Wikimedia/© Julo/public domain, Wikimedia/© Takkk/ Creative Commons Attribution-Share Alike 3.0 Unported, Wikimedia/© China Crisis/ Creative Commons Attribution-Share Alike 3.0 Unported, Wikimedia/ © pzk net/ Creative Commons Attribution-ShareAlike 3.0., 60 Wikimedia/ © Achim Raschka (talk)/C.C by S.A 4.0, Wikimedia/© Ikar.us (talk)/ Creative Commons Attribution 3.0 Germany, Wikimedia/© Anne-Madeleine Plum/ GNU Free Documentation License, Wikimedia/ © Achim Raschka (talk)/C.C by S.A 4.0, 63 Wikimedia/© Jar.ciurus/Creative Commons Attribution-ShareAlike 3.0 Poland, Wikimedia/ © Kobretti/ Creative Commons Attribution-ShareAlike 3.0 Poland, Wikimedia/ © Vincent de Groot/ license CC BY-SA

4. ST. HEDWIG, QUEEN OF POLAND

Wikimedia/public domain, © Alicja Marchewicz, © Poznaniak/Creative Commons Attribution-ShareAlike 2.5

5. ST. JOHN OF RICE (MACÍAS)

Wikimedia/© Ingo Mehling/ Creative Commons Attribution-Share Alike 3.0 Unported, Wikimedia/Cicero Moraes/ Creative Commons Attribution-Share Alike 4.0 International license, Wikimedia/© Alfonso24/public domain, Wikimedia/© Miguel Chong / Creative Commons Attribution-Share Alike 3.0 Unported, Wikimedia/ © Alfonso24/public domain, Wikimedia/public domain, Wikimedia/© Diego Delso/ Attribution-Share Alike 4.0 International, Wikimedia/ , © Diego Delso/ Attribution-Share Alike 4.0 International, © Garciadelosbarros/ Creative Commons Attribution-Share Alike 4.0 International/Wikimedia/public domain, Wikimedia

6. ST. LAURA MONTOYA

Wikimedia/©Raomir Ramirez Morales/ Creative Commons Attribution-Share Alike 3.0 Unported, Wikimedia public domain. Wikimedia/©Melissa Sanchez A. Creative Commons Attribution-Share Alike 4.0 International, Wikimedia/ © Santiago Pareja Echeveri Creative Commons Attribution--Share Alike 3.0 Unported. Wikimedia/©Santiago Pareja Echeveri/Creative Commons Attribution-Share Alike 3.0 Unported

7. ST. MAXIMILIAN MARIA KOLBE

Wikimedia/public domain, Wikimedia/CC0 1.0 , Wikimedia/CC0 1.0 , 105 © Alicja Marchewicz, Wikimedia/© czarnowski/CC BY-SA 3.0, 107 Narodowe Archiwum Cyfrowe [National Digital Archives], Wikimedia/ ©Dnalor 01 / CC-BY-SA 3.0, @cesscasawin/fotolia.com, Wikimedia/©Jean-Christophe BENOIST/ Creative Commons Attribution-Share Alike 3.0 Unported, Wikimedia/©Gianni Careddu / Creative Commons Attribution-Share Alike 4.0 International, Wikimedia/©Jakub Halun / GNU Free Documentation License, Wikimedia/©czarnowski/CC BY-SA 3.0, © www.pastoralcentre.pl

8. MIRACULOUS RESURRECTORS

Wikimedia/public domain, Wikimedia/ ©Wladyslaw/Creative Commons Attribution-ShareAlike 3.0, Wikimedia/ ©Andreas F. Borchert/ Creative Commons Attribution- Share Alike 3.0 Germany license, Wikimedia/© Patricia Drury/ Creative Commons Attribution-ShareAlike 2.0. Wikimedia/©615-Columbano / Creative Commons Attribution-Share Alike 4.0 International license, Wikimedia/© Philippe Alès / Creative Commons Attribution-Share Alike 3.0 Unported license. Wikimedia/ Creative Commons CC0 1.0 Universal Wikimedia/© Utente:Dd11/ Creative Commons Attribution-ShareAlike 3.0. courtesy of Custodian of Sanktuarium Świętego Ojca Świętego Ojca Papczyńskiego[Sanctuary of the Saint Father Papczyński] in Marianki, Góra Kalwaria, courtesy of Custodian of Sanktuarium Świętego Ojca Świętego Ojca Papczyńskiego[Sanctuary of the Saint Father Papczyński] in Marianki, Góra Kalwaria.

9. ST. PATRICK

Wikimedia/public domain, Wikimedia/ ©Eckhard Pecher / Creative Commons Attribution 2.5 Generic license. Wikimedia/©Patnac/ GNU Free Documentation License, Wikimedia/GNU Free Documentation License, Wikimedia/ ©Mike Boehmer/ Creative Commons Attribution-ShareAlike 2.0, Wikimedia/uggboy Creative Commons Attribution-ShareAlike 2.0, 148 Wikimedia/©J.M. Luijt. cropped by MathKnight/Creative Commons Attribution-ShareAlike 2.5. Andrew Fleck/Flickr.com, Wikimedia/ ©Ardfern/Creative Commons Attribution-Share Alike 3.0 Unported license, Wikimedia/©N-heyob/Creative Commons Attribution-Share Alike 4.0 International license, Wikimedia/ ©Elkington & Co. /Creative Commons CCO 1.0 Universal Public Domain Dedication, Wikimedia/ Sicarr/Creative Commons Attribution 2.0 Generic license. Wikimedia/ ©August Schwerdfeger / Creative Commons Attribution-Share Alike 4.0 International license, 151 Wikimedia/ ©Chmee2/ Creative Commons Attribution-ShareAlike 3.0. Wikimedia/ ©Self / Creative Commons Attribution-ShareAlike 3.0, Wikimedia/ Amockens / Creative Commons Attribution-Share Alike 4.0 International, Wikimedia/ ©Chmee2 or Mates/Creative Commons Attribution-ShareAlike 3.0., Wikimedia/ ©Alan James Croagh Patrick Pilgrim Sunday / CC BY-SA 2.0, Wikimedia/ ©Paul Mcllroy Croagh Patrick / CC BY-SA 2.0, Wikimedia/© rann áirtí anai nid Creative Commons Attribution-Share Alike 3.0 Unported license.

LIST OF ILLUSTRATION SOURCES

10. ST. RAPHAEL KALINOWSKI

Wikimedia, public domain, courtesy of Monastery of Discalced Carmelite Friars in Czerna.

11. ST. JOSÉ SÁNCHEZ DEL RÍO

Wikimedia/public domain, Wikimedia/ ©Alejandro Linares Garcia/Creative Commons Attribution-Share Alike 3.0 Unported license, ©Wdrdp/ Wikimedia/public domain, Wikimedia/ ©Luisalvaz/Creative Commons Attribution-Share Alike 4.0 International license, Wikimedia/© thor Thelmadatter/Creative Commons Attribution-Share Alike 3.0 Unported license, Wikimedia/ AlexandLeigh/Creative Commons Attribution-ShareAlike 3.0/ Wikimedia/public domain

12. ST. TERESA OF JESUS OF THE ANDES

Wikimedia/public domain, Wikimedia/© Marqués de la Force/ Creative Commons Attribution- Share Alike 3.0 Unported license, Wikimedia/ ©refractor/Creative Commons Attribution 2.0 Generic license, ©Luis Roteli/ Flickr.com, • ©Fundacion mi parque/Flickr.com, ©fotohbeens/Flickr.com, 222 Wikimedia/public domain, ©Space Ghots/Flickr.com/ 223 ©kcidyaguirre campos/Flickr.com, ©La de Azabache Cabellera/Flickr.com, ©gripspix/ Flickr.com.

13. ST. MOTHER TERESA

Wikimedia/ ©Kumar Rajendran/public domain, Wikimedia/ ©Vikramjit Kakati/ CC BY-SA 3.0, 225 Wikimedia ©Kingkongphoto & www.celebrity-photos.com/ CC BY-SA 2.0, Wikimedia/ ©M.Peinado/ CC BY 3.0 es, Wikimedia/©-flowcomm - Flickr.com: ©Missionaries of Charity Mother House/CC BY 2.0, ©NicPic/Flickr.com, Wikimedia/ ©Thamizhpparithi Maari/ CC BY-SA 4.0, ©Darkone, MichaelJanich, Hph on de.Wikimedia/CC BY-SA 3.0, Wikimedia ©Fennec/ public domain, Wikimedia/public domain, ©NicPic/Flickr.com, Archives and Records Administration/public domain, Wikimedia/ ©Manfredo Ferrari/ CC BY-SA 4.0, Wikimedia/ ©Steve Browne & John Verkleir/ CC BY 2.0, 231 Wikimedia/ ©Danielmkd/ Public Domain, Wikimedia/ ©thotfulspot/ CC BY 2.0, Wikimedia/ ©Arianit/CC BY-SA 4.0

14. ST. ANDREW BOBOLA

Wikimedia/© Lowdown/ CC BY-SA 4.0, Wikimedia/public domain, Wikimedia/ ©Hubert Śmietanka/ CC BY-SA 2.5, Wikimedia/ Lowdown/ CC BY-SA 4.0, Wikimedia/ Lowdown/ CC BY-SA 4.0, Wikimedia/© Albertus teolog CC BY-SA 4.0, ©Przemysław Jahr Wikimedia Commons//public domain, ©Przemysław Jahr / Wikimedia Commons/public domain

15. ST. CONRAD OF PARZHAM

Wikimedia/public domain, ©S. Finner: Siddhartha Finner, Dipl. Ing.-Architektur/CC BY-SA 3.0, Wikimedia/ ©MOs810/CC BY-SA 4.0, 257 Marchal/Flickr.com, Wikimedia/ Konrad Lackerbeck/ CC BY-SA 2.5 Wikimedia/ ©Aconcagua/ CC BY-SA 3.0, Wikimedia/© Konrad Lackerbeck / CC BY 3.0, Wikimedia/ public domain, © S. Finner: Siddhartha Finner, Dipl. Ing.-Architektur/ CC BY-SA 3.0, Wikimedia © Konrad Lackerbeck / CC BY 3.0, ©kfrauenbundhausimwald/Flickr.com, ©HEN MAGONZA/Flickr.com, ©Croagh Patrick Pilgrim Sunday / CC BY-SA 2.0, Wikimedia/© Paul McIlroy/Croagh Patrick / CC BY-SA 2.0, Wikimedia/© rann áirtí anai nid/Creative Commons Attribution-Share Alike 3.0 Unported license. * Wikimedia/© Bene16/CC BY 2.5, Wikimedia/© MOs810/CC BY-SA 4.0, Wikimedia/© Frank/ CC BY-SA 3.0, Wikimedia/ ©Kirchenfan//public domain, Wikimedia/© Andreas Janik/ CC BY-SA 3.0, Wikimedia/©ekpah/CC0

16. ST. NICHOLAS OF FLÜE

Wikimedia/ Wolkenkratzer/ CC BY-SA 4.0, Wikimedia/© Lutz Fischer-Lamprecht/ CC BY-SA 4.0, © https://www.erzbistum-koeln. de/thema/auszeit/ blogs/Bruder-Klaus-der-Volks-Heilige, Wikimedia/ ©Wandervogel/ CC BY-SA 3.0, Wikimedia/public domain, ©ben ter mull/Flickr.com, Wikimedia/public domain, Wikimedia/© PaterMcFly/ CC BY-SA 3.0, Wikimedia/ ©Berthold Werner /public domain, Wikimedia/© Ikiwaner/ CC BY-SA 3.0, ALVIER / Flickr.com, Wikimedia/© Ginkgo2g/ CC BY-SA 4.0, 281 Wikimedia/© Roland Zumbühl of Picswiss/ CC BY-SA 3.0

17. ST. KATERI TEKAKWITHA

©Jean-Guy Duc/Flickr.com, Wikimedia/public domain, Fahrenheit 451, © Library of Congress/ public domain, https://quizlet.com, ©Fr. Shawn Tunink/ Flickr.com,Wikimedia/© Eden, Janine and Jim / CC BY 2.0, 292 Wikimedia/ ©Nheyob/ CC BY-SA 3.0, Wikimedia/ ©Dieterkaupp/ CC BY-SA 4.0, 293 Wikimedia/© Andrew Balet/ CC BY 2.5, ©Pat//Flickr.com,

18. ST. BERNADETTE SOUBIROUS

Clamon/Fotolia.com, Wikimedia/public domain, Wikimedia/© Charnoff/ CC BY-SA 4.0, Wikimedia/© Milorad Pavlek/ CC BY-SA 3.0, Wikimedia/ Moreau. henri/ CC BY-SA 3.0, Wikimedia/public domain, Manolo Guallart/Flickr.com, 301 Wikimedia/public domain, Wikimedia/public domain, ©Roock at Polish Wikimedia/ CC BY-SA 3.0, Wikimedia /©José Luiz Bernardes Ribeiro/ CC BY-SA 3.0, Wikimedia/ ©Ireneed/ CC BY-SA 3.0

19. ST. MARIA ELISABETH HASSELBLAD

Wikimedia/public domain, Wikimedia/ ©AngleAndDawn/CC BY-SA 4.0, Wikimedia/ ©Boston at English Wikimedia & John Stephen Dwyer/ CC BY-SA 3.0, Wikimedia/ ©Vitaly repin/ CC BY-SA 4.0, Wikimedia/© Jerzy Strzelecki/ CC BY 3.0, Wikimedia/ ©Eoghanacht/ CC0, Wikimedia/© Eupe/ CC BY-SA 3.0

20. LARGE-SCALE MIRACLES

Wikimedia/public domain, Wikimedia/© Didier Descouens/CC BY-SA 4.0, Wikimedia/ ©Quodvultdeus/CC BY 3.0, www.bialystok.naszemiasto.pl, Wikimedia/© Bonio/ CC BY-SA 3.0, Wikimedia/© Sailko/ CC BY 3.0, Wikimedia/ public domain

21. ST. ANTHONY OF PADUA

Wikimedia/ ©Cicero Moraes/ CC BY 3.0, Wikimedia/public domain. Wikimedia/© Didier Descouens/ CC BY-SA 4.0 Wikimedia ©nanabou/ CC BY 2.0, Wikimedia/ ©Chris Light/ CC BY-SA 4.0, Wikimedia/ www.tanogabo.it/public domain, Wikimedia/ ©Didier Descouens/ CC BY-SA 4.0, Wikimedia/© Aldiaz di Wikimedia in italiano/ CC BY-SA 3.0, Wikimedia/ ©Didier Descouens/ CC BY-SA 4.0, Wikimedia/© Lovio - mia foto/ public domain, ©Richard Orr/Flickr.com, Wikimedia/© Didier Descouens/CC BY-SA 4.0, Wikimedia/ ©Lovio - mia foto/ public domain, Wikimedia/© Mfran22/CC BY-SA 4.0, 353 Wikimedia/ ©Didier Descouens/ CC BY-SA 4.0, Wikimedia/public domain, ©Reliquiarian, 354 Wikimedia/ ©Nheyob/ CC BY-SA 4.0, Wikimedia/© Caramo/ CC BY-SA 3.0, Wikimedia ©Kazimierz Mendlik/ CC BY-SA 3.0

22. ST. MARIA GORETTI

Wikimedia/public domain, Sharon molierus/Flickr.com, Wikimedia/public domain, © orene rangel torres/Flickr.com, Wikimedia/ ©Torvindus--commonswiki/ CC BY-SA 3.0, Wikimedia/© Stefano. nicolucci at Italian Wikimedia/ CC BY-SA 3.0, ©conly marie /Flickr.com. ©Santa Maria Goretti 2010/ Flickr.com, Wikimedia/ ©Nheyob/ CC BY-SA 4.0, Pinterest, ©www. worthpoint.com/, ©Beati e santi / Flickr.com

23. STS. JACINTA AND FRANCISCO MARTO

all photos © Wincenty Łaszewski, archival photos are the courtesy of Wincenty Łaszewskiego, colorized photos are from Fahrenheit 451

24. ST. CHRISTOPHER MAGELLANES

Jara and His Twenty-Four Companions

Wikimedia/public domain

25. ST. JEAN MARIE VIANNEY

© Daily Breakfast/Flickr.com, Wikimedia/public domain, © milton mic/Flickr.com, Christine Petitjean/Flickr.com, © Fr. Patrick Anderson/Flickr.com Wikimedia/ © Paul C. Maurice/ CC BY-SA 3.0, Wikimedia/©Herwig Reidlinger/ CC BY-SA 3.0, Francisco/Flickr.com, © sandomars / Flickr.com, © Megara Liancourt/Flickr.com, © Pater JPM/Flickr.com, © Anne L56/Flickr.com

26. MIRACULOUS GIFTS, CHARISMS, AND OTHER PHENOMENA

Wikimedia/public domain, Wikimedia/ © Denys3200/public domain, ©Combusken/Wikimedia/public domain, Wikimedia/Sailko/ CC BY 3.0, ©adam dal pozzo/Flickr.com, © stigmata 175/ Pinterest, Wikimedia/ ©Zarateman/Creative Commons CC0 1.0 Universal Public Domain Dedication

27. ST. ALPHONSA OF THE IMMACULATE CONCEPTION

Wikimedia/© Wouter Hagens/public domain, Wikimedia/©Jovianeye/ CC BY-SA 3.0, Wikimedia/public domain, Wikimedia/ ©Mathen Payyappilly Palakkappilly (User:Achayan)/ CC BY-SA 3.0, Wikimedia/ ©Achayan / CC BY 3.0, Wikimedia/©Simynazareth/ CC BY 2.5, Wikimedia/© Rojypala/ CC BY-SA 3.0, Wikimedia/© Simynazareth/ CC BY 2.5

28. ST. PIUS X

Wikimedia/public domain, Catawiki, Wikimedia/ Biser Todorov/ CC BY 4.0, Riccardov/ Wikimedia/public domain, https://www.digitalcommonwealth.org,

29. ST. FREI GALVÃO

Wikimedia/© Zééh.mané/ CC BY-SA 3.0, © Márcia/Flickr.com, Wikimedia/ Carolina de Barros / CC BY-SA 4.0 Wikimedia/ © Valter Campanato/ABr - Agência Brasil (ABr/RadioBrás) / CC BY 3.0 br, https://conventodapenha.org.br/dia-de-santo-antonio-de-santana-galvao- o-primeiro-santo-brasileiro/, Wikimedia/© Alexandre Giesbrecht/ CC BY 3.0, © sandra castanhato/Flickr.com, Wikimedia/public domain, Wikimedia/ Carolina de Barros / CC BY-SA 4.0, Wikimedia/ ©Carolina de Barros / CC BY-SA 4.0, Wikimedia/ © Valter Campanato/ ©ABr - Agência Brasil/ CC BY 3.0 br, 500 eraquel heidrich/ Flickr.com 501 Wikimedia/ ©Fabio Pozzebom/ABr - Agência Brasil/ CC BY 3.0, Wikimedia/© Fabio Pozzebom/ABr - Agência Brasil/ CC BY 3.0

30. ST. JOSEPH VAZ

Wikimedia/public domain, ©joegoauk20/Flickr.com, Wikimedia/ ©Anuradha ©Ratnaweera/ CC BY-SA 2.0 Wikimedia/ public domain, 510 © A.Savin (WikiCommons) / FAL, Wikimedia/ ©Bleuchoi/ CC BY-SA 2.0, Wikimedia/ ©Nima Sareh/CC BY 2.0, Wikimedia/© Danny Burke/ CC BY-SA 2.5

31. ST. CHARLES OF MOUNT ARGUS

Wikimedia/public domain, Wikimedia/© Hohenloh/ CC BY- SA 3.0, Wikimedia/© Arch/ public domain, Wikimedia/© Mijnwerker/ CC BY-SA 4.0, © Nik Morris (van Leiden)/Flickr.com, Wikimedia/© Jeroenvan Veen/ CC BY-SA 3.0, Wikimedia/© Otter/ CC BY-SA 3.0, Wiwikwand

33. ST. JOAN OF ARC

Wikimedia/public domain, United States Library of Congress›s Prints and Photographs division, Wikimedia/© Francis MONTIGNON Creative Commons Attribution-ShareAlike 3.0,

34. ST. JANUARIUS

Wikimedia/© Wantay/ CC BY-SA 4.0, Wikimedia/public domain, © MAX Fridman/Flickr.com, Wikimedia/ © Berthold Werner/ CC BY-SA 3.0, © blue st/Flickr.com, hasian flercetiger/Flickr.com © Alerto Cervantes/Flickr.com, Wikimedia/ Wantay/ CC BY-SA 4.0, Piotr Karczewski, © Christian lagat/Flickr.com,© Stefano Flore / Flickr.com,

35. ST. GREGORY THAUMATURGAS

Wikimedia/public domain, Wikimedia/Licencja 3.0, © Georgios Kollidas/ Fotolia.com, Wikimedia/ © Pvasiliadis/ CC BY-SA 3.0

36. ST. GIUSEPPE MOSCATI

Wikimedia/© José Luiz Bernardes Ribeiro / CC BY-SA 4.0, Wikimedia/public domain, Giank/Flickr.com, Wikimedia/© Guybrush Threepwood/ CC BY-SA 3.0, 574 Wikimedia/ public domain, Wikimedia/© Lady of a times/ CC BY-SA 4.0, Wikimedia/ Fiore Silvestro Barbato/ CC BY-SA 2.0, Wikimedia/ © Palickap/ CC BY-SA 4.0 Wikimedia/© IlSistemone/CC BY-SA 3.0, Wikimedia/© Decan/ CC BY-SA 3.0, © Richmond Lim/Flickr.com, © sarah hollowood/ Flickr.com, © jonfholl/Flickr.com, © Cam- Tu Huynh/Flickr.com, © RELIQUIE SANCTORUM OMNIUM/Flickr. com, Wikimedia/© Heinz-Josef Lücking/ CC BY 3.0, Wikimedia/ © Rei Momo/public domain.

37. ST. JOHN BOSCO

Wikimedia/ public domain, Wikimedia/ © Stebunik/ CC BY-SA 3.0

38. MIRACULOUS CHILDREN

Wikimedia/public domain, Wikimedia/© Desconhecido (CNS photo/ courtesy Sainthood Cause of Carlo Acutis), © Imelda Lambortini/Flickr.com, Worthpoint.com, Wikimedia/© Rama/ Creative Commons Attribution--ShareAlike 2.0 Francja, www.Florianskaz.pl, findgrave.com, catholicweekly.com.au, Pinterest.com, Wikimedia/ © Michaelphillipr/Creative Commons Attribution-ShareAlike 3.0, Pep padula/Flickr.com, Wikimedia/ Pascal Bart/ Creative Commons Attribution-Share Alike 4.0 International license, http:// gentedicalabria.blogspot.com/

39. ST. CLARE OF ASSISI

Wikimedia/public domain, Wikimedia/ © Sailko / Creative Commons Attribution-Share Alike 3.0 Unported license, Wikimedia/ © Ludwig Schneider/ CC BY-SA 3.0, © PD/Wikimedia/ public domain, © Bocachete/Wikimedia/ public domain, Wikimedia/© Radomil /CC BY-SA 3.0 catholicsaintmedals.com

40. ST. JOSÉ GABRIEL DEL ROSARIO BROCHERO

Wikimedia public domain, Wikimedia/© Jiròni B. /CC BY-SA 4.0, 610 Wikimedia/ Jofrigerio/ CC BY-SA 4.0, Wikimedia/© Adriel anvoo/ CC BY-SA 4.0

41. ST. GABRIEL POSSENTI

Generic, 2.0 Generic and 1.0 Generic license, Wikimedia/© Miyska/ Creative Commons Attribution-Share Alike 4.0 International license,© Patafisik/ Wikimedia/ public domain, Wikimedia/public domain, ©Patafisik/Wikimedia/ public domain, Wikimedia/ ©Wolfgang Sauber/ CC BY-SA 4.0, Wikimedia/ public domain, adeste.org © Patafisik/ Wikimedia/public domain,Torsten Henning/Wikimedia/public domain, Wikimedia/ ©freegiampi/Creative Commons Attribution-ShareAlike 2.5., Wikimedia/CC0

42. ST. MARTIN DE PORRES

© FAVPNG, © jupiterius/Flickr.com, Pustyniaserca.wordpress. com, drdoom--1618798967103-cathopic/Flickr.com, Wikimedia/public domain, © Magda House/Flickr.com, © rafael reyes /Flickr.com, © Mara/Flickr.com, Mike Davis/ Flickr.com, toshiki/Flickr.com © flannery s./Flickr.com, © Michael/ Flickr.com, www.hanhtrinhductin.com/Flickr.com, ©the gathering place/Flickr.com, hiltonography/Flickr.com, © James/Flickr.com

43. ST. PADRE PIO

Wikimedia/public domain, © Vincenzo De Maria/Flickr.com, © pasquale vitale /Flickr.com, packy 1976/Flickr.com, roberto acuna/ Flickr.com, © Giovanni Cingolani/Fotolia.com, defendero6/Fotolia. com, © angelospeed/ Fotolia.com, Christa Eder/Fotolia.com, Wikimedia/© Mazaki/ CC BY-SA 4.0, © Stanisław Marciniak, Wikimedia/© Lino M - Flickr.com/ CC BY-SA 2.0, © LianeM/Fotolia.com, franciscan universiti pilgrimage/Flickr.com, diegobib/ fotolia.com, © MiTi/fotolia.com, michele masiero /Flickr. com, © valeria2valeria/Flickr.com, Wikimedia/© Itto Ogami/ CC BY 3.0, © saginaw/Flickr.com, © saginaw/Flickr.com, © saginaw/Flickr. com, © indiadiaz/Flickr.com,

44. ST. STANISLAUS KOSTKA

Wikimedia/ Danielkwiat/Creative Commons Attribution-Share Alike 4.0 International, 3.0 Unported, 2.5 Generic, 2.0 Generic and 1.0 Generic license, Wikimedia/ © Danielkwiat/Creative Commons Attribution-Share Alike 4.0 International, 3.0 Unported, 2.5 Generic, 2.0 Generic and 1.0 Generic license, Wikimedia/ © Mariusz82// public domain, Wikimedia/ Bestbudbrian/ Creative Commons Attribution-Share Alike 4.0 International license, Wikimedia/© Sailko/ Creative Commons Attribution-ShareAlike 3.0., Wikimedia/© © Wolfgang Sauber/ Creative Commons Attribution-Share Alike 3.0 Unported, 2.5 Generic, 2.0 Generic and 1.0 Generic license, 678 Wikimedia/ © Luigi Santoro//public domain, Wikimedia/© Tango7174/ Creative Commons Attribution-Share Alike 4.0 International, 3.0 Unported, 2.5 Generic, 2.0 Generic and 1.0 Generic license, ikonografia-sw-stanislawa- kostki/© Opiekun. Kalisz.pl, Wikimedia/ © Sailko/ Creative Commons Attribution-ShareAlike 3.0, Wikimedia/© Sailko/ Creative Commons Attribution-ShareAlike 3.0., Wikimedia/ © Jakub Halun/GFDL ver. 1.2 or CC-by-sa ver. 2.5, 2.0, and 1.0, 681 ikonografia-sw-stanislawa-kostki/Opiekun.Kalisz.pl, ikonografia-sw- stanislawa-kostki/ © Opiekun.Kalisz.pl

45. ST. MARY OF JESUS CRUCIFIED

© Papadimitriou/Fotolia.com Diak/Fotolia.com Wikimedia/ public domain, Worthpoint, Parafia w Strzygach, Wikimedia/public domain, Wikimedia/public domain, Wikimedia/ Dobroš/Creative Commons Attribution-Share Alike 4.0 International license, © https:// karmelduchaswietego.pl

46. POWERFUL EXORCISTS

Wikimedia/ public domain, ©Emmedi 1979/Flickr.com, Del Alberico/ Wikimedia/public domain, Wikimedia/ ©Andreas Tille/Creative Commons Attribution-ShareAlike 4.0 International

47. ST. HYACINTH

Wikimedia/public domain, Wikimedia/© Zygmunt Put/Creative Commons Attribution-Share Alike 4.0 International, 3.0 Unported, 2.5 Generic, 2.0 Generic and 1.0 Generic license, Wikimedia/ Praca własna Creative Commons CC0 1.0 Universal. PD/Wikimedia/public domain. © Dominican Foundation/ Flickr.com, Wikimedia/ © IvoShandor/Creative Commons Attribution-ShareAlike 3.0 USA

48. ST. RITA OF CASCIA

all photos from Fr. Zbigniew Sobolewski, Fundacja [Foundation] Ad Gentes,

49. ST. FRANCIS OF ASSISI

Wikimedia/public domain, Wikimedia/Tetraktys/ Creative Commons Attribution-Share Alike 3.0 Unported license, 783 Wikimedia/ Roberto Ferrari/ Creative Commons Attribution-Share Alike 2.0 Generic license, © Gunnar Bach Pedersen / Wikimedia/ public domain, Wikimedia/ © José Luiz Bernardes Ribeiro / CC BY-SA 4.0 Wikimedia/ © Tetraktys/Creative Commons Attribution-Share Alike 3.0 Unported license, Wikimedia/ © Nheyob/ Creative Commons Attribution-Share Alike 4.0 International license. © Berthold Werner/Wikimedia/ public domain, © Gunnar Bach Pedersen/Wikimedia/ public domain, Wikimedia/© Laurajsi / Creative Commons Attribution-Share Alike 3.0 Unported license, © © Gunnar Bach Pedersen/Wikimedia/public domain, Wikimedia/ © Georges Jansoone/ Creative Commons - Atribuição-Compartilhalgual 3.0 © Não Adaptada, Wikimedia/ Georges Jansoone / Georges Jansoone / Creative Commons - Atribuição-Compartilhalgual 3.0 Não Adaptada, Wikimedia/ © Starlight modified by Gunnar Bach/Creative Commons Attribution-Share Alike 3.0 Unported license, © Starlight/Wikimedia/ public domain, © Starlight/Wikimedia/ public domain

50. ST. PHILIP NERI

Wikimedia/public domain, Wikimedia/ ©sailko/ Attribution- Share Alike 3.0 Unported license, Wikimedia/ public domain, Zgromadzenie Braci Serca Jezusowego [Congregatio Fratrum *Cordis Iesu* – CFCI], Wikimedia/© Lalupa/public domain, ©H. Marco- Flickr.com, Wikimedia/© Stefano Bolognini/public domain, ©Wikimedia/Jensens/public domain, Worthpoint, Wikimedia/ public domain

The original Polish publisher informs that it has exercised due diligence within the meaning of Article 335 paragraph 2 of the Civil Code (Kodeks Cywilny) in order to find the current holder of the proprietary copyrights to the photograph. In the event of a possible mistake in the spelling of the nickname, first name, surname of the author, or the type of license, we guarantee to correct the errors in future editions of the book.

About Sophia Institute

Sophia Institute is a nonprofit institution that seeks to nurture the spiritual, moral, and cultural life of souls and to spread the gospel of Christ in conformity with the authentic teachings of the Roman Catholic Church.

Sophia Institute Press fulfills this mission by offering translations, reprints, and new publications that afford readers a rich source of the enduring wisdom of mankind.

Sophia Institute also operates the popular online resource CatholicExchange.com. Catholic Exchange provides world news from a Catholic perspective as well as daily devotionals and articles that will help readers to grow in holiness and live a life consistent with the teachings of the Church.

In 2013, Sophia Institute launched Sophia Institute for Teachers to renew and rebuild Catholic culture through service to Catholic education. With the goal of nurturing the spiritual, moral, and cultural life of souls, and an abiding respect for the role and work of teachers, we strive to provide materials and programs that are at once enlightening to the mind and ennobling to the heart; faithful and complete, as well as useful and practical.

Sophia Institute gratefully recognizes the Solidarity Association for preserving and encouraging the growth of our apostolate over the course of many years. Without their generous and timely support, this book would not be in your hands.

www.SophiaInstitute.com
www.CatholicExchange.com
www.SophiaTeachers.org